EQUAL EMPLOYMENT POLICY FOR WOMEN

TEMPLE UNIVERSITY PRESS   Philadelphia

EQUAL EMPLOYMENT POLICY FOR WOMEN

Strategies for
Implementation in
the United States, Canada,
and Western Europe

Edited by
Ronnie Steinberg Ratner

Library of Congress Cataloging in Publication Data

Main entry under title:

Equal employment policy for women.

   Revised papers prepared for conference convened May 1978 by Wellesley
College Center for Research on Women.
   Bibliography: p.
   Includes index.
   1. Women—Employment—Congresses. 2. Sex discrimination in
employment—Congresses. I. Ratner, Ronnie Steinberg, 1947– II. Wellesley
College. Center for Research on Women.
HD6052.E6   331.4   79-19509
ISBN 0-87722-156-1

Temple University Press, Philadelphia 19122
© 1980 by Temple University. All rights reserved
Published 1980
Printed in the United States of America

To
ALICE H. COOK

CONTENTS

ACKNOWLEDGMENTS

The German Marshall Fund of the United States, the Social Fund of the European Economic Community, and the Women's Bureau of the U.S. Department of Labor generously sponsored the completion of this book and the Report of the Wellesley Conference on Equal Pay and Equal Opportunity Policy for Women.

Many current and former colleagues contributed to the organization of the Wellesley Conference. The involvement of Mary Jo Bane, Carolyn M. Elliott, Norman Jackman, and Brigid O'Farrell in the conference pre-dated my own. They joined me in forming a Program Advisory Committee, where together we made the major decisions about the conference. Judith Paquette, administrative assistant and secretary, worked tirelessly and imaginatively on all facets of the conference from start to finish. Judith Inker coordinated the conference arrangements by combining a concern with detail with a creative understanding of the distinctive needs of conference participants. Several members of the conference Advisory Committee were especially helpful in identifying key persons in the area of equal employment policy. Barbara Bergmann, Mai-Britt Carlsson, Alvin Golub, Elisabeth Haines, Christine Jackson, Betty Lockwood, and Nancy Seear steered me to many of the authors in this volume.

Many individuals contributed generously of their time and knowledge in their insightful reading of all or some of this book, especially Alice H. Cook, Carolyn M. Elliott, Judith Hybels, Brigid O'Farrell, Irene Little, and Barbara M. Wertheimer. Constance Sorrentino and Joyanna Moy of the Bureau of Labor Statistics generously made available labor force data that they had collected and made comparable across countries. Claire Loranz, reference librarian at Wellesley College, assisted in locating facts and figures, often at a moment's notice.

I am extremely grateful to several people for their irreplaceable contribution to this enterprise. To Françoise J. Carré, who shared in and facilitated the completion of this project in many ways—in the collection of statistics, in the preparation of tables and figures, in the compilation of the bibliography, and in coordinating correspondence with authors and assisting many of them with the notes to their chapters. To Christina Graf of the German Marshall Fund and Jacqueline Nonon of the European Economic Community for their constant support of my work on this project. To Michael Ames and Doris Braendel of Temple University Press, two imaginative and remarkable editors, whose sustained involvement with this book added enormously to its shape and quality. To Jonathan B. Ratner, whose patience, support, intelligence, and sense of humor helped me to smooth over the inevitable problems along the way. And to Alice H. Cook, to whom this book is dedicated, not only because she freely shared of her knowledge and contacts in helping me to organize the conference, but also because of her endeavors to improve the position of women by stimulating a cross-national dialogue to which she, herself, has contributed so much.

PREFACE

Employment policies affecting women have been a central focus of the Wellesley College Center for Research on Women program since its inception in 1974. The development of research, innovative programs, and publications at the Center have continually been informed by conferences. The Center's focus on employment policies designed to expand opportunities for women began with a conference on occupational segregation. Researchers pointed out the need for studies of employment practices within specific institutions and in relation to the employment structures of regional economies. This was followed by a series of workshops which examined obstacles to equal employment in various occupational categories in New England and a conference on restructuring the world of work which emphasized the relationship between work and family over the woman's life cycle.

With this background we began an empirical research program on both the mobility of women within organizations and the relationship between work and family roles. We began to explore the implementation of equal employment laws for women managers, professionals, and blue collar workers in private corporations, universities, and government; to look at the relationship between volunteer and paid work; to better understand the interaction between work and family timing patterns, child care, community services, and men's changing family roles. As Affirmative Action emerged as a central part of equal employment policy for women we brought together government policy-makers and enforcement officers, corporate personnel officers, and representatives of women's organizations to discuss the strengths and weaknesses of what had become a cumbersome and controversial administrative process.

Through our strategy of research and communication we saw the need to assess more fully the United States' legal and administrative policies and procedures for achieving equal opportunity for women in the workplace. Despite fourteen years of equal employment and equal pay legislation, occupational segregation continued, the wage gap between women and men had widened, and there was evidence of complex implementation problems for both employers and government enforcement agencies. A national family policy had yet to be articulated. We naturally looked to other western, industrialized countries as a source of experience and alternative approaches to expanding employment opportunities for women. The idea for an international conference on equal pay and equal opportunity therefore was firmly grounded in an evaluation of United States policy from the critical perspectives of research, policy, and action.

When an international advisory committee first came together to plan a conference on Equal Pay and Equal Opportunity for Women, we proposed an agenda focusing on administrative remedies and litigation to eliminate sex discrimination. These are the major routes for bringing about equality in the labor market and settling disputes with employers that are available to women workers in the United States. We thought the U.S. story of success and failure in using these measures could inform other nations now planning equal opportunity policy. In return, we could learn from Europeans and Canadians, particularly in the area of Equal Pay policy, because of the progress in some countries in reducing the wage gap between men and women.

Our European advisers raised doubts about what they perceived to be the litigious orientation of U.S. policy. More useful to them would be an increased emphasis on collective bargaining and trade union activities, for so many more European women are organized. They asked also that we give major attention to the family, which plays a primary constraining role on women's opportunities to work. Because European societies have explicit policies toward family life, these policies often become the embodiment of societal attitudes toward working women. Finally, since the recession pressed everyone and unemployment was a major concern for all leaders dealing with opportunities to work, they urged that we address the economic context of equal opportunity policy.

The discussions which began in this meeting continued over several months of conference planning. With colleagues at Wellesley, we identified an array of institutional mechanisms utilized in different countries to implement equal opportunity for women. We also determined that the conference must discuss frankly the experiences of each country in utilizing its institutions, to see how such problems as employee harassment during litigation or lack of women leaders in collective bargaining might be averted.

The conference enriched us all. Participants from Europe, Canada, and the United States brought many strong but different areas of expertise. Some Europeans left with plans to consult with other European colleagues about details of proposed legislation, while the trade union women made plans to gather and develop strategies for making presentations to a major U.N. conference. As Americans, we came away with an expanded sense of the many levels of equal opportunity policy. European perceptions of how family and labor market policies govern access to jobs provided a context for our longer experience with modes of redressing sex discrimination in the workplace itself. At the same time, many Europeans in countries just now contemplating legislation developed a new appreciation of how law may augment the other modes already available to them.

Finally, we developed a heightened appreciation of the women's movement in all of the countries. The time, courage, and commitment which so many women have given to formulating, implementing, and fighting for equal pay and equal opportunity policies are the bedrock of the successes that have been achieved. Many of these women attended the conference, and we are grateful to them for their insights.

We are particularly pleased that the knowledge shared and insights gained through the conference are now available to a much wider audience. This volume reflects both the substance and the spirit of the conference which contributes to all our continuing efforts to eliminate sex discrimination in employment and expand work opportunities for women throughout the world.

Carolyn M. Elliott
Brigid O'Farrell
Wellesley College Center
for Research on Women

INTRODUCTION

Equal employment policy for women stands at an historic juncture in the advanced industrial democracies. In Western Europe, a directive of the European Economic Community, effective August 1978, requires each of its nine member states to develop a policy instrument to further the equal treatment of women in the labor market. In Canada, a federal Human Rights Act went into effect March 1, 1978. It not only established a commission to handle complaints of discrimination but also introduced the principle of equal pay for work of equal value, making possible the adjustment upward of women's wages based on a comparison of the rates of pay for women who work in dissimilar jobs. This represents a radical departure from similar policy in other countries.

In Sweden and the United States, policies instituted in the 1960s to eliminate sex discrimination are undergoing serious attack and reassessment by supporters and opponents alike. The Swedish approach of coordinating selective and general labor market policies with collectively bargained contract rights has received its most serious challenge to date from the small but vocal Liberal party of the majority coalition in Parliament. This party has been the major force behind an anti-discrimination law enacted in early 1979. The law has been sharply criticized by both employers and employees, and receives only modest support from the Social Democratic party. It constitutes the first attempt to reform the labor market through a law opposed by these social partners.

United States policy, long based on legislation and its enforcement through the courts and administrative agencies, also is at a turning point. The 1979 Reorganization Act consolidated the enforcement of equal opportunity and equal pay under the Equal Employment Opportunity Commission. The Commission, moreover, is overhauling its processing of individual complaints through a newly developed rapid-processing system and is activating its powers to initiate complaints against major corporate offenders of the law through targeting what has been called "systemic" discrimination. Despite this move toward greater administrative efficiency, many believe that current and pending court decisions will establish precedents that strictly delimit what can be accomplished under existing legislation.

Equal pay and equal employment opportunity policies thus are high priorities on the political agenda in the United States, Canada, and Western Europe. While the development of policies in these countries is at varying stages, the issue has moved from a concern with *whether* to expand the employment opportunities of women to a preoccupation with *how* best to accomplish this change. As a consequence of this heightened interest in policy implementation, policy-makers and others concerned with women workers are grappling with the difficulties and dilemmas that arise in the selection of specific goals and concrete means for achieving women's labor market equality.

These concerns spurred the Wellesley College Center for Research on Women to convene an international conference in May 1978 to discuss the implementation of equal pay and equal opportunity policy for women. The conference brought together over sixty-five government and corporate policy-makers, lawyers, trade unionists, feminists, and researchers from twelve advanced industrial democracies to assess progress on equal employment policies and to discuss alternative strategies for better implementing them.[1] The conference agenda addressed five related themes: the economic and social context of equal pay and equal opportunity; strategies for implementing equal employment policy; the impact of these policies on employment procedures in work organizations; the role of trade unions and women's organizations in facilitating EEP; and technical issues in implementing these policies.

More than twenty papers on seven countries were commissioned specifically for this conference. They explore equal employment policy in Austria, Canada, the Federal Republic of Germany, France, Sweden, the United Kingdom, and the United States. These papers together constitute a coherent set of analytic case studies and critical essays on the evolution, implementation, and impact of equal employment policy for women. Rather than providing general background material, the papers treat some theme of equal employment policy in one country. These experiences are juxtaposed with those described in papers on other countries to highlight the contrasts or similarities between countries. Moreover, the papers do not dwell on the idiosyncrasies of each country's policies. Rather, they address issues that transcend the more narrow concerns peculiar to any country. The chapters of this book are revised versions of the papers prepared for the Wellesley Conference.

This book comprises the first cross-national discussion of equal pay and equal opportunity policy for women. But the materials it draws together are unique in several other respects as well. First, all of the chapters are original. Several present as yet unpublished data on the effects of equal opportunity or equal pay policy in private firms. Others document some of the contradictions in policy implementation with information that has been, up until this time, accessible only to policy-makers. Yet others treat for the first time in English a set of equal opportunity and equal pay policies in continental Europe. Second, the authors write from first-hand experience in developing, implementing, or evaluating equal opportunity and equal pay policy. Most, currently or in the recent past, have been in major policy-making positions. Some have received government contracts to evaluate existing programs. In addition, they are also people whose writing experience extends to both academic and lay audiences.

The book addresses four aspects of equal employment policy development and implementation: the strengths and limitations of different strategies for achieving EEP, and the linkage of such strategies to organized political action among women; the impact of equal employment policy in work organizations; the ways in which economic conditions and other public policies constrain or facilitate policy implementation; and equal employment policy goals for the future. (In addition, two topics are taken up in the Appendixes: the range of statistics necessary to monitor equal opportunity policy and the applicability of job evaluation schemes to equal pay policy.)

The opening chapter examines, for the seven countries discussed in this volume, the labor market position of women, the historical development of EEP, and the policy actions actually being undertaken currently in seven countries. It sets the stage for Parts II and III, which explore the conditions under which institutional strategies are likely to be effective in achieving labor market equality for women. Four approaches to equal opportunity and equal pay policy stand out: collective agreements between trade unions and employers; a legal strategy emphasizing litigation; a legal strategy involving administrative enforcement; and general employment and training programs. The activities of women's organizations and of women in trade unions facilitate the achievement of EEP through these means. Policy in most countries encompasses multiple approaches for achieving equal opportunity and equal pay for women. At the same time, one or two institutional means appear to dominate each country's approach.

Part II deals with legislation and collective agreements as means of attaining equal pay and equal employment opportunity. Legislation provides for enforcement through an administrative agency, the courts, or both. Collective agreements are upheld through grievance procedures, conciliation or arbitration, or the courts. Laws and agreements are means by which disputes that arise over an accusation of discriminatory behavior can be resolved. They can establish machinery for identifying "systemic" discrimination—that is, actions by gatekeepers that systematically restrict job opportunities—as well as institute procedures for monitoring the elimination of this behavior. Consequently, while laws and collective agreements are not necessarily synonymous with one another, the purposes they serve overlap to some extent. The chapters on these strategies explore these and other issues for Sweden, the Federal Republic of Germany (West Germany), France, the United States, and the United Kingdom.

Part III deals with training and organizing women for equal employment. The lack of opportunities for pre-employment and on-the-job training contributes greatly to keeping women in poorly paid, deadened jobs. Training programs, therefore, are an integral part of a coherent equal employment policy. The Labor Market Boards in a number of Western European countries, for example, have developed training programs to provide women with the skills necessary to take advantage of blue-collar and professional jobs traditionally held by men. The 1979 regulations issued to prime sponsors under the Comprehensive Employment and Training Act suggest that the United States is beginning to follow the European lead. Furthermore, in Sweden, training programs are supplemented by other labor market policies designed to stimulate employers to hire these women. Two chapters describe and assess the innovative programs of several Western European countries.

Moreover, policies are enacted and implemented when supported by visible, articulate, and effective interest groups. It is the political actions of women that prompt governments to pass laws and design programs, and trade unions to reach agreements with employers. Furthermore, it is the sustained pressure by women that causes these plans to be put into effect. This is true whether an action takes the form of supporting an individual complaint or grievance, initiating court proceedings, or lobbying. The experience of the Canadian National Action Committee on the issue of equal pay for work of equal value, discussed at length, is an important case in point. Whether action is undertaken by autonomous women's organizations or by women members of trade unions or political parties may be a function of the strength of existing interest groups, especially the extent of unionization. In Sweden, for instance, where most of the labor force is unionized, women work within trade unions to achieve the same goals that the NAC is working for in Canada. In Canada and the United States, on the other hand, few working women belong to unions. In these cases, the first order of priority would be to organize women and to train them to assume positions of leadership. Therefore, women must not only be trained for skilled jobs; they must be trained to participate in trade union and other activities. One such program of worker education is the Trade Union Women's Studies Program at the Cornell School of Labor and Industrial Relations. Its objectives, program, and impact are discussed in the final chapter of Part III. Such training enables women to participate in a plurality of organizations, including trade unions, community groups, women's organizations, and political parties. It has specific benefits within trade unions in that it broadens the range of responsibilities that women are able to assume within their unions, especially those relating to participation in bargaining.

Part IV focuses on the impact of government policies on personnel procedures and on employment patterns in private companies. Equal pay and equal opportunity policy has been in effect for almost fifteen years in the United States, and almost five years in the United Kingdom. Original data on the effect of these policies on women's positions and on personnel procedures within private firms in these two countries are presented from two large-scale surveys of major corporations. Using aggregated data, one study measures changes in the range of jobs available to women in the United States, and the second study measures changes in the gap in wages between men and women for Great Britain. Both studies are restricted to 1970–1975. Attention must not be limited to change that can be measured with aggregate data, however. Also relevant are many subtle but nonetheless significant modifications that have been introduced in the environment of work organizations as a result of equal opportunity policy. Based on extensive analysis of the process of change within major firms, case material on changes in the perception and treatment of women in private companies is presented and their implications for other change efforts are drawn out.

Part V explores the economic and social context of equal employment policy, particularly the impact of the current recession on women's position in the labor market and the planned coordination of equal employment opportunity policy and family policy. Women's employment is closely tied to the ebb and flow of the national economy in each country. High levels of unemployment appear to constrain severely programs to expand the employment opportunities of women. The effects of the recession and of other macroeconomic conditions are explored for the United States and West Germany. Important differences between these two countries exist in how the state of the economy curtails the employment options of women.

The successful implementation of equal employment policy not only requires an expanding economy but also a sensitivity on the part of policymakers to the dual role of working women. Women have entered the labor market in unprecedented numbers without having yet relinquished their primary responsibility for the family. Obviously, equal employment policy must take into account women's family responsibilities even if only to create incentives that will lead to a more equal division of these responsibilities between women and men. It is all the more startling, then, to note the considerable variation among countries in the degree to which policies that affect the family are made consistent with the goals implicit in equal employment policy. Nowhere are these differences more apparent than in

Great Britain and Sweden, for which the case material presented in two chapters is rich in detail.

Part VI looks at future directions in equal employment policy. The evolution of equal pay and equal opportunity policy reflects a continuing reassessment both of the sources of inequality between men and women in the labor market and of the realities of pratcical politics in a recessionary economy. The early experience of enforcing legislation providing equal pay for equal work exposed to policy-makers and activists the link between occupational segregation and the wage gap. They responded to these insights in the 1970s by redirecting their energies from equal pay policy to equal opportunity laws and agreements. The resistance to implementing equal opportunity in a period of high unemployment is amply documented in many of the papers included in this volume. As a consequence of this and other difficulties in policy implementation, attention is again returning to equal pay. The goal, however, has been broadened considerably from equal pay for identical or similar work to equal pay for work of comparable worth. Conventional job evaluation techniques are being used to compare jobs traditionally held by men with jobs traditionally held by women. Discrepancies in the rate of pay for male jobs and female jobs judged as equivalent must then be justified. A comparable worth study carried out in the United States (state of Washington) is described. The similarities between its findings and in the political reactions to it and those of a similar study undertaken in West Germany (described in Appendix B) are striking.

A final chapter draws on but moves beyond the case material from the preceding chapters to arrive at some general conclusions about several themes and issues in equal employment policy for women. It then identifies a number of unresolved issues and offers specific suggestions for the future development of these policies in three areas: changing women's family responsibilities as an integral part of equal employment policy; increasing the role of organized interest groups in the policy-implementation process, and broadening the goals of equal employment policy to encompass both affirmative action and equal pay for work of comparable worth.

NOTES

1. A list of participants and other information on the conference is included in Ronnie Steinberg Ratner, *Report on Wellesley Conference on Equal Pay and Equal Opportunity Policy in the United States, Canada, and Western Europe* (Wellesley, Mass.: Wellesley College Center for Research on Women, 1979).

I

Background

1   *Ronnie Steinberg Ratner*

THE POLICY AND PROBLEM: OVERVIEW OF SEVEN COUNTRIES

Equal employment policy for women, which encompasses the goals of equal pay and equal opportunity, has become one of the salient political issues of the late 1970s. A critical mass of women has exerted pressure on governments, trade unions, and employers to develop laws, collective bargaining agreements, and other government regulations to rectify the acknowledged unequal labor market situation of women. This volume assesses cross-nationally the variety of institutional means by which equal employment policies have been implemented in seven countries: Austria, Canada, the Federal Republic of Germany, France, Sweden, the United Kingdom, and the United States. While the development of policy in these countries is at differing stages, the concern in all of them has moved from *whether* to expand the employment opportunities of women to *how* best to accomplish this change. The issue of how to achieve labor market equality for women involves, in turn, both the choice of an implementation strategy and the selection of specific policy goals.

This chapter will provide an overview of the alternative goals and particular means associated with current approaches to equal employment policies in the advanced industrial democracies. First, I will examine the

Françoise J. Carré provided invaluable assistance in the collection of statistical information and the preparation of tables and figures. I would like to thank Alice Cook, Carolyn Elliott, Judith Hybels, Brigid O'Farrell, Joseph Pleck, Jonathan Ratner, and Barbara Wertheimer for comments on drafts of this chapter.

trends in female labor force participation in these seven countries and trace the historical development of equal employment policy; then I will look at the present alternatives. This cross-national review of the problem and the policy will set the stage for the case material about and policy analyses of specific countries provided by the contributors to the volume.

TRENDS IN THE LABOR FORCE PARTICIPATION OF WOMEN

In the advanced industrial democracies, women comprise a large, permanent, and growing constituency in the labor market. In the mid-1970s, the female labor force participation rate in the seven countries under discussion ranged from a high of 55 percent in Sweden to a low of almost 38 percent in West Germany (Table 1-1). In four of the seven countries, there has been a sharp rise in the labor force participation rate (LFPR) since 1960. In Canada, for instance, the rate for all females fifteen years of age or older has increased by over fifteen percentage points between 1960 and 1977, from 30 to 46 percent. Moreover, the entrance of women into paid employment in unprecedented numbers has occurred at the same time that the labor force participation rate for men is undergoing a modest, but noticeable decline. In Canada, during those

TABLE 1-1
Labor Force Participation Rate, by Sex, 1960–1977 (selected years)

Year, by country	LABOR FORCE PARTICIPATION		
	Total	*Female*	*Male*
Austria			
1975	58.4	42.4	76.3
Canada*			
1960	56.2	30.2	82.2
1964	56.2	32.9	79.7
1968	57.6	37.1	78.7
1972	58.6	40.2	77.5
1976	61.1	45.0	77.7
1977	61.5	45.9	77.7
Federal Republic of Germany*			
1960	60.0	41.2	82.7
1964	59.0	40.3	81.4
1968	57.1	38.6	79.1
1972	55.8	38.1	76.4
1976	53.2	37.7	72.1

TABLE 1-1—(*Continued*)

Year, by country	LABOR FORCE PARTICIPATION		
	Total	*Female*	*Male*
France†			
1960	62.0	43.3	84.2
1964	60.5	41.7	82.5
1968	58.8	41.4	78.5
1972	58.0	41.9	76.3
1976	58.7	43.8	75.3
Sweden			
1960	63.2	43.4	83.3
1964	63.0	45.6	81.2
1968	62.4	46.9	78.9
1972	63.1	50.5	76.1
1976	65.3	55.2	75.8
United Kingdom‡			
1960	60.7	38.7	86.0
1964	60.9	40.2	84.1
1968	60.2	40.8	81.7
1972	59.4	41.9	78.8
1976	61.5	45.8	79.0
United States†			
1960	59.4	37.7	83.3
1964	58.7	38.7	81.0
1968	59.6	41.6	80.1
1972	60.4	43.9	70.0
1976	61.6	47.3	77.5
1977	62.3	48.4	77.7

NOTE: Data related to the civilian labor force of working age is given as a percent of the civilian population. Austria is an exception: Civilian labor force of working age is given as a percent of the population 14–70 years of age.

*Working age is 15 and over.

†Working age is 16 and over.

‡Working age was raised from 15 to 16 in 1973.

SOURCE: Statistics Canada, Labour Force Survey Division, *Statistics Canada: The Labour Force* (Ottawa: Ministry of Industry, Trade and Commerce, Dec. 1977); United States Department of Labor, Bureau of Labor Statistics, Division of Foreign Labor Statistics and Trade, Office of Productivity and Technology, "International Comparison of Unemployment" (preliminary draft), Sept. 1977; United States, Department of Labor, United States Department of Health, Education and Welfare, *Employment and Training Report of the President, 1977* (Washington, D.C.: GPO, 1977); and personal communication.

same seventeen years, men's rates dropped by over four percentage points. The pattern of increasing female and decreasing male labor force participation holds for Sweden, the United Kingdom, and the United States as well.

At first glance it would appear that the continental European countries of Austria, France, and West Germany deviate from this pattern. The female rate in West Germany declined between 1960 and 1976 from 41 percent to almost 38 percent, or by approximately 7 percent. In France, the proportion of employed women remained quite stable over this same sixteen-year period. Yet, because of the greater decline in the LFPR for men in both countries (of almost 13 percentage points), the proportion of the total labor force made up of women has increased. In West Germany, between 1968 and 1976, women's share of the total labor force grew from 37 to 38 percent. In France, between 1972 and 1976, their share increased from 38 to 39 percent.[1]

Not only are *more* women working than ever before, but there also has been a noteworthy change during the twentieth century in *which* groups of women are working. Of course, farm women have always worked alongside their husbands. Historically, women worked in their homes as laundresses and seamstresses, for example, or by taking in boarders.[2] It is only in the last thirty-five to forty years that married women separated home responsibilities from their economic contribution to the family by entering the paid labor market. In Sweden in 1976, 67.7 percent of married women were in the paid labor force.[3] The 1977 Canadian Census reports that 44 percent of all married women and 49 percent of unmarried women worked for pay.[4] In the European Economic Community countries, with the exception of the Netherlands, slightly over one-half of all working women are married.[5] In France and West Germany, in 1969, for example, 58.1 and 56.4 percent of married women were employed in France and West Germany respectively.[6]

This shift in the distribution of the labor force by marital status seems to have taken place during the Second World War, at least in the United States (Table 1-2). As recently as 1940, the female labor force was predominantly made up of single women. By 1960, well over half of all employed women were married and living with their husbands.

In addition, as Hilary Land and Rita Liljeström point out in their chapters, the increase in the LFPR of married women has been accompanied by an increase in the number and proportion of working mothers.[7] In the United States, between 1950 and 1976, the LFPR for married women with children increased by almost 150 percent, 90 percent, and 215 percent, for those with children under eighteen, with children between the ages of six and seventeen, and with children under six respectively (Figure 1-1). In

TABLE 1-2

Numbers and Distribution of the Female Labor Force in the United States,
by Marital Status, 1940–1976 (selected years)

| Marital status | NUMBER (IN THOUSANDS) | | | | | DISTRIBUTION (%) | | | | |
	March 1940	April 1950	March 1960	March 1970	March 1976	March 1940	April 1950	March 1960	March 1970	March 1976
Never married	6,710	4,304	4,233	6,965	9,083	48.5	27.7	19.8	22.3	24.3
Married, husband present	4,200	7,682	12,244	18,377	21,554	30.3	49.4	57.4	58.8	57.0
Married, husband absent	840	933	1,224	1,422	1,801	6.1	6.0	5.7	4.6	4.8
Widowed	} 2,090	} 2,641	2,406	2,542	2,233	} 15.1	} 17.0	11.3	8.1	5.9
Divorced			1,222	1,927	3,146			5.7	6.2	8.3
TOTAL	13,840	15,560	21,329	31,233	37,817	100.0	100.0	100.0	100.0	100.0

SOURCE: United States Department of Labor, Bureau of Labor Statistics, *United States Working Women: A Databook* (Bulletin no. 1977; Washington, D.C.: GPO, 1977), table 18, p. 19; United States Department of Labor, Employment Standards Administration, Women's Bureau, *1975 Handbook on Women Workers* (Bulletin no. 297; Washington, D.C.: GPO, 1975), table 4, p. 17.

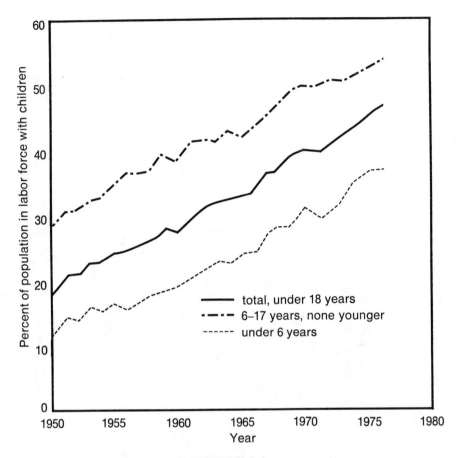

FIGURE 1-1

Labor Force Participation Rates of Married Women, Husband Present
by Age of Own Children, 1950–1976*

*Children are defined as "own children of the family head and include never-married sons and daughters, stepchildren, and adopted children. Excluded are other related children such as grandchildren, nieces, nephews, and cousins, and unrelated children.

†Data were collected in April of 1951–1955 and in March of all other years.

SOURCE: United States Department of Labor, Bureau of Labor Statistics, *U.S. Working Women: A Data Book, Bulletin, 1977* (Washington, D.C.: GPO, 1977), table 22, p. 22.

Germany and France, in 1968, more than half of all employed married women under the age of forty-five had at least one child (Table 1–3).

In a report prepared for the European Economic Community on women's employment, Evelyne Sullerot points to a number of reasons for the dramatic increase in female labor force participation, especially among married women with children. These include demographic influences, such as the decrease in the birth rate, which leaves women free from the constraints of child-rearing and able to engage in paid employment for most of their married lives (Figures 1-2 and 1-3). They also include socioeconomic influences, such as the increase in the standard of living, which necessitates two-earner families, and in the educational level of women.[8] Changes in labor demand have also stimulated the entrance of women into the labor force, most notably the increase in the proportion of service and clerical jobs.[9] Describing the trends in the labor market, the *U.S. 1975 Handbook on Women Workers* reports:

> The coming of World War II, with its greatly expanded need for labor, provided the impetus for the rapid growth in the labor force of women. Following the war, continued prosperity and the swift growth in the service sector of the economy meant substantial increases in women's employment. The year 1956 marked the switch over from a predominantly blue-collar to a white-collar economy in which women had greater opportunities.[10]

TABLE 1-3

Distribution of Employed Married Women Less Than 45 Years of Age in France and the Federal Republic of Germany, by Number of Children, 1968

Number of children	Federal Republic of Germany (%)	France (%)
0	47.8	39.7
1	28.0	34.9
2	15.6	17.2
3	5.8	5.6
4 or more	2.8	2.6
TOTAL	2,751,600	2,523,800

SOURCE: Evelyne Sullerot, *L'Emploi des Femmes et ses Problèmes dans les Etats Membres de la Communeauté Européenne* (Bruxelles: Commission des Communeautés Européennes, 1972).

FIGURE 1-2
Crude Birth Rate, 1950–1970 (selected years)

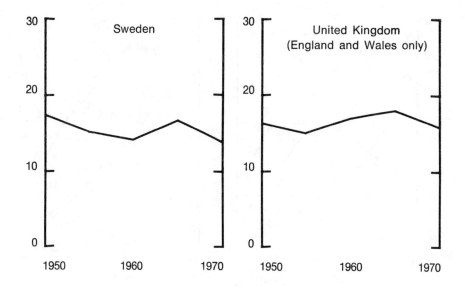

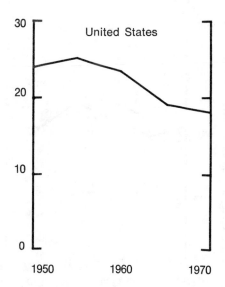

Source (all countries): United Nations, Department of Economic and Social Affairs, Statistical Office, *Levels and Trends of Fertility throughout the World, 1950–1970* (Population Studies no. 59; New York: United Nations, 1977).

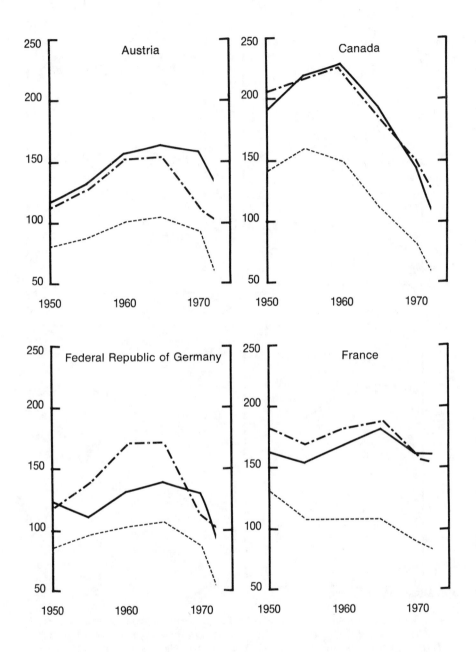

FIGURE 1-3
Age-Specific Fertility Rates, 1950–1974 (selected years)

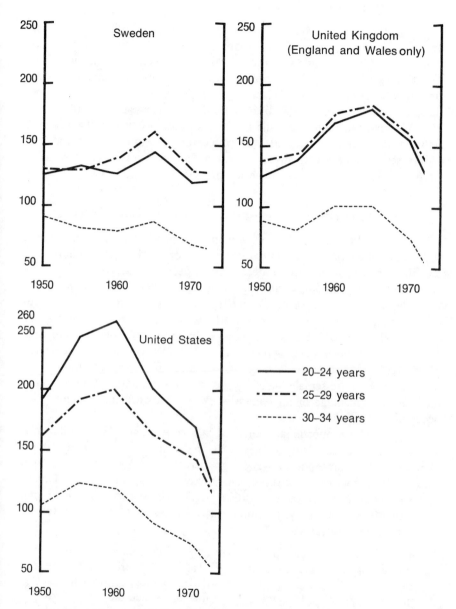

SOURCE (all countries): United Nations, Department of Economic and Social Affairs, Statistical Office, *Demographic Yearbook 1975, 27th Issue* (New York: United Nations, 1976); United Nations, Department of Economic and Social Affairs, Statistical Office, *Levels and Trends of Fertility throughout the World, 1950–1970* (Population Studies no. 59; New York; United Nations, 1977).

The experience in the United States is typical of other countries as well. For the four countries other than the United States for which data is available, the clear trend over the twentieth century has been away from the primary (that is, agriculture and extractive industries) and secondary (industrial) sectors toward the tertiary (service and clerical) sector, especially for women workers (Table 1-4). More recent data for France and West Germany indicate that this trend has continued up to the present: between 1960 and 1975, while the proportion of employees in the secondary sector remained relatively constant, there was a marked increase in the proportion of employees in the tertiary sector (Table 1-5).

CONCENTRATION AND INEQUALITY OF WOMEN WORKERS

Despite this rapid influx of women in general, and married women with children in particular, into the paid labor market, their integration remains far from complete. Indeed, few aspects of socal life display as much uniformity among countries as do the patterns that indicate the separate and restricted position of women workers. Women are overrepresented among part-time workers (Table 1-6). They are also segregated into a small range of occupations within a limited set of industries (Figures 1-4 and 1-5). This sex segregation is measured in two ways: by the degree of sex-typing—that is, the percentage of all workers in an industry or occupation who are female—and by the degree of female concentration— that is, the percentage of all female workers who work in an industry or occupation.[11]

Men are disproportionally engaged in a wide range of blue-collar jobs in the industrial sector. By contrast, as the chapters by Land, Däubler-Gmelin, and Seear report, a very high percentage of women work in a very small number of occupations. One study of occupations in the United States concluded that, in the late 1960s, "of the 100 occupations employing over 100,000 people, only 46 employ as many as 35,000 of each sex."[12] This sex-typing also exists in Canada:

> By 1961, women made up more than 70 percent of the workers in all but two of the selected occupations in [Table 1-7]. Moreover, in these two jobs—sales clerks and janitors—the proportion of women was growing rapidly. In fact, the only occupations which did not experience substantial increases in their female proportions were school teachers, graduate nurses, and "domestics." In other words, the female percentages dropped in the only two professional occupations that were significant for women workers.[13]

In addition, Table 1-7 points to the extent of female concentration in a small range of occupations and industries in Canada. During the

TABLE 1-4

Percentage Distribution of the Labor Force in Selected Countries, by Industrial Sector and Sex, 1920–1960

Sector, by country	ABOUT 1920		ABOUT 1930		ABOUT 1950		ABOUT 1960	
	Female	Male	Female	Male	Female	Male	Female	Male
Canada								
Primary	3.7	42.9	3.9	41.1	3.5	26.8	5.1	18.4
Secondary	21.6	26.9	17.3	26.5	24.8	36.2	18.8	35.9
Tertiary	74.7	30.2	78.8	32.4	71.7	37.0	76.1	45.7
Federal Republic of Germany								
Primary	43.7	27.8	40.8	26.3	11.4	18.0	4.7	11.1
Secondary	25.0	46.7	24.0	46.3	36.4	51.8	40.3	56.6
Tertiary	31.3	25.5	35.2	27.4	52.2	30.2	55.0	32.3
France								
Primary	46.2	41.9	40.6	36.9	28.6	31.9	18.9	25.1
Secondary	25.3	32.6	26.9	36.3	26.2	40.3	27.0	43.1
Tertiary	28.5	25.5	32.5	26.8	45.2	27.8	54.1	31.8
United Kingdom								
Primary	1.9	19.5	1.2	16.6	1.8	12.2	1.5	9.2
Secondary	39.4	43.5	37.2	40.3	38.8	48.5	36.1	50.9
Tertiary	58.7	37.0	61.6	43.1	59.4	37.3	62.4	39.9
United States								
Primary	12.7	33.1	8.9	30.0	4.1	18.4	2.2	10.9
Secondary	28.8	34.9	23.1	33.9	24.9	37.4	23.2	41.9
Tertiary	58.5	32.0	68.0	36.1	71.0	44.2	74.6	47.2

SOURCE: Joachim Singelman, "The Sectoral Transformation of the Labor Force in Seven Industrialized Countries, 1920–1960" (unpub. Ph.D. diss., University of Texas, 1974).

TABLE 1-5

Percentage Distribution of the Labor Force in the Federal Republic of Germany and France, by Industrial Sector, for All Employees and Females, 1960–1975 (selected years)

Sector, by country	1960		1968		1970		1973		1975	
	Total	Female	Total	Female	Total	Female	Total	Female	Total	Female
Federal Republic of Germany										
Primary	14.2	20.8	9.4	14.4	8.3	12.6	6.8	9.8	6.3	8.8
Secondary	50.1	34.9	49.6	34.7	50.8	36.5	47.3	33.1	45.7	30.9
Tertiary	35.7	44.3	41.1	50.9	40.9	50.9	45.8	57.1	48.0	60.3
France										
Primary	23.8	25.0	14.7	13.9	12.3	11.0	10.9	10.0	10.2	8.8
Secondary	38.3	25.7	39.8	25.9	40.3	26.6	39.1	26.0	38.2	25.1
Tertiary	37.9	49.3	45.5	60.3	47.4	62.5	50.0	64.1	51.6	66.2

SOURCE: Statistical Office of the European Community, *Labour Force Sample Survey, 1975* (Luxembourg: Eurostat, 1976), table VIII/4, p. 168.

period 1941 to 1971, more than 50 percent of all women in the labor market in Canada were employed in ten occupations. (The decline in the total percentage over the twenty-year period of 1941–1961 from 62.1 to 52.8 percent is accounted for almost entirely by the decline in domestic labor.)[14] Once the category of domestic labor is removed, this concentration appears to be increasing. In a study of sex segregation in employment in Canada, Pat and Hugh Armstrong point out that, in 1951, "the female participation rate was on the point of rising steadily and quickly, two-thirds of all women in the labor force held jobs in just four industries: trade; finance and real estate; community, business, and personal services; and public administration and defence. By 1971, over three-quarters were concentrated in these industries."[15]

TABLE 1-6

Percentage of the Labor Force Employed Full and Part Time,
by sex (selected years)

Country	Year	PART TIME	FULL TIME	
		% female labor force	*% female labor force*	*% male labor force*
Austria*	1975	14.0	86.0	99.0
Canada†	1977	22.1	77.9	94.5
Federal Republic of Germany‡	1975	22.8	77.2	98.9
France‡	1975	14.0	86.0	97.9
Sweden*	1977	45.2	54.6	94.0§
United Kingdom‡	1975	40.9	59.1	97.8
United States*	1975	33.0	67.0	87.6

*Part time = less than 35 hours per week.

†Full time = those who work more than 30 hours per week + those who work less but consider themselves to be working full time.

‡Part time = approximately 30 hours per week or less.

§1976 data.

SOURCE: National Labor Market Board (AMS), "Equality in the Labor Market: Statistics," unpub. ms (Stockholm: AMS, 1977); Statistical Office of the European Community, *Labour Force Sample Survey 1975* (Luxembourg: Eurostat, 1976); Statistics Canada, Labour Force Survey Division, *Statistics Canada: The Labour Force, 1977* (Ottawa: Ministry of Industry, Trade and Commerce, Dec. 1977); Statistiska Centralbyran, Utredningsinstitutet, *Arbetskrafts Undersökningén Arsmedeltal, 1976* (Stockholm, 1977); personal communication.

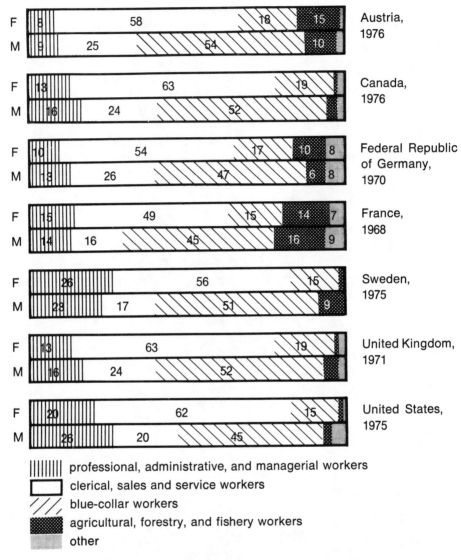

FIGURE 1-4

Percentage Distribution of the Labor Force for Broad Occupational
Categories, by Sex, Selected Years

Source: International Labor Organization, *Yearbook of Labor Statistics* (Geneva: ILO, 1976) and *Yearbook of Labor Statistics* (Geneva: ILO, 1977).

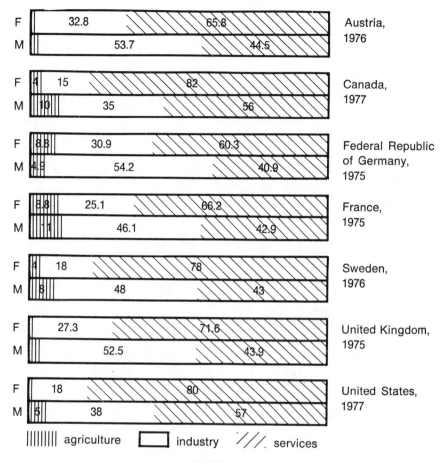

F	32.8	65.8	Austria,
M	53.7	44.5	1976

F	4 15	82	Canada,
M	10 35	56	1977

F	8.8 30.9	60.3	Federal Republic
M	4.9 54.2	40.9	of Germany, 1975

F	8.8 25.1	66.2	France,
M	11 46.1	42.9	1975

F	4 18	78	Sweden,
M	8 48	43	1976

F	27.3	71.6	United Kingdom,
M	52.5	43.9	1975

F	18	80	United States,
M	5 38	57	1977

|||||||| agriculture   ☐ industry   /// services

FIGURE 1–5
Percentage Distribution of the Labor Force by Broad Industry
Categories, by Sex, Selected Years

Source: International Labor Organization, *Yearbook of Labor Statistics* (Geneva: ILO, 1976); Statistics Canada, Labour Force Survey Division, *Statistics Canada: The Labour Force, 1977* (Ottawa: Ministry of Industry, Trade and Commerce, Dec. 1977) Statistiska Centralbyran Utredningsinstitutet, *Arbetskrafts Undersökningén Arsmedeltal, 1976* (Stockholm, 1977); United States Department of Labor, Department of Health, Education and Welfare, *Employment and Training Report of the President, 1977* (Washington, D.C.: GPO, 1977).

TABLE 1-7
Sex-Typing and Female Concentration in Ten Occupations with Greatest Number of Women Workers in Canada, 1941–1971

Occupation	1941		1951		1961		1971	
	Sex-typing*	Female concen-tration†	Sex-typing	Female concen-tration	Sex-typing	Female concen-tration	Sex-typing	Female concen-tration
Stenographers and typists	95.9	9.4	96.4	11.6	96.8	12.2	96.9	12.3
Sales clerks	41.4	6.8	52.9	8.3	53.6	7.8	51.0	6.7
Baby-sitters, maids, and related service workers	96.1	22.8	90.8	9.3	88.9	7.7	93.5	3.4
School teachers	74.6	7.8	72.5	6.5	70.7	6.9	66.0	6.4
Tailoresses, furriers, and related workers	67.8	6.2	73.7	6.4	76.2	4.5	76.0	3.4
Waitresses and bartenders	62.5	2.8	66.7	3.5	70.5	3.6	76.6	4.1
Graduate nurses	99.4	3.2	97.5	3.0	96.2	3.4	95.4	3.9
Nursing assistants and aides	71.0	1.0	72.4	1.6	78.9	2.9	79.2	2.9

Telephone operators	92.6	1.5	96.5	2.6	95.2	2.0	95.9	1.2
Janitors and cleaners	19.7	0.6	27.5	1.2	31.5	1.8	32.4	2.1
TOTAL	74.3	62.1	73.7	54.0	73.6	52.8	72.0	46.4

*Percentage of all workers who are female.
†Percentage of all women workers engaged in a specific occupation.
SOURCE: Pat Armstrong and Hugh Armstrong, *The Double Ghetto* (Toronto: McClelland and Stewart, 1978), tables 6–7, pp. 32–33.

Regardless of the country studied, jobs in which females are concentrated share several common characteristics: they command low wages despite the fact that they require a considerable amount of schooling; they call for skills, such as manual dexterity, or qualities, such as nurturance, associated with stereotypes about female capabilities or capacities; they require pre-employment rather than on-the-job training; and they include little supervision of other employees.[16]

This sex-typing of jobs and the concentration of women workers into a small range of jobs places them in an unequal position in three important respects. Women workers earn significantly less than their male counterparts, suggesting that women's work is systematically undervalued. Women workers suffer differentially high unemployment compared to men during economic downturns, suggesting that they have not yet lost their status as a reserve army. As part-time workers, women rarely receive the fringe benefits, or the training and job opportunities, accorded to (disproportionately male) full-time workers. Let us consider each of these dimensions of inequality in turn.

The wage gap

In the early 1970s, full-time year-round women workers in these seven countries earned, on average, about two-thirds of the amount men did (see Table 1-8). In 1973, the ratio of women's to men's salaries in Sweden was 86 percent, which is the lowest differential in salary by sex of the advanced industrial countries. This is the result of the wage solidarity policy of the Swedish trade unions (elaborated upon by Alice Cook in Chapter 2), in which conscious effort was made to equalize wages without reference to sex. At the other extreme is the United States, where evidence suggests that the gap is larger than it was twenty years ago, even though the United States has had a federal equal pay law since 1963.

> The $2,827 median wage or salary income of women employed full time year round in 1956 was 63 percent of the $4,466 median income of men. Although women's median income rose to $6,488 in 1973, men's income rose even faster—to $11,468. Thus, full-time year-round wage and salary income of women fell to 57 percent of men's income.[17]

The gap in wages by sex in the United States not only has increased but also varies markedly by occupation: In 1973, full-time women sales workers who worked year round earned 37.8 percent of men sales workers. At the other extreme were women professional and technical workers, who earned 63.6 percent of their male counterparts.[18]

TABLE 1-8

Indicators of Wage Gaps between Men and Women, 1970–1976
(selected years)

		WAGES*		
Country	Year	Standardized wage gap† (%)	Year	Average wage rate disparity‡ (%)
Austria	1975	64.4		
Canada	1971	59		
Federal Republic of Germany			1976	72
France	1972	66.6	1976	77
Sweden	1974	86	1970	80
United Kingdom			1976	71
United States	1973	57		

*Data collected from different sources—not fully comparable.

†Ratio of average female to average male salary for full-time, full-year employees, all occupations.

‡Ratio of average female to average male hourly wages, industrial workers.

SOURCE: Gail C. A. Cook, ed., *Opportunity for Choice: A Goal for Women in Canada* (Ottawa: Statistics Canada, 1976); The Joint Female Labor Council, *Women in Sweden in the Light of Statistics* (Stockholm: Arbetsmarknadens Kvinnonämnd, Aug. 1973); Statistical Office of the European Community, *Hourly Earnings: Hours of Work, 1976* (Luxembourg: Eurostat, 1976); Evelyne Sullerot, *L'Emploi des Femmes et Ses Problèmes dans les Etats Membres de la Communeauté Européenne* (Bruxelles: Commission des Communeautés Européennes, 1972); United States Department of Labor, Employment Standards Administration, Women's Bureau, *1975 Handbook of Women Workers* (Bulletin no. 279; Washington, D.C.: GPO, 1976); and personal communication.

In countries other than the United States, women are also systematically paid less than men. In a study of wages in the industrial sector, Evelyne Sullerot found that there were, in general, systematic differences in wage dispersion by sex in France and West Germany. The dispersion of wages is always more compressed for women than for men (Figure 1-6). Women receive, on average, lower wages than men. This varies by skill level, however; the higher the skill level, the lower the wage gap between women and men: in France, as of 1968, women in skilled, semi-skilled, and unskilled jobs earned 74.2, 80.6, and 84.4 percent of men in these

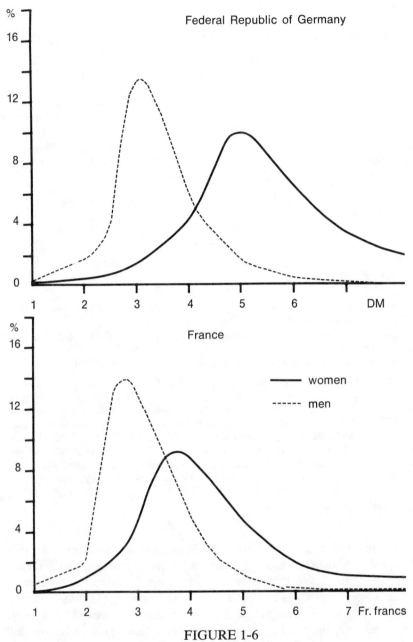

FIGURE 1-6
Dispersion of Pay Rates by Sex, about 1972

SOURCE: Evelyne Sullerot, "Equality of Remuneration for Men and Women in the Member States of the EEC," *Women Workers and Society* (Geneva: International Labour Office, 1976), p. 95.

skill levels respectively; in West Germany, in 1968, the comparable wage ratios were 73.2 percent for skilled workers, 74.4 percent for semi-skilled workers, and 78.2 percent for unskilled workers.[19]

U.S. and Canadian studies have found that the gap in wages persists even when adjustments are made for differences in schooling, in skill level, in hours of work, or in occupational groupings.[20] Only when women and men work on exactly the same job within the same firm do their earnings become approximately equal.[21] These studies suggest that the most important factor contributing to the gap in wages is sex segregation by occupation and industry. Women are found in jobs "characterized by relatively low capital investment, and . . . low productivity per worker, by low pay, and by the absence of unions."[22] Economist Barbara Bergmann maintains that the crowding of women into a small number of occupations increases the supply of labor for these positions, and since more applicants compete for fewer jobs, wages are depressed.[23] Thus does occupational segregation translate into wage inequality between men and women.[24]

Female unemployment

With few exceptions, and despite the fact that unemployment statistics understate the actual number of women who would accept jobs if they were available, women in general suffer a higher rate of unemployment than men (Figure 1-7). It also takes women a longer time than men to find new employment.[25] The differential effect of the economic downturn of the 1970s on the level of female unemployment, however, varied by country: in the United States, while a higher proportion of women are unemployed than men, Ralph Smith reports (in Chapter 16) that the level of unemploymen for women is less sensitive to changes in the business cycle than is men's. Women are insulated from these cyclical fluctuations because of occupational segregation; yet their higher rate of unemployment is, in part, also a function of occupational segregation. The impact of the current recession on women's unemployment in Great Britain and France is different from its impact in the United States. A recent study concluded that women workers appear to have experienced more difficulties than men during the economic downturn:

> In the recessionary phase both men and women appeared to experience increasing unemployment except in Sweden where the policy measures implemented greatly curtailed the effect of the cycle on the labour market. For men, however, the increase was largely due to lay-offs, whereas among women the rise in [unemployment] . . . was attributable . . . to continued entry into the labour market in an unsuccessful search for employment. In the recovery phase, which

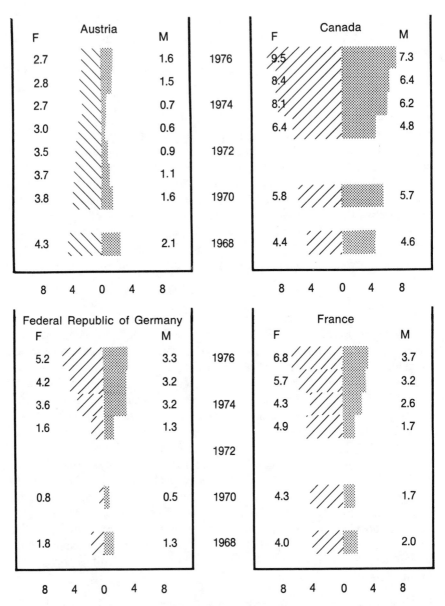

FIGURE 1-7
Unemployment Rate by Sex, 1968–1977

NOTE: Estimates of unemployment computed independently of number of registrations in unemployment offices. They are comparable across countries.

SOURCE: Bearbeitet im Osterreichischen Statistischen Zentralamt, *Sozialstatistische Daten 1977* (Vienna: Druck, Herausgeber und Eigentümer, 1977) Statistical Office of the European Community, Demographic and Social Statistics, *Statistical*

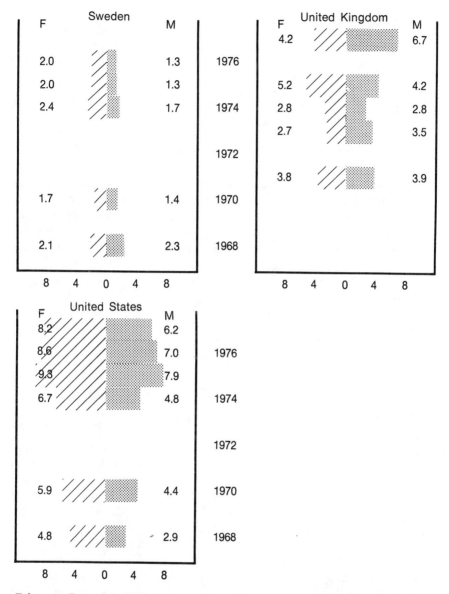

Telegram, December 1977 (Luxembourg: Eurostat, Jan. 1978) and *Labour Force Sample Survey, 1975* (Luxembourg: Eurostat, 1976); Statistics Canada, Labour Force Survey Division, *Statistics Canada: The Labour Force, 1977* (Ottawa: Ministry of Industry, Trade and Commerce, 1977); United States Department of Labor, Department of Health, Education and Welfare, *Employment and Training Report of the President, 1977* (Washington, D.C.: GPO, 1977); United States Department of Labor, Bureau of Labor Statistics, Division of Foreign Labor Statistics and Trade, Office of Productivity and Technology, *International Comparisons of Unemployment* (Bulletin no. 1979; Washington, D.C.: GPO, 1978).

was characterized by a slow and uneven improvement in conditions, men were the chief beneficiaries . . . ; women, in contrast, continued to experience an increase in unemployment as the growth of employment in traditionally feminine domains was too slow to accommodate all those seeking work.[26]

In Chapter 15, Herta Däubler-Gmelin describes a similar pattern of female unemployment in West Germany.

The link between occupational segregation, women's unemployment, and women workers' second-class status is nowhere more clearly demonstrated than in the response of governments to the economic downturn. As the chapters by Berit Rollén and Herta Däubler-Gmelin show, public works and job-training programs to put the unemployed back to work are, for the most part, designed around the needs and skills of male workers. Indeed, as Ralph Smith points out, policy-makers in the United States are blaming "women's increased commitment to paid work . . . for part of the nation's unemployment." Some policy-makers and their economic advisors contend that if women would only leave the paid labor force, we would be able to return to the "full employment economy" of the early sixties. As economist Nancy Barrett has remarked of this mentality: "Women are viewed as a reserve army of labor whose interests should be given the lowest priority in hard times."[27]

Part-time work

As indicated above, most part-time workers are women. Not surprisingly, part-time work disproportionately occurs in female-concentrated occupations. In the United Kingdom in 1974, 70.4 percent of all full-time employed women worked in four broad occupational categories; 80.4 percent of all part-time employed women worked in these same occupations.[28] In Sweden in 1976, between one-third to one-half, on average, of all women in typically female jobs worked less than thirty-five hours per week.[29] Women with children are more likely to work either part-time or part-year, as 1973 data listed in Table 1-9 for the United States indicates.

Part-time work is what Nancy Barrett has called a compromise solution to the conflicting demands faced by married women with children in industrial societies that require women's labor force participation but refuse to provide the costly social programs, such as day care and services for the aged, which would make it possible for them to display the same level of commitment to paid employment as men.[30] This compromise solution became the explicit goal of the trade unions, the employer's confederation, and the Labor Market Board in Sweden in the 1960s, for instance, when they faced a situation in which there was a severe labor short-

TABLE 1-9

Percentage Distribution of Work Experience for Married Women, Husband Present, in the United States, 1973*

Presence and age of children	% DISTRIBUTION OF FULL-TIME WORK EXPERIENCE†			% DISTRIBUTION OF PART-TIME WORK EXPERIENCE‡		
	Total	50–52 weeks	27–49 weeks	1–26 weeks	Total	27 weeks or more	1–26 weeks

Presence and age of children	Total	50–52 weeks	27–49 weeks	1–26 weeks	Total	27 weeks or more	1–26 weeks
No children under 18	75.1	52.4	12.7	10.0	24.9	16.4	8.5
Children 6–17 only	62.6	41.5	11.1	10.0	37.4	23.5	13.9
Children 3–5 only	62.7	32.6	13.0	17.0	37.3	20.4	16.9
Children under 3	68.1	19.6	18.1	30.4	31.9	12.0	19.9
TOTAL	69.0	42.6	13.0	13.4	31.0	18.5	12.5

*Women 16 years of age and over.
†Worked 35 hours or more a week during a majority of the weeks worked.
‡Worked less than 35 hours a week during a majority of the weeks worked.
SOURCE: United States Department of Labor, Employment Standards Administration, Women's Bureau, *1975 Handbook on Women Workers* (Bulletin no. 297; Washington, D.C.: GPO, 1975).

age. They were extremely successful in their efforts: in 1977, over 45 percent of all employed women in Sweden worked between one and thirty-five hours per week as compared with 6 percent of employed men. While no other country except the United Kingdom approaches this level of part-time work among women, the pattern observed for Sweden prevails in all the advanced industrial democracies. (It should be noted, however, that the increase in part-time work continues despite the opposition of trade unions in countries such as France and Austria.)

Part-time work is disadvantageous to women in at least two respects. First, as Hilary Land discusses in Chapter 17, part-time work is, perhaps, the most concrete expression of the prevailing assumption that women's commitment to the labor market is tenuous *because of* their primary commitment to their husbands, their children, and their parents and in-laws. Second, as Herta Däubler-Gmelin points out in her chapter, part-time work brings with it fewer opportunities for advancement and offers lower hourly wages and fewer fringe benefits.[31]

In summary, women have simultaneously become permanent members of the labor market and been restricted in their access to certain jobs and opportunities. The sex-typing of jobs means that women who are entering and staying in the labor market are offered limited choices, low pay, and second-class status. They are channeled into jobs where there is very little likelihood of mobility, and are paid less than men performing jobs with comparable levels of skill. Over the last fifteen years, the insistence of large numbers of women that this labor market inequality is no longer acceptable and must be eliminated has stimulated major policy changes in the area of equal pay and equal opportunity. Their political agitation has also led to the creation of national commissions to deal with women's issues in general and of women's bureaus in many government agencies to address the particular concerns of women workers. These policy developments deserve a brief review.

EVOLUTION OF EQUAL PAY AND EQUAL OPPORTUNITY POLICY

The history of how equal employment policy evolved demonstrates the integral link between equal opportunity and equal pay policy. Both policies aim at nothing less than equality for women in the labor market. In large measure, it was the growing awareness of the limitations of equal pay as a policy for achieving equality for working women that prompted and continues to prompt women activists and policy-makers to turn their energies to the development of equal opportunity policy. This shift in emphasis from equal pay to equal opportunity policy can only be pointed to in retrospect, at least for certain countries such as the United States, because national legislation on equal pay and equal opportunity were adopted within one year of each other, in 1963 and 1964 respectively. Yet, despite the similar dates of enactment, equal pay policy for women was enforced several years earlier than equal employment opportunity policy for women. As Ruth Shaeffer notes in Chapter 13, it was only when a number of significant developments occurred in the early 1970s that the serious implementation of equal opportunity policy began.[32] In other words, the disillusionment with equal pay policy came about after equal employment opportunity laws had been in existence for several years but before they had been enforced to any great extent. By contrast, in the countries of Western Europe, equal employment opportunity policy grew out of this deeper understanding of the ways in which equal pay policy is inadequate. In their chapters, Marguerite Lorée and Nancy Seear discuss this point as it applies to France and the United Kingdom.

More recently, the difficulty of eliminating the wage gap through existing equal pay legislation has led to a reassessment of the scope of these laws, especially the definition of equal pay. As we shall see below and in several other chapters, it is proposed that equal pay or equal employment opportunity legislation, or both, be reinterpreted by the courts or amended by legislatures to allow for comparisons of wages for men and women in dissimilar jobs. Keeping this basic connection between equal pay and equal opportunity policy in mind, let us turn to a more detailed history of the evolution of equal employment policies in general.

The goal of "equal pay" was first articulated by three distinct groups in the late nineteenth and early twentieth centuries: by "the socialist movement in its striving to realize equality generally, . . . [by] trade unions, whether socialist or pragmatic, who viewed with consternation and alarm the increasing number of women in all kinds of employment, . . . [and by] middle class women's rights movements, shocked at conditions of their working class sisters, whom they saw caught between 'white slavery' and 'wage slavery.' "[33] Alice Cook has noted in her comprehensive, cross-national survey of equal pay policy that, while equal pay periodically surfaced as an issue in various countries, most notably during World War I, equal pay for equal work did not become a serious political demand until World War II, when certain countries, including the United States, passed regulations requiring that women receive equal pay for equal work.[34] That this policy goal was even placed on the political agenda was largely due to the efforts of a small minority of trade union women who continued to press for equal pay because of their commitment to women workers. The general support of the trade unions, and especially the industrial unions, which led to enactment of these laws and other regulations during and after World War II was not, however, motivated by a commitment to equal treatment of women and men in the labor market. Rather, equal pay as a political demand was taken seriously for two reasons:

> In one circumstance, it arises out of men's anxiety that because women receive lower wages they threaten men's rates and perhaps even their jobs. The concern here is less that women may be underpaid than for the men who may lose out in favor of women's cheaper labor. . . . In a second circumstance, men have been called up to war service and their jobs have had to be filled by women. The absent men then are concerned that if women are paid lower rates for their jobs they may not automatically be restored to men when they return and the old hard-won battles will have to be refought. . . . In both cases men are presumed to have the first claim on jobs; women are a reserve force and the determination of their rightful wage rates will be made largely in the light of how their pay will affect men's chances to retain their prior and original rights.[35]

Not until the post–World War II period did sustained political lobbying for equal pay on the part of this small group of women activists and their trade unions bear fruit. In 1951, the International Labor Organization (ILO) adopted Convention 100, stating that "each member shall . . . promote and . . . ensure the application to all workers of the principle of equal remuneration for men and women workers for work of equal value."[36] In 1961, Article 119 of the Treaty of Rome, the basic document establishing the European Economic Community, contained a non-binding clause on equal remuneration. It is interesting to note that even Article 119 of the Treaty of Rome came about not only out of a concern for women workers but also out of the concern of those countries where there was a small wage gap that they suffered a comparative disadvantage to countries with a large wage gap.

> France made the inclusion of Article 119 a condition of signing the Treaty of Rome. Although humanitarian principles were also invoked, the French demand seems to have been inspired mainly by the fact that the country's competitive capacity was diminished because, unlike its neighbours, it did not underpay women workers. The Treaty instituted a means of combating sex-based discrimination with regard to pay in the six [original] EEC countries, and this certainly produced results. However, although in countries where differentials of 30–40 per cent had existed these were reduced to 10–15 per cent, there was no spectacular improvement in France. . . . It was as though once the differences in discrimination had been reduced, the EEC countries were settling for a situation in which they would continue to practise discrimination on a uniform if more modest scale.[37]

After these international resolutions were passed, it took many years for countries to adopt a specific national policy instrument. Sweden was among the first to adopt a policy on equal pay. In Sweden, where wage-related issues are settled through national collective bargaining between a confederation of employers and confederations of unions—that is, what Europeans have come to call the social partners—a 1961 agreement required the elimination within five years of all contract provisions sustaining pay differentials between men and women engaged in the same work.[38] Similarly, the wage solidarity policy mentioned above was recognized in the early 1960s as relevant to the issue of equal pay.[39] As Alice Cook discusses in Chapter 2, "solidary wage policy" became the primary route in Sweden to equal pay. Equal pay policy crystalized in Sweden less because of women's activism than because the appearance of the issue "coincided with important political events marking the increased power of the Social Democratic Party, closer alignments between the unions and the party, and the unions' adoption of a full employment program."[40] It also emerged at a time when there was a serious shortage of labor and when women were seen as the means to rectify this situation.

Other Western countries approved the ILO resolution quickly, but were slow to institute changes in the wage determination policy as it related to women workers. The resistance to implementing these policies is recounted in the chapters by Lorée on France and by Cook and Däubler-Gmelin on West Germany. Austria, which has long had among the highest female labor force participation rate of a non-Communist European country, made only the most modest of commitments to equal pay. It introduced the principle of equal pay into its constitution in 1958; yet even in the late 1970s Austria has not drafted implementing legislation.

Except for the United States and Sweden, Western democracies only began to pay more than lip service to the goal of equal pay in the 1970s. This shift in position was caused by the rise of the women's movement, nationally and internationally, starting in the United States in the mid-1960s. (The early gains made in equal pay and equal opportunity policy for women in the United States are to a large extent the product of the relatively early development of the modern women's movement and of the civil rights movement of the late 1950s. A major goal of the civil rights movement was to change the treatment of individuals in the labor market through the extension to all workers of legal rights backed by strong sanctions. Hence, the adoption in 1964 of Title VII of the Civil Rights Act. Among the many women active in the civil rights movement were early adherents of the new feminist movement. They brought their concern for political and legal change with them into the new women's rights organizations.)

The women's movement spoke with a political voice that could not be ignored. With an awakened awareness of the extent to which they were treated as the subordinates of men in all domains of life, large numbers of women asserted for the first time that they wanted nothing less than full equality. This demand expressed politically became one for equal rights before the law. The U.S. government responded. Other countries followed, and, as Table 1-10 indicates, six of the seven countries treated here established national commissions to deal with women's issues between 1969 and 1976; the U.S. Commission on the Status of Women had commenced its work earlier, in 1961. Most countries also created special bureaus or task forces to deal specifically with questions related to women's employment.

Equal pay, long one of these women's issues (albeit for reasons having less to do with women than with the anxieties of male workers), took on a new meaning consistent with the new interests of women workers. Government reports and independent studies responding to the growing concern about women workers documented the large gap in wages between men and women. ILO Convention 100 assumed a new importance in this context, as Lorna Marsden points out for Canada in Chapter 11. New policy was drafted. Some of the Western democracies enacted laws providing for equal pay by the early 1970s, notably the United Kingdom, Canada, and the United States (see Table 1-11). In France, inadequate measures to deal with equal pay for equal work established in the mid-1940s and early 1950s were replaced by the Equal Pay Act of 1972, which, for the first time, "clarified the nature of equal renumeration, establish[ed] a clear basis for appeals in the court and provid[ed] for enforcement."[41] The fact that Article 119 of the Treaty of Rome was made binding through the promulgation of the 1975 Directive on Equal Pay of the European Economic Community (EEC) can be interpreted as an attempt to consolidate these policy developments throughout the nine member states. In non-EEC countries such as Austria, however, legislation remains only in preparation, and proponents of equal pay must rely on informal pressure on the social partners to include clauses on equal pay in their collective bargaining agreements.[42]

Thus, policy to combat the differential in earnings between men and women working on the same jobs had been making significant progress. But at the same time, it was becoming increasingly clear that equal pay policy would have only a modest impact on equalizing male and female earnings across the entire labor market. As long as equal pay policy specified that comparisons between the wages of men and women workers be limited to those performing the same or essentially similar jobs within the same firm, few women workers could take advantage of their right to equal pay. Beginning in the late 1960s, government commissions, study groups, and agencies thoroughly documented the extensiveness of job segregation, and concluded that it was the result of deeply rooted attitudes that led to pervasive labor market discrimination against women. The 1973 *U.S. Economic Report of the President* stated:

> Women have gained much more access to market employment than they used to have, but they have not gained full equality within the market in the choice of jobs, opportunities for advancement, and other matters related to employment and compensation. To some extent the cause of this discrepancy is direct discrimination. But it is also the result of more subtle and complex factors originating in cultural patterns that have grown up in most societies, . . . [what has come to be called systemic discrimination].[43]

An ILO Committee of Experts addressing the issue of employment discrimination surveyed 130 countries. In their 1971 report, they noted that, although many measures had been taken since their last survey in 1963, much remained to be done. The committee concluded that:

> Discrimination based on sex is another form of discrimination whose elimination calls for constant attention and the development of a series of positive measures in various fields. One view which is often implicit in governments' reports is that such discrimination as may exist in this respect may be ascribed to sociological factors which must be left to evolve. Nevertheless, the efforts that have been made in some countries show that it is possible in the end to secure acceptance of the fact that many of the distinctions between the sexes which it has become customary to accept as "normal" are really discriminatory; and there is a risk that sociological practices and circumstances may not evolve in the desired direction unless specific efforts are made with this end in view.[44]

The Council of Europe, the European Economic Community, and the Organization for Economic Cooperation and Development (OECD) also compiled evidence documenting the pervasiveness of employment discrimination in their affiliated countries.[45]

If women were to achieve equality in the labor market, equal pay policy needed to be supplemented by other governmental policy and nongovernmental activity including: laws and collective agreements mandating equal employment opportunity and its enforcement; vocational training programs and other labor market policies to promote the entrance of women into traditionally male occupations; family policy such as day care programs and provisions for parental leaves to enable women and men to balance work and family obligations; and efforts by trade unions and other organizations to incorporate women and to seek and sustain the elimination of employment discrimination.

TABLE 1-10

Constitutional Clauses and Government Offices Concerned with Women's Issues

Country	NATIONAL COMMISSIONS OR COMMITTEES TO DEAL COMPREHENSIVELY WITH WOMEN'S ISSUES		WOMEN'S BUREAUS IN ESTABLISHED MINISTRIES	
	Year	*Title*	*Year*	*Title*
Austria	1969	Committee for Labor Market Affairs of Women	1966	Women's Division, Federal Ministry of Social Affairs
Canada*	1970	Royal Commission on the Status of Women	1954	Women's Bureau, Labour Canada
	1973	Advisory Council on the Status of Women		
	1976	Office of the Coordinator on the Status of Women		
Federal Republic of Germany*	1973†	Commission of Inquiry for Women and Society, Ad Hoc Commission to German Bundestag		Ministry of Youth, Family, and Health (general questions about women) Women's Division of the Ministry of the Interior
France*	1976	Delegation on the Condition of Women (formally State Secretary to the Condition of Women)	1965	Committee on Women's Work, Ministry of Labor
Sweden*	1972‡	Advisory Council on Equality between Men and Women	1976	Committee on Equality between Men and Women (a parliamentary committee within the Ministry of Labor)

United Kingdom	1969	Women's National Commission of Great Britain
United States	1961	Commission on the Status of Women
	1920	Women's Bureau, Department of Labor
	1978	National Commission on Working Women, Department of Health, Education and Welfare

*Clause on equality in Constitution.
†Newly constituted, 1977.
‡Reorganized within the Ministry of Labor in 1976.

SOURCE: Camille Pichault, "The Belgian Commission on the Employment of Women," *International Labour Review* vol. 115, no. 2 (March-April 1977); United Nations, Secretariat of the Interregional Seminar on National Machinery to Accelerate the Integration of Women in Development and to Eliminate Discrimination on Grounds of Sex, "Countries Having National Commissions or Similar Machinery to Accelerate the Integration of Women in Development and to Eliminate Discrimination on Grounds of Sex: Background Paper" (unpub. ms, Ottawa, Aug. 26, 1974); and personal communication.

TABLE 1-11
Current Principal Machinery for Implementing National Equal Pay and Equal Opportunity Policy, 1978

Policy, by country	DOMINANT MEANS OF IMPLEMENTATION			PRINCIPAL IMPLEMENTING MEASURES		
	Constitution	Legislation	Collective agreement	Year	Title	Enforcement machinery*
Austria						
Equal pay	X	(in prep.)		1958	European Convention on Human Rights, Art. 23(2) Part of constitution	None
Equal opportunity	X	(in prep.)			(in prep.)	
Canada						
Equal pay		X		1971	Equal pay provisions incorporated into Canadian Labour Code	Labour Standards Branch, Canadian Department of Labour
				1977	Canadian Human Rights Act	Canadian Human Rights Commission
Equal opportunity		X		1977	Canadian Human Rights Act	Canadian Human Rights Commission
Federal Republic of Germany						
Equal pay	X			1949 1952	Basic Law (Constitution) Law of Enterprises	None

Equal opportunity	X	(in prep.)	1949	Basic Law (Constitution)	None
France					
Equal pay	X		1972	Act No. 72-1143 respecting equal renumeration for men and women, implemented through directive in 1973	Labor and Manpower Inspectors in Ministry of Labor
Equal opportunity	X		1975	Act No. 76-625, part of article 416 of the penal code; fine for discriminating in hiring or firing because of sex or race	None
Sweden					
Equal pay	X			Wage Solidarity Agreement	Appropriate trade union officials
Equal opportunity	X	(bill intro. in Parl.)	1977	Equality agreements between Employers' Association (SAF) and each of two major trade unions (PTK) and (LO)	Committee for Sex Equality (final dispute resolving method is arbitration)
			1976	Ordinance on Equality between women and men in Government Service	Government Employee Administration Board

TABLE 1-11—*Continued*

PRINCIPAL IMPLEMENTING MEASURES

Policy, by country	DOMINANT MEANS OF IMPLEMENTATION			Year	Title	Enforcement machinery*
	Consti- tution	*Legislation*	*Collective agreement*			
United Kingdom						
Equal pay		X		1970	Equal Pay Act (came into force in 1975)	Central Arbitration Committee for complaints by member of trade union; industrial tribunal for individual complaints
Equal op- portunity		X		1975	Sex Discrimination Act	Equal Opportunities Commission; industrial tribunals for individual complaints
United States						
Equal pay		X		1963	Equal Pay Act of the Fair Labor Standards Act	Equal Employment Opportunity Commission (formerly the Wage and Hour Division, Department of Labor)

| Equal op-portunity | X | 1964 | Title VII of the Civil Rights Act | Equal Employment Opportunity Commission |
| | | 1968 | Executive Order 11375, which extended Executive Order 11246 to include sex | Office of Federal Contract Compliance Programs |

*All countries except Sweden provide final resolution of disputes in courts.

SOURCE: Directorate General of Social Affairs, Commission of the European Communities, "Egalité de Traitement entre Travailleurs Masculins et Féminins" (preliminary draft, Jan. 13, 1978); Camille Pichault, "The Belgian Commission on the Employment of Women," *International Labour Review* vol. 115, no. 2 (March-April 1977); Swedish Ministry of Foreign Affairs, "Ordinance on Equality between Men and Women in Government Service," Aug. 19, 1978 (unofficial trans., Aug. 31, 1978); United Nations, Secretariat of the Interregional Seminar on National Machinery to Accelerate the Integration of Women in Development and to Eliminate Discrimination on Grounds of Sex, "Countries Having National Commissions or Similar Machinery to Accelerate the Integration of Women in Development and to Eliminate Discrimination on Grounds of Sex: Background Paper" (unpub. ms, Ottawa, Aug. 26, 1974); and personal communication, copies of laws.

When ILO Convention 111 on Employment Discrimination was originally promulgated in 1958, it was largely ignored. In 1964, the United States enacted the Civil Rights Act, Title VII of which prohibited employment discrimination on the basis of race, color, religion, national origin, and, as an afterthought, sex.[46] As indicated above, this statute had less to do with the international convention than with the influence of the civil rights movement within the U.S. Apart from these two early actions, explicit policy instruments on the national and international level mandating equal employment opportunity policy for women are recent phenomena. In 1975, during International Women's Year, the ILO reinforced its 1958 Convention through its Declaration on Equality of Opportunity and Treatment for Women Workers. In 1976, the European Economic Community issued its Directive on Equal Treatment for Men and Women, effective in mid-1978. Canada, France, and the United Kingdom each enacted some piece of legislation prohibiting discrimination between 1975 and 1977. The social partners in Sweden developed a national collective agreement on equality covering most private employees in 1977. An ordinance covering public employees was enacted in the prior year. Equal employment opportunity legislation is currently in preparation in Austria and in West Germany (see table 1-11). The stories behind the enactment of specific policies in different countries is the subject of many of the chapters of this book.

In the remainder of this chapter, I want to focus instead on what I regard as the three general policy approaches to equal employment opportunity policy. After delineating these approaches, I will indicate which ones dominate actual strategies currently underway in each country and discuss, in broad terms, why countries adopt one or another approach. Finally, I will turn from a discussion of equal opportunity policy to address a new equal employment policy goal that promises to receive increased attention over the next five years—namely, equal pay for work of comparable worth.

EQUAL EMPLOYMENT OPPORTUNITY POLICY: THREE APPROACHES

In some countries, and especially in the United States and Canada, equal employment opportunity policy (EEOW) typically is equated with legislation that guarantees employees certain rights and establishes procedures for handling complaints and resolving disputes. To a lesser extent, it is associated with positive action to expand the opportunities of women. Yet legislation is merely one of several means for accomplishing one of a number of intermediate tasks involved in attaining EEOW for women.

Moreover, those who equate EEOW with legislation and are critical of the direction such policy has taken in the United States over the last decade oftentimes categorize such policy in terms of the seemingly inconsistent goals of either equality of opportunity or equality of results. Nathan

Glazer has argued in *Affirmative Discrimination*, for example, that policies that were originally intended to equalize opportunities turned into what might be called "equal outcomes policies."[47] A concern with protecting an individual's right to equal treatment—that is, a concern with *process*—turned in the late 1960s into a preoccupation with the position of groups relative to other groups—a concern with *outcomes*. While process and outcome are relatively easy to separate in theory, they are more difficult to disentangle in practice. Given the current state of knowledge, statistics about outcomes remain the most expedient and feasible indicator of process, at least in the area of employment. In other words, the attention given to outcomes does not reflect a change in ultimate objective, but rather points to the difficulty of obtaining an operational indicator of process.[48]

This explicit acknowledgment that a change in outcome reflects a change in process is evident in Swedish policy. As Chapter 8 discusses, both the equality program of the Labor Market Board and a draft anti-discrimination bill define EEOW specifically in terms of outcome. In these documents, equal employment opportunity exists when at least 40 percent of all those doing a particular job are male and at least 40 percent are female. (To be sure, the ease with which Swedish officials state a standard in terms of outcomes no doubt largely depends on the legitimacy accorded to the Social Democratic party's general program for equality.)

A different way of conceptualizing EEOW is in terms of *mechanisms for mandating policy*, such as legislation and collective agreements, and alternative *institutional means for implementing policy*, such as litigation, arbitration and conciliation, and administrative agency regulation, as well as in terms of *what has to be accomplished in the labor market* in particular *and in society* in general in order to eliminate occupational segregation and decrease the gap in wages between men and women. Once policy approaches are grouped in functional, rather than institutional, terms, the implicit strategy underlying a set of programs is more easily understood and clearly identified.

Equal employment opportunity policy for women encompasses those policies and programs that aim at the removal of barriers preventing the full integration of women into the paid labor market. These barriers primarily operate within the labor market and consist of adverse decisions made by gatekeepers at employee career-junctures: decisions about education and training to obtain marketable skills, about hiring and job selection, and, once on the job, about further training and job mobility. EEOW, in this sense, seeks to incorporate women into the labor market by changing the behavior of gatekeepers. If EEOW policy is to be effective, however, it must also take into account and act—directly and indirectly—upon barriers that operate outside the labor market. These barriers are associated with women's home and family responsibilities, and with the more intangible, yet crucial effects of prior socialization of men and women in appropriate expectations and patterns of behavior.

Countries have focused on different barriers—that is, on different sources of female labor market inequality—in the development of policies. In addition, they have selected different institutional mechanisms through which to implement programs and enforce policy. The selection of policy instruments is, to a certain extent, conditioned by many features of a country's social, political, and economic landscape: for example, the composition and relative power positions of different interest groups on the labor market; the legal framework; the character of women's organizations; and the dominant approach to solving general problems on the labor market. Yet, in spite of the importance of these country-specific factors to the evolution of policy, it is possible to identify three general approaches that link institutions and policy-goals to different assumptions about the sources of female labor market equality: a "discrimination" model, an "affirmative action" model, and an "expanding opportunities" model.

In the *discrimination* model, labor market inequality is perceived to result from the specific behavior of employers and others toward employees. These actions constitute unfair treatment or discrimination. Policy, then, is formulated in terms of what employers and others are to be prohibited from doing. A major activity of this approach would be the resolution of disputes between those who discriminate and those who are discriminated against. Strategies for resolving disputes include litigation in the courts, complaints made to administrative agencies, or conciliation and arbitration associated with collective bargaining.

In the *affirmative action* model, indicators of labor market inequality such as the extent of occupational segregation and the male-female wage gap constitute sufficient evidence that discrimination is an inherent feature of the normal operation of the labor market, regardless of whether any individual or group of employees has registered a complaint of unfair treatment. The emphasis of policy is to formulate and implement new personnel procedures within work organizations—in other words, to change the ways firms recruit, select, assign, train, or promote employees. Strategies for implementing this approach to EEOW are carried out by administrative agencies, by other governmental agencies, and by firms, as well as through the activities of trade unions and women's organizations.

Finally, in the *expanding opportunities* approach, the sources of women's labor market equality is located outside the boundaries of the labor market. It flows from three interrelated handicaps women suffer that make it impossible for them to perform in the labor market as the equals of men. These are their lack of training for higher-paying jobs, their home and family responsibilities, and their tenuous commitment to full-time, continuous employment. If these impediments were removed, the labor market would be relatively sex-blind in its processing of employees. From this analysis of the problem follows a strategy emphasizing pre-employment training programs, as well as the development of day care programs and social service programs for the aged. In addition, this approach calls for the modification of existing social policies that work to the advantage of the one-earner family.

Most countries have adopted multiple strategies for achieving equal employment policies for women. At the same time, one or two institutional strategies appear to dominate each country's approach to policy. In the United States, a combined discrimination–affirmative action strategy is being pursued. United States policy has long been based on legislation allowing for the resolution of disputes through the courts and administrative agencies. EEOW is at a crucial turning point, however. The enforcement of equal opportunity and equal pay has been consolidated under the Equal Employment Opportunity Commission. The commission is overhauling its processing of individual complaints, through a newly developed rapid-processing system, and is activating its powers to initiate complaints against what was identified above as "systemic" discrimination through the targeting of major corporate offenders of the law. Along with this move toward greater administrative efficiency is the disturbing likelihood that current and pending court decisions will establish precedents that strictly delimit what can be accomplished in terms of affirmative action under existing legislation. Chapters 4 and 5 assess the strengths, limitations, and dilemmas inherent in the dominant approach to EEOW in the United States.

Sweden combines an expanding opportunities approach, which places heavy emphasis on training programs and day care policy, with a less well-developed affirmative action strategy. Positive action to change the way women are processed in the labor market has been undertaken in many firms through joint union-employer affirmative action plans, largely in reaction to government incentives. In addition, the threat of having their power undercut by an anti-discrimination law has led the social partners to create many affirmative action–type programs within private firms.

EEOW in West Germany, France, and Austria is only just beginning to evolve. In West Germany, as Chapters 2 and 15 document, almost all attempts to develop equal opportunity policy—either through collective agreements and trade unions or through legislation and government enforcement—have met with little success. At the same time, impressive reforms in the area of family law and family policy, which policy-makers regard as highly relevant to EEOW, have been carried out.[49] Moreover, an anti-discrimination law currently is being drafted. Thus, it appears that West Germany is moving in the direction of a combined discrimination and expanding opportunities strategy. In France, a variety of related labor market policies are regarded as consistent with the goal of equal employment policy. Specifically, policy-makers are exploring the possibility of creating special training programs for women and strengthening family policies in order to remove some of the non–labor market impediments to women's employment. Both of these moves in the direction of an expanding opportunities approach are geared to enabling women to take advantage of existing opportunities on the labor market. In Austria, there is little at present in the way of a coherent and explicit equal employment opportunity policy for women. This is especially surprising, given the fact that Austria and Sweden share some important structural similarities: both are highly unionized, both have maintained low levels of unemployment relative to other countries during the current economic downturn, both have well-developed labor market policies, and both have been governed by democratic socialist majorities in the recent past. Despite these similarities, there remain important differences in their government policies for integrating women into the labor market. Nowhere are these differences more clear than in the use of training programs in Austria and Sweden; Chapters 8 and 9 offer considerable detail about what programs exist in each country.

The United Kingdom and Canada both follow a discrimination approach. The strategy in the United Kingdom is distinctive in that it allows for several institutional mechanisms for dispute resolution, including conciliation and arbitration, as well as the settlement of complaints in special labor courts called "industrial tribunals." This unique constellation of mechanisms for dispute resolution came about for several reasons, which are developed at length in Chapters 6 and 7. The government of Canada recently enacted a Human Rights Act covering federal employees. In addition, many of the provinces have laws providing for the resolution of disputes through conciliation by government agencies or judicial procedures. These laws bear a striking resemblance to early versions of Title VII of the U.S. Civil Rights Act, which is perhaps the classic statement of the discrimination approach.[50] Thus, the discrimination approach predominates in the United States, the United Kingdom, and Canada, while the expanding opportunities approach is pursued in Sweden, France, and West Germany. The affirmative action approach has only been tried in the United States and Sweden; in both of these countries, it has been combined with another approach.

It appears, therefore, that most countries initially adopt either a discrimination or an expanding opportunities approach to equal employment opportunity policy. In deciding between these two, countries choose the approach that is least threatening to the power relationships among existing groups in the labor market and most consistent with past labor market policy. Consequently, the Anglo-Saxon countries, where the extent of unionization among women workers is relatively low, where an ideology of individualism prevails, and where courts and administrative agencies are legitimate arenas for the resolution of labor disputes, the discrimination approach becomes, in certain respects, a simple extension of the right of an individual employee to file a grievance or complaint to a government agency when her or his rights are abridged. In countries such as Sweden, where the extent of unionization is relatively high, where an ideology of collectivism prevails, and where negotiations between the social partners is the predominant way in which labor market policy is formulated, a policy strategy develops in which the source of the problem is located outside the labor market. This is further reinforced by the fact that trade unions tend to maintain explicit ties to political parties. Trade unions thus have a strong say in the political priorities of these parties. They can pressure for political and social reforms to remove the non–labor market impediments suffered by women without resorting to significant changes in the way labor markets operate.

As the preceding discussion suggests, the affirmative action model is only beginning to become explicit, even in the two countries that already employ it. This is not surprising, since the affirmative action model implies a fundamental reassessment of the source of inequality within the labor market. In particular, it shifts the locus of discrimination from individual behavior inside and outside the labor market to the structure of the labor market—in particular, to the systematic behavior of all parties acting in it. This new definition has implications for power relationships in the market. Both employers and organized employees have a stake in maintaining that structure in its current form. Each will resist large-scale changes unless such changes will enhance their power position relative to the other social partner. Therefore, a necessary precondition for introducing an affirmative action approach may be a greater understanding of the sources of inequality in the labor market, which can only come about as a result of implementing less threatening strategies that locate the source of labor market inequality in factors unconnected to the normal operation of the labor market. In part, this understanding is a function of the emergence of new groups committed to the broader definition of the source of inequality associated with the affirmative action approach. In the United States these new groups have been autonomous women's organizations; in Sweden women have worked through the existing political party and trade union structure.

CONCLUSION

The scope and character of women's labor force participation has undergone considerable change since World War II. Recent projections of trends in the labor force suggest that, over the next twenty years, the rate of labor force participation for women in the United States and the United Kingdom will continue to increase, especially for married women with children.[51] Perhaps more important, women's labor force attachment is and will continue to increase; in other words, more women will be engaged in continuous paid employment throughout their lives.[52] Consequently, increasingly strong evidence of women's commitment to paid employment should make it more difficult to sustain the ideological justifications and rationalizations that rest so heavily on apparent evidence to the contrary. These labor market trends are a good sign that decreasing occupational segregation and eliminating the associated labor market inequalities of women will continue to rank as a high priority for some time to come. But the goals of integrating and equalizing women's position in the labor market will only be realized when there is a conscious, concerted, and multifaceted policy effort.

While equal pay for equal work carries a long history as a political *demand*, equal employment *policy* for women is a recent product of a confluence of forces that emerged in the 1960s and 1970s. Even in the short time since these policies were implemented, however, they have produced significant changes in women's labor market position, as Nancy Seear and Ruth Shaeffer point out in later chapters, and important insights into the strengths and limitations of the policies that exist. Many of the following chapters assess the policy efforts to date in specific countries. Yet a number of general points about the evolution of policy warrant consideration here as a concluding note. First, policy appears to change when enough people organize around a new definition of what problem must be solved through policy intervention. This leads, in turn, to a new definition of policy. Equal pay for equal work seemed an adequate policy goal in the early 1960s, at least to all but a few prescient trade union women. Perhaps because its implementation coincided with the resurgence of the women's movement, however, it has been subject to close examination and evaluation. As studies were completed, the new information fostered a greater understanding of how occupational segregation was the central determinant of women's labor market inequality. The end result was that the goal of equal employment policy shifted from equal pay to equal opportunity as the most direct way of integrating women workers and, hence, equalizing their position.

Second, in this context, it is important to realize that there are significant variations among equal opportunity policies currently being implemented in the advanced industrial democracies. While it is too soon to arrive at a definite conclusion, these differences in policy approach may carry important implications for the policies' potential effectiveness. To be sure, the sources of occupational segregation and its translation into labor market inequality are multidimensional and complex. It is likely that all three sources of inequality associated with the three policy approaches outlined above—specific discriminatory behavior of gatekeepers, the normal and basic procedures by which individuals are processed on the labor market, and non–labor market factors—contribute to the subordinate position of employed women. As equal opportunity policy evolves over the next decade, it will either be modified to encompass remedies directed at the multiple sources of inequality, and therefore have a greater likelihood of effectiveness, or revert to what one political scientist has labeled a symbolic reform.[53]

Finally, equal opportunity policy has been enacted not only to decrease occupational segregation but also to eliminate the gap in wages by sex. At the same time that equal opportunity policies are beginning to be implemented, many policy-makers and activists are questioning the extent to which equal opportunity policy is an effective strategy for reducing the wage gap. Instead, it is being suggested that equal opportunity policy needs to be supplemented by other policies specifically designed to attack that problem head-on. Hence, equal pay for work of comparable worth (or equal value) is emerging in several countries as another goal of equal employment policy for women. Broadening the scope of equal pay policy to allow for comparisons of the wages paid to men in traditionally male jobs with the wages paid to women in traditionally female jobs is regarded as a more direct approach to removing the systematic undervaluation of women's work than equal pay for equal work. The new federal Human Rights law in Canada, for example, makes it illegal to pay different wages to men and women workers when it is proven, through job analysis and job evaluation, that the tasks they perform in dissimilar jobs are of "equal value" (Chapter 11). Other attempts to enact some policy instrument mandating this policy have met with less success, most notably in West Germany and in the United States, in the state of Washington (Chapters 2 and 19 and Appendix B).

Proponents of this broadened definition of equal pay argue its merits as follows: Since most women work in traditionally female jobs, raising the wage rates in those jobs is the most expedient way to eliminate the gap in wages. Furthermore, if the wages for these jobs increase, men will be more likely to enter these traditionally female jobs, leaving women free to enter traditionally male jobs. Therefore, they contend, equal pay for work of equal value can simultaneously reduce the wage gap and decrease occupational segregation. Equal pay for work of equal value appears to many to be the next plateau in the larger journey toward equality for women in the labor market.

NOTES

1. United States Department of Labor, Bureau of Labor Statistics, *International Comparisons of Unemployment* (Bulletin no. 1979; Washington, D.C.: GPO, 1978). Calculated from unpublished data provided by Constance Sorrentino and Joyanna Moy of the Office of Productivity and Technology, Bureau of Labor Statistics.

2. Ann Oakley, *Women's Work* (New York: Pantheon, 1974); Ann Oakley, *The Sociology of Housework* (New York: Pantheon, 1974); Robert Smuts, *Women and Work in America* (New York: Columbia University Press, 1959).

3. National Labor Market Board (AMS), "Equality in the Labour Market, Statistics" (unp. ms), table 4.

4. Statistics Canada, Labour Force Survey Division, *Statistics Canada: The Labor Force, 1977* (Ottawa: Ministry of Industry, Trade, and Commerce, Dec. 1977).

5. International Labor Office, *Equality of Opportunity and Treatment of Women Workers* (Report VIII; Geneva: International Labor Office, 1974), p. 14.

6. Evelyne Sullerot, *L'Emploi des Femmes et Ses Problèmes dans Les Etats Membres de la Communeauté Européenne* (Bruxelles: Commission des Communeautés Européennes, 1972), p. 71.

7. International Labor Office, *Equality of Opportunity and Treatment of Women Workers*, p. 14.

8. Sullerot, *L'Emploi des Femmes*, p. 72.

9. William G. Bowen and T. Aldrich Finegan, *The Economics of Labor Force Participation* (Princeton, N.J.: Princeton University Press, 1969); Valerie Kincade Oppenheimer, *The Female Labor Force in the United States* (Population Monograph Series No. 5; Berkeley: University of California Press, 1970); Robert W. Bednarzik and Deborah P. Klein, "Labor Force Trends: A Synthesis and Analysis," *Monthly Labor Review* 100, no. 10 (Oct. 1977): 3–15; Francine D. Blau, "The Data on Women Workers, Past, Present, and Future," in Ann H. Stromberg and Shirley Harkness, eds., *Women Working: Theories and Facts in Perspective* (Palo Alto, Calif.: Mayfield Publishing Co., 1978), pp. 29–62.

10. United States Department of Labor, Employment Standards Administration, Women's Bureau, *1975 Handbook on Women Workers* (Bulletin 297; Washington, D.C.: GPO, 1975), p. 10.

11. Pat Armstrong and Hugh Armstrong, *The Double Ghetto: Canadian Women and Their Segregated Work* (Toronto: McClelland and Stewart, 1978), p. 23.

12. Patricia Cayo Sexton, *Women and Work* (Employment and Training Administration, R & D Monograph No. 46; Washington, D.C.: GPO, 1977), p. 5.

13. Armstrong and Armstrong, *The Double Ghetto*, pp. 34–35.

14. Ibid., p. 34.

15. Ibid., pp. 23, 26.

16. Jerolyn R. Lyle and Jane L. Ross, *Women in Industry: Employment Patterns of Women in Corporate America* (Lexington, Mass.: D. C. Heath, Lexington Books, 1974), p. 3; Valerie Kincade Oppenheimer, *The Female Labor Force* (Westport, Conn.: Greenwood Press, 1977).

17. Women's Bureau, *1975 Handbook*, pp. 129, 131.

18. Ibid., p. 130.

19. Evelyne Sullerot, "Equality of Remuneration for Men and Women in the Member States of the EEC," *Women Workers and Society: International Perspectives* (Geneva: International Labor Office, 1976), pp. 94–97.

20. Sylvia Ostry, *The Female Worker in Canada* (Ottawa: Queen's Printer, 1968); U.S. Department of Labor, Manpower Administration, *Manpower Report of the President, April 1975* (Washington, D.C.: GPO, 1975), p. 62.

21. Francine D. Blau, *Equal Pay in the Office* (Lexington, Mass.: D. C. Heath, Lexington Books, 1977).

22. Armstrong and Armstrong, *The Double Ghetto*, p. 22.

23. Barbara Bergmann, "Occupational Segregation, Wages, and Profits When Employers Discriminate by Race or Sex," *Eastern Economic Journal* 1 (April/July 1974): 103–110; Carol L. Jusenius, "The Influence of Work Experience, Skill Requirement, and Occupational Segregation on Women's Earnings," *Journal of Economics and Business* 29, no. 2 (Winter 1977): 107–115; Mary Huff Stevenson, "Wage Differences between Men and Women: Economic Theories," in Stromberg and Harkness, *Women Working*, pp. 89–107.

24. It has been suggested that equal pay legislation, supposedly designed to eliminate the wage gap, actually exacerbates it by reinforcing and even increasing occupational segregation. The argument runs as follows: if legislation requires equal pay for men and women engaged in the same or similar work, it serves as a disincentive for hiring men and women to perform the same jobs. Instead employers will hire women (and no men) to perform certain jobs, and pay them a substantially lower wage. As Armstrong and Armstrong conclude, "Rather than raise women's wages to match those of their male counterparts, employers may simply hire women only and pay them all the same low rate. And, of course, the legislation is largely irrelevant for the many women working in jobs where virtually no men work. Occupational segregation and wage differentials go hand in hand" (*The Double Ghetto*, p. 40).

25. Stuart Garfinkel, "The Outcome of a Spell of Unemployment," *Monthly Labor Review* vol. 100, no. 10 (Jan. 1977); Diane Werneke, "The Impact of the Recent Economic Slowdown on the Employment Opportunities of Women," Working Paper, World Employment Programme Research, International Labor Office, May 1977.

26. Werneke, "Recent Economic Slowdown," pp. iii–iv.

27. Nancy Smith Barrett, "Women in Industrial Society: An International Perspective," in Jane Roberts Chapman, ed., *Economic Independence for Women: The Foundation for Equal Rights* (Beverly Hills, Calif.: Sage Publications, 1976), p. 83.

28. *New Earnings Survey, 1974* (London: HMSO, 1974).

29. National Labor Market Board, "Statistics," table 6.

30. Barrett, "Women in Industrial Society," pp. 95–97.

31. Ibid.

32. In part, the delay in the enforcement of Title VII of the 1964 Civil Rights Act for women was a function of the controversy over its effect on state labor laws regulating the employment of women, such as maximum hours laws, nightwork laws, and weightlifting laws. In particular, those who had been opposing these so-called protective labor laws saw the enactment of Title VII as an opportunity to invalidate the laws. Thus, after 1964, the discriminatory effect of protective legislation became a major issue. At first, the Equal Employment Opportunity Commission (EEOC) avoided the issue; the forum in which the controversy was played out shifted to the courts. The federal courts also were initially hesitant to face the issue. After much hesitation and long delay, the EEOC issued regulations on August 19, 1969, stating that state protective laws were inconsistent with the general objectives of Title VII. One of the major casebooks on sex-discrimination law concluded that "1968 marked a turning point" in the history of invalidating these laws," and by mid-1973, the decision of the highest courts to rule on each case had found state hours, weight, and job prohibition laws invalid under Title VII. . . . The laws . . . were also attacked in other ways. . . . By 1973, 14 states had repealed their hours laws, the attorneys general of 21 jurisdictions had ruled that the laws did not apply to employees covered by Title VII, 3 states had amended the laws to provide for voluntary overtime for women, and 3 states had exempted employees from maximum hour coverage if they were protected by [the federal hours law]. This left only one state maximum hours law" (Barbara Allen Babcock, Ann E. Freedman, Eleanor Holmes Norton, and Susan C. Ross, *Sex Discrimination and the Law: Causes and Remedies* [Boston: Little, Brown, 1975], pp. 270–271). See also Judith Baer, *The Chains of Protection* (Westport, Conn.: Greenwood Press, 1978), esp. chs. 4 and 5.

It is interesting to note that, while the long legal battle over protective laws in the United States invalidated these laws because of their discriminatory effect, it may have had an opposite impact on the controversy over these same laws in the United Kingdom: The 1975 Sex Discrimination Act in the United Kingdom explicitly exempts protective laws from the effects of the law. This decision not to repeal the laws received considerable support from many of the same groups who supported the Sex Discrimination Act. See Anna Coote and Tess Gill, *Women's Rights: A Practical Guide* (2nd ed.; Middlesex, England: Penguin Books, 1977), and Jean Coussins, *The Equality Report* (London: National Civil Liberties League, 1976).

33. Alice Cook, "Equal Pay: A Multi-National History and Comparison" (unpub. MS, Jan. 1975), pp. 7–8.

34. Ibid., chs. 3 and 4.

35. Ibid., pp. 97–98. See also Theresa Wolfson, "Aprons and Overalls in War," *Annals* 229 (Sept. 1943): pp. 46–55.

36. International Labor Office, *Equal Remuneration: General Survey by the Committee of Experts on the Application of Conventions and Recommendations* (Report III, Part 4B; Geneva: International Labor Office, 1975).

37. Sullerot, "Equality of Remuneration," p. 104.

38. Cook, "Equal Pay," p. 180.

39. A forward-thinking group of rank-and-file trade union women supported the efforts of Sven Jonassen, then of the National Confederation of White-Collar Workers (TCO), to use the wage solidarity policy to differentially benefit women workers (personal communication, Stockholm, 1978).

40. Cook, "Equal Pay," p. 96.

41. Sullerot, "Equality of Remuneration," p. 99.

42. Helga Stubianek, "Collective Agreement Developments for Salaried Employees in Austria: Their Importance for Women," paper prepared for International Symposium on Women and Industrial Relations, Vienna, Sept. 1978; Edith Krebs, "Women Workers and Trade Unions in Austria: An Interim Report," in *Women Workers and Society*, pp. 185–198.

43. Council of Economic Advisors, *U.S. Economic Report of the President* (Washington, D.C.: GPO, 1973), p. 90.

44. *Equality of Opportunity and Treatment of Women Workers*, pp. 39–40.

45. Ibid., p. 38.

46. Caroline Bird, *Born Female* (New York: D. McKay Co., 1968).

47. Nathan Glazer, *Affirmative Discrimination: Ethnic Inequality and Public Policy* (New York: Basic Books, 1975). For a philosophical critique of these basic distinctions, see Onora O'Neill, "How Do We Know When Opportunities Are Equal," in Mary Vetterling-Braggin, Frederick A. Elliston, and Jane English, eds., *Feminism and Philosophy*, (Totowa, N.J.: Littlefield, Adams, 1977), pp. 177–189.

48. It appears that even Glazer is unable to suggest a better way to measure changes in treatment. In the chapter of *Affirmative Discrimination* addressed to racial discrimination, he resorts to using indicators of outcomes to support his contention that blacks advanced more prior to the enactment of Title VII than subsequent to it. In an attempt to refute the existence of "institutional racism," Glazer contends that the argument that it exists "became institutionalized and strengthened at a time when very substantial progress had been made, and was being made, in the *upgrading* of black *employment and income*" (italics addd). His proof of such improvements is the distribution of black families by income level and the distribution of blacks by occupation (pp. 41–43, 69). These are the same type of statistics used by courts to determine the existence of discrimination.

49. Max Rheinstein and Mary Ann Glendon, "West German Marriage and Family Law Reform," *University of Chicago Law Review* 45 (Spring 1978): 519–552.

50. Section 703 of Title VII of the Civil Rights Act of 1964 reads:

It shall be an unlawful employment practice for an employer—

(1) to fail or refuse to hire or to discharge any individual, or otherwise to discriminate against any individual with respect to his compensation, terms, conditions, or privileges of employment, because of such individual's race, color, religion, sex, or national origin; or

(2) to limit, segregate, or classify his employees or applicants for employment in any way which would deprive or tend to deprive any individual of employment opportunities or otherwise adversely affect his status as an employee, because of such individual's race, color, sex, or national origin. . . .

(c) It shall be an unlawful employment practice for a labor organization—

(1) to exclude or to expel from its membership or applicants for membership, or otherwise to discriminate against, any individual because of his race, color, religion, sex, or national origin;

(2) to limit, segregate, or classify its membership or applicants for membership or to classify or fail or refuse to refer for employment any individual, in any way which would deprive or tend to deprive any individual of employment opportunities or otherwise adversely affect his status as an employee or as an applicant for employment, because of such individual's race, color, religion, sex, or national origin; or

(3) to cause or attempt to cause an employer to discriminate against an individual in violation of this section.

51. Ralph E. Smith, *Women in the Labor Force in 1990* (Washington, D.C.: the Urban Institute, March 1979); Department of Employment, *Gazette* 85, no. 6 (June 1977): 590; United States Department of Labor, Bureau of Labor Statistics, "New Labor Force Projections to 1990: Three Possible Paths," *News*, Aug. 16, 1978, table 3.

52. Martin Rein has suggested that women's labor force participation can be assessed in terms of three dimensions: participation, attachment, and contribution to family income. He has characterized the post–World War II increase in women's employment as a revolution in participation. Even though participation has risen dramatically, however, only a very small percentage of employed women work continuously throughout their lives. Indeed, very little is known about the dimensions of women's labor force attachment. See Lee Rainwater, "Mother's Role in the Family Money Economy in Europe and the United States," Working Paper, Joint Center, Sept. 1978. Rein and Rainwater are exploring these and other issues in a forthcoming book on the dynamics of the family economy in several countries.

53. Murray Edelman, *The Symbolic Uses of Politics* (Urbana, Ill.: University of Illinois Press, 1967).

II

Legislation and Collective Bargaining: Strategies for Change

2 *Alice H. Cook*

COLLECTIVE BARGAINING AS A STRATEGY FOR ACHIEVING EQUAL OPPORTUNITY AND EQUAL PAY: SWEDEN AND WEST GERMANY

Collective bargaining is the major function of unions in Western Europe as it is in the United States. Item one on the bargaining agendas is almost invariably improvement in wages. Governments in these countries hold these truths to be so evident that freedom of unions and employers to bargain is a cardinal point of public policy; and governments, however much they may regulate the bargaining process in terms of scope and the parties' respective rights, only exceptionally attempt to regulate wages.

Bargaining being what it is, it is the unions which formulate demands and the employers who seek to bring these demands down to an acceptable level. Unions are thus the initiators of wage scales. The policy underlying wage systems is conceived in the research bureaus of the unions, defended

Note: The data and evaluative judgments included in this paper are the product of a project, "Women and Trade Unions in Four European Countries," the field research on which was conducted in Sweden, Britain, Germany, and Austria between October 1976 and June 1977 by Profs. Alice H. Cook (Cornell) and Val R. Lorwin (Oregon) with the assistance of Dr. Roberta Till-Retz (Oregon). The project was supported by the German Marshall Fund of the United States, Washington, D.C. This paper relies heavily on the chapter entitled "Collective Bargaining, Equal Pay and Equal Opportunity," drafted as part of the final report on the project.

by union representatives at the bargaining table, and, once an agreement is struck, administered by union staffs and shop stewards dealing with personnel officers at the worksite.

Equal pay has long been a subject of both legal and union policy in Sweden and in Germany, although its full achievement is considerably closer in the former than in the latter country, as we will discuss in detail below. Equal work opportunity has not been the subject of legislation in either country—in Sweden because the unions and the Social-Democratic party believe it can be better handled through collective bargaining; in Germany, because the issue has not yet been very widely considered.

As for collective bargaining on equal opportunity, the Swedish unions, both blue-collar (LO) and white-collar (TCO) federations, negotiated a special agreement on equality with the employers' federation (SAF) in private employment early in 1977. The German unions, however, have not yet embodied this issue into their structure and practice, although policy discussions and resolutions have often dealt with the issue peripherally and even assumptively. We shall follow these actions in both countries in detail.

For a better understanding of what has been going on in Sweden and Germany it is useful to outline the framework of the collective bargaining structures in each country. A special characteristic of both is the high degree of centralization of bargaining as compared with either Britain or the United States, a matter of concern in policy-making on women's issues to which we shall return. In this respect Sweden is considerably more centralized than Germany.[1]

In Sweden at intervals of about three years the national federations of unions (LO for production workers and TCO-PTK for the alliance of white-collar unions in the private sector) bargain with SAF, mainly for wages.[2] The agreement they reach regulates the amounts of wage increase. It is binding on affiliated national unions, which in their turn negotiate agreements with their national employers' associations in the various industry branches, all of which are affiliated with SAF. And finally local unions ("factory clubs") and individual managements negotiate the assignment of the rates arrived at in the national agreements and additional increments to cover wage drift.

Despite this centralized process, the Swedes' law on codetermination effective January 1977 provides for decentralized administration of bargaining agreements. Moreover, the "factory club" negotiates with local employers and managers before the latter make any important changes in production or personnel procedures, and management must inform the union of all company decisions. Indeed, the "clubs" are to work out collective agreements at plant level on union participation in a new decision-making pattern.[3] Thus, in spite of the high degree of centralization on wage bargaining, which is not to be disturbed, Swedish unions have, or will shortly have, perhaps more power at the local level than is true in the labor relations systems of other countries.[4]

In Germany the national industrial unions are in charge of all bargaining in their jurisdictions. Their agents negotiate with counterpart representatives of employers' associations organized in each industry branch, in turn divided by regions of the country. Thus any single national union is responsible for administering through its subindustry and regional offices a great variety of contracts and wage rates. Yet no more than in Sweden do agreements exist with individual employers.

Administration of German argreements at the worksite is in the hands not of subordinate bodies of the unions but of Works Councils, bodies established by law in each workplace employing more than five workers and made up of elected representatives of all employees, organized and unorganized, blue- and white-collar workers. The function of the Works Councils as laid down under recent revisions of the Basic Works Council Law (1972 and 1976) is to deal with the employer on "social," as distinct from "basic economic," issues within the plant. What this means is that the individual Council is responsible for the enforcement of the regional union contract with the employers' association of which its own employer is a member. This contract has set up a wage scale which is binding on the Council and the local employer, but the Council is allowed to negotiate plant agreements on a great many matters closely related to wages: management must inform and consult with the Council on questions of plant wage classification conforming to the contractual scale, especially the setting up of rules of payment and the introduction and use of new systems of payment, including piecework, premium pay plans, and related payments based on productivity. The Council may even agree with management on bonuses, or productivity payments above the union scale. The "social" issues include making plant agreements on such matters as schedules and vacations, the introduction of new machinery and processes, and safety and health measures and employer health and social services for employees. The Council coadministers canteens, vacation homes, company housing, and other amenities which may be furnished by the employer. The Council must be consulted and agree to layoffs including giving approval or veto to the list of persons to be laid off, and does so on the basis of "social indicators" measuring mainly personal need.

At this point arises a major concern of German trade union women, affecting their access to equal opportunity. Unemployment among German women is absolutely higher than among men and the proportion of women workers who are unemployed is greatly above that of men.[5] Since no workers can be laid off without the consent of the Works Council, it is clear that the administration of the "social indicators" justifying dismissal operates generally to permit layoffs of women over men.

The unions endeavor, of course, to have the Works Council in their hands.[6] They run active campaigns on behalf of union candidates before the triennial elections. The Councils, however, can end up having representatives of more than one union and even representatives of unorganized workers on them.

The grievance system functions through the Works Council, culminating in a state industrial court with appeal to a Supreme Federal Labor Court when settlement cannot be achieved at the plant. The court may conciliate disputes or deal with them by decision.[7]

The question now is how these systems deal with the two issues of equal pay and equal opportunity for working women.

THE ISSUES OF EQUAL PAY AND EQUAL OPPORTUNITY

While a good many other issues are of concern to women and the subjects of collective bargaining,[8] this chapter limits its considerations to the questions of equal pay and equal opportunity. Historically these two questions have become actual at considerably different times, and as a consequence when these issues are embodied in law, they are usually separate pieces of legislation and assigned to separate agencies for enforcement. Unions, similarly, though for quite different reasons, deal with these issues separately. In their case an important reason is that wages and wage policy are their chief concern. Employment opportunity, on the other hand, has only exceptionally been the subject of collective bargaining or indeed of union control or consultation. Employment opportunity in all its phases—guidance and choice of occupation, pre-employment apprenticeship and training, recruiting, placement, on-the-job and released time training, lateral transfers and promotion, the delineation of career ladders—has been the prerogative of nonlabor institutions: of schools in their prevocational curriculum and of vocational schools, of labor market boards and specifically of labor exchanges, and most commonly of employers. Only unions which operate under some form of the closed shop—and the American building and maritime trades are among the few examples of such organizations—take on the function of controlling admission to the trade and of employment within it.

In both Sweden and Germany a Labor Market Board[9] functions as an independent national institution with broad statutory powers and substantial budgets to regulate the labor market in respect to training, retraining, and advancement training as well as placement for new entries to the labor market and those threatened with unemployment. The boards in both countries are governed by advisory commissions made up of representatives of unions, employers, and the government.[10] (German law requires that the board include representatives of women at every level of its operation, but this requirement has on the whole been honored in the breach. Certainly no trade union or employer representative on the Board has been a woman.) The unions have important influence on labor market policy through their representatives on these boards, even if they do not take these issues up in collective bargaining.

We could anticipate then that unions for the most part have not dealt very extensively or directly with the questions of equal opportunity in the labor market. Where legislation may have seemed advisable, they have used their close relationship with the social-democratic parties and in some cases with the liberal or center parties or some of their labor-friendly factions.

EQUAL PAY AND THE UNIONS

Historically, unions as well as labor and socialist parties were so concerned with the low-wage competition of women that they wanted women excluded from working in any but the "women's trades" and advocated therefore their exclusion from the labor market and their return to their womanly duties in the family.[11] When this approach demonstrated itself as unrealistic in view of the increasing number of women working for wages and with the appearance of August Bebel's *Women and Socialism* in 1879, trade unionists came to adopt a defensive position in behalf of equal pay where men and women were engaged in the same work, so as to protect men's hard-won gains. But employer resistance to paying women men's wages resulted in compromise agreements with the unions to the effect that since women were physically weaker than men and could not therefore produce as much as they, and women were presumably not the breadwinners, they should be paid at an agreed-upon percentage—usually 60–75 percent—of the male scale. These special women's wages appeared in union contracts both in Sweden and Germany, and in many other countries until very recent years.

In Germany the change came in 1955, when the Supreme Labor Court in a case involving a woman worker in a chair factory ruled that the guarantees of equality in Article 3 of the Constitution applied to labor contracts. Its ruling read in part:

> A clause in a collective agreement which allows payment to women generally and as a part of the wage pattern, in terms of percentage of the contract wage for the same work as men runs counter to the equal pay principle and is null and void.[12]

German unions began to abolish these explicit scales almost immediately but the last of them disappeared only with the 1970s.

In Sweden special women's rates were not abandoned until 1960 in the private sector although public employment had done away with them considerably earlier.

Both Sweden and Germany have ratified the International Labor Organization's Convention 100 on equal pay for work of equal value. Germany is additionally bound by Article 119 in the Treaty of Rome, the Charter of the Common Market (EEC).[13] Although these ratifications have the presumable effect of law in both countries and have been the basis of court decisions in equal pay cases, neither country has an administrative statute which allows for inspection or enforcement of alleged violations of these prescriptions. (Sweden points to the fact that Convention No. 100 allows for its application through collective agreements, a principle which has been fully honored there since 1960. Individual workers may take cases to the labor courts and win redress there, but only for their own grievances.)

It is the responsibility of the unions so to shape collective bargaining policy that women are paid more equitably and to train councilors or stewards, local officers, and staff to deal consistently and aggressively with grievances embodying this issue. This latter task is on the whole assigned to the unions' education departments and carried out in the course programs provided for and even required of union officers.[14]

In bargaining for wages, unions typically subscribe to certain understandings. These have been stated by two Swedish economists in the following terms:

1. to assure wage earners a reasonable part of the national product;
2. to create "just" and reasonable relationships between the wages of various groups and wage earners; and
3. to heed, as far as possible, the demands of the national economy.[15]

Rarely do unions perceive continuation of the already-gained as acceptable or even reasonable. At the same time, in demanding improvement in each succeeding contract, they start from the existing discriminatory differentials. Hence as initiators of wage demands in bargaining they assume that "gaining a reasonable part of the national product" under no circumstances allows for any lowering of real wages nor indeed, under principle 2, of any adjustments as between workers which will diminish the income of any individual workers. Finally, there is an understanding among unions in the Western democracies that their demands, to be "reasonable," must not "rock the boat." The meaning of this is that no radical or sudden change is going to take place at any single negotiation which will bring women's low wages up to the average levels of men's and that whatever adjustments do take place over time will not be achieved at the expense of fellow workers. At the same time they will not be so excessive in terms of the national economy as to place undue burdens on employers or consumers. Demands are thus shaped into agreements based on what the domestic market and the nation's export interests will bear.

All of these constraints operate to make progress toward wage equality for women at best extremely slow and to halt it altogether in periods of recession. To the extent that unions and employers subscribe in any degree to some kind of "wages fund" assumption, women's absolute gains are subtracted from, or call for sacrifices on the part of, men. Thus demands for equal pay, when put forward aggressively, raise the male anxiety level and operate to create resistance from the very persons within the union who are often its staunchest supporters and most dependable activists, men whose skills and seniority push them into positions of leadership.

The history of the German and Swedish unions' approaches to wage equity for women varies sharply in approach and accomplishment and will be reported therefore in separate sections.

Germany

Following the Labor Court decision, employers maintained that the costs of raising women's wages to the level even of the lowest-paid male workers, usually classified as helpers, constituted an undue burden and a danger to the economy. The unions showed understanding. A series of negotiations took place which produced a revision of the wage scales[16] such that they introduced into generally four-step scales a new category designated as "light work." At the 1957 congress of the Trade Union Federation (the DGB), a number of women leaders, notably Lisel Winkelstraeter of the Chemical Workers, warned that this reclassification of wages would fundamentally affect the entire scale and adversely for women.

A word about the German wage system as it is presently shaped is necessary to make clear where the issues lie. In production a seven- to ten-step scale has evolved out of the old four steps. It is built, as was the old one, around an *Ecklohn,* a "cornerstone" wage set at the amount paid the average qualified skilled worker.[17] The "light-work" groups introduced after 1955 were set in at the bottom of the scale, usually designated as Groups 1, 2, and 3. They were then, and still are, occupied almost entirely by women who receive the lowest rates in the scale. These rates are paid on the assumption that they remunerate for "light" as contrasted with "heavy" work of men and that the work done in this category calls for minimal or no skill qualifications.

Never were these classifications designated as "women's work"—that would have been unconstitutional after the court decree—but no one needed to be told that this indeed was the case. Of the workers assigned to these grades, 70 to 85 percent and more, depending on the industry, were women. Thus these categories in effect took the place of the abolished and explicitly specified women's wage scale.

The Women's Division of the DGB began very soon to call attention to this discriminatory classification.[18] By the mid-sixties a number of unions in negotiations were raising the question of removing the light-wage groups from the wage scales. The employers were obdurate, and the unions with many other pressing items on their agendas allowed this question to drop off their priority list. By 1969, however, the issue reappeared, this time in political discussion and in the form of parliamentary inquiries to the minister of labor. This new minister (the Social Democrats came into the government in that year), a prominent trade unionist, set up a committee of union and employer representatives urging them to sponsor jointly a study of the light-wage groups. The study which emerged raised more questions than it addressed, and the committee ceased its activity. Once again the Women's Division persisted in bringing the issue to the forefront. It succeeded in having the DGB designate the year 1972 as the Year of the Working Women *(Das Jahr der Arbeitnehmerinnen)* and launched a campaign inside the Federation and outside it among other women's groups to abolish the light-wage categories and to bring more women into membership and positions of leadership within the unions.

In respect to wages, the women's demands were twofold: first, for a re-evaluation of these jobs, using factors which would objectify and measure other dimensions than that of "light-heavy"; and, second, for increases in pay for the designated groups or alternatively for their abolition. These efforts produced a powerful ripple effect, one which now seems to have exhausted itself on the rocky shores of the recession. It is, nevertheless, worth recording in detail for the movement could take off again in more favorable waters.

The DGB and its national unions without exception took up the women's claims. The minister reactivated his committee. His aim was to respond to the first of the women's demands for a revised job evaluation system which could be realistically and equitably applied to persons now in the light-wage groups. Months of discussion followed, but in the summer of 1973 the parties declared themselves at an impasse. Renewed parliamentary inquiries followed. The minister called meetings of his Parliamentary Committee. In the opinion of the Committee the impasse of the "social partners" (a term the Germans apply to the representatives of employers and unions in collective bargaining) on this issue arose not only from the problem of assigning these jobs to other appropriate wage groups but to the fact that payment for these jobs was to some degree a product of the supply and demand for labor on the market. (In other words, the pressure of women entering the labor market willing to take low-paid work acted as a disincentive for employers to move from their position opposing any revisions in respect to the light-wage groups.)

The minister believed, however, that an expert study of job evaluation in these groups would offer the social partners a scientific base from which they could negotiate more equitable job classifications and job assignments. He commissioned two experts, one in industrial medicine, Dr. J. Rutenfranz, and the other an engineer, Prof. W. Rohmert, and charged them as follows:

> through scientific experimental research to test the stress and demands put on workers in various industrial jobs, to see whether—as is today generally anticipated—it is possible scientifically to describe certain work as "heavy" if it is related to heavy physical demands on the musculature, or in contrast, whether work is to be described as "light" when it calls for less demand on the musculature solely, but where the stress is psychic-nervous in nature.[19]

During 1974, while this expert report was in progress, the minister commissioned another study of the status of light-wage groups in German collective agreements.[20] Of the 346 wage agreements which went into effect that year covering nearly 11,000,000 workers, or 90 percent of all wage earners covered by contracts, 104 contracts contained definable wage groups characterized as engaged in "light" or "simple" work. Under these contracts the difference in wages between jobs in the light-work groups and the nearest helpers' (male) wages varied by between 1.5 percent and 25 percent with average differences, depending on the wage category, of 2 to 10 percent. At the end of 1974, when this study was made, some 500,000 women and men were still classified in the light-wage groups. For this reason alone, the two authors concluded that the "problem" of the "light-wage groups will not find solution in the forseeable future."[21]

The expert report was ready in early 1975.[22] The authors believed that they had provided industry with guidelines on stress and demands on workers which could be used to make objective job classifications and job assignments. They cautioned, however, that

> the contribution of the scientist to a solution of wage equity lies solely in the development of methods which can deal with such matters as demands upon workers, their qualification for the work and their level of production. The setting of equivalencies in money to any of these elements, and beyond that, the problem of assignment of a wage rate to any particular job and its relative position on a wage scale are matters which exceed scientific capability.[23]

In other words, the scientists can only provide data for the bargainers; these data may influence the process but they cannot determine it.

Both unions and employers were slow to respond to the report. They complained that it was filled with scientific jargon and almost impossible to explain in plain German to their constituents. The DGB and the Metalworkers did, however, after some months prepare official responses in which they accepted the report's findings.[24] The employers postponed their reply until early 1977 and then wrote what constituted a rejection. During 1977 word reached me from the Ministry that in view of the recession in Germany and of the wide division in views between the "social partners" the Ministry was unwilling to push the matter further at that time. Even in the inactive files, the report has nevertheless been useful simply by throwing the existing justification of the light-wage groups into considerable doubt.

Almost all unions have taken the issue into consideration, although approaches and solutions vary considerably from union to union.[25] The Metalworkers began by eliminating Class 1 entirely, and in some contracts Class 2 has similarly disappeared. The effect has been to lift women's minimum wage by one or more grades. However, because in some contracts a new grade 11 has appeared at the top of the scale, the differential between men and women has probably not disappeared; indeed, it may even have increased. The effect nonetheless has been to raise the rate of pay to individual women and to increase their proportion of the *Ecklohn.*

A second approach has been to work toward revision of job evaluation schemes and a reconstruction of the wage scale so as to apply new measurements to women's jobs which call for higher values expressed in higher wages. A committee of the DGB Women's Division working with the Collective Bargaining and Research Divisions is working under the chairmanship of Ruth Koehn of the Foodworkers on this aspect of the problem. The work of this committee is important if for no other reason than that women's average earnings in German factories are still about 30 percent below those of men and in white-collar employment almost 40 percent below their male colleagues'.

It must be noted that while this approach through job evaluation is aimed at paying women more justly for the kinds of work they do, it is not directed toward changing their access to work for higher pay based on higher skill. Nevertheless, since it is important for unions to have both short-range and long-range goals, these approaches continue to be useful. Their effect is to reward many women immediately with better wages for the work they do. They also call the attention of employers and fellow workers to the fact that women's wages have been set by standards of hidden discrimination which require exposure and open treatment.

Sweden

Beginning as early as the 1930s and actively in the 1950s and 1960s, the Swedish unions showed their concern for the low-wage categories among their members. They determined on what they call the "solidary wage policy" to narrow the gap between high and low wage earners. That meant in effect that women, who make up the bulk of the low wage recipients, would receive special consideration. Adoption of the policy, as the historians of Swedish wage policy point out, meant, in short, that

> groups with high relative pay held back their demands for the benefit of the lowest paid. Efforts were directed particularly at reducing differences between industries, but other problems were also underlined, particularly differences in pay between men and women.[26]

Central negotiations insured implementation of the policy. Over the years and with the use of a variety of measures the unions worked persistently in the direction of raising women's wages to the levels of those of men.

In the negotiations of 1957–1958, LO insisted on special consideration of the low-wage categories and reached an understanding with its affiliates as to which groups were to be included. It is worth noting that women's wage scales had been eliminated in government employment as early as 1939 in the hope that this would provide a model for the private sphere. Twenty-one years elapsed, however, before the bargaining parties agreed in 1960 to eliminate women's wage scales for a trial period of five years. The temporary agreement was never later abrogated nor indeed called into question. In each of the next three agreements the central bargainers named the groups that were to receive special treatment. The usual approach was to divide the wage settlement into three parts: (1) a "low wage supplement" in the form of an öre-per-hour increase to be applied to the workers earning less than 96 percent of the average male worker's wage; (2) "a wage increase guarantee" or "guarantee of growth of earnings" which gave to every group not getting wage drift of a certain amount a supplement to bring them up to that amount; and (3) the "social package," including such improvements as accident insurance or pensions, working hours and holidays, and compensation for undesirable hours of labor.[27]

After several years during which wage drift—the increase in actual earnings above the central union scale—often exceeded the amounts assigned to equalization, LO in 1969 proposed to bargain for no general increase at all and instead to assign all raises to persons with earnings below the 96 percent average. The agreement actually reached with the employers was somewhat less drastic: everybody got a flat increase of at least 15 öre but low wage recipients received as much as 45 öre per hour. In 1971, LO approached the matter from still another angle. It established an average hourly earning of 12.50 Skr as its norm, and worked out an agreement to bring all persons below that rate up to it in not less than four years.

LO throughout, while keenly cognizant of women's special wage inequities, has preferred not to single out women's wages as a subject of bargaining. Instead, the unions have treated them as a significant element of the problem of low wages. As a consequence, the rate of wage increase for women has been noticeably higher than that for most men. Each year the gap between men's and women's earnings has narrowed and, as of 1977, it stands at less than 12 percent, women earning 88.7 percent of men's incomes, the highest comparative rate in any country. The wage differences which still exist are mainly a product of the differential distribution of women among industries and jobs, a matter on which the Swedes are taking positive corrective measures as well. "What is needed now is equality of recruiting and choice of occupation," say the experts of the two main labor federations and of the employers in their joint book on wage policy.[28]

Among the three labor union federations in Sweden—LO, TCO, and the professional unions affiliated in SACO/SR—decided differences exist in respect to wage policy, with the white-collar and professional unions to varying degrees supporting wages based on merit, a position hard to align with LO's solidary wage policy. Nevertheless, LO-SAF agreements are usually patternmakers for white-collar and government wage settlements.[29] TCO agreements, for example, provide for setting aside a certain share of the margin in the total wage agreement for special increases for those women whose rates are still, for historic reasons, below the standard.

The two approaches compared

The contrast between German and Swedish efforts to achieve equal pay is great. The German unions approach the problem with the recognition that the rates between men and women have been set on probably spurious grounds that deserve correction. Finding corrective measures begins with the development of a scientific method of job evaluation with the expectation that weighting of factors hitherto neglected or seriously undervalued will more equitably remunerate women's efforts in the work force.

If the important steps so far undertaken with union and government backing were to be negotiated into contracts, women would undoubtedly appear in higher wage categories in substantial numbers, though almost certainly not in classifications above 6 or 7, where the *Ecklohn* is presently established. Their continuing deficient education and vocational training will not place them even under revised job evaluation schemes in the upper earnings levels and the incomes of men and women will continue to show a wide discrepancy.

The Swedish approach, on the other hand, is one which defines equality as much in social as in economic terms. The goal is to abolish low incomes and to do so by narrowing the gap between low and high earnings. Since studies have clearly shown that women make up the largest proportion of low wage earners, the effect of the unions' consistent devotion to the solidary wage has been to raise women's wages in relation to men's and in doing so to narrow the gap between low and high wages. Equality in Sweden means accepting a system under which all workers earn a reasonable but not a widely differentiated standard of living.

While the Swedes are to some extent concerned with job evaluation, the effect of its introduction into the present scales would probably not greatly affect income or relative standing of men and women workers as such. For example, the production workers' scale in metal, the largest sector of private employment in Sweden, has four steps. The difference between the lowest and highest steps of the scale is about $1.00 an hour, something under 5 Skr. While my own observation in factory visits is that all, or nearly all, women are in the lowest or A category and that men working side by side with them are frequently rated B, a circumstance strongly suggesting overt discrimination in job classification, the difference in income between them is often not over 20 cents per hour on a wage of about $4.00. An equitable job evaluation scheme would unquestionably make a difference to many women, but the difference will not be as great as German women hope for by a correction of their light-wage categories.

By placing emphasis on narrowing the wage gap through the solidary wage policy, the Swedes have actually achieved more pay equity than the Germans can arrive at through job evaluation unless the Germans attach to their schemes a consistent programmatic attempt to bring women into the better-skilled and more highly rated jobs.

The fact is that in both countries, the major problems lie elsewhere. Equal opportunity in access to training and to better paying jobs and equal treatment on the job from both supervisors and fellow-workers are more important than all the efforts to achieve equal pay.

EQUAL OPPORTUNITY AND EQUAL TREATMENT

Neither Germany nor Sweden has an equal opportunity statute.[30] In Germany the view is that Article 3 of the Constitution, guaranteeing equal treatment to all citizens regardless of sex, provides all the legal protection that is necessary. The Swedish unions and the Social Democratic party, which governed Sweden for forty-four years until the fall of 1976, are chary of legislation, believing that the unions can much better police equal opportunity at the workplace than can government commissions and inspectors, and that collective bargaining offers a more flexible instrument than does law for dealing with industry's ever-changing conditions. The Conservative-Liberal government which replaced the Social Democratic government in 1976, however, is committed to adopting equality legislation and the parliamentary Equality Commission has produced a draft for the legislative hopper. A closer examination of the experience and programs in the two countries will be informative.

Germany

Despite the guarantees of the Basic Law on equality, many German statutes were defective in this regard. In the past few years the German legislatures have been busy bringing such laws as those governing marriage and divorce, property rights, parental control of children, vocational education and general education, social security and health insurance[31] into conformity with the intent of the Constitution. Equal access to apprenticeships in all occupations, training, and employment opportunities have received less specific attention.

Speaker of Parliament Annemarie Renger, during her term of office, invited German women workers to write her of cases of discrimination in employment. She has put together a white paper on the subject in her book *Gleiche Chancen fuer Frauen? (Equal Opportunity for Women?)*, in which she publishes many of these letters.[32] Its gloomy picture to be sure reflects not a scientifically selected sample but rather the self-selection of her correspondents. A careful study of the attitudes and experience of some two hundred working women in the chemical industry in Bavaria, however, confirms the Renger picture.[33] The percentage of those women who reported themselves as disadvantaged when compared with men in respect to wages related to promotion was 65 percent, related to further training was 53 percent, related to influence was 36 percent, and related to job security was 18 percent. When asked whether this disadvantagement was specifically due to sex discrimination, they designated the following issues as particularly subject to it: wages, 34 percent; education and training, 30 percent; promotion, 28 percent; possibility of influence, 21 percent; and job security, 12 percent.[34]

The practical stuff of labor market equal opportunity consists of many elements: recruitment, employment, job assignment, training and promotion, all matters which lie outside the usual subject matter of German contract negotiations primarily because they are in the jurisdiction of the labor market board. The chief role of the unions in affecting these matters is played by works councillors, most of whom are trade unionists and who under the law have to be consulted on several of these matters. The critical issue then is their sensitivity and commitment to the issues of women's equal opportunity in employment. The outlook at present is not hopeful. The cases which Renger presents, for example, refer repeatedly to women's frustrated attempts to gain assistance from their works councillors or to reach their employers with evidence of their qualifications for further training, higher classification, and promotion. The letters suggest and Renger herself appears to believe that, with the exception of a few token women whom private firms and public agencies place in high positions in order to be able to point to them as evidence of nondiscrimination, women have to work years longer, present greatly superior qualifications and experience, and face repeated disappointments before—perhaps—achieving at the end of their careers a few months' recognition in rank and salaries which less qualified men have long enjoyed. The old adage that a woman has to be twice as good as a man to achieve advancement in competition with him is borne out again and again.

Leading German jurists who advocate equal opportunity insist that "the equalization of opportunity for men and women must not be achieved at the expense of the legal position of men but rather only in the improvement of the position of women."[35] Can this be done, and especially in a period of recession? Two German feminists believe not. In their view equal opportunity invitably must disrupt the status quo:

> [The jurists' position] means in practice nothing other than that the present legal status will be firmly established as the norm. Disadvantagement of women in work life permits of improvement only if promotional and earning possibilities can be divided more justly than has yet been the case.

Like the Swedish labor groups, these women have little faith in direct improvement in women's status through law. The approaches they see as useful are

> indirect ones, somewhat analagous to the study commissioned by the Federal Government on the wage issue. If in the future we should have a comparable report on the "Principles of Promotion," public pressure could be mobilized strongly enough to affect the private employer and lend more weight to the demands of working women.[36]

Sweden

In Sweden the unions have been considerably more aggressive than their counterparts in Germany in dealing with the question of equal job opportunity. Early in 1977 two agreements were entered into with the employers, one by LO for blue-collar workers, the other by TCO-PTK for white-collar workers in private industry. These are agreements to agree. The next step is for the national unions to include in their contracts the provisions contained in the peak agreements. The most important statements in both agreements include the following:

- Planned and purposeful measures to further equality between the sexes at work to be undertaken at plant level. All forms of discrimination to be opposed.

- The objective shall be to eliminate sex-biased recruitment to jobs and to provide women and men with equal recruitment and training conditions by drawing up and applying in practice a consciously objective personnel policy in respect of internal and external recruitment, further training, etc.
- The purpose should be to plan the work organization and environment of the individual company so as to eliminate obstacles to equal employment of men and women.
- All measures taken are to be evaluated and further developed on a continuing basis.[37]

In addition, the SAF-TCO agreement includes equal opportunity in promotion as one of its objectives.[38]

The two documents differ chiefly in the way disputes arising under them are to be settled. In the case of the SAF-LO agreement, they are to be treated as grievances, and like grievances they may find their final determination in the industrial court. The SAF-TCO agreement, on the other hand, creates a joint arbitration committee which shall work out settlements through channels of direct negotiation and finally, if necessary, with the aid of a neutral umpire.

In addition to these agreements in the private sector, the state service operates under similar conditions as the result of an ordinance issued by the minister of finance in August 1976. The circular which elaborates the ordinance states that

> the work people do shall not only give them a livelihood and independence, it must also contribute to their development and self-confidence. But this approach places great demands on work content and working conditions. Having a chance is not enough. Working life and the conditions under which people work must also be such that a man or a woman can make the most of their talents and not be checked in their development by the inflexible categorization of employees. . . . The goal should be to abolish the system of allocating men and women to particular categories, to create the same working conditions for all and the same training and promotion opportunities for both sexes.[39]

The circular further prescribes that the agency "where jobs are mainly of the routine type must try to find new ways of organizing work allocation . . . so that work meets employees' needs of stimulus, variety and personal development." And further,

> delegation of executive tasks, exchange and broadening of work tasks and projects should also be tested, together with extended in-service training. A greater number of places in the further training of staff should be reserved for lower-bracket employees and for employees of the sex which is under-represented in the service category training is intended for.[40]

Each agency must budget for the costs of the equality measures it finds necessary and appropriate and must report to the minister of finance each year on its plans and accomplishments.

Both the agreements and the ordinance make clear that much of the practical work of achieving equality at work has to take place in the shops and offices with the active participation and initiative of the local unions. Under the new codetermination law,[41] shop stewards and local factory clubs are given a great deal more power over personnel matters including hiring and layoffs, training, and the selection of trainees than was the case in the past. Moreover the employer is bound to keep the local union officers "continuously informed of the development of the production and economy of his business and of the guidelines for his personnel policy." The unions see the implementation of the equality agreements as greatly aided by this law with its emphasis on plant-level bargaining.

Some Swedish unions, but notably SIF and SKTF,[42] have for some time had a policy calling for setting up shop level, branch, and district equality committees. Under the new agreements such committees will probably be established in all areas of Swedish employment.[43] Several committees including those already in operation under union initiative have established a notable record of activity.

One such committee is already working in the Swedish Broadcasting Corporation. It began operations in December 1976. Made up of four persons each from the union and the company, it has a full-time secretary provided at company expense. The committee began to assemble information on recruitment, on training and promotional programs, and on planning for company development. It early agreed that sex-labeled jobs were a major barrier to upward movement within the corporation. It recommended that each job should be carefully described in an occupational dictionary covering the 730 jobs in the organization. When new openings occur candidates other than those from the dominant sex ought to be sought out. (An enterprise in Sweden is deemed to be in sex balance when it has a not greater than 60/40 division of the sexes.)

The Committee noted that men on the whole had been receiving training in expert technical work whereas most training for women had been in improvement of already acquired skills, without attention to further development. On-the-job training is now to be structured so as to provide training for each sex in proportion to its numbers in a given department or occupation. Departments are asked to survey their practices and conditions in respect to sex equality and to propose training programs to correct inequities.

The Committee is reluctant to go into job evaluation unless old attitudes on the values to be attached to job elements radically change. It expects to engage in about a year and a half of experiment and planning before going to departments with recommended programs and with offers of assistance.

Under the ordinance operating in state employment, similar committees are to be established in each of the more than two hundred agencies, and each must report annually to the appropriate office in the Ministry of Finance. At the end of the program's first year, this office had assembled and evaluated the first reports and listed a number of innovative practices worth replication in other agencies of the national government. Among these were: an emphasis on vocational training especially for women in low pay categories; introduction of a shorter working day and flextime for both sexes; a more positive view on paternal leave for child care (as of the mid-1970s, only about 8 percent of fathers take advantage of the fact that either parent or both in rotation is eligible for child care leave); an effort by men in higher-grade posts to learn typing with a view to doing some of their own routine work; the application of equality criteria to content and participation in managerial training programs (in some programs places are reserved for low-level employees interested in upward movement); discussions preliminary to introducing self-management for work groups set up in departments and sections (these work groups will include everyone in the department from typists to program officers and directors); and rotating chairmanships and group participation in agenda planning in committees and work teams.

However, one agency warned that the enunciation of new policies on equality and the granting of new powers to the trade union do not in themselves guarantee smooth going. Of seventeen proposals which the union made to management in that agency, only one was accepted, and then only after long and stubborn bargaining. Even after the union publicized agency recalcitrance, it was able to achieve agreement on only four additional points.

Of equal interest and importance has been the work of locally initiated women's committees in some of the unions, despite the fact that both LO and TCO would prefer work on equality to be carried on under the unions' family councils or in the still-to-be-established joint labor-management equality committees. In both SIF and ST (unions affiliated with TCO), we interviewed women who had been responsible for setting up committees dedicated to bringing union women together at the shop or district level specifically to discuss women's problems, present proposals to the appropriate union decision-making bodies, and over time raise the level of consciousness not only of the women but of their male colleagues about women's problems and possible solutions to them.

The approach of the Swedish unions is clearly to use collective bargaining as the medium for achieving equal opportunity on the job. The resort to a national agreement rather than to a law is a matter of explicit policy. They are committed to building the equality agreement into the collective bargaining system, placing heavy emphasis on administration by local union officers within the shops and using the established grievance system to correct allegations of discrimination. The local family councils and equality committees will have the responsibility for studying local practices and conditions and recommending changes to appropriate bargaining units.

WOMEN AS UNION OFFICERS

Women trade unionists believe that many of their difficulties arise from the fact that men alone do the bargaining. These men, they say, are on the whole indifferent to women's special problems and either discard their issues from the agenda or eliminate them early in bargaining by pairing them with unpopular employer demands. An answer to this fateful neglect, women believe, is to have more women on the bargaining committees. While there is no received opinion that women at the bargaining table necessarily do better than men, the view persists that if they were there, the female constituency would be better served.

To some degree this assumption rests on the consideration that women are gaining not only self-consciousness but power in the unions. It is important to note that, first, their numbers in the union are everywhere increasing—most of the new membership gains are made up of women. Second, the number of women in union training programs is steadily increasing and thus adding to the available number of women who can be union officers and staff members. Third, the number of women elected to union office, particularly at the plant and local union level, is rising. Fourth, women's voices are more audible than they have been in the past —they are proposing resolutions, formulating demands, and exerting pressure on union leaders and staff for consideration of their problems. Fifth, the growing concern in society for sex equality as expressed in new legislation on equal pay and against discrimination in the workplace is reflected in the unions in the increasing number of items appearing in collective agreements on this subject, as well as in the establishment of special committees and divisions within the unions charged with the monitoring of equality measures.

To what extent are women appearing on bargaining committees? A few reported figures also suggest an upward trend. A partial tabulation by the DGB Women's Division in 1974 showed that among unions reporting, women made up 12.8 percent of the bargaining commission members at the district level where most of the contractual bargaining is done. (Women make up 17 percent of the total membership of the DGB.) In textiles, where women make up 80 percent of the membership, some local commissions, particularly in the clothing branch, are over 50 percent women. The Chemical Workers report participation at about the national average. The Metalworkers, however, with 25 percent of their membership among women, reported in 1976 only 4.7 percent women on the bargaining commissions.

In Sweden the federation of white-collar unions, with about 35 percent of its membership female, learned in a recent survey that thirty-two women and sixty-five men were on negotiating committees. Only one woman sits, however, on the central bargaining committee. In LO no woman holds such a position.

However much women's activity may be increasing in union affairs, the increase is primarily in the shops and local unions. For all the reasons which tie working women to their homes and families, trade union women are rarely free to accept union office far from their localities. Nor are they free to accept full-time union office with its heavy demand of travel, long hours, and night work. The result is that very few women appear in the district and national union rosters of staff and activists. Women are further handicapped in taking on these functions in that union training courses which qualify trade unionists for these posts are for the most part held in residential schools where the courses last several weeks or even months. The proportion of women attending these programs falls rapidly when compared with the women enrolled in local evening or weekend programs of a more elementary nature.[44] Thus the outlook for bringing women into more posts in the upper levels of the unions is not bright.

CENTRALIZATION VS. DECENTRALIZATION IN UNION FUNCTIONING

Although both Germany and Sweden represent high degrees of centralized bargaining, at least in comparison with the U.S. pattern, both are moving toward decentralization of many aspects of union-employer relations. The issue for us is what structural form is likely to favor the improvement of women's status.

The arguments in favor of centralization rest on the degree to which top officers and organs of the union are committed to a policy of sex equality. Both Swedish and German federations when measured by this test would earn high marks. Sweden with its history of the negotiation of the solidary wage has, however, a considerably more impressive record of achievement. Could this policy have been as successfully worked out under a less centralized system of bargaining? The feeble and varying efforts of the German unions in dealing with the light-wage groups under considerably less centralized systems of bargaining suggest that it could not.

Indeed, I would contend that the more decentralized the bargaining, the more powerfully local factors press to form varying decisions on pay and opportunity. Such factors have to do both with conditions within the firm and within the union. Individual firm profitability becomes the major determinant of decisions on pay, pay systems, and the distribution among worker categories of improvements or cuts. Final decisions will bear little necessary relation to national trends, guidelines, and pronouncements. Even high degrees of centralization in wage setting cannot control for this factor, as witness the runaway wage drift, particularly for skilled male workers in Sweden in boom times. Furthermore, the more decentralized the bargaining, the more powerful the play of internal union political forces. Here it is not the larger numbers of the unskilled who mobilize powerfully and effectively to improve their positions. They are typically the transient and politically indifferent members of the union. Rather, union power lies with the craft- and status-conscious skilled workers, whose ranks furnish most of the officers and delegates who make up union leadership.[45] These groups contain few if any women. Many men earning at or near the top of the scale take pride in being able to support their wives at home and have little personal contact with the needs and lives of women who work in the same shops with them. They share the rhetoric of their union superiors on equality, but they have no commitment born of experience to drive them to realize those goals.

Rutenfranz and Rohmert saw clearly in their report that, however objective a system of job classification might be, the job assignments made with it and the wages attached to classifications would be products of the interplay of political forces and subjective judgments on both sides of the bargaining table. They might have added that the more decentralized the bargaining, the more local and varied these pressures shaping the union contract can become. Yet exactly these manipulations of systems and agreements must take place locally. They must accommodate themselves to individual jobs, individual plant conditions, and individual workers. The trend toward decentralization is in fact a response to these necessities as is the new legislation on workplace democracy.

The impressions we gained from interviews with women workers, works councillors, and shop stewards in both countries are that the pronouncements of top-level union policy on equality in work life are only dimly reflected in actual working life. While local officers may express concern for overt discrimination, they are often blind to the covert biases of company personnel policy and practice.[46] Indeed, generally they share these biases, for workers, like managers, are imprinted with the patterns of the social fabric in which they are swaddled at birth. One hopes that as women's participation in Works Councils and local union office and meetings increases, they can correct inequities of job assignment, job classification, and wages.

Collective bargaining is a key strategy for achieving equal opportunity and equal pay. Without it the outlook would be quite hopeless. But it is not an invincible weapon, for the hands and heads which direct it are often no stronger or clearer than those in other sectors of our muddled and confounded economy.

NOTES

1. See Karl Olof Andersson, "Collective Bargaining in Sweden," *Current Sweden* no. 134 (Oct. 1976). For a fuller description of the Swedish system, see Lennart Forsebäck, *Industrial Relations and Employment in Sweden* (Stockholm: The Swedish Institute, 1976), and LO, *The Swedish Trade Union Federation* (Stockholm: Prisma, 1976).

2. Other issues are left to individual national union bargaining. LO and TCO have not always bargained jointly. Indeed, the 1977 bargaining round was the first in which the two federations succeeded in carrying through to conclusion a single national agreement which satisfied their respective needs and somewhat differing wage policies.

SAF and LO, and to a lesser degree SAF and TCO, over the years have also entered into special agreements on broad issues, beginning with a basic agreement in 1938 at Saltsjöbaden that has carried that name and substantially governed relations between management and workers ever since. The special agreements have covered such matters as health and safety, rights of shop stewards, the introduction of rationalization methods, employer-union training programs, and, most recently, the agreement on sex equality.

3. See Andersson, "Collective Bargaining," as well as Ministry of Labor, *Towards Democracy at the Workplace: New Legislation on the Joint Regulation of Working Life* (N.p.: The Ministry, March 1977), especially the text of the law, and Å. Bouvin, "New Swedish Legislation on Democracy at the Workplace," *International Labour Review* vol. 115, no. 2 (March–April 1977).

4. A period of wildcat strikes in 1969–1970 threatened the stability of the Swedish system of national union monopoly of policy-making, particularly in respect to wages and forms of wage payment. The present practice and the new legislation are undoubtedly responses to the dissatisfactions expressed in those episodes.

5. For a thorough and incisive discussion of women's unemployment in Germany, see the study by Dr. Herta Däubler-Gmelin, *Frauenarbeitslosigkeit oder Frauen zurueck an den Herd? (Women Unemployment or Women Back to the Kitchen?)* (Hamburg: Rowohlt Taschenbuch, 1977).

6. Of the roughly 200,000 works councillors in Germany, about 80 percent are trade unionists. Similar relationships exist within the public service, where worker representatives carry the title "personnel councillors." German unions also have their direct representatives in most plants (union delegates—*Vertrauensleute*), but these do not deal with management. Instead they handle union business, such as dues collection, organizing, passing out union information, and campaigning for the union ticket in Council elections.

7. See Benjamin Aaron, ed., *Labor Courts and Grievance Settlements in Western Europe* (Berkeley and Los Angeles: University of California Press, 1971), with chapters on both Germany and Sweden.

8. In our report we set up six major categories of subjects on bargaining of concern to women. In addition to equal pay and equal opportunity, we treat the subjects of part-time workers, hours and schedules, social services granted by the employer, and women's representation in the union at the workplace.

9. In Germany, the Bundesanstalt fuer Arbeit (BFA) (the Federal Institution for Labor), and in Sweden, the Arbetsmarknadsstyrelsen (AMS) (the National Labor Market Board).

10. In fact, the Swedish Board has a majority of union representatives—six out of eleven Board members, assigned three to LO, two to TCO and one to the Federation of Professional and Supervisory Employees, SACO.

11. For this history see, among others, Werner Thoennessen, *Fraueneman-zipation: Politik und Literatur der deutschen Sozialdemokratie zur Frauenbewe-gung, 1863–1933 (Women's Emancipation: Policy and Literature of the German Social Democracy on the Women's Movement, 1863–1933)* (Frankfurt, 1969).

12. Translation of this and other passages from the German are by the author.

13. The wording of the Treaty of Rome in Article 119 actually called for "equal pay for equal work," a formulation which has been even less useful than the ILO's. As pressure rose within Common Market countries to align the two international actions, EEC adopted ILO's broader phrasing.

14. Both in Sweden and in Germany, national unions as well as the federations maintain elaborate educational systems for this training. Beginning with evening and weekend courses offered by local and regional union bodies, students move in their advanced training to residential labor schools for longer, full-time intensive programs for which released time is usually provided by law or by union contract and for which the union typically carries the full costs of teaching and teaching materials, board, and room. The amount of time and attention which unions devote generally to women's issues and specifically to issues of equal pay and equal opportunity varies considerably from union to union. On the whole it makes up a very insubstantial part of the education program.

15. Rudolf Meidner and Berndt Öhman, *Fifteen Years of Wage Policy* (Stockholm: LO, 1972).

16. For a detailed and critical summary of these events, see Claudia Pinl, *Das Arbeitnehmer Patriarchat: Die Frauenpolitik der Gewerkschaften (The Worker Patriarchy: Trade Union Policy on Women)* (Cologne: Kiepenheuer und Witsch, 1977).

17. Formerly this represented the step at the top or next to the top of the scale. The radical changes which Winkelstraeter foresaw have now placed it at about position 6 on a scale of 10.

18. The Women's Division is a statutory section not only of the DGB but of each of the affiliated industrial unions. (In a few unions, notably the Textile

Workers, where women make up 80 percent of the membership, the title has been changed in recent years to the Division on Family Policy in order to encourage the inclusion of men in its program.) The Division has its own officers and organization at every level of union structure with full-time staff at national and regional levels. Its purpose is to discuss women's problems and formulate resolutions for adoption by the policy-making bodies of the unions. It holds a national convention every three years in advance of the DGB Congress for the purpose of adopting such a program and passing it on to the DGB. The national director of the Women's Division sits on the DGB Executive Board and her counterpart in the individual unions on their Boards. Indeed, the present head of the DGB Women is first vice president of the Federation.

19. Herman Boedler, "Leichtlohngruppen unter die Lupe ("Light-wage Groups under the Magnifying Glass"), *Bundesarbeitsblatt* vol. 10 (1975).

20. *Bericht der Bundesregierung ueber die Art, den Umfang und den Erfolg der von ihr oder den Laenderregierungen vorgenommenen Beanstandungen betreffend die Anwendung des Artikels 119 des EWG-Vertrages* (*Extent and Success of the Requirements of Article 119 of the Common Market Treaty on the Federal and State Government*, Federal Printing) (Bericht und Antrag des Ausschusses fuer Arbeit und Sozialordnung, Bundestagsdrucksachen 7/534 und 7/3782).

21. Marie Schlei and Dorothea Brueck, *Wege zur Selbstbestimmung: Sozialpolitik als Mittel der Emanzipation* (*Roads to Self-determination: Social Policy as Means to Emancipation*) (Cologne and Frankfurt: Europaeische Verlagsanstalt, 1976), p. 126. Both women are friends of the unions and Social-Democratic party officials. Schlei is state secretary in the office of the prime minister.

22. J. Rutenfranz and W. Rohmert, *Arbeitswissenschaftliche Beurteilung der Belastung und Beanspruchung an unterschiedlichen industriellen Arbeitsplaetzen* (*Scientific Analysis of Stress and Demands in Varying Industrial Workplaces*) (Bonn: Bundesminister fuer Arbeit und Sozialordnung, 1975); hereinafter referred to as *The Report*.

23. Rutenfranz and Rohmert, *The Report*, p. 22.

24. See particularly the critique and commentary prepared by Hans K. Weng, I.G. Metall, Frankfurt, August 1975, in which he analyzes a number of metalworkers' contracts for their early recognition of factors emphasized in the report.

25. One of the most careful studies of women's wages in trade unions has been done by Lisel Winkelstraeter of I.G. Chemie, *Frauenentlohnung kritisch betrachtet* (*A Critical View of Women's Wages*) (Hannover, 1975).

26. Meidner and Öhman, *Fifteen Years*.

27. These matters are discussed both in Andersson, "Collective Bargaining," and with somewhat differing terminology—at least as translated—in Edgren et al., *Wage Formation*.

28. Gösta Edgren, Karol-Olof Faxén, Clas-Erik Odhner, *Wage Formation and the Economy* (London: George Allen & Unwin, 1973), p. 47.

29. In 1969 the white-collar unions in private industry (TCO-PTK) broke away from the LO pattern and negotiated a five-year agreement with SAF. The 1977 negotiations saw them, however, sitting side by side for the first time with LO in central negotiations. At one point in the early years a settlement for government workers also upset the course of LO bargaining by instituting new wage scales which in effect in their turn became the pattern for LO-SAF.

30. Sweden has an Equality Commission established by former Prime Minister Olof Palme as part of his office in 1972. With the change in government in 1976, the Commission was reorganized as a parliamentary body representing all the parties. Its function is to study and report on present practice of equality in all phases of society and to recommend legislation which may correct inequities. It is not an administrative agency. The present chairperson of the Commission, a prominent member of one of the government parties, and other women in the coalition are committed to drafting a law and bringing it through under the present government. Women of this persuasion with whom I talked promised that by 1979 Sweden will have such a law.

31. One important piece of legislation affecting women was the extension of health insurance to cover five days a year of paid leave for care of sick members of the family, a right extended to male as well as female workers. The unions are generally credited with having provided the example as well as the pressure to bring about this legislation. For details see, Schlei and Brueck, *Wege zur Selbstbestimmung*, pp. 70–71.

32. *Gleiche Chancen fuer Frauen? Berichte und Erfahrungen in Briefen an die Praesidentin des Deutschen Bundestages* (Heidelberg and Karlsruhe: G. F. Mueller, Juristischer Verlag, 1977).

33. Barbara Stigler, *Die Mitbestimmung der Arbeiterin: Frauen zwischen traditioneller Familienbindung und gewerkschaftlichem Engagement im Betrieb* (*Codetermination of Women Workers: Women between Traditional Family Ties and Trade Union Engagement in the Plant*) (Schriftenreihe des Forschungsinstituts der Friedrich-Ebert Stiftung, vol. 123; Bonn and Bad Godesberg: Verlag Neue Gesellschaft, 1976). Although the group as a whole can be described as inclining strongly to traditional views, Stigler finds a significant difference in attitudes between women who are union or works council functionaries or are ready to take on such functions and those who are disinterested in such activity. The differences are measurable in terms of commitment to work, interest in having more information in matters affecting the plant and work, and of sensitivity to the disadvantagement of women in respect to their male colleagues, as well as of disapproval of sex differentiation in job assignment, traditional ideology about the family, and male dominance in the plant and in the family (see particularly pp. 200–201).

34. Ibid., p. 164.

35. W. Loewisch, W. Gitter, and A. Mennel, "Welche rechtlichen Massnahmen sind vordringlich um die tatsaechliche Gleichstellung der Frauen mit den Maennern im Arbeitsleben zu gewaehrleisten?" *Gutachten fuer den 50. Deutschen Juristentag.* (What Legal Steps Are Necessary to Assure Actual

Equality of Men and Women in Work Life?" *White Paper for the 50th Meeting of the Juridical Association*) (Muenchen: C. H. Beck'sche Verlagsbuchhandlung, 1974).

36. Schlei and Brueck, *Wege zur Selbstbestimmung*, p. 135.

37. SAF-LO, *Agreement on Action to Further Equality between Men and Women at Work* (SAF Doc. No. 166; mimeo.).

38. SAF-LO-PTK, *Agreement Concerning Actions Intended to Further Equality between Men and Women at Work* (SAF Doc. No. 121; mimeo.).

39. Ministry of Finance, *Circular*, Aug. 19, 1976 (mimeo.).

40. Ibid.

41. *Act on Codetermination at Work* (SAF Doc. No. 1532, effective Jan. 1, 1977; mimeo.).

42. These affiliates of TCO represent white-collar workers respectively in private industry and in local government.

43. One area of public service is not yet included under a specific equality policy. Local government employees have no such ordinance. SKTF operates, however, under an agreement similar to that for private industry (interview with Eva Falkenberg, SKTF, Stockholm, May 16, 1977).

44. In consequence of these facts, Swedish unions have introduced child care in one of their major training centers, Brunsvik, and considered it in others. More significantly, however, the unions are already moving to decentralize their schools, placing major emphasis on providing training programs at district or even local levels in mainly nonresidential sequences. German unions have on the whole dropped the child care issue and are not discussing decentralization of their education programs.

45. "The policy of wage solidarity . . . gets more support from the high income earners who lose by it, than from the low income earners, who gain by it. This is because it is chiefly LO's high income members who take part in the extremely wide-ranging program of study courses which inculcate the unionistic ideology" (Leif Lewin, "Union Democracy," *Working Life in Sweden* no. 3 [Dec. 1977]).

For a realistic analysis of the persuasiveness of these elements in German collective bargaining, see Claudia Pinl, *Das Arbeitnehmer Patriarchat*, pp. 30–63.

46. Renger repeatedly notes that women meet a blank wall when taking complaints to their works councillors. Pinl in her chapter on "Der Betriebstrat als Pascha" ("The Works Councillor as Pasha") quotes verbatim from an interview with such a councillor at a plant in the Rhineland. He speaks of "typical women's work for which men are not suitable" (p. 66); "outdoor cleaning is physically heavy work which women ought not to be asked to do" (p. 67); "women are not employed in weaving for a special reason—the male workers were clever enough to make clear to them that often the weaver has to bend over the shaft in such a way that the upper body touches it; that would mean that certain parts of the female body would be brought into contact with it. In order not to get involved in such a possibility, the women on the advice of their male colleagues withdrew their applications for consideration for this work" (pp. 67–68).

3 Marguerite J. Lorée

EQUAL PAY AND EQUAL OPPORTUNITY LAW IN FRANCE

The package of law reforms on equal pay and equal opportunity enacted since the Second World War—most of them in the 1970s—is part of the century-long struggle French women fought to establish their right to equality under the law. The laws were passed in response to several economic and political changes, including the growth of the paid female labor force and the existence of a majority female electorate. But still more important were the attitudinal changes among the younger generation, especially their dramatic reassessment of sex-role dichotomies and traditional values and lifestyles.

We cannot yet fully assess the effectiveness of all the reforms. Complete equality through the enforcement of legislation invalidating unequal pay and unequal access and opportunity is far from being achieved. Nevertheless, it is possible to evaluate the impact of some of the reforms. This chapter will focus on two sets of reforms that are related to the evolution of the principle of equal rights as it gradually has come to encompass women, first in the public sector—the revision of the civil service statutory legislation—and then in the private sector—the 1972 Equal Pay Act.

In addition, the chapter will outline some of the major reforms aimed at ending discriminatory practices in equal access and equal opportunity for women in the labor market. The problem of occupational segregation remains one of the most acute labor issues, and the attempts to implement equal pay legislation have proved that equal opportunity and equal access are necessary preconditions to achieving equal pay.

Ultimately, however, the question is whether the law can actually change attitudes. (I will discuss this in the concluding section.) Certainly, French women are reluctant to wait another century for full integration in social, political, and economic life. But are they themselves ready to fight for the enforcement of legislation that though limited and sometimes inefficient has the merit of being available and that can be improved?

EQUALITY UNDER THE LAW: THE HISTORICAL FRAMEWORK

When the French Revolution ushered in a new egalitarian era in 1789, French women took the opportunity to claim the right to "better education as a major means that would provide them at least some way to become less totally dependent on men."[1] The men of the revolution called them dangerous revolutionaries and, in 1793, sent them to the scaffold, or back to their homes.

The 1804 Civil Code, often referred to as the Code Napoléon, an amended version of which is still in force, likewise denied women any rights as citizens. The only gains women had made during the revolutionary era that were kept in the Civil Code were legal age of majority (set at twenty-one for both girls and boys) and equal inheritance rights for brothers and sisters. Only childless widows and single women over twenty-one were recognized under civil law. A woman was expected to obey her husband or nearest male kin. For her, marriage was "civil death"; her person and her property were owned by her husband, while he lived, and by her male children after he died. Women were legally held in tutelage, and their fathers, husbands, and sons were held responsible for their actions. Though according to the Penal Code they could be tried and sentenced by the courts, the Civil Code sanctioned the superiority of men over women from cradle to grave.

The long struggle for the principle of equality under the law, which encompasses the extension to women of such rights as the right to work, equal pay, and civil rights, has been closely linked with the history of the struggle for women's rights since the 1789 Revolution. Both the 1848 and 1871 revolutions were felt by feminist pioneers of the time to be a revival of the egalitarian spirit that would enable women to be acknowledged at last as equal beings and citizens. But their hopes were dashed when they failed to convince their contemporaries that they were entitled to equal rights.

Between 1830 and 1870, the female labor force increased dramatically. Though the short-lived revolutionary government of the Commune de Paris (March 18–May 27, 1871) defined the right to the equal pay–equal work principle as a right that should apply to all workers, this concept was only enacted piecemeal. For instance, the 1907 Labor Code was an attempt to protect the individual worker from employers' reprisals; the growth of a unionized labor movement was acknowledged through such acts as those of March 21, 1884, and March 12, 1920, which enabled workers to organize collectively. Even for male workers, the equal pay–equal work principle started to be applied only after 1936, when it became part of the collective bargaining issues.[2]

Meanwhile, between 1871 and 1945, women's movements and associations started to fight for reforms that would provide better coverage to women workers and improve the status of women in society. Their aims can be listed under a few headings: the right to work, as an alternative to prostitution, stressing as a corollary equal pay for male and female workers; civil rights, with an emphasis on the rights of married women to control their own property; the right to equality in education and career opportunities; the right to vote (though such a right was considered less important than the redress of the social, legal, and economic grievances suffered by women).

The achievements of these pioneers improved the status of women workers and allowed women to enter professional careers. The enacting of "protective legislation," for instance, dramatically improved the conditions of women workers.[3] The 1892 Act still grouped them with children and apprentices, but it acknowledged their existence as workers, which meant granting them the right to work. In 1907, they gained the right to the free disposal of their earnings.

Yet women were barred from equal access. The reforms of the educational system, for example, granted women access only to sex-segregated education. Though they were finally granted "civil capacity" in 1938, they acquired full citizenship only when they finally received the right to vote and eligibility to run for office on April 21, 1944. Finally, on October 27, 1946, the Preamble to the Constitution stated the principle of the right to equality under the law with its corollary principle prohibiting sex discrimination.

Equal Pay. On December 10, 1952, France ratified the Equal Remuneration Convention 100 of the International Labor Organization. On March 25, 1957, it ratified Article 119 of the Treaty of Rome setting up the Economic European Community. In 1965, three years after the EEC Council urged its members to take steps to enforce the equal pay principle for women and men, the Ministry of Labor under Labor Minister Granval created a study committee on women's work, which was reorganized in 1971 as a joint committee on women's work (a division of the Ministry of Labor with a specific status and enlarged powers). The committee gave priority to issues concerning the status of working women with a view to promoting such principles as equal pay and equal opportunity. Among the results were the 1972 Equal Pay Act, which outlawed discriminatory practices in earnings, and the 1975 Act, which outlawed discriminatory practices in hiring and firing policies based on sex.

Equal access. Married women were still handicapped by their civil status. They had to wait until 1965 to be totally emancipated from a marital status that prevented them from becoming breadwinners without their husband's authorization (though tacit agreement became the rule in most cases after the Second World War) and from managing their own property. They had to wait still longer for a revision of the "paternal authority" principle. (Since June 4, 1970, it has been replaced in legislation by the principle of "parental authority," though the notion of "male head of family" has not yet been completely abolished.) Though birth control was made legal in 1967, women were not granted the right to reproductive freedom and responsible choice until the June 28, 1974, Abortion Act (to be reassessed in 1979).

Since the appointment of a secretary of state for the status of women in July 1974 (replaced by a delegate for the status of women from September 1976 to September 1978 and reappointed with extended powers in September 1978), priority has been given to equal employment opportunity through revision of educational and professional training systems, readjustment of working schedules compatible with family commitments such as maternity and child-rearing, job desegregation, and reassessment of parental roles. Legislation has been reviewed in order to reconcile family and professional activities for both men and women. By 1981, in accordance with the VII Plan's forecast set up by the Commissariat au Plan (the government agency in charge of the overall policy guidelines for a given period, in this case 1976–1981), the proposed package of reforms concerning the legislation dealing with the status of women should be implemented. Steps to reduce remaining inequalities in order to promote the entry of woman at all levels of public life, including employment are being taken.

EQUAL PAY

The Preamble to the 1946 Constitution (and later the Preamble to the 1958 Constitution) proclaimed that "the law guarantees to women the same equal rights as to men."[4] It places women on an equal footing with men in all spheres of economic and social life. In the area of labor, this meant that women should be granted equal pay for generally equal work. In the public sector, the Civil Service Statute of October 19, 1946, which covers all salaried state employees, was the first legal instrument to apply the principle. In the private sector, the major legal instrument was to be the Equal Pay Act of December 22, 1972.

The public sector

For career civil servants, and those government employees classified by statute as equivalent to civil servants, the merit system prevented pay discrimination at least in the lower grades: the equal pay principle was applied *ipso facto* since salaries were based on an index classification and grade rating for each occupation. The salary structure of the public sector, therefore, appeared to be relatively simple. The real discrimination began at the entry level (for those jobs where qualification requirements made women ineligible—for instance, military training) and in the area of promotion. Earnings gaps, therefore, were mostly linked with the exclusion of women from the higher grades and positions.

The 1946 General Statute of the Civil Service, as amended by the 1959 General Statute of the Civil Service, covers about 20 percent of the labor force. Numerically, the proportion of women entering the civil service has steadily grown, from 30 percent in 1936, to 42 percent in 1967, to roughly 50 percent in 1975.[5] But this numerical parity does not take into account the disparities in categories and grades. There are fewer female career civil servants, and those who do exist are concentrated in the lower grades, which has a direct effect on their earnings, as well as in specific professional groupings (such as education) and specific functions (such as clerical tasks).

In general, civil servants are paid according to the pay scale for their grade in the hierarchy. In addition, salaries may differ on account of a number of factors: the *base salary*, corresponding to the employee's rating, out of which contributions to pension plans and social security coverage are deducted; a *housing allowance*, which may vary according to the base salary and the area; a *family allowance*; and *specific allowances and benefits* such as incentive bonuses, overtime, risk bonuses (police), or compensations attached to the nature of the function (magistrates, higher civil servants).

Civil service employees are distributed into four main categories, labeled A, B, C, and D. The categories correspond roughly to the American rating system, D being the equivalent of GS-1 to GS-8 and A corresponding to GS-16 to GS-18. Within the categories, classification indexes are set up according to a general salary scale: net rating is from 100 to 650 for most categories; at the higher senior levels, civil servants are rated according to letter coefficients corresponding to a ranking of earnings from 1 to 10.8. Categories depend on the level of education required of applicants.

Career civil servants are recruited by the civil service through a system of entrance examinations. Applicants must fulfill certain conditions for eligibility (French citizenship, a clean police record, a given level of studies and degrees, an age limit, and so on). Upward mobility takes place within the administration that recruited the employee, and according to requisites of the category. Within the category, employees may be promoted either through choice[6] (appointment to a higher grade) or by seniority (grade rating). They may change from one category to a higher one provided that they take the internal examinations or are eligible under certain conditions set up in the specific statutes of their administrations in accordance with the rules of the General Statute of the Civil Service. In addition, no career civil servant can be dismissed or discharged unless found guilty of a "serious offense" before reaching retirement age. Actually, this ruling guarantees employment security and explains the relatively high number of non-career civil servants (most of them female) in the public sector.

In spite of its drawbacks, the Civil Service Statute of 1946 did set an example by enforcing the equal pay principle in an area of labor that had a reputation for occupational segregation. The statute stated explicitly that any discrimination between male and female civil servants was unlawful. In this regard, it represented a major step forward, especially when compared with the private sector at that time.

The private sector

Within the scope of this chapter, it is nearly impossible to take into consideration all the aspects of unequal pay for work of equal value in privately owned businesses. Nevertheless, this sector employs the majority of the labor force, at least 50 percent of them women, so we must attempt a summary.[7]

In most areas of the private sector (industry, services, the professions) and for most white-collar and blue-collar employees, disparities in earnings are due to indirect sex discrimination, reinforced by such factors as occupation, age, and qualifications. The female labor force is still concentrated in lower-skilled, low-paying occupations, in lower-status positions. Girls still choose patterns of employment that do not put them on an equal footing with boys. Occupational segregation has a direct impact on earnings; equality would require setting up a comparative job-evaluation and job-grading system that would not be systematically detrimental to female occupations and qualifications. Compounding all this are the intricacies of the various pay systems and the complexity of the criteria that determine a given pay-scale structure within a specific plant, workshop or department—criteria whose distinctions vary from one occupation to another and from one industrial sector to another.[8]

Before the enacting of the 1972 Equal Pay Act, other laws had dealt with the issue of equal pay for women. On July 30, 1946, the Ambroise Croizat Decree rescinded provisions that had enabled employers to apply deductions to women's wages and salaries. The Act of February 11, 1950, as amended on July 13, 1971, provided for specific measures to be taken in collective agreements regarding the enforcement of equal pay for equal work for women and young employees. After 1946, and especially after 1952, when France ratified ILO Convention 100, and 1957, when France entered the European Economic Community, more bills were drafted. But these were either killed or pigeonholed.

The equal pay bill was debated and approved on November 21, 1972, by the House of Representatives in one sitting. It was then sent to the Senate, which discussed and approved it on December 13, 1972. All amendments were rejected by both houses. Most amendments aimed at providing more drastic punishment for offenders (the employers) and at securing concrete means of enforcement, such as the objective criteria to be used in order to adjust earnings to the "value" of the task performed. One amendment proposed that paying unequal wages be punished, like theft, by imprisonment. Most representatives opposed this suggestion; they felt that employers guilty of nonwillful discrimination should only be deemed "guilty of neglect."

Opponents of the bill contended that female labor would prove too costly. They argued that employers hiring a majority of women would be penalized by being put on an unequal footing with their European competitors not subject to similar legal constraints. The litany of prejudices against female employment also were reiterated: women gave priority to their family responsibilities; their rate of absenteeism was higher; the gap on earnings was, after all, "normal" since women were not main breadwinners once they married.

Representative Michel Rocard (Socialist party) pointed out, the text of the bill outlawed discrimination, but did not provide any means for detecting discriminatory practices, thus allowing the subtle discriminations produced by job evaluation. As long as work evaluation systems attributed lower ratings to the so-called female work characteristics (speed, manual dexterity, and the like) while attributing higher ratings to so-called male characteristics (physical strength, unpleasant working conditions), job evaluations and wage practices would undervalue women.

Supporters of the bill viewed it as a means of ending the gross inequities and inherent sexism reflected in unequal pay practices. Lengthy preparatory studies had revealed the intricacies of unequal pay scales—for instance, the existence of sex discrimination in occupational titles, the need for reviewing traditional job classification criteria,[9] the need for reassessing women's work in order to improve the status of the female labor force. The bill was also seen as compatible with the equal-rights reforms being enacted for other areas (for instance, the revision of marriage legislation in 1965). Besides, they said, it was a matter of public policy and a response to the pressures of the female electorate as well as those of the growing female labor force.[10]

Hope was expressed that such legislation would provide women, and men, with a legal tool to combat deeply ingrained sexist attitudes in labor practices as a whole. So far, the main tool had been the Act of February 11, 1950, which had institutionalized collectively bargained settlements.

Actually, such agreements were not devoid of discriminatory effects: agreements that provided for a 10 cent hourly increase for labor grades containing mostly women (generally jobs with lower skill ratings) and a 14 cent an hour increase for grades containing mostly men were current practice.

There were some misgivings about the practicality of implementing the bill's legal machinery. It had already been noted in a previous report released by management representatives that "work of equal value" could give rise to "misinterpretation."[11] On the other hand, the text implied that women were placed on equal footing with men as regards access to employment, training, and opportunity, which was far from reality.

The Equal Pay Act (loi sur l'égalité de rémunération entre hommes et femmes) went into effect December 22, 1972. The act and its implementation decree were hailed as a breakthrough by working women. Women accounted for nearly three-fourths of the growth of the overall labor force between 1968 and 1975, and since the majority of them were on payroll, as the 1975 Population Census revealed, they were covered by the legislation. This meant that six and a half million women out of the eight and a half million in the labor force, or 38.5 percent of the entire labor force, would be affected by the act.[12]

The final provisions established a definition of "remuneration" that was consistent with ILO Convention 100: it not only covered base wage and salary but such components as fringe benefits and bonuses. Title 2 extended coverage to all types of wage systems, operating in private firms, and provided that each of these systems must be applied identically for men and women. In other words, the pay rate for women would be determined according to the same measuring unit used in determining the rate of earnings for men. Female pay rates would be based on such criteria as degrees, seniority rights, and any other rights entering into the definition of the task performed, as set up in job classification systems and occupational analysis systems, and would no longer take into account such elements as an individual's on-the-job training experience. The focus was on job classification and not on individual performance.

Title 3 of the law nullified prior clauses mentioned in contracts, collective settlements, conventions, and any other documents that might transgress the principle of equal pay for work of equal value. Readjustments of the rates of pay were to be based on the higher rate given. The same treatment was to be applied to both sexes.

Title 4 extended the enforcement of the act to those relations between employers and paid employees that were not covered by the Industrial Relations Labor Code provisions. This ensured coverage for farm workers and for other types of employer-employee contracts.

The March 27 implementation decree defined the tasks of investigators and the litigation process established in Title 1. It set up the amount of the fines and specified the various departments in charge of enforcing the provisions. It also required employers to cooperate with the investigators, and to produce all documents relevant to the assessment of pay scales. With respect to enforcement, the law compelled employers to post the act and its implementation decree on the premises of any establishment hiring or employing female personnel.

Title 5 assigned the authority to enforce the act to manpower and labor inspectors, rural social-legislation investigators, and investigators from other areas of competence, aided by the police if necessary. Such officers are career civil servants. Investigators handle complaints as well as enforce the provisions. If the investigators find against them and move towards legal proceedings, employers and employees may choose to get assistance (for instance, by engaging private counsel).

Violators are subject to a criminal penalty—a fine of 600–1,000 French francs (approximately $150–250) for each injured party. For a subsequent offense within a year, the penalty is 2,000 French francs (about $450) and a ten-day jail term. Employers who fail to post the act or refused to disclose pay scales and related documents are liable to smaller fines.

The scope of the act was broadened in two significant respects: first, the equal pay principle was extended to all sectors, including semi-public and private sectors, and the concept of equal work understood as work of equal value was emphasized, which implied the standard of "comparable worth" as the basis for comparing men's and women's jobs. On the other hand, the law was not as strong as it could have been had it taken into account other enforcement amendments.

The effects of litigation

The 1972 Equal Pay Act and its implementation decree did not change overnight the gross disparities of earnings between men and women. In September 1976, in fact, the Department of Labor's Committee on Women's Work called the act a relative failure. It also recommended a few remedies.[13]

One set of shortcomings concerned the difficulty of enforcing the law, both through administrative agency investigation and through court proceedings. Indeed, the machinery of enforcement was crucial to the law's success or failure. Extensive powers were given to the Labor Department inspectors; the fact that they (or the complainant) could seek legal redress showed the government's determination to encourage positive action through the combination of litigation and administrative enforcement mechanisms. But the intricate maze of pay structures made it difficult to trace discriminatory practices with regard to equal pay. That and the lack of any clear-cut definition of "work of equal value" meant that formal inquiries could hardly secure any proof that would stand up in judicial proceedings.

As we saw, provisions are to be enforced by inspectors who are alerted to potential violations through routine investigations or when aggrieved employees apply to their shopstewards, who in turn inform the labor inspector. An investigation is then conducted. If the officer concludes that the act has been violated, the employer may request a counterinvestigation. If the officer concludes that there has not been any legal discrimination, the employee may request a counterinvestigation. Either party may seek legal aid. Investigators seek to reconcile the parties. If conciliation or voluntary compliance fails, a suit can be filed by the aggrieved party before the industrial tribunals, whose judgment can be appealed in the higher courts.

Neither the act nor its implementation decree specified a time limit for resolution. The length of time needed to settle a case might vary considerably, depending on the enforcement process and the backlog of cases; if a suit is filed, it may take years to reach conclusion. The only time specification was that a repetition of the offense within the year was punishable by a higher fine and jail penalty.

The first lawsuit to be filed and prosecuted under the 1972 Equal Pay Act was judged on December 6, 1974, by a local industrial court. Fifty-three female employees of a department store complained they had been subject to illegal pay discrimination. The court ruled that the employer had violated the act: he had failed to apply the provisions of the collective agreement, which set up job classifications and stipulated that each of the categories defined in the settlement could cover different types of occupations. Since the same salaries should apply to all jobs within the same category "unless otherwise provided," the court granted back pay and attorney's fees to the employees. The employer appealed to a higher court, which annulled the judgment.[14] The ruling may be considered a breakthrough, but one should also bear in mind that the ruling of an industrial court is not precedent-setting.

As of February 1975, only eighteen complaints had been acted upon.[15] The very fact that so few cases were registered by the Department of Labor in three years illustrates the difficulties investigators met in spite of their extensive powers. Most cases were settled out of court: employers were willing to readjust pay scales gradually. But such readjustment did not eliminate earnings gaps resulting from disparities only indirectly linked to sex. Seen in this light, the law proved inefficient, the more so when the findings proved inconclusive in twelve of the cases. In those twelve cases, earnings disparities did exist between men and women but did not fall within the scope of the law. In two of the cases, this was caused by the complexity of the wage structure and policy, which depended in part on subjective criteria such as incentive schemes based upon individual performance or job evaluation systems including individual performance appraisals.

The limited scope of the law was further revealed when the courts attempted to harmonize the policy differences existing under the assortment of laws covering pay and employment practices—the Labor Code provisions regarding female work, collective settlements as set up by the February 11, 1950, Act, not to mention such legislation as private law, social security and health regulations, and statute laws covering specific occupational categories. Since the 1972 law was stronger, more inclusive, and of greater benefit to women than these other laws, it should have contained some provision guaranteeing that it superseded earlier statutes when there were contradictory provisions.

Moreover, the compliance officers had been given very little guidance. They could only take into account certain norms and the enforcement of those norms. In most cases, the very notion of "identical norms" and "objective criteria" was absent. Because conditions of violation could not be established, or because of lack of convincing evidence, such cases were unsuitable for litigation—hence the small number of complaints filed and their inconclusive results.

A second problem with the law had to do with how narrowly it defined the basis for making comparisons for purposes of determining equal pay. Actually the Equal Pay Act could only be interpreted as applying to very specific cases. For instance, the labor inspectors can enforce the law if they are able to prove that unequal pay results from unequal evaluation ratings assigned to identical jobs. But the reverse is not necessarily true— that earnings must be the same for different occupations that receive the same job evaluation ratings. In other words, if two dissimilar jobs receive the same evaluation score, and if the wage rate for one job, primarily held by men, is higher than the wage rate for a second job, primarily held by women, this would not be illegal under the equal pay law. Moreover, since the basis of proof is not specified in the law, the courts were often reluctant to interpret strictly the vague terminology of the act.[16]

The main criticism that can be leveled at the enforcement of the 1972 Equal Pay Act is that it does not deal with the fact that job evaluation schemes are themselves discriminatory. In one plant, a small plastic processing company with 180 employees, only one division employed female and male workers in occupational activities that were, on their face, essentially the same. Since men were earning more than women, the labor officer initiated inquiry proceedings in compliance with the act (after

March 1973). The investigation found that, although the tasks performed by female and male employees might look the same, it could be proven that the women actually worked on simpler assembly lines. Therefore, their jobs could be considered as requiring fewer skills and the tasks performed could be termed dissimilar. According to an article of the Labor Code, it is unlawful to hire women in potentially dangerous jobs. Consequently, it was found that it was in fact legal for the employer to use a wage system that resulted in unequal rates of pay. Such a finding underscores how presumably scientific job evaluation systems include criteria that are sex-biased, a subject dealt with by Christof Helberger in Appendix B.

Another significant case dealing with the "comparable worth" problem is *Marcoux et Sté Marcoux-Laffay* v. *X* . . . (a small textile firm). The firm's employer had granted "industriousness bonuses" to his thirteen male knitters; his fifteen female skein examiners felt discriminated against and filed a complaint. On June 11, 1976, the Lyon Court of Appeals upheld the industrial court's award by enjoining the employer to pay fines of 600 French francs (approximately $150) for each female employee. The employer's appeal to the higher Court of Appeals was dismissed on June 22, 1977. Unlike the earlier case, this decision may be considered precedent-setting. It was assumed that, though the employees performed dissimilar tasks, their jobs were to be appraised according to the same performance criteria. Though dissimilar, they could be evaluated as "jobs of comparable worth" and paid the same.

What about higher-level positions that require applicants to possess identical degrees and qualifications? If men and women with identical qualifications hold different jobs, the Equal Pay Act would legally entitle the employer to treat female employees differently, and pay them less. In one semi-public business, for instance, two female applicants were hired for a traditionally male position. Since the original job description of the function called for male employees only, however, a new job classification was created and the women were hired. The subtle differences in titles resulted in a wide disparity in earnings and in access to promotion. (The salary differential was 13 percent in the first years of employment, averaging 24 percent by retirement.) The complainants argued that the classification violated the Equal Pay Act since the scope of responsibility and the tasks assigned were identical for both female and male employees. Due to lengthy judicial proceedings, the case was still pending in 1978.[17]

In short, because of the way equal pay was defined, the Equal Pay Act did not touch upon the fundamental reason for wage gaps—occupational segregation. In one large corporation, some female operators complained that they were not paid according to the same pay scale as men in the same category. Actually, the pay differential resulted from unequal incentive bonuses and different individual working schedules. The inquiry revealed that male operators and some female operators had benefited from an incentive bonus tied to a shortening of working hours. While the benefit had been integrated into the salary of operators hired afterwards, a disparity remained between the newly hired male operators and some of the female operators who had been hired earlier. Readjustment forced the corporation to change its pay-scale structure. It was decided to standardize the incentive bonuses, but nevertheless to grant certain categories special bonuses, in accordance with the collective agreements that created distortions in the pay scale by entitling some operators to get bonuses on account of special duties.

The issue raised by this example shows that the shortening of work hours in conjunction with extra compensation can prove discriminatory in the long run. But according to the investigators' findings, disparities in earnings associated with the performance of jobs classified as different could not be interpreted as discriminatory under the law.

Limitations and remedies

Over the period 1973–1975, it was proved that the equal pay for work of equal value principle could not be applied as long as the comparable worth of jobs was still rated according to male and female stereotypes. Gaps in earnings reflected the overall job segregation of the labor force, with women concentrated in the low-prestige, low-skilled, low-pay categories of the economy. Women were still considering "secondary" workers, and second-class citizens in the labor market.

Biased job evaluation systems might reflect the effect of labor market trends. A small parachemical corporation, for example, which was having increasing difficulty attracting male applicants, decided to upgrade job classifications for positions held by men, while maintaining its female employees at a lower job classification within the same category. This may be an extreme example, but even in the case of fair job evaluation systems, women often can not get into the better jobs because of the lack of equal opportunities.

Current trends of employment opportunity, in fact, provide one of the main obstacles to enforcing equal pay legislation. Stratification and the high differentiation of roles have increasingly produced sex-based segregation. The law of supply and demand has assured that this "double-tier" market based on the segregation of male and female occupations has had a direct or indirect effect on earnings: for one thing, women applying for "male" jobs would not ordinarily have the same degrees or qualifications as men and therefore would get lower wages.

Since the majority of the female labor force has fewer professional degrees, or has degrees that are not always adjusted to the job requirements (for instance, a degree in needlework for a job requiring a degree in electricity), a woman might receive lower earnings even if she performs exactly the same job as her male counterpart. Moreover, in "female" occupations, the higher level of competition among women would result in lower earnings. The first step to achieving equal pay, therefore, must be to ensure women equal access to the labor market by enacting legislation to create the *de facto* conditions enabling women to choose their status according to their own priorities, to harmonize family and professional life, and to break down the barriers of occupational segregation.

In short, equal opportunity is a major prerequisite to equal pay. As long as women were not given equal opportunity in apprenticeship, training, and skills and were covered by protective labor legislation based on a nineteenth-century image of labor conditions, they would remain concentrated in the low-skilled, low-paying jobs. Most cases would then appear unsuitable for litigation since there would appear to be no violation of the equal pay principle.

Recommendations for improving implementation by incorporating equal opportunity legislation were made by the public authorities as well as by representatives of both employers and labor unions. In 1975 and 1976, for example, the Department of Labor's Committee on Women's Work recommended, among other measures, the enactment of some instrument to provide equality of opportunity and treatment for women through professional training, help for women re-entering the labor market, and the like. (This would be in accordance with Convention 111, Resolution on Equality of Opportunity and Treatment for Women Workers, established by the ILO Conference on June 25, 1975, and would be in compliance with the EEC directive.) Similarly, employers have agreed with the need to revise and update job classification structures, and to set up flexible work hours and day-care facilities to reduce the difficulties faced by female employees who are trying to harmonize professional and family life.[18]

THE CIVIL SERVICE EXAMPLE

The historical background

We can get a clearer picture of the status of equal opportunity policy in France if we take civil service reforms as an example. The tradition of female employment in the civil service dates back to the late eighteenth century, when women began taking jobs as post office employees and teachers. Legally, of course, special exceptions were needed for such employment, since women had neither civil nor political rights, which were prerequisites to civil service employment. The status of French women in the civil service has often been proposed as an example of access to equal opportunity, at least in the traditional female fields and positions. In 1880, women worked mostly in education, in girls' schools. At the turn of the century and during the First World War, they filtered into the lower ranks of the civil service administrations as typists and secretaries. In 1936, they constituted about 30 percent of the 510,000 civil service employees. After 1920, a few female civil servants reached relatively high positions, but most were employed in minor positions in sex-segregated occupations and fields (the post office, health, education, social services, and of course in educational and penal institutions for women).

Though the civil service regulations did not specifically require women to remain single, most career women did not marry. Since women were not legally citizens until 1944, access to civil service employment depended on the goodwill of both the administration, and if they were married, on their husbands. A husband could prevent his wife from entering the civil service or could compel her to resign. In 1939, a famous case went all the way from the administrative courts and courts of appeal to the Supreme State Council, which upheld the husband's right to prevent his wife from staying away from her household. Mme Pagès had to resign from the post office administration, thus losing her rights to promotion and to a retirement pension.[19]

Under the Vichy regime (1940–1945), the French government undertook to eliminate women from the civil service. According to the executive orders of October 11, 1940, and September 14, 1941, in order "to fight against unemployment and to promote family policies," an administration was forbidden to hire or recruit married women or women with an "acknowledged quasi-marital status."[20] Employment quotas were set up in each category that required female personnel.

Women were granted full civil and political rights on April 21, 1944, by an act of the provisional government. On April 11, 1945, legislation entitled them to become judges and public prosecutors. On October 9, 1945, an ordinance created the Ecole Nationale d'Administration (National School of Administration), which has become one of the most prestigious institutions of higher education; it opened up to women access to the higher civil service positions. These rights were reiterated in the 1946 French Constitution. Thus, women became eligible for public office and could have access to the higher levels of the civil service hierarchy in most fields and administrations, the major exemption being the Interior and War departments, where military service was statutorily required.

Article 7

The General Statute of the Civil Service of October 19, 1946, was quite explicit about equal pay and equal access practices. According to the rigid civil service pay structure, which was based on the coded grade and merit system, salaried employees' earnings must be the same, provided that they fulfilled the requirements for entry (civil service entrance examinations, academic credentials, age limit, and so on). But even the apparently sex-neutral policies did not mean that women actually had equal access to occupations because those very requirements barred many women from such access.

In addition, Article 7 provided that "no distinction for the enactment of this Statute is established between male and female civil servants, *except when otherwise provided for in special provisions.*"[21] This meant that, although women had the same formal rights to access, equality of access depended on the discretionary power of administrations, which could set up bylaws defining the "nature" of the function in such a way that women could be excluded from higher-status, decision-making, more financially rewarding positions.

The Civil Service Commission as well as the Supreme State Council could bar women from certain occupations and categories by arguing that the position was inappropriate for women because of the "nature" of the commitments and duties involved. As a matter of course, the civil service discriminated against married women simply on account of their marital and family status; the assumption was that a woman could not commit herself fully to a higher function because, of course, it was "natural" for her primary commitment to be to her family. But though single women had more opportunities, they too were discriminated against. For one thing, the argument ran, their "feminine nature" would make them more easily influenced and would undermine their authority. For another, the traditional dichotomy of roles meant that some positions—prefects, the diplomatic corps—should be held only by men, because such fields required a "male image," while others—health, education, social services—should be held by women. This attitude thus circumscribed female civil servants into relatively few sectors of public life, excluding them from the more powerful and prestigious positions.

Litigation before the Supreme State Council reveals the latent sexism and ambiguity prevailing in Article 7. On January 23, 1950, a woman was appointed by decree to the position of administrative officer (which corresponds to an executive-level position in the top category of the civil service). The all-male administrative officers' national union of the department requested the State Council (the supreme judiciary authority) to rescind the decree. On January 6, 1956, the State Council annuled the decree; its precedent-setting decision was based on the grounds that "the prerequisite conditions to carry out the duties required by the position as defined by the statutory bylaws of this Administration are of a nature which legally entitle the exclusion of female applicants from the said position."[22]

The State Council interpreted the General Statute of the Civil Service as subject to governmental override: "If, as a rule, women have had access to all public offices in the same conditions as men since 1946, it was only without prejudice of the lawful right of the government to bring out exemptions to the said rule."[23] In other words, women could be legally barred from positions if the government or the State Council decided to rescind a departmental order.

To be fair, some other rulings of the State Council have not been detrimental to women. But such litigation is lengthy, and sometimes the final ruling is pronounced after years of judicial procedure.

Article 7 was revised on February 4, 1959, in the Civil Service General Statute. The revision made more explicit the meaning of the terminology prohibiting sex discrimination "except when otherwise provided for." The revised version stated that "exceptions" depended on the specific statutory bylaws defining the "nature of functions," thus introducing the concept of "bona fide occupational qualifications."[24] In other words, the various statutory laws of the different administrations would set up criteria for eligibility based on the duties and performance relevant to the position and should not disqualify persons of one sex on account of their sexual characteristics. It did, however, leave open the possibility of requirements related to, but not defined by, gender (physical capabilities, discretionary promotions, marital and family status, geographic mobility, military service).

Despite the revision, the civil service still reflected the societal patterns of occupational segregation. Women were concentrated in the lower ranks in clerical occupations and in fields traditionally related to their stereotyped sex roles: health, education, social services, women's affairs in the departments of Labor or Justice. Eligibility for higher levels was made particularly difficult for married women because family laws interfered with their professional status. In numerical terms, male civil servants had become the minority, but they still dominated the decision-making levels and key positions,[25] since private law, domestic relations law, and labor law impeded the progress that women might have made through numbers.

Until 1965, domestic relations laws restricted the professional ambitions of married female civil servants. As was mentioned above, their husbands could prevent them from entering a profession or from applying for a job. They were not available for transfer or travel, since, as the legal head of the household, the husband could dictate the legal place of residence. In fact, the administrations had to provide transfer for married female civil servants whenever their husbands moved for professional reasons. The rule applied until 1970, when reform of the domestic relations law provided that both partners were entitled to choose the legal place of residence. In the case of two married civil servants, the "transfer rule" was then applied for either spouse, since in accordance to the Family Code, the administration had to provide married employees with jobs that would "enable them to share the same place of residence."[26] The updating of family law therefore, had a special impact for women in the civil service.

Other changes in private law also created improvements for female civil servants. On July 9, 1970, for example, the National Service Act introduced as an experiment "voluntary female national service," thereby allowing a few women to become eligible for jobs requiring that background. As another example, the updating of the Act of December 23, 1972, allowed reversion of the retirement pension to all spouses of civil servants, not just widows.

Article 7 was revamped again on July 10, 1975. According to this revision, only a very few positions could specifically be reserved for one sex or the other. The State Council was entitled to set up a list of occupational activities open to men or women only in accordance with the recommendations of the Civil Service Commission and the joint technical committees. Once men and women were free to enter the same administration, access to promotion and thus to equal earnings was open to all employees according to the merit system and seniority rights.[27]

The updating of Article 7 resulted from constant pressure by the female civil servants themselves, who felt discriminated against in areas and positions that had remained male strongholds. A June 1974 report from the Committee on Women's Work had exposed the unequal opportunities for female civil servants in the higher ranks and in decision-making positions.[28] The report noted that some positive results had been achieved regarding better access at the entry level and the upgrading of the lower grades in the lower-level and mid-level ranges. But in spite of some recent career breakthroughs, female civil servants were effectively barred from the higher grade levels and positions. Moreover, they remained clustered in stereotypical occupational categories and professional groupings.

Priority was to be given to eliminating the sex-discriminatory aspects of the legislation covering employment practices in the civil service. The updating of Article 7 was one major step toward achieving this goal. It was still necessary, however, to change the attitudes of personnel management and the commissions in charge of promotions as well as to motivate women themselves.[29]

FROM EQUAL ACCESS TO EQUAL OPPORTUNITY:
LEGAL REFORMS IN THE 1970s

The civil service experience had helped to identify the problem—the need for a strategy and for reforms that could change basic conditions of employment, thus allowing women to operate differently in the labor market. That meant a drastic reassessment of policies regarding equal access to education, professional training, promotion and careers, re-entry into the labor market, seniority rights, and pension plans.

In the past, occupational segregation had been reinforced by the law either directly or indirectly. There has been a gradual updating and rescinding of protective legislation that barred equal access in occupational categories requiring night work, overtime, heavy lifting, and so on. Legal prohibitions against employment of women in certain occupations (policing, bartending) have been challenged and revoked. The recent domestic relations laws view marriage as a contractual agreement between equal partners and no longer support stereotyped definitons of marital roles.

Unequal access to education and training had also helped to reinforce sex-segregated occupational choices. By 1980, however, the French educational system should be completely integrated, providing equal access to employment through the same placement examinations open to girls and boys.

Legal prohibitions against occupational segregation did not automatically imply that women could have access to the labor market on an equal footing with men. The civil service example proved that point: Its system had not denied women admission, since it applied on apparently sex-neutral employment policy. But the requirements were clearly such that very few women could meet them. So the new sets of reforms were geared toward giving women better means of access.

Access to entry and to the higher levels of the hierarchy were facilitated for women through a series of reforms initiated in the seventies. The plan of action submitted by the secretary of state in charge of Women's Status, Françoise Giroud, recommended the implementation of 111 measures over the years 1976–1981 designed to improve the status of women.

The civil service

Age-limit requirements had proved a handicap for women who wished to apply for jobs in the civil service because the entrance examinations were open only to applicants under thirty, or thirty-five, or forty, depending on the satutory bylaws of the various administrations.

On January 3, 1975 legislation was passed rescinding age-limit requirements for widows compelled to work.

On May 20, 1975, access to public employment was extended to women who have raised their children; they receive a one-year extension of the age limit for each dependent child under sixteen (or over nine). The provision also applies for handicapped dependents.

On August 14, 1975, age limits for access to entrance examinations were extended to forty-five for all applicants to the lower- and mid-level categories. Since the majority of the clerical and secretarial applicants were women, such a measure benefited them especially.

On December 17, 1975, men were granted the legal leave of absence granted to employees who wished to stay at home in order to raise a child, thus updating the 1959 Decree which had granted such leaves of absence to female employees only.

The Act of July 9, 1976, and its July 12, 1976, implementation decree was a major breakthrough for female civil servants. Access to the entrance examinations for the higher categories was open to women up to forty-five years of age provided that they had raised one child. In this case, child-rearing could no longer be considered as jeopardizing equal access, at least at the entry level.

On March 25, 1977, a decree set up a list of civil service categories open to one sex only, as well as a list of administrations and departments providing different entrance examinations and job specifications for men and women. This listing made it more difficult for the administrations to practice sex discrimination in their employment policies.[30]

The private sector

Similar reforms were enacted in the private sector. On January 3, 1975, female heads of family were granted priority of access to professional training. Regarding access to employment, statutes were passed (July 10, 1975, May 20, 1975, and July 9, 1976) giving preference to women whose familial responsibilities had prevented them either from applying for a job on account of age limit or from re-entering their occupation; this meant that maternity and child-rearing were seen as a "national service" that should not interfere with the professional status of female workers.[31]

The most important legal prohibition regarding equality of access was probably the Act of July 11, 1975, which specifically forbade an employer to discriminate on the basis of sex and family status, thus extending to sex discrimination the penalties provided for race discrimination. According to the act, employers are forbidden to refuse to hire or to terminate the legal training period of an employee on account of pregnancy. Violators are subject to a fine and a two-month to one-year imprisonment.

One example may serve to illustrate the importance this law. On July 31, 1976, a restaurant manager dismissed one of the waitresses, who was then pregnant. She brought her case before the conciliation board, which dismissed her claim on the grounds that she could not prove her employer knew about her pregnancy. Moreover, the employer argued that she had been dismissed for professional reasons; he brought proof that she had slapped a kitchen-boy.

The complainant filed an appeal. On May 28, 1978—nearly two years after the firing—the district court of appeals re-examined the case. According to the judges, the 1975 act covered the state of pregnancy, so the complainant was entitled to the benefits of this legislation and her employer had violated the law by dismissing her. But, the court continued, if her dismissal was due to misbehavior, her employer had been legally entitled to dismiss her. The court then recommended further inquiry into the professional offense.

On October 23, 1978, the case came back before the court of appeals. The employer's counsel attempted to prove that the slap was indeed a professional offense justifying dismissal; the complainant's counsel contended that the slap had been a mere jostling and that the vague and contradictory statements of the kitchen-boy and the witnesses did not prove otherwise.

On November 10, 1978, the court of appeals granted the complainant compensatory damages and interest equal to the back pay award and nullified the dismissal. Nevertheless, the judges ruled against reinstatement because of the "incident" between the two employees. The employer is entitled to lodge an appeal.[32]

The controversy over part-time work

The Act of December 27, 1973, institutionalized flexibility of work schedules and part-time work, thus "normalizing" the work discontinuity that had penalized women during the child-rearing years. (In the civil service, part-time work provisions had been the same for both female and male employees since the Act of June 19, 1970, and the implementation decrees of December 23, 1970, and December 23, 1975.)[33] This act and the Decree of June 9, 1975, which modified the implementation of social security systems for part-time workers on payroll, applied to all salaried employees, female and male, although a 1975 official document[34] recommended that priority for enforcing the act should be given to corporations and businesses employing at least 50 percent salaried women. This sex-neutral policy was also applied to working conditions.

One example may serve to illustrate the kind of practices the act could legally prohibit: in November 1975, a textile company required its married female employees to accept reducing their work schedules to part time as an alternative to layoffs.[35]

Though the legislation was not geared specifically to women, it seemed obvious that few men would consider taking part-time employment. (According to the 1975 Population Census, male salaried part-time work was practically nonexistent before age sixty.)[36] Women themselves felt a reluctance to take part-time jobs, since in France part-time work had always been regarded as marginal and unrewarding. Therefore, the public felt some resentment toward regularizing part-time employment. Many thought it was itself discriminatory, allowing employers to hire part-time workers only when needed. Besides, they argued it might create structural segregation and encourage unequal pay practices.

Toward a strategy for change

The best legal strategies for changing the occupational system are geared to specific situations. The numerous reforms enacted in the mid- and late 1970s reflect the emergence of attitudes and lifestyles that question traditional sex and work roles. On the one hand, individuals wish to reconcile their commitments to professional and family life; on the other hand, people increasingly seek a high quality of life, including the freedom to choose their own orientations, which may vary at different life stages. The main difficulty lay in reconciling the "double" status of women as mothers and workers. Maternity and child-rearing had excluded women from equal access whenever employment practices implied that a marital or family status would interfere with professional status. Women were expected to choose between marriage and higher education, between childlessness and a maternity leave that would jeopardize upward occupational mobility. In addition, they were expected to carry out the double burden of job and family responsibilities. As a result, most women felt too drained of energy and ability by such a hectic life to aspire to anything beyond a lower occupational status.

The Act of July 12, 1977, on parental-education leaves went still further in responding to the wishes of men and women for equal commitment to family and occupational roles. Though the mother was to be granted priority, the father would be legally entitled to take such a leave if she could not or would not take it. The act provided that the salaried employee who had chosen the leave would be rehired or be given priority of access to training paid for by the state government.

Toward a reduction of working time

Since the Act of June 21, 1936, the median legal work time has been set at 40 hours per week over a twelve-week period. Extra work hours were to be paid at overtime rates. The maximum length of the work day could not exceed eight hours per day (i.e., a 48-hour week) as established by 1919 acts, but an absolute maximum length of weekly hour schedules could vary. Those absolute maximums have been gradually reduced, from

60 hours per week as of June 18, 1966, decree to 57 hours per week in 1971 to 52 hours per week in 1975. The December 12, 1978, Act (Decree 78.1155) was a further step toward reducing the length of weekly work-hour schedules in a number of occupations requiring specific time-schedules (especially retail businesses, hairdressers, catering, and the like).

The unions have been pressing for a more thorough replanning of work schedules. According to public authorities (see the statement by the labor secretary commenting on this act), the January 2, 1979, Act (*Official Journal*, Jan. 3, 1979) constitutes a first step toward the actual reduction of work schedules and should be geared specifically to women workers. The act sets up a 50-hour-per-week maximum without changing the median 48-hour schedules. But these schedules may be reduced by decree to a 46-hour week though this is still far from the unions' demand for a 35-hour week without reducing pay.

The act also affects the nature of working time. The most positive step may well be the provision regarding the distribution of the schedules. It is no longer unlawful to allow workers and employers to distribute work hours over a four-day period or a four-and-a-half-day period (though the daily work-hour schedule should not exceed ten hours per day) provided that such provisions do not interfere with other specific clauses, such as legal provisions concerning women and youth and collective agreements. Another provision concerns female night work: women executives as well as employees (excluding female manual workers) working in health and welfare establishments and services are entitled to avail themselves of this provision, which gives them the right to work during night hours.

It should be noted, of course, that such replanning of work-time schedules is not a panacea. According to the government, for instance, such planning must be dealt with at a European level so that the measures do not prevent French business and industry from remaining competitive. And, according to economic experts, it cannot be expected to solve the unemployment issue.[37] But its benefits for women are obvious.

CONCLUSION

For all their limitations, the attempts to implement equal pay legislation in the private sector prove at least that equal opportunity and equal access were necessary prerequisites to achieving equal pay. The civil service example shows that earlier laws (in this case, from the mid-1940s) designed to promote equal access and equal pay lacked the deeper understanding of the nature and extent of occupational segregation needed to remove those aspects of the law that in fact invalidate equal access. It took approximately thirty years to discover that unequal access and occupational segregation were linked in some way.

Moreover, the civil service experience illustrates that the real problem confronting women in French society is lack of power. Apart from a few visible cases of tokenism, a dramatically small number of women hold positions where policy is either made or implemented. As in other areas of labor, and perhaps more so on account of its rigid, hierarchical system and the use of "discretionary choice" for appointments to top-level positions, the civil service has been ruled by two sets of laws and principles: a written general statutory legislation, which provides guidelines for the setting up of statute law specific to each administration, and an unwritten code of behavior inherited from the sexist tradition that barred women from "the bastions of male chauvinism." The moot point is whether the legal remedies now being enacted will result in change.

Legislators and jurists have provided legislation that may be used by the pioneering minority of working women who are attempting to break down gender-related barriers in the workforce. It is still too early to judge whether the economic and occupational status of women in our society will be changed dramatically.

While glaring, overt discrimination is slowly being dealt with, much remains to be done to eradicate disparate treatment of women and latent discriminatory attitudes. Theoretically, it would require deep-rooted sociopsychological changes in order to overcome the reluctance of women themselves as well as of men to accept a redefinition of sex-stereotyped roles within the occupational system and the family system.

Legally, structural changes in the occupational system are feasible. The setting up of a flexible occupational structure institutionalizing a paid leave available to all parents during child-rearing years may help individuals who wish to reconcile their commitments to family and job. Encouraging girls and women to enter nontraditional careers may also change the pattern of occupational segregation. The enforcement of the legislation forbidding sex discrimination may prove powerful enough to compel employers to change their employment policies.

But changes in occupational segregation may be legislated only if individuals agree to the societal changes implied. It means that jobs should no longer be associated with sex-role stereotyping. This problem is particularly noticeable when women try to enter occupations traditionally held by men. For instance, managerial positions and male-dominated occupations are still associated with male sex-stereotypes. If a female applicant does not possess the "necessary" attributes—from sheer physical strength to leadership drive—she is likely to be rejected; if she does possess them, she may be rejected as well on the theory that her lack of adjustment to her sex role raises doubts as to her general psychological health.

Within the scope of this chapter, we could not possibly deal with all those degrees of inequality that vary according to the economic and social status of women within the sociocultural framework of society as a whole. Though unequal access and unequal opportunity are reflected at all levels of working life, women do not constitute a homogenous social group. Therefore, it is not easy to lay down provisions that guarantee equality of opportunity and treatment in every case. In a number of cases, the law has proved limited by the very details of the case. That does not mean that the legal remedies are not adequate or cannot be improved, but social reality is far too complex to be reflected adequately and changed by laws. Legislation can in fact help women identify their unequal status by emphasizing their equal rights and giving them the chance to avail themselves of the tools provided; but the implementation of the legislation may depend a lot on the energy and pressure women are ready to muster in order to fight for the achievement of equal opportunities through time- and money-consuming precedent-setting litigation.

In spite of the limitations of the legal approach to equal pay and equal opportunity, and the relatively limited use of litigation, women workers have at least gained the recognition that they are entitled to equal pay and equal access and should no longer be treated as second-class citizens. The reforms have focused attention on the attitudinal changes of the female labor force. Though flexible and part-time scheduling is still a highly controversial issue, mostly because it raises basic questions about the reallocation of parental and occupational roles within the family, it may be considered as a long-term strategy for change eventually beneficial to women.

Women have become aware of their power as a pressure group. Media are currently giving wide publicity to the rights of women at the workplace, describing discriminatory practices and warning against them. It may be hoped that this new awareness will not be undermined by the contradictions still inherent in the sociocultural framework, reinforced by the differences in social and economic status among women themselves. The priorities of a female worker may not seem the same as those of a female executive, unless both come to realize that they are facing the same problem of sex discrimination and that implementing an overall legal strategy will improve their own positions.

NOTES

1. Mme B. B., "Cahier de Doléances et Réclamation des Femmes," and Olympe de Gouges," Les Droits de la Femme et de la Citoyenne" (Sept. 1791), quoted by Maïté Albistur Daniel Armogathe in *Histoire du Féminisme Français* Paris: Editions des Femmes, 1977), p. 2, ch. 1 ("Le Féminisme sous la Révolution").

2. See L. H. Parias, ed., *Histoire Générale du Travail* (Paris: Nouvelle Librairie de France, 1962); and on French unions, see J. D. Raynaud, *Les Syndicats en France* (Paris: Seuil, 1975).

3. For fuller particulars, see the well-documented " 'Le Féminisme Réformiste' les Acquis" in *Histoire du Féminisme Français*, pt. 3, pp. 391–397.

4. "La Loi Garantit à la Femme, dans Tous les Domaines, des Droits Egaux à Ceux de l'Homme," quoted in Comité du Travail Féminin, *Bilan de l'Application de la Loi du 22 Décembre 1972 sur l'Égalité de Rémunération entre Hommes et Femmes: Actualités du Travail Féminin* (Paris: Ministère du Travail, Sept. 1976), p. 2; for fuller particulars on the French Constitutions, see M. Duverger, *Les Constitutions de la France* (Paris: Presses Universitaires de France, coll. "Que sais-je?" 1971), quoted in *Constitutions et Documents Politiques* Paris: Presses Universitaires de France, coll. "Thémis," 1968) p. 138; on women's rights as guaranteed by the Constitution, see O. Dhavernas, *Droits des Femmes, Pouvoir des Hommes* (Paris: Seuil, 1978), for the legal controversies and parliamentary debates raised by this issue.

5. See Comité due Travail Féminin, assisted by G. Becane-Pascaud, *Les Femmes aux Postes de Direction de la Fonction Publique* (Paris: Ministère du Travail, June 1974), pp. 1–18. Figures were updated according to the data of the 1975 population census analyzed by Laurent Thévenot, "Les Catégories Sociales en 1975: L'Extension du Salariat," *Economie et Statistique* 91 (1977): 3–31.

6. "Choice" in this acceptance (Promotion au *choix*) has a specific meaning: Employees are graded according to their merit criteria as rated by supervisors. Their direct hierarchical heads may thus exercise a discretionary choice and speed up promotion by granting them a higher score with a note explaining this highly satisfactory upscoring. On the other hand, their heads are also entitled to downscore, thus slowing the promotion process. The focus is laid on the performance of the individual as well as on other job components.

7. For an analysis of overall employment in France, see *Economie et Statistique* 81–82 (1976), special issue. On female work and employment, see *Travail Féminin: Un Point de Vue* by Andrée Michel (Paris: La Documentation Française, 1975). Statistical data are available and updated in the regular publications of the Institut National de Statistiques et Etudes Economiques and in the reports of the Comité du Travail Féminin.

8. *Bilan de l'Application de la Loi du 22 Décembre 1972*, p. 7, dealing with "les difficultés d'application de la loi."

9. A system of job analysis and classification known as "nomenclature des métiers et des activités individuelles" (NAI) was set up in 1947 after the publishing of the Parodi Agreements (1945–1946), which defined a hierarchy in job qualifications based on similar training within the industrial sector and according to each sector of activity. A listing of occupational titles had been established as early as 1872. Since 1974, the Labor Department has used the newly established "Répertoire Opérationnel des Métiers et des Emplois (ROME), the equivalent of the U.S. dictionary of occupational titles. See C.

Taffin, "Les Nomenclatures de Professions et de Formations," *Economie et Statistique,* 81–82 (1976): 95–99, and J. C. Foubert, "Le Répertoire Français des Emplois," *Economie et Statistique* 81–82 (1976): 105–111.

10. This is a summary of the controversial debate that took place during the session of the French House of Representatives (Assemblée Nationale, Nov. 21, 1972) and published in the *Journal Officiel* as quoted by Dhavernas, *Droit des Femmes, Pouvoir des Hommes,* pp. 271–274.

11. The "Conseil National du Patronat Français" had pointed out in various reports and in the media the difficulties of applying the broader concept of "equal pay for work of equal value" because of the lack of job evaluation systems (i.e., work of comparable worth was difficult to translate in terms of earnings). Later, in a press conference held on October 21, 1975, on "Femmes et Entreprise," the C.N.P.F. published policy guidelines aiming at a better integration of women at the workplace.

12. See Comité du Travail Féminin, *Les Femmes aux Postes de Direction,* pp. 1–18; *Economie et Statistique* 81–82 (1976), special issue; and Michel, *Travail Féminin.*

13. *Bilan de l'Application de la Loi du 22 Décembre 1972,* pt. 3 ("Les Voies de Réalisation de l'Egalité"), pp. 20–25, recommended focusing on better career-counseling and stricter enforcement of the legislation on female professional training as well as revision of job classifications, thus advocating a better system of comparative job evaluation.

14. *Droit social,* n. 3, March 1978, *Galeries Lafayette de Montpellier* v. *Dame Bachelas et al.* The department store was staffed by 120 female shop assistants and 25 male shop assistants distributed into nine job classifications. Out of the 120 female employees, 53 complained; the complaint was filed and the Montpellier Industrial Court granted back pay awards and attorney's fees to aggrieved employees (May 23, 1975). On November 24, 1976, the Court of Appeals annulled the judgement. A conciliatory agreement was reached nevertheless; the employer agreed to grant back pay to employees who were earning lower salaries (Jan. 1, 1973—Aug. 31, 1974). Actually, it raised the issue of the wording of the collective agreement, which did not specifically state criteria regarding "job evaluation on performance difficulties." The aggrieved employees had convinced the industrial court that their jobs were as difficult as those of other employees enjoying higher salaries. But the appellate court did not uphold the decision, since the employer had not discriminated against his employees under the terms of the collective agreement covering the employees.

15. *Bilan de l'Application de la Loi du 22 Décembre 1972,* p. 4.

16. Ibid., p. 8; the law did not define the contents of the "identical norms" to be respected in job evaluation.

17. Girelle Halimi, ed., *Choisir la cause des femmes* (Paris: Grasset, 1978), p. 115.

18. Press conference, "Femmes et Entreprise."

19. Pagès, *Recueil Lebon* 44, Feb. 19, 1943. This case and others are mentioned in Dhavernas, *Droit des Femmes, Pouvoir des Hommes,* pt. 4, ch.

3 ("L'Accès à la Fonction publique"). Among other sources for more particulars, see Comité due Travail Féminin, "Les Femmes aux Postes de Direction dans la Fonction Publique."

20. Dhavernas, *Droit des Femmes, Pouvoir des Hommes*, p. 288, 2, "Loi relative au travail féminin, D.P. 40, IV, 336."

21. Ibid., p. 291, quotation from the legal text as published in *Gazette du Palais*, 46, II, 384: "Aucune distinction pour l'application du présent statut n'est faite entre les deux sexes, sous réserve des dispositions spéciales qu'il prévoit." For fuller particulars and an analysis of women and the civil service, see Catherine Bersani, "La Femme et la Fonction Publique," *Droit Social* 1 (Jan. 1976): 51–52, and G. Bécane-Pascaud, "Les Femmes dans la Fonction Publique," *Notes et Etudes Documentaires: Documentation Française* no. 4056–4057, Jan. 25, 1974, and Comité du Travail Féminin, *Les Femmes aux Postes de Direction*.

22. Ibid., p. 294, quoted from *Recueil Lebon* 4, Jan. 6, 1956, "Syndicat National Autonome des Cadres d'Administration Générale des Colonies." The State Council (Conseil d'Etat) stated that "les conditions d'exercice (de la fonction en cause) sont de nature à justifier légalement l'exclusion des candidats de sexe féminin de l'accès de ces fonctions."

23. Ibid.: "si, depuis 1946, les femmes ont désormais, en règle générale, vocation à tous les emplois publics dans les mêmes conditions que les hommes, c'est seulement sous réserve du droit du gouvernement, dans l'exercice du pouvoir règlementaire qui lui est reconnu . . . d'apporter, sous le contrôle du juge, des dérogations à la règle ci-dessus définie."

24. Statut Général de la Fonction Publique, ordonnance du 4 février 1959, Article 7, quoted in Dhavernas, *Droit des Femmes, Pouvoir des Hommes*, p. 292: "Pour l'application de la présente ordonnance, aucune distinction n'est faite entre les deux sexes, sous réserve des mesures exceptionnelles prévues dans les statuts particuliers et commandés par la nature des fonctions."

25. Comité du Travail Féminin, *Les Femmes aux Postes de Direction*, p. 4 and statistical annex.

26. Halimi, ed., *Choisir la Cause des Femmes*, p. 109: "La loi Roustan du 30 décembre 1921, dite "loi sur le rapprochement des ménages" [literally, "drawing together both spouses"] a été étendue aux hommes le 4 juin 1970." The 1921 clause was extended to men by the 1970 act.

27. Revised version of Article 7 as quoted in *Choisir la Cause des Femmes*, p. 118: "Cependant, lorsque la nature des fonctions ou les conditions de leur exercice le justifient, il peut être prévu pour certains corps, dont la liste est établie par décret en Conseil d'Etat, après avis du conseil supérieur de la Fonction Publique et des comités paritaires, un recrutement exclusif d'hommes ou de femmes ou, à titre exceptionnel, selon les modalités prévues dans le même décret, des recrutements et conditions d'accès distincts pour les hommes et les femmes."

28. *"Les Femmes aux Postes de Direction*, pp. 16–18.

29. The June 1978 report *Les Femmes dans la Fonction Publique*, published by the Comité du Travail Féminin, updated the former reports and the

statistical data. Its conclusions remained pessimistic, stressing the fact that there are still discriminatory practices regarding equal opportunities. Some piecemeal reforms have been undertaken: For example, access has been opened up for female applicants to state examinations formerly open to male police officers only (Decree no. 78-794, July 26, 1978). Similarly, a sex quota was set up in the recruitment of elementary schoolteachers to help put a stop to the dramatic feminization of this occupation (Decree no. 78-389, March 25, 1977, Annex II, enforcing Article 7 of the Civil Service General Statute, completed by Decree no. 78-872, Aug. 22, 1978).

The Comité pointed out the relative failure of part-time work in the civil service, and the denying to male civil servants of leaves in order to stay at home and take care of sick children even though, legally, they are entitled to such leaves in accordance with Act 70-459 relative to parental authority (excerpts from Comité du Travail Féminin, *Actualités du Travail des Femmes* 21 [Dec. 1978]: 6, 7, 8).

30. Act 78-753, July 17, 1978 (*Journal Officiel*, July 18, 1978, p. 2853), improving some social, fiscal, and administrative statutory provisions. To date, there are still about twenty-five state examinations (internal or external) that are not open equally to both male and female applicants (Comité du Travail Féminin, *Actualité du Travail des Femmes*, p. 7). The Post Office Department seems to use extensively the provisions of Article 7 allowing "BFOQ" (Bona Fied Occupational Classification).

31. *Le Monde*, April 21, 1978, p. 10. A major debate took place in the House of Representatives (Assemblée nationale) on the prime minister's program and policy guidelines. Regarding the family and the status of women, Prime Minister Raymond Barre stated that family policy had always been and would remain a top priority: emphasis was laid on the family as "cellule de base de la société" (the basic unit upon which society is founded) and on the necessity to give mothers and homemakers a social status. The government was to enact measures that would entitle large families to a guaranteed minimum income (families of three are supposed to get such an income by the end of 1979). The prime minister wished that "women be given the means to reconcile family and occupational activities by being granted priority access to part-time schedules" (as quoted in *Le Monde*).

32. *France-Soir* Nov. 12, 1978, p. 6.

33. See note 29 above on the follow-up.

34. Comité du Travail Féminin, file (document issued by the Ministry of Labor).

35. Halimi, ed., *Choisir la Cause des Femmes*, p. 118.

36. Institut National de la Statistique et des Etudes Economiques, *Census de la Population, 1975* (Paris: INSEE, 1975).

37. "Information Emploi," *France-Soir* Jan. 4, 1979, p. 16.

4 *Marcia Greenberger*

THE EFFECTIVENESS OF FEDERAL LAWS PROHIBITING SEX DISCRIMINATION IN EMPLOYMENT IN THE UNITED STATES

Given the fact that sex discrimination in employment has been widespread, and that pervasive sex discrimination in the workplace is still a critical problem,[1] it is important to assess the effectiveness of the major legal remedies available to combat sex discrimination in employment in order to determine whether they adequately serve their intended purposes.

Title VII of the 1964 Civil Rights Act[2] has been the leading vehicle through which courts have defined employment practices that are considered sex discriminatory, and through which relief has been provided to those discriminated against. There are other federal laws, however, which prohibit sex discrimination in employment, and which provide alternate or supplementary options to Title VII. In certain respects, these laws have advantages over Title VII, either because of the sanctions they provide or because of the agencies charged with their enforcement. This chapter will review the relationship among all these laws, their strengths and their weaknesses.[3]

TITLE VII OF THE 1964 CIVIL RIGHTS ACT

Title VII prohibits discrimination by employers in their employment practices on the basis of sex. It is interpreted and enforced by the Equal Employment Opportunity Commission (EEOC). The EEOC has the authority to investigate complaints, to make a finding as to whether unlawful discrimination occurred, and, if so, to seek a remedy in court. If after a specified time period EEOC has not investigated a complaint, a complainant may seek a "right to sue letter" from the agency, go to court directly, and sue the employer. If successful, the individual discriminated against can receive relief for the discrimination suffered as well as reimbursement of the costs of the suit, including attorney's fees. This right to court redress as individuals or through class actions, including the possibility of recovering attorneys' fees, has been the critical reason why Title VII has been one of the most effective tools available.

Legal interpretation of Title VII

Although it was enacted in 1964, there were relatively few sex-discrimination cases brought under Title VII until the 1970s. In fact, the first Supreme Court Title VII case concerning sex discrimination was *Phillips* v. *Martin Marietta Corp.*, 400 U.S. 542 (1971). In that case, the Supreme Court in a per curiam opinion found that excluding mothers of preschool-age children violated Title VII. The employer agreed that the exclusion was *not* sex discrimination because it was excluding only women with preschool-age children, not all women. The Supreme Court rejected the employer's argument that a "sex plus" requirement fell outside the scope of Title VII, thereby establishing a very important principle for Title VII coverage—adding extra burdens just on women violates Title VII, even if all women are not affected by the extra burden.

It was not until 1976 that the next major sex discrimination Title VII case was decided by the Supreme Court—*General Electric* v. *Gilbert*, 429 U.S. 125 (1976). In that case, the court held that GE's exclusion of pregnancy-related disabilities from its employee fringe benefit plan, while all other disabilities were included, was not sex discrimination and therefore not a violation of Title VII. The full ramifications of this decision, and the reasoning used, have yet to be discerned. The court indicated that pregnancy is sui generis. Under that analysis, different treatment on the basis of pregnancy is not necessarily sex discrimination because pregnancy can be compared to no other condition. But at the root of sex discrimination in employment is women's childbearing role, and employers' views that women are not valuable employees because they will become pregnant and leave the workforce. The refusal to hire a pregnant woman, firing a woman who becomes pregnant, or refusing to promote a woman who is or may become pregnant arguably all fall outside the scope of Title VII if the *Gilbert* reasoning were applied in the extreme.

More recently, the Supreme Court dealt with the issue again in *Nashville Gas Co.* v. *Satty*, 98 S.Ct. 347 (1977). The confusion wrought by *Gilbert* was evident in the various opinions written in that case. What seemed to be emerging is the notion that if a burden is placed on the employee because of pregnancy, Title VII may be violated. If, on the other hand, a benefit is simply not extended, then no Title VII violation occurs. Needless to say, how one decides whether an employer's disparate treatment results in a burden or just a withholding of a benefit is far from clear.

On October 31, 1978, legislation passed Congress overturning the *Gilbert* decision and including discrimination on the basis of pregnancy within the scope of Title VII (Pub.L. No. 95-555, 92 Stat. 2076). It is to be hoped that, because of this bill, the legacy of *Gilbert* will be diminished.

There are other troubling aspects of *Gilbert*. Since the GE policy was not sex-discriminatory on its face, sex-discriminatory impact was to be gleaned from looking at the total benefits which went to the female as opposed to male employees. Called into question through this reasoning is the relationship between the Equal Pay Act (discussed below) and Title VII, and whether the limitations of the Equal Pay Act will also serve to limit the scope of Title VII.

This issue was addressed by the Supreme Court again in *City of Los Angeles* v. *Manhart*, 98 S.Ct. 1370 (1978). This case concerns the city's policy of withholding additional amounts from the pay of its female employees to cover the added costs of providing pensions to women on the grounds that since women as a group live longer than men they will ultimately collect more and therefore should pay more for the pensions. Guidelines under the Equal Pay Act stated that employers can provide equal benefits or make equal contributions. The EEOC guidelines, however, state that employers must provide equal benefits—thereby treating each employee on the basis of individual rather than class characteristics. However, the facts in *Manhart* did not require the court to choose between the two interpretations. It was argued that there was a violation of both laws since the pay itself is reduced for women, and the court so held. The court struck down the policy as violating Title VII. Some have argued that this holding further weakens any precedential effect of the *Gilbert* case.

Another key case, of concern for all civil rights laws, is *Bakke* v. *Regents of University of California*, 98 S.Ct. 2733 (1978). In this case, the court dealt with affirmative action requirements in the context of race discrimination, and the point at which "reverse discrimination" becomes an overriding countervailing consideration. There is no question that without a strong affirmative action requirement, progress in eradicating sex discrimination will be slow indeed. The court, by a five to four split, upheld the constitutionality of affirmative action in the context of another civil rights law, Title VI of the 1964 Civil Rights Act, 42 U.S.C. § 2000d, which prohibits discrimination in programs receiving federal funds, but struck down the plan at issue as involving unjustified rigid quotas. Left to later cases is the task of drawing the precise line between permissible affirmative action programs and programs that are too rigid. Significantly, Justice Powell, in his opinion, drew a distinction between race and sex discrimination, indicating that sex discrimination is less odious. The impact of this reasoning on developing case law is difficult to assess.

Effectiveness of Title VII

As we discussed above, it is only recently that the Supreme Court has started making key decisions on sex discrimination cases, and they are being made by a court becoming increasingly conservative and restrictive on the relief it will afford victims of discrimination. But even before these decisions, Title VII had only limited success. In part, the effectiveness of Title VII is hampered because an insufficient budget and administrative ineptitude have limited EEOC's ability to mount an aggressive enforcement campaign. It is hoped that major reorganization efforts and increased budget allotments will bring substantial improvements to EEOC's capabilities. It is too soon to judge these results, however. Enforcement continues to be left to the private individuals who have been discriminated against, through private lawsuits in courts.

Private groups and individuals are ill-equipped to shoulder the enforcement burden alone. While the provision of an award of attorneys' fees to successful plaintiffs has facilitated access to courts, at least to some degree, those discriminated against are often unable, for financial and other reasons, to secure lawyers and to press their claims in court. In addition, the harassment and intimidation suffered by complainants is a further hindrance to their willingness and ability to go to court. Therefore, since EEOC plays such a limited role, and those discriminated against face serious obstacles in going to court for redress, very few instances of discrimination are ever exposed and remedied.

Moreover, where private cases are brought, they result in the most sweeping and effective remedies if brought as a class action—that is, on behalf of all those similarly situated to the plaintiffs in the case (which can include past and future employees). A study shows, however, that for the Title VII cases reported for the years 1965 through mid-1975, courts ordered class relief in only 13 percent of all sex discrimination cases. In contrast, courts ordered class relief in 24 percent of all reported race discrimination cases brought during this period.[4] Again it is hoped that EEOC's new efforts to bring systemic cases will redress this problem at least to some extent.

Moreover, because of the design of Title VII, little incentive is given to employers to eliminate discriminatory practices before they are sued. In large part, this is because Title VII remedies are mainly prospective in nature, with back pay as the major exception. There are no penalties available under the Act. An employer therefore has little to lose by waiting to change discriminatory practices until forced to do so by a court. Back salary would have been paid by a nondiscriminating employer in any event, and any future changes ordered by a court presumably also would have been instituted by an employer seeking voluntarily to eliminate discriminatory practices. By waiting for a court to order back pay, the company has the use of the funds in the meantime. And, of course, there are good possibilities of settling a case on a compromise basis, or of a company's winning even if it has discriminated. This virtual absence of any sanction for noncompliance, coupled with the small number of cases ever brought to court, accounts for the relative ineffectiveness of Title VII.

THE EQUAL PAY ACT OF 1963

The Equal Pay Act (EPA),[5] passed in 1963, was the first federal law to prohibit wage discrimination by sex, despite the fact that many such bills had been introduced prior to that time. Unlike Title VII, passed the following year, the EPA does not touch upon any area of employment discrimination outside the realm of compensation. Its enactment was deemed necessary in light of the fact that women, who then constituted one-third of the labor force, were earning an average of only 60 percent of the average wage of men.[6] It is a sad commentary that fourteen years after the passage of the act, women were earning only 57 percent of the average wages for men.

The EPA mandates equal pay for equal work on jobs requiring equal skill, effort, and responsibility that are performed under similar working conditions within any establishment. Differentials are permissible, however, if based upon seniority, merit, or incentive systems, or any factor other than sex. Employers may not bring their establishments into compliance by lowering the wages earned by any group of employees.

EPA does not cover as large a number of employees as does Title VII. However, the exemptions to coverage have been narrowed in recent years.[7] Originally, eleven categories of employees were not subject to the act.[8] Taking 1972 as a sample year, there were an estimated 2 million enterprises covered, with more than 46 million employees affected.[9] The EPA was amended by the Education Amendments Act of 1972 to include executive, administrative, and professional employees and outside salespersons.[10] Moreover, in 1974, further amendments included additional state and local government employees, most federal employees, and others.[11]

Employees who feel they have a claim under the EPA may opt to bring suit for back wages,[12] liquidated damages including double damages for willful violations,[13] attorney fees, and court costs through a private attorney. Unlike Title VII, however, no class actions may be brought. Alternatively, the employee may seek the assistance of the Wage and Hour Division of the Department of Labor by filing a complaint with the division. If merit is found, the Labor Department itself may go to court to seek an injunction to restrain continued violations and prevent withholding of back wages legally due.

Moreover, the Wage and Hour Division is empowered to conduct investigations of employers' compliance with the act, whether or not complaints were received. In contrast, the EEOC acts only on the basis of complaints. There are currently approximately one thousand compliance officers across the country, but it has been estimated that only 15–20 percent of their time is devoted to enforcement of the EPA.[14]

It should be noted that President Carter's reorganization plan has shifted the responsibility for enforcement of EPA to the EEOC. The effects of this shift are hard to predict.

Most of the compliance investigations conducted are not made in response to a complaint filed by an employee.[15] These general, routine compliance investigations are crucial to allowing for an overall strategy for enforcement. In addition, they facilitate the ability of the investigator to keep complaints confidential, for an employer does not know whether or not the investigation stemmed from a complaint. As a result, harassment and retaliation are kept to a minimum.

Upon a finding by the Wage and Hour Division of a violation of the EPA, voluntary compliance is usually obtained, including an agreement to pay back wages. It has been estimated that more than 95 percent of equal pay cases are settled out of the courts.[16] Table 4-1 indicates the amounts found due by the Labor Department in 1965–1972. As can be seen from this table, the 1,115 establishments investigated in 1972 were found to have underpaid more than 29,000 employees under the EPA.[17] The De-

TABLE 4-1

Equal Pay Investigations Conducted by U.S. Department of Labor,
1965–1974

Fiscal year	No. of establishments investigated	No. of employees underpaid under the EPA	Amounts found due
1965		960	$ 156,202
1966		6,633	2,097,600
1967		5,931	3,252,319
1968		6,622	2,488,405
1969	385	16,100	4,585,344
1970	736	17,719	6,119,265
1971	1,203	29,992	14,842,994
1972	1,115	29,022	14,030,889
1973		29,619	18,005,582
1974 (6 mo.)		16,507	11,043,833

Source: Memorandum of Morag Simchak, Chief, Branch of Equal Pay Discrimination, U.S. Department of Labor (Jan. 1974), and Albert A. Ross and Frank V. McDermott, Jr., "The Equal Protection Act of 1963: A Decade of Enforcement," *Boston College Industrial and Commercial Law Review* 16 (Nov. 1974): 1–73.

partment of Labor more recently announced that during the first quarter of fiscal 1978, over $4.7 million was found to be due to 6,346 employees.

A well-publicized settlement leading to substantial wage adjustments in part under the EPA was that entered into with American Telephone & Telegraph. In 1970, the EEOC conducted an investigation of the employment practices of AT&T, and found race and sex discrimination in their nonmanagement employee programs. Because at the time the EEOC did not have the power to go to court, the agency petitioned the Federal Communications Commission (FCC) to order the elimination of these sex and race discriminatory practices pursuant to AT&T's request for a rate increase. An extensive hearing was conducted by the FCC, and the Department of Labor joined the effort. In January 1973, a settlement with AT&T was reached whereby $15 million in adjustments was to be paid to 15,000 employees discriminated against on the basis of race and sex. Moreover, an adjustment in wage rates estimated at $23 million each year was agreed to. Finally, AT&T agreed to adopt an affirmative action plan requiring serious modifications in its policies and practices.[18] Questions have been raised, however, about whether AT&T has been meeting the goals set forth in the plan.

A second aspect of the settlement took the form of a consent decree entered in U.S. district court on May 30, 1974, covering management employees. The decree involved changing the wage structure for promotions, and it was estimated that approximately 17,000 employees (10,000 women) would receive wage adjustments of $14.9 million under the decree. Moreover, 7,000 employees (4,200 women) would receive $7 million in back pay awards. This was the first major settlement reached under the 1972 amendments to the Equal Pay Act which extended coverage to professional and managerial employees.[19]

The large sums found due resulting from these investigations strongly indicate the pervasive nature of sex discrimination in wage rates and the need to reach all of the other establishments with a much more widespread campaign than the Wage and Hour Division has thus far undertaken. One distressing fact is that as of February 22, 1976, the Wage and Hour Division had a backlog of 1,800 complaints received under EPA but unresolved, as indicated in Table 4-2. It is hoped that a more vigorous enforcement effort will be undertaken in the future.

Legal interpretation of the act

In order to establish a violation of EPA, a showing must be made that the "employer pays different wages to employees of opposite sexes 'for equal work on jobs the performance of which requires equal skill, effort, and responsibility and which are performed under similar conditions.' "[20]

TABLE 4-2
Complaints Filed against Establishments

Fiscal year	Total	New coverage	Old coverage	Complaint backlog
1969	385			
1970	738			
1971	1,203			456
1972	1,122			432
1973	2,095			1,201
1974	2,864			1,487
1975	2,727	375	2,352	1,790
1976	2,311	253	2,058	1,860
1976*	444	77	370	1,798
Sept. 21, 1976– Jan. 20, 1977	454	77	377	1,800

*Transition quarter, June 21–Sept. 20, 1976.
NOTE: Over 1,024 cases have been filed since the act's effective date in June 1964.

Failure to prove each of these elements results in dismissal since the act is brought into play only when the jobs in question are equal. That is to say, the EPA is not relevant to determining reasonable differentials for unequal work.

A significant amount of litigation has dealt with the meaning of "equal work." Equality does not require that the jobs be identical, but they must be "substantially equal,"[21] even if the nature of the jobs makes it impractical for both sexes to work interchangeably.[22] The doctrine of substantial equality was discussed by the Court of Appeals for the Fifth Circuit in *Hodgson* v. *Brookhaven Hospital*:

> As the doctrine is emerging, jobs do not entail most of the same routine duties, if the more highly paid job involves additional tasks which (1) require extra effort [skill and responsibility], (2) consume a significant amount of the time of all those whose pay differentials are to be justified in terms of them, and (3) are of an economic value commensurate with the pay differential."[23]

It is important to note that the skill, effort, and responsibility involved are to be determined by the actual demands of the position and not from the job classification or description. For example, where the employer justifies a higher male salary because he has some special ability which the female in the comparable job does not, a showing that the job does not in reality require that skill will result in a finding of an EPA violation.

Following this reasoning the Third Circuit in *Usery* v. *Allegheny County Hospital* recently held that beauticians and barbers held equal jobs for purposes of EPA and were entitled to equal wages.

Many employers arbitrarily try to accord greater weight to physical effort required on the job than to skill, job responsibility, and working conditions, but the court in *Hodgson* v. *Daisy Mfg. Co.*[24] struck down that reasoning as a means of characterizing jobs as unequal. That court also made it clear that "effort" entails both physical and mental labor, with neither automatically commanding higher wages if the degree of effort expended is comparable.

Another issue often raised concerns additional tasks performed by male employees and whether such tasks justify a higher salary. In order to justify the differential wage under such circumstances, the employer must demonstrate that every employee receiving the higher wage is performing the extra task and that everyone performing the extra task is receiving the higher wage. Further, the employer must show that the primary job functions of the two groups are somehow made qualitatively different by the presence of the additional duty. Differential wages have been struck down when based upon extra jobs which do not in fact exist[25] or which consume minimal time and are of little significance.[26]

In examining the employee's responsibilities (described as the "degree of accountability required in the performance of the job, with emphasis on the importance of the job obligation"[27]), higher wages have been deemed justified for employees in supervisory roles or in positions requiring that they make decisions materially affecting the employer's business operations.[28] The EPA has also been held inapplicable where a group of higher paid employees had accident prevention duties[29] or security responsibilities.[30]

Even if unequal pay for an "equal" job is shown, however, the employer may still justify wage differentials if they result from a system of seniority, merit, or incentive or any other factor other than sex, provided the system is "a systematic normal system" based upon "objective, written standards."[31] The ascertainable criteria for these systems must be known, available, and equally applied to all employees.[32]

An employer must justify paying even one member of one sex at a different rate than members of the opposite sex performing equal work by showing that sex factors provided no part of the differential basis. For example, night shift workers might legally receive higher wages because of the undesirability of the work, even if the shift is comprised solely of one sex. However, if that shift also receives a higher base rate than the shift staffed by the opposite sex performing the same work or the sex-differentiated shift employees are the only ones on those shifts earning more than their corresponding day workers, a violation of EPA would occur.[33]

"Red circle" rates (higher rates legitimately paid to one set of employees because of some special circumstances which are not sex-related) may be permissible in recognition of prior achievement and experience if relevant to the job requirements and evenhandedly applied to both sexes. For example, they may be allowable for a bona fide training program:

> In summary, the cases suggest that the courts look to the following factors as tests for the legitimacy of such programs: whether the trainee is aware of the program's existence; whether the employee is actually hired as a trainee; whether the work performed by the trainee and the regular employees is substantially the same; whether the program entails any instruction, courses or supervision; whether there is a written, formalized program; whether trainees are actually rotated through various jobs to get a better comprehension of the employer's business operations; whether rotation occurs due to completion of the training program rather than the employer's personnel needs; and whether the program is available to members of both sexes.[34]

Temporary assignments may also serve as a permissible reason to pay an employee at a different rate than others performing the work, as is true for temporary or part-time employees, as long as the practice is applied without discrimination against either sex.[35]

Differential wage treatment cannot be justified by claiming that it is costlier to employ women,[36] nor may employers rely on the "market force" theory that women will work for less money than men,[37] since it is just this sort of discrimination that the EPA was designed to remedy. It is not clear, however, whether an employer may, because of some "economic benefit," pay higher wages to one group of employees. In *Hodgson* v. *Robert Hall* the Court of Appeals for the Third Circuit allowed higher wages for all the male employee groups in the men's department than were being paid to the female employees who worked in the women's department, in part because of the greater profits realized in the men's department and the fact that the court found the sex segregation was justifiable. The court held that under those circumstances wage differentials not related to actual job performance could be maintained for the economic benefit of the employer. The Fifth Circuit held differently, finding in a similar situation that the differential was based on sex, although there was no proof in the case that the men's department was more profitable for the employer.[38] The implications of the *Robert Hall* case are quite disturbing. If employers can look to profitability as a basis for wage rates, the effectiveness of the EPA in many circumstances might be seriously undermined.

Effectiveness of the Equal Pay Act

As can be seen by the number and size of back pay awards made under the EPA, the statute has had a significant impact on remedying discrimination in wage rates. It should be noted, however, that as of January 1977 the Wage and Hour Division had found $135,590,752 due but only $29,562,135 restored, as indicated in Table 4-3.[39]

Several explanations have been advanced concerning the mounting backlog of complaints. The answer lies in part in the fact that investigators have been given additional responsibilities, including age discrimination and the expanded coverage of the EPA and Fair Labor Standards Act (FLSA), yet the number of investigators has not been expanded accordingly. Moreover, the professional employment cases are more complex and more difficult for investigators to understand and resolve. Finally, there are those who raise the question that the commitment to enforce EPA may not be as strong as it should be.

Even if more vigorous enforcement were secured, the effectiveness of EPA will continue to be limited. A serious drawback is that even where virtually identical jobs are at issue, there are exceptions in the act which allow differences in wage rates if they are based on factors other than sex. Decisions such as that in *Robert Hall* underscore the limitations of EPA because of these exceptions.

Further, the EPA has no effect on the critical problem of women clustered in low-status, low-paying jobs where there are no male counterparts. And it should be noted that most women working outside the home work in such jobs. EPA does not provide a vehicle for moving women into nontraditional jobs, nor does it address the need to upgrade the status and pay of jobs traditionally held by women. For example, it has long been suggested that traditionally female positions such as nurse or secretary have been undervalued in relationship to positions such as "salesman."[40] The EPA cannot be used to address this issue. It is precisely because the great bulk of women in paid employment work in "women's jobs"[41] that the Equal Pay Act, even if enforced to its full potential, is of important but limited utility.

EXECUTIVE ORDER 11246

In 1964, President Johnson issued Executive Order 11246 (32 Fed. Reg. 12319), which prohibits federal contract funds from going to employers who discriminate in their employment policies or practices on the basis of race, color, religion, or national origin. In 1968, the order was amended to include sex by Executive Order 11375 (32 Fed. Reg. 14303). For the most part, the employment practices prohibited by Title VII are also prohibited by Executive Order 11246. Therefore its scope is broader than the Equal Pay Act. The employers covered, however, are limited to those receiving federal contracts.

The Executive Order is enforced by the Office of Federal Contract Compliance Programs (OFCCP) within the Labor Department. Originally, OFCCP delegated enforcement responsibilities to federal agencies which

TABLE 4-3
Equal Pay Findings

Fiscal year	No. of employees underpaid under the Equal Pay Act	Amounts found due	INCOME RESTORED	
			Employees	Amount
1965	960	$ 156,202		
1966	6,633	2,097,600		
1967	5,931	3,252,319		
1968	6,622	2,448,405		
1969	16,100	4,585,344		
1970	17,719	6,119,265		
1971	29,992	14,842,994		
1972	29,022	14,030,889		
1973	29,619*	18,005,582*	17,331*	$4,626,251*
1974	32,792†	20,623,830†	16,768†	6,841,443†
1975	31,843	26,484,860	17,889	7,474,163
1976	24,610	17,052,212	16,728	7,881,502
1976‡	2,402	1,487,464	1,765	650,217
Sept. 21, 1976– Jan. 20, 1977	4,930	3,503,786	4,297	2,088,559
TOTAL	239,175	135,590,752	74,778	29,562,135
Sept. 21, 1975– Jan. 20, 1976	9,182	7,963,667	5,777	3,074,046

*Not included in these figures is $6,300,000 paid under the Equal Pay Act by American Telephone & Telegraph to 6,100 of its employees. While the violative practice was originally disclosed by several wage-hour investigations, the resolution of the problem throughout the entire American Telegraph operating system was secured through litigation by the Solicitor's Office but was not based on individual compliance actions. This amount is thus not included in wage-hour compliance statistics.

†Not included in these figures is $7,000,000 which AT&T agreed to restore to 7,000 employees. This is the second consent decree which was entered into with AT&T covering equal pay violations at management level.

‡Transition quarter, June 21–Sept. 20, 1976.

each focus on different industries.[42] However, under the President's Reorganization Plan, as of October 1, 1978, all compliance responsibilities were consolidated within the Department of Labor. The program is divided into construction and nonconstruction contractors.

The approach of the Executive Order differs from that of the Equal Pay Act or Title VII in that the major remedy is not direct relief to the individuals discriminated against in the form of back pay, promotion, reinstatement, or the like. Instead, the sanction is termination of federal contract funds[43] if the discrimination is not remedied. Of course, back pay, promotion, and the like can be secured by OFCCP in order that the fund cutoff remedy not be used.

Moreover, Executive Order 11246 has a unique and critical aspect which could be its greatest strength. Pursuant to regulations issued under the Executive Order, contractors must develop affirmative action plans in order to remain eligible for federal contracts. With the development of and adherence to good affirmative action plans, enormous progress could be made in the eradication of sex discrimination in employment.[44]

In addition, unlike Title VII or the Equal Pay Act, there is no express provision under Executive Order 11246 for a private right of action, and there has yet to be established a clear right of individuals to go to court and sue the federal contractor if it has sex-discriminatory employment practices. As a result, individuals discriminated against have tended to rely upon OFCCP and the delegated federal contract compliance agencies to enforce the Executive Order and to investigate complaints filed by the aggrieved individuals or groups.[45] The agencies can conduct investigations either pursuant to a complaint or in the course of their own plan of spot checks of contractors for compliance with the provisions of the Executive Order.[46] It is expected that employers will agree to remedy discrimination under the threat of fund termination.

Unfortunately, on the whole this reliance upon OFCCP for enforcement has been misplaced. Most of the compliance agencies have yet to develop vigorous enforcement efforts, and OFCCP has failed to exercise its authority to require that such efforts be made. Moreover, since there have been so few enforcement efforts, there has been very little case law interpreting the Executive Order. Whether the situation will change after the reorganization remains to be seen.

Enforcement of the Executive Order

A series of reports by the General Accounting Office (GAO) have reviewed the enforcement efforts under Executive Order 11246 and found those efforts to be seriously wanting.[47] Moreover, enforcement has been particularly inadequate in the area of sex discrimination.

For example, GAO has found that compliance agencies often did not investigate to see if discrimination was systemic and affected a class of employees. Similarly, they did not review whether there was a need for back pay.[48] It was not until March 1975 that OFCCP published proposed guidelines on back pay for affected class employees. Yet it is through back pay and class relief that the most effective remedies to discrimination can be achieved.

In addition, GAO has found that during fiscal years 1972–1974, virtually all efforts of the OFCCP regional staffs were devoted to monitoring the construction program. Yet the construction program is not geared to the problems of sex discrimination, and until early 1978 required affirmative action through goals and timetables to be developed for race and national origin, not for sex.[49]

The weaknesses in the enforcement program were summarized as follows:

> At least two compliance agencies were approving affirmative action programs that did not meet department guidelines. Some agencies were reluctant to initiate enforcement actions and therefore they extended conciliation efforts with contractors beyond department time limits. Some compliance agencies did not always conduct the required preaward reviews. Of the 13 compliance agencies, 12 had not identified all contractors for which they were responsible, and most agencies were not reviewing an adequate portion of the contractors for which they were responsible.[50]

Moreover, enforcement of Executive Order 11246 has not improved dramatically since the Ahart article and the GAO report dated May 5, 1975. A GAO report dated August 25, 1975, dealt with enforcement of the order by the Department of Health, Education, and Welfare (HEW) and was entitled "More Assurances Needed That Colleges and Universities with Government Contracts Provide Equal Employment Opportunity." The report concluded, for example, that sanctions for noncompliance were not initiated and affirmative action plans not approved. Significantly, in its published annual operating plan for fiscal year 1977 (41 Fed. Reg. 41776 and the following [September 23, 1976]), the Office for Civil Rights (OCR) in HEW—the office charged with the responsibility of enforcing the Executive Order—announced it would investigate virtually no new sex discrimination complaints filed under Executive Order 11246 and would conduct no general reviews of compliance with this order. In short, OCR announced its enforcement of the order had come to a standstill. Under a recent consent order, this policy has been changed.[51] Finally, GAO prepared a report dated March 30, 1977, concerning the Office for Civil Rights in HEW. This report repeated the distressing conclusions of the earlier reports prepared.

There are several possible explanations for this dramatic lack of enforcement of Executive Order 11246. OCR itself claims that it lacks sufficient resources to do a better job, an explanation which appears to lack credibility. Women's groups have been shocked to learn that during the last several years OCR has returned, unspent, millions of dollars to the Treasury. As of May 1977, there were over two hundred authorized slots in OCR which were unfilled. These unfilled positions represented more than one-fourth of all OCR positions. Given these hard facts, coupled with lack of training of the personnel which OCR does have and the absence of established routine procedures for enforcement, it is clear that OCR has been either unwilling or unable to develop a serious enforcement effort of the Executive Order.

GAO has also prepared a report on the enforcement of Executive Order 11246 by the Treasury Department against financial institutions dated June 24, 1976, and entitled "More Action Needed to Insure That Financial Institutions Provide Equal Employment Opportunity." The summary on the cover page of the report stated:

> Treasury has made limited progress in insuring that financial institutions follow equal employment opportunity practices. The program's credibility has been seriously impaired by Treasury's record of nonenforcement—even in instances of financial institutions' deliberate refusal to comply with requirements.[52]

Effectiveness of the Order

The unique aspect of Executive Order 11246 is its sanction of federal fund cutoff and its requirement that affirmative action plans be developed.[53] Because individual lawsuits are not encouraged by the structure of the Executive Order, however, enforcement of its provisions has depended upon the efforts of the OFCCP and the compliance agencies. As discussed above, government agencies to date have been unwilling or unable to provide effective enforcement of this order. Since the Executive Order was amended to include sex in 1968, virtually no federal funds have ever been terminated or contractors debarred because of their sex-discriminatory practices. And because the sanction of the Executive Order is for practical purposes never invoked, there is little compliance with it on the part of employers receiving federal contracts.

That is not to say, however, that the Executive Order has secured no gains for women at all. Some employers have been willing to develop effective affirmative action plans or enter into settlements providing some remedies for past discrimination. For example, under the Executive Order in a settlement with the Veterans' Administration, McNeil Laboratories, a subsidiary of Johnson & Johnson, has adopted a maternity leave policy guaranteeing workers reinstatement without loss of pay, job status, and seniority after childbirth, miscarriage, and abortion.[54] Until the government indicates its willingness to impose sanctions when necessary, however, recalcitrant employers can continue to refuse to change sex-discriminatory employment practices without fear of losing government contracts.

There have been some signs that improvement in enforcement of the Executive Order can be expected. Enforcement proceedings have been started against the St. Regis Paper Company, Harris Trust and Savings Bank of Chicago, and John Hancock Life Insurance Company.[55] In addition, because the Executive Order is based on the government's power to contract, its authority to require affirmative action may prove broader than that under Title VII. If there is now a willingness to use this authority, the Executive Order may prove to be a major tool.

CONCLUSION

In sum, there are several major federal laws prohibiting sex discrimination in employment. Each has its own advantages and disadvantages. However, all of the laws require strengthening. For example, more stringent sanctions to correct discriminatory practices should be available under Title VII. Furthermore, it is extremely important that existing laws either be interpreted by courts or expressly defined by Congress so as to require review of traditional female jobs in order to see whether they are rated fairly compared to traditional men's jobs.

Because most women who work outside the home do so in "women's" jobs, it is critical that the pay, status, and benefits of these jobs be assessed according to neutral principles. Should jobs requiring manual dexterity, often held by women, be paid less than jobs requiring physical strength, often held by men? Are the tasks performed by secretaries worth less than those performed by "salesmen"? To date, existing sex-discrimination laws have not been used in any major way to address these questions. Yet, since most women are employed in these "women's" jobs, a fair resolution of these questions is essential.

But even with deficiencies in the design of the present laws, together with the problem of lack of resources to press cases, inability to find lawyers, and fear of retaliation, important gains have come from lawsuits of private citizens. Unfortunately, not as much can be said for government efforts to spearhead enforcement. In no case is the responsible federal agency fully meeting the expectations of the law; it is not implementing regulations by aggressively bringing suits or seeking far-reaching settlements that will change sex discriminatory employment policies of employers across the country. At the moment, we can point only to isolated government victories. Yet the private sector cannot carry the burden alone.

It is only with more vigorous, widespread and consistent government enforcement and a willingness to use available sanctions that we will see a widespread movement which will significantly change the employment picture for women.

NOTES

1. Women who worked at year-round full-time jobs in 1974 earned only 57 cents for every dollar earned by men. Just as startling, in 1974 women with four years of college education had lower incomes than men who had completed only eighth grade (U.S. Department of Labor, Employment Standards Administration, Women's Bureau, "The Earnings Gap between Women and Men" [Washington, D.C.: GPO, 1976]).

2. 42 U.S.C. sec. 2000e.

3. Much of this paper is based upon an article published by the Joint Economic Committee, Marcia Greenberger and Dianne Gutmann, "Legal Remedies beyond Title VII to Combat Sex Discrimination in Employment," *American Workers in a Full Employment Economy* (95th Cong., 1st sess., Sept. 15, 1977, p. 75.

4. See Mary C. Dunlap, "The Legal Road to Equal Employment Opportunity: A Critical View," *American Workers in a Full Employment Economy*, pp. 61–63.

5. 29 U.S.C. sec. 206(d).

6. Statement made by President Kennedy upon signing the EPA on June 10, 1963, cited in Albert A. Ross and Frank V. McDermott, Jr., "The Equal Protection Act of 1963: A Decade of Enforcement," *Boston College Industrial and Commercial Law Review* 16 (Nov. 1974): 1–73.

7. It has been estimated that three-fourths of the employed nonsupervisory workforce, excluding outside sales workers, and almost seven-eighths of the nonsupervisory employees, excluding outside sales workers in the private sector, were covered by the act. See *Minimum Wage and Maximum Hours Standards under the Fair Labor Standards Act*, an economic effects study submitted to Congress, 1977 (Washington, D.C.: U.S. Department of Labor, Employment Standards Administration, 1977), p. 55.

8. Sec. 213, supp. 1975, enumerates eleven categories of employees who are exempt if they are employed "in a bona fide executive, administrative, or professional capacity"; "in the capacity of outside salesman"; by any retail or service establishment if more than 50 percent of the annual dollar volume for sales of goods and services is made within the state; by an amusement or recreational establishment; by certain manufacturing retailers; in certain fishing and seafood operations; in certain types of agricultural activities; by a local newspaper; by a small independently owned public telephone company; as a seaman on a vessel other than an American vessel; or on a casual basis in domestic service to provide babysitting or companionship services for individuals unable to care for themselves.

9. John E. Burns and Catherine G. Burns, "An Analysis of the Equal Pay Act," *Labor Law Journal* 24, (Feb. 1973): 92.

10. Since 1972, Wage and Hour Division investigations showed higher education institutions owed some 8,000 employees, many professional, about $10 million in back pay. Several institutions have paid more than $100,000 in back wages to employees. However, not all of the back wages found due have yet been paid ("Equal Opportunity in Higher Education" [biweekly newsletter; Washington, D.C.: Education News Services Division of Capitol Publications, Inc.], Feb. 4, 1977, p. 8).

11. 1974 amendments to Fair Labor Standards Act of April 8, 1974, Public Law 93-259, 88 Stat. 58, amending 29 U.S.C. sec. 201 et seq. (1970). In *Brown* v. *City of Santa Barbara*, 45 U.S.L.W. 2351, Jan. 14, 1977, D.C. Cal. the court held that the 1974 amendments to the Fair Labor Standards Act (which applied the equal pay provisions to federal and state employees) constituted a valid exercise of congressional power, notwithstanding the Supreme Court's earlier decision in *National League of Cities* v. *Usery*, 44 U.S.L.W. ¶ 4674 (1976). In *Usery* it was found that the amendments' extension of minimum wage and hour protection to state and local government employees constituted invalid federal regulation of state governmental activities. The court decided that the 1974 extension of the Equal Pay Act would not impinge on the states' sovereignty since "the argument that decision to discriminate in pay on the basis of sex is an essential and integral State function is both asinine and an affront to human dignity" (45 U.S.L.W. at 2352). See also *Christensen* v. *Iowa*, 45 U.S.L.W. 2086, Aug. 14, 1976 (U.S.D.C. N. Iowa), and *Usery* v. *Allegheny City Institution Dist.*, 45 U.S.L.W. 2251, Oct. 28, 1976.

12. It is important to note that back pay may be recovered for two years for nonwillful violations and three years for willful. In Title VII, the limit is two years.

13. Prior to the enactment of the 1974 amendments, sec. 16(c) prevented the secretary from bringing an action to recover back wages in a case involving a question of first impression, essentially rendering the remedy of sec. 16 (3) totally ineffective (Ross and McDermott, "Equal Protection Act," p. 11).

14. Telephone conversation with Mr. Michael McCarthy of the Department of Labor Standards Office of Equal Pay and Employment Standards, April 20, 1977.

15. Burns and Burns, "An Analysis," p. 92.

16. Ibid., p. 95.

17. There have been amounts recovered under the Equal Pay Act pursuant to private suits as well. For example, in 1973 a settlement was reached pursuant to a case filed in the northern district of Indiana, *Burry* v. *General Electric*, whereby the company paid $300,000 in back pay and agreed to a $1 million increase in wages (Winn Newman, "Policy Issues," *Signs: Journal of Women in Culture and Society* 1 [spring 1976]: 270, table 2).

18. Significantly, no changes in the employment policies related to pregnancy were adopted.

19. *The Spokeswoman* 5 (July 15, 1974): 1.

20. *Corning Glass Works* v. *Brennan,* 417 U.S. 188, 195 (1974). Janet A. Johnson, "The Equal Pay Act of 1963: A Practical Analysis," *Drake Law Review* 24 (1975): 591.

21. *Schultz* v. *Wheaton Glass Co.,* 421 F.2d 250 (3rd Cir.), cert. denied, 398 U.S. 905 (1970).

22. *Hodgson* v. *Robert Hall Clothes, Inc.,* 473 F.2d 589 (3rd Cir. 1973), cert. denied, 414 U.S. 866 (1973).

23. *Hodgson* v. *Brookhaven General Hospital,* 436 F.2d 719, 725 (5th Cir. 1970).

24. *Hodgson* v. *Daisy Mfg. Co.,* 317 F.Supp. 538, 544 (W.D. Ark. 1970), affirmed in part, reversed in part, and remanded per curiam, 445 F.2d 823 (8th Cir. 1971).

25. *Brennan* v. *Goose Creek Consolidated Ind. Sch. Dist.,* 519 F.2d 53 (5th Cir. 1975); *Brennan* v. *Woodbridge School District,* 8 CCH Empl. Prac. Dec. 4719 (D.Del. 1974).

26. *Brennan* v. *Bd. of Ed.,* 374 F.Supp. 817 (D.N.J. 1974). In *Brennan* v. *Owensboro-Davies Cty. Hosp.* (6th Cir. 1975), No. 73-1261, 10 EPD para. 19, 404, the court struck down a wage differential between nurses' aides and orderlies upon finding that they performed much the same work. Although generally only orderlies set up traction and assisted in removing casts, these duties were found to have been performed "so infrequently that they did not render the jobs of aides and orderlies substantially different." The average additional postmortem work done by orderlies was deemed to constitute a "modest difference" which did not justify the existing wage differential (10 EPD, p. 5709).

27. 29 CFR 800.129 (1974).

28. *Brennan* v. *Victoria Bank and Trust Co.,* 493 F.2d. 896, 899 (5th Cir. 1974).

29. *Hodgson* v. *Daisy Mfg. Co.,* supra.

30. *Schulz* v. *Ky. Baptist Hospital,* 62 CCH Lab. Cas. 44 (W.D.Ky., 1969).

31. *Brennan* v. *Victoria Bank and Trust Co.,* supra.

32. 29 CFR 800.144 (1974).

33. *Corning Glass Works* v. *Brennan,* supra at 204–205.

34. Johnson, "Equal Pay Act," pp. 570, 596.

35. 29 CFR 800.147 (1974).

36. See U.S. Department of Labor, Employment Standards Administration, Women's Bureau, "The Myth and the Reality" (Washington, D.C.: GPO, April 1973), for discussion of absentee rates, work-life expectancy, and job rates.

37. *Brennan* v. *Victoria Bank and Trust Co.,* supra at 896.

38. *Hodgson* v. *City Stores, Inc.,* 332 F.Supp. 942 (M.D. Ala. 1971), affirmed sub nom. *Brennan* v. *City Stores, Inc.,* 479 F.2d 235 (5th Cir. 1973).

39. Although the moneys found due are only estimates of what is owed and may, therefore, be inflated, the large disparity with the amounts actually restored is disturbing.

40. In California, a clerk-typist II must have a high school education, knowledge of office machines and equipment, grammar, spelling, and so forth.

A warehouse worker must have the ability to read and write English; there are no educational or specialized skills required. Warehouse workers, virtually always male, make $199 more per month than clerk-typists, a 97 percent female class (*The Spokeswoman* 7 [March 15, 1977]:4).

41. "Although the future may hold more options, the largest proportion of women with paid employment currently work in clerical/sales occupations. These typists, clerks, secretaries, and office machine operators comprise . . . 38 percent of those in the paid labor force.

"Twelve percent of all women are in professional, technical, and managerial jobs, but half of this group work in education or health fields, principally in teaching and nursing. Only 9 percent of women are members of labor unions" (Barbara Bryant, *American Women Today and Tomorrow* [Washington, D.C.: National Commission on the Observance of International Women's Year, March 1977]).

42. The eleven compliance agencies are the Atomic Energy Commission, Department of Agriculture, Department of Commerce, Department of Defense, Department of Health, Education, and Welfare, Department of the Interior, Department of the Treasury, Department of Transportation, General Services Administration, U.S. Postal Service, Veterans' Administration.

43. A further sanction is referral of the case to the Justice Department for suit.

44. As discussed above, the whole operation of affirmative action plans is being reviewed by the courts, in light of charges of "reverse discrimination." See, for example *Cramer* v. *Virginia Commonwealth University*, 415 F.Supp. 673 (E.D. Va. 1976), for a case involving Executive Order 11246, presently on appeal to the Fourth Circuit Court of Appeals.

45. In a 1978 change in its regulations, OFCCP will retain only limited responsibility for investigating complaints.

46. Unfortunately, compliance agencies responsible for enforcing Executive Order 11246 do not have the same record of success in keeping the identity of complainants confidential as the Wage and Hours Division under the EPA.

47. "EEO Program for Federal Nonconstruction Contractors Can Be Improved," MWD-75-63 (Washington, D.C.: General Accounting Office, April 19, 1975); "Colleges and Universities with Government Contracts Provide Equal Employment Opportunity," MWD-75-72 (Washington, D.C.: General Accounting Office, Aug. 25, 1975); "Report to Congressman Jones on the Federal Equal Employment Program for Northeast Oklahoma Construction Project Is Weak," MWD-76-86 (Washington, D.C.: General Accounting Office, May 28, 1976); "More Action Needed to Insure That Financial Institutions Provide Equal Employment Opportunity," MWD-76-95 (Washington, D.C.: General Accounting Office, June 24, 1976).

48. Gregory J. Ahart, testimony and prepared statement on the evaluation of the contract compliance program in non-construction industry, hearings, U.S. Congress, Subcommittee on Fiscal Policy, Joint Economic Committee, 93d Cong., 2d sess. (Washington, D.C.: GPO, Sept. 11, 12, 1974). The Ahart article summarizes the findings of the GAO report, "EEO Programs for Federal

Nonconstruction Contractors Can Be Improved," prepared for the U.S. Congress, Subcommittee on Fiscal Policy of the Joint Economic Committee, April 29, 1975.

49. *Advocates for Women* v. *Marshall*, Civ. Action No. 76-0862, presently pending D.D.C., challenges this omission.

50. Ahart, testimony and statement, p. 568.

51. See *Women's Equity Action League et al.* v. *Califano et al.*, D.D.C. (Civ. Action No. 74-1720), Order issued Dec. 29, 1977.

52. See also report on the "Treasury Department's Contract Compliance Program for Financial Institutions," U.S. Senate, Committee on Banking, Housing, and Urban Affairs, 94th Cong., 2d sess. (Washington, D.C.: GPO, 1976).

53. In the area of construction contracts, the failure to require goals and timetables for sex severely impaired this effectiveness.

54. *The Spokeswoman* 7 (March 15, 1977): 3.

55. *Women Today* 111, no. 2 (Jan. 23, 1978): 1.

5 *Peter C. Robertson*

STRATEGIES FOR IMPROVING THE ECONOMIC SITUATION OF WOMEN: SYSTEMIC THINKING, SYSTEMIC DISCRIMINATION, AND SYSTEMIC ENFORCEMENT

The original congressional strategy for combatting discrimination in the United States was based upon voluntary compliance with the law. This strategy was legislated as Title VII of the Civil Rights Act in 1964. The problem of discrimination was perceived as an essentially human problem in which employers who were biased against minorities or women would yield their prejudices to skillful government persuasion though conciliation. This voluntary compliance strategy had the following elements:

Filing complaints. Any individual who believed that he or she had been discriminated against could file a complaint alleging discrimination. Any one of the five members of the Equal Employment Opportunity Commission (EEOC) could also initiate a complaint if he or she had reason to believe that there was discrimination.

Conducting an investigation. EEOC could conduct an investigation and gather facts concerning the discrimination alleged. The commission was given the power to require an employer to produce documents, records, and files for inspection and copying, a power without which no law of this type can ultimately be effective.

Finding "cause." After the investigation was completed, EEOC was given the power to make a finding as to whether there was "cause" to believe that discrimination existed.

Voluntary conciliation mechanism. If a finding of cause was made, the law gave EEOC the responsibility for attempting to eliminate the discrimination through voluntary methods of conference, conciliation, and persuasion.

Enforcement mechanism. EEOC did not have the power to file lawsuits. If the voluntary conciliation failed, further action was up to the individual or the Department of Justice.

When any individual who filed a complaint was dissatisfied with the results of the voluntary conciliation effort which the government had made, they could, after a minimal waiting period, file a private lawsuit. The Equal Employment Opportunity Commission could intervene in these lawsuits, but EEOC could not file a suit on its own motion.

The U.S. Department of Justice could file a lawsuit on two grounds. If the voluntary mechanism failed, EEOC could refer the case to the Department of Justice. If the Department of Justice found that there was a *pattern or practice* of violating Title VII, they could initiate a lawsuit on their own motion.

Other provisions of Title VII. In addition to the power to attempt to eliminate discrimination through the voluntary conciliation mechanism or by referring a case to the Department of Justice for a lawsuit, EEOC was given several other powers in the law: Section 709 of the statute gave EEOC the power to require that those covered by the statute maintain records and file reports that might be relevant to a determination as to whether discrimination existed. EEOC could also hold public hearings and could subpoena witnesses to testify concerning the possible existence of discrimination and ways to eliminate it. Finally, EEOC had the power to issue guidelines and other documents interpreting the statute for whose enforcement it was responsible. While we did not realize it when the law was first adopted by Congress, it was this power that was, ultimately, to develop into one of its most important elements.

SYSTEMIC THINKING ABOUT DISCRIMINATION

The most important aspect of the Equal Employment Opportunity Commission strategy involved the way in which it defined discrimination—

or more specifically the way in which it thought about discrimination. Americans had traditionally perceived discrimination in a nonlegal context as involving the evil state of mind of an employer who did not want to hire blacks or women or some other group. The Equal Employment Opportunity Commission studied the legislative history of the congressional debates that had led to the passage of Title VII. It appeared obvious that, while Congress was concerned with bias, bigotry, and prejudice in the workplace, the bulk of the legislative hearings preceding passage of the law focused on statistical facts showing the historic exclusion of minorities and women. The relative unemployment rates, the relative rates of pay, the relative participation in different types of jobs, all were outlined with careful charts and tables. An enforcement approach which thought only of eliminating bias, bigotry, and prejudice would fail to change those basic facts which had led Congress to pass the law. EEOC began to think about strategies for enforcement that would enable it to change those facts—that is, to improve the economic situation of women and of minorities. The law enforcement approach designed to eliminate discrimination was the overall method chosen. But within that method the strategies had to focus on the economic situation which gave rise to the law in the first place.

The major strategy was to define discrimination objectively in terms of the statistical impact of employment practices and to require the justification of such practices by a business necessity standard instead of focusing only on subjective proof that the state of mind of the employer was deliberately to exclude blacks or women or some other group. Unfortunately, EEOC's strategy for changing unnecessary practices which excluded minorities and women was very difficult to implement using the congressional strategy of voluntary compliance. The process by which the EEOC definition and strategy was ultimately approved by the U.S. Supreme Court and later (in a reexamination of Title VII) by Congress, when it changed its own strategies in order to make it possible to implement the EEOC strategies, deserves examination.

In 1972, Congress decided that the original "voluntary compliance" strategy had failed. The discussion in the congressional report analyzing the reason for the failure is instructive. Committees in both houses of Congress hypothesized that voluntary conciliations often reached an "impasse" because a major participant—employers—simply did not agree with the way in which the government was thinking about discrimination and defining it as a matter of law. Obviously, employers will not eliminate an employment practice voluntarily if they do not believe that it constitutes discrimination. In 1972, Congress pointed out that the average employer—its personnel staff and its legal staff—lacked the "technical perception" to recognize discriminatory employment systems and therefore often thought there was no discrimination to remedy.

Because it agreed with the EEOC strategy and with its perception of discrimination, Congress in 1972 adopted a compulsory compliance strategy and gave EEOC enforcement power, specifying that such power was needed to make the EEOC perception of discrimination prevail even where employers disagreed with it. According to the Senate Committee:

> In 1964, employment discrimination tended to be viewed as a series of isolated and distinguishable events, for the most part due to ill-will on the part of some identifiable individual or organization. It was thought that a scheme that stressed conciliation rather than compulsory processes would be most appropriate for the resolution of the essentially "human" problem, and that litigation would be necessary only on an occasional basis. Experience has shown this view to be false.
>
> Employment discrimination as viewed today is a far more complex and pervasive phenomenon. Experts familiar with the subject now generally describe the problem in terms of "systems" and "effects" rather than simply intentional wrongs, and the literature on the subject is replete with discussions of, for example, the mechanics of seniority and lines of progression, perpetuation of the present effect of preact discriminatory practices through various institutional devices, and testing and validation requirements. [fn]
>
> In short, the problem is one whose resolution in many instances requires not only expert assistance, but also the technical perception that the problem exists in the first instance, and that the system complained of is unlawful. This kind of expertise normally is not found in either the personnel or legal arms of corporations, and the result in terms of conciliations is often an impasse, with the respondent unwilling or unable to understand the problem in the same way that the Commission perceives it.[1]

THE TECHNICAL PERCEPTION OF DISCRIMINATION

What did Congress mean when it suggested that eliminating employment discrimination "requires . . . the technical perception that the . . . system complained of is unlawful"? Historically, we thought about the workplace when we were dealing with discrimination in terms of identifying blame or fault—bias or prejudice. Today under the current technical perception of discrimination we think about the workplace systemically.

As I see it, there has been a three-stage evolution in thinking.[2] Congress suggested that it was absolutely essential in dealing with employment discrimination to have the correct technical perception, and footnoted a series of court decisions spelling out a particular technical perception of systemic discrimination. The major case which they cited is, of course, the Supreme Court case of *Griggs* v. *Duke Power Co.*, 401 U.S. 424, 3 EPD 8137 (1971).

The *Griggs* case summarizes three historical stages in the development of a legal thinking about "discrimination":

Motivation or "ill-will." As the committees pointed out, in 1964 "employment discrimination tended to be viewed as a series of isolated and distinguishable events . . . due to ill-will on the part of some identifiable individual or organization."[3] In *Griggs*, Chief Justice Burger specifically rejected this as the only definition, saying Congress directed Title VII at the "consequences" not the "motivation" of employment practices. He specifically said that "good intent or absence of discriminatory intent does not redeem employment procedures or testing mechanisms that operate as 'built-in head winds' for minority groups and are unrelated to measuring job capability."

Unequal treatment. At Stage 2, discrimination was defined by reference to the actions of the employer, union, or employment agency but focused on identifying only those actions in which blacks and whites similarly situated were treated differently; in which male and females similarly situated were treated differently; in which anglos and chicanos similarly situated were treated differently, on so on. For example, the mandate to federal government investigators contained in the now outdated U.S. Civil Service Commission's pamphlet "Investigating Complaints of Discrimination in Federal Employment" says:

> The ultimate issue in most discrimination complaint cases is whether or not the agency's action or failure to act in the matter complained of was free from discrimination. Direct evidence of discrimination is very rare. Discrimination, when present, is usually revealed by evidence which establishes a *difference of treatment* because of race, color, religion, sex, age, or national origin between the complainant or members of his group, or both, and the person or group alleged to have discriminated. For this reason, the investigator must assemble evidence which will enable the agency official making a decision on the case to determine (1) whether or not there was *disparate treatment* of the complainant and, if so, (2) whether or not the disparate treatment was based on the complainant's race, color, religion, sex, age, or national origin. [Emphasis added.][4]

"Consequences" or "effects." Stage 3 shifts the nature of a governmental inquiry substantially. It shifts how we think about the workplace. The chief justice specifically looks, in *Griggs*, at the two earlier definitions and concludes that, under Title VII, "practices, procedures, or tests

neutral on their face [Stage 2—equal treatment was the standard] and even neutral in terms of intent [Stage 1—the intent or motivation would be the standard] cannot be maintained if they operate to 'freeze' the status quo."

In dealing with the *Griggs* situation (whites registered far better on the company's requirements—written tests and high school diploma— than Negroes), however, the court did not rule out all employment "practices, procedures, and tests" simply because they have an adverse impact. In fact, it provided guidance in determining which tests are to be rejected and which tests can be retained: "The touchstone is business necessity. If an employment practice which operates to exclude Negroes cannot be shown to be related to job performance, the practice is prohibited."

This language focuses us not on a "series of isolated and distinguishable events . . . due to ill-will" but to a description of the problem "in terms of systems and effects." As I understand the *Griggs* case, the initial inquiry in determining whether a system is discriminatory is to look at its effects in terms of race, sex, national origin. If the statistics show that an employment practice or system "operates to exclude," in Burger's words, and if the practice or system in question "cannot be shown" by the employer to be job related *and* a business necessity then "the practice is prohibited."

BUSINESS NECESSITY

The Supreme Court has recognized the difficulty of achieving the special "technical perception" needed to see discriminatory effects, for it later observed that the unequal treatment way of thinking "is the most easily understood type of discrimination."[5] The *Griggs* case established a whole new way of thinking about the workplace. The following concepts are helpful in that thinking and in the development of a strategy to improve the economic position of minorities and/or women:

Statistical factual data. Ample statistics are available to demonstrate that existing employment systems have operated to exclude women from full participation. In all countries and in all types of employment women are, with a few exceptions, concentrated in lower-paying jobs and do not participate fully in employment opportunities. At the national level, decisions must be made on overall strategies; at the level of individual employers, statistics can be used to identify employers whose practices must be examined in greater detail. If an employer's practices indicate that women participate at rates disproportionate to their availability in the labor force (including women who may have excluded themselves because they are discouraged by artificial barriers), then it must justify the practices by a business necessity standard.

An individual employer who wants to engage in "systemic thinking" about his employment practices should first define the nature of his employment system and then examine its precise statistical impact on minorities and women. This awareness of the impact of systems on these groups is the first step in systemic thinking.

The nature of the employment selection process—making predictions. The first step in understanding the nature of the business necessity doctrine is to focus on the concept of "job relatedness." Historically, the first discussion of business necessity occurred when written tests excluding a disproportionate number of minorities were required to be job related. That concept, in turn, can best be understood by looking at the selection process. Let us assume that I have never met you and am considering hiring you. Whether I interviewed you, called your references, looked at your educational background, asked you to take a written test, or timed your running a mile with a stop watch, my goal would be to make a prediction. I want to predict which individuals would be able to perform the job.

Job relatedness—validation. If I use a test which does, in fact, help me to make a prediction as to which individuals will perform on the job I say that the test is "job related." That is, there is a statistical relationship between positive performance on the test and positive performance on the job. I say that the test has been "validated" if someone has actually analyzed the way people perform on the test and compared it with the way they perform on the job and determined that it is useful in making predictions. I cannot talk about a "valid" test because that implies it will make predictions for all types of jobs. I can only talk about "validation" of a test where a study has been performed indicating that it does in fact enable me to make predictions for a *particular* job. Thus, if I had you run around the track, that might help me make predictions about your potential as a messenger but not about your potential as an attorney. The *Griggs* principle in the United States was first enunciated in this context: the court ruled against the Duke Power Company for using a written test which excluded blacks in disproportionate numbers but did not, in fact, predict ability to do the job.

Other systems. While the *Griggs* principle was first enunciated in looking at systems for selecting individuals and making predictions about their performance, the principle applies to all other employment systems. One of the most important things a practitioner must do in this field is to learn how to identify the nature of the employment system he is dealing with—and this is what I call "systemic thinking." For example, applicants for jobs in your company learn about vacancies from friends who work for the company. Your workforce is all male. First, you would ask, What is the nature of the employment system?—it is a "word of mouth recruitment system." Second, you learn that the predictable effect of a word of mouth recruitment system is that it tends to perpetuate the existing nature of the workforce. Third, you would have to question its business necessity.

Business necessity. Under American law the business necessity standard involves a two-stage analysis. First, we ask whether the practice in question is necessary to the safe and efficient operation of the business. Second, and more importantly in dealing with employment discrimination, we ask whether there are available alternative systems which do not have as great an impact on minorities and women. If such alternative systems exist, the employer has an affirmative obligation to utilize those systems. If he fails to do so, discrimination exists.

The term "business necessity" has been discussed in the court decisions. As early as July 28, 1969, one U.S. court[6] looked not only at "safe and efficient" operation of the business but also at the question of whether there were "alternatives" available with a lesser racial impact. In discussing whether a certain job seniority system as it was then functioning was "so necessary . . . as to justify" its adverse impact on Negroes, the court looked at expert testimony suggesting that there was an alternative system available (a fractional seniority credit system for victims of discrimination) that would meet the employer's legitimate business needs while eliminating the exclusionary impact on blacks.

In *Robinson* v. *Lorillard*,[7] Judge Sobeloff discussed the evolution of such cases as *Papermakers* and *Griggs*. He suggested:

> Collectively these cases conclusively establish that the applicable test is not merely whether there exists a business purpose for adhering to a challenged practice. The test is whether there exists an overriding legitimate business purpose such that the practice is necessary to the safe and efficient operation of the business. Thus, the business purpose must be sufficiently compelling to override any racial impact; the challenged practice must effectively carry out the business purpose it is alleged to serve; and there must be available no available acceptable alternative policy or practices which would better accomplish the business purpose advanced, or accomplish it equally well with a lesser differential racial impact.[8]

Judge Sobeloff explains the final phrase with a footnote: "It should go without saying that a practice is hardly 'necessary' if an alternative practice better effectuates the intended purpose or is equally effective but less discriminatory."[9] Significantly, it was Sobeloff who wrote a dissenting opinion when the appeals court hearing *Griggs* refused to adopt the Stage 3 impact theory of discrimination. His language there appears to have played a role in the thinking of the Supreme Court in *Griggs*. Specifically Sobeloff said:

the statute interdicts practices that are fair in form but discriminatory in substance. Thus, it has become well settled that "objective" or "neutral" standards that favor whites but do not serve business needs are undoubtively unlawful employment practices. The critical inquiry is *business necessity* and if it cannot be shown that an employment practice which excludes Blacks stems from legitimate needs, the practices must end.[10]

What the *Robinson* case required has critically been called a "no alternative" approach to business necessity. In the case of *Crockett* v. *Green*,[11] Judge Reynolds of the U.S. District Court for the Eastern District of Wisconsin recognized that there are two steps. According to him, "professional validation is but a part" of the business necessity justification which an employer must demonstrate to retain employment practices with an adverse impact on blacks. He cites *Robinson* v. *Lorillard* for the proposition that business necessity requires "not only validation of requirements and tests but also a demonstration by the employer that there are not available alternatives to the tests or requirements which have a lesser racial impact."[12]

Judge Reynolds suggests, however, that if the "no alternative" approach were to be "literally applied" it would give the employer the "practically impossible burden" of proving an absolute negative—that is, the "nonexistence of any alternative procedures." Judge Reynolds suggests that be believes:

> A fair and preferable allocation of the burden of proof on the existence of alternatives would place upon the plaintiff the burden of initially *proposing or suggesting* reasonable alternative practices while leaving to the employer the ultimate burden of demonstrating that any *suggested* alternatives are not adequate substitutes for its present practices. [Emphasis added.][13]

The Supreme Court in the *Moody* case[14] confronted a related issue and makes it clear that it, also, believes there is a two-step process. The court accepts the position that there are two separate elements which must be dealt with, but it may accept Judge Reynolds' requirement that the plaintiff must "suggest" the alternative when it states:

> If an employer does . . . meet the burden of proving that its tests are "job related," it remains open to the complaining party to show that other tests or selection devices, without a similarly undesirable racial effect, would also serve the employer's legitimate interest in "efficient and trustworthy workmanship."[15]

Is the court suggesting the possibility that, even if an employer can show the written test or high school diploma requirement to be validated and job related, it would still be illegal under Title VII if some other "selection device" would also serve the employer's legitimate interest "without a similarly undesirable racial effect"? The Fifth Circuit Court of Appeals obviously thinks so, for they quoted *Moody* ("other tests or selection devices without a similarly undesirable racial effect") to make it clear that there are two steps, that a validated test can be illegal. Specifically, Judge Wisdom said: "It is clear that business necessity is limited to those cases where an employer has no other choice. Here, even if the diploma requirement is job related, it is likely that its abrogation will not result in unqualified employees being thrown into impossible situations."[16]

Clearly, the Supreme Court believes that business necessity and job relatedness are two different and separate steps in the obligation of an employer to deal with employment practices and systems which "operate to exclude." The court removes any ambiguity on this issue at the end of the *Albemarle* opinion when it re-emphasizes the charging party's opportunity "to present evidence that even validated tests might be" discriminatory in light of "alternate selection procedures available to the company."[17]

As for sex discrimination—this concept from *Moody* was accepted by Justice Rehnquist in his concurring opinion in *Dothard* v. *Rawlinson*.[18] There, a height-weight requirement having a nationwide disparate impact on women had been found illegal when the employer failed to justify it. He concurred with the conclusion on the facts of the case, but he said he was not prepared to state that "all or even many of the height and weight requirements imposed by states" are illegal. He suggested that employers might on the facts in other cases be able to prove that "height and weight requirements" were job related. He went on to stress that even this would not end the inquiry but that "under our cases, the burden would shift back to [the government or charging party] to demonstrate that other tests, without such disparate effect, would also meet that concern."[19]

There is nothing in the cases I have quoted concerning the intent, motivation, bias, bigotry, or prejudices of the employer. As I suggested earlier, this is not just a change in the definition of the word "discrimination" but a major change in how we think about the workplace. Thus, when we investigate a case we are no longer thinking about identifying a person whose evil motivation or state of mind was responsible for the exclusion of blacks and women. We are, instead, thinking about the statistical facts, the existence of alternatives, and the business necessity for the practice in question. I believe that this way of thinking about the workplace is perhaps the most important contribution that the United States has made during the fifteen years that it has been struggling with strategies for the effective enforcement of anti-discrimination legislation.

Moreover, a definition of discrimination based on objective standards would not just improve the economic position of women or minorities. A subjective standard which focuses investigations and law enforcement efforts on proof of employer motive has the predictable result of increasing anxiety in the workplace. The workers are trying to prove that the boss is prejudiced and the boss is trying to prove his good faith. Neither effort is designed to increase productivity. Both efforts increase anxiety. Productivity falls. Adoption of the objective, job-relatedness standard would mean all employment decisions will be increasingly made on an objective and production-oriented basis, and productivity will rise both within countries and worldwide.

A RECOMMENDED STRATEGY FOR DEALING WITH THE ECONOMIC POSITION OF WOMEN

As other chapters point out, women participate in the economic opportunities of various countries less than do their male counterparts. Some of these gaps are due to education, training, background, child care obligations, and so forth. I believe that a large part of the gap is caused by what we now describe as "discrimination." I believe that a strategy to close these gaps should focus in part on changing how we think about the gaps. That strategy would define many of these gaps (or the systems which lead to the gaps) as "discrimination" and it would focus on closing them by the implementation and enforcement of anti-discrimination legislation. Such a strategy should have, at a minimum, six elements:

Make it illegal to discriminate in employment. An appropriate law should be passed making it illegal to discriminate in employment.

Define discrimination in terms of the effect of employment systems and evaluate that effect under the business necessity standard. Discrimination should be defined in "objective" rather than "subjective" terms. It would still be illegal to exclude women (or other sex, racial, and ethnic groups) because one was motivated by an exclusionary state of mind, and it would still be illegal to treat them unequally. The major focus of the law would, however, be on employment systems which had an exclusionary impact and could not be justified.

Convention 111 of the International Labor Organization dealing with employment discrimination defines the term "discrimination" as early as 1958 in language broad enough to encompass this definition of employment discrimination:

> For the purpose of this convention, the term "discrimination" includes . . . any distinction, exclusion, or preference made on the basis of race, colour, sex, religion, political opinion, national extraction or social origin which has the effect of nullifying or impairing the quality of opportunity or treatment in employment or occupation.

It further provides that "any distinction, exclusion, or preference in respect to a particular job based on the inherent requirements thereof shall not be deemed to be discrimination."

In jurisdictions which permit a law to be interpreted once it has been passed, all that needs to be done is to pass a law outlawing "discrimination" and to interpret it in the *Griggs*–business necessity fashion. In other jurisdictions where courts and administrative agencies do not have this interpretive flexibility it is essential that the law be drafted in such a fashion as to include the *Griggs* or objective standard. Language similar to that in Convention 111 could be used.

Establish a specific authority to enforce this law. Because of the systemic nature of employment discrimination, many of the existing institutions both in government and in society are involved in the implementation and maintenance of systems which have the exclusionary impact on women or minorities. These institutions are inappropriate for enforcing a new law designed to change those systems. It is recommended that an appropriate enforcement strategy normally would include the establishment of some independent enforcing agency within the government or, at a minimum (if enforcement is to be assigned to an existing agency, bureau, or department), that a separate subsection be established and that this subsection, subbureau, or subdivision have its own lawyers and its own enforcement power.

Give the enforcement agency adequate power. An anti-discrimination enforcement strategy will not work if the agency given responsibility for its administration does not have adequate powers. At a minimum, those powers should include the power to gather statistical data, to initiate enforcement action, to subpoena data, to enforce compliance, and to issue guidelines.

The agency should have the power to gather reports and statistical data from employers, labor unions, and other entities which may be operating systems which have an exclusionary impact on women. The goal of these statistics would be to measure the extent of the exclusionary practices and to pinpoint them for justification or elimination.

It is important that the enforcement agency have the power to receive and investigate individual complaints. The most important power, however, will be the power to initiate its own investigations and its own enforcement actions. In the early days, EEOC blurred these two powers. The result was a substantial backlog of complaints. A study of the American experience shows the importance of separating the processing of individual complaints where the focus is on a rapid remedy for the individual from the processing of initiated systemic complaints where the focus is on changing an entire employment system which has an exclusionary impact and replacing it with a nonexclusionary system.

An investigation of an individual charge or an initiated systemic charge will never be adequate unless the investigating agency has broad power to gather factual and statistical data concerning all aspects of the employment system and the power to compel employers, labor unions, and others to supply this data when they do not wish to do so.

The agency administering the law must have the power to bring law suits or take other action within the framework of its country's legal system to compel employers to change and eliminate the employment systems which have an exclusionary impact on women and minorities and to require the implementation of alternative systems in their place. This power must include power to require reports on compliance.

If possible, consistent with the legal system of the country or jurisdiction in question, the enforcing agency should have the power to issue interpretive guidelines.

Set up an agency program. The agency program must separate the processing of individual grievances from agency-initiated investigations. Agency investigations should be initiated using the statistics gathered pursuant to the reporting and data-gathering power. Specifically, employers whose statistical reports indicate that their systems have an exclusionary impact on minorities and women should be the subject of investigation. The focus of those investigations will provide the employer an opportunity to submit his or her justification, which can then be evaluated by the job relatedness–business necessity standard.

Set up a voluntary compliance strategy. I believe only a law with a strong enforcement mechanism will work to change unnecessary exclusionary employment systems. Once such a law has been passed, implemented, and enforced, however, some of the greatest changes will occur through voluntary compliance. This requires that the staff of the enforcing agency and personnel in the legal and enforcement arms of companies, unions, and others get expertise in what I have called, throughout this chapter, "systemic thinking." Every time an individual thinks about his or her employment system, he must be aware of two questions: What is the impact of this system? If the system is exclusionary, is there an alternative system available? When both government and private institutions begin to think about employment systems in this fashion, changes will begin to occur that will assure that women and minorities and others now excluded are included and which will do so in a fashion which will contribute to the country's productivity constructively. It is a strategy which, I believe, will have the maximum impact in the long run on improving the economic situation of women and which will, secondly, have the maximum impact on increasing the world's productivity to the benefit of us all.

NOTES

1. *Legislative History of the Equal Employment Opportunity Act of 1972* (House of Representatives 1746, P.L. 92-261) Amending Title VII of the Civil Rights Act of 1964 (Washington, D.C.: GPO, Nov. 1972), p. 414. Footnote in the original reads: "See e.g., 'Developments in Law'—Employment Discrimination and Title VII of the Civil Rights Act of 1964,' 84 Harv. L. Rev. 1109 (1971); Cooper and Sobol, 'Seniority and Testing Under Fair Employment Laws: A General Approach to Objective Criteria of Hiring and Promotion,' 82 Harv. L. Rev. 1623 (1969); Blumrosen, 'The Duty of Fair Recruitment Under the Civil Rights Act of 1964,' 22 Rutgers L. Rev. 465 (1968). See also M. Sovern, Legal Restraints on Racial Discrimination in Employment (1966), and decisions in *Griggs* v. *Duke Power Co.*, 401 U.S. 424 (1971); *Asbestos Workers, Local 53* v. *Vogler*, 407 F.2d 1047 (C.A. 5 1969); *Quarles* v. *Phillip Morris*, 279 F. Supp. 505 (E.D. va. 1968); *U.S.* v. *Local 138 United Papermakers*, 282 F. Supp. 39 (E.D. La., 1968) and cases cited therein."

2. The three-stage analysis was first suggested to me by Al Blumrosen in his landmark article "Strangers in Paradise: *Griggs* v. *Duke Power* and the Concept of Employment Discrimination," *Michigan Law Review* 71 (1972): 59. The Supreme Court acknowledges the different theoretical ways of thinking about discrimination when it cites Professor Blumrosen's article in *Teamsters* v. *U.S.*, 14 FEP Cases 1514, 431 U.S. 324 (1977), 1519 n. 15. Another analysis suggests that there are four ways of thinking about discrimination. In the same footnote the court cites Barbara Lindemann Schlei and Paul Grossman, *Employment Discrimination Law* (Washington, D.C.: Bureau of National Affairs, 1976), pp. 1–12. Schlei and Grossman suggest that there are *four* ways of thinking about discrimination. They split the third one (which I call the *Griggs* theory and the Supreme Court calls the "disparate impact theory") into two for discussion purposes—one focusing on employment systems with a present disparate impact and another focusing on present effects of past discrimination. For my purposes I perceive those as basically the same way of thinking about the world—in "systemic" terms—although, for some purposes, the subdivision may be useful.

3. *Legislative History*, p. 414. The committees were the Senate Committee on Labor and Public Welfare and the House Committee on Labor and Education.

4. U.S. Civil Service Commission, *Personnel Message Series No. 17* . . . (rev. ed.; Washington, D.C.: GPO, March 1975), p. 21. See also the same book (p. 25), which mandates that an investigative file contain information showing "how the complainant's group has been treated compared with other groups over which the alleged discriminatory official has exercise [discretion] in personnel matters." For additional analysis on the technical perception of the pre-1977 Civil Service Commission concerning employment discrimination, see "Statement Recommending a Constant Federal Approach to Class

and Systemic Discrimination under Title VII." This analysis and comment on proposed CSC rules was transmitted to CSC Chairman Hampton with a cover letter from EEOC Vice Chairman Ethel Bent Walsh, June 22, 1976.

5. 14 FEP Cases 1514, 1519 n. 15 (1977).

6. *Local 189, United Papermakers and Paperworkers* v. *U.S.*, 417 F.2d 980, 2 EPD 10,047 (5th Cir. 1969).

7. 444 F.2d 791, 3 EPD 8267 (4th Cir. 1971).

8. Ibid., 3 EPD 8267 at p. 6901.

9. Ibid., n. 7.

10. 2 EPD 10,143, p. 548.

11. 388 F. Supp. 912, 9 EPD 10,029 (D. C. Wis. 1975).

12. Ibid., 9 EPD 10,029, p. 7258.

13. Ibid., p. 7259.

14. *Albemarle Paper Co.* v. *Moody*, 422 U. S. 407, 9 EPD §10,230 (1975).

15. Ibid., 9 EPD 10,230, p. 8006.

16. *Watkins* v. *Scott Paper Co.*, 530 F.2d 1159, 11 EPD 10,880 (5th Cir. 1976).

17. 422 U. S. 407.

18. 14 EPD 7632, 15 FEP Cases 10 (1977).

19. Ibid., 14 EPD 7632, p. 5109.

6 *Dipak Nandy*

ADMINISTERING ANTI-DISCRIMINATION LEGISLATION IN GREAT BRITAIN

Assessing the administration of a social policy is an essential part of describing that policy. The conception of a policy and its implementation are not two separate entities. What a policy is cannot be divorced from how it is implemented. How good a policy is cannot be divorced from whether it can be implemented effectively. Whether a policy can be effectively implemented depends on whether the design of its implementation mechanism matches the strategic aims of the policy—the development of a new warhead is a pretty useless exercise unless an adequate delivery system is also planned simultaneously. Good ideas, in this as in other fields, live or die in the administration.

This chapter deals with the administration of anti-discrimination legislation relating to equal pay and sex discrimination in Great Britain

(England, Wales, and Scotland; Northern Ireland has its own parallel legislation and its own Equal Opportunities Commission). To understand the nature of the enforcement agency, the Equal Opportunities Commission, and the other relevant agencies, we need to understand the evolution of anti-discrimination legislation as such in Great Britain. Only in this context are the powers, duties, and limitations of the enforcement agency fully intelligible.

In Britain there are four stages, broadly speaking, in translating a social goal into operational policy. The first stage is a campaign or lobby to get social recognition for an issue or a social problem (homelessness, the position of one-parent families, equality for women). The emphasis at this stage is on the long-term social ideal; the object of the campaign is to create a coalition behind the issue and to generate momentum for governmental action.

If the campaign succeeds, the issue is taken up by a government department. This is the second stage. A White Paper, outlining the government's proposals, is placed before Parliament. A social ideal is now in process of being translated into the language of statute. In addition, the policy proposals are inevitably affected by the other commitments of the government. When a conservative government deals with homelessness, it is likely to find that its commitment to private home ownership as a form of tenure and its championing of the private landlord considerably dilute any tendency towards a radical policy. A Labour government, even in the best of circumstances, is unlikely to champion a proposal which places it at odds with the Trades Union Congress and the unions. These are the facts of political life, but to those who campaigned for the social ideal, the vision has already begun to fade.

The third stage is the passage of a bill through Parliament—the most important part of the process being the committee stage, in which MPs drawn from the major parties debate the clauses of the bill and amendments proposed in the light of the preceding public debate. Here, from the point of view of the campaigners, is room for more horse-trading, more compromises, further dilution.

Finally, after the act has been passed, an agency is set up, or existing agencies are extended, to implement the act's provisions. These agencies are generally para-governmental agencies, so they inevitably adopt a civil-service approach to their task. To the campaigners the cause seems to have been taken over by faceless bureaucrats.

It is important to be explicit about these four stages. If enough care is not devoted from the start—the *campaigning* stage—to the last and, some would argue, most crucial stage—the machinery for implementation—then disenchantment is inevitable.

THE EVOLUTION OF ANTI-DISCRIMINATION LEGISLATION

Two separate streams of lobbying came together to produce the Sex Discrimination Act of 1975. First of all, there was the pressure to develop some official measures to promote equality of opportunity for women. Between 1967 and 1969, Christopher Norwood, MP, introduced an equal pay bill on three occasions. During roughly the same period, between May 1968 and February 1971, Joyce Butler, MP, introduced four bills against sex discrimination, and similar bills were introduced by William Hamilton, MP, in December 1971 and November 1972. Baroness Seear introduced similar bills in the House of Lords in 1972. Thus, from the latter half of the 1960s there was growing pressure to introduce legislation in this field, the first product of which was the Equal Pay Act, 1970. The pressure to extend legislation to cover discrimination in matters other than pay and terms and conditions of work was carried forward in the report of a Labour Party study group, *Discrimination against Women*, in November 1972. In September 1973, the then home secretary, Robert Carr, MP, presented a consultative document to Parliament, *Equal Opportunities for Men and Women*, in which a set of legislative measures to promote equality of opportunity in employment and education was put forward. In March 1974, however, before any legislation of this kind could be presented to Parliament, a new Labour administration came into office, with a commitment to introducing legislation of a more radical kind than the Conservative government had envisaged.

The second influence on the development of the Sex Discrimination Act was the growing pressure from the early 1950s to enact anti-discrimination legislation dealing with discrimination on the grounds of race or color. In that process, three features were especially important. One was the considerable and continuing debt to the United States experience in this field and, at the same time, a continuing problem of relating legislation and enforcement models drawn from one country to the legal and economic institutions of another. The second was the trade-off needed between conciliation and wider, strategic powers of an enforcement agency. In Chapter 7 of this volume, Jeffrey Jowell traces the implications of these two features for anti-discrimination legislation in Great Britain.

The third historical feature—the separation of enforcement in the employment field from enforcement in other forms of discrimination—is especially important, and therefore, requires elaboration. For the pressure for strengthened anti-discrimination legislation, with stronger enforcement powers, took place at just that historical point when the trade union movement was most resistant to the idea of any form of legal intervention whatsoever in industrial relations. Industrial relations in Britain have been characterized by what has come to be known as the "abstention of the law."[1] From 1967 to the present, however, the need to control inflation has become the major priority of successive governments, of both parties, and the pressure on governments for some form of statutory incomes policy ran into severe opposition from the trade union movement. In January 1969, the then Labour government produced a White Paper, *In Place of Strife*, whose proposals became an issue of major contention between the government and the unions. The Conservative government of 1970–74 pressed forward with their plans and enacted the Industrial Relations Act, 1972, against severe opposition from the unions and the Labour party. The enforcement agency was a specially constituted court, the National Industrial Relations Court, a body which never succeeded in shaking off its controversial origins. As soon as Labour took office in 1974, the Industrial Relations Act was replaced by the Trade Union and Labour Relations Act (TULRA), 1974, and the NIRC disappeared.

The trade union movement, however, was also committed to the principle of an effective attack on discrimination on the grounds of both sex and race. The only feasible compromise was to separate the enforcement of the legislation's employment provisions from that of the other provisions. In the case of the Sex Discrimination Act, this was all the more necessary because the Equal Pay Act had been enacted in the last months of the Labour government of 1964–1970, and the enforcement of this act was entrusted to industrial tribunals and the Central Arbitration Committee (described below). From the point of view of the individual complainant, therefore, the present anti-discrimination legislation provides two routes: in matters of equal pay, the complainant seeks redress through an industrial tribunal, with the possibility of appeal to the Employment Appeal Tribunal, while collective agreements between employers and unions can be scrutinized by the Central Arbitration Committee; in matters of discrimination other than pay, the complainant seeks redress through the county courts. This is not an ideal solution. Indeed, Americans might well find it unintelligible. But this is the shape taken by the plant when transplanted from American to British soil.

One further innovation in British anti-discrimination legislation that owed much to the American experience was the prohibiting of "indirect discrimination." Experience in the administration of British legislation had already demonstrated (as successive reports of the Race Relations Board bear out) that a legal attack on direct discrimination was by itself of limited effectiveness. Some acceptable method had to be found for dealing with the effects of past discrimination on both the disadvantaged group in question (lowered expectations, lower demands, etc.) and on social institutions (lowered provisions, the maintenance of conditions or requirements which assumed lower demand). Here the case of *Griggs* v. *Duke Power Co.* was crucial. In a lecture delivered to the Race Relations

Board's annual conference in 1973, Professor Louis Pollak, dean of the University of Pennsylvania Law School, highlighted the significance of this case in enabling Americans to come to grips, through the law, with rules, conditions, or requirements which were fair in form but discriminatory in operation.[2] This was the origin of the concept of "indirect discrimination," which section 1(1)(b) of the Sex Discrimination Act declares to be unlawful. The effect of this innovation is not merely that it specifies more precisely what constitutes unlawful discrimination but, much more, that it brings the statutory definition of "discrimination" closer to the reality of the social and institutional processes that enable acts of overt discrimination to resonate, so to speak, through the social system. To that extent, the Sex Discrimination Act, 1975, and the closely allied Race Relations Act, 1976,[3] comprise a body of anti-discrimination legislation as comprehensive in scope and powerful in remedies as can be found anywhere in the world.

INSTITUTIONS, PROCEDURES, AND PROBLEMS

Apart from the Equal Opportunities Commission itself, there are three national institutions involved in the process of law enforcement. These are: the ACAS, the Advisory, Conciliation and Arbitration Service, set up under the Trade Union and Labour Relations Act, 1974; the industrial tribunals and the Employment Appeal Tribunal (EAT); and the Central Arbitration Committee (CAC).

ACAS

The Advisory, Conciliation and Arbitration Service, set up under the TULRA, 1974, does not, as its name implies, possess any law enforcement powers. It is, however, an important agency. It can be called into any industrial dispute to undertake conciliation and arbitration functions, none of which prevents the parties in a dispute from taking such further legal action as they please. The central role of ACAS is to prevent disputes from escalating to the point where they require the intervention either of the courts or of the government. Many private settlements in equal pay and sex discrimination cases are reached through the intervention of ACAS. (See Tables 6-1, 6-2, 6-3, and 6-4.) Previous experience of anti-discrimination legislation suggests that it may be desirable to split the conciliation and law enforcement roles in this way, for it is logistically difficult for the same agency to attempt to perform the tasks of conciliation and law enforcement in succession, as Jeffrey Jowell points out in Chapter 7. It is possible that the emphasis on conciliation may lead ACAS to per-

TABLE 6-1
Outcome of Applications, Equal Pay Act (1976)

Outcome		COMPLAINTS	
		No.	*%*
Conciliated settlements and withdrawals where conciliation attempted			
Settlements		106	6.1
Withdrawals			
Private settlement	180	854	49.0
Reasons not known*	674		
Other withdrawals			
Private settlement	4	73	4.2
Reasons not known*	69		
Tribunal hearings			
Complaints upheld		213	12.2
Dismissals			
Not like or equivalent work	366		
Not same employment	10	496	28.5
Material difference	78		
Other reasons	42		
TOTAL		1,742	100.0

*These will include cases where the parties reached a private settlement but ACAS were not informed and cases where the applicant found the complaint to be out of scope.

TABLE 6-2
Outcome of Applications, Sex Discrimination Act (1976)

Outcome	Male	Female	Total
Conciliated settlements	9	26	35
Withdrawn			
Private settlement	3	18	21
Reasons not known*	19	49	68
Tribunal decisions			
Application upheld	6	18	24
Applications dismissed	22	73	95
TOTAL	59	184	243

*These will include cases where the parties reached a private settlement but ACAS were not informed and cases where the applicant found the complaint to be out of scope.

TABLE 6-3
Outcome of Applications, Equal Pay Act (1977)

Outcome	Males	Females	Total	%
Conciliated settlements and withdrawals where conciliation attempted				
Settlements	5	51	56	7.5
Withdrawals				
Private settlement	3	93	96	12.8
Reasons not known*	9	226	235	31.3
Other withdrawals				
Private settlement				
Reasons not known*	1		1	0.1
Tribunal hearings				
Complaints upheld	35	56	91	12.1
Dismissals				
Not like or equivalent work	1	133	134	17.8
Not same employment		2	2	0.3
Material difference	7	79	86	11.5
Other reasons	11	39	50	6.6
TOTAL	72	679	751	100.0

*These will include cases where the parties reached a private settlement but ACAS were not informed and cases where the applicant found the complaint to be out of scope.

TABLE 6-4
Outcome of Applications, Sex Discrimination Act (1977)

Outcome	Males	Females	Total	%
Conciliated settlements	24	39	63	27.5
Withdrawn				
Private settlement	4	9	13	5.7
Reasons not known*	23	53	76	33.2
Tribunal decisions				
Order declaring rights	1	5	6	2.6
Awards of compensation	2	6	8	3.5
Recommended course of action	1	2	3	1.3
Dismissal	12	48	60	26.2
TOTAL	67	162	229	100.0

*These will include cases where the parties reached a private settlement but ACAS were not informed and cases where the applicant found the complaint to be out of scope.

suade complainants to accept "soft settlements" in the interests of industrial harmony, but to my knowledge such a complaint has not been lodged against ACAS. On the contrary, what complaints there are, are broadly to the effect that the agency is required to do too much and, because of the absence of sanctions, is unable to influence the course of events. It is thus in the unenviable position of being accused at once of interference and impotence, accusations which pay scant regard to its many silent successes.

Industrial tribunals and the Employment Appeal Tribunal

Industrial tribunals were first set up in 1911. Their main current functions derive, first, from the Industrial Relations Act, 1971, which required the tribunals to hear unfair dismissal cases, and from the TULRA, 1974, which gave them a wider jurisdiction to hear cases on health and safety at work, employment protection, sex discrimination, and equal pay. Although either or both parties are entitled to legal representation before an industrial tribunal, the intention is to discourage excessive legalism. Most important, the finding of an industrial tribunal does not create case law. The relative informality of the tribunals is, therefore, balanced by the fact that the findings of industrial tribunals on similar cases may show wide variations.

The finding of an industrial tribunal may be appealed to the Employment Appeal Tribunal. The President of the EAT is a high court judge nominated by the lord chancellor, who also nominates a number of other high court judges to direct the progress of EAT cases. At least one further judge is nominated by the lord president of the court of session to act in the same capacity. The legally qualified member of the tribunal is assisted by two or four lay members, appointed by the queen, on the joint recommendation of the lord chancellor and the secretary of state for employment. These lay members must possess a practical knowledge of industrial relations, as representatives of either employers or workers. The decisions of the Employment Appeal Tribunal, unlike those of industrial tribunals, do create case law, and they are therefore particularly important in clarifying the provisions of the law.[*] (The tribunals' decisions on sex discrimination are discussed at length in Chapter 12.)

The Central Arbitration Committee

Where there are collective agreements between employers and unions, the responsibility for cleaning up discriminatory clauses rests with the Central Arbitration Committee. In its present form, its origin lies in the

Industrial Arbitration Board (IAB) set up under the Industrial Relations Act, 1971. Under the Employment Protection Act, 1975, it took over the functions of the IAB, with its present title, as of February 1, 1976. Constitutionally it is a committee of ACAS, and is headed by a chairman appointed by the secretary of state for employment after consultation with ACAS.

Under the 1975 Act the Committee has responsibilities relating to the workings of collective agreements, pay structures, wage regulation orders, and agricultural wage orders that contain any provision applying specifically to men only or women only. References to the CAC can be made by either party to the agreement or by the secretary of state for employment. The Committee may then declare what amendments need to be made in the agreement, order, or pay structure so as to remove discriminatory provisions. The Committee does not deal with complaints from individuals.

At mid-1976 there were about 8,000 collective agreements affecting more than 100 employees each. Approximately 350 of these determined the pay of 4.5 million employees. Additionally, there were large numbers of small companies where pay was determined by collective bargaining for much smaller groups than 100.

The main powers of the CAC are dealt with in section 3(4) of the Equal Pay Act, 1970 (as amended by schedule 1 of the Sex Discrimination Act, 1975). According to that section, amendments are required in a collective agreement

(a) to extend to both men and women any provision applying to men only or to women only; and

(b) to eliminate any resulting duplication in the provisions of the agreement in such a way as not to make the terms and conditions agreed for men, or those agreed for women, less favourable in any respect than they would have been without the amendment.

The approach of the CAC is best set out in its own words: "The Committee's chief aim is to approach its various tasks in an informal way. The legal framework covering a particular type of case is acknowledged and respected but the work of the Committee, within that framework, is industrial arbitration."[5] The Committee does not operate on precedent. The facts of each case are looked at afresh and, in applying the rules, most chairmen tend to look at good industrial relations practice as much as to the letter of the law. There is no machinery for appeals within the CAC, and serious errors of fact or mistakes of law can be brought before the regular courts, by the use of prerogative writs, particularly certiorari. Several such cases have been brought, and have enabled the framework of law to be clarified, as the Committee acknowledges.[6]

The Committee's approach to equal pay and the degree of its success are lucidly set out in its annual report for 1977:

> The legislative provisions in S.3 of the Act are somewhat obscurely drafted. The Committee sees its first task as that of identifying existing discrimination. The task is not always easy. Discrimination does not always appear on the face of the agreement. For example an agreement may have been re-negotiated or altered with Grade 1 and Grade 2 replacing the previous male clerks and female clerks with no other change. Such a change cannot be said to have ended the matter. The Committee has to ensure that discrimination has been truly removed and replaced with unisex grades bearing appropriate rates. Distribution of sexes amongst the grades forms an interesting pointer. Significant representation of both sexes will often be dependent upon changes in historical attitudes and social custom, which do not occur quickly. Very uneven distribution may indicate that real discrimination has not been eliminated. Each case requires special attention.
>
> Once discrimination is seen to exist, the Committee has found that its informal approach and its determination to use the goodwill of the parties to achieve a sound solution are invaluable. Joint job evaluation is very often an essential prerequisite to settlement and it has been found that there is usually willingness to undertake this. Often all that is needed from the Committee is advice, although not surprisingly the final settlement of grade rates does lead to disagreements that the Committee can resolve.
>
> There are those who have constructed the provisions of the Act as meaning that those rates in an agreement or structure which are female only must be raised to the lowest male rate irrespective of job content. This is a view which is hard to reconcile with the concept of equality and leads to the extinction of differentials which may still be necessary if a grading structure showing the relative assessment of jobs free from discrimination based on sex is to be maintained. It has been found possible by means of the procedures set out in the last paragraph to achieve solutions which are perceived as fair and reflect true equality.
>
> It is the involvement of the parties that gives the Committee most satisfaction. Solutions have to be operated successfully and those that are jointly evolved, albeit with guidance, stand the best change of success—certainly more so than those arbitrably imposed.
>
> An analysis of our awards on equal pay shows the overwhelming majority of applications alleging discriminatory collective agreements were upheld. The total number dealt with by the Committee since full implementation of the Equal Pay Act is, of course, too small to represent a significant proportion, but may well be indicative of many more such agreements and pay structures operating in a discriminatory manner in British industry.[7]

The Equal Opportunities Commission

The Equal Opportunities Commission, which began operation in December 1975, has, along with its educational and persuasional activities, the strategic role of enforcing the law in the public interest. The Commission has a wide variety of powers and considerable discretion (subject to appeal to the ordinary courts) in the exercise of these powers. The Sex Discrimination Act, 1975, gives the Commission powers to deal with discriminatory advertisements (sec. 38), with instructions and pressure to discriminate (sec. 39, 40), and with discrimination by way of victimization (sec. 4).

By far the most important of its powers are: (1) to assist individual complainants (sec. 75); (2) to undertake formal investigations into any purpose connected with the carrying out of its statutory duties; and (3) to take action against persistent discriminators (sec. 71). Although the Act places the main responsibility of seeking redress on the individuals who felt themselves to be aggrieved, it recognizes that there will be circumstances in which it would not be reasonable to expect an individual to embark on legal action unaided. In the absence of legal aid for proceedings before industrial tribunals, but given the general problem of proving discrimination, the section 75 powers of assistance are in fact part of the Commission's strategic role of helping to clarify the law. Assistance under this section includes: giving informal legal advice to individuals or their advisers; visiting both complainants and respondents where there have been complaints; briefing the applicant's own counsel; providing counsel to represent an applicant; and supporting appeals against an industrial tribunal decision.

The Commission is required to consider all such applications for assistance, though the decision to grant assistance is discretionary. The main grounds on which assistance can be granted are three: where the case raises a question of principle; where it is unreasonable to expect an individual complainant to deal with the case unaided, whether because of the complexity of the case or because of the applicant's position in relation to the respondent or to other involved persons; and where other special considerations arise. It will be seen that the discretion given to the Commission is very broad indeed. (Statistics of assistance granted under section 75 are set out in Table 6-5.) At the heart of the Commission's strategic role as envisaged by Parliament is the power to conduct formal investigations into suspected unlawful acts or discriminatory practices in the absence of individual complaints. By 1978, the Commission had undertaken two formal investigations, one in the field of education and the other in employment, relevant details of which can be found in the Commission's annual reports.[8]

TABLE 6-5
Assistance Granted under Section 75 of the Sex Discrimination
Act, 1976 and 1977

Judicial body	*Number of requests*	*Legal assistance granted*	*Advice granted*	*No assistance granted*	*Withdrawn*
1976					
Industrial tribunals and county courts	30	5	15	10	
Employment Appeal Tribunal	8	5	2	1	
Court of Appeal					
House of Lords					
TOTAL	38	10	17	11	
1977					
Industrial tribunals and county courts	59	29	7	16	7
Employment Appeal Tribunal	21	15		4	2
Court of Appeal	3	1		2	
House of Lords	1	1			
TOTAL	84	46	7	22	9

The concept of a formal investigation is a broad one: it can be confined to the activities of a single firm or organization or to an entire industry or to practices common to a number of industries. The intention was to give the Commission as much discretion as possible in taking a strategic overview of the pattern and incidence of sex discrimination in society generally and to determine its own priorities. This broad, discretionary power is, of course, accompanied by a number of constraints. Very broadly, the outline of a formal investigation is as follows.

The Commission decides to conduct a formal investigation and appoints new commissioners or nominates existing commissioners to conduct it (sec. 57); terms of reference are drawn up and, where they allege that a particular person has behaved unlawfully, an opportunity must be given to that person to make representations to the Commission about the allegation before the formal investigation begins (sec. 58); evidence within the terms of reference is then collected by the Commission, if necessary, with the aid of the Commission's statutory powers to compel information to be given (sec. 59); at the end of an investigation the Commission must draw up a report of its findings and may, either during or at the end of an investigation, make recommendations based on the findings that have been made (sec. 60); finally, commissioners and Commission employees are required to keep information gained in the course of an investigation confidential, except in specified circumstances, although this restriction does not apply to the person being investigated (sec. 61).

In conducting a formal investigation, the Commission must have careful regard not only to the strict and explicit requirements of the statute but also to the wider common law requirements imposed upon any statutory body which exercises statutory powers—for example, the rule of natural justice that requires that every person should know what allegations are made against him or her and be given an adequate opportunity to state his or her own case in reply. The Commission must take care to ensure that it always acts within the scope of the powers given to it. The terms of reference of an investigation must relate to the Commission's duties as set out in section 53 of the Sex Discrimination Act. Where those terms of reference allege that a person has behaved unlawfully, the Commission must ensure that it has sufficient evidence on which to base those allegations. The Commission can only require such evidence as is relevant to the terms of reference that it has set itself.

Nondiscrimination notices may be issued by the Commission only after a formal investigation has been completed and only if that investigation has disclosed evidence of unlawful acts within either the Sex Discrimination Act or Equal Pay Act. Nondiscrimination notices may not be issued under any other circumstances. The statute requires that notice must be given to the person that the Commission are minded to issue a nondiscrimination notice in his or her case, specifying the grounds on which they contemplate doing so.[9] The person then has a period, specified in the notice, of not less than twenty-eight days within which to make oral and/or written representation. A nondiscrimination notice may require a person to stop doing certain things and may require information to be given for a period of time. This notice by itself cannot compel anybody to do anything. The Sex Discrimination Act provides that a person against whom a nondiscrimination notice is issued may appeal against it, or any part of it, to an industrial tribunal or county court, whichever is appropriate.

If a person on whom a nondiscrimination notice has been served seems likely to contravene either act, or commit a discriminatory practice within the following five years, this might be shown to be "persistent discrimination" and the Commission may apply for an injunction to stop him. The Commission is required to keep a register of nondiscrimination notices.

It will be seen that although formal investigations are an extremely powerful weapon, they are, for that reason, subject to severe constraints in order to ensure that the requirements of natural justice are met.

Persistent discriminators are those who have failed to comply with the award of an industrial tribunal or a nondiscrimination notice issued by the Commission. So far the Commission has not had occasion to take action against persistent discriminators, although, as a result of the monitoring of the awards of industrial tribunals and the issuing of nondiscrimination notices (if any) by the Commission, such action is expected to develop as the Commission's work progresses.

THE ADMINISTRATIVE MACHINERY AS SEEN BY INDIVIDUALS

It may be useful to examine what the administrative machinery and its procedures look like to ordinary individuals—the ultimate beneficiaries of the system.

Equal pay: ACAS, industrial tribunals, CAC

It is at the initial stages that individuals are in greatest need of assistance. All applications to industrial tribunals are automatically sent to ACAS, which endeavors to secure a settlement without recourse to a tribunal hearing. The procedures followed are set out succinctly in the ACAS *Annual Report* for 1976.

> Equal pay cases are more complex than most of the complaints with which ACAS is concerned. In each case the conciliation officer draws the attention of the applicant to the services of the Equal Opportunities Commission which is ready to advise individuals on their cases. The conciliation officer may become involved in problems of pay structure and questions of job evaluation.[10]

One reason for the complexity of equal pay cases lies in the heavy burden of proof placed upon the applicant in the initial stages of a claim. Figure 6-1 shows the successive stages of an equal pay claim. As the figure indicates, there is a substantial burden of proof on the applicant until the stage is reached where the burden shifts to the employer to show that there is a material difference between a woman's work and that of a comparable man.

The work of the Central Arbitration Committee is less visible to individuals, although its record to date shows clearly that its decisions have

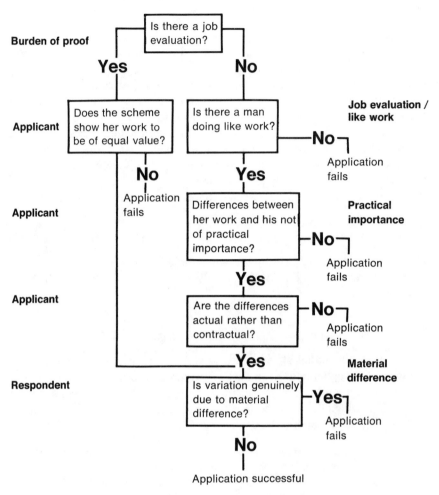

FIGURE 6-1
Procedure for Establishing Claim to Equal Pay

had a substantial impact on a large number of individuals who are never likely to come into contact with it. The one weakness which may need remedying is the fact that an agreement can be referred to the CAC only by the bargaining parties in a dispute or by the secretary of state for employment and not by individual complainants. The Equal Opportunities Commission has suggested in its second *Annual Report* that industrial tribunals, who are often confronted with cases requiring the sort of expertise which the CAC provides, should also be entitled to refer cases to that committee.

A basic problem in the whole field of equal pay stems from the fact that the Equal Pay Act, 1970, was constructed on different premises from the Sex Discrimination Act. As Nancy Seear discusses in Chapter 12, when the Equal Pay Bill was being debated in Parliament, the CBI proposed the definition of "equal pay" in terms of the Treaty of Rome, "equal pay for the same work," while the Trades Union Congress (TUC) rejected this as inadequate and preferred the ILO Convention definition, "equal pay for work of equal value." Both of these were rejected by the then secretary of state, Barbara Castle, the first on the ground that it was too limited in scope and the second because it was too abstract and would require continuing interpretation.[11] The weakness of the present definition is twofold: first, it requires that there should be a man doing comparable work before an equal pay claim can be registered; secondly, it makes no provision for indirect discrimination in the area which arguably matters most, namely pay. On these and other grounds there is a clear and pressing need for harmonizing the two pieces of legislation. (In Chapter 12, Nancy Seear assesses "equal pay" and discusses its limitations.) This may have the added advantage of making what is a complex act more readily intelligible to individuals.

The Equal Opportunities Commission

It will be seen from the statistics presented in Table 6-5 that the Commission has considerably increased the assistance provided to individuals, and it is the Commission's intention to give greater emphasis to section 75 assistance in the near future. The possibility that increasing emphasis on assistance to individuals might turn the Commission into a complaints-processing agency, the very thing that Parliament wished to avoid, is at present so remote as to be negligible.

The Commission has also adopted a five-year strategy that envisages a program of five formal investigations each year. Given the legal and logistical complexities of the formal investigation procedure, this is the maximum that the Commission can reasonably undertake. What it means in practice, however, is that over a decade the Commission will have a maximum of fifty formal investigations with which to cover the entire field of sex discrimination. Each formal investigation will have to be carefully chosen therefore so as to exert maximum leverage.

CONCLUSION

The administrative machinery for the implementation of equal pay and opportunities in Britain has been extensively redesigned in recent years. The experience of earlier methods of implementing anti-discrimination legislation has been a shaping influence in this process, as has the American experience in the field. This machinery has to work in a context in which the paramount desire is to avoid the undue intervention of the law in industrial relations and, more positively, to create an informal climate in which claims can be met and disputes settled without excessive legalism.

The present machinery is still at an early stage of operation, and it remains to be seen whether it will meet the expectation of Parliament of enforcing the law vigorously in the public interest. All those concerned with the implementation of the present equal pay and opportunities legislation are conscious of the warning of the Race Relations Board that a vicious circle can develop too easily in which "lack of confidence in the Act may initially cause a reluctance to complain; this may result in less complaints being sustained, which will lead, in turn, to a further decrease in confidence."[12] It is clear from present trends that as more women enter the labor force, the pressure towards the elimination of discrimination, towards a breakdown in occupational segregation, and towards the supporting provisions necessary to enable women to take advantage of widening opportunities will increase dramatically. This pressure will be felt primarily, but not exclusively, by the agencies responsible for the implementation of the legislation.

NOTES

1. Kenneth William Wedderburn, *The Worker and the Law* (London: Longmans, 1965). Fenner Brockway, in *This Shrinking, Explosive World: A Study of Race Relations* (London: Epworth Press, 1967), p. 81, indicates why he omitted employment matters from the scope of his Private Member's Bills from 1960 onwards.

2. Louis H. Pollak, *Discrimination in Employment: The American Response* (London: The Runnymede Trust, 1974), p. 18.

3. Race Relations Board, *Annual Report for 1969–70* (London: HMSO, 1971), p. 22.

4. Fuller details of the most significant EAT decisions may be found in the *First Annual Report of the EOC* for 1976 (London: HMSO, 1977), pp. 27–29.

5. Central Arbitration Committee, *Annual Report, 1977* (London: HMSO, 1978), para. 4.12, p. 22.

6. Central Arbitration Committee, *Annual Report, 1977*, para. 4.13, p. 22.

7. Central Arbitration Committee, *Annual Report, 1977*, paras. 2.16–2.20, pp. 16–17.

8. Equal Opportunities Commission, *First Annual Report of the EOC, 1976* (London: HMSO, 1977), and *Second Annual Report of the EOC, 1977* (London: HMSO, 1978).

9. The Home Office, *Sex Discrimination: A Guide to the Sex Discrimination Act, 1975* (London: HMSO, 1975).

10. *Department of Employment Gazette* 85, no. 5 (May 1977): 462.

11. *Hansard* (House of Commons), vol. 795, cols. 915–916, Feb. 9, 1970.

12. Race Relations Board, *Annual Report for 1969–70*, p. 22.

7 *Jeffrey Jowell*

THE ENFORCEMENT OF LAWS AGAINST SEX DISCRIMINATION IN ENGLAND: PROBLEMS OF INSTITUTIONAL DESIGN

In deciding whether to prohibit one or other form of behavior, legislators tend to consider the matter largely disposed of once they have decided that "there ought to be a law." Some attention is naturally given to the scope of the law and the extent of the prohibition, but relatively little time is given to designing the machinery of the law's enforcement.

Anti-discrimination legislation attempt to affect entrenched patterns of behavior and also to change deeply engrained attitudes. The machinery of enforcement is thus crucial to the law's success or failure. Ought the law to prohibit discrimination through the imposition of a criminal penalty for its breach? Or ought the law to be enforced through the mediation of a public agency which attempts to affect a conciliation between the parties? Ought this agency to be able to act on its own initiative without the application of an aggrieved individual? Ought aggrieved individuals be permitted to institute civil proceedings against the discriminator? Ought they to be aided by the public agency?

These are some of the complex questions of institutional design that have faced sex-discrimination legislation in Britain. This chapter will outline the machinery eventually chosen in the light of its evolution, and will ask whether the balance struck will ensure the effective reduction of sex discrimination in Britain, or anywhere else.

THE HERITAGE OF RACE-RELATIONS LEGISLATION AND THE CONCILIATION MODEL

In September 1974 the Labour Government published a consultative document[1] that made it clear that the aim in proposing legislation to outlaw sex discrimination was to harmonize the powers and procedures dealing with sex and race discrimination. The model of legislation that then emerged in the Sex Discrimination Act, 1975, was reflected in a remodeled Race Relations Act, 1976. The machinery for the enforcement of sex-discrimination laws in Britain is thus greatly influenced by the experiments of the previous decade in laws prohibiting race discrimination. To understand the genesis of the 1975 act it is therefore necessary to look at the history of race-relations legislation from 1965, when the first attempt was made in the U.K. to use law to promote equality of opportunity.[2]

The first government bill to outlaw racial discrimination was published on April 8, 1965. The bill sought to outlaw racial discrimination in public places ("places of public resort") and also to make racial restrictions on the disposal of tenancies unenforceable.[3] This bill was modeled on a similar bill that had been introduced in Parliament in each of the previous nine years by a pioneering member of Parliament, Fenner Brockway. The machinery for enforcement of the proposed legislation was blunt: violators would be subjected to a criminal penalty ([£50 fine [$92] for a first offense, £100 [$184] for a subsequent offense]). No agency was to be established and no personal remedy granted to an individual victim of discrimination.

The various pressure groups in favor of anti-discrimination legislation found the proposals disappointing. For a start, the scope of the bill was far too narrow, excluding the important areas of employment, housing, discrimination in credit facilities, insurance, and so on. These pressure groups began to look at anti-discrimination laws elsewhere for an example, and focused particularly on state laws against discrimination in the United States. Here they saw that sophisticated machinery had been established with the central feature neither criminal nor civil actions but conciliation in the first instance, through an official anti-discrimination agency, followed by adjudication only as a last resort.

United States and Canadian anti-discrimination laws had rejected a criminal approach for both philosophical and practical reasons: A criminal prosecution was seen as primarily geared to working retribution upon the offender and did not contain machinery to eliminate the various and subtle forms of discrimination except insofar as would-be offenders might be deterred by the fear of a criminal sanction. The prosecutor may not easily take action, and juries, perhaps not sympathetic with the aims of the law, may prove reluctant to convict. Proof "beyond reasonable doubt," the standard of proof necessary for criminal cases, would be difficult to secure.

Civil actions were also regarded as deficient to achieve the law's aims. Damages in a civil action were likely to prove neither sufficient compensation nor an adequate remedy to a person whose primary interest was in securing the service, accommodation, employment, or housing now, or the opportunity to do so (for himself and his race) in the future. In suing for monetary compensation, individuals would ask for damages as a substitute for their rights. And a person who discriminates might well be prepared to pay damages (or even a fine in criminal cases) as the price for continuing to discriminate.

Another reason for rejecting the criminal sanction and the civil remedy was the fear that an immediate public airing of the issue, without formal preliminary attempts at a settlement, and the consequent publicity given to cases brought with the object of extracting monetary revenge or criminal sanctions, could exacerbate racial tensions. There was some apprehension too that the courtroom would be used cynically by those with little other opportunity of obtaining an audience for demonstrating their prejudices.

In view of the deficiencies attached to criminal and civil remedies, the lobbyists pressed for a change in the legislation. They wanted the establishment of a statutory body empowered to investigate, conciliate, hold hearings, and make legally enforceable orders against those found to have violated the law. The object of the legislation should be to alter conduct rather than to punish, and to provide the complainant with the facility he sought.

With an official agency charged with the enforcement of anti-discrimination legislation, the main expense of enforcement would be borne by the government and not the individual, as in a civil suit. The investigations would be conducted not by a court or lay jury but by officials who become experts in the subtle and insidious forms that discrimination can take. Proof of discrimination would be on the balance of probabilities.

In addition to dealing with complaints, the official agency could conduct its own research into patterns of discrimination and, if given the power, could lay its own complaints in strategic areas. It would become a clearing house for information on the problems of minorities, and evolve techniques of education to encourage voluntary compliance with the law.

The conciliation procedure was favored as a means of attaining remedies more flexible than those of monetary compensation and criminal sanctions. As in civil proceedings, the complainant may still be compensated— for example, by the award of back pay—and, as in criminal proceedings, the respondent may be deterred from breaking the law by the threat of adverse publicity or the consequences of breach of the agency's order, but the principal purpose of conciliation would be to provide the opportunity sought to the complainant and, in the future, to members of his or her race similarly situated.

Finally, it was considered that an official agency would be in a position to check on recalcitrant respondents, either by ordering periodic "compliance reports" or by following up conciliation agreements or other orders.

The government accepts the conciliation approach

It is unusual for a bill that has passed its "second reading" in the British House of Commons to be radically amended thereafter. The Race Relations Bill was an exception. The home secretary bowed to the pressure groups and agreed to remove criminal penalties and to substitute instead conciliation procedures. In a sense this move was designed also to ensure the bill's survival in the face of Conservative opposition to the attempt "to import the taint of criminality into this aspect of our affairs".[4] Conciliation was probably seen by the Conservatives as a softer way of dealing with discriminators than the criminal approach.

Under the Race Relations Act, 1965, a Race Relations Board was created to secure compliance with the legislation. The Board would appoint local conciliation committees to investigate individual complaints of discrimination. If conciliation failed to achieve compliance with the law, the local committee would report to the Board. In cases in which the Board considered it likely that discrimination would continue, it would refer the matter to the attorney-general, who would be empowered to bring court proceedings seeking an injunction to restrain further acts of discrimination from being committed. Sanction against disobedience of an injunction would be the usual one of a fine or contempt of court. If the attorney-general did not, in his discretion, seek enforcement through the courts, however, the individual complainant was not granted the right to sue on his own. The Home Secretary explained that "the remedy is still a public remedy. . . . This is a question of a general public relationship which should be asserted in the name of the public at large by the Attorney-General resorting to the county court."[5]

The 1968 act

The 1965 act was not permitted to rest undisturbed for long. A bitter debate on immigration, followed by restrictive measures, intensified the pressure for further and better anti-discrimination legislation. The structure of enforcement was, in the interim, given careful consideration by a committee chaired by Professor Harry Street.[6] The Street Committee looked at the experience of American anti-discrimination commissions and noted many of their defects. The Committee did not regard these defects as irremediable, however; with some differences they recommended the wholesale adoption of the American model in Britain.

The Street Report recommended that the Race Relations Board and its local committees continue to be responsible for securing compliance through conciliation, but suggested that, where conciliation failed, the Board should be empowered to bring enforcement proceedings before an independent tribunal, chosen from a special panel of judges and lay experts. The Board would also have the power to compel witnesses to attend before a local committee and produce relevant documents during the conciliation process. The parties would be entitled to legal representation at hearings before the tribunal. The tribunal would make findings of fact and law, assess damages (if requested to do so by the Board), and recommend the form of any order which might be made against the respondent. The statute would contain a list of the types of orders, the final choice of which would be left to the Board. The list would include orders requiring the respondent to cease and desist from further unlawful practices, or, positively, to sell or lease property, or offer employment, to the complainant, or to report to the Board the steps taken to comply with the law. In cases of emergency, the Board would be able to obtain temporary injunctions to prevent the respondent from disposing of property or filling a job vacancy before it was able to investigate the alleged discrimination. It was also recommended that nondiscrimination conditions should be inserted into all government contracts, and that a special division of the Race Relations Board should supervise the proper performance of these conditions.

The aggregate of these proposals would have given the Board as much power as is possessed by any of the North American state commissions. They would not, however, have given the individual victim any right to bring proceedings on his own behalf in the courts. The Street Committee hoped that

> speedy determination of complaints, together with interlocutory relief and the power to award damages proposed to be conferred on the Board, should make it unnecessary to create new causes of action for damages. We do not seek a proliferation of proceedings: the enactment in the public interest of laws restraining discrimination does not entail the creation of new remedies in tort.[7]

Here the Street Committee did not go as far as Title VII of the U.S. Civil Rights Act of 1964, which did permit complaints to the Equal Opportunity Commission to bring civil actions in the federal courts.[8] Nor were the Street Committee able to recommend judicial remedies equivalent to those available in the United States for violations of the "equal protection" clause of the Fourteenth Amendment to the U.S. Constitution, because there is no written constitution protecting fundamental rights in British law. The Street Committee thus sought effective persuasion through a Board possessing strong powers. Where persuasion failed, the Board itself would attempt to achieve an adequate judicial remedy for the victim of discrimination.

On April 9, 1968 the Race Relations Bill was published, making it unlawful to discriminate on racial grounds in employment, housing, and the provision of commercial and other services. The Race Relations Board was given the duty of securing compliance with its provisions and a new Community Relations Commission was established to promote "harmonious community relations" and to act in an advisory capacity to the home secretary.

In some respects the powers of the Race Relations Board were widened along the lines suggested by the Street Committee. The Board would now have the power itself to bring legal proceedings in the courts (thereby obviating the necessity of having to proceed through the attorney-general), but judicial enforcement was to be considered only as a final resort. The emphasis of the act was firmly upon conciliation, which was also expanded so as to contain dual functions. Conciliation was to remove both the private wrong done to the victim of discrimination and the public wrong which was an offense to the well-being of the community. An individual discriminated against could not himself sue to remedy his private wrong, but was compelled to use the statutory machinery which, if conciliation failed, had absolute discretion in deciding whether to take the case to court.

The functions of the Board were also greatly expanded. It retained the duty to appoint conciliation committees to help the Board to discharge its functions locally, but now retained a parallel jurisdiction to deal with the investigation and conciliation itself, at its own discretion. It was thus able itself to deal with certain classes of complaint, such as those against government and local authorities or the police.

A particularly significant expansion of the Board's power, suggested too by the Street Committee, was the power to investigate suspected unlawful discrimination upon its own initiative, even in the absence of a formal complaint. This power, however, was severely qualified. The Board had to have reason to suspect that there had been unlawful conduct during the two months before the matter came to its notice (or longer period in special circumstances). This meant that in practice the act of discrimination had to involve an identifiable victim. The Board could not draw conclusions from patterns of the work force (for example, an all-white work force in a black neighborhood) unless it also suspected that someone had been discriminated against.

One of Street's major recommendations was not accepted in the 1968 act. The Board was given no power to compel witnesses to attend or to produce relevant documents. In the absence of these powers the Board and its committees would have to rely upon information provided by the complainant or other witnesses or upon the voluntary cooperation of those against whom complaints were made.

The procedure to be followed by the Board is familiar to those with knowledge of state anti-discrimination commissions in North America: After a complaint has been lodged, the Board (or the conciliation committee dealing with the complaint) makes inquiries with regard to the alleged facts of the complaint. Next, the Board "forms its opinion" as to whether the person has performed an act of unlawful discrimination (this procedure corresponding to the "probable cause" finding in state commissions, except without the subpoena powers possessed by some). Thirdly, where it considers that there has been unlawful discrimination, the Board must attempt both to secure a settlement of any difference between the parties and, where appropriate, to secure a written assurance against the repetition of the act considered unlawful or acts of a similar kind. The act did not specify what settlements were permissible, and so an apology or compensation in varying degrees would satisfy the law. Nor was the written assurance against repetition of discrimination specified and so a bare promise to obey the law would satisfy the law.

It should be mentioned that where complaints related to employment, or to membership of facilities provided by a trade union or employers' association, the Board was not empowered immediately to investigate. These complaints had to be referred to the secretary of state for employment, who would then decide whether nonstatutory machinery existed to deal with the complaint and, if such machinery did exist, refer the complaint to that machinery to investigate and conciliate the dispute. If the industrial machinery should fail to complete the investigation in time, however, or should fail to obtain a settlement or assurance, the complaint would be referred to the Board, which would investigate the matter afresh. An additional safeguard provided a party aggrieved by a decision of the voluntary machinery with the right to appeal to the Board, which might reject the appeal, refer it back to the voluntary machinery, or investigate the complaint itself.

This special procedure dealing with employment cases arises from the initial opposition of both sides of British industry to any form of intervention to deal with complaints of racial discrimination in employment. Trade unions in Britain have always had a distrust of legal intervention, which has been seen as largely unsympathetic to the trade union position. The reference of disputes to industry itself, at least initially, was therefore a means for the government to win industry's grudging approval for the 1968 act.

Finally, if the Board failed to secure a settlement of any differences between the parties, or a satisfactory written assurance, or where there has been a breach of a written assurance, the Board (but not the complainant) possessed discretion whether to institute judicial proceedings. In these proceedings no evidence could be given of any matter said or written to the Board, its committees, or to voluntary industrial machinery. The remedies that could be sought were not the flexible remedies that the Street Committee recommended the Board itself should be empowered to order, but the traditional legal remedies of injunction, declaration, damages, or the revision of discriminatory contracts. Injunctions contained a further restriction in that they could only be negative in form (thus enabling the court to restrain the defendant, say from disposing of jobs or property) but not positive or mandatory (which would enable the defendant to offer a house or job to the complainant, or to widen his sources of recruitment). In addition, the act required that the Board had to satisfy the court not only that the act complained of was unlawful, and was likely to be repeated unless restrained (normal matters under proceedings for an injunction), but also the surprising provision that the defendant had previously engaged in conduct which was of the same kind or similar to the act complained of and was unlawful.

In summary, then, in 1965 the British Government moved to outlaw one form of discrimination, race discrimination. The move was prefaced by virtually no thought about the machinery most suitable to achieve the law's objectives. A criminal penalty first introduced was quickly withdrawn as the virtues of conciliation procedures became apparent.

In 1968 the Labour Government reaffirmed its commitment to equality of opportunity by extending the areas of prohibited racial discrimination, and adopted in large measure the model of the American state antidiscrimination commissions. The Race Relations Board was firmly established as the relevant regulatory agency, with a directive to settle the dispute wherever possible by a process of conciliation rather than compulsion. Although hampered in its powers to investigate complaints by the lack of power to require the disclosure of information, the Board possessed power to initiate judicial enforcement of the law as a last resort, even to the exclusion of the individual complainant.

LEGISLATION AGAINST SEX DISCRIMINATION: THE SHIFT
FROM CONCILIATION

We shall now move from race to sex discrimination, and from 1968 to September 1974, when the Labour Government, elected that year, published a consultative document (known in England as a "White Paper") entitled *Equality for Women*.[9] The White Paper was published by the Home Office, whose minister was Roy Jenkins, who had been home secretary during the formative stages of the preparation of the Race Relations Bill, 1968. Jenkins was assisted by a special adviser, Anthony Lester, who was perhaps the chief lobbyist behind the move to the conciliation proceedings in 1965 and 1968.

It is particularly surprising, therefore, that the White Paper clearly indicated the government's intention to move away from the conciliation model in important respects. This section will outline the development and provisions of the Sex Discrimination Act, 1975, which implemented the intentions of *Equality for Women* and was, incidentally, then followed closely by the Race Relations Act, 1976, which mirrored a similar shift away from conciliation in the enforcement of the law against racial discrimination. The next section will then examine the reasons for this relatively sudden move.

A new strategy

Equality for Women suggested firmly that the government intended to enact legislation to prohibit discrimination on the grounds of sex, and maintained that the use of law to provide equality of opportunity was effective. It quoted with approval the summary of the role of law previously expressed by the Race Relations Board:

1. A law is an unequivocal declaration of public policy.
2. A law gives support to those who do not wish to discriminate, but who feel compelled to do so by social pressure.
3. A law gives protection and redress for minority groups.
4. A law provides for the peaceful and orderly adjustment of grievances and the release of tensions.
5. A law reduces prejudice by discouraging the behaviour in which prejudice finds expression.[10]

Although acknowledging that the consequences and nature of racial and sex discrimination differ, the White Paper considered the similarities more important than the differences for the purpose of enforcement machinery, and resolved to harmonize the machinery for both areas of discrimination.

The White Paper then outlined two possible approaches to enforcement machinery. The first was that reflected in the Equal Pay Act, 1970, which was, from 1975, to prohibit sex discrimination in contractual conditions of employment. This legislation would be enforced without the intervention of any public agency; complainants would themselves bring proceedings in industrial tribunals. The second possible approach was the conciliation model contained in the Race Relations Act, 1968, as outlined above.

The first model was considered inadequate "because it would depend too heavily on the initiative of individuals in presenting and pursuing complaints, and would therefore tend to be random in its operation and impact."[11] This was well understood during the genesis of the Race Relations Act in 1965. In 1974, however, the government also rejected wholesale reliance on the second, conciliation model. It was felt that "a requirement that the enforcement body should investigate all individual complaints would create a vast, costly and wasteful administrative burden." In addition, "the complainant would feel justifiably aggrieved at being denied the right to seek legal redress while his or her complaint was waiting to be processed." Third, the agency would be distracted by "an ever-increasing backlog of individual complaints from playing its crucial general role in changing discriminatory practices and encouraging positive action to secure equal opportunity."[12]

For those reasons, the government proposed to combine the two approaches. A new public body would be created, but this body would be concerned in major part not with the conciliation of complaints laid before it but with strategic action on its own initiative so as to enforce the law "in the public interest on behalf of the community as a whole."[13] Individuals would seek redress of their own grievances largely through traditional legal channels.

The Sex Discrimination Act, 1975

The Sex Discrimination Act, 1975, faithfully enacted the intentions of the White Paper, and set up the Equal Opportunities Commission as the principal agency concerned with furthering the objectives of the legislation. Unlike the Race Relations Board, the Commission would not itself normally deal with individual complaints, and would have no conciliation functions. The principal enforcement function of the EOC is, at its discretion or as directed by the home secretary, to embark upon a formal investigation in areas covered by the act.

To assist in these investigations the Commission has what the Race Relations Board lacked, namely, enforceable powers to obtain information. After its investigations, the Commission may make recommendations or, if it is satisfied that there has been a breach of the act, issue a "non-discrimination notice"[14] requiring the recipient to cease the discriminatory practice and alter it so as to comply with the law (this might include "affirmative action"). The Commission is also empowered to undertake a further investigation after a year to check compliance with the terms of the notice. Breach of nondiscrimination notices and "persistent discrimination" may be restrained by judicial enforcement through general injunctive relief (or through an industrial tribunal in employment cases). The Commission has exclusive power to deal with discriminatory advertisements and pressure and instructions to discriminate. Here it can also institute investigations, issue nondiscrimination notices, and institute legal proceedings where a breach has occurred.

The individual who has been the object of unlawful discrimination would not normally seek enforcement through the Commission (except in regard to advertising or pressure or instructions to discriminate). The individual has the right to institute proceedings in the ordinary courts (county or sheriff court), where legal aid is available or, in the field of employment, in an industrial tribunal.[15]

Industrial tribunals, established in 1964, have experienced a continued growth in their jurisdiction, which now ranges from appeals under the Redundancy Payments Act, 1965, to the determination of disputes arising from the operation of the Race Relations Act, 1976 (section 54), and the Equal Pay Act, 1970. The hearings of industrial tribunals, held before a lawyer chairman and two lay members representing both sides of industry selected by the secretary of state, are less formal than court proceedings although both applicant and respondent may be legally represented. Legal aid, however, is not available. Appeal from a decision of the tribunal on a point of law lies to the Employment Appeal Tribunal (and thence to the Court of Appeal), which, unlike the individual tribunals, creates binding case law.

The individual litigant is not, however, totally without official assistance. He may be considerably assisted in proving his case by prescribed forms (now known as "section 74 forms"), which, if put in the prescribed time, pose questions to respondents that are admissible in evidence in court or tribunal proceedings. The courts may also draw any inference from evasive or equivocal replies. This novel procedure may well help to avoid unnecessary litigation as well as assist the complainant, although it appears to fall short of shifting the burden of proof (or disproof) to the respondent.[16]

Second, the individual complainant may be assisted by the Commission. The Commission, however, may only assist an individual where the case raises a question of principle, or where it is unreasonable (because of the complexity of the case or the relationship between the complainant and other party) to expect the individual to deal with the case unaided, or where some special consideration applies. In these cases the assistance may include advice, legal advice or assistance, or seeking a settlement.

It would be untrue to say that the concept of conciliation is entirely absent from the act. Where a complaint has been made to an industrial tribunal, it is passed automatically to the Advisory, Conciliation and Arbitration Service (ACAS).[17] A conciliation officer of the Service then has responsibility for assisting in settling the dispute between employer and complainant. Provided both parties are willing, the officer attempts conciliation by talking with each party separately to clarify the individual's point of view and to explain the parties' rights under the law. If a settlement is possible, the conciliation officer helps to frame the agreement, which is then signed by both parties and registered at the office of industrial tribunals as a formal resolution of the dispute. Should either party not wish to conciliate, however, or conciliation proves to be impossible, ACAS withdraws from the process and the dispute returns to the tribunal.

Despite the growth in individual conciliation, the main concern of ACAS is with collective arbitration and conciliation. Even within the individual conciliation sector complaints arising from the Sex Discrimination and Equal Pay Acts form only a small minority of the total; the major part being complaints of unfair dismissal.[18] The 1977 ACAS report shows that the majority of disputes are either withdrawn or referred back to the industrial tribunal.[19] In this report the Commission expresses concern at the large number of withdrawals of cases from industrial tribunals without conciliation.

At a collective level, the Central Arbitration Committee (CAC) established under the Employment Protection Act, 1975, can examine collective agreements referred to it by either party or by the secretary of state for employment and may declare what amendments have to be made to the agreement to remove discriminatory sections. The CAC does not deal with individual complaints.

The remedies available when discrimination has been established are an order declaring the rights of the parties, an order of compensation (including compensation for injury to feelings), and a recommendation of action practicable for the purpose of reducing the adverse effect on the complainant of discrimination (such as giving a job to the complainant).

The Sex Discrimination Act, 1975, then, adopts and strengthens some of the features of the race relations legislation of the previous decade, but dispenses with others. The Commission is given greater powers of investigation, access to information, and enforcement of "strategic" matters. It is largely divested of the task of the settlement of individual complaints, although it can help in important or deserving cases.

The individual complainant has little use for the Commission. Help may be forthcoming in complex or strategic cases, and some attempt at conciliation is provided in cases before industrial tribunals. By and large, however, the individual complainant is abandoned to the pursuit of his or her remedy through traditional legal channels.

CONCILIATION ABANDONED: THE REASONS

What were the reasons for the quick shift in the design of anti-discrimination laws in Britain?

The first possible reason is perhaps cynical and is based on political considerations alone: The conciliation model was introduced partially to mollify opponents of governmental intervention in race relations. Regulatory agencies are unusual in Britain, with its centralized public administration. Opposed to strict judicial enforcement of the law, conciliation was thus seen by the opposition as introducing a bargaining element instead of coercion, which made the new agency more acceptable. Now that time had allowed the law to become accepted, however, and the Board, using its conciliation powers, had established its legitimacy, it became possible to move to blunt judicial enforcement of the law.

There is some truth in this proposition, but not the whole truth.[20] Even those most firmly committed to anti-discrimination legislation in the 1960s[21] were committed also to the concept of conciliation as a preferred method of institutional design, both because of the positive virtues of conciliation as a method of attaining flexible remedies that would enhance all aspects of the law's purpose, and because of the inherent limitations of civil or criminal enforcement of the law in the courts that we have discussed. The government's view in the mid-1970s, therefore, was one that recognized defects in the conciliation model that had not been fully appreciated in the early years.

The first defect was one that had been pointed out as early as 1952 in New York by Morroe Berger in his classic *Equality by Statute*: namely, that response to individually initiated complaints would not eradicate patterns of discrimination; that it was unlikely that these complaints would be laid in strategic areas, where enforcement would lead to the toppling of discrimination in other areas, and thus significantly widen opportunities.[22] In his study of the Massachusetts Commission Against Discrimination, Leon Mayhew similarly pointed out that the individualistic approach was to "treat anti-discrimination law as a system of private law, designed to adjust disagreements that arise within the established social order."[23] Other commentators have said more colloquially that reliance on the individual complaint to enforce the law is like trying "to drain a swamp with a teaspoon."[24]

The reason for this lies in social-structural forces and attitudes that prevent people from exposing themselves to a potentially discriminatory situation in the first place. It is not easy to be a pioneer. Even where a person may have been discriminated against, he or she may still not recognize that discrimination has occurred. Where discrimination is recognized, the person may not know about the law, or may not know where to complain, or how to complain, or even be willing to invest the time, effort, and cost in complaining. Those complaints that are eventually translated into enforcement action may, finally, not be strategically significant in widening opportunities for similarly situated people. It is a matter of chance, but the odds are stacked against effective and strategic enforcement through individually initiated complaints.[25]

This is the reason why the new model gives the official agency more effective powers to investigate discriminatory practices and enforce the law. Now the agency has the means to concentrate on strategic enforcement. But why, in the attempt to convert the agency from a relatively passive receptacle to an active strategist, is the individual victim of discrimination largely abandoned to the mercy of judicial enforcement?

The first reason lies in the tension that results from an agency charged with performing a variety of roles. When an individual complaint is laid, the body seeks first to achieve a remedy for the complainant, as if he were a plaintiff in a tort action. This kind of exercise normally requires relatively judicialized procedures, since the defendant in the action is in the end required to respond to the complainant with some kind of offer of compensation. Yet the body charged with conciliation is also in a didactic role, educating the defendant in the law's objectives, persuading him to open his doors in the future, to widen his recruitment, and so on. Here the judicialized model and emphasis on proof of discrimination is less appropriate; the agency wants to coax the defendant into doing better in the future, rather than to exact punishment for his previous wrongs.

The individual complainant may or may not be interested in the longer-term aspect of the defendant's practices. If he wants remedial action toward himself, however, he will have no sympathy with the coaxing tactics of the agency. The agency in turn may find that the retributive aims of the complainant interfere with their bargaining strategy.[26]

Ultimately, for the agency, the problem becomes one of a diffusion of aims and goals, some of them mutually inhibiting. The role of response to wronged individuals often lies uneasily with those of education and persuasion on the one hand and strategic enforcement of the law on the other. The victim is unlikely to sympathize with these organizational tensions, and may lose faith in the agency and in the enforcement of the law. The matter was clearly put in the White Paper that presaged the Race Relations

Act, 1976, which said that the denial of individual access to legal remedies "suffers from a double disadvantage. It distracts the statutory agency from playing its crucial strategic role whilst leaving many complainants dissatisfied with what has been done on their behalf by means of procedures which may seem cumbersome, ineffective or unduly paternalistic."[27]

EVALUATION AND CONCLUSIONS

The machinery of enforcement of equal opportunity legislation in Britain centers on a Commission with strong powers of investigation and enforcement. Such Commissions and powers are unusual in Britain. The structure thus represents a significant achievement in itself.

The hiving off of most individual complaints allows the Commission to concentrate on aims and strategic enforcement of the law unhampered by the conflicting goals that were presented by the necessity of dealing with individual complaints. What is not clear, however, is to what extent the individual complaints themselves presented the agency with an important source of knowledge about the kind and extent of discrimination. Nor is it known whether the Commission will perhaps be missing an important source of strategic complaint. However haphazardly initiated, some individual complaints may have triggered important strategic enforcement.[28] The Commission may still become aware of strategic complaints when individuals approach them for help, or when they hear of cases in the County Court. Once it becomes known that the Commission is not in the business of processing individual complaints, however, it is unlikely to be frequently approached.

Many questions hang over the position of the individual complainant and the move away from conciliation. We have considered the material and psychological obstacles facing a potential complainant. Would that complainant be better placed by having the option of approaching an agency committed to the enforcement of the law (with perhaps the alternative of bringing a civil action on his own)? In complaints before industrial tribunals, legal aid is not available (although trade union representation may be provided). Proof of discrimination, despite the help of section 74 questions procedure, may be seen as an insurmountable difficulty.[29] Finally, it may well be that the law is seen as a hostile maze by would-be complainants. Whether this applies to victims of sex discrimination as much as it does to victims of race discrimination is doubtful. Nevertheless, recent studies in England have shown that the obstacles to the use of the legal process are considerable.[30] The 1977 Annual Report of the Commission shows concern that only a handful of cases were brought in the County Court.

Nor has the British judiciary shown itself at all sympathetic to equal opportunity legislation, at least that concerning race discrimination. Under the 1968 act county courts proved very unwilling to find discrimination. Even with these powers now to award wide remedies, it seems unlikely that the remedies will be as flexible as imaginative conciliation might achieve, and most doubtful that they will aim their remedies wider than the complainant, at "strategic" discrimination.

In its last report the Race Relations Board reported that the experiment of the use of industry panels in employment complaints "has failed and ought not to be repeated."[31] Since 1973, when industrial tribunals were given the jurisdiction of dealing with cases of unfair dismissal on racial grounds, not one of 119 cases made a determination in favor of the complainant. Yet the tribunals will now hear cases of unlawful discrimination in industry. Hetherington's criticisms of the voluntary industrial machinery which formerly heard complaints about discrimination in employment seems apposite here too:

> Representatives of management and union, both of whom have a vested interest in preserving the good name of the industry and both of whom may be hostile to the complainant, sit in judgment on a complaint from an individual who is almost certainly not represented by anyone with an understanding either of industry or of the procedures followed by the machinery.[32]

The Race Relations Act, 1968, was given its narrowest interpretation by the House of Lords, Britain's highest court. The judges made clear their view that Parliament should intervene as little as possible in matters about which people differ in great numbers, and statutes should be so interpreted. As Lord Diplock put it: "This is a statute which, however admirable its motives, restricts the liberty which the citizen has previously enjoyed at common law to differentiate between one person and another in entering or declining to enter into transactions with them."[33] Very few English judges have expressed themselves on discrimination in a way that makes clear that it is more a social wrong than an individual right.

Does the 1975 act strike the right balance? Is the machinery correctly adjusted? With skilful manipulation in the years ahead, could it prove successful in Britain, and a useful model to adapt elsewhere? The powers of the Commission are unusual for Britain and have been won in a hard political struggle. They will surely be used to great effect by the existing able personnel. The worry is that the individual victim of discrimination has been abandoned, too early and too completely, to a judicial and industrial system of dispute-settlement that is not wholly in sympathy with the aims of the law.

NOTES

1. *Equality for Women* (CMD 5724; London: HMSO, Sept. 1974).

2. See Anthony Lester and Geoffrey Bindman, *Race and Law in Great Britain* (Cambridge: Harvard University Press, 1972), esp. ch. 3.

3. Race Relations Bill (Bill 125 43/1, 1965). The bill also sought to penalize "encitement to racial hatred."

4. For the debate on the second reading of the bill see *Hansard* (House of Commons), vol. 711, cols. 926–1060, May 3, 1965.

5. *Official Report*, Standing Committee B, May 25, 1965–July 1, 1965, cols. 3–412.

6. Harry Street and others, *Anti-Discrimination Legislation: The Street Report* (sponsored by the Race Relations Board and the National Committee for Commonwealth Immigrants; London: Political and Economic Planning, 1967).

7. Ibid., p. 128.

8. S.706(e).

9. CMD 5724, Sept. 1974.

10. Ibid., para. 19.

11. Ibid., para. 28.

12. Ibid.

13. Ibid., para. 81.

14. Except with regard to educational bodies, where the minister of education must be informed of any breach (s.67[6]), persons affected by nondiscrimination notices must be given notice that they may be imposed and the opportunity to make representations (s.67[5]).

15. Under s.66(5) alleged discrimination in educational establishments must first be referred to the minister of education.

16. S.74 of the act. See S.I. 1975 no. 2048.

17. The Advisory, Conciliation and Arbitration Service was established by the Employment Protection Act, 1975, and has a general duty to "promote the improvement of industrial relations and in particular to encourage the extension of collective bargaining and the development and, where necessary, reform of collective bargaining" (ACAS, Annual Report, 1977, p. 5).

18. Of the 43,899 cases received by ACAS in 1977, only 984 arose from the Equal Pay Act, 1970, and 367 from the Sex Discrimination Act, 1975. This represented a further decline from the figures for 1976, which were 2,517 and 401 respectively.

19. Cases arising under sex discrimination law for 1977 (from ACAS, Annual Report, 1977, p. 30):

	Equal Pay Act		Sex Discrimination Act	
	No.	%	No.	%
Received by ACAS for conciliation	984		367	
Total processed by ACAS in 1977	983	100	355	100
Settled by ACAS conciliation	64	7	66	19
Settled privately	33	3	9	2
Withdrawn	307	31	81	23
Sent forward to industrial tribunal	579	51	199	56

20. I have discussed the problem of establishing the legitimacy of the Massachusetts Commission Against Discrimination in *Law and Bureaucracy* (New York: Dunellen Pub. Co., and Port Washington, N.Y.: Kennikat Press, 1975), esp. ch. 6.

21. See Lester and Bindman, *Race and Law*, ch. 3, n. 2.

22. Morroe Berger, *Equality by Statute: Legal Controls over Group Discrimination* (New York: Columbia University Press, 1952).

23. Leon Mayhew, *Law and Equal Opportunity: A Study of the Massachusetts Commission Against Discrimination* (1969). See my review of Mayhew, especially on the definition of a "strategic" complaint in *Harvard Law Review* 83 (1969): 283. See also Jowell, *Law and Bureaucracy*, pp. 76–77 and 202.

24. Robert A. Girard and Louis L. Jaffe, "Some General Observations on Administration of State Fair Employment Practice Laws," *Buffalo Law Review* 14 (1964): 114, 115.

25. See Jowell, *Law and Bureaucracy*, ch. 3.

26. Vilhem Aubert has shown how a "dyadic structure" is suitable for bargaining, whereas the "triadic structure" is suitable for classic judicial situations ("Competition and Dissensus: Two Types of Conflict and Conflict Resolution," *Journal of Conflict Resolution* 11, no. 1 [1967]: 40). When the agency resolves an individual complaint, a triadic situation exists; when they negotiate with the respondent a dyadic situation exists. This dichotomy may also account for the strain on the agency's structure when combining these roles.

27. *Racial Discrimination* (CMD 6234; London: HMSO, Sept. 1975), para. 41.

28. The Commission seeks to gain knowledge of court proceedings by a stipulation in the County Court Rules which provides that individuals who institute proceedings under the Sex Discrimination Act in the County Court are required to give notice to the Commission of their intention to proceed.

29. The first annual report of the Commission states that these forms have not been widely used in industrial tribunal proceedings (para. 4–6). See also Laurence S. Lustgarten, "Problems of Proof in Employment Discrimination Cases," *Industrial Law Journal* (Dec. 1977), pp. 213–214.

30. Michael Zander, Brian Abel-Smith, and Rosalind Brooke, *Legal Problems and the Citizen* (London: Heinemann, 1973).

31. Report of the Race Relations Board, Jan. 1975–June 1976, para. 60.

32. *Race Today*, Nov. 1971, p. 381. In 1975–1979 over 80 percent of cases heard by industrial tribunals under the Sex Discrimination Act were dismissed (EOC, Annual Report, 1977, p. 46).

33. *Dockers' Labour Club* v. *Race Relations Board* (1974) 3 W.L.R. 533. See J. A. G. Griffith, *The Politics of the Judiciary* (Political Issues of Modern Britain; Manchester: Humanities Press, Manchester University Press, 1977), esp. pp. 87–93.

III

Training and Organizing for Equal Employment

8 *Berit Rollén*

EQUALITY BETWEEN MEN AND WOMEN IN THE LABOR MARKET: THE SWEDISH NATIONAL LABOR MARKET BOARD

Swedes are not particularly religious, but one thing we do hold almost sacred is everyone's right to work. One of our more radical professors of economics tried to question the foundations for Swedish policy in general and Swedish labor market policy in particular by arguing that work has no intrinsic value and should be kept to a minimum. From what I have seen he has found little support for this view.

The right to a job for everyone throughout his or her active life is thus an overriding goal for all the political parties. It would in fact be political suicide for any politician to question this right for any group, such as the elderly, the handicapped, or married women. (At the same time, there are still people who write to the papers about the need for earlier retirement to make way for the younger generation, about the wrongness of married women taking jobs from others, about immigrants competing with "true Swedes" or the feeling that there should be a limit to the public money that is spent on technical aids at work for the handicapped.)

It is in fact only in recent decades that society in general has recognized the individual's right to work and the public obligation that this entails. At the beginning of this century it was assumed that the unemployed had only themselves to blame and that the community was being charitable in providing a place in the poorhouse. In time the authorities did deign to provide relief work, but there was no question of paying anything like a full wage for this or of arranging work that was either important or meaningful—the unemployed should not be tempted to remain on relief work.

The breakthrough for modern Swedish labor market policy is considered to have come in the thirties, when the theories of Keynes were put into practice and there was a lively discussion about the part to be played by employment services, relief work, and unemployment insurance. A nationwide organization for employment services was built up during and after the war years and served as the foundation for the present National Labor Market Board (NLMB). During the sixties this organization was extended rapidly on a wide front, as were the funds and instruments at its disposal. This evolution was particularly marked for the series of selective instruments that smoothed the inevitable process of adjustment and helped to maintain and boost employment. It is this aspect of Swedish labor market policy here, however, I shall be referring both to selective and to more general measures. In other words I shall be talking about the public employment service, labor market training, removal assistance, special measures for the handicapped, relief work, regional development support, various grants to employers who retain their work force during a recession, vocational guidance, and so on. In Sweden we are particularly concerned to emphasize the importance of a virile(!) organization that is ready at any time to wield the various instruments of labor market policy.

ORGANIZATION AND TASKS OF THE NATIONAL LABOR MARKET BOARD

Sweden's labor market policy is directed in the final analysis by the government and Parliament. The Labor Market Administration is composed of the Labor Market Board, the county labor boards, and the public Employment Service (see Figure 8-1). In the United States, and perhaps in most countries in Europe, the National Labor Market Board would form part of the Labor Department or the Ministry of Labor. In Sweden, however, the Ministry of Labor has a staff of less than one hundred, whereas the NLMB with its regional and local organizations has some eight thousand employees. It should be noted here that the ministries in Sweden are very small bodies, engaged on policy-making, drafting parliamentary bills, and issuing directives to the agencies (such as the National Labor Market Board), which are then left to interpret and execute the current policy within the framework of specific guidelines and budgets. In practice, moreover, the NLMB plays a large part in planning and up-dating labor market policy.

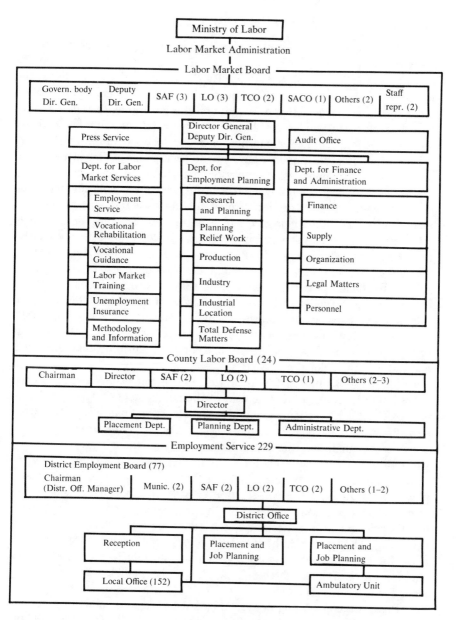

FIGURE 8-1
Organization of the National Labor Market Board

The National Labor Market Board

The Board is the central administrative authority for general labor market matters and the supervisory authority for the county labor boards and the public Employment Service. By the terms of its instructions, the Board leads planning and initiates measures to cope with unemployment or labor shortages; leads activities to do with the government's policy for regional development; undertakes legislated responsibilities and other advisory and information activities connected with the location of business enterprises; supervises the public Employment Service (including activities in accordance with employers' statutory obligations to register vacancies with the Service); inspects employment agencies which are not run by public authorities; directs the vocational rehabilitation activities; directs national activities for vocational guidance which are not the responsibility of some other authority; undertakes responsibilities in accordance with the legislation concerning aliens, with the Promotion of Employment Act, and with the Unemployment Insurance Act and the Act on Cash Unemployment Assistance; handles certain matters to do with investment funds and working environment funds; and plans the utilization of labor in the event of war or comparable circumstances, including matters to do with the postponement, delay, or other leave from military service during a state of war or emergency as well as certain matters to do with noncombatant conscripts and the voluntary defense service.

The NLMB's budget for fiscal 1977/1978 totaled 8.9 billion kronor ($1.9 billion), representing 7 percent of the government budget and 3 percent of GDP. The National Labor Market Board is financed entirely from government funds via the annual budget. But in the Board's governing body, as we shall see, the representatives of the three largest labor organizations and the employers form a majority. It is in this context particularly important to note the major part that is played by union and employer organizations. The construction of Swedish labor market policy has been and still is a joint undertaking by these three parties, though their enthusiasm obviously varies and it can take time for certain ideas to gain a hearing. The governing body also includes representatives for the staff and—for historical reasons—for agriculture and female occupations. The chairman is the Board's director-general, who is appointed by the government for a term of six years.

Besides the governing body, the Board has regional offices (under the Production Division), workplaces for industrial relief work (under the Industry Division), and a machine workshop and central store in Ghesta (under the Supply Division). The regional offices undertake the regional direction and follow-up of relief work under the auspices of the Board (as a rule, what is known as special relief work) besides assisting the Board and the county labor boards in technical matters. The staff of the National Labor Market Board and its regional offices in 1973–1977 is shown in Table 8-1.

TABLE 8-1
Staff of the Labor Market Board and Its Regional Offices

	NLMB			
Year	*Executive staff*	*Other staff*	*Total*	*Regional staff*
July 1, 1973	477	359	836	1,110
July 1, 1974	503	367	870	1,010
July 1, 1975	538	343	881	1,486
July 1, 1976	541	343	884	1,414
July 1, 1977	543	342	885	1,388

The county labor boards

The regional organization has a similar structure, with county labor boards composed of representatives from the interested parties.

A county labor board is the provincial authority for general labor market matters and for the Employment Service. In its area it follows labor market developments and plans and undertakes such measures as these developments may call for; directs the public Employment Service and occupational rehabilitation; collaborates with schools and authorities in planning and supervising public vocational guidance; undertakes responsibilities laid down in the Promotion of Employment Act; undertakes responsibilities laid down in the Act on Cash Unemployment Assistance and in accordance with instructions from the Labor Market Board and supervises assistance connected with unemployment; cooperates with private organizations in the areas affected by its activities; and, in accordance with regulations and instructions from the Board, plans the utilization of labor in the event of war or comparable circumstances and also assists the Board in coordinating the voluntary defense service within the civilian part of total defense.

Recently (January, 1977) composite boards of this type were set up for the local employment offices.

The Employment Service

The provincial organization of the Employment Service consists of one or more district offices, local offices, and ambulatory units. There are 77 district offices and 152 local offices in Sweden. A district employment board is attached to every district office representing the municipality and the labor market parties. The district office manager acts as chairman.

An employment office is the local authority for general labor market matters and within its area it undertakes the activities of the public Employment Service, including vocational guidance and vocational rehabilitation, in keeping with the labor market regulations and other relevant statutes; assesses matters to do with individual labor market training, vocational rehabilitation, unemployment assistance, removal assistance, and other measures that are taken for reasons of employment, insofar as such matters do not have to be submitted to the National Labor Market Board or the County Labor Board; and follows labor market developments and proposes or undertakes such measures as these developments may call for.

The large employment offices are made up of a reception section plus sections for placement and job planning services. As a rule each of the latter sections has eight to twenty executive staff, including any officials for vocational guidance and rehabilitation. In fiscal 1976/77 most of the employment offices had less than five placement officers. Staff of the county labor boards and the employment offices are given in Table 8-2.

TABLE 8-2

Staff at County Labor Boards, Employment Offices, Centers for Office Work and Relief Work Projects, etc.

Year	COUNTY LABOR BOARDS		EMPLOYMENT OFFICES		OFFICE WORK CENTERS, RELIEF WORK, ETC.		Total
	Executive staff	Other staff	Executive staff	Other staff	Executive staff	Other staff	
July 1, 1973	636	620	3,034	408	266	112	5,076
July 1, 1974	688	722	3,141	437	267	127	5,382
July 1, 1975	712	704	3,345	585	244	116	5,706
July 1, 1976	746	724	3,469	644	241	122	5,946
July 1, 1977	747	726	3,562	649	243	131	6,068

Central, regional, and local coordination

The way in which the central, regional, and local organizations collaborate can be illustrated by a survey of the planning and execution of relief work.

The local and regional organizations keep a continuous check on developments on the labor market, labor requirements, and the need for measures of labor market policy. These assessments are made by the county and the district labor boards in cooperation with firms, union organizations, and the local authorities. The county labor boards report regularly to the National Board, which assesses the need for various measures, including relief work, and allocates funds to the twenty-four counties in accordance with the state and needs of the labor market. These allocations are accompanied by instructions from the National Board as to how the funds are to be used—that is to say, the main categories to be catered to. The instructions may state, for instance, that consideration is to be paid to the large proportion of young women among the unemployed or to the particularly high level of unemployment among construction workers. This procedure is backed up by the existence of a reserve of projects of various kinds that can be started at short notice. This bank of projects is drawn from the central government, local authority, and private sectors, and it covers investment activity as well as work in nursing and the like and in administration. Briefly, then, the entire process is initiated locally and regionally, where officials know most about who is feeling the pinch. It is there that responsibility also lies for maintaining preparedness in the form of planned projects. The need for assistance is aggregated centrally at the National Board, which then distributes funds to its regional and local bodies. These bodies decide which projects to start up from the reserve and which unemployed persons to assign to them. The funds allocated by the National Board are accompanied by instructions for their use.

Cooperation with labor market organizations

The parties in the labor market are represented on the National Labor Market Board and the county labor boards and on the district employment boards. Eleven members of the Board's governing body are appointed by the government. Three come from the Confederation of Trade Unions (LO), two represent the Central Organization of Salaried Employees (TCO), and one the Confederation of Professional Associations (SACO). In addition there is a member representing female labor and a member for agriculture as well as representatives for the staff. The labor market organizations are represented in a similar manner on the county labor boards and on the district employment boards.

This representation, however, is not confined to the decision-making bodies. The principal is also applied to the more or less permanent working groups that are continuously engaged on investigations and development work in the sphere of the Labor Market Administration. An example of this is the Central Committee for Construction Work, which is made up of representatives for the Federation of Building Employers, the Construction Workers Union, the Central Organization of Salaried Employees, and the Board itself. Similarly, various labor market organizations are represented in many other groups such as the Joint Committee for Semi-sheltered Employment, the Working Group for Agriculture and Market Gardening, the Working Group for Labor Matters in Forestry, the Joint Advisory Delegation for Labor Market Training Courses, and the Working Group for Certain Matters to Do with Trainees. This composition of primary preparatory bodies in important fields ensures that the Board obtains an insight into conditions in the labor market and at workplaces, besides obtaining a realistic foundation for assessing the possibility of implementing measures of labor market policy.

ROLES OF WOMEN AND MEN

Large groups of women in Sweden have always had to work for a living. Yet it is only recently that official policy and public opinion started to recognize the existence of more than one category of women—those who married, were supported by their husbands, and remained married for the rest of their life. The right of women to take up various occupations was restricted until well into the present century. And throughout history the work done by women has been arduous—washing clothes out on the ice, carrying mortar, catering work—and they have been paid much less than men.

A new way of looking at a woman's life started to catch on after the war. People like Alva Myrdal started talking about a woman's twin roles, and it became acceptable for a woman to arrange her life accordingly: training first and employment for a brief period, then marriage, children and some years at home, followed by re-entry to the labor market when the children started to grow up. Female labor was in demand and instruments of labor market policy were used to stimulate women to leave their homes, train, and take a job.[1]

By the sixties the time was ripe for the next step, when Eva Moberg questioned the "conditional liberation of women"[2]—that is, the circumstance that women were permitted to train and work provided they saw to the supervision of their children and the running of the home. This more radical view was likewise supported by economic conditions in that labor demand was still strong and women represented the only major source of supply. By that time it had been found that large-scale immigration, such as had occurred during the sixties, raised problems, and costs, of its own.

It was in 1968 that Sweden established its present official attitude to women's work and the concept of equality between women and men in working life, the home, and society. In the report on the status of women that all member countries of the United Nations were to submit that year, the government laid down its goal as follows:

> The aim of a *long-term* programme for women must be that every individual, irrespective of sex, shall have the same *practical* opportunities, not only for education and employment, but also in principle the same responsibility for his or her own maintenance as well as a shared responsibility for the upbringing of children and the upkeep of the home. Eventually to achieve complete equality in these rights and obligations, a radical change in deep-rooted traditions and attitudes must be brought about among both women and men, and active steps must be taken by the community to encourage a change in the roles played by both. The view that women ought to be economically supported by marriage must be effectively refuted—also in the legislative field—as this view is a direct obstacle to the economic independence of women and their ability to compete on equal terms in the labour market. Similarly, the husband's traditional obligation to support his wife must be modified to constitute a responsibility, shared with her, for the support of the children. This concern for the children should also be manifested in a greater degree of participation in the supervision and care of the children on the husband's part.
>
> The Government is well aware that this view appears revolutionary and unrealistic in the eyes of the representatives of many other countries. A growing opinion in Sweden has however rallied to its support. In Sweden, as in the other Scandinavian countries, a lively debate has been going on for the past six or seven years in mass media, in organizations and in public bodies concerning the tasks of men and women in society and the home. This debate has brought forth a new approach which involves a departure from the traditional habit of regarding these problems as "women's questions."[3]

The goal—equality

In keeping with this general development in society, the tasks of the National Labor Market Board have been modified from boosting female employment and supporting the re-entry of women to promoting equality between men and women in the labor market. The latter goal naturally includes improved employment opportunities for women in general, but it also represents a desire to do away with sex patterns on the whole, so that both men and women are stimulated to choose occupations that have been dominated traditionally by the opposite sex.

A program for the National Board's work for equality, entitled *Equality in the Labor Market—a Task for the Labor Market Administration,* was adopted in June 1977. In the foreword, the director-general noted that in working for equality in the labor market, the Labor Market Administration has the following tasks: to have regard in job placement to the qualifications and wishes of the individual irrespective of traditional sex demarcations in the labor market; to encourage individuals to select occupations and training without regard to sex; to harness and develop the individual capacities of men and women through labor market training; and to encourage employers to recruit without regard to sex.

Further on, under the heading "Responsibilities of the Labor Market Administration," the program states "equality cannot be achieved solely through policies directed at working life. Nevertheless, the situation in employment is a powerful determinant of people's whole life style. Labour market policy is accordingly of great moment in advancing the cause of equality, and the Labour Market Administration has an important role in and a particular responsibility for this activity."[4]

An attitude in our daily work

When it comes to describing how the Board tries to promote equality, we usually say that this aspect of our work must not be treated like a train that runs along a track all by itself. On the contrary, our motto—Equality: A Task for the Labor Market Administration—means that equality is a facet of our daily work that has to be considered and applied in every field at all times. It calls for a specific attitude or response to every task. We are still having some difficulty in getting this attitude across to all the eight thousand members of our staff. Many still tend to equate work for equality with stimulating housewives to take an outside job or with special measures for reactivating middle-aged women. But this is hardly surprising—one cannot expect attitudes to change over night.

What we expect of our placement officers, then, is that when faced with a job applicant, they discard traditional attitudes about what is suitable work for men and women. They should find it reasonable to discuss an industrial job with a girl or a woman, just as they should be able to suggest a day nursery or hospital job to a man or a boy.

We also expect our employment offices to think in terms of equality when planning relief work and assigning persons to these projects, which are started when work is lacking on the open market. If a majority of the unemployed are women, something is wrong if most of those on relief work are men. Similarly, if a majority of the unemployed are young women or elderly persons, relief work should not be mostly road construction and the like.

In its instructions to the county labor boards concerning relief work, the National Labor Market Board writes,

In their planning the county labour boards shall heed the Labour Market Administration's equality programme and strive to allocate women and men to relief work in a manner that really corresponds to each sex's share of unemployment. Considering the level of unemployment among young women, it is important that the Employment Service take active steps to ensure that their opportunities for relief work are extended and utilized, too.[5]

If these mild exhortations do not produce the desired result, we have threatened to introduce stricter regulations—that is, quotas.

Table 8-3 illustrates the way in which this new attitude has gradually affected the composition of relief work. The growing proportion of women in relief work has in fact been accompanied by an increased number of relief projects in nursing and allied occupations, but I need hardly say that our policy is not to extend traditional sex roles to relief work. On the contrary, we strive to use relief work so that girls and women get a chance to try untraditional occupations, while boys and men have an opportunity of doing traditional female work—for example, at a day nursery or a hospital.

LABOR MARKET TRAINING

One of the Employment Service's chief means of counteracting unemployment is labor market training, which is now provided for more than 100,000 persons a year. This is roughly the same as the number of students at our universities. Indeed, we tend to refer to labor market training as our alternative university.

There are two purposes to labor market training. The first is to support those who are unemployed and in a position to improve their situation via such training. The second is to generate a supply of trained labor—that is, to help the labor market function more smoothly.

Labor market training generally aims at an occupation, lasts for anywhere from two weeks up to about a year, and is undertaken at special centers. But in some cases it lasts longer than this, is arranged in the regular school system, and covers general subjects. We can thus provide a basic education for persons whose schooling was inadequate, and we can teach the Swedish language to immigrants. Persons attending labor market training receive a taxable training grant, roughly on a par with the regular wage for a fairly unqualified industrial job.

Labor market training is available for persons over twenty who are or run the risk of becoming unemployed. In the case of occupations with a labor shortage, labor market training can be extended to persons who are not in danger of becoming unemployed. Furthermore, the govern-

TABLE 8-3
Persons on Relief Work, Annual Averages

	1972/73			1973/74		
Type of work	*Total number*	*No. of women*	*% **	*Total number*	*No. of women*	*% **
Roads	4,564	87	1.9	3,507	86	2.5
Water and drainage	2,728	45	1.6	2,058	27	1.3
Housebuilding	4,545	62	1.4	3,047	33	1.1
Forestry	4,585	163	3.6	4,294	183	4.3
Nature conservation	1,904	98	5.1	1,501	101	6.7
Culture and monuments	797	35	4.4	576	27	4.7
Military work	214	13	6.1	117	5	4.3
Tourism and recreation	916	12	1.3	636	13	2.0
Industrial	1,865	909	48.7	2,051	1,004	49.0
Service	3,630	1,541	42.5	3,827	1,673	43.7
Nursing	645	537	83.3	817	721	88.2
Other	6,251	296	4.7	5,646	361	6.4
TOTAL	32,644	3,798	11.6	28,077	4,234	15.1

*Percentages are rounded.

ment's proposals for 1978/79 will enable us to reserve some places in labor market training for men and women who are not unemployed but who wish to change their occupation for one that is dominated by the opposite sex.

Clearly, then, labor market training is an important instrument in the work for equality. Indeed, our program states:

> "one of the objectives for an expansion of labour market train-
> ing must be that it can contribute to reducing divisions in the labour
> market. Labour market training should be used as a medium for
> training men for traditional women's occupations and vice versa.
> County Labour Boards are already empowered, in consultation with
> the labour market parties, to give priority in training for which there
> are both male and female applicants, to applicants from the sex which
> is underrepresented in the occupation concerned."[6]

Unfortunately we cannot yet claim that labor market training has become the instrument for equality that we would like it to be. Figure 8-2
and 8-3 show that, in the aggregate, we are still training women and men
in a very traditional manner. But there are certain areas and certain occupations where labor market training can function as we would like it

TABLE 8-3
(Continued)

	1974/75			1975/76			1976/77	
Total number	*No. of women*	*% **	*Total number*	*No. of women*	*% **	*Total number*	*No. of women*	*% **
1,893	78	4.1	2,255	78	3.5	1,949	73	3.7
1,292	26	2.0	1,392	29	2.1	1,180	30	2.5
1,176	15	1.3	889	25	2.8	694	9	1.3
3,339	144	4.3	3,688	158	4.3	3,400	141	4.1
937	76	8.1	1,069	140	13.1	1,089	145	13.3
331	22	6.6	317	34	10.7	315	36	11.4
61	2	3.3	144	4	2.8	118	1	0.8
226	3	1.3	220	9	4.1	168	4	2.4
1,938	947	48.9	1,812	932	51.4	1,776	934	52.6
1,331	662	49.7	4,299	2,284	53.1	8,219	4,655	56.6
454	398	87.7	760	649	85.4	1,452	1,210	83.3
4,089	159	3.9	4,435	277	6.2	7,139	1,187	16.6
17,067	2,532	14.8	21,280	4,619	21.7	27,499	8,425	30.6

to for equality. The following figures show the proportion of women who have received labor market training in mechanical engineering in the four nothernmost counties. In March 1975, of 351 people trained, 42 percent were women. In March 1976, 44 percent (of 359) were women, and in March 1977, 39 percent (of 338) were women.

ORGANIZATION

Even though equality is to be promoted by all our staff in their daily work, we are well aware that the desired result will not be achieved unless organizational measures are taken to provide a driving force to get things going and routines for following up and checking results. When the governing body of the National Labor Market Board adopted the equality program, it also appointed a central working group comprised of a number of heads of divisions chaired by the director-general. This group is to keep a continuous eye on equality work. It discusses the aids and instruments at our disposal and the ways in which they need to be developed. We also apply the equality criterion to the need for improvements to, for instance, our regular statistics or the organization of the employment offices. In passing, it can be mentioned that the appointment of high-ranking officials

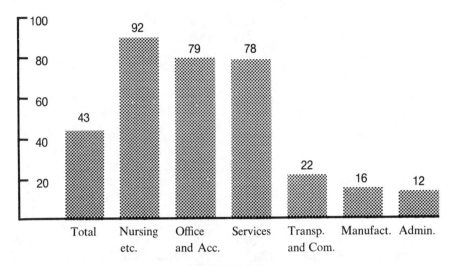

FIGURE 8-2
Women's Share of Employment in Some Occupational Areas,
1976 (percent)

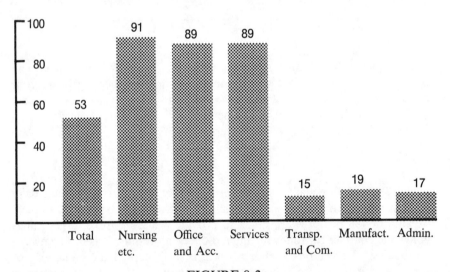

FIGURE 8-3
Women's Share of Labor Market Training for Some Occupational Areas,
1976 (percent)

to this group is considered most important as a means of indicating the weight of this issue at a time when it has not yet been accepted fully by all our staff.

At the county labor boards an official has been assigned special responsibility for equality questions. This post is known as activation inspector, a relic of the fifties, when it was mainly a question of "activating" housewives. Then at each district office there is an official for the coordination of equality questions. These officials cooperate with the county's activation inspector and have the task of following the public debate, stimulating discussion among their colleagues, encouraging the latter to participate in further training to do with equality, and continuously ensuring that equality aspects are not overlooked in daily work. The activation inspector and the coordinators are to keep the county and district labor boards continuously informed about work for equality. Similarly, questions concerning equality are taken up regularly by the governing body of the National Labor Market Board and at the annual conferences with county labor directors.

SPECIAL INSTRUMENTS

Although the concept of equality, as already emphasized, should leave its mark on everything we do, it naturally needs to be reinforced with special instruments and pilot projects for promoting equality on the labor market. I should like to describe some of these—namely sex quotas in regional development policy, what is known as the Kristianstad model, courses on working life and training, the equality grant, and guidance groups.

Sex quotas

There are certain areas in Sweden where state support is available to new enterprises or to firms that expand their operations. This support is provided for investments in buildings and machinery as well as for the training of personnel. Its purpose is to boost employment in places where the labor market is weak, thereby reducing differences in the level of employment between different parts of the country. Since 1974 there has been a pilot scheme with sex quotas for the new jobs that are created through this regional development support. The scheme, which is to run until July 1979, means that a firm obtaining this state support has to recruit at least 40 percent from each sex.

A preliminary evaluation is available of experience and statistics for the first two years. During this period the proportion of women in the firms receiving support rose two percentage points, from 19 to 21 percent.

Women accounted for 35 percent of new recruits; this is lower than the statutory level of 40 percent, the difference being due to the granting of exemptions—a general exemption has been made for the recruitment of fewer than three persons and additional exemptions have been allowed in the case of staff with special skills. Compared with firms in corresponding branches in Sweden as a whole, women increased their share of employment in the firms receiving support somewhat more rapidly. The share of women in the national labor force has risen during the trial period, but it has done so to a greater extent in the counties where regional development support can be obtained.

From the statistics alone it might therefore be asked whether the sex quotas have achieved very much. At the National Board, however, we regard it as our best instrument for equality and hope to establish it on a regular footing. This assessment is based on the experience of our personnel in the field. They have provided numerous examples where the sex-quota stipulation has meant that premises have been planned from the start for the employment of both sexes; this means for instance, that they have been equipped with the necessary washrooms and changing rooms. And when the firms have applied for the grant, it has been possible to assess the chances of finding, say, women with suitable training for the new jobs; if no such women have been available, this gave the Employment Service time to arrange suitable training.

When evaluating the result of the sex quotas, it should be pointed out once more that they apply to parts of the country where the level of employment is below the national average for men, too, and where the traditional view is that any work should be reserved in the first place for men, the "family providers." It seems reasonable to suppose that the sex quotas have given women a better chance of asserting their right to employment in the face of prejudice and traditions.

I should like to mention in passing that the idea of quotas is gaining ground in many contexts in Sweden. It is being discussed in connection with education, for young persons as well as for adults. As already mentioned, the National Board instructs the county labor boards in terms of quotas as regards women's share of relief work. In politics, moreover, large groups of women are strongly in favor of quotas when appointing representatives to Parliament, municipal assemblies, committees, and so on. A similar discussion has also started in the trade union movement.

The Kristianstad model

In 1973 a pilot scheme was started in the county of Kristianstad with the aim of encouraging women to choose traditionally male occupations in industry. The resultant model was then applied all over the country. The project was arranged as follows.

Advertisements and leaflets were used to invite female job-seekers to an information day at the employment service, where they were told about the local labor market, the opportunities in industry, training facilities, and so on. Transportation and child-minding were arranged for this day.

The women who then wanted to go a step further were invited to take a course lasting four to six weeks, known as Working Life and Training; after one week of theory the rest of the course was devoted to practical experience at ordinary workplaces. Having completed the course, the women were generally able to choose a regular job at one of the places where they had practiced. During the course they received a training grant on the same scale as that for labor market training—a fairly low wage on the open market.

We know that projects based on the Kristianstad model in six counties in the early years enabled two thousand women to find jobs. At the same time, however, a far greater number of women took up traditionally male jobs directly in the country as a whole, and it is therefore difficult to measure the impact of these particular pilot projects.

Rita Liljeström and some colleagues have studied a group of women who entered traditionally male jobs in Kristianstad itself (see Chapter 18). They also interviewed the husbands, children, workmates, and employers. An English summary of a preliminary version of their report is available, entitled *Roles in Transition*.[7]

Working life and education

The course employed in the Kristianstad model is a standard course that the Employment Service uses to inform uncertain and inexperienced job-seekers about the various forms of employment and training that are available. The practical experience can be concentrated on one or several industries, but it can also cover work of different kinds—for example, in industry, nursing, and commerce. The duration of practical experience can be extended individually. This is done as a general rule, for instance, in the case of young persons with social handicaps. A course can be arranged for men and women together or separately. Courses in nursing and allied occupations, for instance, have been arranged for men only, just as courses concerning industry have been confined to women.

In our view this course performs important functions in breaking down traditional occupational choices. People in much the same life situation meet one another and are able to talk together about their situation with an official from the employment service. They are able to go as a group to a workplace and gain practical experience without committing themselves to employment there. This is reassuring both for the person who is breaking a sex barrier and for the housewife who wants to join the labor market after many years at home.

Equality grant

The equality grant is an example of a selective measure for equality at work that we do not consider to have been particularly effective. The grant has been used for only about 250 persons a year, and in only one case for a man. The grant is available for employers who take on and train men and women in a job that is untraditional for their sex. The grant amounts to eight kronor an hour for six months (fourteen kronor in some counties). The range of occupations for which the grant is available is limited, though it is wider in the pilot counties (where the rate is fourteen kronor) than in other counties.

The National Board has tried—so far without result—to get the government to alter this grant's construction, which seems to be one reason why it has been used so little. We would like the size of the grant to be the same everywhere—fifteen kronor—and we also want to remove the restriction to certain occupations, making the grant available instead whenever an employer takes on someone in an untraditional job (the criterion of this being a sex bias of more than 40–60 percent).

At present, moreover, there is a regulation that excludes the grant if unemployed persons of the traditional sex are available for the occupation in question. This means, for instance, that in most parts of the country the equality grant cannot be used to increase the proportion of men in nursing because there is an almost universal supply of unemployed female nursing aides.

Guidance groups

A guidance group is a fairly new instrument that is being used on a trial basis in certain parts of the country. It is designed for those who need more information and support than can be provided by an employment official over the counter or during a short talk. It is used in particular for young persons and those who have worked in the home for a considerable period. These job-seekers are often very vague about their choice of occupation or training and their expectations on the labor market tend to be rather unrealistic.

A guidance group is a means of bringing together people in the same situation so that they can help and support each other and realize that there are others with similar problems. At the same time it is naturally more efficient for the employment officials to talk with people in a group instead of individually. A group is comprised of a placement officer, a psychologist, and about ten job-seekers. The activity of guidance groups is arranged preliminarily as follows: introduction; what to consider when choosing an occupation; occupations and forms of training; the labor market; personal qualifications and limitations; functioning in a work situation; arriving at a decision. The meetings generally last two days, but there are instances of groups meeting for half a day each week over a period of several weeks.

CONCLUSION

Sweden has attracted interest for many years because of its approach to labor relations and its labor market policy. In the early sixties, for instance, the heads of the Employers' Confederation and the Confederation of Trade Unions toured the United States together to talk about their collective agreements and general air of cooperation. Indeed, the spirit of cooperation in the Swedish labor market is usually traced back to the Saltsjobaden Agreements of 1938.

Since then, employers and employees have negotiated numerous agreements about wages, hours of work, the working environment, and much besides. The traditional approach to problems in the Swedish labor market has in fact been to negotiate an agreement. Only when this proved unfeasible and a request was made by one of the parties (usually the employees) has the government intervened with legislation.

In recent years this pattern has been broken to some extent, even though everyone still affirms the principle. Several labor laws were introduced in the early seventies to increase security of employment and to strengthen the influence of workers on job safety and on the management of the enterprise in general. Several of these laws constitute a foundation for more detailed regulations which are formulated in collective agreements.

In the case of wage agreements, the parties have been adamant in dismissing a wages policy in any form. But here, too, it can be argued that the tradition is being eroded. In the early seventies, for instance, the government reached agreements with the employee organizations about state tax cuts on the implicit understanding that demands would be lowered correspondingly in the current wage negotiations (the aim being to check inflation).

This background helps to explain why the labor market organizations and the Social Democrat party are opposed to a sex discrimination law. Two sex-equality agreements that cover most employees in the private sector were in fact concluded by employers and the unions in the spring of 1977. And in the central government all agencies already have a statutory obligation to draw up an equality plan each year and report the previous year's measures. In spite of this, the bourgeois coalition government presented a bill on the subject in the spring of 1978. This law proposal has been commented on by over sixty organizations, and should be voted on in Parliament before the upcoming elections in the fall of 1979.

An interesting question is to what extent the agreements and a law can be coordinated to form an effective whole. Experience in many fields has shown that legislation is not sufficient by itself to generate changes in practice. It has to be accompanied by organizational resources, funds, and many people's enthusiasm and determination. A law, suitably drafted, may perhaps get things going or help keep them rolling by providing psychological support. But any real equalization of conditions for men and for women on the Swedish labor market calls for major changes in society in general (in residential planning, communications, day nurseries, and so on) as well as in the attitudes of both sexes concerning what is feminine and masculine, and in conditions of working life. In addition, it is essential that the employees at every place of work put their weight behind demands for changes and that the unions are actively prepared to initiate and implement reforms. A law drafted in collaboration with the labor market organizations might perhaps serve to back up agreements. But a law that does not correspond to their wishes is liable to render agreements inoperative and paralyze local initiatives at workplaces. One should not underestimate the moral force that an agreement—in Sweden—exerts on the union organization that has signed it.

NOTES

1. Alva Myrdal, in Viola Klein, *Women's Two Roles* (London: Routledge and Kegan Paul, 1956).
2. Eva Moberg, *Kvinnor och Människor* (Stockholm, 1962).
3. Stockholm, Department of State, *Report to the U.N. on the Status of Women in Sweden* (Stockholm, 1968).
4. National Labor Market Board, *Equality in the Labour Market* (Solna, Sweden, Sept. 1977), p. 10.
5. Ordinary letter, 1978 Yearly Instructions.
6. *Equality in the Labour Market*, pp. 15–16.
7. Rita Liljeström, Gunilla Fürst Mellström, and Gillan Liljeström Svensson, *Roles in Transition: Report of an Investigation Made for the Advisory Council on Equality between Men and Women* (Stockholm: Liber Förlag / Allmänna Förlaget, 1978).

9 *Alice H. Cook*

VOCATIONAL TRAINING, THE LABOR MARKET, AND THE UNIONS

Women's achievement of equal opportunity in the labor market and the availability of vocational training are closely linked. Almost every study of women's place in the labor market points out that women receive less pay than men, work more generally in deadend jobs, occupy a segregated section of the labor market, and have little upward mobility. And the thread which ties these fateful facts together is women's lack of vocational training.

In part this lack rests on conceptions widely held by parents, employers, labor market specialists, and, yes, by women themselves, namely that they will not remain long within the labor market because marriage is their destiny and career. Parents may see training for their daughter as unrewarding because, since she will work only a few years, she may as well enjoy the earnings she can make during that time, rather than spending a substantial part of those few years in nonremunerative training, an investment which will presumably never pay off.

Employers often say that they cannot afford an investment in women's training either, but their reason is that the trainee becomes an undependable worker. A woman, they complain, is both mobile and immobile; mobile in the sense that she must leave if her husband moves; immobile in the sense that she is tied to her family and is not available to go to other locations, to take on overtime, or to travel on the job. She will always place family ahead of job, and this means taking time off to care for sick children or older people; she will insist on getting home promptly from work to care for children and to take on household responsibilities. As a consequence, women's absenteeism rate is high; they have little interest in entering more responsible jobs; they may leave at any time to have another baby, and so on. The consequence is that employers rarely think of investing in women's training.

Vocational counsellors in schools and labor offices, we assume, have access to all the information available today which shows that a large and growing percentage of women work most of their adult lives, that the number of women whose divorce or separation makes them their families' sole support grows amazingly fast, and that the number of working mothers of young children is steadily increasing—all these facts point to women's increasing tendency and need to work and work uninterruptedly even during their early adult years. Yet these counsellors tend still to direct women into the typical women's trades, deadend and low paid as they are. Many of them do this in good conscience because they cannot seriously urge them to climb the barriers erected against women's entering the men's trades.

Women are caught in the vortex of this circular thinking and indeed tend to take on the characteristics which they are alleged inherently to possess. Open opportunities are few and their own time so limited that they remain frustrated in their jobs without an effective way to challenge the fate which society has designed for them.

So long as these attitudes influence official policy on the one hand and women entrants on the other, in their choice of work, so long will women continue to crowd the ranks of unskilled and semi-skilled workers. Women's work has become so stigmatized as being of low value that it is particularly difficult for women in these occupations to gain entry to training for other jobs.

This vicious circle in which attitude shapes reality and reality reinforces attitude must be broken through. The critical point is access to vocational training. So immediate is the linkage between vocational training and equal labor market opportunity that the Seminar on Vocational Guidance and Training for Women Workers, sponsored by the European Communities a few years ago, found that "most of the problems encountered by women of the European Communities in their work or their desire to find employment are grounded in vocational guidance and training."[1]

Not many countries have embarked on a thoroughgoing policy of labor market equality. The most usual assumption, more implicit than explicit, is that women are a reserve army which can be called up when the supply of men is short and which will retreat without question when they are no longer needed. Such is the history of both world wars, when all the interested parties—mobilized men, the women who filled their vacated jobs, employers, and government—assumed that the period during which women would work would be no more than a few years; the jobs, they all agreed, belonged to the men. Although at that time women were actually invited into men's jobs, which had been highly skilled, from which they had previously been totally barred, training was simplified as much as possible so as to reduce time and costs. For the most part, crafts were diluted into easily learned occupations and tasks, and women emerged from that experience often only partially qualified for the jobs they had taken over from men. Given this foreshortened training devised for them by the war industry, those who continued work were not able to compete with men in the postwar job market. Small wonder that even these women, when they were fired, retreated to their homes and to the women's trades.

The boom of the sixties and seventies again saw employers actively recruiting women for a wide variety of jobs not previously open to them. The period coincided with the rebirth of the women's movement, a movement identified not just with equality at the ballot box, as had been the case in World War I, but equality on the job. Women themselves were just beginning to imagine and articulate what this might mean. "Equal pay for equal work" or "work of equal value" or "work of substantially equal value" were the terms in which the discussion for the most part ran. But women and their organizations slowly began to understand that equal pay was not enough unless women could have equal job opportunities. They stated their demands more and more in terms of training and placement, of full rights to skills and full use of skills. Labor market boards encouraged employers to offer women training and assisted women with grants-in-aid to pursue training which would equip them for the new openings. Women began to penetrate the skilled trades.

The test of these approaches came with the recession. As it deepened, the mask of equality fell. Employers, public boards, legislators, and unions were revealed again as adherents of the "reserve army" concept. The figures of women's unemployment as compared with men's provide the basic evidence. In Germany, in 1978, women made up, as they had for several years, 52 percent of the unemployed although they were only 37 percent of the labor force. In the U.S. unemployment among white women was half again as high as among white men. In Sweden, although unemployment was the lowest in Western Europe, women's unemployment was well above that of men. And so it goes.

The reasons employers often give for laying off women more readily than men is that they will suffer less from loss of wages, particularly if their husbands are employed. But it is clear that women's lack of skill makes them dispensable. Labor market boards cut down on training programs or raise requirements for admission to them such that the number of women who can participate is seriously curtailed. As jobs vanish, training opportunities, particularly for women, diminish.

As Berit Rollén makes clear in Chapter 8, Sweden is one of the few countries where, as the depression has continued, the labor market board has increased programs and subsidies both to women and to employers to encourage further training. It is true of course that Sweden is a small and relatively wealthy and homogeneous country, and that in such a setting central planning and programming are more workable than in the United States or even Germany. Nevertheless, it is important to see what kinds of experiments are going on there and in other countries, too, that may offer models adaptable to similar needs in different circumstances.

WOMEN'S SPECIAL NEED FOR TRAINING

Training institutions have been designed to accommodate themselves to men's working life cycle. Whether the programs are public or private, on the job or off the job, pre-employment or post-employment, offering further training or retraining, they assume—except for Sweden and one or two other Scandinavian countries—an uninterrupted life of work from school-leaving to retirement.[2] When the war broke this pattern for millions of men, most countries recognized a special, new need and provided programs such as the GI Bill in the United States which encouraged men who had lost several years of work experience or training to go back to school before starting off again in work life. Yet, although such an interruption is a standard part of women's adult experience, few if any labor market institutions respond to their need. Training opportunities are not geared to this massive problem of withdrawal from the labor force and re-entry.

This is not women's only exceptional circumstance. Boys all through school are prepared to think in terms of work and to begin to prepare for it in their later school years. They move from school into training as an important and necessary preliminary step to entry into lifetime occupations. Girls have been treated very differently both at school and at home. Work, they are told, is a means of filling a presumably short interval between school and marriage; marriage is their career; when work is undertaken, it is a supplement to the responsibilities of homemaking and child-rearing. Women who combine marriage and work do so under two major handicaps. They interrupt their work experience at a time usually in their mid-twenties, when men are being selected for advanced training on or off the job. Having missed these opportunities they are considered, by the standards applied to men, to be too old for the programs leading to advancement. The result is that upward movement on otherwise promising career ladders in, for example, the professions and paraprofessions is cut off. The second problem which all the world accepts as almost immutable is that they carry home responsibilities as well as job responsibilities. Part-time work is a desideratum, and yet part-time work is an absolute handicap to on-the-job training and advancement. A man who wants to get ahead is expected not only to work full time but to spend his nonworking hours studying for the next step up the ladder. A woman who cannot do this is hardly worth consideration for the position of supervisor or lead worker.

And perhaps most constricting and different from men's experience is the circumstance that when women do work it is understood they will go into the "women's occupations": "light" work—assembly, sewing, typing, filing, reception; work to which women have traditionally been judged as particularly suited—nurturing, caring, cleaning, laundering, food service—all of them jobs which are low paid, most of them low-ceiling, and most of them low skilled.

Women's problems in the labor market are that most of them will interrupt their work for shorter or longer periods, though as the birthrate falls, these interruptions are of less and less duration and frequency. Many of them come into the market not expecting to remain or to make their work a central interest in their lives. They come doubly burdened. The nature of their educational and vocational training is different from that of the men with whom they are expected to compete, unless, of course, they are in the typical women's jobs where competition scarcely exists and remuneration is on quite another level from that of men's work. Their opportunities for on-the-job training hardly exist.

What we need to consider then are the points at which women must be given special attention in providing vocational training. The first, of course, is in school itself in terms of curriculum, counselling, and pre-vocational set. Second is at school-leaving and initial entry to work. Third is on-the-job training opportunities designed to allow for learning skills and to prepare for upward movement, including into at least the lower levels of management. The fourth has to do with training opportunities at re-entry into the work force after some period away from work.

A further consideration is that of the agencies which best meet these needs. They include the schools, employers, labor market institutions, and the trade unions organized in many of the fields women enter or would like to enter. We look first at the organization of the labor market and then turn to programs presently in operation in three European countries which have recently been studied.[3]

LABOR MARKET REGULATION AND TRAINING

Each country has its own labor market policies covering a wide range of functions. We shall here concern ourselves simply with training and the degree to which women are provided for. These policies are administered by a statutory governmental board made up, in addition to government officials, by representatives of employers and trade unions, along with experts. Some boards, notably the German Federal Institution for Work (Bundesanstalt fuer Arbeit), are financed by the contributions to the unemployment insurance fund which the Board also administers. In others, as in Britain and Sweden, the board is a state agency financed out of the central budget.

Most of these boards with the exception of Sweden's operate under policies and powers which are quite inadequate to deal vigorously with labor market problems. Instead, they administer a series of statutory programs, often not closely integrated with one another and often designed to respond more to political pressures from special interest groups than to meet needs of the changing structure of the labor force and the changing nature of work.

A major responsibility in all cases is that the boards carry out programs to combat unemployment and thus, insofar as training is concerned, men and women threatened with unemployment or actually unemployed are retrained for available jobs. Re-entering women may well be fitted more or less wisely into these programs.

The needs of school leavers as they enter the labor market may be handled by the schools or by the employment service working closely with the schools. Where apprenticeship is a standard means of training young people for work, however, responsibility for recruiting apprentices and contracting with them for training becomes an employer function and the number of places available will depend upon the employers' estimates of their needs for trained personnel over the long haul. More and more, labor market boards are endeavoring to fill the gaps between available openings and the many applications from young people by setting up board-sponsored training centers or assisting such organizations as unions and chambers of labor (in Austria) to establish youth training centers. These public (supra-firm—*ueberbetriebliche*) centers are relatively new in Europe. Finally, the boards encourage employers, unions, chambers, public enterprises, and private entrepreneurs to offer on-the-job and off-the-job programs of further training for the upward bound. In some cases, as we shall see, the boards support likely candidates in limited programs of general education as well, where that is needed as a base for specific vocational courses. Thus, initially there are apprenticeship and youth training, almost never available to adults. Adult training falls into the three categories of entry, on-the-job training, or off-the-job refresher training; retraining for persons who have become redundant; and further or advanced training for people seeking to acquire higher levels of skill or credentials for promotion. At each of these stages the boards or their sub-agencies offer vocational information and counselling and in a number of countries have a statutory monopoly on counselling and placement.

Counselling is of special importance to women, who often know little about labor market or training opportunities. Moreover, many women face discrimination in the hiring interview itself and need help in understanding how and where to apply for work.[4] The critical question about counselling is whether women seeking guidance in their search for jobs are directed mainly or only to the typical women's trades. If so, advice on training will of course be related to them, and the woman's chances for adequate earnings, upward mobility, and high levels of job satisfaction are correspondingly narrowly circumscribed.

So far as these kinds of training opportunities are concerned, women often are ruled out because they have passed the age when training is open to them, as is the case with all apprenticeships, or because they do not have the requisite grounding in math or mechanical drawing or basic science.

Frequently they cannot meet labor market board requirements for previous employment over a given number of years—six is fairly standard—and work at home is rarely recognized as an equivalent. Moreover, as one Swedish group pointed out after an investigation of the training programs in a major public corporation, training for men is frequently stated in terms of promotion whereas women are offered not skill advancement but skill improvement training: they can become better stenographers able to deal with more types of office machines, but not supervisors or managers. Even in the boom period, when women were very much in demand in most European countries, training for them was ad hoc and piecemeal, accommodating not to the circumstance of women entering or re-entering the labor market as permanent workers, but rather to the immediate needs of local employers at a given time.

In the late 1970s, in the recession, labor market boards are all too sensitive to the real shortage of jobs and are reluctant to train either women or men for work that is not likely to be available. Moreover, their own funds are depleted, particularly when they derive mainly from unemployment insurance contributions.

Given these circumstances and given the pervasive notion that women constitute a reserve army of workers, where can we look for the kind of change necessary to meet working women's special needs for training? Certainly not to the proprietary schools, which exist to make a profit out of the status quo whether in boom or recession. Probably not to employers, whose risk-taking propensities rarely direct them to take new directions in advancing women. Perhaps to the unions, whose goals are stated in terms of commitment to full employment. But in the short run, union men in a period of depression can only feel that women moving out of the congested female trades and acquiring skills and supervisory status are a threat to their own security and hopes. Rhetoric and practice in the unions tend to fall widely apart. If, however, unions can and do demand the changes women need, they will do so for several sound reasons: First, they are political institutions in every sense of the word. Internally they form their policies and choose their officers by political means—pressure, elections, interest representation. Women make up a growing number of their members. Since the late 1960s, in many countries, more women have joined unions than have men. Women are becoming more articulate and vocal. The existence of special union departments attending to their problems provides a political base for their organization within the unions where they discuss their special problems, formulate demands, and place them before the union's decision-making bodies. Second, unions are the only institution in the labor market made up of workers. They wield great influence with employers with whom they bargain, and they can to a great extent determine the degree to which the employer responds to women's needs. Beyond that they are invariably represented on the labor market boards and represent the major constituency of the labor ministries. So far as training is concerned, it is not only the labor market boards, but vocational schools, adult education institutions, technical colleges, and apprenticeship programs which are the targets of their concern. The role of the unions alone is seldom decisive, but it is essential and powerful as it interplays with employers and national political interests in the formulation and administration of labor market policy.

But it is the public agencies, the labor market boards, and their equivalents which must bear the major burden of producing change. They are the legal institutions charged with administering and supervising training, and they have the financial resources to realize new attacks on old problems. As Berit Rollén has demonstrated in Chapter 8, Sweden provides in this respect a model far in advance of any other country, both as to policies favoring women's entry into the labor market and their continued presence there, even in recession, on equal terms with men, and as to the individual programs designed to implement these policies. But labor market boards in Great Britain, Germany, and Austria are also endeavoring to open access to equal opportunity in the labor market. Each has a different approach to the problems we have raised here.

GREAT BRITAIN

As a British expert sees it,

> Women are poorly distributed throughout the range of training provided. Many would argue this is not a training problem. Quite right: women's training opportunities are limited by a complex network of social, economic and cultural problems in which the effect of attitudes is particularly significant.[5]

The agency concerned with labor market problems and specifically with women's training in Great Britain is the British Manpower Services Commission (MSC), which in turn has created the Training Services Administration (TSA) as its executive arm. One of TSA's functions is to encourage industries to set up training boards to bring young women into their employment and training programs. Twenty-seven boards had been created by 1971, made up of union and management representatives from the industry together with some education specialists. We shall look mainly at the Engineering Industries Training Board (EITB), which has made the first attempt to open craft jobs to women.

The Employment and Training Act of 1973 provides, as did its predecessor, the Industrial Training Act of 1964, for the labor minister to set up industrial training boards such as the EITB. Most of these industry boards have concentrated on youth training, but the Chemical ITB is in process (1977) of setting up a course in business studies for women with university science degrees so that they can move into management. This was a landmark undertaking because, until then, training—at least in peacetime—had been left entirely to employers.

Within the engineering field, the National Women's Sub-Committee of TASS, the white-collar division of AUEW, after 1974 took an active role in trying to increase training opportunities for women in skills. Its leaders met with the general secretary of the Union and a representative of TSA to discuss possible programs. Among them was one for upgrading training for women tracers (a low grade of draftsmanship), leading to full qualifications as drafters. By December 1975, the Sub-Committee had decided to make training and retraining of women one of its main priorities.

After several studies of women in the labor market had unmistakably noted that women are handicapped by wide differences in early education between boys and girls and that women as a consequence tend to be directed and indeed to flow into low-skilled, low-paid jobs mainly in "the women's trades," the Manpower Services Commission called attention to the need to "reduce curricular differences between boys and girls in schools" and stressed "the need to train careers teachers (school vocational counsellors) to help [girls] take a wider view of the developing opportunities for female employment." It wants to "direct expansion of women's training to parts of the economy which are growing and to shortage occupations." More particularly, it wants to provide "gateway courses" for young people entering new occupations and "early priority or pilot courses to benefit girls." At the same time, it plans "to provide new incentives to employers for first-year off-the-job training for a number of girl engineering technician trainees and to encourage girls to go into craft training by providing incentives to employers to open up training opportunities for women."[6]

A study of women in the engineering industry[7] points out that of the 650,000 women in that industry in 1975 (of a total of 2,827,300 workers), 95 percent, or 615,000, were in three low-skilled job categories, chiefly operators and clerical workers. At the same time, women made up only 2 percent of the craft, managerial, scientist, and technologist personnel in the industry. Although training is an important industry undertaking, female trainees represented a low proportion of the total, much lower than their proportion in the industry's labor force.

Although the EITB was established in 1965, it was only in 1976 that it put together a program of training for school-leaving girls in three areas of England. Pat Turner, representing the General and Municipal Workers (G&M), was a member of the special working party set up to examine training opportunities for women in the industry, and is generally credited with propelling the scheme into operation. This committee was to monitor the scholarship scheme for girls as it progressed.

TASS, Technical, Administrative and Supervisory Section of the Amalgamated Union of Engineering Workers (AUEW), also named a woman staff member to the EITB steering committee. She urged from the beginning wider publicity than just shipping materials to the schools, the main approach decided upon originally for reaching girls and one which later had to be abandoned in favor of more popular and direct methods. (Later TASS commissioned a popular English singer, Peggy Seeger, to cut a record for the union, "I'm Gonna Be an Engineer!"[8] which narrated the difficulties of a woman trying to enter this all-male field. The record quickly sold out.) Another woman representative of TASS served on a similar steering committee in Croydon, one of the program's three locations.

The occupations opened to women under this scheme are in the mechanical and electronic trades, which call for four years of training. The first year is spent in industrial training in a company workshop, coupled with block-released time for twenty weeks of courses at a local technical college. This is the standard first-year off-the-job craft/technician course, based on EITB's training manual. The second year is on-the-job training in a plant. EITB covers the students' cost of these two years in the form of "scholarship awards." In the final two years, EITB expects, firms will take the girls onto their payrolls as full employees for the standard period of in-service training and development. EITB hopes that employers who take them on will commit themselves to released time to allow the girls to complete their college training, but at this point, which represents the beginning of the third year, responsibility for program content passes from EITB to the firms.

In 1977, when our study was made, every indication pointed to high interest on the part of employers, who, after all, were going to receive trainees whose first two years of schooling would have been paid for and who would already have proved their capacity to handle the work. Moreover, despite massive unemployment in Britain, the fields selected for training were ones in which there were labor shortages. In fact, one firm had offered to take all the trainees who completed the first two years, but EITB rejected this offer because it wanted to send these young women in small groups of two or three into as many firms as possible rather than to concentrate them in one enterprise.

The greatest difficulty this scheme had in getting going was in finding girls to participate. The story of the ultimate success of that endeavor is therefore worth repeating for the suggestions it has for other experiments of a similar kind.

You prepare a brochure and full supporting literature and use it to try to sell the scheme through the schools and the various career counselling outlets. What the EITB found was that this conventional, time-honored approach was a sure-fire recipe for banging your head against the brick wall. . . . The first shot in November 1975 had been to invite headmasters [school principals] to a seminar in a Birmingham hotel, an occasion that proved to be positively lukewarm. . . . One headmaster actually got up and said that he would not encourage any of his girls to enter engineering. That was a good start! . . . The EITB then tried to involve the careers people by sending literature to the schools for distribution to possible takers, or at least, for it to be made available for any girl who might show an interest. This approach produced very little return and can best be described as passive in the sense that any response must come from the school staff, the counsellors or the girls themselves. What the board staff wanted . . . was to get inside the schools so that they could speak directly to groups of girls. This the schools just wouldn't allow.

With the schools closed to them, the EITB staff then tried to contact girls and their parents directly by appearing on local radio and TV. The measure of the problem can be seen from the fact that at that stage, after some seven months of intense effort, a mere fifty applications, suitable or unsuitable, had come in for the twenty-five available Birmingham places.

What produced the breakthrough was newspaper advertisements aiming to attract both the girls and their parents. Indeed, the form of the wording was such that it was directed mainly at the parent. After all, the offer represents a fine opportunity—it is a scholarship award in a very real sense. It is backed by the EITB, a body which packs a punch when it comes to training for a career. It's not just the firm down the road behind it. If Bloggs and Sons pack up, you can be sure that the EITB award holders will be looked after; they'll be transferred. An EITB award holder is a member of a favored elite and parents are quick to see the advantage. What did the trick was getting into the family environment as opposed to the school environment. Within four days, the 50 applications, which had represented the first seven months of effort, rose to a dramatic 150 and it was from this number that the 21 successful applicants were chosen.[9]

In interviews with our team, several of the applicants told us how they had had difficulty in getting any information whatever in school about the technical trades. One girl had traded off with a boy, who was likewise having difficulty learning about opportunities in cooking, his loose-leaf binder on technical trades for one given her on occupations suitable for girls.

Because women applying for jobs often have difficulty getting serious consideration even when they qualify for the available jobs, G&M proposed a procedure to its shop stewards and local (branch) officers to meet this situation. First they were to get reports on the numbers of applicants and of hirings of men and women. When the percentage of women being turned down was much higher than that of men, they were to demand that the personnel office give the reasons for the rejection of each woman applicant. This procedure presumes some kind of equal opportunity agreement at plant or company level with provisions for monitoring compliance, but it would surely call the attention of the company to the unions' concern for a reasonable proportion of women in the workforce.

The Employment Service Agency (ESA) and TSA decided about 1975 to institute a special training program for unemployed women. Their aim was to train 100,000 persons a year, and in the first year, 1976, they actually enrolled 80,000. The Training Opportunities Scheme (TOPS), which has had the most success in numbers of any of the MSC programs, was designated the responsible scheme for carrying out this training. It is able to pay allowances to trainees and it uses training places in the so-called Government Skill Centers and in local polytechnic colleges. While all of its programs had been open to women, it now planned certain ones particularly for women—"New Careers in Office Work" and "A New Career in Management."

In an early study, "Training Opportunities for Women," it noted that "women are breaking into some new types of employment which have very largely been closed to them in the past" and therefore "more varied training opportunities will be needed to keep pace with and reinforce these changes." Among other recommendations of its report on training for women are the following dealing particularly with adult women job-seekers:

- give mature women some support to enable them to get necessary educational qualifications before training can start;
- direct expansion of women's training to parts of the economy which are growing and to shortage occupations;
- increase the staff of Industry Training Boards and TSA by at least one person who will have specific responsibility for women's training;
- continue to encourage women to take the TOPS courses leading to managerial qualifications;
- stimulate interest in training for mature women and develop basic and refresher training for mature women;
- offer Wider Opportunities Courses to women re-entering the labor market or seeking a change of occupation and provide preliminary training courses to help women participate later with men in standard programs of career development.[10]

AUSTRIA

The Austrian labor market agency in the late 1960s developed what it called an "active labor market policy." Under it, vocational training emerged as a major instrument of government efforts to achieve full employment. All apprenticeship training is the responsibility of employers, with whom parents sign an agreement for the training of their children in a two- to four-year program of practical work supplemented by a day a week of "theoretical schooling in a vocational school." These apprenticeships are regulated by the Vocational Training Law.[11] The vocational schools are usually public, although in some cases large employers are certified to set up their own schools.

Austria has a unique institution in the Chamber of Labor (Kammer der Arbeiter und Angestellten), a quasi-governmental agency set up under law to represent the interests of labor to government and society.[12] Every worker has a fraction of a percent of his income deducted as tax to the Chamber, which in turn operates training institutions for youth and adults, does research on a variety of labor problems, works intimately with the trade unions on legislative and social programs, deals with the employers' comparable institutions—the Chambers of Commerce, of Handcraft, and of Agriculture—takes the lead in setting up a variety of social welfare programs for workers, and operates schools to train workers elected to Works' Councils. The Chamber of Labor has a women's division which maintains close contact with the women's divisions of the unions and with professional organizations of employed women. It is concerned among many other matters with apprenticeship, vocational guidance, and training.

The Chamber has set up a number of trades committees (Fachausschüsse), in which the unions play a large role, to monitor and influence the nature of apprenticeship programs. One problem the labor market faces is the growing number of children coming out of school and into the labor market—a demographic trend in the mid-seventies which will continue for several years to come—and their predilection for a narrow and traditional range of occupational choices. Both boys and girls tend to opt for "fad" occupations, but the crowding of girls into a few occupations is far worse than among boys. Among male apprentices, 95 percent are enrolled in seventy-two training programs, while 90 percent of girls are found in only ten programs and 40 percent of these are crowded into the retail trades alone.

The women's division of the metal workers union has been endeavoring with the cooperation of the Chamber of Labor to draft legislation to change the curriculum in the final compulsory school year, when boys and girls are fourteen or fifteen years of age. These women see an inherent sex bias in this "polytechnic year" and want teachers at this stage to notice technically gifted girls and give them special encouragement to enroll in the schools' technical vocational track. They want further to have vocational guidance begin as early as twelve years of age instead of at the present age of fifteen, in order to help girls attain the same kind of realistic view of their participation in work life that boys acquire in growing up. In pursuit of these aims the women's division carried on an intensive education program among their own union's officers, works councillors, and activists generally about their report and its implications both for men and for women.

They talked with the minister for social affairs about women's limited access to occupations, with the result that he agreed not just to encourage, but to put pressure on employers applying for aid under the 1973 Employment Promotion Act to accept specific quotas of girls in vocational training not traditionally available to them. He went further and supported a supplementary study by the Institute for Vocational Training Research, which he asked to examine the degree to which girls can be introduced into about fifteen traditionally male occupations (among them, welders, fitters, turners, high and low voltage electrical workers, plumbers, toolmakers, radio and television technicians, electrical and mechanical engineers—all branches in which the labor market administration sees promise of expansion).

Another chance for girls to move into a wider range of apprenticeships in the metal trades came with the opening in 1978 of Austria's first nonemployer training workshop for apprentices. This project, sponsored by the metal union and the Chamber, combined practical and theoretical training. The program has had international repercussions: At one stage the International Metal Trades Secretariat (IMF) in Geneva as well as the German Metalworkers' Union joined the Austrians in working with their research institute to adapt the study to a wider audience abroad.

In upper Austria, the labor office has for several years made a special effort to reach school girls early with materials about careers including occupations which do not normally come within the girls' range of consideration. A pamphlet entitled "Some Trades You Perhaps Have Not Thought About" is widely circulated.[13]

When mature women are ready to return to the labor market, they often face severe difficulties born of their lack of self-confidence and lack of information about available work. To meet this circumstance, the Vienna labor office began several years ago to invite women up to fifty years of age who would like to go to work to phone or mail in a simple statement of their age, education, and desire for work. After some selection and screening by interviews, forty or so women at a time are invited for a week's seminar for which the women receive a small remuneration to cover transportation and midday meals. Mornings are taken up with lectures and other informational meetings on such matters as how to prepare for an employment interview, the coverage of social security and protective legislation, the kinds of jobs available and the training and qualifications necessary to hold them, what applicants may expect in terms of wages, fringes, and services. Afternoons are filled with visits to offices and plants and with talks there with personnel officers about openings, conditions, and compensation. At the end of the week, they may apply through the labor office for work and may either be sent out directly to jobs or first seek counselling interviews about the range of work available to them and the training they may want to undertake for desirable jobs.

Training programs for Austrian women are assisted in two categories of government subsidy. The first are subsidies to employers to take on women, train them on the job, and pay them full wages while learning; the payments to employers then diminish as the training period progresses and the women are presumably producing nearer and nearer the norm for a skilled worker on the job. The second type of subsidy goes to women themselves to reimburse them in a variety of ways for taking training at an approved training institute under employer, provincial, or Chamber of Labor auspices.

Like Sweden, Austria has had a low unemployment rate throughout the recession, a fact which in both countries is traceable to policies of the labor market boards and their emphasis on retraining of redundant workers. Yet unlike Sweden in this regard, Austria has constructed its program mainly to accommodate men and to keep them at work. As a consequence, the proportion of women in labor market training has fallen from its peak in 1974. The drop in the first years was from 55 percent of all enrollees in training to 40 percent in 1975. Employers similarly cut back their training commitment to women, and the percentage of women in on-the-job programs declined sharply from 70 percent in 1974 to 34 percent in 1975.

Yet all this time, women continued to enter the labor market. Their participation rate increased from 37.1 percent in 1971 to 38.8 percent in 1975.[14] Despite the drop in enrollment in the various training programs, however, women did not fall entirely out of consideration. In 1977 the administration of the training programs stated a priority policy to be one of "qualitative improvement" of the position of women, both school-leavers and adults, with particular emphasis on improved training and increased aid for child care to enable women to enter training.

The Women's Bureau of the Ministry of Social Affairs has been especially active in urging such a policy by calling attention through its series of studies to the facts of women's employment and particularly of the barriers to advancement for women. The Bureau was established to deal with problems of equality for girls and women in all areas, including the labor market. Its director was deeply involved in producing the national study on the position of women in Austria.[15] And the facts laid down in this study, particularly in its Section 5, "Women at Work,"[16] in turn set off the studies and programs reported above that the women in the Austrian metal workers union undertook to remove sex bias in the vocational schools and in apprenticeships. The Bureau, after studying the German report on "women's work in the light-wage categories,"[17] has focused on exposing "disguised discrimination" as it exists in limited promotional opportunities, unfair job classfications, and discriminatory job evaluation systems. Several important government publications have paved the way for this development, notably the recently reissued brochure, "Women at Work: A New Start."[18]

The union of white collar workers in private industry (GPA) is endeavoring to serve its large constituency of low-wage earners in the routine, deadend office jobs. Its approach has been twofold: it actively supports a program of disseminating detailed vocational information on a wide range of occupations for girls leaving school and for women re-entering the labor force and promotes the idea of women spending more time in training in order to attain qualification for higher grades of employment. It supports paid educational leave for women to get both on- and off-the-job training. The women's division of the union is taking an energetic stand with works counsellors in helping them to understand the importance of recruiting women for further training. At present, women members of GPA have a somewhat higher participation rate in these labor market programs than do men.

GERMANY

Vocational training for girl school-leavers tends to be limited to the traditional women's jobs in retailing, office work, child care, and the various health services. Girls coming out of German schools still suffer from differential requirements for boys and girls in the elementary curriculum. In Bavaria, for example, girls at the high school level are required to spend so much time on their home economics subjects that general preparation for higher education is slighted to their disadvantage in gaining admission to a university and even to many of the skilled trades. A provincial government report in Hesse on vocational training notes that "the number of apprenticeships available to girls is very limited and in industry and handwork is about three times as many for boys as for girls." In a study of girls' education throughout the Federal Republic, Maria Borris found decided differences in the instruction of boys and girls in the natural sciences and in practical handwork (such as sewing and home economics), areas in which the traditional concepts of separate education for girls are still very widely held. "In most of the provinces, a basis is laid in elementary school for sex-role typed activities." For example, "boys are directed to 'creative patterns,' the girls to order, cleanliness and discipline." As to vocational education, while only 6.7 percent of the boys reject training and become unskilled workers, more than 20.9 percent of the girls are in this category.[19]

Although a number of studies, including government-sponsored ones, make these kind of facts eminently clear, it is difficult to find programs of any scope actually in operation to correct the deficiencies so plentifully documented.[20]

The unions in Germany operate schools offering both general education and vocational education for their members, and many young workers, particularly among the unemployed and those who have had problems in finding apprenticeships, enroll in them. The unions have made no particular effort, however, to meet the special needs of girl school-leavers and to introduce them to skilled trades aside from the typical clerical trades. As in Austria, the public vocational schools are designed to supplement vocational training at the workplace. Apprentices and other young workers in job training come one day a week—some provinces are now requiring two days of "theoretical schooling" per week—to these schools. They tend, however, to be segregated, as the jobs are segregated, by sex and relatively fewer young women than young men attend.

The German school system still tracks its students into separate groups depending upon whether they are simply completing the compulsory nine-year elementary school, going on to middle school, where they finish at fifteen years of age, or attending academic preparatory schools. While this tracking is much less rigid than it was a few years ago because general schools (Gesamtschulen) have been introduced in many cities, the system still tends to encourage families to plan an educational program for their girls different from that of the boys with the result that girls generally have a lower educational level than their brothers. Institutions affiliated with the adult education programs in many places have for some time been offering a bridge program for young people who in their late teens or early twenties wish to pick up their education where they broke it off and prepare for skilled work in the higher vocational schools (Fachschulen) or even to go on to higher education.

One such program exists at the Frankfurt Seminar fuer Politik,[21] an institute established soon after the war to awaken and support the political education of women who had in this regard been totally neglected under the Nazi regime. It has developed a number of programs since that time, one of which will be described below, but its most sought-out one has been in preparing young working women for university entrance in a program lasting several years, depending upon the point at which the students left elementary, middle, or high school, but concentrating on general education geared to adult motivations and abilities. The rate of success among these women in gaining university admission is very high.

The People's High School is a long-established German institution offering noncredit programs in a wide variety of subjects to adults in evening courses. (Some residential schools on the Scandinavian model also exist and operate longer courses.) In the 1950s the trade unions and these adult education schools formed a joint body known as Arbeit und Leben (Work and Life), aimed particularly at young workers though trade unionists of all ages were welcome to its programs. Again it was an attempt to provide the general education which in so many instances accentuates the rigid lines between the middle and working classes within the country as well as between the sexes. Special programs in a wide variety of subjects were written by the union educators who participated in this undertaking, and some of these were particularly designed for young women workers. The Chemical Workers Union was a pioneer in setting up some of these courses.[22]

As unemployment has deepened since 1974, the Labor Market Board and the individual labor offices of the nine provinces turned their attention to the special problem of youth employment and supported a variety of schemes for encouraging employers to increase the number of apprenticeships and youth training positions. In exceptional cases, some of these are set up particularly for young women, though attention is mainly directed to young men. The Conti firm (Continental Rubber) has set up twenty-seven apprenticeships in the metal trades particularly for girls with the express purpose of increasing the openings for women in the typical "men's trades." The firm plans to open a number of new occupations to women in metal and chemistry.

In 1977, the province of North-Rhine–Westphalia, in a joint undertaking of the Women's Division of the Ministry on Federal Affairs and the Labor Ministry, issued a proposal for promoting training opportunities for women and girls. Included was a study of the possibilities for bringing women into occupations in heavy industry (the province is the center of the Ruhr coal and steel basin), among them warehousing, stores, transport within the firm, crane operation, toolmaking, and production control, all occupations which, at least at the time of the study, seemed to be expanding and thus to allow for the introduction of new trained workers without in any way endangering the jobs of men already attached to the industry. The project developed on the basis of this proposal is described below.

Among the proposals were schemes for subsidizing employers who would agree to provide on-the-job training for re-entrants. Under this rubric, Germany has provided a rich fare of training opportunities for older women, dating back at least to the founding of the present Labor

Market Board, the Federal Institute for Work, created by the Employment Promotion Act in 1969. Among the tasks the law assigned to the Board was to regulate the labor market in such a way as to maintain a high level of employment. As for women, they were to be specifically assisted "in cases where their employment is made difficult under the going conditions of the market, or because they are married or are, or have been, for other reasons tied down with household duties."[23]

The law gives the Labor Market Board a monopoly on vocational counselling and placement. It sends its own staff into the schools to reach children in the last (polytechnic) year. It occasionally conducts training itself, or, more frequently, it approves public and private training programs to which it directs would-be trainees. The Board's statistics on its adult training program show women's participation at the beginning of the recession and for the two following years (Table 9-1). One notes at once a sharp falloff in the number of enrollees as the recession deepened in about the same proportion both for men and women.[24] Training of three kinds is identified in the statistics. In 1976, about 80 percent of the men and 70 percent of the women were in advancement training; 11 percent of the men and 18 percent of the women were learning new jobs; and 9 percent of the men and 12 percent of the women were in on-the-job training. A considerably higher percentage of both men and women had been in advancement training the previous year and considerably fewer in on-the-job training. Women have characteristically chosen training programs of shorter duration than men and have consequently emerged in the labor market with a lower level of skill training. Figures for the trainee entrants in July 1976 showed a continuance of this trend. A further breakdown of women's participation in the programs by trades shows that in the skilled category they are training in larger numbers in office work, next in social and educational occupations, and then in the service trades, whereas the highest number of men were enrolled in technical trades, in administration, machinist, and electrical trades, and in metal work. About two-thirds of all the women in training already had completed basic vocational training in their chosen occupation, suggesting that those who already possess some skills are the ones most likely to move ahead professionally.

TABLE 9-1
Participants by Sex in Vocational Training
Programs for 1974, 1975, and 1976

Sex	1974	1975	1976
Men	172,000	168,143	91,731
Women	60,500	57,819	32,401

Beginning in 1974, a wave of layoffs rolled over the labor market. The number of entrants, not surprisingly, fell, and the percentage of women seeking training at re-entry or first entry sank from 8.4 percent of all women reporting for work to 6.2 percent.

As we noted earlier, in 1976 women made up more than half of the unemployed (52 percent), a figure which has continued throughout 1977 and 1978, although they comprise only about 37 percent of the labor force. The high amount of unemployment benefits which the Labor Market Board had to expend out of its income from unemployment insurance contributions so cut into its budget for training and other countermeasures that programs were cut and rules about admission to the existing programs were tightened. Parliament amended the Employment Promotion Law in January 1976 in a way that seriously affected women's access to these programs. Only persons with six years of work experience (including time spent in training) received support, and at lowered rates than existed previously. Moreover, the Labor Office was not to endeavor to find work

> for unemployed persons who because of the hours of work of the spouse or the demands of the household can only work between 11 and 17 o'clock, although unemployed who can work between 8 and 13 o'clock because of caring for a child will be placed *if* work is available in reasonable distance from home.[25]

Despite these distressing developments, two programs have been undertaken—one in the city of Frankfurt by its Seminar fuer Politik, and another in the province of North-Rhine–Westphalia, to both of which we have referred briefly above. Both are supported by grants from the Federal Ministry of Family, Youth, and Health as well as by grants and in the Frankfurt case by aid from the city. Both aim to recruit and train adult women lacking in vocational education for jobs which are regularly advertised and yet rarely filled by women. In both cases the unions were consulted, and the programs are going forward with the active interest and participation of women trade union representatives.

The program in North-Rhine–Westphalia grew out of the special labor market conditions in the Ruhr basin. Women make up a relatively small proportion of the work force in this area, which is heavily devoted to mining and basic steel. Unemployment rates among women are high and women's outlook for work is even less bright than in other parts of the country. Of the women in this labor market, 75 percent are unskilled and their jobs are rapidly disappearing as technology displaces them with automated processes.

The program began in late 1976 with an introductory session to give the applicants information about the kinds of occupations for which training would be available and the conditions of training. That was followed by six weeks of general courses during which the women participants would make their occupational choices and then enter on a two-year training period in the trade they selected in the metal industry. In the first period, employers and works' councillors in the area were brought in to meet the women, see what their interests were, and suggest how they might find work.

To set up the program, the Essen labor office interviewed some eight hundred candidates, of whom forty showed genuine interest. These women were then invited to the introductory session. It included a visit to the Training Center and to some of its on-going classes, a discussion of the occupations in electro-technics, and a discussion of occupations in the metal trades, followed by a closing summary session. An observer who participated in the day's meetings reported:

> By the summing up session, the earlier atmosphere of anxiety and diffidence had changed dramatically. Women began to ask practical questions: what about child care during classes (the Center offered to help here); transportation to classes (they would be held in Essen, a centrally located city but not where all the women lived); the subsidy they would receive during the period of study (the equivalent of unemployment insurance); vacations during the two years of study; beginning date of the program. Towards the end of this session more personal problems and questions of content began to surface: opposition of husbands to time for training and to later work mainly with men, lack of math background, lack of self-confidence in dealing with theoretical subjects and with the machines, questions about the actual content of the courses and their structure and development.

Following that introduction, thirty-three trainees entered the three-months' orientation phase of the program. Of these, twenty-seven actually entered the training phase and nineteen continued in electronics and metal work. The problems which these women faced in endeavoring to undertake training were related to their lack of general education, the lack or incompletion of earlier vocational training, heavy home burdens, serious problems of personal adjustment to study and to concentration on technical and theoretical matters to which they were unaccustomed. Fortunately the sponsors of the program had anticipated many of their needs and had built assistance from tutors and social workers into staffing and curriculum. These people acted as counsellors and teachers. The results justified the sponsors' planning. The high levels of motivation, the demonstrated improvement in learning, and the strong cohesion of the group in its mutual support of members all received high marks in the evaluation. As a result a second course was organized even before the first group passed its final qualifying tests. This second group will benefit from the careful analysis of teaching methods, support systems, and students' critiques. Changes will include more time spent on introducing applicants to the purposes and plans for the program—a week instead of a single day—a somewhat shorter orientation phase, and a lengthened period of study and training.[26]

The Frankfurt program began a few months earlier. As we noted above, the Seminar fuer Politik had for some time been providing several kinds of "bridge programs" for school dropouts who wished now to go to the university, in addition to a program for former women prisoners who were facing release from jail. Dissimilar as these programs were, they had demonstrated the need for general education as well as vocational training among adult women entering the labor market. The aim in the new program was to reach women who were first coming into the labor market whether after divorce or separation or because, though married, they now had to go to work. Since a two-year vocational program was planned, trades were selected which would pay well once women qualified for them. The selected trades were laboratory assistant in chemical firms, gardener, cook, outdoor advertiser, and furrier. Attempts to include some metal trades in this list broke down when works councillors and firms recommended by the Metal Union were dubious or downright opposed to bringing women into their workplaces.

The seminar teachers interviewed about a hundred unemployed women in selecting the forty-five who were eventually enrolled. They wanted to take the most distressed cases, since this was to be a demonstration, an experimental program which would hope to help the most difficult kind of applicant for skilled work.

This program had a somewhat larger number enrolled than was the case in Essen; fifty-nine women showed interest and forty-nine were in the group which began study in the first, the motivational, stage. Of these, slightly more than half were over thirty; thirty-three were widowed, separated, divorced, or engaged in divorce proceedings. Thirty-four had completed only elementary school and six more had not even won their diplomas. Nine had had some previous vocational training but none of it was any longer acceptable. Thirty-two women had one or more children. Twenty-nine were unemployed and eight were housewives. The prerequisite for enrollment was that they should have worked at least six years, but time spent as housewives counted toward this requirement. (Housewives could only be accepted, however, if their financial situation had drastically changed for the worse, as might have been the case after divorce or desertion.)

This program, too, was divided into two parts. First came a three months' introductory session that was mainly a refresher program in general education. During these months, the women talked with representatives both of employers and of unions about training available in firms where later employment would be possible. The second part of the program lasted two years and was so designed that women completing them would have their high school equivalency plus the training normally given in a three-year apprenticeship. It is hoped that any woman who does not pass the final examination can still be given a helper's certificate in the occupation for which she studies. A typical week of school includes three days of on-the-job training, one day in a special class in vocational school for theoretical instruction in the trade, and one day at the seminar working on general education subjects such as history, civics, and German.

Both the Essen and Frankfurt programs were staffed with social workers to assist women in solving personal and family problems which might interfere with their continuing through the two years of training.

A thoroughgoing evaluation of the first three months, the motivational phase, of the program[27] showed that of the forty-nine women who began work, twenty-seven decided for training. The dropouts during the program occurred at various points in time and were all due to outside circumstances either in the participants' families or because some of the planned training was canceled by employers who withdrew from the program. The sponsors of the program used the degree to which participants could find and decide upon a trade as an important criterion of success both for the program and the participants. About 50 percent of those who began training had no trade in mind when they entered. Of those who completed the first phase and moved into training seven dropped out, leaving twenty women who stayed through the vocational training. It is worth noting that while the majority of this number had not finished compulsory school, only two dropped out because they were unable to handle the instruction.

The conclusion of the evaluators was that

> a simple vocational counselling is not sufficient for our group; instead only an integrative offering of information, counselling and social and educational support can make possible a considered and enduring decision about vocational choice. . . . Women of this sort need such a preparatory program in which the objective conditions for a successful training program can be created, and in which their often very diffuse and unrealistic vocational wishes and images can become concrete. They especially need the financial support and the organization of child care together with the support system of group work, teaching aids, individual assistance from tutors and personal counselling which allows them to develop their ability to study and achieve self-confidence.

Another kind of program sponsored by a union is worth considering for its possibilities as a model of advancement training as well as preparation for re-entry. The independent union of white-collar workers, Deutsche

Angestellten Gewerkschaft (DAG), has for many years operated schools for its members and prospective members in office skills. These schools exist in nearly every city in Germany and are a recognized and certified training institution eligible for Labor Market Board subsidy.

In 1972 the union's research department undertook a study of the special needs of women in their membership returning to work after a considerable absence.[28] The purpose of the study was to organize a curriculum which would allow women to study systematically for successful re-employment. The resulting curriculum covered five fields: economic and social theory, office organization and data processing, accounting and bookkeeping, written German, and shorthand and typing. Each of these was planned for forty teaching hours, except the course in office organization and data processing, which runs eighty hours.

This curriculum was to be introduced into the existing schools with emphasis on the needs of re-entry women. In a handbook developed for this purpose, directors of these schools as well as teachers are reminded of the special difficulties older women face when they have been out of their occupation for some time, are unfamiliar with new machines and processes, have probably had inadequate vocational training in their youth, and whose skills are rusty. The handbook cautions:

> In a curriculum whose purpose is to re-integrate women into work life, these . . . problems have to be dealt with not only intellectually but [in confronting and overcoming their conflict situations] these women have to receive practical help.

CONCLUSION

These reports on experience and experiment have been introduced to demonstrate the kinds of approaches being undertaken in these three countries to deal with the presence of very large numbers of unskilled women in the labor market. Each country recognizes to some degree that vocational training is the key to equality of opportunity both in wages and in kinds of work. At the same time, powerful vestiges remain of the "reserve army" assumption and its bias operates to make it difficult to carry on these programs in more than a tentative and temporary way.

The most discouraging and difficult aspect of the movement toward equality in job opportunity is the depressing effect of the recession which not only diminishes the number of available jobs overall just at a time when ever-larger numbers of young people and women are looking for work,[29] but produces an anxiety among planners, employers, unions, and male employees that strongly inhibits bold and radical programs. Sweden is one of the very few countries that accepted the depression as a challenge to increase the number and kinds of programs offered and to enhance the incentives to employers to accept and train women.

Of the three countries examined in this chapter, only Great Britain has anti-discrimination legislation affecting both training and employment. The one form of positive discrimination allowed under the law is in specialized training for either women or men in fields in which the sex imbalance is conspicuous. Britain is, however, still in the process of testing its law, and it is not yet clear how effective it will be in dealing with what the Americans see as societal inequity that may be handled through class actions, since they are not allowed for in British law. In fact it permits only individuals to bring grievances to industrial tribunals, which may then redress the single complaint brought before the bench. Unions who might take such cases—not many have done so—may complain through other channels.

Union pressure will be more effective when women members become powerful enough to influence policies of the organizations, to seek representation in the decision-making bodies, and to gain membership in union delegations to such agencies as the labor market boards. Resolutions, pronouncements, pledges exist in plenty. Remedies, however, suffer continuing postponement under the pressure of outside economic circumstances and of traditional concepts of women's place as secondary and their worklife as spasmodic.

Government and specifically the labor market boards must play the central role in providing women the kinds of training that will open access to equal status and at locations and times where they can take advantage of the opportunities. Jenny Dorling argues the case for special consideration of women not just in terms of women's improved position and earnings, but of the benefit to the national economy.

> The fact that women tend to be concentrated in occupations requiring little skill or responsibility implies an enormous waste of ability. . . . Can we afford in the long term to employ women in menial jobs? In economic terms we need to insure that training is available to men and women based on merit, and to ensure optimum use of the nation's best talents as an aid to economic recovery. . . . Equity demands that women should not only be granted equal opportunities to training but also that they should be *actively* assisted to make balanced judgments about available opportunities.[30]

NOTES

1. Commission of the European Communities, European Seminar, "Vocational Training for Women," Nov. 24–28, 1975 (Paris, 1976), p. 5.

2. Some writers are considering that men, too, might well enjoy and indeed profit from breaks in their long, uninterrupted work life that might be periods of rest and relaxation, of study, of movement into new careers or occupations, or development of talents, skills, and hobbies. In this sense a work life cycle not unlike women's might become a model for men. See, for example, the proposal of Gösta Rehn, the director of Sweden's economic research institute and former chief of the Labor Market Board, who proposes a kind of leave bank on which every individual could draw as he/she wishes during various periods of adult life. The leaves would be backed by "a general income insurance with individual access to drawing rights" ("Lifelong Allocation of Time," a draft of an Ad Hoc Group of Experts for OECD, Paris, Sept. 6, 1974, MS/S 74.4).

3. In 1976–1977, the author and two colleagues, Professor Val R. Lorwin and Dr. Roberta Till-Retz (both of the University of Oregon), studied women in trade unions in four European countries. We were looking for programs operating there which might be of assistance to trade union women in the United States. To a considerable degree this chapter is a product of that study, although earlier investigations by the author into problems of working mothers in these and other countries have also been drawn upon.

4. A British writer has noted that women go through a two-stage selection system: first a social selection and then a job selection. The employment office asks questions about their family situation, their husbands' jobs and their chances of moving to another locality, the ages of children and the arrangements for their care—questions never addressed to men, but which have the effect often of providing grounds for rejecting a woman with no consideration for her job suitability or qualifications. See Sheila Green, in Nickie Fonda and Peter Moss, eds., *Mothers in Employment* (Uxbridge: Brunel University, 1976), p. 99.

5. Jenny Dorling, "Making a Start on Training for Women," *Personnel Management* 7 (Dec. 1975): 18.

6. Manpower Services Commission, "Training Opportunities for Women" (London, Dec. 1975), pp. 26–27.

7. "Employment and Training of Women in the Engineering Industry," in EITB, "Statistics, 1971–1975" (processed, Jan. 10, 1977).

8. An "engineer" in British parlance is, literally, a person working with or on engines or machines. "Machinist" is a rough American equivalent.

9. John Wellens, "Girl Technicians for Engineering," *Industrial and Commercial Training* 9 (March 1977): 105–111.

10. Manpower Services Commission, "Training Opportunities for Women," pp. 26–27.

11. BGB, NR. 142/1969, Berufsausbildungsgesetz.

12. Outside Austria a few states and provinces, chiefly the city-state of Bremen, have established similar institutions.

13. Landesarbeitsamt, Oberösterreich, "Diese Lehrberufe kennst Du vielleicht nicht? Berufsinformation für Mädchen" (Linz, 1977).

14. Bundesministerium fuer soziale Verwaltung, Abteilung V/4, "Die Situation der Frau auf dem oesterreichischen Arbeitsmarkt, Beteiligung der Frau an dem Foerderungsmassnahmen aus Mitteln der Arbeitsmarktfoerderung: Analyse 1971 bis 1975" (Vienna, March 29, 1976).

15. Bundeskanzleramt, *Der Bericht ueber die Situation der Frau in Oesterreich* (Vienna, 1975).

16. Ibid., Heft 5, "Frau im Beruf."

17. Drs. J. Rutenfranz and W. Rohmert, *Arbeitswissenschaftliche Beurteilung der Belastung und Beanspruchung an unterschiedlichen industriellen Arbeitspaetzen* (Bonn: Bundesministerium fuer Arbeit und Sozialordnung, 1975).

18. See, among others, D. Gaudart and W. Schultz, *Maedchenbildung-Wozu?* Bd. 1 (Vienna, 1971); H. Kreutz and G. Fuernschuss, *Chancen der Weiterbildung*, Bd. 2 (Vienna, 1971); D. Gaudart, *Zugang von Maedchen und Frauen zu technischen Berufen* (Vienna, 1975); all in the Schriftenreihe des Bundesministeriums fuer Unterricht und Kunst, *Schriften zur Frauen und Maedchenbildung*.

19. Maria Borris, *Die Benachteiligung der Maedchen in Schulen der Bundes-Republik* (Frankfurt-am-Main: Europaeischer Verlagsanstalt, 1972).

20. H. J. Niemann, *Arbeitsmotivation und Arbeitschaltung bei Auszubildenden: Eine empirische Leitstudie* (Frankfurt: Rationalisierungs-Kuratorium der Deutschen Wirtschaft [RKW], 1976); Sibylle Diekershoff and Karl Heinz Diekershoff, *Bildungs und Weiterbildungsbereitschaft von Frauen bis zu 45 Jahren* (Schriftenreihe des Bundesministers fuer Jugend, Familie und Gesundheit, Bd. 42; Stuttgart/Berlin/Koeln/Mainz: Verlag W. Kohlhammer, 1976); Gisela Helwig, *Zwischen Familie und Beruf: Die Stellung der Frau in beiden deutschen Staaten* (Bibliothek Wissenschaft und Politik, Bd. 10; Koeln, 1974).

21. Seminar fuer Politik, "Das Seminar fuer Politik stellt sich vor" (Frankfurt), Sept. 9, 1976.

22. The union put out a series of pamphlets under the general title "Partnerschaft von Mann und Frau." Among them, for example, is Gabrielle Witting, "Rolle und Einfluss der Frau in der Politik der Bundesrepublik."

23. Arbeitsfoerderungsgesetz (AFG), Part I, par. 2(5).

24. Bundesanstalt fuer Arbeit, "Eintritte in berufliche Bildungsmassnahmen in der Zeit von 1. Januar 1974 bis 31. Oktober, 1974, von 1. Januar 1975 bis 31. Oktober 1975, von 1. Januar 1976 bis 31. Oktober 1976" (Nuernberg, 1977).

25. As quoted in Karl Luecking, *Frauen und Arbeit* 1/2 (1976): 7–8.

26. Berufsförderungszentrum (BFZ) Essen, "Qualifizierung von arbeitslosen Frauen in gewerblich-technischen Bereich (Metall- und Elektroberufe) mit sozialpaedagogisher Begleitung," *Berichte*, Heft 9, Neue Berufe fuer Frauen (Essen: Modellehrgang Zwischenbericht, Ende 1977).

27. Modellversuch, "Berufliche Wiedereingliederung von Arbeitslosen/Berufslosen Frauen," Werkstattberich ueber die erste Projektphase zur Motivierung und Berufsfindung, durchgefuehrt von der Abteilung "Seminar fuer Politik" beim Amt fuer Volksbildung, Volkshochschule der Stadt Frankfurt, im Auftrag des Bundesministers fuer Jugend, Familie und Gesundheit (Jan. 1978).

28. Deutsche Angestellten Gewerkschaft (DAG), *Wiedereingliederung weiblicher Angestellten in das Berufsleben* (Hamburg: DAB Forschungsstelle, Dec. 1972).

29. For the macro-data in this regard within the United States, see Ralph E. Smith, "The Impact of Macroeconomic Conditions on Employment Opportunities for Women," in *Achieving the Goals of the Employment Act of 1946— Thirtieth Anniversary Review,* a study prepared for use of the Joint Economic Committee, Congress of the United States, Jan. 3, 1977.

30. Jenny Dorling, "Making a Start on Training for Women," *Personnel Management* (Dec. 1975), p. 17.

10 *Barbara M. Wertheimer*

LEADERSHIP TRAINING FOR UNION WOMEN IN THE UNITED STATES: ROUTE TO EQUAL OPPORTUNITY

"There's got to be more to life than wrapping meat," one trade union woman stated when asked why she was participating in the year-long labor studies and leadership training program for union women sponsored by Cornell's School of Industrial and Labor Relations. Another student, describing the trepidation with which working women return to school, begins an essay submitted for her writing course like this:

> The school bell figuratively rings at 5:00 P.M. tonight at Cornell. I'm like the old fire horse pulling the milk wagon, going berserk when the fire alarm sounds. School again *at my age*, with my commitments, lunacy, but still the gong is sounding. Opening night jitters. The other students are probably younger and smarter. The teachers probably are expecting more than I can deliver in one 12-week course.

What is the rationale for a program that requires such strong motivation on the part of its students, as well as time, effort, and money from them and from the educational institution, all focused on developing self-confidence and leadership skills and encouraging union women's educational goals? How does informing women about the labor movement in general and problems relating to their role and participation in unions in particular lead to changes in their status? What is the relation of this kind of workers' education program to achieving equal pay and opportunity?

To shed light on these problems, this chapter will examine four questions: What are the barriers to the participation of women in labor unions?

What is the impact of the labor studies and leadership training program for union women that evolved from study findings, based on a three-year longitudinal assessment? What are the multiplier effects of this program in terms of education for working women? Can workers' education for union and other employed women serve as a tool for achieving equal job opportunity and pay?

BARRIERS TO WOMEN'S PARTICIPATION IN LABOR UNIONS

Unionization impacts positively on women's earnings. The U.S. Bureau of Labor Statistics estimates that women in unionized jobs average $1,500 a year more in wages and fringe benefits than women in nonunion plants or offices. Yet, as of 1974, only 4.6 million women (of the more than 38 million then in the work force) belonged to labor unions, compounding their disadvantaged status as workers.

Women and the labor movement

Some 28 out of 175 national unions reported no women members at all in 1974—down, however, from 39 so reporting two years earlier.[1] If we add 1.5 million women members of employee associations to the total, just 12 percent of the female labor force in the United States is organized. Nonetheless, women compose 21.3 percent of all union members, and make up at least one-half the membership in twenty-one different unions. Seven unions account for 40 percent of all women members:[2]

International union	*No. of women members*
Amalgamated Clothing and Textile Workers	337,650
International Ladies Garment Workers	324,000
International Brotherhood of Electrical Workers	297,368
Retail Clerks International Union	292,894
Communication Workers of America	264,334
American Federation of State, County, and Municipal Employees	239,819
United Automobile Workers	216,280

Overall, unions report that their membership in the United States is declining, with an absolute loss of 600,000 reported between 1975 and 1977 (though the workforce, 87.5 million in 1976, will increase to 93 million by 1985). One of the key problems facing labor leadership is how to organize the millions of unorganized women workers. Huge segments of the workforce, largely female, remain virtually union-free. The insurance and banking industries and office work are three. A majority of workers in the service trades and in hospitals are unorganized. By their own estimates, the two largest garment unions could triple their memberships if they were able to organize their jurisdictions more fully.

Where are women in the governance of labor unions? Do they influence policy decisions, for example, concerning what proportion of the union budgets should go toward organizing the unorganized? Women in labor leadership in America do not fare any better in terms of power and influence than they do elsewhere. In 1974, only 7 percent of the national executive board members of unions were women, although women composed 21.3 percent of all union members. Twelve percent of the boards of employee associations were women, but here 55 percent of the total membership is female. No woman sits on the executive council of the American Federation of Labor–Congress of Industrial Organizations (this council at present is made up entirely of union presidents) and the only woman to head a department at the AFL-CIO headquarters is the librarian.

Just two small national unions in the AFL-CIO, both in the performing arts, have women presidents. Only a few women who hold posts as international vice presidents have real input at the collective bargaining table, where basic decisions are made on wages, fringes, and other benefits. Nor do very many women have a strong voice in shaping basic union policies.

This is not to say that women do not hold increasing numbers of posts on the local and regional levels, as stewards and union officers. They do. But women's concerns and issues, voiced more strongly than ever before, still are those traded off at the bargaining table, if they get there at all.

Barriers to participation

Several national unions have taken a look at where women are in the power structure of the unions. The earliest of these surveys, that of the United Automobile Workers, was conducted back in 1962. It found that of the union's 150,000 women members, only 800, or less than one-half of one percent, held elective office, although thousands more were active as committee members, in political action, community services, and grievance work. The union's Women's Division had its assignment cut out for it.

The Packinghouse Workers, the Bakery Workers, and the International Union of Electrical Workers have queried their locals to determine the extent of women's participation. All found women holding few of the key leadership jobs. Where women were local union presidents, more often than not it was in the smaller locals (or, in the case of the Automobile Workers, in locals where the president's post is unpaid rather than a full-time paid job). On the local level, women office holders most frequently are executive board members, with the major elected office that of secretary or trustee. Even in unions with predominantly female members, where the whole range of union jobs tends to open up for women, still women are not found in the top positions, and few are international vice presidents.

What are the barriers to women's participation at the higher levels of their labor union organizations? In 1972, Anne Nelson and I sought to examine that question.[3] We believed the answers might lead to designing and testing a program to help overcome some of the barriers. With a grant from the Ford Foundation and with New York City as our laboratory, we studied what held women back at every level of union activity. We also looked at attitudes: of men in the union toward the women and of the women toward themselves. Of course, some women compete successfully for union leadership posts. But why do so many others hold back? Do women see themselves differently in relation to their union than men do?

This research project, sponsored by the metropolitan office of Cornell's School of Industrial and Labor Relations, was a natural outgrowth of courses and conferences conducted for blue-collar and other working women since 1970 and of the growing interest of women in increasing their participation at decision-making levels in their unions.

Research project

Our first step was to survey all local unions in New York City having substantial numbers of women members. One hundred and eight responded, representing over 500,000 workers, of whom 254,000 were women. We found that most of the women held semi-skilled or unskilled jobs offering little or no up-grading possibilities. The union leaders who reported stated that women were less likely to run for office where they had to compete against men and were more likely to do so where large numbers of women composed their memberships. However, in 10 percent of locals where women were in a majority, no women held executive board positions.

The study's second stage focused on seven locals constituting a cross section of New York's unionized workforce: one each in retail sales, city government, federal employment, assembly line electronics, hospital work, supermarket meatwrapping, and garment work. It sought to identify barriers to the involvement of women workers in union activity. From the study we learned that women's union participation is held back more by lack of information and experience than by lack of interest. While family responsibilities constitute a barrier for both men and women, they fall most heavily on women.

Close to one in five of the women studied, however, stated that no barriers hold them back. These women form a potential untapped reservoir for their labor organizations. On the job, women viewed their supervisors as hard on active women unionists, a problem that can be addressed through training in grievance handling and assertiveness. Finally, women more than men wanted education and leadership training if they were to become more active in their unions, with minority women wanting it most of all.

Thus a profile of the union woman emerges: She is a seeker of information; she wants to know why it matters to the union whether she is active. She wants education and leadership training. She views the union as a helping agent, and seeks roles where she can assist others. Yet the union is seen as hierarchical, and she feels closed out of decision-making, sensing a lack of encouragement in terms of her deeper participation in other than traditional nurturing roles. While she does not like to compete with men, she believes overwhelmingly that more women should run for union office at every level. Her need is for greater self-confidence and feelings of competency, for training in labor-related and leadership skill areas, and for a chance to fulfill individual educational goals.

A LABOR STUDIES AND LEADERSHIP TRAINING PROGRAM FOR UNION WOMEN

Out of this study a pilot program known as Trade Union Women's Studies emerged, designed to provide the labor and leadership courses union women wanted and college credit that would enable them to continue toward what often were long-delayed educational goals.[4] Core courses were developed: Written Communication; Oral Communication and Logic; and the Psychology of Leadership, all in the skill areas; Union Organization and Administration, Collective Bargaining, and Women in Labor History on the content side. New material was prepared, and texts culled to find any that might be useful. In labor history, for example, available material totally ignored the contribution of women to the economy or to the growth of the labor movement from the seventeenth century to the present.[5] Each new course we developed included problems reviewed from a union woman's point of view, whether it was bargaining issues, the legal responsibility of the union administrator for enforcing Title VII of the Civil Rights Act in terms of women and equal job opportunity, or legislative issues of special concern to working women.

These core issues, then, were offered (starting in the fall of 1974) in a year-long program where students attended three twelve-week terms a year, one night a week, and took two courses each term (a skill course paired with a content course). The package of six courses was, upon successful completion, worth nine Cornell college credits, which the students could take to any institution of higher education in the city on a transfer basis.

Who are the students?

In its fourth year, most of the students of this college credit program were between the ages of thirty-five and fifty, with half forty years or younger. Two-thirds were minority women, Afro-American and Hispanic. Two-thirds were single, divorced, separated, or widowed and supported themselves and their families through full-time work. Forty percent had no children. Most, though not all, had completed high school. Perhaps one in five had had some college work, usually done years ago. Common to all the women were the same fears that the student whose essay was quoted earlier voiced: their study skills were rusty, their high school training completed in less-than-adequate schools. Their motivation, however, was sky high.

Here are women who work all day, fulfill family and home responsibilities, are active in their unions, and come to school one night a week for three and a half hours, undertaking two hours of homework for every hour in the classroom. How do they do it? Something has to give. We asked them, one time, what *did* give, and found that it was sleep. Few women got more than four and a half to six hours of sleep a night. But they went to great lengths not to miss a night of classes, and developed a strong supportive network during their year together as students that extended into the Alumnae Association that they join upon program completion.

Importance of teacher role models

A program that serves women with such a high degree of motivation, who are willing to sacrifice not only hard-earned money but also the most valuable thing they have—their time—must provide the best in the way of teachers and services. Teachers are recruited who have an interest in the total program and are experts in their particular field. It may be the first time that union women have the chance to meet and talk with women who have achieved success in labor-related fields such as collective bargaining or are top union administrators. It becomes an inspiring experience. But we expect a great deal of the teachers: to come to class early and stay late, to talk with students about courses or personal problems, to work with the program's tutor/counselor in helping individual students, to be willing to integrate content and skill course assignments for overall relevance for the class. Teachers must know their subject and also how to teach it. They must tap the rich life experience students bring to the classroom. To assist teachers, the program conducts developmental sessions which include teaching methods and practice in designing and implementing course outlines. All courses strive to relate directly to the life, work, and trade union experience of the students. This is a necessity. Adult students who work all day come to class at night only because they *want* to. The dropout rate can be astronomical for programs that are not seen as relevant or where the lecture method induces drowsiness.

In the U.S. there is a shortage of women in labor education, in industrial relations fields, and in union administration to serve as teachers and role models. It is sometimes difficult in New York City to recruit the kind of teachers needed; it is much harder outside the metropolitan area. However, increasing numbers of women enter these fields every year, and our recruiting and training techniques are improving. Once teachers have been trained for Trade Union Women's Studies, they are recommended for teaching in Cornell's labor studies program, which reaches men as well as women. Union men need the exposure to women teachers who are experts in these fields: it builds their respect for women in a profession traditionally seen as a male province and helps to change attitudes.

Financing the program

Tuition charges, based on the State University of New York system, are modest. Unions finance about one in three of the women in Trade Union Women's Studies, providing scholarship help. In other cases, negotiated tuition reimbursement plans cover the cost. The Institute for Education and Research on Women and Work, of which Trade Union Women's Studies is an integral part, maintains a special scholarship fund to assist women not covered by any tuition plan for whom payment would be difficult. Scholarships are given on request. We are always impressed with the extent to which women will try to go it alone before they seek assistance.

Since the first year-long course opened in 1974, the New York State School of Industrial and Labor Relations has gradually institutionalized its support, and contributes a good portion of the administrative costs. The Ford Foundation grant has been instrumental in helping to launch the program, to develop a materials center and library on working women, and to prepare and produce course syllabi and related materials and conference proceedings that have made replication of this program or portions of it possible elsewhere. It has meant staff support that was essential.

Longitudinal assessment of program impact

More than thirty different unions have students attending Trade Union Women's Studies, most of the unions those with the largest proportions of women members. Program graduates responding to questionnaires that were part of the longitudinal assessment indicated an awakened interest in and appreciation of the rewards of learning and a discovery of their own capacities:

"I became more confident and more determined."

"I've learned I'm better qualified than I thought."

"I thought before, 'my absence won't make any difference.' Now I want to involve myself in the leadership of my union."

"Now I understand the importance of women striving for recognition of their needs. I'm not going to wait for others to do it for me."[6]

Of the thirty-six union women who graduated our first year, twenty-seven elected to continue in the Labor/Liberal Arts program offered by the metropolitan office of Cornell's School of Industrial and Labor Relations, a program that had been predominantly for men, but which the union women have thoroughly integrated. In an informal tally of the number of times these women participated in the mixed classes the second year, compared to the women students who had not been through Trade Union Women's Studies, TUWS graduates were found to contribute in class twice as often as the other women, indicating that much of their fear of participating where men were in the majority had been overcome. At entry into TUWS, one in five union women specified no specific educational goals; upon graduation at the end of the year, the figure was one in twelve.

Students were asked to evaluate their own progress, and recorded gains in every category were measured. For example, they showed an increased willingness to write a report, something they had shown great reluctance to do upon entering the program and a skill that is essential in union leadership. They also indicated a sharp improvement in the degree of poise they felt they had when speaking in public and a greater ability to outline oral and written presentations.

Some 77 percent of the students were involved in some form of union activity when they entered the program. But 31 percent stated upon completing the year that they had a new interest in running for union office. Fifty-five percent had changed their union goals in some way. For many it meant an understanding and acceptance of the risk of running and losing, overcoming the fear of failure. More than two in five graduates now have a union career in one form or another as a goal and have stated that they believe they have found the courage and self-confidence to reach for these goals. They see this as an outgrowth of the program.[7]

While it is difficult to separate out which accomplishments of program graduates are attributable to their year of study together and which they would have done in any event, the list of their achievements is impressive:

- Thirteen have made radio, television, or other public appearances, spoken at the New York State IWY meeting, testified at hearings on women's issues, spoken at union conventions

- Eight have moved up in their job, or into new jobs
- Six now work full time in labor union jobs
- Five write for their union papers
- Three edit publications
- Seven have been involved in organizing campaigns
- One won an essay contest her union sponsored
- One was invited to a White House gathering based on a write-up of her activities appearing in the U.S. Commission for IWY report
- One won a district school board election
- One won the annual Community Services Award from the National Council of Negro Women
- One was elected to her union's International Executive Board and made chairperson of its National Civil Rights Committee
- Fourteen have been active in the Coalition of Labor Union Women, NYC Chapter
- Eight are unit or chapter officers in their unions
- Three chair standing committees of NYC CLUW (out of four committees)
- One has been elected to the statewide board of her union
- One is organizational vice president of her union; for three months, when the president was ill, she served as acting president of a union of 25,000
- One is secretary-treasurer of her union

In summary, the longitudinal assessment points to program impact on goal change, risk acceptance, skill development and reinforcement, union-career orientation, educational aims, and individual self-confidence. Central to each woman's feeling more capable and secure is the network of trust and support of which she is a part because of her continuing relationship with the forty or so women with whom she has studied for a year. As one student said: "I am no longer afraid of my future for I know that I have one."[8]

PROGRAM MULTIPLIER EFFECT

What is the multiplier effect of the program that has been described? As a pilot model, does Trade Union Women's Studies have an impact beyond the women it serves? What is its potential for expanding education options for union and other working women?

The credibility of programming for employed women

The *New York Times* of April 7, 1978, reported that for the first time women outnumbered men in this country's two-year colleges: 52 percent of all full-time and part-time students are women. However, these are not, in the main, the women in blue-collar, service, and clerical jobs who are the audience that university and union labor education programs seek to reach. Still, over 70 percent of women entering the workforce today have high school diplomas, compared to only 50 percent in 1952. The potential exists for reaching these working adults.

Trade Union Women's Studies is a viable approach for delivering to union women the kind of programs that they want and need. The short courses and conferences which are part of the not-for-credit programming of the Institute on Women and Work have proven their value as "ticklers" to stimulate the interest of working women in getting information they need and to prove to them that they are able to do the course work that is involved in returning to school.

Over the past few years we have seen universities with labor extension programs, some of whom we have advised, begin to include programs for union and other working women in their regular offerings. A number of state federations of labor now work with universities in conducting conferences either for union women or centering on problems of women in the workforce today. The response to these programs has been greater than anticipated, thus encouraging the state federations to do more, while university extension programs have begun to take women's education interests seriously.

An illustration of this interest is the Task Force on Programs for Union Women, which has been set up as regular activity of the University and College Labor Education Association. More than twenty universities are represented on this Task Force, which is the largest of all the committees and task forces in the Association. It publishes a national newsletter as a regular feature of the *Labor Studies Journal*, and sponsors regional residential institutes for union women. In this endeavor it has the cooperation of the AFL-CIO Department of Education and of union as well as university women in labor education. So far more than five hundred union women have attended one or more of the nine schools that have been held, and the enthusiasm engendered there must be experienced to be believed. The newest effort of the Task Force is the establishment of a clearinghouse for women candidates for labor education jobs, an effort to alert women to the jobs available and increase the ranks of women in labor education.

Career development and public service women's studies

Cornell's Institute on Women and Work now is testing two new programs based on the Trade Union Women's Studies model. Funded by a grant from Carnegie Corporation of New York, the project is known as Education for Equal Opportunity. It reaches two different audiences. One is women in private-sector white-collar jobs, where the courses focus on career development and personal skills and the company sees the program as potentially useful in spotting women to tap for promotion, an aid in meeting its affirmative action goals. The other is women in the public sector who hold state clerical jobs in grades three to twelve. Designed to build personal, human relations and technical skills, it also provides a working knowledge of the civil service system that enables women to operate more effectively within it.

Both these programs grant nine college credits for the year's work, transferrable to two- or four-year institutions of higher education, should these students move on toward degree work. These two models, both spin-offs of the format that proved successful with Trade Union Women's Studies, also utilize women teachers, provide support services and counseling, and develop linkages with colleges in the communities in which the programs take place, so that transition to these institutions can proceed with a minimum of red tape. The Career Development Women's Studies has the added advantage of being offered on company property, maximizing convenience for the students. Both programs utilize tuition refund plans that constitute employee fringe benefits, lessening the financial burden of a return to school.

While these programs are too new to assess results, if attendance records are an indicator of student interest, it is high for both Career Development and Public Service Women's Studies.

Still another spin-off of the pilot model is the branch program of Trade Union Women's Studies which is conducted by the Institute on Women and Work at the invitation of a particular union, in this case District Council 37 of the American Federation of State, County, and Municipal Employees. The program is offered at its own headquarters, where the union offers a host of education programs to city workers of New York, most of them available through an education fund negotiated by the union with the city. Each year between forty and fifty women members of this union study at our branch program, where the curriculum is altered to focus more sharply on the special concerns of women in city jobs.

International interest in trade union women's studies

Almost since the inception of this program, we have been receiving requests for information about it from women in a number of Western European countries, and from Israel, Australia, and New Zealand, to mention others. At New Zealand's University of Otago researchers have replicated the study described here, although since results have not yet been made available, no comparative work has been done.

The associate director of the Institute on Women and Work attended and led several sessions at the only international conference conducted specifically for union women during International Women's Year, held in Tel Aviv in December of 1975 and sponsored by Histradut. The International Labor Organization journal, *Labour Education*, in its June 1976 issue, carried articles describing both Trade Union Women's Studies and the Tel Aviv Conference.

Additional vectors of growing interest in programs for union women

For reasons elaborated earlier relating to the need to encourage women's participation in labor union organizations, a number of unions have initiated special programs for women members. Sometimes this responsibility is assigned to special women's divisions as in the United Automobile Workers, the International Union of Electrical Workers, and the Amalgamated Meatcutters. Sometimes it is carried out through training of women staff (such as programs conducted annually at the George Meany Labor Studies Center, or by the Communications Workers of America). Or programs may focus on special concerns of women workers but be directed to the entire membership (such as those sponsored by the Amalgamated Clothing and Textile Workers, the United Storeworkers, or the American Federation of State, County, and Municipal Employees). Union women support all these approaches, realizing that it is important to reach men as well as women if progress is to be achieved.

Another indication of the rising self-awareness of working women is the formation of the Coalition of Labor Union Women (CLUW), open to union women—and men—across all union lines. Operating within the framework of the trade union movement, its goals include: increasing affirmative action on the job and through women's involvement in their unions at all levels; passage of legislation important to women workers; encouraging women's participation in the political process; and organizing unorganized women workers. With a structure that to some degree parallels that of the labor movement itself, it functions through chapters that afford opportunities for leadership experience to individual union women, and nationally through an elected executive board.

For all its initial enthusiasm when it was founded in March of 1974, the organization has not grown beyond a membership high of five thousand scattered in perhaps thirty chapters across the country. However, CLUW has spoken effectively with a new voice for union women. Instrumental in moving the AFL-CIO to support the Equal Rights Amendment, it also urged the appointment of a woman as associate director of the federation's Civil Rights Department with special responsibility for Women's Activities, and achieved the appointment of four women union leaders to the Civil Rights Committee of the AFL-CIO. In the past, only national union presidents held these committee posts.

CLUW has the potential for effecting change, particularly if it can develop effective methods for reaching union women on issues such as job discrimination and equal pay, and demonstrate how to use the union to take up complaints in these areas. In the rough and tumble of its own political structure women will get good training which they can transfer to their own union structures.

While CLUW to some extent substitutes for women's caucuses within local unions, these, too, have emerged and are growing in effectiveness, especially in their support of candidates for union office who take positions promoting women's rights on the job and encouraging their participation.

None of the above diminishes in importance the value of direct, job-related education that prepares women for widening the range of occupations and jobs in which they work. Every effort is needed to overcome the effect of generations of ghettoized "women's work" and to compensate for the intermittent workforce experience of many younger women. Not only do the latter miss out on job training and apprenticeship opportunities, but also on chances to develop their trade union leadership roles.

The International Labor Organization position is a positive one: it calls for counselling and retraining for women to accommodate for job obsolescence and new technology, to allow for changes in women's own interests or work needs, and to make up for any lack of direction and motivation carried over from an earlier sex-role stereotyped education.

EDUCATION: TOOL FOR ACHIEVING EQUAL JOB OPPORTUNITY AND PAY

Worker's education is action-oriented and always has been linked to effecting change. In this chapter I have discussed how education directed to the needs of working women can develop leadership skills, encourage women's participation in their trade unions, and contribute to a higher and more effective level of information on issues of direct concern to them. These skills are transferrable, and should lead to greater involvement in political, legislative, and community areas as well. They should lead to gains in achieving equal pay and job opportunity.

In concrete terms, on the union level, women must get to the bargaining table to ensure that changes that lead to these goals are incorporated into union contracts. They must attain positions of sufficient power in their unions to insist on the three steps that Winn Newman, General Counsel for the International Union of Electrical Workers, outlines for putting this into effect: (1) stop the assignment of new employees to the lowest-paying jobs; (2) survey the rates for all so-called "women's jobs" and raise them to what they are worth; (3) insist on non-discriminatory job posting and bidding based solely on seniority and qualifications.[9]

It is difficult to get to the bargaining table. In American unions, as elsewhere, this is a long, hard road and a political one. It becomes critical to develop the understanding that those issues that concern women workers so deeply—parental leave, flextime, released time for education, pregnancy disability, legislation for health insurance—are equally vital for men. They are human issues. A job that is considered unsafe for a woman of child-bearing age probably is not safe for a man either, and our goal should be jobs safe for people.

To incorporate affirmative action plans into collective bargaining agreements will demand all the know-how and energy and skill that we have indicated women need. Only as women are educated and trained to move these into place will they seek the power they need. The importance of this is underscored in a report issued in February 1978 by the U.S. Commission on Civil Rights, which found that economic gains for minorities and women lagged in 1977, even with an administration in Washington that had put forth efforts that it hoped would move these groups forward.[10]

This is attributable in no small measure to the declining economy and the difficulty of implementing equality on the job in a period of job scarcity. Nonetheless, the force of statistics are with women: a report issued by the Work in America Institute indicates that in the twelve months between October 1976 and October 1977 women obtained "more than one-half of the 3.3 million new jobs created by the U.S. economy. By 1980 fifty percent of women over 16 are expected to be working, accounting for six out of every ten net additions to the work force."[11] These women, and women already holding jobs, gain in seniority every day. As women increase in numbers in the workforce, so does their realization that they are there to stay—unless laid off—and that employment is a permanent part of their lives. We must ensure that the higher level of education that new entrants to the workforce bring with them includes education on their job rights and an understanding of what the job world can offer, including their potential as a force to improve this situation. It may be that women are on the threshold of a push for equal opportunity that we can only begin to imagine.

We should not underestimate the growing interest in education that workers are evincing. Education is seen as the key that unlocks many doors: to employment (college graduates have a 3 percent unemployment rate compared to 15 percent for those with a high school diploma); to higher earnings (college graduates earn in a lifetime almost twice what workers with no more than a high school degree earn). More union leaders than in the past hold college and even graduate degrees.[12] The message is not lost.

Women must be provided with information and trained in leadership skills. Creative new programs in worker education must be designed to accomplish this. I am thinking, for example, of the national women's conference that the Institute on Women and Work will be conducting for a major union, which will bring together some five hundred of its women members—and some men—from across the country. The conference will combine skill training workshops with the chance to put these skills to work in a Mock Convention built around issues. The goal is to increase the ability of the women of that union to take more active roles in their own national union conventions. It is also to develop women's committees in each region of the union. If these committees use the Mock Convention idea on a smaller scale, the participation skills of an even wider level of union women will be developed. Certainly, the risk is there: the idea may not work. But we will turn whatever skills we have to offer as labor educators to giving it every chance to succeed.

Ultimately, the speed with which women move toward these goals depends on women themselves. The basic change necessary is one of attitude. In a British Department of Employment paper entitled "Women at Work—a Survey," Margaret McCarthy indicates that workers, employers and British society must all change their attitudes about what constitutes the role of women. "If there is to be a major breakthrough in attitude," she writes, "it will only happen because of an increased, and an increasingly active, women's membership, strong enough to insist that such changes be brought about."[13] That "active women's membership" has been the focus of this chapter. Women must gain the power to bring about these changes in attitude and in status. That is what education for working women can— and must—help to achieve.

NOTES

1. The statistics in this section are drawn in large part from the U.S. Department of Labor, Bureau of Labor Statistics, *Directory of National Unions and Employee Associations* (Washington, D.C.: GPO, 1977), pp. 65, 66.

2. Ibid., p. 103. These figures were gathered by the U.S. Bureau of Labor Statistics in 1974. The International Brotherhood of Teamsters, which did not report its female membership that year, had 255,000 women members in 1970.

3. For a fuller discussion see Barbara Wertheimer and Anne Nelson, *Trade Union Women: A Study of Their Participation in New York City Locals* (New York: Praeger, 1975).

4. For women not wanting to make the year-long commitment, a variety of conferences and short (six-week) courses of direct and immediate usefulness were designed and offered. Here, too, all materials had to be prepared from scratch, building women into the curriculum, developing self-confidence and awareness of their roles as women workers and unionists.

5. This finally led the author to write *We Were There: The Story of Working Women in America* (New York: Pantheon, 1977) to fill this gap.

6. Barbara Wertheimer and Anne Nelson, "Longitudinal Report of Trade Union Women's Studies, 1974–1977," prepared for the Ford Foundation, August 1977, p. 27.

7. Ibid., p. 27. 28. See the New York *Daily News*, Feb. 13, 1978, p. 34, for an article about a graduate of Trade Union Women's Studies who now is secretary-treasurer of the largest postal local in the country.

8. Grace Weiner, alumna of Trade Union Women's Studies and panel speaker at a conference sponsored by the New York State School of Industrial and Labor Relations, Cornell University, in "Toward a State-Wide Network of Programs for Working Women," March 1976. Quoted in the conference proceedings published by the Institute for Education and Research on Women and Work, Cornell University.

9. *Union Labor Report*, Sept. 27, 1973, p. 2.

10. *Women Today* 8, no. 6 (March 20, 1978): 1.

11. *Christian Science Monitor*, March 24, 1978.

12. Barbara Wertheimer, "New Programmes for Union Women through University Labour Education," *Labour Education* no. 31 (International Labour Office, Geneva, June 1976): p. 13.

13. Margaret McCarthy, "Women in Trade Unions Today," in *Women in the Labour Movement*, ed. Lucy Middleton (London: Croom Helm, 1977), p. 174.

11 *Lorna R. Marsden*

THE ROLE OF THE NATIONAL ACTION COMMITTEE ON THE STATUS OF WOMEN IN FACILITATING EQUAL PAY POLICY IN CANADA

The improvement of equal pay laws in Canada owes much to a voluntary organization called the National Action Committee on the Status of Women (NAC). An umbrella organization with a membership consisting of approximately 130 Canadian organizations, NAC has a combined membership of about 5 million women. Since its inception in 1972, the organization has been active in the struggle for improved labor legislation, including the enactment into Canadian federal law of the ILO Convention 100 concept of equal remuneration for work of equal value. This chapter will examine the environment in which the organization was formed and the chronology of actions surrounding NAC's pressure for equal pay and especially Convention 100 in order to analyze the effectiveness of the organization and its possible usefulness as a model elsewhere.

HISTORY AND STRUCTURE

The contemporary women's movement in Canada has benefited immeasurably from a long tradition of women's voluntary associations. Religious groups such as the Anglican Church Women, the United Church Women, and the Catholic Women's League, and other groups such as the National Women's Institutes (a national organization of largely rural and small town women), the National Council of Women, the Canadian Federation of University Women, the Imperial Orders of Daughters of the Empire, and the Fédération des femmes de Québec, have been in existence long enough to have built national networks of women with some interlocking memberships and considerable ongoing exchange of information.

NOTE: I am grateful to Marjorie Cohen of the OCSW and NAC for her detailed review of an earlier version of this paper and to other colleagues in the Movement for their help in preparing sections of the paper. I am especially grateful to Ronnie Ratner for her help, patience, and clarity of mind in preparing this version of the paper.

The National Action Committee on the Status of Women developed from a coalition of these and other trade union and professional women.

The formation of NAC

The main impetus for NAC's formation came out of the pressure put on the prime minister of Canada and his cabinet by a group of leading Canadian women to create a Royal Commission on the Status of Women (RCSW). According to a story told in the women's movement about the tactics for securing this particular commission, Laura Sabia, a fiery radio broadcaster from a small town in Ontario, threatened to march one million women to the "Hill" (the Parliament of Canada in Ottawa) if the prime minister didn't act. (This story amuses Laura's colleagues, since it might have been hard to turn out two hundred women for such an occasion.) Whatever Prime Minister Pearson's reasons for agreeing to a commission, the RCSW was established in February 1967 under the chairmanship of Florence Bird, another radio broadcaster. Thirty-four research projects were commissioned and public hearings were held across the country. The commission's report was submitted in December 1970, complete with 167 recommendations, 85 of which applied directly or indirectly at the provincial level.

Royal commissions in Canada perform an important role in the study of special issues—from taxation, to the relations of labor and capital, to national security. The commissions vary widely in their composition and goals but the approach of most is similar. They research the issue, hold public hearings across the country, receive briefs, and make recommendations for legislative and administrative reform. On the matter of equal pay, this commission's recommendations were strong and sweeping:

> To ensure universal observance of equal pay for equal work in Canada, legislation is obviously needed that will be realistic enough not to demand unreasonable proof. We urge legislators to find a more appropriate way of defining the situation in which pay rates for women and men must be the same. In the meantime, . . . the most practical definition developed so far . . . speaks of "equal work on jobs the performance of which requires equal skill, effort and responsibility and which are performed under similar working conditions." The present use in legislation in Canada of such terms as "same" and "identical" is much too restrictive. The term "equal" is more within the intent of the International Labour Organization Convention 100 which speaks of "work of equal value". We also strongly urge that legislation should recognize the responsibilities of unions as well as those of employers. Therefore, we recommend that the federal Female Employees Equal Pay Act, the federal Fair Wages and Hours of

Work Regulations[1] and equal pay legislation of provinces and territories require that (a) the concept of skill, effort and responsibility be
used as objective factors in determining what is equal work, with the
understanding that pay rates thus established will be subject to such
factors as seniority provisions; (b) an employee who feels aggrieved as
a result of an alleged violation of the relevant legislation, or a party
acting on her behalf, be able to refer the grievance to the agency
designated for that purpose by the government administering the
legislation; (c) the onus of investigating violations of the legislation be
placed in the hands of the agency administering the equal pay legislation which will be free to investigate, whether or not complaints
have been laid; (d) to the extent possible, the anonymity of the complainant be maintained; (e) provision be made for authority to render
a decision on whether or not the terms of the legislation have been
violated to specify action to be taken and to prosecute if the orders
are not followed; (f) where someone has presented the aggrieved
with the decision, she has the opportunity to present her case herself
to the person or persons rendering the decision who may change
the decision; (g) the employee's employment status be in no way
adversely affected by application of the law to her case; (h) where the
law has been violated, the employee be compensated for any losses
in pay, vacation, and other fringe benefits; (i) unions and employee
organizations, as well as employers and employer organizations, be
subject to this law; (j) penalties be sufficiently heavy to be an effective
deterrent; and (k) the legislation specify that it is applicable to part-
time as well as to full-time workers.[2]

The commission having made its recommendations, the question became whether the government had any intention of implementing them.
Laura Sabia, among others, was inclined to think not. Using her excellent
contacts and her magic tongue, Laura and some friends induced Minister of
Manpower and Immigration Bryce MacKasey to give them enough money
to bring women from across Canada for a conference on the future of the
recommendations of the Royal Commission.

In April 1972, the Strategy for Change Conference was held at the
King Edward Hotel in downtown Toronto. Five hundred women came
from across the country, including members of the Royal Commission on
the Status of Women; Senator Therese Casgrain; and Madeleine Parent, a
distinguished nationalist trade unionist woman who had run for Parliament and lost. Women from the west and the east, from the poor and the
rich, from the radical and the conservative, turned out. It was an exciting
meeting and, fortunately enough, recorded on film.

From it emerged, in addition to a set of resolutions and recommendations, formal recognition for the newly formed National Action Committee

on the Status of Women. This was designed to be a coalition of women's groups with the aims of maintaining communication with women across the country and getting the RCSW recommendations implemented. Although intended as a national organization, for all intents and purposes NAC was a group of Toronto women. A couple of annual and midyear meetings attracted women from across the country, but most communication was by newsletter, personal letter, or visits from women fortunate enough to move around the country on business. Status-of-women groups affiliated to NAC formed in every province and territory and in many cities as well.

Laura Sabia became the first president, and it was her leadership, to a large extent, that kept the organization going. The second president (1974–1975), Grace Hartman, was a high-ranking member of the Canadian Union of Public Employees (CUPE), the largest public sector union in the country and the union with the most women. I succeeded her as president in 1975.

The National Action Committee presses for legislative and administrative change at the federal level. The membership of about 130 separate organizations is represented by about twenty women who compose the national executive and approximately two hundred women who attend the annual meeting. While several thousand subscribe to *Status of Women News,* the NAC newspaper, and while the member organizations are supportive, the millions of women NAC represents are not necessarily knowledgable about our issues or work.

The executive of NAC consists of a president, secretary, and treasurer, three vice-presidents, and twelve members at large, along with a few "consultants," people who are too busy to attend general meetings but who give us valuable advice and often do a lot of work. All are volunteers working in evenings and on weekends. The executive has two major functions. One is to prepare briefs to government and to apply pressure for change. The other is to build and maintain communications across the country. NAC is funded by grants from the federal government, one for organization and one for *Status of Women News.* We raise modest affiliation fees (fifteen dollars annually in 1977) and subscription fees and accept donations.

In July 1975 we visited the government for the first time and presented a brief on our issues. In 1976 we held our annual meeting in Ottawa and organized a day of lobbying on Parliament Hill. Women came from across the country to a rather grimy hotel (the cheapest we could find), and we passed a series of resolutions dealing with our major concerns. In 1977 we again met in Ottawa (this time at a rather more respectable establishment) with a larger turnout than ever before and again lobbied Parliament. That evening on the national news broadcast, we were described as "the most powerful lobby in Canada." We repeated this Ottawa meeting and lobby in 1978, with an even larger turnout.

Equal pay for work of equal value was one of our chief concerns from the beginning. It still is. Other issues have been child care (primarily a provincial matter except that the federal government has money directed to this concern), changes in the criminal code (especially concerning rape and abortion-education), training and job opportunities, and other aspects of labor legislation. While we participated in International Women's Year and in the Mexico meetings and keep up on the International Decade for Women, our chief concern remains national and provincial policy and legislation.

The complexity of Canadian society

In examining any pressure group or social movement in Canada it is important to understand the political context. Canada is a confederation of ten provinces and two territories under the jurisdiction of the federal government. According to our constitution, the British North American Act of 1867, responsibility is divided between the federal government and the provinces. The relationships are complex, but in general the provinces have jurisdiction over most social policy—education, health, welfare, and community and social services—and "all matters of a merely local or private nature in the Province."[3] The federal government retains control over the obvious matters of defense, monetary and fiscal policy, international trade and tariffs, international relations, and all matters pertaining to the "peace, order and good government" of the country.[4] But the federal government also has a department of labor with control over all federal government employees (about 10 percent of the Canadian labor force), a department of health and welfare, and a department (Secretary of State) which supplies about half the funding for post-secondary education. The area of justice is equally fragmented. Divorce, rape, and abortion fall under the federal criminal code, while family property law is under provincial jurisdiction. Notwithstanding federal jurisdiction over abortion law, it is the provinces that provide the services.

In spite of the jurisdictional division of powers, however, a number of arrangements exist which interlock federal and provincial governments. In particular, cost-sharing arrangements, through which the federal government hands back dollars or tax points to the provincial governments for particular projects or within particular guidelines (such as education and child care), are common. In some instances federal legislation passed by the House of Commons and the Senate can only be enacted with the agreement of two-thirds of the provinces having two-thirds of the population. This gives Ontario and Quebec, which together have over 60 percent of the population, a de facto veto. Where Quebec does not join a federal program, Ontario alone can and does veto changes.

The problem of divided jurisdiction goes well beyond administration and the legislative differences. The provinces vary considerably in their economic base and interests as well as in their ethnic, cultural, and language composition. Central Canada (the provinces of Ontario and Quebec) is the industrial base of the country, with vested interests in the continuation of tariff walls protecting their industries, good industrial wages, and work opportunities, while the Atlantic region, whose economy is based primarily on fishing, farming, and forestry, has interests in the redistribution of economic benefits, including industry, and the creation of new jobs and opportunities. The rate of unemployment in Newfoundland is especially high, notably among women, who are not involved in the indigenous industries. The three prairie provinces of Manitoba, Saskatchewan, and Alberta depend on the wheat economy, oil, and potash, although the wheat farming industry no longer supplies a great deal of direct employment. These provinces are quite dissimilar, especially in terms of opportunities for women. British Columbia, cut off by the Rocky Mountains, is rich in forests, fishing, and mining and has a long political tradition of dissatisfaction with any central government. Such economic interests are felt as keenly by women as anyone else, and women are divided on these grounds.

Quebec is a French-language province with many constitutional and political arrangements different from those in the rest of the country and a long tradition of tense French-English relations. Most postwar immigrants in Canada have come to Montreal and Toronto, but most have learned English, rather than French. Eastern European traditions have been strong in the prairie provinces since just after the turn of the century. The British have dominated the Atlantic provinces and British Columbia, although there is a large francophone population (the Acadians) in New Brunswick and Nova Scotia.

The existence of two official languages in the country, and many cultural traditions, is a hard social fact which affects every social organization. Most Canadians relate most closely to regional interests which are often religious and cultural as well as economic. This is reflected in voting patterns, in the formation and composition of political parties, and in the different systems of education and civil law. These differences are found as much in social movements, such as the women's movement, as anywhere else.

Any group trying to bring about social change in the country—whether it is the government, unions, professional or business groups, or voluntary organizations of citizens—has to face these divided loyalties. An attempt to build a national network of people often breaks down under the pull of regional concerns. It is also incredibly expensive in money and time to canvass a country over three thousand miles wide with five times zones.

A voluntary movement, like the women's movement, is hard hit by these divisions. On issues of major concern, Canadian women must address themselves to both federal and provincial legislation and administrations, usually with different political parties in charge. An attempt to built consensus on any issue implies building a compromise position that will take into account the sensibilities of French and English, Catholics, Protestants, and Jews, the economic interests of the various regions, the dominance of Central Canada, especially much-hated Toronto, and the dependent position of the economically poor regions such as much of the Maritimes. On matters of equal pay certain differences are particularly noteworthy. The Canadian women's movement faces eleven jurisdictions of government, a regionally and industrially divided labor movement, a largely nonunionized labor force, and a powerful business sector. In the late 1970s, it is facing a downturn in the economy involving both inflation and high rates of unemployment. For all these reasons, it is easier for a group of women to form around a municipal or provincial matter than a federal one, and it is usually more attractive.

THE STRUGGLE FOR EQUAL PAY FOR WORK OF EQUAL VALUE

Equal pay legislation did not come into law in any Canadian jurisdiction until 1951, and only in 1973 did the Yukon Territory enact such a law. Although the wording varies slightly in each jurisdiction, the approach is "to require equal wages for women and men only when the women perform the 'same' or 'identical' work as men in the same establishment."[5]

While sex-based pay discrepancies are obvious to those women who have male colleagues with whom to compare salaries, the majority of women in the Canadian labor force have no such comparisons. Women work largely in job ghettos where the only comparisons possible are to other women.[6]

Despite the inadequate historical series of wage data, several studies have documented the wage gap and the reasons for it.[7] All studies find evidence that discrimination is a major factor in wage differences although differences in productivity between the jobs done by women and those by men are also considered important. That is, job segmentation which keeps women from the jobs with the most return to the firm is reflected in productivity differences.[8] What historical material there is suggests that the male-female earnings gap widened between 1951 and 1961 and 1978 evidence shows that the gap has increased further. We can use the case of a national news-reporter to illustrate both the working of the old equal pay law under federal jurisdiction and the role that NAC, and its member organization in Ontario, the Ontario Committee on the Status of Women (OCSW), have played in exerting pressure for change.

In March 1972, Joan McLellan filed a complaint with the Canada Department of Labour alleging discrimination on the basis of sex. At that time Ms. McLellan had been employed by the CTV network for five years. and had been a reporter on the National News for two-and-a-half years. She was CTV's only female reporter and was being paid considerably less than any male reporter in the network, although she was one of the senior staff members. The complaint was duly investigated by officers of the Department of Labour, who reported to CTV in July 1972:

> Our investigation to date indicates that Miss McLellan performs, under similar working conditions, comparable work on the job, requiring the same skills, effort and responsibility as that performed by your male news reporters and writers. These circumstances would appear to entitle her to equal wages as set out in Division 2.1 Section 38.1 of the Canada Labour Code, part 3.

CTV was instructed to adjust Ms. McLellan's salary from July 1, 1971, unless they could provide more direct and conclusive information to support their position.

In August 1972, a month later, Ms. McLellan was dismissed for performing in a television commercial without consulting the network. Ms. McLellan had not been notified that she could not do this, nor of any company policy on the matter. Since the employer failed to comply with the Department of Labour recommendation, the Canadian government was required to take steps to prosecute the employer. After nine months of bureaucratic wrangling, Ms. McLellan was informed by the minister of labor that he had been advised by the Justice Department: "The weight of evidence was insufficient to prosecute." Even though cases involving equal pay complaints seldom get to court in Canada, Ms. McLellan decided to fight on her own. The case came to trial in February 1974. NAC and OCSW were instrumental in getting women to court, raising funds, and helping with publicity in the case, but the case was lost.

Inequalities in pay persist despite legislation for several reasons. First, the structure of the economy has created work ghettos in certain sectors of the economy and low pay in many of those sectors. Second, both government and the private sector are often unresponsive to change (as the preceding case illustrates). The equal pay laws have been ineffective, and even where they could be used governments have proved unwilling to take initiatory action or pursue cases in the courts.[9] Employers do not come to grips with the problem in their own establishments nor do they take pains to understand the legislation and programs. This situation has been compounded in the late 1970s by concern over inflation and "uncompetitive" wage rates. What laws exist are incredibly complex for those attempting to appeal discrimination in hiring, opportunity, or pay, and a complainant gets little help in trying to find her way through the provincial acts, the various agencies which deal with discrimination or pay issues, and matters of investigation and appeal.

It was in this climate that the NAC intensified its effort to improve legislation and, especially, to have put into law the controversial equal pay for work of equal value concept recommended by the International Labour Organization.[10]

Equal pay for work of equal value

As we saw earlier, in 1970 the Royal Commission had urged support of ILO Convention 100's principle of equal pay for work of equal value, recommending that a federal-provincial conference on labor legislation affecting women in Canada be called to prepare for ratification of the Convention. Both federal and Ontario jurisdictions had been, or were contemplating, tinkering with their laws respecting pay. But in 1971, when the federal jurisdiction changed the wording of its Female Employees Equal Pay Act it used a section in the Canada Labour Code which read:

> No employer shall establish or maintain differences in wages between male and female employees employed in the same industrial establishment, who are performing, under the same or similar working conditions the same or similar work on jobs requiring the same or similar skill, effort and responsibility.

This wording proved no more effective than the earlier version in breaking job ghettos.

NAC and the OCSW, while concerned with the equal pay problem, did not stress the usefulness of the equal value concept embodied in ILO Convention 100 until late in 1972. For example, on March 9, 1972, the OCSW presented a brief to Premier Davis of Ontario in which labor legislation and the problems of equal pay for equal work as a wording in the Employment Standards Act governing pay legislation was a key issue. No mention was made of Convention 100.[11]

Toward the end of 1972, however, we began to realize how job ghettos made any existing legislation unworkable. Groups of us were engaged in various specific actions such as supporting a group of women on strike against a discriminatory pay settlement at a biscuit factory; sending representatives to the head office of Air Canada, the nationally owned airline, to protest discrimination against female flight attendants; and mounting a massive compaign directed toward women in banking, which is also a federal jurisdiction. But others started to point out the potential contained in ILO Convention 100.

On February 7, 1973, a public meeting and panel discussion on women's rights, chaired by Grace Hartman, was held at the Town Hall in Toronto. Federal and provincial legislators were present. The Honorable John Munro, federal minister of labor and minister responsible for the status of women, a provincial minister, three union leaders, a member of the Toronto Board of Education, and a federal Conservative member of Parliament spoke, along with Laura Sabia, who was then president of the National Action Committee. Among the topics was "equal pay for work of equal value." Since the concept was not widely understood, ministers were able to argue that it was unworkable and would lead to the need to evaluate jobs across the country. Nonetheless, the topic was on record, and NAC and the OCSW also were on record as firmly committed to its implementation.

On April 2, 1973, however, Munro revealed that Canada was officially committed to Convention 100. In answer to numerous questions put to him in the House of Commons by Frank Howard, the New Democratic Party critic for the status of women, Munro reported that "Canada deposited with the ILO the Instrument of Ratification of Convention 100 on November 16, 1972," something not realized at the public meeting in February.[12]

Although Canada had ratified the Convention, it apparently meant little in terms of implementation. At the provincial level, for instance, Ontario was amending its equal pay section to conform with the federal government's legislation on equal pay for the same or similar work. The Ontario government introduced amendments to the Employment Standards Act in late 1973. The OCSW appeared before the subcommittee of the legislature dealing with these amendments to argue for an amendment to section 33(1). Our proposal was:

> No employer or person acting on behalf of an employer shall differentiate between his male and female employees by paying a female employee in the same establishment, less than *equal pay,* paid to a male employee, or vice versa, for work of equal value, to be appraised by job evaluation on the basis of the criteria of skill, training, effort, responsibility and working conditions, except where such payment is made pursuant to: (a) a seniority system; or (b) a system that measures earnings by quantity or quality of production.[13]

Our amendment was accepted by the two opposition parties, but at the same hearing, to our consternation, representatives of the United Steelworkers spoke against the equal value concept on the grounds that it could not be implemented. They were supported by other male union representatives. The government voted against the amendment, and the government amendments involving the concept of same or similar work became law in late 1974 despite an additional brief we presented to the Ontario government in support of the concept of equal value.

During 1974, prior to the general election, the OCSW with NAC members held a news conference to review and evaluate the platforms of the three major parties concerning our issues. Then, on January 13, 1975, the OCSW sponsored another public Town Hall meeting specifically on the equal pay issue. The leader of the Ontario NDP Party, the leader of the Liberal Party, and union leader Madeleine Parent were the speakers, together with a representative of the premier. The quantity of evidence introduced on the large and increasing pay gap clearly put the government representative on the defensive; the papers picked up this fact.

The coverage was a good kick-off to IWY (1975), which was a great year for publicity for the women's movement in Canada. In comparison to campaigns on advertising, marital property law, and so on, of course, the equal pay issue received relatively little notice, but several important events did take place. For example, the Ontario government held a conference for leading businessmen to explain the law, the problem, and a new program of voluntary attempts to improve the status of women in their firms. Members of the OCSW and NAC showed up with a fact sheet entitled "Captains of Industry—Which Way's the Wind Blowing?" which set out a few facts, asked a few hard questions, and called explicitly for "equal pay for work of equal value."

The conference provides a good example of how the OCSW and, to a lesser extent NAC, work. The conference began at 9 A.M. in a posh downtown hotel. We turned up just after eight, wearing our business suits and looking respectable. Although none of us had been invited to the conference, we stationed ourselves at the registration area and quietly handed our fact sheet to the participants, engaging them in conversation when we could. Many of our feminist friends who work for the Ontario government were somewhat embarrassed by our presence, but they didn't want to make a scene. Since we looked as if we might be government officials, the guest businessmen tried to charm and disarm us. We pressed for the equal pay for work of equal value concept which the Ontario government had rejected. The government only learned later what we had done.

The media began to pick up our concern both at the time of our presentation to the legislative subcommittee and at a later meeting with the Ontario minister of labor. For example, the Toronto *Globe and Mail* reported our meeting with the Honorable John MacBeth on January 6, 1975, as follows:

Toronto sociologist Lynn McDonald, another member of the delegation, told Mr. MacBeth that the average differential between men and women in Ontario doing the same job was $767 a year in 1973. She said the difference was $494 in 1969, and said this indicates the wage spread between men and women is increasing, despite legal requirements for equal pay. The delegation called for equal pay for work of equal value, even though job titles and descriptions may differ between men and women, and called for job evaluation and enforcement by government inspectors.[14]

Finally on July 21, 1975, five years after the RCSW recommendations, the minister of justice, the Honorable Otto Lang, introduced Bill C-72, the Canadian Human Rights Act, into the federal Parliament. This was "an Act to extend the present laws in Canada that proscribe discrimination and that protect the privacy of individuals." This bill signaled the opening of NAC's greatest campaign on the equal value question. We had a lot of quarrels with this act, especially it proposal to remove the equal pay section from the Canada Labour Code and replace it in the Human Rights Act with a section as follows:

(1) It is discriminatory practice for an employer to establish or maintain differences in wages between male or female employees employed in the same establishment who are performing under similar conditions, similar work requiring similar skill, effort and responsibility; (2) Notwithstanding subsection (1), it is not a discriminatory practice to pay to male and female employees different wages if the difference is based on a reasonable factor, other than sex, that justifies the difference.[15]

Because human rights laws have at present no constitutional basis, they can be superseded by other legislation. We took the position that the equal wages legislation should remain in the Canada Labour Code, since the Department of Labour already had the machinery for implementation and the necessary initiatory and monitoring powers. Furthermore, we wanted the existing labor legislation changed and strengthened in line with our principles. Of course, we rejected subsection (1) quoted above in favor of "equal remuneration for work of equal value, to be assessed by the criteria of skill, effort, responsibility and conditions of work." Further, we worried about the "reasonable factor" wording, which might justify wage differences. The only factors we were prepared to endorse as reasonable were seniority and piecework.

In this struggle to change the situs and principles of the legislation and to introduce the equal value wording we had allies. The government-appointed Federal Advisory Council on the Status of Women performed an invaluable service to our cause by quickly issuing a discussion paper on the legislation. Well-written and informative, it was free on request to people across the country. Although the paper did not come out in support of equal pay for work of equal value, at that time favoring the weaker "similar work" concept, and members of the Council continued to have reservations about the implementation of the concept, nonetheless NAC's lobby was more effective because of their general support.

In addition, one of the founding members of the OCSW, Aideen Nicholson, was by now a member of Parliament, and she worked with members of Parliament on our behalf both behind the scenes and openly. At the April 6, 1976, meeting of the Standing Committee on Labour, Manpower and Immigration of the House of Commons, for example, Ms. Nicholson asked pointed questions about the study of the equal value concept which the minister of labor, John Munro, declared had been begun in December 1975 and about the Department of Labour's and the minister's knowledge and views of the concept.[16]

Such questioning revealed what became apparent to NAC members in our meetings with the ministers and members of Parliament. There was a wrangle within the cabinet about whether the equal wages provision should go into the Human Rights Commission or should remain in Labour. Since we favoured its remaining in Labour, we contacted Munro and his officials to put forward that view.

Our contact took two forms. At our annual meeting and lobby in Ottawa in April 1976, we invited the ministers and representatives to come to appear on a panel. Our members that evening included well-informed women from across the country. Our anger and distress at the ill-informed responses from the members of Parliament and their representatives had quite an impact on some members of Parliament and government. Subsequently, we were invited to several long meetings in both Toronto and Ottawa with representatives of both the minister of labor and the minister of justice concerning our point of view.

In addition, informal contacts took place. Some of us visited the minister of labor in his constituency office in Hamilton. Finally, when Otto Lang was replaced as minister of justice with someone more congenial to our point of view, we presented a brief to the new minister.

In the meantime, several of us inside the Government party (Liberal) had been lobbying with the prime minister and his assistants, the party leaders, and the minister responsible for the status of women, using NAC materials and positions. Women in the other parties had been lobbying with their members of Parliament and party leaders. Questions were asked in the House and in party meetings.

The bill was withdrawn for amendments in 1975 and for a long time we had to rely on inside information and our contacts for news of what was going on. Influential people, such as the former head of the Women's Bureau in the Department of Labour, were reported to be against the equal value concept on "practical" grounds. Several of us knew lawyers inside the ministry and asked them to get us news. "Anonymous" brown paper envelopes came our way. At social gatherings we pressed for news and questions. Officials in town on other business would stop off for a chat in our offices. A newly formed and highly effective organization of women lawyers and women legal secretaries made presentations and briefs and accompanied us on lobbying visits. The Ontario government formed a study group on which one of our members sat. Officials in the Ontario government, while remaining officially neutral, unofficially pressed us to continue, fed us information, and warned us of pending developments.

The lobbying had some impact although our view that equal pay for work of equal value be included in existing labor legislation was not sustained. The federal government reintroduced the issue as a new bill (C-25) in November 1976, complete with the equal value section added. Section 11 reads in part:

> (1) It is discriminatory practice for an employer to establish or maintain differences in wage between male and female employees employed in the same establishment who are performing work of equal value. (2) In assessing the value of work performed by employees employed in the same establishment, the criteria to be applied are the skill, effort and responsibility required in the performance of the work and the conditions under which the work is performed; (3) Notwithstanding subsection (1), it is not a discriminatory practice to pay to male and female employees different wages if the difference is based on a reasonable factor that justifies the differences.[17]

The bill received Royal Assent on July 14, 1977. The section dealing with the establishment of a Human Rights Commission was proclaimed, and such a commission was established.

AN ASSESSMENT OF OUR STRATEGY FOR OTHER JURISDICTIONS

Two further questions remain: to the extent that we have been successful in pressing the federal government to implement Convention 100, why have we succeeded? And could the action or the organization exist fruitfully elsewhere?

To answer the first question, we will look at the principles which Jo Freeman cites as crucial to the formation of any social movement: a network of communication through which information about an issue may flow; a network cooptable to the new ideas of the incipient movement; and some precipitant to start the movement growing.[18] In the case of the equal value issue and NAC, the conditions were clearly met. We have already described the network of communication. Not only was the contemporary women's movement (and NAC) formed through such an active network but that network had grown and flourished during the process of organizing the Royal Commission on the Status of Women and the Strategy for Change Conference in 1972. In addition to the network of people, there was a sudden and dramatic flow of publishing in the women's movements in Canada. Literally hundreds of newsletters, little magazines, journals, and newspapers appeared, often reprinting reports from groups across the country. While conferences were expensive, in fact the governments were providing more and more funding for this and other organizational action.

The network was not comprised entirely of people interested in the equal pay issue. In fact, probably most women in the movement in Canada do not understand the equal pay issue in detail. Given the sponsorship of the issue, however, and a general willingness to espouse anything which led to economic equality, there was widespread support for the idea from across the country and from many different groups. Our support did not only come from women. A March 4, 1978, newspaper poll reported that 58 percent of Canadians (62 percent of women and 56 percent of men) said that women are not treated as equals to men in terms of wages; and 56 percent said that women are not treated as equals in terms of job opportunities.[19]

There were some tradeoffs. The equal pay issue was accompanied in the NAC priorities with other issues such as law reform and child care, abortion and birth control. In essence, these were presented as a package which made all issues more palatable to a broad range of people.

The precipitant is more important. Freeman poses two alternatives: a crisis of one or more events which galvanizes people; or one or more people who begin organizing in terms of an idea.[20] Clearly there were those on the Royal Commission on the Status of Women who recognized the importance of the equal value concept. Clearly also there were those in the government who organized the ratification of ILO Convention 100 soon after the report of the RCSW. But in the voluntary sector, the pressure for implementing Convention 100 came from two or three people who not only had analyzed the data on equal pay but also understood in practical details the difficulties of implementing laws and regulations. Two women in the labor movement, in particular, provided regular, persistent, and highly informed commentary on the equal pay laws. Several others in NAC and the OCSW who were generally informed about the economic issues became early advocates of these ideas within NAC and promoted the equal value concept. Therefore, in Freeman's terms, the precipitant was a few women organizing within the labor movement and the women's movement.

What allowed the work to expand and persist was the membership of the OCSW and NAC. Like-minded, hard-working, for the most part highly educated, and solution-oriented, these women understood the issue and pressed hard wherever possible. There was no attempt to build mass support for the concept, to sell it to the private sector or even unions. All the focus was on changing the law.

One must ask, if most of the women involved in this came from or were working in Ontario, why did the federal law and not the provincial law change? Why is Ontario in fact hostile to the equal value concept? Part of the answer is that the government of Canada is Liberal and the government of Ontario Conservative, so the two are supported by rather different constituencies. But probably more important is the proportion of the labor force in each jurisdiction. Under federal jurisdiction, which encompasses approximately 10 percent of the Canadian labor force, covers mostly white-collar workers in highly segregated parts of the labor force. Most of the private sector force comes under provincial law, and therefore the private sector lobby, while present in the federal case, is not so forceful. Knowing this, the federal government is probably more willing to innovate. Their role is primarily one of leadership.

In addition, we have to acknowledge that our relationship with the ministers of the federal government has been much closer than with the provincial government, largely because of the party affiliation of many of our members, but also because of ministers' assistants and influential civil servants who have an intelligent dedication to the cause inside the federal civil service and agencies. Women both inside government and in the movement have made major contributions to the analysis of statistics on the equal pay question, on the workings of the labor law, and on the study of how the equal value concept might work. This constant documentation and analysis has been the mainstay of our arguments with government. Finally, the tremendous support we received from the majority of women in the country when the issue finally became popularly accepted came, I believe, because it posed no moral dilemmas for anyone. Everyone is in favor of equality in the workplace and even the most resistant do not oppose the principle but only the practical aspects of wages. In the movement, we are almost unanimous in our dismissal of the consideration of what the establishment defines as "practical" problems.

How would this type of selective lobbying work elsewhere? Earlier in the chapter we saw what characteristics of our political, economic, and social structures affect the way the women's movement must operate in Canada. To the extent that these are reproduced, the NAC strategy may work. On the other hand, only if the federal leadership on this issue influences provincial action will the strategy have been effective.

Clearly the concept is of little interest in a nonindustrialized country. It may also be of less interest in a country such as Sweden where a large majority of the women workers are unionized. Collective agreements might take precedence in terms of the struggle for equal pay, but only if male and female union leaders understand and support the concept of equal value at the bargaining table.

On an issue as complex as this, however, I am prepared to recommend any strategy which puts a group of well-prepared, articulate, and pragmatic women together with those who actually implement law in a face-to-face negotiation. The important point of a social movement is to get a concept accepted. It is then up to the parties, governed by the principle of law, to work out the details in their particular circumstances. Social movers are not social planners. We should not try to respond to the demand for detailed blueprints. It diffuses the issue, and the supporters. Any attempt to draw into the detailed debate a mass movement with demonstrations, the private sector with its enormous resources and vested interests, or particular industrial or occupational groups will only decimate attempts to discuss such a complex issue as equal pay for work of equal value, and lead to failure.

NOTES

1. Regulations applicable to companies under contract to the federal government. [Footnote in original.]

2. Canada, *Report of the Royal Commission on the Status of Women* (Ottawa, 1970).

3. BNA Act, sec. 92

4. Ibid., sec. 91.

5. Gail C. A. Cook and Mary Eberts, "Policies Affecting Work," in Gail Cook, *Opportunity for Choice: A Goal for Women in Canada* (Ottawa: Statistics Canada and C. D. Howe, 1976), p. 174.

6. At present there are just over four million women in the labor force representing just over two-fifths of the Canadian work force. Three-quarters of all working women are employed in only five occupations: clerical (1,290,000), services (629,000), sales (380,000), all forms of nursing (266,000), and elementary and kindergarten teaching (155,000) (Sylvia Gelber, "Unemployment and the Woman Worker: The Facts," Address to the Rotary Club of Ottawa, Jan. 30, 1978).

7. Pay discrepancies can be seen to exist anywhere women are gathered in even small numbers in the labor force. The situation is worst among women paid on piece rates, those whose contracts gain percentage increases rather than across the board increases, and those who bargain individually rather than collectively for their wages.

8. Morley Gunderson, in an article summarizing the problems, finds a pattern of earnings in which women earn 50–80 percent of male earnings and "when adjustments are made for productivity differences they typically earn 80–90 percent of male earnings. The extent of the differential that can be attributed to discrimination depends on the extent to which productivity differences

themselves arise from sex discrimination. If one argues that current productivity differences are due to past discrimination, then all of the unadjusted wage gap can be attributed to discrimination" (Work Patterns," in Cook, *Opportunity for Choice,* p. 120). Even so, his most "conservative productivity-adjusted wage gap" is still 10 percent.

9. As Cook and Eberts have stated: "Equal pay legislation does not, in fact, hold much threat that an employer will be required to pay equal pay to individual women because of the narrowness of the legislative standards, the possible exceptions, the inability of equal pay legislation to combat employer segregation of employees, and the problems of enforcing the legislation" ("Policies Affecting Work," p. 176). This was written before the equal value concept was introduced into the federal law.

10. NAC and the Ontario Committee on the Status of Women are both centered in Toronto and have overlapping executive membership. This account of the Canadian equal pay struggle focuses on Toronto and these two groups. Others were working toward the issue elsewhere—for example, women in the Canadian Textile and Chemical Union, led by Madeleine Parent, and the Equal Pay Coalition in Toronto—but NAC has been officially credited by the minister of justice, who finally introduced the concept into legislation, with successfully making the case for the equal value concept.

I make no claim to a definitive version of the struggle for equal pay for work of equal value. It is impossible at the present time to reconstruct the records of the thousands of women and dozens of organizations that were actively engaged in study and in pressing for this concept. Nor is the battle won yet. Since the recommendation of the Royal Commission in 1970 and after three bills at the federal level since 1972 dealing with the issue of equal pay, C-25, establishing a Human Rights Commission with the equal pay for work of equal value concept as part of its mandate, was passed in 1977, to be implemented March 1, 1978. Pressing for implementation and effective monitoring are still ahead.

11. As another example of why we became diverted from the equal pay issue: In May 1972, John Munro introduced Bill C-206 into Parliament. The purpose of the bill was to amend the Canada Labour Code and the Public Service Employment Act to ensure that there be no discrimination on the basis of sex or marital status. There was, however, a limitation clause excluding pensions and life insurance plans from the amendments, thus permitting discrimination in those areas. NAC's attention turned from equal pay to those aspects of remuneration. Parliament dissolved for a general election shortly thereafter and the bill died. The Liberal government was returned with a minority during the summer of 1972.

12. *Hansard,* House of Commons, vol. 117, no. 63, 29th Parl., 1st sess., April 2, 1973, p. 2828.

13. OCSW Brief to the Ontario Legislature on Proposed Amendments to the Ontario Employment Standards Act, 1974.

14. Jan. 7, 1975, p. 11. Dr. Lynn MacDonald published an article in May 1975 in *Canadian Forum,* a journal for intellectuals, documenting the wage gap

between men and women workers in Canada. Based on the government's own figures she estimated that women in Canada earned on average 60 percent of the wages of men and further that half of the wage difference could be accounted for by the ghettoization of women in the labor force and the other half by sheer discrimination. Her article was based on material circulated earlier in the form of a fact sheet to meetings of women in Ontario and elsewhere.

15. C-72. The Canadian Human Rights Act, Parliament of Canada, July 21, 1975.

16. Minutes of Proceedings and Evidence of the Standing Committee on Labour, Manpower and Immigration, Main Estimates, 1975–76, April 6, 1976.

17. Canadian Human Rights Act, 1977, sec. 11.

18. Jo Freeman, *The Politics of Women's Liberation* (New York: David MacKay, 1975), pp. 48–49.

19. *Weekend Magazine,* March 4, 1978.

20. Freeman, *Politics of Women's Liberation,* pp. 48–49.

IV

Implementing Equal Pay and Equal Opportunity Policy Inside Work Organizations

12 *Nancy Seear*

IMPLEMENTING EQUAL PAY AND EQUAL OPPORTUNITY LEGISLATION IN GREAT BRITAIN

The movement in Great Britain for equal rights for men and women stretches back at least to 1792, when Mary Wollstonecraft published "A Vindication of the Rights of Women." It developed slowly but steadily in the nineteenth century with the support of a small number of middle-class women helped by a handful of dedicated men of whom John Stuart Mill was the most well known. Their energies were devoted mainly to educational and political aims: to establishing girls' schools and women's colleges and to obtaining the right to vote, a right not finally achieved until the passing of the Representation of the People (Equal Franchise) Act in 1928.

At that date little progress had been made toward equality in the world of work. In 1888, the Trades Union Congress had passed a resolution supporting the principle of equal pay for equal work, but for decades little action was taken to translate the principle into practice. The wide gap between men's and women's pay was apparently accepted as a law of nature by the vast majority of women as well as men.

By custom and practice women were restricted to a very narrow range of jobs assumed to be women's work. Married women had always worked in the textile industry, but elsewhere, not only in industry but also in teaching and the civil service, women were required to leave employment on marriage. In 1921 the activity rate for married women was 8.7 percent.[1]

In many sectors of society attitudes had changed little since 1864, when in a paper given to the National Association for the Promotion of Social Sciences a Mrs. Bayley declared "the wife and mother going abroad for work is, with few exceptions, a waste of time, a waste of property, a waste of morals and a waste of health and life and ought in every way to be prevented."[2]

During the First World War, women entered a very wide range of occupations from which they had previously been excluded. Though this was "for the duration only," nothing could erase that wartime evidence of women's grossly underutilized capacity, or put into reverse the psychological and social changes flowing from the shattering impact of war. The Second World War made even heavier demands on women, some of whom carried extremely responsible jobs in the armed forces, in industry, and in the civil service. On the factory floor, as in many types of employment, women took over the jobs normally done by men. Yet, at the end of the war, to a very large extent women vacated these jobs as men returned from the armed forces, not because there were too few jobs to go around, but because of the power of traditional attitudes. As late as 1945, it was possible for the Royal Commission on Equal Pay to produce a majority report unfavorable to a policy for equal pay.[3]

Up to this time there was in fact little mass support for women's rights. Not until the 1950s, as a result of pressure from women in the Civil Service Unions, was the principle of equal pay accepted in the civil service, the policy being implemented over a period of seven years. The movement gathered momentum in the sixties. Developments in the United States stimulated interest. British legislation to outlaw discrimination on grounds of race or ethnic origin prompted the question "Why not on grounds of sex?" The widespread acceptance and practice of birth control led to an upsurge in the activity rate of married women, which by 1971 had risen to 42.2 percent. Women began to join trade unions in increasing numbers, the figures rising from 926,000 in 1938 to 2,208,000 in 1965, and trade union support for equal pay became more active.[4]

There was much to be done. In 1964/1965, median earnings per annum for men were £934 compared with £466 for women. Even more important, women were employed in a narrow range of predominantly low-paid jobs. In 1971, about 30 percent of all women were in manufacturing industries, but half of these were to be found in a small number of industrial categories—food, drink, and tobacco; electrical engineering; clothing; footwear and textiles—clearly overrepresented, in fact, in declining industries. Of all school leavers entering apprenticeships in manufacturing, only 2.5 percent were girls and only 12.1 percent in trade, although 17 percent of all working women were in this area. About 40 percent of girl school leavers took up office work, often with little or no training. In jobs at a more responsible and better-paid level in industry, women constituted only 8.4 percent of managers, 15.3 percent of all supervisors, 1.7 percent of all engineers, scientists, and technologists, and only 12.5 percent of all technicians. These figures are reflected in membership of professional institutes —a qualification essential for many senior appointments. In the Institute of Chartered Secretaries and Administrators, 2.6 percent were women; in the Institute of Bankers, 1.2 percent; in the Institute of Chartered Accountants in England and Wales, 1.6 percent; in the Institute of Electrical Engineers, 0.1 percent; in the Law Society, 3.2 percent; and in the Royal Institute of British Architects, 4.2 percent.[5]

Given the absence of strong public feeling on women's rights, the lack of political activity both at Westminster and in the country at large is not surprising. A Labour backbencher, Mrs. Joyce Butler, introduced a private member's bill in favor of equal opportunities in 1968. The bill failed, attracting little attention, a result which can scarcely have surprised her in view of her comment some years later: "If anyone had told me in 1967 that equal pay would be one of the major political issues of 1973, I would not have believed them."[6] But when Barbara Castle became first secretary of state at the Department of Employment and Productivity, she seized the initiative, and after much heated argument the Equal Pay Act was passed in 1970, a few weeks before the Labour Government fell.

THE EQUAL PAY ACT

The Equal Pay Act of 1970 set out "to prevent discrimination as regards terms and conditions of employment between men and women." It did not lay down the principle of "equal pay for work of equal value"— the principle enunciated in the ILO Convention 100—nor the principle of "equal pay for equal work" stated in Article 119 of the Treaty of Rome. (Britain did not ratify the ILO Convention until 1971.) When Barbara Castle was pressed to accept the principle of equal pay for work of equal value, she argued, no doubt correctly, that its implementation would require British employers to operate a job evaluation system, which, in her view, was not practical. The Equal Pay Act does, however, cover terms and conditions of employment as well as pay and so includes all aspects of bonus and redundancy payments and fringe benefits such as sick pay and vacation pay. Retirement and pension rights are excluded, though pension rights in occupational pension schemes have subsequently been covered by the Social Security (Pensions) Act of 1975. Because of the extensive nature of the changes required, their costs, and possible industrial-relations repercussions, a period of five-and-a-half years was allowed between the passing of the act and its full implementation, which was to be completed by December 29, 1975.

The act contains a three-pronged attack on inequality between the sexes. In relation to collective agreements at both industry and company levels, Section 3 lays down that any agreement containing any discriminatory element can be referred to the Central Arbitration Committee, which has the power to require the removal of the discriminatory clauses and the substitution of clauses ensuring equal treatment. Such agreements, normally negotiated at the national level for a whole industry, usually cover minimum time rates for the lowest level in the job hierarchy and rates for one or more higher grades; standard hours; overtime; shift and incentive premiums; sick pay and vacation provisions. They thus establish a framework of terms and conditions of employment, but a framework that has to be filled in at the level of the company or plant where the collective agreement is applied. It is here that rates of pay for individual jobs are settled. Industry-wide agreements form the basis of company pay structures, but there is nonetheless considerable variation between different companies within the same industry as a result of local labor market conditions and local trade union bargaining power. It is the decisions taken at company and plant level which are the most important determinants of pay and of the way in which the equal pay and equal opportunity policies are actually applied.

The Equal Pay Act also lays down that a woman can claim equal pay with men "if, but only if, her job and their job have been given an equal value, in terms of the demands made on the worker under various headings [for instance, effort, skill, decision], on a study undertaken with a view to evaluating in those terms the jobs to be done by all or any of the employees in an undertaking or group of undertakings." Where a job evaluation scheme exists, the same criteria must be applied to all jobs whatever the sex of the worker. Properly used, this section of the act introduces the concept of equal pay for work of equal value. But when the act came into force, probably fewer than one-third of all employed persons were covered by job evaluation schemes, so only a minority of women stood to benefit from its provisions. For the remainder, their entitlement to equal pay rests on Section 1(4), which states that a woman can claim to be "employed on like work with men if, but only if, her work and theirs is of the same or of a broadly similar nature."

This section in practice imposes important limitations on the extension of equal pay since by tradition men and women are mainly employed on different work. These serious limitations make it all the more important that a woman be able to establish that her work is "broadly similar" to work being performed by men. But "broadly similar" is a very loose term. The act gives some limited clues to its interpretation. Work is to be treated as broadly similar where the differences between jobs are not of practical importance, regard being paid to the nature, extent, and frequency of the differences between the women's and the men's jobs. When it has been established on these grounds that the woman's claim is justified, it is still possible for an employer to maintain that a material difference in circumstances exists between the man's job and the woman's job sufficient to justify differences in pay.

Clearly, the Equal Pay Act, as drafted, though a genuine step in direction of equality, would have only limited effect. In addition it was feared that it might even have an adverse effect on the position of some women, since employers might prefer to replace women by men or by machines once women ceased to be cheaper to employ. To some it seemed that equal pay was in fact a symptom of unequal opportunity since the restriction of women to a limited range of jobs could be expected to depress the price of their labor, especially at a time when increasing numbers of women were entering the labor market. Equal pay, if unaccompanied by equal opportunities, seemed likely to prove a mixed blessing. At once, women's organizations began to press for the inclusion of an equal opportunities clause in the Equal Pay Act. Robert Carr, the shadow minister for employment and productivity, voiced these views when he spoke in the second reading debate in the House of Commons:

> The Bill is intended to prevent discrimination in the terms and conditions of employment between men and women, but it leaves untouched some of the most important aspects of discrimination, for example, it does not apply to freedom of opportunity to apply for or to enter any form of employment, or to be admitted to training courses.[7]

The proposal was not accepted. After the act was passed, however, the movement for equal opportunities gathered the support of a wide variety of women's organizations, from the most traditional to the most avant garde.

By 1973 all political parties were committed to some form of equal opportunities legislation, and in 1975 the Labour Government passed the Sex Discrimination Act, which came into force, together with the Equal Pay Act, on December 29, 1975.

THE SEX DISCRIMINATION ACT

The Equal Pay Act relies on the industrial tribunals, the employment appeal tribunals, and the Central Arbitration Committee to enforce the act. The Sex Discrimination Act allowed aggrieved individuals to bring their complaints before the industrial tribunals and set up an Equal Opportunities Commission with the responsibility of working toward the elimination of discrimination, of producing equality of opportunity between the sexes, and of keeping under review the working of both the Sex Discrimination and the Equal Pay Acts. Dipak Nandy's and Jeffrey Jowell's chapters in this volume describe the content and enforcement of the Sex Discrimination Act in great detail.

IMPACT OF EQUAL PAY AND SEX DISCRIMINATION LAWS

It is extremely difficult to isolate the impact of legislation from the many other variables affecting the position of women. In the first two years that the legislation was in force, Great Britain experienced the most serious recession in nearly fifty years. Rising unemployment figures were accompanied by an unprecedented level of inflation. Very little new recruitment took place. Moreover, as women's pay levels rose and redundancy increased, a small number of men took advantage of their legal rights and applied for and obtained jobs previously held by women. Similarly, the cost of equal pay—a subject much discussed before the legislation was passed—attracted little attention in relation to the huge addition to the wage bills arising from inflation and from the high pay settlements of 1974 and early 1975. It is against this background of uncertainty that a tentative appraisal of the effects of the legislation must be attempted.

Earnings gap

Figures of changes in pay are available, however they are interpreted. In 1970, the year in which the Equal Pay Act was passed, women's average gross weekly earnings were 54.3 percent of men's average earnings. This figure rose to 61.5 percent in 1975 and to 64.3 percent in 1976. For hourly earnings in 1970, excluding the effects of overtime, women were receiving 63.1 percent of the men's figure. This increased to 72.1 percent in 1975. and 75.1 percent in 1976.[8]

The relative pay position of women has undoubtedly improved. But there is still a long way to go. Probably the most important single reason for the continuing differential between men's and women's pay is the continuing practice of job segregation, despite the requirements of the Sex Discrimination Act. In Great Britain, as elsewhere, women are traditionally concentrated in a relatively small number of jobs at the lower level of the employment hierarchy. So far, the Sex Discrimination Act has done little to alter this position. Research findings suggest that there is widespread knowledge among employers, trade unions, and women of the existence of the Equal Pay Act, though accurate knowledge of its content is less extensive. But knowledge of the Sex Discrimination Act is at a very low level indeed. This comment is supported by the small number of applications submitted to industrial tribunals. Where action was completed in the period from December 20, 1975, to December 31, 1976, applications under the Equal Pay Act amounted to 1,742, but under the Sex Discrimination Act there were only 243 and, of these, 59 came from men.[9]

Court cases

In attempting to assess the effectiveness of the legislation, some analysis of the outcome of the cases brought forward is needed. Of the Equal Pay cases, over half were withdrawn—a minority because settlements were reached privately and the rest for reasons unknown. In part, this reflects ignorance of the legislation among complainants, leading to cases which never had a chance of success. (Such faux pas were unfortunately occasionally encouraged by sections of the press which bewailed the failure to achieve radical change after six months.) Just over 6 percent of equal pay cases were settled by formal conciliation—a long-established and valued method of handling industrial conflict in Great Britain. Of the cases which reached tribunals, over 40 percent were won by the complainant—a rate which compares well from the point of view of the complainant with cases of unfair dismissal also handled by tribunals. Of the 184 cases taken under the Sex Discrimination Act, 26 were officially abandoned and 18 were settled privately. But of the 91 cases which finally reached a tribunal, only 18, or just under 20 percent, were settled in favor of the applicant—a result which bears out the contention that the Sex Discrimination Act is too little understood.

In considering these cases it is important to take into account the decisions handed down by the Employment Appeal Tribunal. In the early months of 1976 some industrial tribunal decisions appeared to be confused and were undoubtedly confusing. Industrial tribunal decisions do not constitute case law, so the results of these decisions were not permanent except when the complainant did not appeal. The Employment Appeal Tribunal, whose decisions do constitute case law, has, however, already gone some way both to correct industrial tribunal decisions and to clarify the law. In general, the Employment Appeal Tribunal has attempted to interpret the intention of Parliament in passing the acts rather than accepting a narrow legalistic construction. In interpreting the employer's defense in an indirect discrimination case, the Employment Tribunal has put a meaning on "justifiable" which brings it closer to the word "necessary"—an altogether tighter interpretation.

One of the most significant cases influenced by the Employment Appeal Tribunal is also one which illustrates the way in which individual cases may have a lasting importance far beyond their immediate circumstances. Ms. Belinda Price, a woman in her thirties, applied for a job at the executive level in the civil service. The Civil Service Department informed her that she was not eligible to apply as jobs in this category were subject to an upper age limit of twenty-eight. Ms. Price appealed, unsuccessfully, to an industrial tribunal with the assistance of the National Council for Civil Liberties, arguing that this condition constituted indirect discrimination since many women, for domestic reasons, were unable to apply for work under that age. On appeal, the Employment Appeal Tribunal agreed that, realistically, women under the age of twenty-eight were in fact not as available as men for employment. The decision will require the civil service to revise its policy on age limits, and it may well have significant results for older women seeking to return to the labor market. Many executive civil service jobs are available all over the country and access to them could ease the mobility problem which so often handicaps married women. Moreover, many other organizations operating upper age limits for recruitment will have to re-examine their practices.

Impact within work organizations

Only so much can be learned by an examination of national earnings figures from reports, from industrial tribunals, from the Employment Appeal Tribunal, and from the first Annual Report of the Equal Opportunities Commission. National figures of this kind tell us relatively little about the legislation's impact at the level of the factories, the shops, and the offices where people work and are paid. It was for this reason that in 1974 the Department of Employment and, to a smaller extent, the Nuffield Foundation financed a study at the London School of Economics to monitor the impact of the Equal Pay legislation, and subsequently the Sex Discrimination legislation, in twenty-six organizations. Though such a small number cannot be regarded as a representative sample of British industry, the ones selected included examples of variables thought likely to be important. Size, skill levels, degree of unionization, predominance of white-collar or of manual workers, proportions of men to women, public or private ownership—all these factors were taken into account when the study was set up.

Over a period of three years a team of four research workers made repeated visits to the organizations to monitor progress. Examinations were carried out of company data on pay (including employer–trade union agreements), paysheets, job evaluation and grading schemes, bonus and performance rates, records of applications for employment, training and promotion, and absenteeism and labor turnover. Interviews were carried out with managers, first- and second-line supervisors of both sexes, shop stewards, and, where possible, male and female workers. These interviews explored formal and informal procedures, how they worked in practice and how they were perceived at different levels of the organization. They were also used to study attitudes toward equal opportunities in general and the changes in attitudes and awareness over the period of the project.

The overall findings are in line with and illustrate the national figures. Real progress has been made toward equal pay. Table 12-1 shows how, in nineteen of the organizations, women's rates of pay had improved in relation to men's. This table deals with rates, since it is the equalization of rates

TABLE 12-1

Organizations Grouped by Manual Women's Pay
before and after Equal Pay
as Compared with Manual Men's Pay within the Same Organization

	NUMBER OF ORGANIZATIONS*	
Category	*Pre-Equal Pay*	*Post-Equal Pay*
A All women paid below lowest male rate	16	3
B Bulk of women paid below lowest male rate	0	1
C Bulk of women paid on or above lowest male rate, but below all other male rates	1	9
D Substantial numbers of women paid as much as or more than substantial numbers of men	2	6
TOTAL, no. of organizations	19	19

*Only nineteen organizations are included because, for three out of the twenty-two where manual implementation was studied, full and reliable pay information was not obtainable.

which is required by the act. But a more informative picture of the changes in women's position can be seen by examining alterations in gross weekly earnings and in hourly earnings. When allowance has been made for women's shorter hours of work, the changes in men's and women's differentials in earnings normally moved in line with the changes in rates. Where this was not the case, the position was affected primarily by alterations in hours worked by men and women and by changes in overtime and shift work influencing differentials and earnings. Men normally worked considerably more overtime and were much more likely to be on shifts than women. But as the economic recession deepened, overtime for men became much less frequent in some organizations. In certain instances, at the same time, the number of women on shifts increased. Where this happened, the gap in men's and women's earnings closed faster than the gap in wage rates. On the other hand, instances were found where management had taken action to maintain the sex differential in earnings. In one case, where women were employed on an incentive system, piece rates on some women's jobs were tightened, while elsewhere men's bonus earnings were adjusted upwards.

The gap between men's and women's rates and earnings would have narrowed even more but for a further finding of some interest. The study showed that, despite the intended coverage of all women in employment, there are still a few women who fall outside the scope of the Equal Pay Act. This occurs where there is neither a collective agreement nor a company pay structure in operation, where pay is in fact fixed by a series of individual ad hoc decisions. If, as was found in several cases, there is also no system of job evaluation in operation and if, further, a woman is unable to identify a man employed on the same or broadly similar work, then such a woman is not legally entitled to a single additional penny as a result of the act.

Table 12-2 shows the extent and range of cases that are covered by the act. In the manual section it was cleaners and canteen workers, especially those employed in small organizations, who did not benefit. A much larger number of white-collar workers in a range of occupations from managerial to clerical were also excluded. In one large white-collar organization, over four thousand women were not covered by any section of the act. In eight cases employers gave increases where they were not legally required to, sometimes in order to continue traditional differentials after equal pay had been given in conformity with the legislation.

It has been suggested that the relative improvement in women's pay springs primarily from national incomes policy and not from the Equal Pay Act. The flat rate increases which were the basis of national policies in 1975 and 1976 clearly benefited the low paid proportionately more than the higher paid. Since the vast majority of women are among the low paid, the improvement in their positions was no doubt in part the result of these policies. But the research findings make it clear that the extent of the improvement cannot be explained solely by incomes policy, and that the Equal Pay Act did in fact contribute to the change.

Genuine though the improvement is, it is also clear that, as a result of action taken by employers, many women have done less well than they might have done. The organizations studied can be classified into four groups according to the extent and nature of their compliance with the requirements of the legislation.

1. Some organizations were found to be clearly in breach of their legal obligation though the numbers affected were small. In one case, twenty cleaners in a large engineering company received less than the lowest male rate in the collective agreement governing their pay. The employers stated that they did not make the required equal pay adjustments for fear of resentment on the part of male cleaners. A second interesting example of breach of the legislation involved the continuation of a practice favorable to women whereby they received larger relaxation allowance than men when bonus performance standards were set.

TABLE 12-2
Women Not Directly Affected by the Equal Pay Act

Type of employment organization	Number of women	Type of work	Equal Pay adjustments
Manual work			
Manufacturing	17	Canteen, cleaning	
Manufacturing*	14	Canteen, cleaning	
Manufacturing*	7	Canteen, cleaning	
Manufacturing	20	Canteen	X
Manufacturing	20	Canteen	
Manufacturing*	8	Cleaning	
White-collar work			
Manufacturing	4	Supervisory, clerical	Y
Service	4	Managerial, secretarial	
Manufacturing	53	Clerical, administrative	Y
Manufacturing	6	Clerical	X
Manufacturing*	22	Clerical	
Manufacturing	2	Administrative, clerical	
Manufacturing	2	Forewoman	X
Manufacturing*	30	Office, administrative	Y
Manufacturing	20	Administrative, clerical	
Manufacturing	10	Manual, supervisory	X
Manufacturing	30	Receptionist, nurses, secretarial	Y
Commercial	4,000+	Typists, secretarial	

*These organizations have both manual and white-collar employees not directly affected.

X = all received adjustments; Y = some received adjustments.

2. Thirteen organizations contained borderline cases of breaches of the law; most of the cases involved the identification of "like work." For example, women managers of small retail outlets were paid on average less than male managers. Analysis by length of service and turnover of store (both used as pay criteria) showed that women on average scored higher than men on both counts. Management admitted that they might well be in breach of the act, but had taken no steps to check the position.

3. In a third group of organizations including no fewer than fourteen of twenty-six studied, employers had taken action prior to the date for the legal enforcement of the act to reduce their legal obligations. One organization, for example, slowed down the increases made on the lowest male rates, while compressing female differentials into the lowest male rate. Other cases included the transfer of men from jobs where "like work" claims might be lodged and alteration of the content of jobs to defeat such claims.

4. The fourth group included all those organizations which implemented the legislation fully. Nine of the organizations studied fall into this category. Some even attempted, not always with success, to go beyond the formal requirements of the law and to carry out the spirit and not merely the letter of the act.

IMPLICATIONS OF THE IMPLEMENTATION OF THE EQUAL PAY AND SEX DISCRIMINATION LAWS

The methods used for implementation raise some interesting issues. Except in the cases discussed above—cases of a type which probably can not be foreseen—Section 3 of the Equal Pay Act has ensured that all women are being paid at least the minimum basic rate, which is now common to both sexes. But, in reality, as the study showed, this has not meant equality, since it is very unusual in these organizations for men to be paid at the lowest rate negotiated in the agreement. Since women frequently were moved to the lowest negotiated rate, but no higher, the gap between men's and women's pay remains. Enforcement bodies are beginning to rectify this defect. The Central Arbitration Committee, to which cases under this section can be referred, now treats very low base rates paid only to women as the virtual continuation of a separate women's rate and, therefore, as not in conformity with the requirements of the legislation.

The "like work" section of the Equal Pay Act was the principal method of implementation in one case only, where it was used for white-collar employees. As we noted earlier, the usefulness of the right to make a claim on grounds of "the same or broadly similar work" is seriously limited by the widespread desegregation of jobs on a sex basis, which makes this section an ineffective instrument for eliminating discrimination. It is, in fact, the section relying on the use of job evaluation that we found to be the most widely used section of the law. Eleven organizations applied this section to manual workers and thirteen to white-collar workers. Three organizations re-evaluated existing job evaluation schemes. One of the companies re-evaluated all its structures out of fear that a structure which had been arrived at by looking at jobs recognized as "women's jobs" might contain discriminatory features based on unchallenged assumptions. Nine organizations introduced new job evaluation schemes or extended existing schemes. Three other organizations used the concept of equal value as a basis for judgment, but did not express it in a formal scheme. Most of the job evaluations were undertaken by joint management-union panels. Most, but not all, of the evaluations were done by men.

This investigation, then, demonstrates the importance of job evaluation in the implementation of equal pay. It is also well known, however, that job evaluation is viewed with considerable suspicion by many trade unions. It undoubtedly relies to a great extent on personal judgment, and tends for understandable reasons to re-establish the status quo. It is a system that can be easily manipulated. Examples were found in this study, side by side with effective schemes, in which job evaluation became an instrument for retarding rather than advancing the application of the principle of equal pay. Nor was it found that the presence of a trade unionist in the job evaluation team was necessarily a safeguard. Only the active involvement in the job evaluation process of well-trained men and women determined to eliminate all aspects of sex discrimination can ensure the proper use of job evaluation schemes.

Despite frequent assertions that equal opportunity was practiced, the investigation found that segregation by sex was common. This arose not so much from deliberate policy as from the results of long-established and unchallenged tradition. With the exception of one organization in which there were a large number of women in professional jobs, women were concentrated in a narrow range of traditional women's jobs, mainly at a low level in the hierarchy. Apart from the inadequacy of systems of comparison between men's and women's jobs, the major block in the path to equality remains the widespread segregation of jobs on grounds of sex.

A small but significant number of changes, however, have been undertaken. In two engineering companies, a female apprentice was taken on for the first time. Another concern appointed a woman graduate engineer. Equally important, especially in regard to the barriers created by conventional career paths, in one enterprise a woman had been promoted from an administrative job to become a supervisor over fifty men.

At the same time, a rather larger number of men moved into traditional women's jobs. An interesting situation arose in an engineering firm which had set up a training scheme for assemblers of electronic circuits.

This job required a high level of dexterity and, as a result of the common belief that women are more dextrous than men, the job had been done exclusively by women. After the passing of the act, dexterity tests were introduced in order to have objective criteria to justify the exclusion of men. In fact, some men applicants performed better in the test than some women applicants. During 1976, eighty-four women and thirty-three men were recruited and trained for the job. Similarly, in one large manufacturing company both management and the trade unions made plans to use the legislation to advance men from low-grade jobs to higher-grade jobs previously done by women.

OBSTACLES TO CHANGE

Why has there been so little progress in establishing equal opportunities in these organizations? The general economic climate from the time that the legislation came into force has undoubtedly been very unfavorable to greater equality. While the development of new techniques combined with widespread shortages of labor undoubtedly can make it easier for women to be considered for jobs which either have not existed before or which have been filled exclusively by men, contraction and redundancy were far more common in the organizations in the study than were innovation and expansion. Where neither men nor women are being recruited and many are being forced to leave, it is hardly surprising that women are not penetrating new areas of work. Even in this economic climate, however, organizations are still frequently short of skilled people. With few exceptions, this has not led to a determined effort to find women as well as men to fill these vacancies.

Probably the biggest obstacles to change are existing organization structures and personnel practices, attitudes about the nature of men's work which are held throughout all levels in the organization, and ignorance of the nature and implications of the legislation. Existing organizational structures certainly have an adverse effect on the implementation of personnel policies. In a number of organizations, after equal opportunity policies were formulated at the center, with, it appeared, a genuine wish to bring about change, little or nothing happened in the divisions away from headquarters. Nor was this merely ineffectiveness on the part of headquarters. Where a company pursues a policy of decentralization, detailed enforcement of headquarter's policies is incompatible with its system of control and style of management. This presents management with an organizational problem for which no satisfactory answer has yet been found.

Traditional personnel policies also hinder the introduction of equal opportunities. In two large white-collar organizations, almost all recruitment was confined to school leavers and to recent university graduates.

But this meant that the doors were closed to women wishing to return to work as their families grew older. Again, partly to avoid raising false hope, training for more responsible jobs was normally given after the candidate had been selected for the post. Prepromotional training might well have helped women who were not considered when selection for promotion was undertaken, but who might well have demonstrated their suitability for higher-level work during the training process.

Inadequate personnel practices also adversely affected women in some organizations. Thorough and regular appraisal schemes geared to management development programs can prevent women from being overlooked. They can give women the opportunity to challenge the stereotypes which certainly appear to prevail in many minds. But in some of the organizations, such schemes are nonexistent or sketchy, and promotion policies seem unrelated to any sound basis of appraisal. Other personnel policies which handicap many women include a requirement that all employees should be geographically mobile and, in other instances, that they should attend quite long residential training courses as a condition for promotion.

A further series of obstacles found in many organizations is the existence of established paths to promotion—a time-served apprenticeship, for example, or experience in a middle management job to which, by custom, women were never appointed. Failure to gain access to such paths meant that subsequent promotion was blocked. Management had not considered the fact that such requirements might, in some cases, constitute indirect discrimination, nor had the issue been raised by the trade unions. Traditional objections, such as the need to lift heavy weights or women's inability to take on shift work, were advanced as reasons for excluding women. But no one had examined whether heavy lifting was really needed or whether a permit to allow women to work shifts had to be obtained, as is sanctioned under the Factories Act, 1961.

The unquestioning acceptance of traditional explanations for limiting women's opportunities reflects widespread views regarding women's employment. There are, of course, exceptions, especially in headquarters, but by and large there is little sign of change in deep-seated attitudes. The feeling is widespread that women should be protected from dirty or heavy jobs; that they are more dextrous; that they accept monotony, but are unsuited to work requiring mechanical ability. Shop stewards and the men they represent also on occasion make it quite clear that they are not prepared to accept women in certain jobs, or in positions of authority over men.

The Sex Discrimination Act has not disturbed these attitudes, partly, no doubt, because many people are almost totally ignorant of it and partly because little pressure has been put on the organizations. In the twenty-six organizations in our study, no single case has been taken to an industrial tribunal under the act; no positive action has been demanded by the trade unions, and the Equal Opportunities Commission has made no impact. Few people realize that the act permits positive discrimination in training where either sex is substantially underrepresented in a particular job. No company has introduced such schemes. Apart from members of personnel departments, the concept of indirect discrimination is not understood, and no systematic examination of job requirements has been carried out to establish whether indirect discrimination is being practiced. Perhaps most disturbing of all in the light of these facts is the widespread belief that once discriminatory advertising has been terminated and, perhaps, a general policy statement on equal opportunities has been made, the organization has fulfilled its obligations and nothing more remains to be done.

There will be many views of the right road ahead. Some will argue for a far more legalistic and punitive approach than has so far been adopted in the United Kingdom. If progress continues to be slow, voices will be raised more loudly in support of such policies. Alternatively, the existing legislation, modified only in detail, must be made to work. For this, two developments seem to be necessary. Existing powers of enforcement need to be used to demonstrate that the law means what it says. One or two well-publicized cases might greatly concentrate the minds of both unions and managements.

But the major developments must come from within the industrial system itself. Joint union-management policies worked out at company level and implemented with determination are much more likely to produce lasting results than changes imposed from without. The more grievances with regard to discrimination are handled by the ordinary industrial-relations machinery, the more likely they are to be redressed. Even more important, the more management accepts the need to incorporate women fully and unreservedly into the enterprise, the more it recognizes that the refusal to make use of abilities women can offer is damaging to the enterprise, the more chance there is that the aims of the acts will be achieved in the not too remote future.

NOTES

1. *Women and Work—a Statistical Survey* (Department of Employment Manpower Paper No. 9; London: HMSO, 1974).

2. Margaret Hewitt, *Wives and Mothers in Victorian Industry* (London: Rockliff, 1958).

3. *Royal Commission on Equal Pay, 1944–46* (CMD 6967; London: HMSO, 1947).

4. "Women Workers," Report of 37th Annual Trade Union Congress Women's Conference (1967), Item 6.

5. *Women and Work—A Review* (Department of Employment Manpower Paper No. 11; London: HMSO, 1975).

6. Nancy Seear, "Equal Opportunities for Men and Women," in *The Year Book of Social Policy in Britain,* ed. Kathleen Jones (1973).

7. Records Hansard, House of Commons, Official Report, Parliamentary Debates, Feb. 22, 1970, vol. 812, 5th ser. (London: HMSO, 1970–1971).

8. Despite this lowering in percentage differences, in cash terms the gap between women's earnings and men's earnings in fact increased in this period, rising from £13.7 in 1970 to £25.6 in 1976. This increase is, however, more apparent than real. In terms of purchasing power £13.7 in 1970 was equal to about £31 in 1976—considerably in excess of the 1976 differential.

9. Equal Opportunities Commission, *The Annual Report of the Equal Opportunities Commission, 1976* (London: HMSO, 1977).

13 *Ruth Gilbert Shaeffer*

IMPROVING JOB OPPORTUNITIES FOR WOMEN FROM A U.S. CORPORATE PERSPECTIVE

The mid-1960s marked a major turning point in the United States' approach to the elimination of invidious discrimination in many aspects of our national life. Voluntarism had failed, and state and local laws had proved ineffective. We moved on to strong federal laws and regulations compelling nondiscrimination on the basis of race, color, religion, sex, national origin, and, a few years later, age. Despite the fact that the first of these new federal laws dealt with equal pay for men and women,[1] during the late 1960s primary attention was given to eliminating overt discrimination against minorities, especially blacks.

But in the early 1970s there were three very significant developments. First, the U.S. Supreme Court unanimously endorsed a results-oriented definition of what constitutes discrimination in employment under Title VII of the Civil Rights Act of 1964. The Court indicated that intent does not matter; it is the *consequences* of an employer's actions that determine whether he has discriminated under Title VII, and he has the burden of justifying any such discrimination on the basis of business necessity.[2] Then, pursuant to Executive Order 11246, as amended, the Office of Federal Contract Compliance (OFCC) issued an order requiring government contractors to have, for each of their establishments, a written affirmative action plan that includes goals and timetables for increasing the representation of women, as well as of minorities, in all job categories where they are currently underutilized.[3]

As a result of these two events, American Telephone and Telegraph Company (AT&T) signed a multimillion-dollar consent agreement in January 1973 with both the Equal Employment Opportunity Commission (the independent agency that administers Title VII) and the Department of Labor (which administers the executive order). AT&T agreed to take many affirmative steps to ensure that equal employment opportunities were provided, especially to women but also to minorities. The cost was estimated to be well over $60 million over a five-year period. The agreement was entered as a court decree, and compliance with it has, therefore, been subject to court supervision.[4] Thus, in the early 1970s all major U.S. corporations were forcefully put on notice that, both as employers and as government contractors, they have significant nondiscrimination obligations not only to minorities but also to women.

These obligations go far beyond the mere evenhanded application of existing agreements, policies, and procedures. With only limited exceptions, companies are required, both independently and through their collective bargaining efforts, to take actions that will yield equal employment opportunity results for both sexes in all parts and at all levels of the organization unless they can demonstrate that business necessity—their legitimate interest in the safe and efficient operation of the business and in trustworthy workmanship—justifies their failure to do so. Women now make up over 40 percent of the U.S. workforce, so it is plain that the implications of this obligation are both broad and profound.

THE CONFERENCE BOARD'S RESEARCH PROGRAM

In 1974, the Conference Board began the planning for a broadly based continuing program to study the efforts of major organizations to change the relative status of working women in the United States.[5] The goals of this study program are (1) to focus greater attention on the problem and (2) to provide key organization leaders in various sectors of the economy with experience-based, results-oriented information they can use to improve their affirmative efforts to provide equal employment opportunity for women.

Given the broad information needs of these decision makers, we decided the following four basic research questions would be appropriate in all phases of the program: Where did matters stand in 1970? What environmental pressures are affecting the situation? What actions have the organization being studied taken to bring about the needed pattern changes? What evidence, if any, is there of change toward greater parity in the status of men and women? We also decided that it made sense to divide the research program into several phases, each directed toward a different sector of the economy, and then within each phase to break the research up into manageable projects.

Our first research project has, quite appropriately, been in the business and industry sector. It has dealt with corporate efforts to increase the representation of women in occupational categories where they have previously been underutilized.[6] The research results reported in this chapter are drawn from this first project. There will also be two regular Conference Board reports covering it that will routinely be disseminated in over four thousand CB Associate organizations and will also be available to others in 1978.[7]

Between 1970 and 1975 measurable changes did occur in the kinds of job opportunities being provided to U.S. women, especially in some of our very large corporations. There are also some remarkably clear-cut and consistent findings to report with respect to how major companies have gone about implementing such changes successfully and how this relates to their overall management of human resource utilization. But it is important to note that our research has not dealt with whether any of these corporations have or have not complied with the law or the executive order. These are matters for the administrative agencies and the courts to determine.

It is also important to note that, because of the nature of the underlying legal situation as well as because of the great amount of overlap in coverage by Title VII and by Executive Order 11246 among major U.S. corporations, it is not possible to separate out the relative impact of the two approaches. (Almost all of the major corporations providing us with measurable data regard themselves as government contractors.) Moreover, many major corporations now say they equate a preventive managerial approach to avoiding difficulties under Title VII with the basic affirmative action approach called for under the executive order. Therefore, unless enforcement has been extremely lax, the only difference between the two is likely to be in the paperwork required for technical compliance and not in the basic nature or substance of their effort.[8]

DESIGN OF THE PROJECT

Most major corporations were well aware of the potential legal and financial liabilities they faced in the area of employment discrimination, and some reported unfortunate experiences in which their previous efforts to cooperate in research projects or information-sharing meetings about such matters had turned out to have serious compliance or public relations implications for them. Considerable thought, consultation, and experimentation were therefore required in order to design a feasible research study that would enable major companies to share useful information about their efforts to improve the job opportunities they provide to women anonymously and confidentially. (The mere fact that such considerations come into play may give observers from other countries some insight into the seriousness with which our major corporations are taking the equal employment opportunity laws and regulations.)

The research design that was ultimately followed consisted of three main parts.

First was a comparison of 1970 and 1975 male-female employment statistics both by industry and by occupational category. The statistics used were from several government sources as well as from very large corporations contacted by mailed survey. The figures do not provide information with respect to any company's compliance with the EEO laws and regulations, but they have enabled us to analyze employment patterns by sex in various settings and to assess the net effects by 1975 of corporate efforts to improve women's job opportunities in various occupational categories, including certain clearly nontraditional jobs.

Second was an analysis of data collected by means of a thirty-two–page mailed survey questionnaire covering corporate experiences with and perspectives on the change process. In addition to yielding some of the figures mentioned above, this aspect of the research addressed six issues: (1) to identify the major job categories at all organization levels for which companies have found efforts to improve opportunities for women to be necessary and to learn where the greatest emphasis has been placed; (2) to describe changes in staffing strategies and approaches that companies have tried in order to increase the representation of women in different job categories, with special emphasis on those they have found either especially effective or especially inappropriate; (3) to determine whether any joint or collaborative efforts have been undertaken with unions, other employers, schools, or other institutions that influence the supply of women who are qualified for various occupational roles; (4) to identify some of the special factors, both within the company and in its environment, that have been found to influence the success of corporate efforts to improve job opportunities for women; (5) to identify some of the perceived consequences, both positive and negative, of such corporate efforts; and (6) to determine whether any changes in compensation, benefit, or layoff and recall practices have had the direct effect of changing the employment patterns of men and women in various job categories.

Our third part consisted of almost two hundred confidential telephone and on-site interviews dealing with examples of successful and unsuccessful experiences. Because even reports of "success stories" in this area have sometimes had unfortunate legal consequences, the only companies mentioned by name in the report are those operating under published agreements with administrative agencies or court decrees.[9]

We regarded our project as an exploratory study rather than one aiming at precise quantification. All told, the 1,015 companies contacted by the mailed survey were among the largest companies in the following broad industry categories: mining, construction, durable and nondurable goods manufacturing, transportation, communications, gas and electric utilities, retailing, wholesale trade, banking, and insurance. The basic sample was largely drawn from the *Fortune* 1,300 lists. Some other industry lists of very large companies were also used, and we were fortunate enough to obtain the cooperation of some industry associations in encouraging their largest members to respond.

The breakdown by industry of those providing useable responses in various parts of the survey effort is shown in Table 13-1. Compared to most Conference Board surveys of corporate policies and practices, the response rate was low, probably due not only to the sensitivity of the topic but also to the length of the questionnaire. However, the quality of the responses was high.

The question of the "purity" of the sample was not deemed of primary importance because there were many reasons why the respondents were not likely to be typical. As this is viewed as an exploratory study, it was considered more important to obtain sufficient responses to permit impressionistic analyses of data about very broad categories than to attempt to find statistically significant differences among groups.

MAJOR FINDINGS REGARDING 1970–1975 CHANGES IN MALE-FEMALE EMPLOYMENT PATTERNS

Because U.S. laws and regulations call for equal employment opportunity and not for instant equal employment results, it is not too surprising that by 1975 no marked shift in the overall configuration of the male-female employment patterns by broad occupational categories in business and industry had occurred. And yet there is clear evidence that changes did occur between 1970 and 1975 in the kinds of job opportunities being provided to women, especially in the female-intensive industries and in some of the very large corporations. If the observed change process continues, there are likely to be some dramatic shifts in the overall male-female patterns shown by our next decennial census in 1980 when compared to the 1970 figures.

TABLE 13-1

Very Large Corporations Responding to the Conference Board Survey

Industry	PROVIDING USEABLE QUESTIONNAIRES		PROVIDING SOME INFORMATION ABOUT NONTRADITIONAL JOBS		PROVIDING USEABLE MATCHED EEO-1 DATA FOR 1970 AND 1975	
	No.	%	No.	%	No.	%†
Durable goods manufacturing	44	17%	33	16%	14	
Nondurable goods manufacturing	50	19	39	19	23	
Transportation	21	8	16	8	*	
Electric and gas utilities	60	23	58	28	32	
Retail trade	14	5	9	4	*	
Banking	27	10	11	5	10	
Insurance	37	14	30	15	16	
Other (e.g., mining, construction, communications, wholesale trade)	12	4	11	5	*	
TOTAL	265	100%	207	100%	111	
Male-intensive industries	158	60%	134	65%	73	
Female-intensive industries	107	40	73	35	38	
TOTAL	265	100%	207	100%	111	

*Fewer than ten companies.
†Because of the known lack of typicality of these companies, it is not appropriate to combine them into an overall sample.

Table 13-2 shows what has been happening to the representation of women in various occupational categories in what we have called the corporate sector (those industries in which there tend to be relatively large profit-making corporations). Since the table uses overall 1970, 1972, and 1975 figures for this sector, they show the share of various kinds of jobs that women held in companies of all sizes. There is a noticeable improvement in the representation of women in two of the better-paying, higher-status categories—in the managerial and administrative jobs (which are growing in numbers) and also in professional and technical occupations —but not in the skilled craft jobs. These changes were occurring at a time

TABLE 13-2
Representation of Women in the Corporate Sector

Occupational category	1970	1972	1975
Managers and administrators	13%	15%	17%
Professional and technical workers	13	13	15
Sales workers	39	42	43
Office and clerical workers	71	74	76
Skilled craft workers	5	3	4
Semiskilled operatives	37	38	38
Unskilled laborers	4	4	5
Service workers	52	53	54
TOTAL	31%	31%	32%

SOURCE: U.S. Bureau of the Census, *Census of Population, 1970: Occupation by Industry, Final Report PC(2)-7C* (Washington, D.C.: GPO, 1972). Adjusted by means of unpublished data from U.S. Bureau of Labor Statistics, ". . . Current Population Survey," *Employment and Earnings* 22, no. 8 (Feb. 1976): 11–27.

when there was a continuing influx of more women into the paid labor force, so there has also been an increase in the representation of women in some of their more traditional occupational roles in business too. The overall representation of women within the corporate sector increased from 31 percent in 1970 to 32 percent in 1975; this compares to an increase from 38 percent in 1970 to 40 percent in 1975 in the representation of women in the labor force of the economy as a whole.

When the data for the corporate sector is disaggregated in various ways, the existing occupational segregation of women becomes even more apparent, but a number of situations also are found in which there has been considerably greater 1970–1975 improvement in the upscale job opportunities being provided to women.

Differences in male-intensive vs. female-intensive industries

As Table 13-3 indicates, there are some industries within the corporate sector—like banking, insurance, retailing, communications, and certain kinds of manufacturing (especially of many nondurable goods)—where women have long constituted a much larger proportion of the workforce than they have in such industries as mining, construction, electric and gas utilities, transportation, wholesale trade, and certain other kinds of manufacturing (especially of many durable goods). The primary reason women constitute such a large percentage of the workforce in the female-intensive industries is that there are certain numerically important low-paying, low-

TABLE 13-3

The Proportion of Women by Industry Group
in the Corporate Sector, 1970

Industry group	Proportion of women in the workforce (corporate sector)
Male-intensive industries	
Construction	6%
Mining	8
Primary metals	9
Lumber and wood, excluding furniture	10
Utilities and sanitary services	13
Transportation equipment	13
Transportation	14
Petroleum and coal products	14
Machinery, excluding electrical	17
Fabricated metals	19
Stone, clay, glass products	19
Paper and allied products	22
Chemicals and allied products	23
Wholesale trade	24
Furniture and fixtures	26
Food and kindred products	26
Ordnance, other durables, misc. manufacturing	30
Rubber and misc. plastic products	31
Female-intensive industries	
Printing, publishing, allied industries	35
Professional, photo equipment, watches	37
Electrical machinery, equipment, supplies	38
Tobacco manufacture	39
Finance, excluding banking	45
Retail trade	46
Textile mill products	46
Insurance	48
Communications	49
Leather and leather products	57
Banking	63
Apparel, fabricated textiles	78
TOTAL, all industries	38%
TOTAL, corporate sector	31
AVERAGE, corporate sector	31
AVERAGE, male-intensive	15
AVERAGE, female-intensive	47

SOURCE: *Census of Population, 1970.*

status jobs in which they predominate. Most work as clerical employees, retail sales clerks, semi-skilled machine operatives, or service workers. In both the male-intensive and the female-intensive industries, men still predominate in all the clearly upscale occupational categories. Regardless of how many women are employed, the men are much more likely to be the managers and administrators, the professionals and technicians, the sales representatives and the skilled craft workers.

Nonetheless, as Table 13-4 shows, even in 1970 the women held a significantly larger proportion of the upscale jobs in the female-intensive industries than they did in the male-intensive ones. Undoubtedly a major reason for these differences is that in 1970 relatively few women had the science or engineering background required for many of the upscale jobs in the male-intensive industries. It is also true that women were more likely to be used as supervisors or managers of other women than of men, and that some of the jobs requiring technical knowledge or craft skills in the female-intensive industries could really be viewed as extensions of certain basic homemaking skills, such as sewing and food preparation.

TABLE 13-4

Representation of Women in Male-intensive
vs. Female-intensive Industries
within the Corporate Sector, 1970 and 1975

Occupational category	MALE-INTENSIVE INDUSTRIES		FEMALE-INTENSIVE INDUSTRIES	
	1970	*1975*	*1970*	*1975*
Managers and administrators	5%	6%	19%	23%
Professional and technical workers	8	10	21	25
Sales workers	7	6	49*	51*
Office and clerical workers	59	64	80	83
Skilled craft workers	2	2	11	12
Semiskilled operatives (including transport operatives)	16	17	51	51
Unskilled laborers	4	5	15	13
Service workers	19	19	60	60
TOTAL	15%	16%	47%	48%

*Includes retailing, where sales work often is not an upscale occupation. If this industry is excluded, the representation of women in sales jobs in female-intensive industries was 13 percent in 1970 and 15 percent in 1975.

SOURCE: *Census of Population, 1970* and "Current Population Survey" (unpublished data for March 1975).

But some observers also point out that companies that have had more experience with women as employees might generally be more likely even to think of hiring or promoting a woman, less likely to assume that all women are very much alike, and/or more likely to be aware that qualified women might be available at lower rates of pay than comparably qualified men. Thus, they would be able to identify women who have the qualifications needed for a broader range of jobs and who also have the potential to fill considerably more responsible roles. In support of their theory, they point out that there are not only differences in the employment of women in the upscale occupations but even in the "traditionally female" clerical occupations—a much higher proportion of women were employed in clerical jobs in female-intensive industries (80 percent) than in the male-intensive industries (59 percent).

By 1975 there had been considerably greater improvement in the representation of women in the upscale job categories in the female-intensive industries. In addition to the possible explanation already noted, two other factors deserve mention. Many of the female-intensive industries are in the service-providing part of the economy where, despite the recession, total employment has been growing quite rapidly—in contrast to the long-term trend of declining employment in goods production. Thus, companies in the female-intensive industries probably had more job openings to fill.[10] Moreover, because these employers have such large numbers of women on their payrolls in lower-level jobs, they may fear they are especially vulnerable to class action lawsuits leading to expensive backpay awards to identifiable victims of prior employment discrimination.

Differences that appear to be related to company size

Even within industries in the corporate sector—whether they are categorized as male-intensive or female-intensive, or whether they are categorized by the kinds of goods or services being produced—there appear to be further differences in the amount of favorable change for women by company size. Some caution in interpretation is needed, however, because we are dealing with three sets of data for the 1970–1975 period that are from different sources and not fully comparable. The Census and Current Population Survey (CPS) data in effect covers companies of all sizes, even the very small ones. The EEOC data was submitted to the Equal Employment Opportunity Commission (EEOC) on the EEO-1 form by somewhat larger employers, those with one hundred or more employees (or fifty or more employees if they were government contractors). The CB Survey data is EEO-1 form information that was submitted directly to us. Exactly the same 111 very large companies are included in both the 1970 and the 1975 samples. These corporations probably are not typical of all the very large companies in their industries. Nonetheless, they are important because they account for a large share of the total employment in these industries.

In 1970, in most of the industries for which we have data, the very large CB Survey corporations appear to have been lagging behind in terms of the representation of women in all their better-paying, higher-status job categories. As Table 13-5 shows, they not only had smaller proportions of women managers and professional technical workers but also fewer women in sales jobs and as skilled craft workers than did their industries overall.

But, in most of the industries, by 1975 the very large corporations in the CB Survey showed the greatest improvement in the proportion of women in their upscale jobs and, as Table 13-6 indicates, in a few cases they even led the industry proportion by a considerable margin. (The 1972–1975 figures for AT&T are shown separately in Table 13-6 because the job categories used under the consent decree do not match the EEO-1 form categories and no 1970 figures are available.) Moreover, over the five-year period these very large corporations also showed high net percentage changes in the numbers of women in their upscale job categories (see Table 13-7).

It is important to note that the 1970–1975 changes in the data have been complex, so the pictures seen from these two different perspectives on the changes in the job opportunities being provided to women do not always match. There was, for example, a significant increase in the size of the managerial workforce in some industries, so that just to maintain the proportion of women in management required a considerable increase in the number of women managers employed. To increase their representation in such a category therefore required even greater growth in their numbers. This is analogous to the situation the Red Queen describes to Alice in Lewis Carroll's *Through the Looking Glass* when she says: "Now, *here*, you see, it takes all the running you can do to keep in the same place."

On the other hand, the seeming "growth" in the representation of women in clerical jobs in the very large corporations in both durable and nondurable goods manufacturing actually turns out to be due to the fact that, on balance, the women did not lose as many clerical jobs as the men did, more of whom were probably laid off in plant shutdowns.

It makes sense that the larger companies might be able to do better at improving the job opportunities they provide for women. They do more internal training of employees. They also have more staff available to help make sure their line managers understand what the EEO law requires and to aid them in making appropriate changes. But it should also be noted that some of our largest companies have really been under the gun both under Title VII and under Executive Order 11246. Stringent enforcement of the

TABLE 13-5
Representation of Women in Upscale Occupations by Size of Company, 1970 and 1975*

Industry	ALL COMPANIES (CENSUS/CPS)		COMPANIES WITH 50–100 OR MORE EMPLOYEES (EEOC)		SOME VERY LARGE CORPORATIONS (CB SURVEY)	
	1970	1975	1970	1975	1970	1975
A. Female managers						
Durable goods mfg.	5%	6%	2%	4%	1%	2%
Nondurable goods mfg.	9	10	5	8	3	6
Transportation	9	11	3	5	5	4
Communications	15	27	35	32	†	†
Electric and gas utilities	4	3	2	3	2	3
Retail trade	21	24	24	28	22	34
Banking	19	29	13	25	17	30
Insurance	17	18	11	17	6	10
B. Female professional and technical workers						
Durable goods mfg.	7	8	6	8	4	7
Nondurable goods mfg.	21	24	14	19	14	20
Transportation	9	10	5	6	4	5
Communications	17	19	16	27	†	†
Electric and gas utilities	4	7	4	7	4	7
Retail trade	28	33	29	36	17	35
Banking	31	39	23	30	24	32
Insurance	29	29	24	37	31	46

C. Female sales workers‡

Durable goods mfg.	6	8	8	15	1	4
Nondurable goods mfg.	13	16	10	16	3	7
Insurance	12	15	5	7	1	3

D. Female craft workers‡

Durable goods mfg.	5	4	3	4	1	2
Nondurable goods mfg.	11	11	20	16	2	2
Transportation	1	§	§	§	§	§
Communications	4	5	1	7	†	†
Electric and gas utilities	1	§	§	§	§	§

*The occupational categories in the Census and Current Population Survey are not precisely comparable with the EEO-1 form categories. Also, the very large corporations are probably not typical.

†Not available. For 1972–1975 AT&T data, see Table 13-6.

‡In industries where this is an important upscale job category.

§Less than 0.5 percent.

SOURCE: *Census of Population, 1970*; "Current Population Survey"; EEOC, *Equal Employment Opportunity Report, 1970*, vol. 1 (Washington, D.C.: GPO, 1971), and *Equal Employment Opportunity Report, 1975*, vol. 1 (Washington, D.C.: GPO, 1977); Conference Board Survey.

TABLE 13-6

Representation of Women in AT&T, 1972–1975

AT&T job categories*	End 1972	End 1975
Middle and upper management (1)	2.2%	4.5%
Second-level management (2)	11.2	15.7
Entry-level management and administrative (3 + 4)	44.4	43.6
All management (1–4)	33.3	33.5
Sales (5)	26.5	37.1
Outside crafts (6 + 9)	0.2	1.5
Inside crafts (7 + 10)	6.0	12.8
Clerical (11–13)	96.0	90.8
Operators (14)	98.6	94.4
AVERAGE, all categories	remained 52–53%	
TOTAL EMPLOYMENT	(793,000)	(782,000)

*Job category 8 no longer exists; 15, service workers, is being limited.
SOURCE: Unpublished data from AT&T.

federal laws and regulations does seem to make a difference. (As many observers have noted, the enforcement effort of the 1970s has been very uneven.)

The combination of the two effects

Table 13-8 shows 1970–1975 male-female employment patterns in the very large CB Survey corporations in male-intensive and female-intensive industries. As would be expected, the net improvements for women are generally larger in the female-intensive industries. The only exception is in the professional category. This may be related to the fact that numerically this is a much more important job category in the male-intensive industries. But it may also reflect a distinction in terminology rather than a meaningful difference. Personnel specialists are aware that in large corporations there is no hard-and-fast line of demarcation between someone who is categorized as an individual contributor or a professional and someone who is categorized as a manager or administrator of a particular body of professional or staff work, but who does not have many subordinates. Custom and usage vary widely from company to company and also from industry to industry.[11]

In the very large CB Survey corporations from male-intensive industries there were about an equal number of professional employees and

TABLE 13-7

Changes in Employment
in Upscale Occupations in Some Very Large Corporations, 1970–1975

| Industry | PROPORTION OF WOMEN | | PERCENTAGE CHANGE, 1970–1975 | |
	1970	1975	Total	Female
A. Officials and managers				
Durable goods mfg.	1%	2%	+ 1%	+111%
Nondurable goods mfg.	3	6	+ 22	+161
Transportation	5	4	+ 38	+ 17
Electric and gas utilities	2	3	+ 14	+ 95
Retail trade	22	34	+ 38	+116
Banking	17	30	+ 47	+150
Insurance	6	10	+ 18	+109
B. Professionals				
Durable goods mfg.	4	7	− 5	+ 65
Nondurable goods mfg.	10	15	+ 5	+ 64
Transportation	3	5	+ 11	+ 69
Electric and gas utilities	6	8	+ 30	+ 77
Retail trade	22	40	+ 19	+118
Banking	27	33	+101	+150
Insurance	23	29	+ 8	+ 37
C. Technicians				
Durable goods mfg.	7	8	+ 6	+ 11
Nondurable goods mfg.	21	29	− 1	+ 34
Transportation	5	6	− 18	− 15
Electric and gas utilities	2	6	+ 20	+200
Retail trade	14	29	− 38	+ 26
Banking	19	30	+ 54	+145
Insurance	39	59	+ 41	+111
D. Sales workers				
Durable goods mfg.	1	4	− 16	+118
Nondurable goods mfg.	3	7	− 6	+157
Insurance	1	3	+ 5	+310
E. Skilled craft workers				
Durable goods mfg.	1	2	− 11	+ 46
Nondurable goods mfg.	2	2	+ 7	+ 27
Transportation	†	†	0	− 32
Electric and gas utilities	†	†	+ 18	+850

*In industries where this is an important upscale job category.
†Less than 0.5 percent.
SOURCE: Conference Board Survey.

TABLE 13-8

1970–1975 Changes in Employment in Upscale Occupations
in Some Very Large Corporations
in Male-intensive vs. Female-intensive Industries

Industry	PROPORTION OF WOMEN		PERCENTAGE CHANGE, 1970–1975	
	1970	*1975*	*Total*	*Female*
A. Officials and managers				
Male-intensive industries	2%	3%	+11%	+111%
Female-intensive industries	17	28	+35	+122
B. Professionals				
Male-intensive industries	4	8	+ 2	+ 75
Female-intensive industries	22	30	+15	+ 56
A. and B. Officials and managers plus professionals				
Male-intensive industries	3	5	+ 7	+ 84
Female-intensive industries	18	28	+31	+105
C. Technicians				
Male-intensive industries	8	10	+ 6	+ 27
Female-intensive industries	28	47	+19	+ 99
D. Sales workers				
Male-intensive industries (excluding transportation)	3	6	−17	+ 38
Female-intensive industries (excluding retailing)	2	6	+ 6	+236
E. Skilled craft workers				
Male-intensive industries	1	1	+ 1	+ 49
Female-intensive industries	3	7	+10	+125

SOURCE: Conference Board Survey.

managerial employees; together they constituted 20 percent of the total workforce in 1970 and 22 percent in 1975. In the very large corporations in the female-intensive industries, on the other hand, there were relatively few professionals (3 percent of the total workforce in both 1970 and 1975) and a larger number of managers (12 percent of the total workforce in 1970 and 15 percent in 1975); thus in these companies the two categories combined included 15 percent of the total workforce in 1970 and 18 percent in 1975. Because the available data do not make it possible to separate out the relatively small numbers of middle- and upper-level managers anyway, it might make better sense to consider the changes for women in the combined managerial and professional categories (A and B in Table 13-8).

When this approach is taken, the data then follow the familiar pattern of showing somewhat greater improvement for women in the female-intensive industries.

There has indeed been something special happening for women in many major U.S. corporations, especially in the female-intensive industries. The observed 1970–1975 percentage increases in their numbers in various upscale job categories become even more impressive when one remembers that much of this change has probably occurred since the signing of the AT&T consent decree in January 1973.

Interpreting the overall change patterns

There are, of course, some critics who may say that perhaps all most companies have really done is to take a few women out of certain traditional job categories and redistribute them into the upscale categories showing gains for women. Indeed this would be one way to describe most of the net results achieved in the male-intensive industries, where total female employment was not increasing very much. But the actual change processes themselves have almost certainly been far more complex. They would necessarily include both input and output staffing flows for hundreds of specific jobs in hundreds of companies at hundreds of locations during the full five-year period. Besides, such critics really would have missed the point. The basic thrust of the EEO laws and regulations is indeed to redistribute the kinds of employment opportunities being provided to various groups, not primarily to provide more jobs to the groups. (But it obviously is true that it will be easier to redistribute the job opportunities if, as was happening in many female-intensive industries from 1970 to 1975, the total number of jobs available is growing.)

On the other hand, the mere fact that there is a much higher percentage change in the employment of women than in total employment in an occupational category does not necessarily mean that companies have been practicing "reverse discrimination" against males. Many job openings that occur are simply to replace persons who have quit, retired, been promoted, and so on, and they do not yield any net change in total employment. Companies are required to provide women with equal employment opportunity in all such "replacement" job openings too, so the percentage increase for women—who had previously been denied access to most of the upscale jobs—can easily be many times the percentage increase in total employment without necessarily indicating any unlawful discrimination against men.

Knowledgable observers do point out that it is likely to be several decades before women (and minorities too) come anywhere near parity of representation in many skilled craft jobs and in jobs at the very top echelons of business, especially in high-technology industries. (Some doubt that it will ever happen for women.) And yet a change process leading toward such a result is now clearly under way, and it has already had an important effect in at least some very large U.S. corporations.

Changes in the representation of women in clearly nontraditional occupations

In 1970 there were many whole occupational categories in various industries within the corporate sector—as well as many relatively common, more specific jobs and job families—that could clearly be classified as "nontraditional" areas for women because women represented 10 percent or less of their workforce. Many of these are in the male-intensive industries and, consistent with the other patterns of change already discussed, they have proved especially resistant to rapid change.

For example, in 1970, the Census data showed that out of a total of fifty-two relevant occupation-by-industry categories there were twenty-two in which women represented 10 percent or less of the employees, and these categories included 47 percent of all the male employees in the corporate sector but only 5 percent of the women. By 1975, CPS estimates show that the number of such nontraditional categories had only dropped to sixteen and that they still included 42 percent of all the male employees.

Among the 111 very large CB Survey companies that provided matched 1970 and 1975 data, the picture was even more gloomy. In 1970, out of a total of fifty-seven relevant occupation-by-industry categories, twenty-eight were nontraditional ones for women. They included 64 percent of all male employees, but only 6 percent of the women. And, despite all the changes that have already been discussed, by 1975 the number of these clearly nontraditional categories had only dropped to twenty-five, and they still included 59 percent of all the men employed.

Information was also provided by 207 CB Survey companies with respect to what had been happening to the representation of women in eighty-two more specific nontraditional jobs and job families—jobs in which, according to the 1970 Census, around 30,000 or more people were employed in the corporate sector and in which women represented 10 percent or less of the workforce. By 1975 the overwhelming majority of these very large companies were still lagging behind the specific 1970 Census figures for women in virtually all the jobs that were relevant to their particular operations. The greatest numbers of companies reporting success in improving the representation of women by at least one full percentage point were for the following nontraditional job categories: sales manager, other manager or administrator (excluding office manager), chemist, engineer, drafting technician, utility meter reader, warehouse laborer, janitor, and guard. Skilled blue-collar jobs, along with semiskilled mine operative jobs and jobs as truck drivers, welders, and flamecutters, and apprentices were rarely mentioned as categories into which any sizeable number of women had been successfully introduced.

Seventy-seven companies, many of them from female-intensive industries, also indicated that there were other, more specific kinds of jobs that had been nontraditional ones in their own companies in which they had managed to increase the representation of women substantially. With the exception of chemical process operator, computer programmer, data processing machine operator, and utility meter tester, almost all the jobs they mentioned were in the managerial, professional, and sales representative categories.

Thus, even in their detail, the CB Survey data confirm the general patterns of change that were discussed above.

MAJOR FINDINGS REGARDING CORPORATE
PERSPECTIVES ON THE CHANGE PROCESS ITSELF

Because there apparently has been improvement in the job opportunities being provided to women, it seems especially worthwhile to examine the nature of the change efforts that very large companies have undertaken and also to consider their views of what has helped or hindered the success of these efforts thus far. The findings are based on the responses of 265 very large corporations to the thirty-two–page survey questionnaire in late 1976 and on follow-up telephone interviews and on-site visits conducted in 1976–1977. It should again be noted that these responses may not be typical of the views of all very large U.S. corporations, but they do come from companies providing employment to several million men and women.

It should also be noted that the findings reflect the perceptions, opinions, and attitudes of those in the personnel function at corporate headquarters and do not necessarily fully cover what has been happening at all the hundreds of establishments such major U.S. corporations may have. The questionnaires were addressed to the senior personnel executives of the companies.[12] It was made plain that they were expected to draw upon their existing fund of knowledge about what had been going on in their company and not to conduct an internal survey of all locations. Similarly, the initial follow-up interviews were with headquarters' personnel executives or staff members, although in some cases additional on-site interviews with line managers or local personnel staff members were arranged. Generally speaking, the employees whose job assignments were being discussed were not interviewed, but a considerable number of them were observed at work.

Consistent with the male-female employment patterns already discussed, most of the companies reported that it has been necessary to try to increase the representation of women in at least some of the jobs in all of their EEO-1 job categories—except for the office and clerical category. The greatest emphasis, however, is clearly being given to improving the opportunities for women as officials and managers and as professionals (especially in male-intensive industries). In a limited number of companies moving more women into certain kinds of sales jobs is receiving the greatest stress. But very few companies employing blue-collar workers are placing the greatest emphasis on increasing the representation of women in this part of their workforce, not even for skilled craft jobs.

Among the reasons commonly offered for the heavy emphasis on the upscale white-collar jobs are the greater availability of qualified, willing candidates both internally and externally; the restricted availability of blue-collar job openings; the higher visibility of the managerial or professional jobs; the importance of providing female role models at higher organization levels in order to encourage women at lower levels to try to move up too; the fact that these are the entry jobs for recent female college graduates who are likely to move on up in management; the greater control exerted by the headquarters personnel group with respect to these jobs; the need for the whole headquarters unit to take a leadership role so that it can then insist on other units following suit; pressure from compliance review officers; and (especially from some companies in male-intensive industries) the fact that these categories are likely to be the most difficult ones in which to make progress in equality.

But even though the greatest emphasis has clearly been placed on only two particular occupational categories, it should not be assumed that most companies have set up special programs to hire and train groups of women for these jobs. The clearest and most important finding with respect to how major companies are going about increasing the representation of women at these organizational levels is that they are relying on working through the organization's basic staffing processes for filling individual job openings and not primarily on special programming.

The problem of improving the job opportunities being provided to women (and minorities as well) is generally being addressed as a problem that the whole organization must solve and not as one that can be delegated to the personnel department. While such staff specialists obviously have important supporting and assisting roles to play in the overall process, in most of the companies it is the line managers who are expected to implement the change process and who are held accountable for making sure it happens. Moreover, it is generally not merely the lower levels of line management that are expected to take appropriate action. Top management is very much involved, especially in the more successful efforts. Interrelated goals and timetables are being established for improving the representation of women in jobs where they are underutilized at these organizational levels, taking realistic account of the expected staffing flows, of the genuine qualifications required to perform the various jobs, and of the maximum present and probable future availability of appropriately qualified women, assuming significant employer effort.

This is, of course, essentially what is called for under the executive order, but the scope of the planning being done is much larger than the regulations require. That is, the planning is being done on an interrelated basis for the whole organization, not merely for each separate establishment. Thus, far from considering a "goals and timetables" approach as a meaningless paperwork exercise needed to satisfy government reporting regulations, most of the companies now say goals and timetables are being used as corporate-wide planning and control tools with respect to the appropriate utilization of human resources, especially at the managerial and professional levels. The fulfillment of these plans is regarded as just as much a part of each line manager's job as any other aspect of managing the work unit. Indeed, some companies note that they have found meeting EEO goals and timetables to be one of the key indicators distinguishing their good line managers from their less successful ones. Thus, those who are constructively and successfully assisting the organization to meet its EEO challenge are reported to be among those most likely to benefit substantially from their managerial performance, both in terms of salary and also in terms of further promotions—even though from now on a larger share of all such promotions will be going to qualified women and minorities.

Consistent evidence was found in the interviews and in the questionnaire responses that the majority of the very large companies taking part in the CB Survey are convinced that an overall management-by-objectives approach to human resource utilization is the most appropriate response to the EEO challenge their organizations face under federal laws and regulations. Some of the questionnaire findings that bear on this point are worth discussing in detail.

Factors contributing to the overall success of the company's efforts to improve job opportunities for women

Those responding to the questionnaire were presented with a list of twenty-three factors (plus room to add more) and were asked to number from 1 to 10 those they considered to have made the greatest contribution to the overall success of their company's efforts. The order of responses, when combined in appropriately weighted form, is:

1. Awareness of federal laws and regulations
2. Commitment on the part of the chief executive officer

3. Establishment of goals and timetables for action
4. Development of an equal employment opportunity policy
5. Analysis of the company's utilization of women
6. Awareness of large back pay awards in class action suits
7. Monitoring of EEO results vs. plans
8. Dissemination of the EEO policy
9. Identification of special problem areas in utilizing women
10. Changes in personnel practices or special programs to improve opportunities for women

The order of the first three items on the list is very clear cut. It is also noteworthy that changes in personnel practices and special programming for women barely made the "Top Ten" list. And, although the general goals and timetables approach called for under the executive order received high marks, the risk of losing government contracts and rigorous compliance reviews as a government contractor both received scant mention, while the risks of a Title VII class action suit were perceived as very real. (Under this law individuals, as well as the EEOC itself, can bring class action lawsuits that may require up to two years' back pay for large groups of employees.) On the other hand, relatively few companies reported that an actual complaint, investigation, or lawsuit alleging sex discrimination had had special importance in spurring their efforts to improve job opportunities for women. An even smaller number reported that the formation of a women's caucus or council within the company or pressure from an outside women's group had made a significant difference.

One of the personnel executives interviewed summed up the situation this way:

> It may seem surprising in these days of Watergate, bribery scandals, and what not, but I really do believe that most large U.S. corporations try very hard to be law-abiding citizens. EEO was an area where it took us a while to understand what the law really meant, but those class action lawsuits proved very effective teachers. And, when the light finally dawned, we really went to work on it. Besides, now we realize that it makes darn good sense.
>
> How do you go about achieving EEO results in a company? The same way you achieve any other results. You analyze the problem carefully, determine what you need to do, and then set up an overall management planning and control system to make very sure it happens—and on schedule.

The importance of a results-oriented management planning and control system

Prior survey research on the changing nature of the corporate personnel function had already indicated that centralized planning and monitoring systems were being developed with respect to EEO matters.[13] Moreover, during the pilot study for this research, a number of companies reported that the single most successful action their organizations had taken to improve job opportunities for women was to set up an overall, results-oriented management planning and control system in order to ensure that the achievement of this objective received the appropriate attention at all levels of the organization on an ongoing basis. To test the current prevalence and perceived effectiveness of such a corporate approach, the companies participating in the full-scale survey were asked for their reactions to it, based on their own experience. The percentages for various corporate responses are shown in the tabulation below:

- We have not established an overall management system in this area —27 percent
- Maybe; it certainly has proved important, but so have other actions we have taken—27 percent
- Yes; this is the single most successful action we have taken too— 22 percent
- Maybe; it's too early to tell because our management system is new —11 percent
- No; we have such a system, but other actions we have taken have proven more important to our success—5 percent
- We have had no real success in improving job opportunities for women—2 percent
- No opinion—5 percent
- No answer—1 percent

This confirms that at least 65 percent of the responding companies relied on such an overall management system in the EEO area and that the vast majority of those that did ascribed important positive value to it. Indeed, fully one-third of the companies indicating experience with such an approach said it was the single most effective action regarding EEO matters their companies had ever taken.

Profiles of successful experiences compared with profiles of disappointing experiences

Companies were asked to describe in considerable detail one of their more successful experiences in improving job opportunities for women. It could be a broad effort or a limited program; the only stipulation was that it must have been in actual operation long enough for them to be able to evaluate its success. Then, in an exactly parallel format, they were asked to describe a disappointing experience. This device permitted comparison of the profiles of the two sets of experiences, sometimes holding constant characteristics, such as the nature of the jobs being filled.

All told, 195 "successful experiences" and 106 "disappointing experiences were reported, with more than three-fourths of each group of experiences reported as beginning in 1973 or later. While it relates only to the examples the companies chose to report and not to the whole of their efforts on behalf of women, this information about timing does tend to confirm that the AT&T consent decree significantly stimulated greater corporate action.

The proportions of the success stories dealing with improving opportunities for women in the various EEO-1 job categories were as follows:

Officials and managers—52 percent
Professionals—48 percent (with a substantial number of the reports also dealing with the managerial category)
Technicians—20 percent (with a substantial number of the reports also dealing with both the professional and managerial category)
Sales workers—20 percent
Office and clerical workers—7 percent
Skilled craft workers—9 percent
Semiskilled operatives—10 percent
Unskilled laborers—9 percent
White-collar trainees—9 percent (especially in banks and insurance companies)
Production trainees—1 percent

This information not only confirmed the emphasis reportedly being given to upscale white-collar occupations, but it is also in conformity with other available information about the typical boundaries of various corporate staffing efforts.[14]

By contrast, the disappointing experiences that were reported tended to be much more evenly spread across the various EEO-1 job categories with much lower proportions of them dealing with the officials and managers category (29 percent), professionals (25 percent), technicians (8 percent), and sales workers (11 percent), and much higher proportions of them dealing with blue-collar jobs (skilled crafts—24 percent; semiskilled operatives —22 percent; unskilled laborers—17 percent). The disappointing experiences reported with blue-collar jobs are more likely to involve unionized employees than the few success stories do, but it seems inappropriate to generalize on this point because the total number of reports is so limited and there are so many other factors, such as the recession, influencing the situation.

There is also a major distinction between the general staffing strategies being followed in the success stories and the disappointing experiences, as Table 13-9 shows. The fact that the emphasis was much more likely to be on both initial hiring and internal movement of women in the success

TABLE 13-9
Basic Approaches Companies Used

Staffing	*Successful experiences*	*Disappointing experiences*
Bringing in women as new employees	24%	44%
Upgrading, transferring, or promoting present female employees	29	26
Both	44	20
Other/NA	3	10
TOTAL, no. of companies	(195)	(106)

stories is compatible with reliance on an ongoing managed process rather than on special programming.

The questionnaire provided a list of twenty-four different activities (plus space to write in others) that companies could indicate were part of each successful or disappointing experience and also, as a separate item, could indicate were crucial to that experience. While many activities, such as recruiting, selection, and job-related training/development, tended to be mentioned with about equal frequency in the success stories and in the disappointing stories, there were certain activities that were much more likely to be mentioned in the success stories and also much more likely to be regarded as crucial to such experiences. These were special preparation of supervisors/managers; career planning/pathing; and job analysis. The follow-up interviews indicated that the supervisory preparation in successful efforts is most likely to deal with the organization's overall EEO obligations and with the basic responsibility of line managers for achieving EEO results. It often includes some guidance with respect to interviewing and evaluating female candidates' qualifications and subsequent job performance fairly. Only in rare instances does it deal with matters of "female psychology." (Indeed, there are experience-based warnings that this kind of emphasis can easily backfire unless it is handled by specially qualified experts. Problems have also been encountered with "consciousness-raising" sessions for male managers which did not take place within the authority structure of the organization and did not offer them a constructive way to release any anxiety generated—for instance, by enlisting their active cooperation in helping the organization to meet its EEO challenge.)

The questionnaire also provided an opportunity for companies to indicate what individuals or groups were involved in various aspects of the successful/disappointing experiences. Once again there was much overlap in what was being reported. But even when the kinds of jobs being filled are held constant, the following differences are found in the successful experiences: Top management and the personnel executive (not merely personnel staff members) were more likely to be crucially involved in the initial planning and organizing. Top management and the personnel executive were more likely to be crucially involved in providing ongoing advice or counsel. The line managers were more likely to be involved in carrying out or doing the activities (but for professional jobs the personnel staff was likely to have major responsibilities for college recruiting). The personnel executive (not merely personnel staff members) was more likely to be officially monitoring the results. Top management was more likely also to be receiving feedback of the results. Top management, line managers, and the personnel executive were all more likely to have the assigned accountability for the success of the program (but for blue-collar jobs members of the local personnel staff are more likely to be among those held accountable than the corporate personnel executive). In short, regardless of the kind of jobs being filled, the successful experiences reported were clearly more likely to be part of a corporate-wide managed effort than the disappointing experiences were. However, because a so much larger proportion of the "successful experiences" than of the "disappointing experiences" deal with improving the job opportunities for women in the officials and managers and professional job categories, this finding may also indicate that few of the CB Survey companies have as yet extended their overall corporate human resource planning and control systems to cover all the EEO-1 job categories. (Indeed, the kind of computer-based information system covering all U.S. employees that is necessary for doing this may not as yet be in place in many of these organizations.)

Efforts to increase the supply of qualified women

The majority of the companies needing to increase the representation of women in their upscale white-collar jobs reported undertaking some joint or cooperative efforts with other organizations for the purpose of increasing the available supply of qualified women. Collaboration with four-year colleges and universities as well as contacts with professional associations were frequently mentioned in relation to increasing the number of women qualified to be officials and managers, professionals, and white-collar trainees.

But when it comes to the blue-collar jobs, the picture seems quite different. Possibly because such efforts exist but are not known to those at corporate headquarters, less than half of the companies needing to increase the representation of women in blue-collar jobs have reported they have been working with other organizations to increase the available supply of qualified women. Those that have done this have worked primarily with unions, community organizations, two-year colleges or private vocational schools, and government agencies.

GENERAL OPINIONS ABOUT CORPORATE EFFORTS TO IMPROVE JOB OPPORTUNITIES

Given the results-oriented thrust of the legal challenge they face, most of the very large companies responding to the CB Survey were understandably cautious in describing their overall success in improving job opportunities for women. Many said their efforts had been somewhat successful (45 percent) or had yielded a mixed bag in terms of success (24 percent, many of them companies from male-intensive industries). Only 10 percent considered their efforts very successful and only 6 percent said they had been either somewhat or very unsuccessful. An additional 8 percent indicated it was too early to tell (some candidly admitted little effort had as yet been made, but others regarded their effort as too complex to be evaluated as yet), and 7 percent did not respond.

The most common comment with respect to the overall success of their corporate efforts was that, while there already was improvement in the company's overall EEO-1 statistics, a considerably longer period of time would be required to achieve good representation of women at the higher levels of responsibility. Sometimes this was attributed to legitimate job experience requirements or to the lack of personnel turnover at higher organization levels, but it was also sometimes noted that it would take time to break down the "typical stereotyped negative attitudes" male managers have about women. On the other hand, a number of the companies do note that many more women are being promoted to much higher-level jobs than ever before in the company's history. The most common comments regarding an overall lack of success dealt with the effect of the recession and the lack of qualified candidates for engineering jobs or for "physical labor" jobs.

As Table 13-10 indicates, most companies volunteered that they have gained some important benefits from their efforts to improve the job opportunities they provide to women—benefits that go far beyond complying with governmental laws and regulations. Their written comments most frequently centered on more appropriate human resource utilization and changed employee attitudes, but there is also mention of improved personnel policies and practices, changed management perceptions, and improved community relations. The following quotation captures the flavor of many of the comments:

> As a corporate program, there has been an overall upgrading of the workforce. Objective criteria for employment decisions have become

TABLE 13-10
Primary Benefits for the Company
from Efforts to Improve Job Opportunities for Women

Benefit	Companies in female-intensive industries	Companies in male-intensive industries
More appropriate human resource utilization		
Better utilization of the talents available within the organization	28%	12%
Women constitute a previously untapped source of competent employees for many jobs	19	33
Better talent employed or promoted when women compete with men for positions	10	2
Women have proved effective, high-caliber, successful employees; productivity is good	8	4
Economies due to promoting from within compared to hiring	3	
Lower turnover		3
Other	2	1
Changed employee attitudes		
Improved morale, especially among the women	13	8
Improved morale of all employees	2	
Greater motivation to improve performance and prepare for promotion; having successful role models has encouraged others to try	7	6
More confidence in personnel function; greater credibility due to correcting past inequities	1	3
Other	1	2
Improved compliance posture		
Reduced chance of lawsuits	6	11
Better EEO statistics	4	
Successful compliance reviews; retained contracts	7	3
Other	1	1

TABLE 13-10 (Continued)

Benefit	Companies in female-intensive industries	Companies in male-intensive industries
Improved personnel policies and practices		
More open, objective personnel practices for all		5
Greater internal movement; more emphasis on training and development; more emphasis on career planning and counselling	3	3
Changed management perceptions		
Myths about "women's work" disspelled; awareness of women's potential for high-ranking positions	5	3
A learning process regarding personnel function	1	1
Improved community relations		
Community approval of efforts	3	3
Appropriate response to social change/needs		2
Other	1	1
TOTAL, no. of companies	(107)	(158)

practice, hence all persons are considered for positions on the basis of merit. Previously untapped human resources are now available. Healthy competition for advancement exists. Legal pressures from the compliance agency have been relieved.

Some of the companies said they have been especially surprised by the remarkably competent performance of women on some nontraditional jobs and also by the rapid acceleration in the number of women expressing interest in career opportunities—and willing to put the time and effort into enhancing their qualifications to advance—once there were a few successful role models. One commentator may have mixed his similes and metaphors a bit, but he certainly got the point across when he wrote: "Getting started was like trying to move a dead elephant with a toothpick. But those first few women were so darned competent they uncorked the whole system."

Generally speaking, companies volunteered far fewer negative comments about their efforts to improve job opportunities for women. Indeed, as Table 13-11 shows, their most common comment was "None." Some did say there had been a negative reaction from some male employees, but they also indicated it had certainly not been an overwhelming problem. Lack of interest on the part of women in the proffered job opportunities was viewed as a special problem by companies in male-intensive industries; there were complaints about high recruiting and training costs from these industries too. Higher turnover was apparently a problem in some non-traditional jobs. And it led to unexpected frustration on the part of line managers when they could not maintain the EEO results they thought they had achieved. The recession, with its massive layoffs based on seniority in some blue-collar jobs, also produced some unexpected pitfalls.

Most of the companies did report that equal employment opportunity considerations (for minorities as well as women) have had real impact on their basic personnel policies and practices. Thirty-nine percent said this impact had been very significant and an additional 36 percent categorized the impact as moderate. Only 14 percent said the impact has been slight

TABLE 13-11

Primary Negatives for the Company
from Efforts to Improve Job Opportunities for Women

Negatives	*Companies in female-intensive industries*	*Companies in male-intensive industries*
None	12%	8%
Male employee reactions		
"Reverse discrimination"	11	
Resentment by those expecting promotions	4	7
Resistance; difficult-to overcome male stereotypes	4	6
Other	4	1
Female employee and applicant reactions		
Lack of interest among present female employees		6
Lack of qualified applicants	1	3
Unrealistic aspirations among some employees	2	2
Unwillingness of women to move	3	2
Disbelief/disillusionment due to slow progress		2
Other	1	1

TABLE 13-11 (Continued)

Negatives	Companies in female-intensive industries	Companies in male-intensive industries
Costs and personnel turnover		
Increased recruiting and training costs	3	6
Higher turnover in some nontraditional jobs	6	3
Increased operating/ facilities costs		2
High costs of paperwork, controls, administration	3	2
Considerable effort for small results		2
Other	1	1
Management problems		
Improper selection of women for some jobs	1	3
Failure to support women who were promoted, encouraging their failure	2	1
Top management slow to accept idea; tokenism	3	1
Other	1	1
Community reactions		
Adverse publicity		1
TOTAL, no. of companies	(107)	(158)

or unimportant, while 11 percent said it is too early to tell or did not answer.

At the same time, the workload of the personnel department has increased very significantly and the nature of its relationship to the rest of the organization has changed. Comments such as these indicate the scope and magnitude of the challenge the EEO effort has posed: "EEO considerations have broadly resulted in a more purposeful and professional personnel practice." "EEO requires more management capability both in the personnel department and throughout the organization." "EEO is a good management tool." "EEO is now one of three corporate goals." Of course, not all companies view the EEO challenge quite so favorably. Most real dissenters probably did not bother to respond to the questionnaire at all, but this partially dissenting view was expressed by a major company in a male-intensive industry: "Government has forced a structural system of employment practices on the private sector. Although there are some benefits, implementation has been costly and disruptive."

Advice as to how senior personnel executives might best help their company avoid unnecessary problems in this area included the following: Clear-cut top management commitment and continuing active, strong support are essential. Proper organization of the effort is also crucial; insist on involvement and accountability from top to bottom. A managed, overall accountability system is necessary. Emphasize quality; tell managers they must expect a good job and a full job from women as well as men. Be realistic and recognize that you must take action *now;* do it voluntarily or your company will be in for a tough time. Develop a long-term approach, not a short-run "crash" solution; be sure to think through the potential problems that may occur, for many of the pitfalls leave difficult-to-modify effects. Make sure the first woman in a nontraditional area is very competent and will be a strong role model; a failure is very hard to overcome. Explain the program to everyone and enlist their active cooperation. Expect and overcome male manager resistance. Encourage the women to think through their own career goals and how the company can help them get there.

Generally speaking, the comments suggest that, due to EEO concerns, a thorough-going review and reassessment of personnel policies and practices has been undertaken which has resulted in: (1) the modification or elimination of many outmoded or unnecessary procedures and practices; (2) the introduction of some new procedures and practices especially with respect to college recruiting for upscale white-collar jobs and also to the operation of the internal labor market; (3) the standardization and wider dissemination of information about all personnel policies and practices; (4) centralized planning, monitoring, and control of their impact at least for managerial and professional employees. There is considerably greater stress on the consistent application of clearly defined personnel policies, including the equal employment opportunity policy, and much greater attention to appropriate personnel record-keeping, not only with respect to individuals but also with respect to the various groups protected by law. In most cases the companies indicated these changes have been of real value to all employees, not just to minorities and women, and also to the company.

Thus, in addition to their direct effects on the job opportunities available to women and minorities, the U.S. EEO laws and regulations have stimulated significant changes in corporate personnel management. Senior personnel executives have been shifting their perspectives. Most no longer focus on administering various personnel activities as a service to the rest of the organization. Instead, recognizing the risks their companies run if they fail to do this, most now focus on the management of outcomes—on monitoring the overall operations of the company's human resource system and on assisting line managers to modify the organization's policies and practices in order to achieve appropriately balanced, nondiscriminatory results that are compatible with the safe and efficient operation of the business.

NOTES

1. The Equal Pay Act of 1963, P. L. 88–38.
2. Griggs *v.* Duke Power Co., 401 U.S. 424 (1971).
3. Revised Order No. 4 was effective December 4, 1971. It has since been further revised in other particulars, most recently effective February 17, 1977. The regulations appear at 41 CFR 60-2. The issuing agency is now known as the Office of Federal Contract Compliance Programs (OFCCP) of the Department of Labor.
4. In signing a consent agreement with an administrative agency a company does not admit to any unlawful acts, but informed observers note that such an agreement is not likely to be signed unless the company feels it risks an even more unfavorable outcome by allowing a lawsuit to proceed. For a fuller discussion of developments under the federal nondiscrimination laws, including the contents of both the AT&T consent decree and the subsequent supplemental order, see *Nondiscrimination in Employment, Changing Perspectives, 1963–1972* (Conference Board Report 589; New York: The Board, 1973) and *Nondiscrimination in Employment, 1973–1975: A Broadening and Deepening National Effort* (Conference Board Report 677; New York: The Board, 1976), both by Ruth Gilbert Shaeffer.
5. The Conference Board is an independent, nonprofit organization established in 1916. It develops and disseminates objective information on a wide variety of management and economic topics in order to improve the quality and effectiveness of business leadership in serving the various publics to which it is accountable and to create broader understanding of business and economic activity. It is supported primarily by annual contributions from organizations, most of whom are large corporations but some of whom are not—for example, government agencies, labor unions, hospitals, colleges and universities.
6. This first project may serve to demonstrate the value of similar studies in other sectors. Partial funding has been provided by the Rockefeller Family Fund, The Ford Foundation, and Mobil Oil Corporation. The bulk of the work has, however, been financed by the Conference Board itself.
7. *Improving Job Opportunities for Women: A Chartbook Focusing on the Progress in Business* (Conference Board Report 744; New York: The Board, 1978) by Ruth Gilbert Shaeffer and Helen Axel has now been published. A companion volume, *Corporate Experiences in Improving Women's Job Opportunities* (Conference Board Report 755), by Ruth Gilbert Shaeffer and Edith F. Lynton, will soon be available.

8. There may turn out to be some limited exceptions to this statement. For example, if a "bona fide seniority system" which has a discriminatory effect exists, actions taken in accordance with it are exempt from Title VII, but they may not be exempt from the executive order. Or a company may, under the executive order, voluntarily set up a very expensive training program lasting several years that it might not be required to provide under Title VII. Matters such as these are currently being litigated.

9. See, for example, *Senter* v. *General Motors Corp.* (Sixth Circuit Court of Appeals), 532 F. 2d 511 (1976). The Supreme Court refused to review this decision.

10. This is not certain because most job openings that occur are not for new jobs; rather, they are to replace employees who have either left the company or moved into different jobs. Voluntary employee turnover is usually lower when employment is declining because people are afraid they may not be able to find other suitable jobs.

11. For a further discussion of such matters see *Monitoring the Human Resource System* (Conference Board Report 717; New York: The Board, 1977) by Ruth Gilbert Shaeffer, pp. 7–18.

12. These executives were asked to respond personally or to turn the questionnaire over to someone else on the corporate staff, such as an affirmative action officer or the EEO coordinator, who was even more knowledgable about the topic.

13. See *The Personnel Function: Changing Objectives and Organization* (Conference Board Report 712; New York: The Board, 1977) by Allen R. Janger.

14. See *Staffing Systems, Managerial and Professional Jobs* (Conference Board Report 558; New York: The Board, 1972) by Ruth Gilbert Shaeffer.

14 *Rosabeth Moss Kanter*

THE IMPACT OF ORGANIZATION STRUCTURE: MODELS AND METHODS FOR CHANGE

For the past five years, my colleagues and I have been developing an approach to the problem of equity for women in employment.[1] The approach has implications both for effective diagnosis of the problem and for effective change strategies. It is based on an examination of the structure of organizations, in both formal and informal senses, and of the ways in which individuals' structural positions affect their relative advantage or disadvantage in the organization, their prospects for further advancement and influence, and their characteristic styles of work behavior and work engagement.

One can not evaluate the question of equality, we suggest, without understanding more fully how positions that appear to be at the same level of authority or status may, in fact, differ in important structural features. What appear to be behavioral predispositions of women in the workplace— at least in the United States, and perhaps in other Western countries— may instead be the characteristic behaviors and styles induced by particular kinds of structural positions in organizations in which women have been disproportionately found, since men in similar structural positions exhibit many of the same tendencies. In fact, our approach permits us to pinpoint those structural features of organizations that, because of the explanatory value of the framework, may represent the most potent targets for change and the intervention possibilities with the most leverage.

Identifying the causes of inequities and perceived limitations to women's equal opportunity cannot be ignored, for the effectiveness of any intervention strategy is inextricably bound up with how adequately one diagnoses the sources of the problem. If the problem is located primarily in women's biology or temperament, their prior socialization, or their role pressures as members of families, then programs and practices oriented at changing something about the women themselves or their social situation will be suggested. But if the problem is analyzed in terms of organizational policies and practices, career paths and access to them, or other features of the design of work systems, then employing organizations themselves should be the target of change efforts. (I will also later point to the strategic advantages of organizational approaches and interventions and suggest some principles that any system-change efforts should follow.)

The model outlined here has been developed from over five years of research in a major U.S. industrial organization and extensive review of the existing research literature, as well as the results of a number of replications in settings ranging from factories to law schools to academic administrations. The interventions are based on several years of activity, in collaboration with colleagues, as an organizational consultant not only on affirmative action but also on more general issues of opportunity and organizational effectiveness. One large systems-change model that is currently being developed and has been in operation for the past nine months in a major corporation will be described in somewhat more detail.

OPPORTUNITY: ITS STRUCTURE AND IMPLICATIONS

Opportunity is the first major structural variable that is central to our approach. Opportunity means access to career development in its fullest sense: to growth, to increased skills, to increased influence and voice in decisions, and to advancement in pay and status. Even though opportunity can have these multiple meanings, in most large corporations it tends to be defined solely in terms of upward mobility, for without advance in status and rank most organizations do not know how to let their employees develop and contribute in other ways. Opportunity is structured and built into the design of jobs and their location in the system in terms of their connection with other jobs and their prospects for mobility. In many corporations the opportunity structure tends to divide jobs into roughly two kinds: those with a great deal of opportunity—with many ladder steps, a high ceiling, frequent promotions, expectation that people will be moving on to better jobs, and attention to training or the development of new skills; and those with low opportunity—short ladders, low ceilings, very few options for movement into other jobs, infrequent promotions, little expectation that people will move on to better jobs, and no attention to training or skill development. It is important to note that what is critical here is not job content or pay, but rather the job's standing in a chain of other jobs.

This differentiation of opportunity has implications for women's position in organizations, since most managerial and professional jobs are designed to be high in opportunity, while practically all clerical jobs and a great many factory jobs—particularly the ones in which women are clustered—tend to be formally low in opportunity. But it is also this difference that explains many of the findings about differences in motivation and work style between women and men. High- and low-opportunity positions tend to breed two very different styles of involvement in work and thus two different "ideal types" of people: what I call "the moving" and "the stuck." Much of the behavior that has been attributed to women in the workplace emerges as behavior characteristics of stuckness, for men who are stuck exhibit the same tendencies. Of course, some differences stem from whether stuckness is an individual or a group experience. Those whose job prospects, and those of their peer group, have always involved limited opportunity are much less likely to exhibit frustration or discontent, and are much more likely to turn to their peers for support and work satisfaction, than are those who become stuck higher up in the corporate hierarchy because they have "reached their level" after prior mobility and find no more openings above them. This distinction—and others which describe in more detail the theoretical framework and the data on which it is based—can be found in *Men and Women of the Corporation.*[2]

The moving tend to differ from the stuck in ways that set self-fulfilling prophecies in motion. Those in moving positions are not only in the formal position of being eligible for advancement, but also tend to behave in ways that confirm their selection as those who should be moving along the corporate ladder. On the other hand, those who are stuck tend, as a result of their situation, to act in ways that confirm the organization's lack of attention to them. These are cycles of advantage and cycles of disadvantage in which individual characteristics and structural position interact to keep the moving moving and the stuck stuck. (In a sense, it does not matter whether the individual characteristics preceded the position the person finds herself in, for the two are mutually reinforcing via a series of feedback loops between individual and position.)

Opportunity affects such key organizational behavior variables as aspirations, self-esteem, work engagement, self-preparation, and style of expressing dissatisfaction. The moving tend to have or develop higher aspirations and to aim for higher positions, in large part because they can already see themselves on a path leading to those positions. The stuck, however, tend to limit and lower their aspirations, and appear to be less motivated to achieve, because they lack a sense that better and higher positions are realistically attainable. (I call this concept—that it takes the experience of being realistically able to reach a position to arouse aspirations for it—the "Gerald Ford Syndrome.")

The moving also have higher self-esteem and tend to recognize in themselves, and use, more skills. Their high opinion of themselves makes it easy for them to volunteer for assignments above their heads or to stretch to meet new challenges, because they are certain they will succeed as a result of being on the high-opportunity tracks. The stuck, in contrast, tend to think less well of themselves and to underrate and devalue their skills and abilities, whether they are in a job category that has always been stuck by design or whether they got stuck after the experience of mobility and begin to question whether they do, indeed, possess the right kinds of skills for success. The stuck, therefore, are much less likely to perceive themselves as skilled, to make their skills or abilities known, or to feel that they can carry out assignments for which they do not already have the experience; they are unlikely to give the organization any indication that they deserve to do more than the job in which they are currently stuck. It is easy to see how attitudes and behavior that develop out of an individual's job experience reinforce the organization's structural differentiation of people into those who are mobile and deserve advancement and those who are not.

The moving are also much more likely than the stuck to become highly work engaged and even committed to the organization, although the commitment is often to the experience of mobility and achievement. They are much more likely to talk about work as a major source of life investment and satisfaction, whereas the stuck, at every level of the organization and almost regardless of how they got stuck, are likely either to become "psychic drops," putting in their time while making their major life investments elsewhere, or actually to dream of escape from the organization into some realm which gives them a greater sense of growth possibilities. To caricature this a bit, if women in clerical jobs dream of escape to run a family, then men in blue-collar jobs tend to dream of escape to run a gas station, and men in professional careers to start a consulting firm. If these situations are all seen as work realms, as they in fact are, then the similarities become apparent.

The greater engagement of the moving also shows up in the extent to which they begin to prepare themselves in advance for their next job— what sociologists call "anticipatory socialization." The moving, anticipating advancement, are likely to train themselves in the skills, attitudes, and even physical appearance styles that they will need for the job into which they are about to move. Organizations, by the way, pay a price for too much mobility, and for too much emphasis on advancement as reward, because the moving often engage in self-training for advancement at the expense of increased competence in the present position. The stuck are much more likely to invest themselves in perfecting details of the present job, in part because they do not see themselves as heading anywhere, and in part because they are interested in competence and mastery. This increased competence in the present job, however, does not help the stuck look better to the organization in advancement terms, but, if anything, only reinforces their stuckness; in a position where mobility is not expected, mastery of the job merely makes someone even more indispensible.

Finally, the moving are likely to be much more active about expressing dissatisfaction and much more constructive in their style of protesting or expressing grievance. They are likely to be more optimistic about being listened to by decision-makers and about the potential or the capacity to change. The stuck, on the other hand, often turn into what they are labeled in many organizations: "dead wood." Much more likely to gripe from the sidelines, they become conservative resisters who are always complaining, interested in getting something more for themselves but rarely constructive when it comes to suggestions for improving the organization.

This analysis reinterprets some classic ideas and research findings: that women have lower aspirations, lower self-esteem, less investment in work, less interest in self-preparation for advancement, and more passive, conservative styles than do men. Aside from the fact that any such findings reflect generalizations that never fit the entire population of men or women, and that a look at the real world provides many examples of women in high-opportunity positions who behave differently, still, it becomes clear that these are not characteristics of women but of stuckness. To the extent that women find themselves more frequently in low-opportunity situations, they are likely to be subject to the same tendencies that men exhibit in similar low-opportunity situations. This then directs us to an organization's opportunity structure as the major target for change efforts.

POWER: ITS STRUCTURE AND IMPLICATIONS

Power is the capacity to mobilize resources, human or material. It refers to influence and resource-access in the organization, in conjunction with, or in addition to, whatever formal authority (accountability for tasks or the actions of others) is contained in the official definition of a job. It derives from the informal system of an organization as much as from its formal definitions of authority, for it is clear that power does not automatically derive from the formal designations of "who is in charge." Relative degrees of actual power, based on one's informal system relationship as well as the potential of one's job, account for who is most likely to be influential in defining and shaping organizational policies and decisions, as well as who is most likely to have the resources needed to gain the cooperation of subordinates and get the job done. In organizational terms, power is defined then as an issue of systemic connections and the degree of influence over the environment both upward and outward, rather than as an attribute of the individual.

Relative organizational power or powerlessness is significant in two ways. First, it impacts directly on the question of which people are in the best position to influence or shape organizational goals, policies, and decisions. Secondly, to the extent that people's location in a power structure contributes to leadership style and capacity and to follower morale, power differences determine who becomes and is seen as effective and is thus given the chance to accumulate more power. As with opportunity, there are cycles of advantage and cycles of disadvantage built into differentiation between the powerful—who are also in a position to accumulate more power—and the relatively powerless—whose behavior is likely to reinforce their situation.

Power is not equivalent to hierarchical position or to such measures of formal authority as number of subordinates. (Elaboration of the concept, its meaning, and its measurement is developed in detail elsewhere.[3]) In general, it is possible to differentiate both a formal and an informal aspect of system location that help determine the accumulation of power: one through job characteristics and the other through alliances in the organization. The analysis of both these makes clear that women are much more likely, by traditional placement and current organizational situation, to be in the more powerless locations in the system, even if formal level and title are roughly equivalent. This again, as with opportunity, has a direct impact on the potential for accumulating more power, or decision-making capacity, and an indirect impact on behavior and effectiveness.

Job activities contribute to power when they are extraordinary—that is, pioneering, nonroutine, discretionary; when they are visible to others—linked to people both inside and outside the work unit, in contact with other activities and functions, central in information flow networks, with clearly identifiable and measurable contributions; and when they are relevant to current organizational problems—handling environmental contingencies, at the center of crisis or problematic activities, considered central to current organizational goals. Historically, even in management and professional positions, women have usually been clustered in the most routinized, least visible, and most peripheral activities, and thus have been most likely to be limited in a formal sense in the accumulation of power. But many men also find themselves in high-routine–low-discretion positions with hidden contributions and away from the mainstream of currently pressing contingencies.

Power also accumulates through alliances—informal network connections. This side of power is more hidden and elusive than the first, since it is not an official part of an organization's operations and may even be masked in the interest of presenting a nondiscriminatory face. In addition, the matter of alliances shades off into friendships, and friendships are considered private and voluntary, not something the organization controls, and therefore not something for which it institutionally can be held accountable. The fact that cliques form in part on the basis of social similarity raises a question of whether this is "natural human preference" or a sign of discriminatory intent. It is also hard, in this domain, to show that alliances have any job-related or official relevance at all, regardless of common sense observations that they do. Does the existence of private men's clubs really handicap executive women? Enough to hurt them in their jobs? What is the evidence? And even if the private clubs are opened, what is to prevent their members from retreating and closing another door? Yet, despite these difficulties in analyzing, measuring, and intervening in the informal network side of organizations, it is still possible and even critical to examine this aspect. It can be shown that organizations, through their policies and job placements, can do some things to put individuals into more favorable or less favorable positions with respect to power-generating alliances.

Three kinds of alliances contribute to organizational power: those with subordinates, those with peers, and those with sponsors. People accumulate power by promoting the careers of subordinates, but this is often based on system location—on whether one is in a position to supervise any subordinates at all, to influence their careers, and to place them. Women in management have often been excluded from this kind of network-building, for they have been clustered in staff positions with few or no subordinates or they have been first-line supervisors of "stuck" subordinates—that is, clerical or factory workers in low-mobility situations where subordinates are not expected to move on and contribute to the organization.

Peer alliances clearly contribute to power; this is the classical source of organizational politics. Since these networks are often preference-based, they tend to be founded on common interests or social similarity, and to the extent that women are rare in organizations, they are likely, as are all people who are "different," to have fewer informal means of entry into these networks. (It should be noted here that there is a prevalent popular view that the reason women are not part of the informal networks in organizations is because they were not educated in team sports, in cooperation and teamwork. My explanation is different—resting on the difficulty of joining a team that does not want one on it.) But despite the heavily informal character of peer alliances, it is also possible to see ways in which formal organizational policy can or cannot facilitate the development of peer networks and individuals' access to peer alliances, so that this, too, can be seen in terms of organizational location and not simply in terms of interpersonal behavior. For example, the likelihood of network membership is facilitated by participation in formal training programs, workshops, or orientations; by cross-department or cross-unit meetings; by "matrix" or project or task force management; by jobs at boundaries or with an extra-department focus; by jobs with high communication content.

Many of these elements, if they involve contact across hierarchical levels, can also facilitate the development of sponsorship—that is, the willingness of influential people in the organization to endorse an individual, thus bestowing reflected power on him or her or supporting his or her career at critical moments by providing recommendations, invitations, or access. Most organizations currently deny the importance of sponsorship as a quite necessary sorting mechanism in large systems and thus leave it to people's informal preferences. Under those conditions, sponsorship systems exist anyway, but they tend to be based not on rational criteria or assessment of competence but on such exclusionary grounds as social similarity. Again, this leaves women in a position of beginning at a disadvantage with respect to power accumulation.

The issue of power is important not only in its direct impact on access to decisions or resources in the system but also because of its impact on leader behavior and style. The more organizationally powerful tend to foster higher group morale. They engender more cooperation and less criticism from subordinates, delegate more control and allow subordinates more latitude and discretion, and provide opportunities for subordinates to move along with them. Naturally, then, they tend to be better liked, talk more often, and receive more communications in meetings. In contrast, the relatively powerless tend to foster lower group morale. They behave in more directive, authoritarian, controlling ways: they supervise too closely; restrict opportunities for subordinates' growth and autonomy; use more coercive than persuasive power; and are often very concerned about threats to their authority and thus engage in a great deal of territorial domination. Consequently, they tend to be less well liked and less talkative in meetings with higher power people.

Some of the characteristics of the powerless have been embedded in occasional research findings and in popular stereotypes about women's tendencies as leaders, and have been used as one explanation for the greater likelihood of men to emerge as preferred leaders. But closer examination of the "bossy woman boss" stereotype, based on the analysis of power and the organizational factors that influence it, makes clear that those characteristics often attributed to women are really characteristics of powerlessness and reflect not necessarily innate sex-linked differences but rather historical differences in women's organizational location. Again, this analysis of what empowering factors are necessary to create effective leaders and managers can be used to determine appropriate organizational interventions.

SOCIAL COMPOSITION: THE EFFECTS OF TOO FEW WOMEN

The third structural variable, the effects of social composition or proportional representation of people of different types, is straightforward and need not be discussed at length. But it is directly relevant to understanding what happens when only a few women are introduced into situations in which men are numerically dominant—or, for that matter, what happens to any "token" or numerically rare groups who are forced to operate among peers of a different social type. It is possible to see that social composition has an impact—and perhaps, in some instances, even a more important impact—above and beyond the effects of attitudes or traditional cultural role definitions. As a structural feature, numbers have importance in and of themselves. What appear to be prejudicial responses on the part of the numerically dominant group may turn out to have less to do with inbred attitudes that are impervious to change (or at least require in-depth psychological work to change) than with the forces and dynamics set in motion by the group's skewed social composition. Similarly, what appear to be ineffective behaviors on the part of people in the token category may say much less about their capacities and abilities or the effect of their cultural heritage than about what they are forced to do because they are scarce and treated as such by the dominants.

The problems of acceptance and effectiveness that many women encounter in managerial and professional occupations many derive primarily from their token status—the fact that there are, as yet, so few women in those positions. In general, people whose social type is represented in very small proportion tend to be more visible, to feel that they are "on display." They feel more pressure to conform, to make fewer mistakes, to try to become "socially invisible," not to stand out so much. They also find it harder to gain "credibility" and trust that they can do the job, particularly in situations involving risk. They are more isolated and peripheral, more likely to be excluded from informal peer networks, and, hence, more limited in this source of power-through-alliances. Similarly, they have fewer opportunities to be "sponsored" because of the rarity of people like them in higher levels. If they are in the very small minority or in the situation of being the "only" ones, they are more likely to turn against other people of their kind as a price of admission to the dominants' group. They often face misperceptions of their identity and role in the organization, and hence they develop a preference for already-established relationships; thus, they are more likely to be stereotyped, to be placed in role traps that limit effectiveness, and to face more personal stress.[4]

It is possible to see cycles of advantage for those in the majority category and cycles of disadvantage for those in the token category set in motion here also. Numbers emerge as important, then, not only as a measure of "results"—that an organization has managed to meet its affirmative action goals—but also as a condition that itself accounts for who is likely to look good in the organization and thus to get further opportunity.

APPLICATIONS

This framework lends itself to a number of immediate applications that conform to some important principles of change efforts. Four principles ought to be critical in any intervention for policy change program:

To fix or rectify the situation

1. It is important to create alternatives without initially disturbing the the conventional hierarchy of an organization. Power is, by definition, operating not out of ill will or prejudice but because of inability to see either the hierarchy's capacity to behave differently or the benefits to them of another mode of doing business. Because of the resistance to change, both by the organization as a system and by individuals, it is often most effective to encourage change by superimposing alternative methods on the conventional structure of the organization, with the goal of eventually moving the conventional form to fit more closely the alternative model. Although the conventional channels remain in place, people are increasingly able to circumvent them, so, over time, they begin to lose their meaning.

2. It is important to develop programs that are not zero-sum in nature, that do not appear to benefit one group at the cost of another. Otherwise, there are risks: first, of generating maximum hostility and resistance; second, of polarizing the system around groups differentiated by characteristics that are relevant not to occupational performance but only to their body type or cultural heritage.

3. It is important to develop and employ strategies that are issue-centered rather than group-type-centered, for not all women are disadvantaged in quite the same way, and some men also suffer from existing system inequities, so that strategies which help some men but benefit the bulk of women are more likely, in the long run, to fulfill the concern for equity and fairness and to win acceptance more broadly in the organization.

4. It is important to stress the *affirmative* side of affirmative action, to generate programs that benefit rather than punish the system and, from the perspective of the individual, that enlarge options rather than increase constraints.

The theoretical framework outlined here, informed by these change principles, can be useful in measurement, education, the identification of small-step interventions, and the development of major projects for systems change that include equality of opportunity as a goal.

Specific measures of access to opportunity and power are detailed elsewhere;[5] the measure of social composition is, of course, straightforward and is built into current affirmative action accountability. The value of the framework presented here, both for measurement and monitoring, lies in two areas. First, examining the opportunity structure, the power capacity of system locations, and the social composition of an organization can provide individuals and policy-makers with a great deal of information both about the functioning of a system and its effectiveness and about its modes of career development. It can permit more informed, if not more rational, decisions by both policy-makers and individuals about more appropriate operating strategies. It permits diagnosis of those characteristics of the system, its design and structure, that are most likely to generate effective or ineffective behavior.

Secondly, including the variables of opportunity and power in any measure of progress toward equal employment opportunity goals can help assess the prospects for long-term change. As has been pointed out, it is not only sheer numbers of women at particular levels of an organization that are important, but also the opportunity and power potential of their positions. More refined ways of collecting information not only on the status and numbers of women but on their functions and job characteristics as well can be very useful in evaluating whether women are, indeed, making progress and if they are in positions where they can grow in and influence the organization in the future. The framework may also help explain why women may find it easier to move into some areas rather than others, depending on the opportunity and power potential of those areas, independent of their rank or pay level. That is, women could be brought into particular jobs in greater numbers now, but if these are jobs from which promotions are made at a much slower rate, eventually they will again fall behind men.

The second application of this framework is to education, both of individuals and of system representatives. For women to see the system in operation, to understand it, to be able to diagnose jobs in terms of power and opportunity, to understand the likely effects of tokenism, has often proved more beneficial than being presented with familiar stereotypes or cliches about "how women are different." But perhaps the greatest educational benefits are for men. Use of a structural framework that does not talk about women and men (or blacks and whites) but rather talks about "the moving" and "the stuck," or the powerful and the powerless, or the "X's" (the numerically dominant) and the "O's" (the tokens), helps men understand not only the organizational position of women but also their own behavior to the extent that they have ever had the experience of stuckness, or powerlessness, or of token status. Moreover, this approach is nonthreatening. It tends to defuse the emotional loading that presently exists around sex or race. It provides an alternative vocabulary for thinking about people in organizations that does not stereotype them based on some ascribed characteristics, but rather defines them in terms of situation and organizational behavior. I cannot emphasize this enough. It is much more effective to present people with an alternative for looking at the situation that does not stereotype them or force them to stereotype others and that also takes away some of the current heat from the issue.

This approach, in a third application, pinpoints direct, small-step interventions that are more broadly useful for an organization but particularly benefit women. It suggests that it is important to enhance opportunity, particularly for people who are blocked (including the male middle managers who are stuck at later stages in their careers), to empower people more widely (to give them greater capacity via access to resources in the environment to get what they need to get their jobs done), and to balance numbers (to avoid tokenism wherever possible). This helps not only in choosing appropriate interventions but also in justifying many of those in current use in organizations as an aid to affirmative action which have little theoretical rationale. For example, we can see the need for career path data and information about actual opportunity structures; for career counseling and career information; for bridging positions out of traditionally "stuck" jobs; and for job stretching that adds responsibility and the chance to exhibit skills without necessarily needing to promote the person into a higher level position immediately. We can also see the need for training managers in people development; for flexibility in policies and practices, such as flexible work hours and leave policies, that permit people to balance in-work and out-of-work obligations; for more formal sponsorship systems, that give everyone some access to higher-level people in the system; and for increased communication content of low-visibility jobs. The approach confirms the importance of cross-functional, cross-hierarchy project teams that permit additional skills to be developed and exercised and people to make contact across the hierarchy; and of more programs that bring people together across the organization and have the function of building relationships between women and men and thus serving as formal mechanisms for bringing women into networks. It also makes clear the importance of clustering women so that they are no longer tokens, rather than spreading them across the organization, but with the goal in mind of eventually increasing numbers everywhere.

While these are among the most significant, there are also other means of reaching the goals of enhanced opportunity, empowerment, and balanced numbers. (Note that the small-step interventions I have chosen to list here all tend to meet the criteria for effective change described above.) In the long run, it will be such systems and procedures that will be the institutional mechanisms for translating stated policies such as equal employment opportunity into operating practice.

A MAJOR PROJECT: SYSTEM CHANGE WITH AFFIRMATIVE ACTION IMPLICATIONS

I have argued that the problem does not lie either in the nature of women or in the discriminatory intent of men (which, in some cases, is an undeniable fact), but rather in the ways in which people are distributed among the system locations and the ways in which opportunity and power are made into scarce commodities. If one sees the problem in this way, then it is also clear that affirmative action will work best in the long run when tied to major system change. There is also the greatest likelihood of success, particularly at this time of retrenchment, when programs for equal employment opportunity are seen as consistent with, rather than unrelated to, the organization's own goals of effective operation. To make a somewhat provocative and controversial statement, I contend that only when affirmative action or EEO officers become change agents in a larger sense, and are seen as resources to the system rather than as agents for punishment, will their efforts truly succeed. Thus, as a final application, I will describe briefly one major change project that is currently serving as a model for other projects in large corporations and government agencies. It has helped change the operation of a large unit of a major basic materials corporation and has both improved the functioning of the unit and increased the direct opportunity of women in junior staff positions and in secretarial jobs.

The project involves developing mechanisms for reallocating the tasks in a seventy-five–person staff department of a Fortune 50 corporation, delegating more professional tasks downward and including lower-level personnel in decisions affecting the department. In effect, it was oriented toward changing the operating structure of the department while the overall official hierarchy remained intact, in such a way that opportunities were expanded for lower-level people and productivity (the amount of work accomplished) increased. Since practically all the lower-level personnel were women (largely secretaries and clerical workers), while 90 percent of the managers and higher-level professionals were men, there were clear affirmative action goals and implications.

The hierarchical structure—a director, two associate directors, managers reporting to them, and professional and clerical staff with rigid top-down communication patterns—was supplemented by a variety of other operating structures: a director's group, consisting of the director and the two associate directors meeting collaboratively; a managers' group, consisting of the directors and all managers; a communications council, consisting of representatives from a variety of positions within the department, making recommendations and passing on information to their constituencies; and a number of task forces and project teams consisting of people at all hierarchical levels. All seventy-five members of the department met together once as an entire group. Overall, there is much more frequent contact among all members of the department at all levels of the organization.

Groundwork for the project began in August of 1976, but the project as outlined here began in about March of 1977. Major project events took place between September 1977 and March 1978.[6] Key steps in the project included nine sets of activities:

The first was building credibility with the director via a series of individual meetings, and helping directly to get the director and the associate directors to work together more effectively and to think about options for managing the department that would be consistent with company goals and affirmative action needs.

The second was gathering data about the operation of the department from all levels of the organization—data that the directors and department members contributed to and, consequently, believed in.

Third, mechanisms were created that involved all levels of the department, both exempt (salaried) and nonexempt (weekly, largely secretarial) personnel, in the process of interpreting the data and making suggestions for their use. The primary vehicle for doing this was a day-long, department-wide meeting.

Next was the development of action steps that all levels could support and that built collaboration, created a sense of belonging, involved limited risk, showed short-term results, and enhanced both opportunity at the bottom and productivity, a need of the top.

Then we encouraged follow-through by the directors, to indicate that they responded to the issues and problems generated by other employees.

The next step was planning for longer-term change in the department's structure, task allocation, decision-making, and operations, on an experimental basis with results to be evaluated after six to eight months and with concrete statements of goals and standards available.

Next we created a process of task analysis (and a series of meetings to train managers to use the process) that would permit managers and professionals to assess their own use of time and to delegate and transfer tasks to others in the organization, thereby freeing themselves for high-priority work and presenting opportunities to lower-level personnel. (The managers' group meetings also developed as vehicles for joint and collaborative problem-solving.)

Having set up the system, we then worked at educating both managers and nonmanagers, professionals and clerical workers, about new ways of communicating, assessing their own skills, and encouraging others to define and use more skills, through formal meetings and workshops, and through counseling and coaching both exempt and nonexempt employees in their own offices. Out of these meetings came two developments that were supported by the outside consultants but "owned" by the department itself. One was the creation of vehicles by which any member of the department could identify undone tasks and "volunteer" to set up a task force to see that they were accomplished, as long as their own managers agreed and their primary tasks were completed. The other was the development by individual managers of new operating procedures and structures with respect to their own people, such as more frequent group-wide meetings, identification of hidden talents, and exchange of functions with other managers.

The final step was to coach and assist the department to take over the management of the project itself, by integrating new structures and processes with the traditional ones defined by the formal organization. This included giving a variety of employees major project responsibilities, on a rotating basis, such as planning teams for the managers' meetings, more frequent and effective communication processes for all employees, posting of tasks that could use volunteers, and posting of accomplishments, thereby making skills visible.

This is necessarily only a sketchy description of a very complex set of activities that has already had a major impact on the climate and effectiveness of the department, as well as changing the opportunity and power structures. At the outset, the directors and then the department management were informed about the theoretical framework that would be the basis for defining the utility of particular project steps. Project elements were specifically designed to enhance opportunity and to be empowering in and of themselves, in addition to their long-range effects on the distribution of these variables. While the project is now supported by internal resources rather than outside consultants, it is still evolving, and most of the planned steps will ensure its institutionalization. Still to come are a major survey of skills in the department, measurement of results to date, and plans for diffusion to other parts of the corporation.

There is currently a hiring freeze inside this corporation. As a result, no new women or minority staff members have been added, and thus, in terms of affirmative action, the overall social composition of the department has not changed. There have already been significant results for women and minorities, however, in terms of their status and position within the department. I think, in any case, that this is a better test of the efficacy of structural change since it is often much easier to solve affirmative action problems by expanding or adding new people than by improving the situation of those women or minorities already in the organization, particularly those women in traditionally "female" jobs such as that of secretary.

The department project has led to several instances of internal change. For example, a young semi-professional woman, who was doing primarily clerical tasks and was not very well known in the department, took advantage of the chance to define new areas that needed work. With the agreement of the managers, she pulled together a task force. She demonstrated so much talent, and became so visible that after a few months she was promoted. The new options at her present level have also encouraged her to seek new opportunities of all kinds, and she is now seen as one of the leaders in the department.

Similarly, a young nonexempt black, who had started out in the mailroom, volunteered to report out the results of the early data collection at the department-wide meeting. He became much more visible and active as a result, seeking people out and becoming more valued. He is now seen as a possibility for promotion to a professional job.

Several secretaries sought out opportunities to participate. They became involved and now have routes—communication channels—to use to give information and feedback to managers. They are being heard and treated differently. Their managers are seeking promotions for them at the first opportunity.

A task force was set up specifically to work with nonexempt employees —primarily women in secretarial and clerical positions—to improve their involvement and their job situation. The task force includes both fairly senior managers and nonexempt personnel, who explore a range of issues and work together collaboratively. The task force was initiated by a senior male manager without any prodding by the outside consultants.

One of the few women in management in the department, an ex-secretary herself, was a supervisor of secretaries, charged with the administration of nonexempt personnel. The project gave her many vehicles for involvement—the managers' meeting (where she was one of two women, the other woman being a professional), the communications council, and task force management. She became very active and demonstrated great skill and capacity. She was often included in the informal gatherings after meetings when the men went for drinks or dinner. She is now a candidate for promotion to one of several professional jobs that represent clear steps up and away from identification with her secretarial past.

These are just a few examples. But many of these results are clearly demonstrated in other, similar projects, such as the organization-wide program of job design at Prudential Insurance. By expanding the ways in which people can be involved and use skills, and by enriching the number of contacts that take place across the hierarchy, it is, indeed, possible not just to equalize opportunity but also to expand it.

CONCLUSION

I have described here my own framework for understanding structural influences on organizational behavior and have indicated some of the applications of this framework not only to diagnosing the problem of equality for women but also to changing strategies. There is certainly value to encouraging a variety of explanations for women's status and a variety of change approaches. Understanding the biological, educational, social, and cultural role pressures that affect women is important in developing complete analyses of the problem. But perhaps there has been too much emphasis on some of these extra-organizational forces and not enough attention to the impact of immediate job conditions and the location of one's job in organizational distributions of opportunity, power, and proportional representation.

I encourage more attention to organizational structure for another reason. For affirmative action and equal employment opportunity programs to have long-range impact and to effect the kinds of changes that are desired, they must be tied in more closely and clearly to issues of organizational effectiveness. If such efforts appear to be imposed from outside and are incongruent with organizational goals—even for those organizations which have accepted social responsibility as one of their obligations—and if such programs prove too punitive and costly, then they will be strenuously resisted. But if they can be designed to benefit women and minorities while also benefiting other organization members, then their chances for success are multiplied.

NOTES

1. This work has been carried out in conjunction with colleagues at the organizational consulting firm of Goodmeasure, 6 Channing Place, Cambridge, Mass. 02138.

2. Rosabeth Moss Kanter, *Men and Women of the Corporation* (New York: Basic Books, 1977).

3. Ibid.; Kanter, "Access to Opportunity and Power: Measuring Racism/Sexism inside Organizations" (paper presented at Research Symposium on Social Indicators of Institutional Racism/Sexism, UCLA, April, 1977), published in R. Alvarez, ed., *Social Indicators of Institutional Discrimination: Management and Research Tools* (San Francisco: Jossey-Bass, 1978).

4. Kanter, *Men and Women of the Corporation* and "Some Effects of Proportions on Group Life: Skewed Sex Ratios and Responses to Token Women," *American Journal of Sociology* 82 (March 1977): 965–990.

5. Kanter, "Access to Opportunity and Power."

6. This project was carried out in collaboration with Barry Stein and Marcy Murninghan of Goodmeasure.

V

The National Context and Equal Opportunity

15 *Herta Däubler-Gmelin*

EQUAL EMPLOYMENT OPPORTUNITY FOR WOMEN IN WEST GERMANY TODAY

Equal rights, equal opportunity for women—these demands have increasingly characterized the discussions of interested and concerned German women in recent years. They are the focus of the work of women's groups and of organizations of women members of German political parties and unions, and they have received growing public attention and coverage in radio, television, and printed media. Even the political parties are expressing renewed interest in these demands, if for totally different reasons.

The Christian Democrats (CDU), a conservatively structured party, emphasizes the value of women as wives and mothers in its position papers as well as in its suggestions for a "solution" to the economic and job crisis of the late 1970s. This view predominates even though the women's organizations of the CDU stress the value of employment for women. In this party and in the public attitude in which it is anchored, being a woman is bound up with a different form of life, distinct from a man's. Women, they say, are more attached to the family; it may be possible to compensate for the detrimental consequences of this fact, but it is not possible to avoid the fact itself.

Among the more liberal Free Democrats (FDP) the question of the *legal* equality of women predominates. But, like the CDU, they too do not question the economic and social framework that they advocate, even when it negates the effect of legal equality. Instead, legal equality is deemed possible within the framework of existing social conditions. This notion reflects

—at least among the women of the FDP—the enlightened opinion of the middle-class wing of the nineteenth-century women's movement.

Social Democrats (SPD) view the problem with more insight. Since approximately 1890 their party platforms, official statements, and theoretical writings have taken the position that the "solution to the problem of women" is part of the socialist striving for emancipation of the human being. Hence, they are aiming for the defeat of illegality and dependence, for participation, and for a present and future based on equality and opportunity. The Godesberg Program and Objectives Statement of 1965 devotes much space to the problem of equality of rights and opportunity for women as well as to the continued striving for emancipation in general.

For several years precedence has been given to putting these accepted principles into practice. Although they did not always do so, Social Democrats are beginning to understand that increased equality of opportunity for women in all areas of life is closely linked to the capacity for reforming society. This is true not only because democratically elected administrations rely on the voice of the majority, and hence on that of women voters, if they wish to remain politically determinate. It is also true because opportunity for women requires the same attitudes and behavior among women that progressive political movements require in their voters in order to obtain support for their change-oriented programs: self-assurance, knowledge, a spirit of independence, the will to change life's oppressive conditions. All these elements and modes of behavior are found less often in women in those societies governed by rigid, tradition-bound, and irrationally fixed definitions of roles according to sex which restrict women to family and home and permits only men to participate in a professional, public life.

The characteristics and modes of behavior which make progressive politics and political change possible are found in those societies in which such sex-determined role definitions are most fully overcome. Recent German history abounds in examples which illustrate that until recently Social Democrats, despite their progressive programs, did not recognize the political implications of relaxing women's political role definitions, with fatal consequences for social progress.

In 1919, after the collapse of imperial Germany and its voting rights based on estates, the Social Democrats put the right to vote "for women" into the Weimar Constitution. The Social Democrats are still proud of this step—and rightly so. But having achieved suffrage, the majority of women in the Weimar period thereupon cast conservative, anti-democratic, and fascist votes. This haunts the Social Democrats as an undeserved personal insult even today. Consequently, many progressive politicians have discounted the support of women because of their apparently conservativepatriarchial voting pattern and have taken only a necessary minimum interest in women's rights and opportunities.

The election results as late as 1969, when the socialists were returned to power, did not prove this assumption wrong. Indeed, the voting behavior of women in the first German Republic becomes clearer if one relates it to another event from the year 1919 that has been largely forgotten. The "demobilization order" issued in that year, which provided that soldiers returning from the front were to be re-employed, became the justification for dismissing all women whose jobs were required for this purpose. Those women who had been taken into war-related industries to fill spaces left when men were drafted were of course dismissed. But the demobilization order went further, loosening up the job market through a drastic eviction of women.

Not only were many women deprived of their economic support, but they seemed to lose their ideological support as well. Due to the overwhelming economic difficulties that appeared shortly after they took office, the leaders of the new government were not able to make good their efforts for more emancipation, education, and equality for women. First, although the new republic claimed to be founded on equality of rights and opportunities, it perpetuated the middle-class family and social model that had existed before the war, with its political representation based on estates and its assignment of traditional roles for women and men. Second, women's employment was viewed as a sort of reserve labor pool, and the idea of an occupation for women was not considered a realistic, emancipating alternative. In short, the provision for equality in the Weimar Constitution was only a paper one.

Viewed in this light, the voting behavior of the majority of women in 1919 makes sense. Women were given little inducement to support parties whose attitudes toward the situation of the majority of women seemed to be only verbally progressive. They had no reason to defend a republic which changed nothing essential in the traditional scope of their function in society. Ultimately, it became apparent that both the slogans of the conservatives and the ideology of the Nazis stressing the role of the mother at hearth and home were only a dirty trick to "solve" economic problems at the expense of women. But by that time it was too late.

Official support for equal employment opportunity continued to decline. The "fight against double income" resulted in dismissal of married women from public service. The campaigns against "emancipated" women continued in the official propaganda even in the years after 1934, when women had been recruited for some time for the defense industries, and later in other war-related areas, to do their part for victory. This propaganda was not without its consequences. Indeed, it is still operative. Among the majority of women and men it was able to extinguish or at least to distort nearly every positive awareness, every constructive assessment of the earlier women's movement, indeed every memory of the courageous fighters for equality and emancipation. The problems with equality of opportunity for women, together with the easing of traditional role prescription, which exist today in Germany life may be explained by the fact that concepts like "emancipation for women," "suffragette," and "women's rightist," which in many countries now have positive connotations, are in Germany still associated negatively with terms like "bluestocking," "crazy," "virago," or other contemptuous expressions. The women's movement in Germany, now that it is once again growing in strength since the middle of the sixties, must combat these prejudices by ensuring that the obscured information about women and their rights is once again awakened in the public memory.

Since the 1969 socialist victory women have become noticeably more active in unions and political parties. In 1969, 1972, and 1976 an above-average percentage of their votes supported the establishment and continuation of the social-liberal coalition in Bonn. Because of these developments, equal opportunity for women has seen decisive progress in many areas of legislation. Perhaps the most important accomplishment took effect July 1, 1977, after years of preliminary work. Not only were equal rights established on the basis of partnerships between men and women, but more actual equality of opportunity was given to women in the areas of marriage, family, and divorce.[1] At the same time, the family-related legal prerequisites set the stage for equal opportunity in occupations.

Since 1949 the Constitution of the Federal Republic of Germany has provided, to be sure, that men and women *are* equal before the law (Art. 3, § 2 German Human Rights Acts); that they have equal rights therefore; and, at the same time, that no one may be *disadvantaged* on the basis of sex; that, therefore, a lessening of opportunities specific to sex is not permitted (Art. 3, § 3 German Human Rights Acts). Despite these guarantees, until 1953, a husband had the right, under certain circumstances, to discontinue his wife's employment, even against her will. And it took until 1977, and required tough negotiations and substantive compromises with the conservative (CDU/CSU) majority in the legislature, to establish that the wife's employment may no longer be admitted as grounds for divorce.

In spite of the existence of this binding constitutional provision on paternal dominance, the social-liberal coalition had to labor between 1953 and 1977 to gain further series of legislative measures—always against the bitter opposition of the conservatives—which would improve the markedly inferior financial and legal situation of the single woman with children, particularly illegitimate children. The objective was to make the rights of this group to support and public assistance conform to the constitutional provisions for equality. Considerable achievements have been attained in this area.

In the area of employment the traditional differences between men and women are equalizing out much more slowly. To be sure, discrimination against women is forbidden *de jure* in the Constitution, in many laws, and in other legal stipulations. Nonetheless, a considerably smaller proportion of women than men is employed outside the home and, women constitute a considerably smaller part of the labor force, compared to their proportion of the population. In 1977 the population of the Federal Republic of Germany was about 65 million. Approximately 25 million men and women were employed outside the home. Women constitute more than half the population. Their proportion of the employed is, however, only about one third. While nearly 60 percent of all employable men are actually working, the corresponding figure for women is only about 34 percent. These dissimilar relations have changed hardly at all since the beginning of the twentieth century except that they sank below this level during the Hitler period.

Not only is the proportion of women working in the Federal Republic low, the statistics also indicate that employment patterns of men and women in West Germany are formed according to sex. For men the normal employment pattern was and is one that has its commencement at the end of the school years and its end only with the attainment of the legal retirement age. With women this rule applies only to those who do not marry or do not have to care for relatives.

For the remaining women—married, widowed, divorced—another pattern is typical. After the school phase comes a period of professional activity. This period—and often all professional activity—ends with marriage or, more often today, with the birth of the first or second child. But the better economic options which women achieved in the wide-open job market of the sixties brought about a wish for a stronger continuity of employment outside the home among more and younger women. Consequently, there has been a rapid increase in the number of working women with children, women who claim to be working not on account of or not only on account of the income. At the same time indications emerged of a third phase in the employment pattern for women: re-entry of mothers to the occupation for which they had originally been trained and in which they had formerly been employed.

Had the favorable economic situation and the labor shortage continued, both options might have had a chance to break the typical discontinuity of women's employment pattern. Possibly too the demonstrable disadvantages of an intermittent employment pattern might have been decisively lessened. Just what these disadvantages are was stated at the sixtieth convention of the International Labor Conference. There it was pointed out that the total employment process in highly industrialized nations is today more than ever geared to continuous presence and participation of the employed. Knowledge and skills become quickly outdated, and must be constantly adapted to changing requirements. This is hardly possible when employment is interrupted for the time required to bring up one or more children.

The temporary absence of the majority of women from the employment process takes its revenge—a point to which we will return. The faulty integration in the total labor force has severe consequences. Length of employment in an industry and continuity of employment play an important role in determining what rights a worker has and how easily they can be realized; they are often crucial to his or her status and to his job security. They affect his or her integration into an operation's core group of employees as well as, for example, his chance to participate in programs of further education, length-of-service bonuses, or fringe benefits. In all these areas, women are at a disadvantage.

It is apparent that the perpetuation of the difference in the employment patterns of men and women is mainly due to the fact that family obligations are still largely left to women and that the socialization of boys and girls still proceeds largely according to traditional patterns. Likewise, there are too few arrangements available to families, at affordable cost, that would relieve this situation. For preschool needs, day-care centers are lacking; for the school age, all-day schools are the rare exception; as for family planning, there is a lack of service facilities at acceptable prices, and day-care concepts are regarded with suspicion.

AREAS OF EMPLOYMENT FOR WOMEN IN GERMANY

Besides the discontinuities in their employment patterns, women are typically employed in areas and in occupations different from those of men. Both of these factors influence the equality of opportunity for women in hiring and in the conditions of their employment outside the home. Women are typically office and clerical workers. They already form more than half of this group. Likewise, the proportion of women among production workers is lower than the proportion of employed women in the population as a whole. The trend away from the woman as blue-collar worker, then, and toward the white-collar employee has become even more noticeable in recent years.

Lines of work for which women are said to be "preferred" are, in reality, open to women because of specific conditions. Most women work in public and private service occupations, in the tertiary sector: in offices, in government, in retailing, in domestic service, health, and education (the helping professions). In production, the secondary sector, women work less frequently. And when they do, their concentration in a few kinds of manufacturing is striking.

Two-thirds of the women in this sector work in the leather, textile, and clothing industries, in electronics, in steel engine and vehicle construction, and in the food and luxury industries. Strikingly different is the occupational structure of men. They are more evenly dispersed, in more and different occupations. The incidence of concentrations is considerably less. They predominate heavily in the production sector and raw materials industries and occupy a subordinate place in the service occupations (including those in the public sector).

The typical differences in men's and women's occupations become still more distinct when one looks more closely at heavy vs. light industry. Food and luxury industries both employ more women than heavy industry. The consumer goods industry has the next largest proportion of women employees with 47 percent, and raw materials and heavy machinery the lowest with 18 percent.

Clear differences in women's employment may also be observed geographically. In the Saar region only about 20 percent of all women able to work are employed; in Bavaria and Baden-Wurttemberg the figure is about 36 percent. The reasons for this lie in the structure of the economy. Where trades, small business, and family businesses predominate, women's share of earnings and the proportion of women among the employed is usually higher. The principal reason for this is the concentrated supply of "jobs for women" that the labor market offers in one place as compared with another.

Further exceptions for women concern the amount of time worked and the place of work. The proportion of women among "part-time employees," those who work less than forty but more than twenty hours, is high—over 80 percent. A still higher proportion of women take part in cottage industry, the so-called "work in the home." More than 90 percent of the people who work at home are women. Both part-time and home work are characterized by substandard legal and social conditions, in spite of the incisive legal changes in 1974. Both are less intensively integrated into the organization of the firm.

Women accept such jobs for several reasons. In some cases other jobs are not available in the region. But usually women are simply not able to accept normal working conditions because of the burden of family obligations, the one-sided process of socialization, and the lack of facilities that would provide relief for these conditions.

QUALIFICATIONS

The education of women even today is inferior to and shorter than that of men. This fact further restricts their work opportunities.

Women are still given lower-caliber academic and vocational education than men. At the beginning of the sixties more than half the women over age fifteen, versus a quarter of the men, had completed only an elementary school education or elementary employment training, the obligatory minimum of schooling. Only one quarter of these women, versus almost half the men, had completed an apprenticeship as well as elementary school education. Thus, almost three out of four people with an elementary school education but no apprenticeship were women, while two-thirds of those with a completed apprenticeship were men. Equally clear disparities exist among those with high school education and advanced vocational training. Among those who completed the Abitur, a qualifying examination necessary for admission to a university or comparable professional training, the proportion of women drops considerably. Only 1 percent of women, versus more than 3 percent of men, completed a university education or a program from a comparable institution. Of degree recipients women comprised only 15 percent.

The educational background of employed women illustrates still more clearly the striking circumstances just noted. Only about 45 percent of employed women can claim even to have completed their education. Among employed men, the figure is three-fourths.

The statistics show that among younger women changes are in progress. Among working women aged thirty to forty, for example, 57 percent have completed an apprenticeship or at least a training program. Among the forty- to fifty-year-olds the corresponding figure is only 39 percent. But the basic impression remains unchanged. Women are more poorly educated than men, even today. The longer and more specialized a course of education, the fewer the women that take it.

Among women, basic qualifications improve as one ascends the social scale, and the ties to the occupation become closer, a peculiarity not found among men, at least as far as the influence on employment behavior is concerned. This makes sense when one also takes into account that motivation for further education is inseparably linked with poor basic qualifications. Analysts, experts in economics and developments in the labor market, and policy-makers are agreed that mobility decisively improves the opportunities of workers. The term is not restricted to regional mobility, but extends also to further education, to retraining, to life-long study.

When the disadvantaged employment situation of women is discussed in Germany, the complaint is often raised that women have no interest in further education, or a lesser interest than men. They are said to have too little initiative, and to be themselves in large part responsible for discrimination. This judgment ignores the correlation between an individual's basic qualifications or skills and the willingness and capacity for life-long continuous study, and for activity and initiative. To improve mobility one must improve occupational qualifications and the capacity for initiative, and thereby the prerequisites that makes it possible for women to attain equality of opportunity. In order to accomplish this goal, it is necessary to stop blaming women for their situation and build countermeasures and suitable solutions which take into account the individual and collective weak points of potential trainees. This applies to all areas of adult education that further mobility and integration: industrial training programs until now have largely bypassed the women employees in the lowest positions just as management programs have also done at their level. Both will be discussed later on.

EMPLOYMENT CONDITIONS

Employment conditions for women are in practice still considerably inferior to those for men. This applies to wages, salaries, and pensions, to opportunities for promotion and further education, to job security and the conditions for dismissal.

Wages

As wage and salary workers, women earn approximately one-third less than their male counterparts. In October 1977 the average gross earnings for men in all industries was 12.04 DM per hour, versus 8.74 DM for women. The average gross monthly earnings of white collar workers in industry and trade was 2.862 DM for men, but only 1.837 DM for women.

Historic wage differences coupled with current disparaties are dragged along into retirement schemes. The standard pension benefit of women is one-third less than for men (this is planned for in tying a women's pension to that for wives and widows of pensioned husbands). This discrimination is quite understandable when women are viewed as dependents: on one hand, the amounts of women's pensions due to them in their own right are computed according to the mandatory insurance contribution paid in by the women themselves and are based on their years of work and the level of their wage; on the other hand, the computation includes the average of the wages and salaries of all women entitled to pensions in the first retirement year of the woman in question. On both counts women fall below men.

In addition, the typical concentration of women's occupations in certain areas of the economy serves to depress wages further. In heavy industry both men and women are paid more on the average than in manufacturing industries. One reason for this is that considerably fewer women work in heavy industry, especially in some areas. Women are everywhere automatically at the bottom of the wage scale because, as we have seen, they always obtain the jobs that pay least.

All this has not been anticipated in the regulations. In addition to the German Human Rights Acts, numerous German and international binding regulations presumably forbid discrimination against women in the area of compensation. Legislators, negotiators in wage agreements, courts, and management are all bound by these legal regulations. Yet "light wage groups" still exist in Germany.

Associated with concepts like "light jobs" or "simple tasks," these light wage groups (usually wage groups I-III) were added to the lower end of the wage scales even below male temporary workers to replace the so-called "women's wage groups," which were declared unlawful by a 1955 decision of the highest German labor court—the BAG. Their origin and partly also their formulation ("which are particularly suitable for women due to their requirements and demands") show that from the beginning they were principally applied to the women temporary employees in industry. They are comparable in every way to the women's wage groups, but the discrimination is covert and therefore *de jure* not forbidden.

The light wage groups were also permitted practically intact in the union wage agreements. The justification put forward for their continuance has been that an immediate introduction of equal pay for women, particularly in the "women's areas," would have led to economic difficulties. One of the real reasons was, most likely, the fear that equal pay would threaten other employee benefits. At least, progress in the areas of vacations, pensions, worker safety, and the shortened work week would have been delayed. Only since the middle of the sixties have the unions made any efforts to eliminate this hidden discrimination in wage agreements.

In major areas of industry, meanwhile, this has already occurred— in the largest parts of the chemical industry and in metal manufacturing, for example. What is remarkable is that the substitution of another system of wage determination, one encompassing all jobs, was implemented earliest and with least friction where the number of male and foreign employees was relatively high. These new systems of wage determination, for example that of an analytical and therefore seemingly rational occupation rating, have not yet been able to narrow the gap in wages. It remains to be seen whether traditional prejudices do not once again penetrate the necessary principles of appraisal and whether disparate requirements according to sex are allowed for. (For further information on wage classification systems in Germany, see Appendix B.)

Further reasons for the wage discrimination lie in the structure and implementation of wage agreements. The assignment of an employee to a position on the wage scale, and therefore to a wage category, has been the prerogative of the employer. According to the new Basic Industrial Statute (BetrVG) 1972, however, employee representatives now have considerable say in the matter. To be sure, these employee representatives do not function fully nor do they exist in all organizations presumably affected by the law. Even when they are elected and functioning as the law prescribes, wage discrimination may only be eliminated when more employed women know their rights. That is the case today only with about 17 percent of women employees, those who are union members.

Promotion

Women work in occupations at the bottom of the organizational hierarchy. They have few chances for advancement. This is true of women in industrial jobs and in the usual female occupational areas as well as in management jobs and highly qualified leadership positions in large companies.

In 1970 less than 3.5 percent of all industrial master-workmen, foremen, and supervisors were women. Less than 10 percent of all women administrators have managerial or supervisory duties. Among the 784 directors' positions of the 150 largest firms in Germany in 1972, there was not one woman. Of the 3,041 top positions in management and administration in the hundred firms with the highest sales, only eight were filled by women. Although women represent 12 percent of independent entrepreneurs and 4 percent of management personnel in public service, they constitute only 1.8 percent leading executives and only .1 percent serve on boards of directors. For example, in 1974 about 14 percent of the employees at Daimler Benz were women. But among the 2,000 section leaders, there were only 91 women; seventeen women among the 1,500 main section leaders and professional assistants; and only two women each among the department heads and professional assistants and among the 200 main section leaders.

These facts and examples are of considerable importance not only for earnings and career opportunities but also in other contexts. In industry as well as in service areas women are concentrated in positions for which professional training is hardly required and in which they perform predominately repetitive, simple, mechanical activities. Such positions are particularly threatened by technical advancements, rising wage costs, or problems of competition. Structurally, they are easily replaced by machines or by unskilled workers. Consequently, companies invest little in such employees, since their dismissal brings about hardly any financial or organizational difficulties.

Despite the recent improvement in the academic and occupational qualifications of women in Germany, professional women too suffer discrimination. Since the beginning of the sixties, for example, many young women completed with honors training in banking and insurance; five years later they had been far outpaced in their occupational positions by their inferior male classmates. In career-track positions or in continuing education programs, one rarely finds women. Positions geared to advancement are not offered even to an outstanding woman. The firm assumes that "she will just get married," so she never receives opportunities for further education for jobs which are not flexible enough for family considerations or which may be subject to an interruption of employment.

Protective legislation

As we mentioned above, there are legal prohibitions against discrimination, and legislators, wage contract negotiators, and other officials have increasingly taken these prohibitions seriously. But there are other legal standards that also conform to the Constitution and are aimed at existing sex disparities and their equalization that themselves have discriminating consequences.

Since the beginning of the first industrial revolution, the proletariat-socialist-oriented women's movement has fought for effective occupational safety regulations for women in order to combat the high mortality rate among women and children and the susceptibility to illness that came about as a result of bad working conditions. But it is possible that the now enormous number of regulations that apply to women's occupational safety could effectively work against women themselves and, to a growing extent, against women's employment as a whole during times of economic crisis. Because of the protective standards, hiring women is more expensive, less profitable, and more complicated for the company, and less convenient for the company organization. So better integration of women into the business world may require a rethinking of protective legislation.

Specifically, we need to examine whether many of the regulations for the protection of women should not apply to all employees, in other words, be extended to include male employees. This is surely true for those regulations designed to safeguard life, health, and physical safety on the job, and especially the present occupational health and safety regulations, which guard against particularly dangerous materials or dangerous work sites.

A second group of rules which are based exclusively on an outdated image of family, marriage, and women must also be adjusted, to the extent that they have a negative effect on women's competition with men. This applies to the "work day at home" provisions incorporated into parts of the wage agreements allowing women industrial employees a day at home a month as well as other regulations. These should apply either to both partners in a marriage or be done away with. Finally, the third group of regulations that should be dismantled are those which pertain directly to women, such as prenatal care and unpaid child care leave.

Job security

The laws that pertain to dismissal and job security presumably apply equally to men and women in Germany. Nevertheless, in practice women are clearly disadvantaged, at least where notice is given on account of "business necessity." In those cases, women are given notice more frequently and earlier than their male colleagues.

The reason for this disadvantage lies once again in the less complete integration of women into the business world. It also dominates the values implicit in the regulations concerning dismissal. According to legal regulations, a dismissal occasioned by business necessity must also, if it is to be valid, be socially justified. The works council has to concur with the employer's nomination for dismissal before notice is given. Failure to consider certain social factors may result in a worker's contesting his or her dismissal before the labor court.

Some of the criteria the court examines are how the employer and the works council have ranked priorities of: age, length of employment in the company, responsibilities for the support of dependents, physical handicaps, and other comparable factors. In length of employment women are already often disadvantaged, since they are rarely considered to be part of the permanent staff, but are instead looked at as a fringe group formed and reformed as the need arises. In the question of dependents they are even more disadvantaged. Until July 1, 1977, statute 1360 of the Civil Code provided that a woman usually fulfilled her obligation to contribute to the support of her family through managing the household, at least as long as her husband's employment provided enough money. So the two-income argument never works against the employed husband, who is after all the "head of the family," but only against the wife who "also" works.

Along with these legal effects, as we have seen, dismissals resulting from conditions within the company more readily affect women, because women, when they go, leave smaller gaps and can be more easily replaced.

Their time is less flexible (family duties often rule out suddenly assigned overtime work), and they cause greater organizational inconvenience.

EQUALITY OF EMPLOYMENT OPPORTUNITY FOR WOMEN IN GERMANY TODAY

Our survey of the peculiarities and problems of women's employment in Germany suggests two major conclusions.

First, although women's employment is important to the German economy, its size and status have hardly changed since the beginning of the century. Neither have women in this long period been more integrated into the business world. They are still "marginal wage earners." The problems of women's employment—their family-oriented socialization, lesser qualifications, lower wages, lack of adequate opportunity for promotion, inferior positions in the work world, concentration in a few areas and occupations, and greater susceptibility to economic vicissitudes and restructuring—all these are interrelated.

Second, since the middle of the sixties a further and different series of interrelated factors has led to a renewed impetus for the improvement of the legal and actual situation of women. Since the SPD/FDP coalition took over the government in Bonn in 1969, long-overdue legislative proposals on the structure of marital partnerships have been passed. The occupational qualifications of girls and women have improved noticeably. The actual and legal improvement of single women with or without children has made great advances.

At this point we should report on recommended proposals for further dismantling the discrimination against women still present in occupational life. We cannot do so, however, for in recent years discussion of this theme in Germany has seen a decisive shift. The impetus for improving opportunities for women began with the favorable economic situation in the mid-sixties, good job market conditions, and the change in government to the SPD and FED. The clouding over of the economic climate subsequently shadowed both official ideology and social policy.

At present, conservative social policy-makers are again trying to tell women that their place is in the home and their happiness is in the care of a family and raising of children; in brief, they wish to turn back that which has been won in the labor market for emancipation. This conservative offensive is receiving growing attention in every kind of media, and it has not failed to have its effect on women, encouraging uncertainty and leading to the suppression of discussion of women's problems just when women had begun to combat their isolation, dependency, and discrimination. The success of the new conservative wave is evidenced in the universal and sometimes growing helplessness of women in pursuit of their own rights and claims in the job market.

This conservatism may be traced to the drastic decline in the economic situation. In Germany, as in the other Western industrial nations, the economy is marked by a deep crisis rooted in many causes, and hence difficult to control. Among the causes is the realization that the supply of fossil fuels, particularly oil and natural gas, is finite. The resulting rise in the cost of energy has intensified the existing symptoms of crisis and generated new ones. Fluctuations in international trade in the West and in the world monetary system have been exacerbated by the fluctuations in the dollar. At the same time, productivity in the German economy is rising faster than demand for goods. In spite of the supply of the necessary capital and the low cost of foreign capital, little is invested in many areas of industry due to the uncertainty of turnover and the lack of new marketable ideas for production. In areas where this has happened it has resulted primarily in a loss of jobs. Problems in the job market also result from the technological restructuring which may be observed in many areas; microprocessors cause as much uncertainty and anxiety in the processing industries as the introduction of data processors and systems in areas of office, management, and organization. Finally, problems in the job market also follow from the justifiable demands of nations in the southern hemisphere for a greater entry into markets for their products.

All these difficulties and uncertainties, together with the altered demographic structure in Germany, have led to widespread unemployment. There were more than a million unemployed in 1977, and that fact is not only an economic and financial factor, but also considerably influences the psychological, social, and political climate. Moreover, most economists believe that this situation will worsen in the 1980s.

In these same next few years considerably larger numbers of people will complete schooling and demand first a professional training and then a job. If one assumes only a steady supply of wage-earners, as has been the case in recent years, then in the next ten to fifteen years about three million new jobs must be created if unemployment is not to exceed the present level.

These problems make progress difficult for women. Programs for improvement cost money. Specialized training programs for women or the expansion of services to relieve the double burden of the working woman, the expansion of all-day school or day care facilities, a more widespread introduction of work hours for parents that would favor the family, or other proposals which aim at an increase in the number of jobs for women and improved integration of women into the business world—all these are met, due to the costs, with no enthusiasm on the part of the economy and company management.

Government financing is also more difficult to obtain under such economic circumstances. In 1978, government payments through the central administration in Bonn, through the Land governments, and through the municipalities are necessary to cover the immensely high costs of ongoing programs—not to speak of new ones—on top of the problems in the job market. One million unemployed cost these institutions a full 20 million DM per year in social services, lost taxes, and lost social insurance contributions. Added to all this is the considerable expense of trying, without much success, to crank up the economy and, indirectly, to improve business conditions. Moreover, such measures as have been undertaken have bypassed unemployed women even more clearly than unemployed men.

This unemployment has hit women much harder than men. Obviously, this has furthered the disintegration of women's employment opportunities, with all the problematic consequences noted above. It has at the same time further emphasized the reserve character of women's employment.

Women constitute approximately 51 percent of the registered unemployed. This proportion has remained stable for some time; indeed, any changes in the trend suggest an increase. If one adds to the officially registered the estimated number of unregistered unemployed in the so-called "quiet reserve" (for example, women who are looking for work but who are not registered with the employment office; young girls who are looking for a training post; women at the end of the so-called family phase who want to return to work but who give up because the prospects are poor; women who lack the legal qualifications for financial support and are therefore no longer registered), then women probably constitute hardly less than two-thirds of the actual unemployed in Germany.

All this comes down to one basic fact: the imperfect integration of women into the economic and employment process, connected to the still-existent one-sided process of socialization of women exclusively toward the family. Besides the factors we have already discussed—women's susceptibility to dismissal for business reasons, their lesser academic and occupational qualifications, their high concentration in women's occupations and in unskilled jobs that are easily replaced by automation—still other elements play a role. Broad areas of industry in which a greater than average number of women—and those in which more women than men work—come increasingly under pressure. When the markets of the industrial states are opened to products from developing countries of the southern hemisphere, as they properly must, the textile industry, jewelry manufacture, leather processing, and the electrotechnical and optics industries will shrink and at the same time "release" labor supplies—of women. Second, the federal, Land, and municipal governments in Germany are no longer hiring at the same rates they were a decade ago, due to financial difficulties. Those most affected by these restrictive hiring policies are graduates of training programs attended primarily by women. Teachers, educators, social workers, professionals in the health fields, all work in Germany almost exclusively in the public sector. A moratorium on hiring in these areas raises the unemployment rate considerably. For the women affected a further development in these areas becomes apparent: sharper competition from men. In a weak economy these occupations become more attractive (more secure jobs, good pay, secure pensions) and attract more male workers. In itself this would be an admirable development, because it loosens up a labor market divided according to sex. Its consequences only become problematic when—as here—the desirable opposing trend is lacking: women are not penetrating to the same extent other secure, promising "reserves for men."

It is against this background that we must consider specific measures to combat women's unemployment. Clearly, efforts must be increased to combat women's unemployment more intensively and effectively. The insight that this is necessary has begun to be more widely accepted, if only in nonconservative camps.

But well-thought-out, realistic proposals are not too plentiful. Particularly in feminist-oriented circles the discussion seems to be dominated by the idea that the problems of unemployment of women—and those of discrimination in general—should and could be solved through hiring quotas and similar individual measures, unconnected in other respects to existing economic and labor market problems. This approach seems unrealistic; in the present climate of conservatism, its success would be doomed by lack of popular support and, specifically, of necessary support among women themselves. For ideological as well as tactical reasons, it seems preferable to continue to treat and understand the problems of equality and unemployment of women as problems of a group that is particularly affected by special circumstances. Since joblessness among women has to do with present conditions, measures to combat this unemployment must—and can—contribute generally to the improvement of opportunities for women within the framework of general labor market policy.

One set of widely discussed proposals concern labor market policies for shortening the work week and/or restructuring the volume of working time. Such policies, on the one hand, would have high withdrawal effects. But they could also improve the educational prerequisites of the girls and women who are working today, of the unemployed, and of those just entering employment since the introduction of a mandatory tenth school year or the introduction of a regular, obligatory leave for education is to be preferred to a shortening of the daily or weekly working time (of at most ½ to 2½ hours) or the lowering of the general retirement age.

Particularly important in our context are proposals which can be realized with the help of the existing mechanisms of the Federal Institution for Employment in Nürnberg, which is the government authority in charge of the labor market, with branches in every larger city. If they were used to set and implement specific goals and calculate cost, the mechanisms already available could contribute considerably to stabilizing women's unemployment, to rectifying the concentration according to sex, and thereby to lowering the high proportion of women among the unemployed. Since 1969 these authorities have had a legal obligation, among others, to contribute to the chances of employees in endangered jobs through forward-looking continuing education or retraining programs. Jobless workers have the right to receive support and assistance to participate in such programs to improve their ability to change occupations and to decrease unemployment.

Women have so far participated insufficiently in these activities. They constitute much too small a proportion of the beneficiaries—far less than their proportion among the employed, or even among the unemployed. Women are most strongly represented in relatively short, unconditional programs of further education and retraining, while one finds fewer women in longer, more comprehensive programs which provide more secure qualifications. Until now the continuing education and retraining programs of the labor administration have done nothing either for workers in threatened jobs or for jobless women to reduce the sex distortions of the labor market.

It is particularly regrettable that this situation affects the assistance of young girls with or without a completed education. The programs are supposed to facilitate their integration into training positions, but the annual report on the advancement and hiring programs for 1973–1974 shows that practically no job changes or planned preparation of young girls for so-called "men's occupations" had occurred or been tenaciously attempted; the programs had produced one woman mechanic trainee as opposed to 383 sales clerks and 118 domestics.

Since January 1, 1976, there has been a marked decrease in the number of women who have taken part in advancement programs or who have wanted to return to their original occupation after completion of the second, family, phase of the three-phase employment pattern. The number of unemployed women who take part in the labor authority's so-called works programs to prepare themselves for new jobs is infinitesimal. The mobility bonuses introduced in recent years to promote regional mobility by encouraging the unemployed to accept lower pay or different occupations than they were originally trained for, have, as expected, almost completely bypassed women.

The fact that all these deficits are recognized today has led to other proposals for improving the employment structure for women and thereby improving women's opportunities. For example, quotas could be introduced according to sex for the assignment of jobless employees in the works programs. Similar quotas could be applied to the labor authority's further education and retraining programs for jobless workers. These quotas would apply not only to the total number of participants in all programs, but also to the individual level of skills. The advancement programs for unemployed women could also be geared to particular content goals to further help equalize concentrations according to sex in the job market. (Such retraining and further education programs should take into account women who, for family reasons, must fall back on part-time work and part-time schooling.) Finally, changes must be made in the procedures concerning referral of job seekers to open positions, counseling of employees, and obtaining and posting job openings with reference to sex.

Such programs are finding growing support in the political and parliamentary party of the SPD. At the last party convention in Hamburg a motion to refer the above-mentioned programs to the Federal Institution for Employment was passed by a large majority. Similarly, the SDP-controlled Land government of Hesse will take up such programs in its new administration. But so far there have been no major attempts to realize these or similar proposals. The financial and policy requirements were present. But until now it has been left up to the—too little—insight and initiative of the Land labor officials whether, in what manner, with what means, and in what scope programs would be introduced. There have been initial attempts to retrain unemployed women for men's occupations and to allow women who want part-time work to participate in continuing education programs of this kind in the Land of North Rhine-Westphalia, but nothing certain about their success can be reported at this time.

A less sensible class of proposals claims to support solutions in the labor market but actually removes, rather than brings closer, the goal of achieving more equality of opportunity. An example is the CDU proposal, increasingly discussed in Germany, to pay "upbringing money" to mothers or, as other groups prefer, the parents of small children to enable them to give up their employment in order to care for their children themselves for a certain time—usually one year; during this period they would receive a kind of compensation for lost wages or salary of approximately 300 DM to 600 DM per month.

However worthy the value of encouraging parental upbringing of children would be in itself, the timing and sociopolitical context of this movement gives pause for thought. Because of the small amount of the government stipend, it might well be accepted only by women, and not by men, certainly not those in a secure employment situation. In fact, the unemployment compensation that could be claimed is much higher. Similarly, the one-year limit raises the question of re-employment. This obligation is completely missing from the CDU proposal. The SPD proposal provides for the parent who claims both the stipend and the right to be rehired after the year's expiration. But it is unclear whether such a right could be realized under existing economic conditions or if such a regulation would not increase the danger that employers might be even more hesitant about hiring young women, who in this proposal, for all practical purposes, are the only ones concerned.

Extending paid maternity leave beyond the biologically necessary recovery time to approximately one year and transforming this period into an option for the parents that would depend upon the interruption of both parents' employment might make rehiring more likely. Collectively, it would require no more resources than would be needed to pay a realistic amount of "upbringing money." It would open up jobs—if only temporarily; it would honor the joint work of bringing up children; it would assure the infant a reference person from its own environment; it would strengthen the father-child relationship; and, finally, it would avoid forcing the mother out of the employment world, with all its negative consequences.

According to the January 1, 1976, version of the employment-promotion law, women are justified in claiming part-time work because of their family responsibilities. Statistics show that the number of women seeking part-time work is steadily increasing every month. In February 1978 the number was almost 200,000 women, of approximately 560,000. The number of jobs available to them was less than 18,000. Consequently, demands for an increase in the number of part-time jobs "for women" are usually prominent in discussions in Germany about overcoming women's unemployment. In particular, conservative factions support such demands strongly. But, as we have seen, from the standpoint of equal opportunity, such a demand must be rated ambivalently; part-time work is too susceptible to pressures from the economy and from rational reorganization and it strengthens the causes of discrimination against women in the working world.

Any actions to create more part-time jobs, therefore, must be linked to additional legal and wage policy measures designed to improve the integation of these jobs into the organization of the firm, and hence to reduce the risk of unemployment and to increase the attractiveness of part-time jobs and the possibility of advancement in such jobs. In the foreseeable future, as an increasing number of both jobless and graduates will be seeking full-time work, the fulfillment of this condition is not likely. Except in branches of public service, in which legal stipulations may balance out some of the disadvantages, part-time work will continue to be characterized by minimal security and attractiveness. It will remain a women's domain, with all the acknowledged consequences of discrimination. Moreover, since part-time work only cements the existing division of function and responsibility into paid work for men versus housework for women, the usefulness of creating more part-time jobs becomes still more questionable. At the least, it would be consistent to create an effective demand for more part-time jobs among men by reducing the amount of working time per day, week, or month, without a wage adjustment. Such a regulation, obviously, could only find application in those job areas where compensation is considerably above the average so that the wage adjustment would not be unbearable. The achievement of such partial regulation would be a step forward in easing the rigid function and role prescriptions between men and women.

Behind the suggestions for "upbringing money" and the proposals to legitimate part-time work for women stands too clearly a trend toward forcing women more strongly than ever out of the business world. At the very least, those who support equal employment opportunity for women must oppose those new policies and proposals, and seek to develop new goals within already existing labor market policies for combatting the high unemployment of women and the continuing discrimination against them.

NOTE

1. Max Rheinstein and Mary Ann Glendon, "West German Marriage and Family Law Reform," *University of Chicago Law Review* 45 (Spring 1978): 519–552.

16 *Ralph E. Smith*

WOMEN'S STAKE IN A HIGH-GROWTH ECONOMY IN THE UNITED STATES

The U.S. economy is currently recovering from the severest recession since that of the 1930s. In the last quarter of 1977, the national unemployment rate was 6.6 percent, compared with almost 9 percent in mid-1975. Women's progress in the labor market in many ways has been closely related to the ebbs and flows of the national economy. The number of women who choose to seek jobs, their success in finding and retaining jobs, and the kinds of job opportunities available to them are all influenced by aggregate economic conditions.

The main theme of this chapter is that a high-growth macroeconomic policy is an essential ingredient in any effective strategy for advancing women's labor market position. A strong economy will not, by itself, generate equality between men and women. But it will provide an environment within which specific equal employment tools are much more likely to be effective.

During the decade prior to 1973, the total number of people employed in the U.S. had been increasing by 1.5 to 2.7 million workers per year.[1] In the two-year period between 1973IV and 1975IV, however, total employment fell by 200,000. In the two-year period between 1975IV and 1977IV, total employment increased by 6.8 million. The progress and setbacks experienced by female workers in the United States between 1973 and 1977 provide an excellent opportunity to analyze the impact on women of fluctuations in the national economy. The sharp contrast in aggregate economic conditions between the adjacent two periods provides the setting for this analysis.

While I would not argue that all of the difference in women's labor market experiences between the two periods is attributable to the economic climate, that seems a more plausible factor than any other that comes to mind. The equal employment opportunity legislation had all been enacted

NOTE: Opinions expressed are those of the author and do not necessarily reflect the views of The Urban Institute or its sponsors. Comments by Nancy Smith Barrett and Ronnie Steinberg Ratner on a previous draft are gratefully acknowledged.

prior to the recession. Although a new administration did take office in January 1977, it is unlikely that any changes in enforcement strategy or commitment would have had a substantial effect in such a short length of time.

The first section of this chapter deals with the issue of how to measure and interpret changes in the labor market for women. The secular growth in the proportion of women in the labor force makes it difficult to interpret changes in employment or unemployment, as conventionally measured. The interpretation of these statistics is facilitated by the presentaion of an additional measure of joblessness, which adjusts for normal labor force growth.

In the second section, labor market data for 1973IV–1977IV are analyzed and interpreted. We will see that there was a substantial reduction in female employment growth during the recession and a substantial increase during the recovery. Much of this cyclical vulnerability was not reflected in the unemployment statistics. The decisions made by many women regarding whether to enter or remain in the labor market were, themselves, influenced by the state of the economy.

A more detailed analysis of this period, reported in the third section, indicates that the kinds of jobs women held strongly influenced their vulnerability to economic fluctuations. The cyclical sensitivity of female workers as a group was less than that of male workers during both the recession and the recovery. This was because the traditionally female sectors of the labor market, such as retail sales, were less affected by the business cycle. On the other hand, in some predominantly male industries, female employees incurred disproportionate losses during the recession and made disproportionate gains during the recovery. Any effects of equal employment opportunity enforcement in these industries were overshadowed by the effects of the recession and recovery.

The fourth section provides a brief assessment of a related issue— the extent to which women are responsible for the higher national unemployment experienced in the U.S. in recent years. Conclusions and speculations are presented in the final section.

MEASURING AND INTERPRETING CHANGE

Some of the important questions asked here ought to be rather easy to answer: How many jobs did women lose due to the recession? How many did they gain from the recovery? How did they fare in each period relative to men? Each month the U.S. Bureau of the Census conducts a comprehensive labor market survey from which estimates of female and male employment and unemployment are calculated.[2] It might seem that the changes in these series would directly answer the questions.

However, changes in employment and unemployment are also related to patterns of labor force growth, which differ between the sexes. The total number of people in the civilian labor force—the sum of employment and unemployment—grows as the population grows. During the four years examined here, the civilian noninstitutional population aged sixteen and over grew by 10.8 million people. With no change in the proportion of the population working or actively seeking work, population growth alone would have caused the labor force to grow by 6.6 million. But the proportion of the female population who are in the labor force has also been increasing, while that of males has been declining. Female labor force participation rates have been increasing for a wide variety of reasons, including changes in sex role attitudes, wages and job opportunities, increases in divorces and separations, and reductions in fertility. Male participation has been gradually declining, probably due to longer education and earlier retirement. The net effects of these opposing participation patterns have generally been to increase the proportion of the total population in the labor force and to increase women's share. In recent years, women have typically accounted for about 60 percent of total labor force growth.[3]

One consequence of these long-term trends is that employment opportunities must continually increase merely to keep up with normal labor force growth. Another consequence is that female employment must increase more rapidly than male employment merely to keep pace with women's growing share of the labor force. As long as these patterns continue, then, period-to-period increases in the number of jobs provided in the labor market do not necessarily signal improvement. The standard against which progress should be measured is continually moving. Since the female labor force has been expanding more rapidly than the male labor force, the norm against which relative progress should be measured is also changing.

In addition, labor force participation rates, especially of women, tend to fall in a recession or increase at a slower than usual rate. This "discouraged worker" phenomenon results from the withdrawal from the labor market of persons losing or unable to find jobs and the failure of some to enter when they feel no job is available. Thus, aggregate employment losses during a recession will be larger than the concurrent unemployment increases and their demographic distributions will differ. Similarly, the employment gains during recovery will be larger than the unemployment reductions and will have a different distribution.

To reflect more accurately the impacts of cyclical fluctuations on the availability of jobs, we use a jobless measure that combines both unemployment and labor force variation. The unemployment rate indicates the percentage of the *actual* labor force without jobs; our jobless rate is an estimate of the percentage of the *potential* labor force without jobs. The difference between the number of people who would be available and the number who are actually working is our estimate of joblessness. Labor force potential size is defined as the number of people who would be working or looking for work if the economy were operating at full employment.[4]

Estimates of the normal growth rates of the female and male labor force vary. In an analysis of the recession's impact prepared in 1976, I used an estimate of 1.35 million per year for the female labor force and 0.8 million for the male labor force.[5] These estimates were based on an econometric model of the U.S. labor market developed at the Urban Institute. Through simulation, the model provides conditional forecasts of the size of the labor force (and other labor market statistics) for sixteen groups, delineated by sex, age, and race. The potential labor force series used here were based on a simulation in which the national unemployment rate was kept to 4.0 percent throughout the 1970s. As shown in the next section, these projections of normal or potential labor force growth were reasonably close to the actual growth that occurred over the four-year period 1973IV–1977IV. For both females and males, however, the recession in the first half of the period caused below-potential growth and the subsequent recovery generated above-potential growth.

The estimates of women's stake in a high-growth economy presented in this chapter all relate to the *numbers* of women in the labor force, employed, or jobless in various periods. Recessions also harm people who do not lose their jobs. Wages, hours, and promotion opportunities are all affected by the state of the economy. These costs are not examined here.

ANALYSIS OF THE RECENT RECESSION AND RECOVERY

In this section I will analyze and interpret the employment and unemployment histories of men and women during the 1973IV–1977IV period, using the jobless concept described in the previous section. The upper part of Figure 16-1 (an extension of the figure reported in my previous analysis of the recession) illustrates the effects of the recession and recovery on each group. For the total noninstitutional civilian population, and for each sex, quarterly averages of the group's actual labor force size and employment are plotted. By definition, the difference between the group's labor force and employment levels, illustrated by the gap between the two lines, measures its unemployment. The straight line plotted for each group is my estimate of the trend in its potential labor force; that is, the growth that would have occurred if the economy had produced enough jobs throughout the entire period to maintain a 4 percent unemployment rate. For the reasons discussed in the previous section, the potential labor force line for females is steeper than that for males. Joblessness is depicted by the shaded area between the potential labor force and employment. The bottom panel of Figure 16-1 provides a plot for the same period of my corresponding

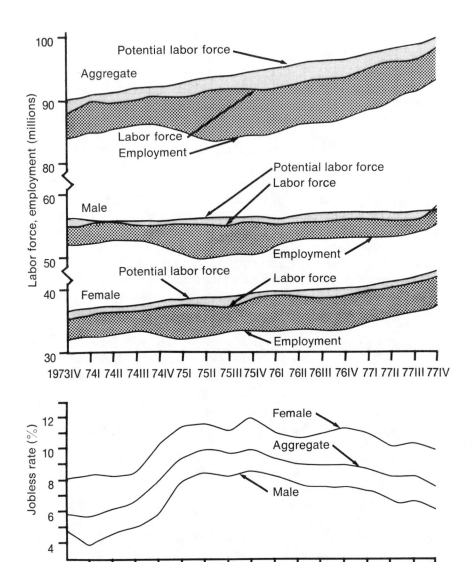

FIGURE 16-1
Labor Market Conditions, by Sex, 1973IV–1977IV

jobless rate estimates for each group. This is the percentage of the group's potential labor force that is without work.

Several patterns can be seen from this figure. First, throughout the first half of the period, the labor force of both groups were not expanding as rapidly as their long-term trends and, throughout the second half, their labor forces were expanding at above-trend growth rates. The size of both groups' labor forces were sensitive to the state of the job market. Hence, the increases in unemployment of both groups understated their job losses and the decreases in unemployment understated their subsequent gains.

Second, throughout the entire period, the female jobless rate was considerably higher than the male jobless rate and a larger fraction of female joblessness was associated with below-potential labor force size, rather than unemployment.

Third, there was a remarkable similarity between the two sexes in the cyclical sensitivity of their jobless rates. Both groups incurred considerable job losses during the recession and have been recovering since. By the end of 1977, the jobless rates of both groups were still well above the rates four years earlier. The lines illustrating the jobless rate paths of the two groups are nearly parallel.

Table 16-1 provides the same data for the beginning and final quarters of the four-year period and for the midpoint, marking the turn-around in the state of the labor market. The last three columns report the changes that occurred in each group's labor market status during the two-year recession period, the two-year recovery period, and the entire year. With these estimates, some of the effects of the economic cycle are brought into sharper focus.

At the start of the recession, in 1973IV, 4.8 percent of the nation's active labor force were unemployed. If 4.0 percent is used as the standard for measuring full employment, then there was some slack in the labor market, even before the recession began. From our model, we estimate that a 4.0 percent unemployment rate would have been associated with a labor force of approximately 90.7 million people, of whom 35.9 million would be female. This potential labor force is about one million larger than the actual size of the labor force in 1973IV, the difference being our estimate of the number of people who were discouraged from active participation; most were female. Our jobless rate estimates, which include both the unemployed and the discouraged, indicate that at the outset of the recession 5.8 percent of the nation's potential labor force were jobless, including 8.1 percent of the females and 4.4 percent of the males.

During the two-year recession period, the nation's jobless rate climbed to 10.3 percent; that of females to 12.2 percent; and that of males to 9.0 percent. By this measure, men did slightly worse than women: a 4.6 percent increase in the male jobless rate, compared with 4.1 percent in the

TABLE 16-1

Employment Status, by Sex, Selected Quarter's

(in thousands, except as indicated)*

Employment status	1973IV	1975IV	1977IV	CHANGE 1973IV–1975IV	1975IV–1977IV	1973IV–1977IV
Aggregate						
Labor force	89,745	93,153	98,616	3,408	5,463	8,871
Employment	85,428	85,241	92,062	−187	6,821	6,634
Unemployment	4,317	7,912	6,554	3,595	−1,358	2,237
Unemployment rate (%)	4.8	8.5	6.6	3.7	−1.9	1.8
Potential labor force	90,716	95,012	99,308	4,296	4,296	8,592
Jobless	5,288	9,771	7,246	4,483	−2,525	1,958
Jobless rate (%)	5.8	10.3	7.3	4.5	−3.0	1.5
Female						
Labor force	35,057	37,339	40,572	2,282	3,233	5,515
Employment	32,978	33,903	37,363	925	3,460	4,385
Unemployment	2,079	3,436	3,209	1,357	−227	1,130
Unemployment rate (%)	5.9	9.2	7.9	3.3	−1.3	2.0
Potential labor force	35,880	38,592	41,304	2,712	2,712	5,424
Jobless	2,902	4,689	3,941	1,787	−748	1,039
Jobless rate (%)	8.1	12.2	9.5	4.1	−2.7	1.4
Male						
Labor force	54,689	55,815	58,044	1,126	2,229	3,355
Employment	52,450	51,338	54,699	−1,112	3,361	2.249
Unemployment	2,238	4,476	3,345	2,238	−1,131	1,107
Unemployment rate (%)	4.1	8.0	5.8	3.9	−2.2	1.7
Potential labor force	54,836	56,420	58,004	1,584	1,584	3,168
Jobless	2,386	5,082	3,305	2,696	−1,777	919
Jobless rate (%)	4.4	9.0	5.7	4.6	−3.3	1.3

*All labor force, employment, and unemployment series are seasonally adjusted and are from *Employment and Earnings* 22 (Feb. 1976): 142–190 for 1973IV through 1975IV and from the *Economic Report of the President* (Washington, D.C.: GPO, 1978) after 1975IV. The potential labor force series are the author's estimates and the jobless series are calculated from the difference between the group's potential labor force and actual employment. Details may not add to totals due to rounding.

female rate. A comparison of conventional unemployment rate increases provides a similar pattern: a 3.9 percent increase for men versus a 3.3 percent increase for women.

Note that a simple comparison of changes in employment during the two-year period would have given a very misleading portrayal of women's labor market progress during the recession. Female employment increased by about 900,000, while male employment decreased by a slightly larger number. In fact, both groups lost relative to the employment levels they would have attained had the recession not occurred. Our jobless estimates indicate the magnitude of the losses relative to the normal growth in the labor force we estimate would have occurred. Since the female labor force has long been increasing more rapidly than that of males, female employment must also expand by a larger amount. The official unemployment statistics, which measure employment losses relative to actual labor force, also show that both groups lost and that the magnitude of the losses were not very different.

The pattern of the recovery observed between 1975 and 1977 has been symmetric to that of the recession. Just as men incurred a slightly larger share of the job losses during the recession, they also are receiving a slightly larger share of the job gains associated with the recovery. As reported in the fifth column of Table 16-1, in the two-year recovery period aggregate unemployment has fallen by almost 1.4 million and the labor force has expanded by about 1.2 million more than normal growth for a two-year period. As a result, the nation's unemployment rate has fallen by 1.9 percentage points and the jobless rate by 3.0 points. The male unemployment rate fell by 0.9 points more than the female unemployment rate and the male jobless rate fell by 0.6 points more than that of females.

After four of the most turbulent years in post–World War II economic history, the relative position of women in the U.S. labor market has barely changed. The growth in the nation's total labor force over the four-year period was a little larger than I had originally estimated to be the underlying trend.[6] The difference, 300,000 more than the 8.6 million anticipated growth in potential labor force, is mostly due to above-trend growth in the male labor force. It seems clear that some potential labor force participants in both sexes timed their participation in accordance with the availability of jobs.

Thus far, the recovery has not brought aggregate unemployment or jobless rates back to their pre-recession rates, but it has evened out the distribution. Between the start of the recession (1973IV) and the end of 1977, the unemployment rates of men and women each increased by about two points and their jobless rates each increased by about 1.4 points.

To summarize this part of the analysis, it is clear that women's progress in the U.S. labor market during the past four years was closely related to the overall state of the labor market. The recession retarded their labor force growth and increased their joblessness; the recovery is providing an economic environment more conducive to their labor force participation and, as one consequence, their joblessness is declining. All of these cyclical patterns were found for men as well. However, the impact of the economic cycle on male joblessness was more pronounced. Why is it that female employment was less cyclical than male employment? To answer this requires an examination of the kinds of jobs women hold.

WHERE WOMEN GAINED AND LOST

In an earlier report, which analyzed the impact of the recession, I sought to explain why women lost fewer jobs than men. Was it because individual employers treated men and women more even-handedly than in the past? Was it because women themselves changed their behavior? Or was it merely because the recession disproportionately hurt industries which employed few women? This last hypothesis presented the least optimistic outlook, since one would expect such gains to be transitory. In fact, this was the hypothesis that appeared most realistic. In that study I concluded that the "major reason that women did not do worse appears to be that the recession struck hardest at industries and occupations in which women are most underrepresented. Hence, during the initial stages of the recovery, the relative employment of women may decline or at least not continue its past rate of increase."[7] An extension of the earlier analysis to the recovery period, reported in this section, suggests that my pessimism was justified.

There is a strong pattern of industrial segregation of women in the U.S. labor market. This is observable even with highly aggregated data. For example, in 1977 women held only 6.4 percent of the jobs in the construction industry and 23.4 percent of the jobs in durable goods manufacturing. By contrast, 86.1 percent of all workers in private household services and 58.9 percent of workers in other service industries were female. This pattern—while harmful to working women in most respects—did make them less vulnerable to the job losses resulting from the recession. Annual averages of employment levels, cross-tabulated by sex and industry, demonstrate this point and can be used to calculate a very rough estimate of the magnitude of this sheltering effect.

The first six columns of Table 16-2 show total and female employment levels in each of the twelve major sectors of the economy in 1973, 1975, and 1977. To estimate the extent to which shifts in the industrial structure of the economy during and after the recession affected total female employment, I began by computing the employment levels in each industry that would have been attained if all industries grew proportionately since 1973. In this hypothetical world total employment in each industry would have increased by 0.45 percent between 1973 and 1975 and by 7.27 percent between 1973 and 1977. The difference between these hypothetical levels shown in columns 7 and 8 and actual employment represent the effects of shifts in the industrial structure on each industry's total employment.

Over the four-year period the effects of recession and recovery were superimposed on an economy that has long been becoming more service-oriented. Notice that between 1973 and 1975 there were major losses in the construction and manufacturing industries. For example, if the durable goods manufacturing sector had kept up with the rest of the economy, employment in that sector would have risen by less than 100,000, rather than declining by nearly one million workers. By contrast, in the service sector (other than private household services) total employment increased by 1.6 million, rather than the 100,000 consistent with proportionate growth.

By 1977 these differential growth rates had considerably narrowed. Partial recovery in durable goods manufacturing increased total employment in that industry by 800,000, about proportionate to the increase in aggregate employment in that period. The service sector grew by another 1.9 million workers, continuing to outpace the rest of the economy.

Total female employment was boosted by the long-run increase in service sector employment and by the specific industrial incidence of the recession. Columns 9 and 10 report the number of women who would have been employed in each industry in 1975 and 1977 if the industry had experienced the hypothetical employment gains indicated in the preceding columns. These were estimated by multiplying the hypothetical employment levels in columns 7 and 8 by women's actual proportion of employment in that industry in 1975 and 1977, respectively.

If the twelve major industries had grown proportionately between 1973 and 1975, 33 million women would have held jobs (column 9), one-half million fewer than actually were employed that year (column 5). That is, because of the favorable shift in industry composition during this two-year period, female employment grew by a half-million more than it might have otherwise. Had it not been for this, the composition of the job losses by sex would have been reversed.

During the recovery, there were very few additional gains from changes in industry mix. By 1977, female employment was 700,000 higher than it would have been in the absence of shifts in industrial structure since 1973 (columns 6 minus 10). The small gain (200,000) between 1975 and 1977 was due to the continued strength of the service sector, which was sufficient to offset the recovery in the predominantly male industries.

Changes in the industrial composition of total employment are probably beyond the scope of equal opportunity policy, although they certainly should influence it. Of more direct concern is women's *share* of employment within each industry. This, too, is influenced by the state of the economy, but in the opposite direction. A recession is an especially bad

TABLE 16-2
Impacts of Shifts in Industrial Structure on Female Employment
(annual averages, in thousands)

Industry	ACTUAL						HYPOTHETICAL			
	(1) Total employment, 1973*	(2) Total employment, 1975*	(3) Total employment, 1977†	(4) Female employment, 1973*	(5) Female employment, 1975*	(6) Female employment, 1977†	(7) Total employment, 1975‡	(8) Total employment, 1977§	(9) Female employment, 1975‖	(10) Female employment, 1977#
Agriculture	3,452	3,381	3,244	619	579	605	3,467	3,703	593	689
Mining	630	732	814	56	70	69	633	676	61	57
Construction	5,514	5,015	5,504	311	311	350	5,538	5,915	343	379
Manufacturing, durables	12,438	11,441	12,274	2,711	2,479	2,867	12,493	13,342	2,711	3,122
Manufacturing, nondurables	8,503	7,834	8,363	3,319	3,031	3,289	8,541	9,121	3,288	3,585
Transportation, public utilities	5,515	5,623	5,833	1,164	1,231	1,303	5,539	5,916	1,213	1,319
Wholesale trade	3,223	3,333	3,597	726	760	848	3,237	3,457	738	816
Retail trade	13,627	14,137	15,109	6,414	6,844	7,440	13,687	14,618	6,625	7,192

Finance, insurance, real estate	4,540	4,665	5,038	2,288	2,396	2,725	4,560	4,870	2,344	2,635
Private household services	1,585	1,378	1,406	1,400	1,213	1,210	1,592	1,700	1,401	1,464
Other services	20,892	22,477	24,391	12,113	13,162	14,345	20,985	22,411	12,297	13,178
Public administration	4,489	4,770	4,972	1,324	1,477	1,635	4,509	4,815	1,398	1,584
TOTAL	84,408	84,786	90,545	32,445	33,553	36,686	84,781	90,544	33,012	36,020

*Employment and Earnings 22 (Feb. 1976): 17, 19.

†Employment and Earnings 24 (Jan. 1978): 157.

‡Column 1 times 1.0045.

§Column 1 times 1.0727.

‖Column 7 times column 5 divided by column 2.

#Column 8 times column 6 divided by column 3.

NOTE: Details may not add to totals due to rounding.

economic enviroment in which to enter or remain in predominantly male sectors.

Between 1973 and 1977 women increased their share of employment within virtually every major industry.[8] This is consistent with the long-run growth in women's share of total employment in the U.S. However, one effect of the recession appears to have been to interrupt this progress, especially within some of the very industries that employed the fewest numbers of women. Columns 1 through 3 of Table 16-3 report the female share of each major industry's employees during 1973, 1975, and 1977. The remaining columns estimate the effects of within-industry changes in female shares on final employment levels. The effects of changes during the recession are reported in column 4, calculated by multiplying the change in the female share within the industry between 1973 and 1975 by the total level of employment in that industry in 1975. The effects of subsequent changes are shown in column 5 and the effects of changes over the entire four-year period in column 6.

The contrast between the two periods provides a vivid illustration of the damage of a recession and the benefit of a recovery in terms of employment integration. During the 1973–1975 period, women actually lost ground in the manufacturing sector, even though their share of total national employment increased. The only industries in which their shares substantially increased were retail trade, services, and public administration. All these industries already had many female workers and were relatively unaffected by the recession.

The recovery seems to have repaired the damage. In virtually every sector—including manufacturing—women's share of employment increased. Nearly half of the net additions to manufacturing employment were female. Hence, between 1975 and 1977, female employment gains from increased industry shares were not only larger than during the recession but they were also more widely distributed.

A DIGRESSION ON WOMEN'S "RESPONSIBILITY" FOR
HIGH UNEMPLOYMENT

Throughout this chapter I have emphasized the impact of aggregate economic conditions on women's success within the labor market. One important impact is on some women's decisions regarding whether even to participate in the paid labor force. Evidence was presented showing that the growth of the female labor force was retarded during the recession and has increased during the recovery. These are fluctuations around a steep trend in female labor force growth which, itself, is alleged to have led to higher national unemployment.

TABLE 16-3
Impacts of Changes in the Female Share of Employment within
Each Industry
(annual averages, in thousands)

	FEMALE SHARE OF INDUSTRY EMPLOYMENT*			IMPACT OF CHANGES†		
	(1)	*(2)*	*(3)*	*(4)* 1973– 1975	*(5)* 1975– 1977	*(6)* 1973– 1977
Industry	*1973*	*1975*	*1977*			
Agriculture	.1793	.1713	.1865	−28	49	23
Mining	.0889	.0956	.0848	5	−9	−3
Construction	.0564	.0620	.0636	29	9	40
Manufacturing, durables	.2180	.2167	.2336	−15	208	192
Manufacturing, nondurables	.3903	.3869	.3933	−27	54	25
Transportation, public utilities	.2111	.2189	.2233	44	26	72
Wholesale trade	.2253	.2280	.2358	9	28	38
Retail trade	.4707	.4841	.4924	190	125	328
Finance, insurance, real estate	.5040	.5136	.5409	45	138	186
Private household services	.8833	.8803	.8606	−4	−28	−32
Other services	.5798	.5856	.5881	131	61	202
Public administration	.2949	.3096	.3288	71	95	169
TOTAL				448	756	1,238

*Proportions computed from female employment and aggregate employment data, by industry, in Table 16-2.

†Estimated impact of change from one period to the next within an industry equals the change in female proportion multiplied by the aggregate industry employment level in the latter year; for example, column 4 equals industry employment in 1975 (from Table 16-2) multiplied by columns 2–1. Note that the impacts of changes over the entire period are slightly different from the sums of the two sub-periods because of the shift in industry mix in the intervening period.

The perception of this linkage—from rising female labor force participation to higher unemployment for everyone—appears to be widespread among economic planners. In effect, women's increased commitment to paid work is being blamed for part of the nation's unemployment. Is this charge justified?

In the narrowest sense, the presence of more women in the labor force *does* translate into higher national unemployment numbers. More people seeking jobs—regardless of their gender—will result in more unemployment if nothing else changes. The total supply of jobs already falls short of the total number of people working plus those seeking work, and additional job-seekers increase the shortfall.

There is no reason to assume, however, that policy-makers should or must be passive. Indeed, it is their responsibility to try to anticipate the number of people who will be in the labor market and their problems and to plan macroeconomic and labor market policies accordingly. I fear that one barrier to their doing so is that women's employment and unemployment are taken less seriously than the jobs and unemployment of men. One function of individuals seeking to bring about equality for women in the labor market is to educate other policy-makers about the seriousness of many women's commitments to and need for paid employment. This task is made much more difficult when jobs are scarce. One further benefit to women of a high growth economy may be to soften the views of those who see each additional woman entering the labor force as a threat to a more deserving man.[9]

CONCLUSIONS

As illustrated by the experience of women in the U.S. during the past four years, women have a large stake in a high-growth economy. The pace of growth in the national labor market is an important determinant of the number of women who participate in the labor force, their ability to find and retain jobs, and the kinds of jobs they get. Without a healthy labor market, it becomes all the more difficult to increase women's share of employment in predominantly male sectors.

Harder to document, but also important, is the atmosphere toward women's work that surrounds a growing versus a declining labor market. When there are few jobs to go around, relative to the number of job-seekers, members of groups that do not have well-recognized roots in the labor force are more likely to be singled out as the ones who should be at the end of the queue. Women, especially if married to men with jobs, often fall into this category. Thus, their labor force participation is resented, all the more so if they seek jobs in occupations or industries that are traditionally male. Also, since they may have developed less seniority in such jobs, they are more vulnerable to layoffs. Within this kind of a divisive atmosphere, policies and programs to achieve equality for women in the labor market may be more difficult to enact and implement and less likely to succeed.

NOTES

1. *Economic Report of the President* (Washington, D.C.: GPO, 1978), p. 288. In 1970 and 1971 the increases were smaller due to the recession in that period.

2. Information is collected from about 47,000 households throughout the U.S. by the Bureau of the Census for the Bureau of Labor Statistics. Tabulations and explanatory notes are published monthly in *Employment and Earnings*.

3. Consequences of anticipated future growth in the female labor force will be examined in Ralph E. Smith, ed., *The Subtle Revolution: Women at Work* (Washington, D.C.: Urban Institute, forthcoming).

4. Ralph E. Smith and Jean E. Vanski, "The Jobless Rate: Another Dimension of the Employment Picture," *Urban Institute Paper 350–76* (1975).

5. Ralph E. Smith, *The Impact of Macroeconomic Conditions on Employment Opportunities for Women* (U.S. Congress, Joint Economic Committee, Series on Achieving the Goals of the Employment Act of 1946; Washington, D.C.: GPO, 1977). Most of the present analysis is based on the methods developed in this study.

6. The trend estimate was from the model simulation in which the national unemployment rate was maintained at 4.0 percent throughout the 1970s. The equations for this model were originally estimated with data from the 1967 to 1973 period. Trends estimated with data covering the period through 1977 are slightly steeper.

7. Smith, *The Impact of Macroeconomic Conditions*, p. 15.

8. The exceptions were mining and private household services.

9. For additional discussion of women's "responsibility," see my "The Effects of the Increased Labor Force Participation of Women on Macroeconomic Goals: A Comment," *American Economic Review, Papers and Proceedings*, 68 (May 1978): 97–98.

17 *Hilary Land*

SOCIAL POLICIES AND THE FAMILY: THEIR EFFECT ON WOMEN'S PAID EMPLOYMENT IN GREAT BRITAIN

"The family does not function in a social vacuum. . . . Its responsibilities have grown: it has been placed in more situations of divided loyalties and conflicting values, it has been forced to choose between kinship and economic progress," wrote Richard Titmuss, one of Britain's most distinguished teachers and students of social policy.[1] This statement is as relevant today as when it was published in 1963; in particular it is still predominantly the women in the family who are pulled most strongly by the tensions between the demands of members of their family and of economic change. This chapter will focus on the conflict between women's responsibilities to their families and their activities in the labor market and show that the assumptions about the nature and division of responsibilities among family members which underpin so many British social policies help to perpetuate this conflict. Moreover, recent developments in various social policies show very little weakening of these assumptions. As a result, although an Equal Pay Act and a Sex Discrimination Act have become law in the 1970s, substantial barriers still prevent women from achieving equal pay and equal employment opportunities. I shall argue that these barriers will not be removed solely by intervention in the labor market; the processes which sustain inequalities within the home and family must be tackled too.

This is not yet happening in Britain. On the contrary, the sex discrimination legislation does not apply to major areas of state policy, namely the social security system, income tax schedules, and family law. In other words, the ways in which the state defines relationships between the sexes within the family do not have to conform to egalitarian principles. Although the definition of marriage contained in the laws concerning divorce and separation now allow for a more equal allocation of rights and responsibilities between spouses, both the Department of Health and

Social Security (DHSS) and the Board of Inland Revenue still treat marriage as an unequal relationship.[2] Furthermore, the marriage contract, although unwritten in this country, remains one which, in practice, has different meanings for men and women.

Upon marriage a man takes on financial obligations, the most important of these being that he must participate in the labor market not only to support himself, like his single brother or sister, but also in order to support his children and his wife. In the last resort he can be sent to prison for failing to do so. Women acquire a set of domestic duties which include caring for their children, elderly or sick relatives, and their husbands. These domestic responsibilities are expected to take precedence over their paid work and their leisure. As a result there is a conflict between a woman's responsibilities towards other members of her family and her activities in the labor market, whereas for men there is not. This definition of the marriage contract, therefore, not only perpetuates a particular division of labor between the sexes within the family, but also, by ensuring that men and women do not compete on equal terms in the labor market, has an impact on the way in which paid work is allocated between the sexes. Men are considered to have a right to paid employment to an extent to which women are not, so at times of high male unemployment—as in 1978, when the overall unemployment rate was over 6 percent—the presence of women, at least married women, in the labor market is questioned.[3] On the other hand, men do not have the right to wages which are high enough to support their families unaided, nor has the British government ever adequately adjusted family income to family size through cash benefits for children. Many married women have had no choice but to make a financial contribution to the family budget even if they wish to devote themselves entirely to their family responsibilities. Moreover, many women do not live with a man with whom they can share financial responsibilities. The 1971 Census showed that one in six households in Britain (excluding pensioner households) depended primarily upon a woman's income, and the majority of these households contained dependents. In return for paid work which fits in with their domestic routine, women accept jobs with considerably lower pay, fewer prospects, and little security.

This chapter will first show how the division of unpaid labor in the home and the different priorities men and women have to accord to participating in the labor market has a considerable impact on women's employment patterns. I shall then examine how social policies sustain an ideology which ascribes to women the primary responsibility for providing domestic services for other members of the family. Recent changes indicate that this ideology is still very strong. Finally, I shall look at various policies which do not necessarily incorporate, in the legislation or administrative rules, assumptions about the division of responsibilities within the home, but nevertheless are being developed and implemented in a way that takes for granted women's primary commitment and availability to their families.

WOMEN'S EMPLOYMENT PATTERNS AND THEIR DOMESTIC RESPONSIBILITIES

For well over a century, women have comprised about a third of the formal labor force in Britain (38.3 percent in 1975), but in the decades prior to the second World War the typical woman worker was young and single. Today she is married and middle-aged. Indeed, one of the most dramatic changes in the composition of the labor force is the increase in the number of married women, particularly older married women who take paid employment outside the home (see Table 17-1). This means that between 1971 and 1975 alone, the number of economically active married women increased by 850,000 to 6.6 million in a total labor force of 25.2 million.

TABLE 17-1
Economic Activity Rates for Married Women by Age

Age	1951	1971	1977	1981*
20–24	36.6	46.7	54.3	55.7
25–34	24.4	38.4	48.8	49.6
35–44	25.7	54.5	68.0	70.3
45–54	23.7	57.0	68.1	70.9
55–59	15.6	45.5	50.8	54.8
TOTAL, all ages	21.7	42.3	50.0	51.9

*Projection.
SOURCE: Department of Employment, *Gazette* 85, no. 6 (June 1977): 590.

By 1981, the Department of Employment estimates that there will be over 7 million married women in a labor force comprising 26.7 million people. Half the projected increase in the labor force will be accounted for by married women, 20 percent by unmarried women, and 30 percent by men.

The Department of Employment attributes the big increase in participation rates to several factors: the fall in the birth rate, which started in 1965 but fell by 25 percent between 1971 and 1975 to 11.9/1,000 population; the change in attitude among men and women towards women's paid employment as reflected in, and affected by, the passing of the Equal Pay Act in 1970; and the big increase in part-time employment opportunities. In 1975, 17 percent of the labor force was working part time (less than 30 hours a week) compared with 14 percent in 1971. So in 1975 there were 4.25 million part-time workers—nearly one million more than in 1971. The majority (3.55 million) were women, and four out of five of them were married.

In Britain, women workers are not spread throughout all sectors of the economy. As a 1974 review of women's employment stated: "The crowding of female employees into a small number of industries is a feature of women's employment which has persisted over many years."[4] Women are heavily concentrated in four occupational groups: clerical workers; service, sports, or recreational workers (mainly cooks, canteen assistants, office cleaners); professional and technical workers (in particular, teachers and nurses); and sales workers. Three-quarters of all female employees were found in these occupational groups in 1971. In the manufacturing sector more than half the women employed are found in electrical engineering, clothing and footwear, textiles or food, drink and tobacco.

As most part-time workers are female, it is not surprising that part-time work is also concentrated in particular occupational groups. In 1971, 74 percent of all women employed part time were found in the service industries. By 1976 this had increased to 79 percent. At the same time the proportion of full-time jobs held by women in this sector decreased (to under 38 percent in 1975). This means that all the increase in female employment in the service sector was due to the increasing proportion in part-time employment. Since 1974, the number of part-time jobs in the manufacturing sector has fallen, and there are now fewer part-time women workers than in 1971. In the previous decade the number of part-time women workers had increased by 85,000. However, the decline in full-time employment here was not limited to men; in 1975 there were 400,000 fewer women working full time in manufacturing industries than in 1967.

There are now clear indications that the economic recession is having a growing impact on unemployment among women as well as men (see Table 17-2).

The actual number of unemployed married women is certain to be substantially higher than the table indicates because the official figures are known to underestimate the numbers probably by as much as half. This is because the official figures are based on the number of people who register for work, which is a prerequisite for receiving a social security benefit. Since the majority of married women are not entitled to unemployment insurance benefits in their own right, having exercised their choice not to

TABLE 17-2
Number of Unemployed by Sex and Marital Status

Year	AVERAGE MONTHLY NO. OF UNEMPLOYED		
	Married females	*Unmarried females*	*Males*
1971	45.7	74.7	655.5
1976	113.5	176.7	975.2
2d quarter, 1977	145.0	185.7	981.5

SOURCE: Office of Population Censuses and Surveys, *Social Trends, 1977* (London: HMSO, 1977), p. 86.

contribute to the program, and since in no circumstances can a woman who is married or cohabiting with a man claim a means-tested benefit, women have little incentive to register.[5] Nevertheless, in July 1977, 10 percent of those registered as out of work were married women compared with 5 percent in 1974. This may be due to a shift in the incidence of unemployment towards those married women who are eligible for benefits. (They are likely to be in the younger age groups.) On the other hand it may represent an increase in overall unemployment among married women. Altogether the number of women registered as out of work increased from 10 percent to 17 percent in the same period, and in 1977 women accounted for one in four of all those who had been unemployed for between six and twelve months.

There are now signs that the number of part-time jobs are declining in some of the service sectors as well as in the manufacturing sector. For example, there is less part-time employment in the distributive trades and in insurance, banking, finance, and business services. Moreover, the growth in part-time employment in the public sector is not expected to continue. Forecasting a slower rate of increase in married women's economic activity rates in future, the Department of Employment stated in the summer of 1977:

> It is assumed that the fall in the birth rate and possible postponement of families will continue but at a slower rate than previously. The Equal Pay Act and other anti-discrimination legislation will continue to have an effect in the future, but it is thought that these measures may have exerted much of their effect by now. The increase in job opportunities, particularly part-time jobs, over the period 1971–75, is assumed not to be matched by similar increases in the future. Specifically, public expenditure controls are assumed to curtail growth of opportunities in the public sector.[6]

This official statement provides an example of how women's paid employment, unlike men's, is seen in the context of their family situation. Moreover, the assumption is not that unemployment among married women will increase if the supply of jobs declines but that fewer of them will join (or rejoin) the labor market. A more detailed examination of the relationship between women's employment patterns and their family responsibilities shows how closely the two are interwoven.

In the past many women left the labor market when they married. Until the end of World War II marriage bars operated in the civil service and teaching as well as in other professions so that upon marriage many professional women lost their right to a job. Although legislation did not directly prevent women from working in industry, a prevalent view, as stated for example by the government's Women's Employment Committee reporting at the end of World War I: "Working women will regard marriage as their proper vocation, . . . in most cases upon marriage, they will leave industry never to return. In so far as the feeling against the employment of married women is based on the view that home and children should be the woman's first concern, it is in line with the interest of the community."[7] Of course the wages of many working-class men were insufficient to support a family, so large numbers of women were compelled to make some economic contribution to the family. Many did so outside of the formal labor market by taking in lodgers, washing, charing, engaging in home work of various kinds or in other seasonal or casual work. Official figures, therefore, underestimated women's economic activities as indeed they still do: the number of women working at home or self-employed is still not known with any accuracy. Nevertheless, if we look at women's past employment patterns, the figures show that marriage ended paid employment for a large number of them. In a national study of the elderly (men and women aged sixty-five and over) conducted in 1976, Audrey Hunt found that over a fifth of elderly women who had had paid work in the past had given up their jobs upon marriage and never returned. A further 3 percent ended their paid employment when their first child was due. Altogether one in eight had never had paid employment. This included nearly one in four of those aged eighty-five or more but only one in ten of those between sixty-five and seventy-five.

Today the vast majority of women participate in the labor market (a national study of women's employment conducted in 1965 showed that only 2.4 percent of women between sixteen and sixty-four had never had paid work),[8] and as the Department of Employment stated in 1974, "it is more usual to remain at work until the first child is due."[9] In other words, motherhood rather than marriage brings about the first interruption in women's employment. This interruption has been getting shorter, however, and the number of mothers of children under five (the age for starting compulsory education) in paid employment increased by 70 percent in the sixties and is still increasing (see Table 17-3).

The increase among those working can be accounted for almost entirely by the increase in the numbers working part time. The mothers with pre-school-age children in full-time work has remained between 5 and 6 percent. Even those with older children are more likely to be working part time; motherhood is associated mainly with part-time employment (see Table 17-4).

Although the presence of children under five constrains women's employment the most, restrictions on the number of hours worked and the timing of paid work continue when the children are in school. We still have a pattern of school terms which may have had some rationale when the agri-

TABLE 17-3

Percentage of Married Women in Paid Employment Outside
the Home by Age of Youngest Child

	PERCENTAGE IN PAID EMPLOYMENT	
Age of youngest child	*(a)* *1966*	*(b)* *1975*
0–4	18	27
5–9	46	62
10–15	56	69

SOURCE: (*a*) Office of Population Censuses and Surveys (OPCS), *Census of Population, 1966* (London: HMSO, 1968), app. 1, table 15 (England and Wales); (*b*) OPCS, *General Household Survey, 1975* (London: HMSO, 1978) (Britain).

TABLE 17-4

Percentage of Women in Paid Employment by Number of Children
in 1975 (Britain)

	NO. OF CHILDREN			
Employment	*0*	*1*	*2*	*3+*
Full-time	51	21	13	11
Part-time	18	32	37	36
TOTAL	69	53	50	47

SOURCE: Office of Population Censuses and Surveys, *General Household Survey, 1975* (London: HMSO, 1978), p. 100.

cultural sector required large numbers of extra hands, including women and children to bring in the harvest. Today the school timetable does not favor the needs of any major sector of the economy. Nevertheless it has remained the same for decades. In addition, the schoolday is shorter than the normal working day. It is therefore not surprising that the 1965 national study referred to above found not only that two-fifths of women who worked part time gave their responsibilities for children as a reason for doing so, but also that a third only worked during school hours and 13 percent gave up paid work during school holidays. A further 6.5 percent of employed mothers responsible for children worked evenings, early mornings, or overnight—times when the father could be home. In contrast, among employed women without children only 1.5 percent confined their paid employment to those times.

Women's family responsibilities do not end once their children have grown up. These responsibilities are extensive and may well affect a woman's availability for paid employment. Apart from an on-going commitment to care for their husbands in health as well as in sickness (the 1965 study found that one in six women said they worked part time and a further one in six of those without paid work did not have paid work at all for this reason), middle-aged women may well acquire the responsibility for caring for a sick or elderly relative. On the basis of a national study of home helps which was conducted in 1967, Audrey Hunt concluded: "Between the ages of 35 and 64 roughly half the housewives can expect at some time or another to give some help to elderly or infirm persons."[10] Her study showed that one in five housewives (that is, the person other than a domestic servant who is responsible for most of the domestic duties) aged between thirty-five and forty-nine years had a disabled person or someone aged over sixty-five in the household, and among those aged between fifty and sixty-four, one in four had an elderly or infirm person present. While not all those aged sixty-five or over were necessarily infirm, many in time would become so, and the more infirm an old person is the more likely they are to be living with one of their children. (In 1970, a national study found that 36 percent of the handicapped elderly and 50 percent of the very handicapped were living with one of their children.[11]) The 1965 study of women's employment found that one fifth of women working part time did so because they had the responsibility for an elderly or infirm person not necessarily living in the same household. Women responsible for an old person who was bedfast were the least likely to have paid employment.

The proportion of women without dependent children but who work part time increases with age, as Table 17-5 shows. This may be because of their responsibilities for caring for other adults. On the other hand it could be that older women have either different attitudes towards working full

TABLE 17-5

Percentage of Married Women without Dependent Children
in Paid Employment by Age in 1975 (Britain)

Employment	16–24	25–34	35–44	45–59
Full-time	65	74	58	34
Part-time	9	10	19	27
TOTAL	74	84	77	61

SOURCE: Office of Population Censuses and Surveys, OPCS, *General Household Survey 1975* (London: HMSO, 1978), p. 100.

time or different skills and expectations. Without good longitudinal data it is not possible to assess the relative importance of these factors.

A more recent study found that nearly a fifth of those women who had given up paid employment altogether between the ages of forty and sixty had done so in order to look after someone other than their husbands. The study concluded that "among women who gave up work between the ages of 40 and 59, the need to look after people other than their husbands comes second only to ill health as a reason for giving up work. The survey therefore provides further evidence that the burden of caring for sick or elderly relatives most often falls on women and makes it impossible for them to work."[12] Altogether nearly half of the women who had given up their paid employment between the ages of forty and sixty would have preferred to have continued. The total number of people over retirement age (which is sixty years for women and sixty-five for men) will remain fairly constant over the last two decades of the twentieth century. However, the number over seventy-five will increase by nearly one-third from 2.75 million to 3.5 million. With only 2 percent of the elderly population in residential accommodation this burden of caring is likely to increase rather than diminish in the near future. Middle-aged married women are therefore likely to have their employment opportunities either curtailed or restricted.

Whether they are caring for children, sick or elderly relatives, or healthy husbands, their domestic responsibilities thus determine when women leave or re-enter the labor market. The number of hours and the times during the day when they can take paid employment are also restricted. Their household duties also place constraints on the location of their work because their place of employment must be sufficiently close at hand to enable them to give attention to such family commitments as taking children to school. How close this is depends on the availability of suitable transportation. A study conducted in 1975 in South East England, in which 86 percent of those households with children under ten had a car, found that altogether only one-third of the mothers had the optional use of a car.[13] Thirty-six percent of married working women walked to work compared with 5 percent of the men. In comparison 23 percent of the women and 73 percent of the men drove themselves to work. Among those women who had full-time employment, half drove to work and a fifth walked. The comparable proportions of those with part-time employment were one in ten-and-a-half. Those with very young children or a chronically sick or disabled person to care for are more likely to do paid work without even leaving their homes. The 1965 study of women's employment found that 16 percent of working women with children under two years of age did homework compared with 8 percent of those with school-age children. Accurate figures of the number of homeworkers do not exist, but it is estimated that there are at least a quarter of a million homeworkers in addition to 130,000 childminders. In other words, there may be something approaching half a million women who do paid work at home.

Many women and those few men who have sole responsibility for the care of dependent children or adults exchange working hours which fit in with their domestic commitments for considerably lower pay and prospects. Part-time employees have fewer rights than full-time employees, and it is only recently that the Employment Protection Act of 1975, which gives certain rights concerning redundancy pay, maternity leave, and so on, has been extended to those working sixteen or more hours a week. (Those working less than this are protected only if they have been with the same employer for five or more years compared with the two years required for full-time workers.) Part-time workers therefore form a more flexible part fo the labor force. As Audrey Hunt's study of management attitudes towards women workers showed, one of the main advantages of part-time workers was that "you can have them when you need them."[14]

Part-time workers are also considerably cheaper. They are less likely to be admitted to employers' sick pay or pension schemes, and those with low earnings (£17.50 in 1978, a quarter of male average earnings) are counted as "nonemployed" and are therefore excluded from the state social insurance system. This means employers need pay no insurance contribution on their behalf, and as an article in the business section of the *Times* entitled "Cost Conscious Approach to Jobs" stated: "Below the national insurance limit . . . there is a very strong incentive to employ part-time."[15] There is evidence that some employers quite deliberately "adjust" part-time worker's pay to keep it below the "nonemployed" limit.[16] In April 1977, one in four part-time women workers had earnings below this limit and would therefore have no entitlement to sickness or unemployment benefits or a pension in their own right. Promotion prospects are very limited. In the study of management attitudes quoted above, only 17 percent of establishments gave part-time workers opportunities for promotion. While employers were sympathetic to women who needed time off to care for sick children, less than 3 percent granted *paid* leave for this reason. Unlike many European countries Britain does not include any provision for paying a social insurance benefit to a parent who takes time off from work to care for a sick child. In 1976, women were absent from work more often than men when aged between twenty-five and forty-four (when they are most likely to have dependent children), but after the age of forty-five are absent *less* than men. On average, part-time workers earn about half of a woman's full-time wage and well under a third of a man's full-time wage (see Table 17-6). Homeworkers, not included in the

TABLE 17-6

Distribution of Gross Weekly Earnings, April 1977

Weekly earnings (£)	Men, full-time	Women, full-time	Women, part-time
Mean	75.9	49.6	21.9
Highest decile	112.0	74.9	34.8
Median	70.7	46.1	20.7
Lowest decile	46.1	30.6	9.5

SOURCE: Department of Employment, *Gazette* 85, no. 10 (Oct. 1977): 1075.

figures listed in Table 17-6 and described by the Trade Union Congress as "probably the most heavily exploited and under-privileged workers in the country," were being paid £ 10 to £ 15 for a thirty- to forty-hour week in 1977.[17]

It is still legal to pay part-time employees at a lower rate than full-time employees because wage rates are not one of the matters to which the Sex Discrimination Act applies, this being the province of the Equal Pay Act. The Equal Pay Act only applies, however, where men and women can be directly compared and can be said to be doing "like work." As we have already seen, many part-time women workers are found in occupations in which women predominate. As the Department of Employment concluded one year after the implementation of the Equal Pay Act: "The extent to which it has been possible to adjust pay structures and jobs to reduce the effects of the act is indeed noteworthy."[18]

There is considerable evidence that women's domestic commitments are being used to prevent diminution of differences between men's and women's work. For example, a report on night work published by the ILO in 1976 argued that bans on night work for women should not be lifted unless there was "an overall reduction of working hours and a *reallocation of household duties*,"[19] because without these, women would be subjected to more strain and their health would suffer. Rather than argue for domestic responsibilities to be shared, the Trades Union Congress, in their evidence to the Equal Opportunities Commission, stated that the restrictions should be maintained. Admittedly, this was put in the context of insufficient child day care provisions but, as I have argued above, the constraints on women's time and energy do not arise solely from their responsibilities for young children. As long as these restrictions remain it can be argued that men and women are not doing "like work," thus enabling employers to pay women less. Neither men nor women should have to work in conditions which are harmful to their health, and while many male trade unionists have a genuine concern not to worsen working conditions for women, there is some truth in the comment of a representative of the Confederation of British Industries: "Some men like the laws because it protects their jobs."[20]

Women's opportunities and pay in the labor market are thus determined to a substantial degree by the division of responsibilities within the family. This is so not only when small children are present but at all stages of the family life cycle. What impact are various social policies having upon the way in which the unpaid work of caring within the family is shared among family members? Is there any evidence that a change in the allocation of duties in which the woman does not have the sole or primary responsibility for caring within the family is thought to be desirable and therefore to be encouraged. I shall look first at recent changes in the social security system and then more broadly at other social policies, including those which provide domicilary care for the young, the sick, and the old.

SOCIAL POLICIES AND DOMESTIC RESPONSIBILITIES

Following legislation passed in 1975, two new social security benefits were introduced. Both are noncontributory, which means that eligibility does not depend on having made the requisite number of national insurance contributions, and neither involve an assessment of income. The first is the noncontributory invalidity pension. Men and single women are eligible for this pension on the basis of "incapacity for work," which in their case means *paid* work, and an inadequate national insurance contribution record. Most men and single women receiving this benefit will have been chronically sick and handicapped for some time and will have had little opportunity to build up rights to a contributory invalidity pension because they have participated in the labor market very little. Their eligibility for benefit is not affected by their ability to plan meals, shop, cook, clean, or do their own and their family's washing. A married woman, or indeed a woman living with a man, only qualifies for this benefit if she is too disabled to take paid employment *and* to perform these "normal household duties." (The legislation actually refers to household "duties." This is the first time these words have been written into social security legislation, which may suggest that the assumptions about the division of labor in the home are not quite as pervasive as they used to be and must therefore be made explicit.) In other words, any woman living with a man, whether legally married to him or not, is first and foremost a housewife, and if she cannot carry out her unpaid work in the home (or only if with "great difficulty or pain") will she be eligible for an invalidity pension.

The second benefit is the invalid care allowance, which is paid to men and women who give up paid employment (meaning earnings of £9 a week) in order to care for a sick or elderly relative. The weekly allowance is currently £10.50, so only those with another source of income other than earnings can afford to claim it. This allowance therefore does not help many who combine paid employment with the care of the sick or the elderly. (In 1965 one in twelve of all women in paid employment had the care of a sick or elderly person. Not surprisingly it is not known how many men were in this situation.) However, married women or a woman cohabitating with a man is not eligible in any circumstances. In the first six months, three-fifths of those claiming this benefit were men, the others being single women. If married women were allowed to claim, the cost of this benefit would increase at least tenfold.

It might have been thought that the EEC social directive which will require that member countries give equal treatment to men and women in their social security programs with respect to benefits concerning loss of earnings through sickness and unemployment, old age, accident or occupational disease, and invalidity would render these two new benefits illegal. To the relief of the British government this is not the case on the grounds that "those who have no connection with paid employment are at present outside the scope of the directive—this applies mainly to housewives." Mr. Vanderweele, a member of the European Parliament, went on to say, when the directive was discussed in November 1977, that "in future it may well also apply to family men who perform domestic tasks instead of women. Though this may seem absurd, we are seeing increasing evidence of women taking a job outside the home and men performing domestic roles."[21]

These benefits, introduced in legislation passed in the same year as the British Sex Discrimination Act, are perhaps two of the most blatant examples of the way in which married women are seen first and foremost as housewives and thus responsible for all domestic duties. There is only one way in which the new legislation neither penalizes nor ignores those couples who have chosen to reverse the traditional roles. Under the 1975 Social Security Pensions Act, women who stay at home to care for children (up to the age of sixteen) or sick or elderly relatives, will have their basic state retirement pension rights protected. It was always clear that single men would be included, but a former minister of social security said in 1975 that the National Insurance Scheme was concerned "merely to provide for the genuine case of involuntary role reversal,"[22] implying that a married man who took paid work would not have his pension protected. However, when the regulations were published in January 1978, married men were included in this new measure, which came into operation six months later. This is the first time voluntary role reversal has been positively recognized in the British social security system. Note that it is men, not women, who benefit.

Further changes in the legislation are required because the wife who has chosen to be the breadwinner, unlike her husband, will have no right to Family Income Supplement (a means-tested supplement for low wage earners with children); no right to additional insurance benefits for her children and her husband when she is sick or unemployed (somehow the family will have to survive on a single person's insurance benefit); and no right even to apply for means-tested supplementary benefits (the equivalent of public assistance). If she should die, her husband will receive no widower's pension, for to receive this pension, introduced in 1978, men under retirement age have to be incapable of paid employment. An adequate system of cash benefits for all children would render many of these extra benefits unnecessary, but that is a long way off. Meanwhile, the British social security system is based firmly on the assumption that men are breadwinners and married women's primary responsibilities lie in the home.[23]

The provision of services for the elderly, the sick, and children are also based on the assumption that women, whether or not they have paid employment outside the home, are, or should be, available to take on the main responsibility for caring for other members of their family. Both residential and domicilary services are allocated in ways which reflect this assumption. For example, the characteristics of the small minority of old people who live in residential institutions are significantly different from those who remain in their own homes or those who live with their children. The majority of the elderly who no longer live in private households are those with no close relatives or whose relatives are infirm or ill. The elderly who remain outside residential care are more likely to live with daughters than sons (a study in the sixties found that three times as many old people lived with a married daughter than a married son).[24] Even when living separately, daughters are the most likely relative to be relied upon for help with housework and other forms of practical support. It is also more common for men to be looked after in their own homes by their wives than the reverse.

Domicilary services, such as home helps, are allocated in a way which reflects family circumstances. For example, Audrey Hunt's 1970 study of the home help services revealed that old people living alone and at a distance from relatives were more likely to receive home help than those living with their families. She found that less than one in ten of the elderly recipients of home help had children living in the same household. (At that time at least one in four of the elderly were living with one of their children.) Three-fifths had children living elsewhere, but these were more likely to be sons than daughters. A similar pattern was found among chronically sick recipients of the service. Her 1976 study of the elderly confirms that female relatives in general and daughters or daughters-in-law in particular still provide much of the regular support and care needed by the elderly living in the community. Although the home help service has expanded considerably in the past decade, in 1976 the service was reaching less than one in ten of the elderly, including one in six of those aged between seventy-five and eighty-four years and just over one in four of those over eighty-five. In January 1978 the prime minister stated that "government policies would be based on the need for older people to stay in the community, active and cared for as long as possible by near treasured friends and family."[25] Between 1975 and 1976, because of the severe restraints on public expenditure, the number of home helps fell by 1.6 percent. In August 1977, local authorities (who employ home helps) were reported to be complaining that they were finding it difficult to implement government policy that field and domicilary services should be protected at the expense of residential care.[26] The growing number of very elderly means that without considerably more extensive domicilary services the women among "treasured friends and family" are going to be shouldering a growing burden and at a time when more and more of them are expected to be in the labor market (see Table 17-1).

The provision of services which either share or replace the care which parents give their young children is based on similar assumptions. Although in the past hundred years the state has gradually taken from parents responsibilities for educating their children, it is not legitimate in Britain for the state to provide preschool child care service either free or on anything approaching a universal basis. The policy is based on the official view stated in 1968 "that early and prolonged separation from the mother is detrimental to the child, that wherever possible the younger preschool child should be at home with his mother and that the needs of older pre-school children should be met by part-time attendance at nursery school or classes."[27] Since 1945, local authority day nurseries have declined in number while nursery education places have doubled, and there are plans to provide sufficient places for all children from three to five years old whose parents wish them to attend. However, these nursery school places will only be provided for the majority on a part-time basis. The extension of nursery education is therefore not considered in the context of enabling mothers to take paid work outside the home but rather as a way of supplementing their skills and expertise.

In contrast, the work of caring is still firmly seen as the responsibility of the mother. Day care facilities do exist, but in 1975, two-thirds of legal day care (nurseries and registered childminders) was provided by voluntary or private organizations. Even when numbers attending playgroups were included in 1974, only about a third of all children under five in England and Wales were known to be receiving some form of organized day care outside their families. This is half the number whose parents would like to use day care services. Access to a local authority day nursery is difficult, if not impossible, for the child from a "normal" two-parent family. Even one-parent families may be refused a place, and some authorities will only accept children who are believed to be in danger of being battered and are therefore on their "at risk" register. Most mothers who do have paid work have to rely on relatives, neighbors, or their own husbands. In particular, grandmothers still provide a significant amount of child care. A national study in 1974 found that 25 percent of children whose mothers worked outside the home were looked after by their grandmothers, but as Audrey Hunt pointed out in 1968, the availability of relatives, especially grandmothers, "does not necessarily correspond with circumstances which may exist in the future. . . . It cannot be assumed that when the present generation of children has grown up, that their mothers will be as willing to accept responsibility for their grandchildren. A grandmother who has worked for many years herself may not feel inclined in her 50's to give up her job to look after her [grandchild]."[28] Unless men's employment patterns change and become more flexible, fathers will not take the place of other relatives. Fathers of young children help mainly when the mother works part time; they rarely give sufficient help to enable the mother to take full-time employment.[29] Indeed men work their longest hours at the time in their working life when they have small children.

The justification for not providing more day care services, particularly nurseries, is often based on concern not to harm the emotional development of young children. However, the evidence that the experience of day care outside the family is inevitably damaging to a child is not convincing. Moreover, as Jack Tizard argued recently:

> The view that young children require constant mothering by the child's own mother or by a single mother substitute is of more than academic interest. It provides the ideological (as opposed to the economic) basis both for the discouragement of day care services, and

for the current enthusiasm for the expansion of child-minding services rather than nursery services for those young children who simply cannot stay at home all day with their mother.[30]

Because the issue of day care for preschool children is discussed predominantly in relation to the mother's employment, the use of such an ideological justification for restricting day care facilities serves to confirm the view that women's attachment to the labor market is, and should be, of secondary importance only.

This is particularly useful in times of high unemployment. It is no coincidence that, in the late 1970s, there is in Britain a growing emphasis on the importance of mothers being at home full time to look after their young children. Proposals for providing positive inducements to stay at home, such as paying a mother's wage, are being more widely discussed, as, for example, at the Conservative Party Conference in 1977. It is interesting to note that a center-page article in the *Times* commented on this with approval, stating that such a measure "could even be quite useful at a time of high industrial unemployment if it helps more women to stay at home."[31] Similarly, the lack of publicly provided child care facilities is seen as an appropriate disincentive for mothers to take paid employment. This, too, is put in the context of the need to leave existing paid jobs for men. The medical correspondent to the *Times*, in December 1977, in an article entitled "Time for Mothering to Come Back into Fashion," wrote: "At a time of high unemployment it makes no sense to encourage women to place their children in nurseries or give them nannies in order to work at jobs that could be done by others."[32]

The school year is still organized in such a way as to pose difficulties for mothers of school children who wish to continue their paid work throughout the year. Play centers for after-school hours and school holidays are not an integral part of the current debate about the education services. Working mothers, rather than the inadequacy of the education service, are blamed for the problem of "latchkey" children. The school meals service, which provided a midday meal for over two out of three school children (a quarter of them getting them free), was not started seventy years ago with the needs of working mothers in mind. Rather, it was a measure to combat poverty. Nevertheless, since World War II, when the provision was considerably expanded, it has become a service which does facilitate mothers' employment outside the home. A study in the late sixties showed that the uptake of school meals in an area is more closely associated with women's economic activity rates than with indicators of poverty.[33] The service is discussed more in the context of children and their nutritional needs, however, than as a means of enabling mothers to work.

The care of sick or handicapped children, like the care of the elderly, takes place mainly outside hospitals and residential institutions. The number of children involved is not insignificant. A government committee on child health services which reported at the end of 1976 estimated that a prevalence of one handicapped child in every seven may be found during the childhood years.[34] Handicap was defined as being a disability which for a substantial period adversely affects normal growth or adjustment to life. The committee stated that "at the root of our thinking on the services for ill-children is the need to reorientate care wherever possible from hospital to home."[35] They therefore argued that "much recurrent and chronic illness can be managed at home and children can often be treated on a day care basis when they do need hospital services."[36] While acknowledging that in order to achieve this objective more nursing support for sick and handicapped children in the community must be developed, much of the committee's discussion about the work of the various staff who could provide this support to parents centered on the need to give advice and education rather than on giving them practical aid. Although one of the early chapters in the report drew attention to the dramatic increase in the number of mothers who now have paid work outside the home, no mention was made of the financial loss to the family incurred when the mother stays home to care for a sick child. Nowhere did they suggest that mothers—or fathers—should be entitled to a social security benefit when their earnings are interrupted for this reason. (Only children who have been sick or disabled for more than six months and require constant attention day and/or night attract an allowance. This is paid irrespective of the employment status of the parents.)

The sheer hard work involved in the daily routine of caring for the sick child, especially those who are physically or mentally handicapped, was underestimated. Research on the families of such children shows how the health of both parents, but especially the mother, is adversely affected by the burden of long-term physical care, and that it is what one study called "the everyday 'slog,' the daily grind,"[37] which is so hard to bear.

In general the health services for all members of the population are making increasing demands on people's time. Changes in organization as a result of increasing specialization and centralization have led to the closing of smaller units and the establishment of fewer, larger units. For example, the number of small hospitals of under 50 beds fell by 15 percent between 1969 and 1976 and those between 50 and 250 beds fell by 12 percent. Changes in the organization of general practitioner services have meant that there are fewer doctors practicing on their own in the community. (In 1959, 31 percent of general practitioners were in solo practices compared with 17 percent in 1973. Conversely, in 1959, only 14 percent of doctors belonged to a group practice of four or more doctors, compared with 37 percent in 1973.) Between 1959 and 1976 the number of general practices declined by 17 percent. This means people have further to travel to reach a doctor and moreover are more likely to have to make an appointment first, which, for those without telephones in their homes, means another trip. Audrey Hunt's study of the elderly found that "the average journey time to the doctor's surgery exceeds that to any of the other amenities investigated."[38] Chemists' shops, where drugs prescribed by doctors must be obtained, are also closing down. The number of chemists' shops fell by over a fifth between 1963 and 1975, and so people are more likely to have to travel further to reach one. Smaller post offices, where social security benefits can be cashed, are also closing down. Women are more likely than men to be responsible for getting their children to the doctor, clinic, or hospital and for collecting prescriptions, and we have already seen that they are more likely to be involved in helping elderly relatives.

Mothers are most likely to be responsible for escorting children to primary school, mainly on foot, and, as the authors of the study on transport cited above commented: "A mother with two children is cast into this tied and potentially unnecessary role for about 8 years of her life. Chaperoning on foot or chauffeuring by car appears to be an added dimension of the function of bringing up children. But this unremitting task is not just a time waster, for the 'chunks' of the day that are spent in this way also reduce the options of many mothers for doing at least part-time work and thereby of leading a less child-centered existence."[39] The fall in the birth rate, particularly in rural or inner-city areas, means schools are being closed. It has been estimated that by 1988 there might be as many as 2 million surplus places. The minister of education said in January 1978, "An awful lot of schools will have to be closed and we will support local authorities who decide this is necessary."[40] Women with young children, therefore, are likely to face longer journeys to school resulting in bigger constraints on the time available for paid employment.

Bigger units, whether these are schools or hospitals, offer a wider range of specialties, but the conflict between choice and proximity is borne disproportionately by women in the family. These decisions are being made on the basis of what is best in narrow educational or health care terms with no reference to their impact on the family. As Beatrice and Sidney Webb said when commenting on the Poor Law Commissioners' inadequate policies for young children in the nineteenth century, "It is only fair to the Poor Law Commissioners to observe that, during their whole reign, their office contained no woman (except the office cleaner)."[41] While it is not true there are no women among senior policy makers in the Department of Health and Social Security and Department of Education, there are very, very few. Perhaps until there are more, and more with children and dependent relatives of their own, these policy decisions will be taken without giving a second thought to their impact on the daily lives of millions of families and in particular the women in those families.

These are a few examples of the ways in which various social policies are based on assumptions which take for granted women's availability and commitment to care for members of their family. The division of responsibilities within the family goes far beyond those associated with the bearing and rearing of children and affects women who are not, and never have been, mothers. Those who argue that the division of labor between men and women within the home arises because it is "natural" for women to rear, as well as bear, children and therefore other domestic responsibilities "naturally" fall to them, must explain why women's work has so little value placed on it. Women are not paid a wage for the work they do caring for children, for the sick and old; they do this in return for their maintenance. Moreover, a woman's experience of being a full-time mother counts for very little when she returns to the labor market. Many are treated as if they had acquired no additional expertise and had lost most, if not all, of the skills they had acquired before having children.[42] The more positive attitude towards returning war veterans (at least until service in Vietnam became associated with drug-taking) makes an interesting comparison with the treatment of mature women returning to the labor market.

As long as women have the primary responsibility for caring for other members of their families and this remains a responsibility which is taken for granted and little valued, their opportunities and their earnings in the labor market will be limited. Only employers faced with labor shortages have made efforts to adjust women's working conditions to take account of their domestic responsibilities. Many have taken advantage of the weak bargaining position women are placed in by the conflict between home and workplace. At the same time, more women have had to make a financial contribution to the family budget by taking paid work outside the home. This is partly a reflection of changes in the real value of men's wages, particularly in middle age; partly a result of changing attitudes towards employment and expectations of higher standards of living; and partly due to the enlargement of the formal labor market and the shrinking of the informal labor market so that women's economic contribution to the maintenance of their families now takes a different form and has become more visible. The proposal to pay mothers a wage at least recognizes that many women seek paid employment out of financial necessity. However, paying mothers a wage, while giving women a measure of financial independence, would tend to reinforce the division of labor in the home both unless the wage was high enough to attract a substantial number of fathers and unless it was realized that they should take their share in the care of their children (or indeed their mothers or grandfathers, for we have seen the work of caring does not end when children become adult).

Little will change in the home or labor market unless the processes, including social policies which sustain and promote gender divisions in the family, are exposed and challenged. A government really committed to equality for women would devise social policies which would make it easier rather than harder for women and men to combine their family responsibilities with paid employment. Women have joined the formal labor market in the last quarter of a century in spite of social policies, which we have seen so often exacerbate, or at best ignore, the tensions between the demands of the home and the workplace. Ideally economic policies would be such as to reduce these tensions, but that requires a more radical restructuring of priorities at the workplace. Nevertheless, if major inequalities between the sexes remain inside the home, then they will not be removed from the world of employment. As Virginia Woolf wrote forty years ago in a feminist essay, *Three Guineas*, "The public and private worlds are inseparably connected. . . . The tyrannies and servilities of the one are the tyrannies and servilities of the other. . . . It is one world, one life."[43]

NOTES

1. R. M. Titmuss, Essays on the Welfare State (2d ed.; London: George Allen and Unwin, 1963), p. 117.

2. See Hilary Land, "Sex Role Stereotyping in the Social Security and Income Tax Systems" in Jane Chetwynd and Oonagh Hartnett, *The Sex Role System* (London: Routledge and Kegan Paul, 1977).

3. For example, a front-page headline in a popular paper said "Tax Wives Out of Jobs." This was based on the comment of a junior Minister in the Department of Employment (*Daily Mail*, March 10, 1977).

4. Manpower [sic] Paper No. 9, *Women's Employment: A Statistical Survey* (London: HMSO, 1974), p. 12.

5. After April 1978, newly married women and married women who have been out of the labor market for two or more years will lose the option of not paying a full contribution to the National Insurance Scheme. About three-quarters of married women in the past have chosen not to be contributors, thus foregoing any right to benefits or pension. Estimates of unemployment rates based on asking women whether they were seeking work are twice as high as the official rate.

6. Department of Employment, *Gazette* 85, no. 6 (June 1977): 592.

7. Ministry of Reconstruction, *Report of the Women's Employment Committee* (Cd. 9239; London: HMSO, 1919), p. 12.

8. Audrey Hunt, *A Survey of Women's Unemployment* (Office of Population Censuses and Surveys [OPCS] publication; London: HMSO, 1968).

9. Department of Employment, *Gazette* 82, no. 1 (Jan. 1974): 8.

10. Audrey Hunt, *The Home Help Service in England and Wales* (OPCS publication; London: HMSO, 1970), p. 424. Home helps are employed by local authority Social Service Departments and do housework, including shopping and cleaning, for the elderly, sick, and handicapped, and mothers during confinement.

11. Ibid.

12. Audrey Hunt, *The Elderly at Home* (OPCS publication; London: HMSO, 1978). This was a study of 2,622 elderly people living in 1,975 households in England, conducted early in 1976.

13. Mayer Hillman, Irwin Henderson, and Ann Whalley, *Transport Realities and Planning Policy* (London: Political and Economic Planning, 1976).

14. Audrey Hunt, *Management Attitudes and Practices towards Women at Work* (OPCS publication; London: HMSO, 1975), p. 14.

15. Eric Whiting, "Cost Conscious Approach to Jobs," *The Times*, May 23, 1977.

16. See forthcoming study of part-time employment to be published by the Low Pay Unit, summer 1978.

17. Trade Union Congress Report on Homeworkers, reported in *The Times*, Jan. 27, 1978.

18. Department of Employment, *Gazette* 84, no. 12 (Dec. 1976): 1340.

19. "Should Women Work Night Shifts?" *The Times* Oct. 25, 1977.

20. Ibid.

21. *Official Journal of the European Community*, Nov. 14, 1977, p. 19.

22. Brian O'Malley, letter to Women's Liberation Campaign for Legal and Financial Independence, May 1975.

23. For a more detailed discussion, see Hilary Land and R. A. Parker, "Family Policies in Britain: The Hidden Dimensions" in Sheila Kamerman and Alfred Kahn, *Family Policies in Fourteen Countries* (New York: Columbia University Press, 1978), and Hilary Land, "Who Cares for the Family?" *Journal of Social Policy* 7, (July 1978), pt. 3.

24. Ethel Shanas et al., *The Old in Three Industrial Societies* (London: Routledge and Kegan Paul, 1968), p. 112.

25. *The Times*, Jan. 28, 1978.

26. *The Times*, Aug. 4, 1977.

27. Ministry of Health Circular 37/68.

28. Hunt, *A Survey of Women's Employment.*

29. Nichola Fonda and Peter Moss, eds., *Mothers in Employment* (London: Brunel University, 1976), p. 24.

30. Jack Tizard, "Effects of Day Care on Young Children," in Fonda and Moss, *Mothers in Employment*, p. 67.

31. *The Times*, Oct. 10, 1977.

32. *The Times*, Dec. 10, 1977.

33. Bleddyn Davies, in association with Mike Reddin, *University Selectivity and Effectiveness in Social Policy* (London: Heinemann, 1978).

34. Committee on Child Health Services, *Fit for the Future* (Cmnd. 6684; London: HMSO, 1976), p. 45.

35. Ibid., p. 181.

36. Ibid., p. 17.

37. Michael Bayley, *Mental Handicap and Community Care* (London: Routledge and Kegan Paul, 1973), p. 307.

38. Hunt, *The Elderly at Home.*

39. Hillman, Henderson, and Whalley, *Transport Realities*, p. 166.

40. "Many Schools Expected to Close by 1988," *The Times*, Jan. 7, 1978.

41. Beatrice and Sydney Webb, *English Poor Law Policy* (London: Cass, 1963), 1: 302.

42. Hunt's study of management attitudes found that one quarter of the establishments surveyed treated married women returners as new entrants. For years the British civil service rarely reinstated anyone in the executive class even when the grade of original entry was executive officer. Instead they had to return at the lowest level as a clerical officer.

43. Virginia Woolf, *Three Guineas* (Harmondsworth: Penguin, 1978).

18 *Rita Liljeström*

INTEGRATION OF FAMILY POLICY AND LABOR MARKET POLICY IN SWEDEN

The interdependence of work and family, production and reproduction, stands out clearly when seen in a sociohistorical perspective. When industrialization separated workplaces from homes, it gave rise to a new family type: the mother-and-breadwinner family. When the need for labor and the movement for women's emancipation returned married women to gainful employment, a new transformation of family patterns was ushered in: the two-breadwinner family.

The British sociologists Young and Willmott have described this evolution in terms of four phases:

1. The family is multi-functional and both spouses combine parental responsibility with participation in production.

2. The family is asymmetric, with a wife-mother and a husband-breadwinner.

3. The woman has two roles, wife and breadwinner, while the man has one main role as breadwinner.

4. The family is symmetric, with two parents and two breadwinners.[1] As we shall see, the model underlying labor market policy in Sweden lags one step behind the model underlying family policy. Present-day Swedish family policy emphasizes a transition from the third to the fourth phase, while labor market policy is still trying to open the door to working-life entry for women in phase 2.

In the course of the last century's phase alternations, both family and working life have changed character: to a growing extent family life has become isolated from the functional contexts of work. Ideologically, the family as an institution has come to compensate with individual solicitude and love for the impoverishment and bureaucratization of working life. This meant that, while men's vocational roles were undergoing a specialization and social stratification that was carried to great lengths, the role of mothers remained more or less traditional. In other words, the expectations put on mothers did not appreciably differ from one social milieu to the next. If anything, the conditions of motherhood became homogenized in that middle- and upper-class mothers lost their domestic servants and were forced to perform chores which they used to supervise, while working-class mothers achieved a higher level of living and were advised to abstain from drudgery in the service of others.

Consequently, it is the father's contributions which give rise to different family situations. We can begin by listing some characteristics of the father's traditional role: (1) Fathers have extremely specialized and highly diverse vocational roles and working conditions. Such variations lead to important differences in the family lives of these men. (2) Society's transformation from patriarchy to equality has resulted in special strains and conflicts for fathers. (3) Fathers determine the family's social position and the children's "ascriptive status" in society. (4) Social aberrations such as alcoholism, criminality, and stress-induced diseases are more common among men than women. Fathers pose a more obvious risk factor for the family. (5) The father's influence in the family comes "from outside," from the job world and the rest of society.

For many decades, then, the man was the crucial link between work and family. His work determined both the family's level of living and the division of labor between the spouses; consequently, his position holds center stage for Swedish family policy, which focuses primarily on equality among children from families with different incomes levels and on equality between the sexes.

All family policy dedicated to social equality must confront the tension between the goal of family policy, which is to create good nurturing patterns for all children, regardless of background, and the incentive structure of the labor market, which presses for performance and efficiency by means of pay differentials. The labor market wants to retain differences in living conditions among adults, to see to it that "it pays to work," that "the leveling-out process is not carried too far."[2] Social welfare and family policy intervene with insurance schemes, child allowances, housing allowances, study funds, and the like, all to counteract the consequences of differential rates of pay. This classic dilemma of Swedish family policy may worsen as equality policy is implemented because the gap between family standards of living risks yawning wider when both the husband's and the wife's incomes contribute to the differentiation; making possible, at the extreme, a gap between the family with one low income and the family with two high incomes.

It is an important principle of Swedish policy that the quest for equality between women and men form an integral part of a quest for social and economic leveling-out in the whole society. Even so, there are differences among political parties about how much emphasis should be put on the element of social leveling-out. In practice this is often a matter of choosing between measures which mainly favor the economically and socially better-off women and measures which favor the worse-off.

SWEDISH FAMILY POLICY

Of children from working-class homes who were born during the first forty years of the twentieth century, eight out of ten had mothers who were housewives throughout the children's growing-up period.[3] Tax and social welfare legislation was enacted, residential areas were built up, and communities were planned exclusively with the mother-and-breadwinner family model in mind. Today, the dominant family pattern is the two-breadwinner family, where both husband and wife work for gain with shorter or longer interruptions when the children come. Statistics show that eight out of ten gainfully employed women rejoin the labor force within twelve months after their children are born.[4]

Swedish family policy has actively contributed to transforming the sex-specialized division of labor associated with the industrial transitional family into a family with shared roles:

1. After prolonged debate the decision was made in 1970 to change over to individual taxation. The tax system now postulates that every adult, irrespective of sex, is self-supporting, whereas the earlier tax system assumed that a married man supports his wife. This reform reduced the tax bite for spouses who both earn income compared with families where only one is an earner. The reform contained separate rules in favor of families with one income-earner so as to cushion the impact of changing over from mother-and-breadwinner families to families with two breadwinners. An-

other effect of the tax reform was to reduce the tax bite in lower income brackets while increasing it in higher brackets, a shift which squared well with the basic policy thrust to achieve greater vertical leveling-out among families with children.

2. On the subject of rendering financial assistance to families with children, the Family Policy Committee argues that the transition to having two incomes involves such a large gain in income that it in no way can be compensated for through child allowances. It therefore becomes a task for labor market policy to open up job opportunities to both parents.

Situations remain, however, in which the parents need to be able to stay at home with their children, as when a child is born or falls ill, for example. To satisfy this need the law on parental insurance came into force in 1974. Gainfully employed parents are entitled to apportion seven months of "child leave" between themselves as they see fit. During this period they receive a daily benefit equal to 90 percent of their regular income.[5] The fathers also share with mothers the right to ten days a year when they can stay at home with sick children. The law makes it easier to uphold the joint responsibility of parents on the labor market.

In this way the principles governing labor market policy, tax policy, financial assistance to families, and social insurance schemes have become adapted to families with two breadwinners, each of whom earns an approximately equal income. In the same spirit, proposals to pay children's allowances to homemaking mothers have been rejected. Therefore, it becomes necessary for labor market policy to afford employment to both parents, and for family policy under the aegis of local authorities to stimulate an expansion of day nurseries and other child care facilities while parents are gainfully employed.

In 1972, in order to coordinate and press for measures to achieve sex equality, the Swedish government appointed a body known as the Advisory Council to the Prime Minister on Equality between Men and Women. The Council was closely attached to the top cabinet level, which gave it opportunities to monitor the work done for equality and to present viewpoints on those proposals for reforms, legislation, and so on which the different ministeries put forward. Its work was dedicated from the outset to strengthening woman's status in the labor market and combatting the division of the labor market by sex. In so doing the Council supported: increasing the number of employment-exchange officials especially assigned to opening up more job opportunities for women; requiring firms to reserve at least 40 percent of newly added jobs for each sex as a condition of eligibility for governmental support of industrial plant location; conducting pilot projects to place women in industrial jobs formerly reserved for men. In partnership with interested firms, the county employment board and the local employment office invite homemaking women to attend "Information

Days" and to make guided plant tours. Interested women are offered one month of employment training with practice in male industrial jobs. Such pilot projects have been successfully implemented in six counties.

OBSTACLES TO COMBINING WORK AND FAMILY OBLIGATIONS

At the behest of the Advisory Council to the Prime Minister on Equality between Men and Women, I undertook a study of families who have been involved with the pilot project which trains women for male industrial jobs. This investigation pitted the model underlying official family policy— that is, of a family with two breadwinners and equal parents, two individuals and two citizens—against the reality of everyday life in fifty working-class families. It analyzed how husbands and wives combined obligations to work and family.[6]

The obstacles men and women have to overcome in combining these two roles have to do with personal identity and with value judgments and ideologies in society; with practical everyday difficulties; and with structural problems in the coordination among different societal sectors. The obstacles faced at these different levels accumulate, but so do the solutions and possibilities.

Psychological obstacles

Some of the obstacles are psychological problems of identity. According to a historical code, the man is responsible for the family. This patriarchal principle still helps form the breadwinner's sense of honor. Many men are convinced that it is up to them to provide for their wives and children and to answer for the future and security of their families. This code is most obvious in the sense of failure most men feel if they cannot give their families the security or the material standards they would like. This code then obtrudes whenever a husband is dead set against his wife's wanting to go out to work for gain. His attitude blends protective solicitude for the wife with a declaration that she is incapable of managing her own affairs: "She's not supposed to have financial worries." "We wouldn't be where we are now if it wasn't for me."

This self-undertaken commitment to the breadwinning role often goes hand in hand with a conviction that one has thereby done one's bit. We see this attitude in men who literally exhaust their energies on the job. Some of them, moreover, suffer work-related injuries. For them the home is the fruit of their labours, the place where they are entitled to relax. We run into the same "I've-already-done-my-job" sentiment among men who pursue leisure interests outside the family circle. Football, fishing, and open-air life are regarded as legitimate forms of relaxation for breadwinners.

Asking them to shoulder new family burdens brought about by their wives' employment seems like an imposition to them. After all, their jobs have not become automatically easier because their wives are now also doing a day's work in a male job.

The wife's wages makes things easier for the husband or for the family: men of insecure status on the labor market are relieved of responsibility and anxiety; husbands have been able to take employment at lower pay in the home town now that the family earns two incomes; families with weak breadwinners (due to illness or drinking) have been given a new kind of economic security; men have been able to cut down on or abstain from their moonlighting; families have been able to buy their own homes; women have been able to obtain divorces to sever marriage ties which for years have had a destructive impact on the family. But many men find it hard to cope with such role changes because they have based their self-confidence on the very aspect that is being changed. The men feel they are threatened by some mysterious force. The wife is often well aware that the situation is delicate for her husband:

> Now that I've got self-confidence I dare to speak out more when I talk to him. But I'm awfully cautious because I'm afraid he'll feel threatened by my new independence. Maybe he doesn't feel the same strength in his relationship with me; in that case he's thinking wrong, but he doesn't know it. And that's such a pity. But we don't talk about it. I've tried to put myself in his situation because it is harder for the man before he's gotten used to the new order. Perhaps it's more difficult in the working class. We're more like machine tools, the men are more tired when they come home and need more personal attention. For that matter, you don't get that sort of encouragement on the job. You stand there in the monotony, stare at the machine parts. You don't think. Besides, how can you with all that noise in the workshop?

Many women, on the other hand, do not take their breadwinning role in complete earnest. Work gives them variety, social stimulation, and money they can call their own. Some women, like the one quoted above, may tone down their breadwinning effort out of deference to the man's self-esteem. Many women, moreover, apparently look on themselves first and foremost as mothers and wives. In general, women's attitude toward the labor market may be described as a desire to combine parenthood with gainful employment. As a rule they do not see homemaking and paid work as alternatives to one another; on the contrary, they are oriented both toward work and toward home. For the majority, in other words, this is not a matter of freedom of choice but of accomplishing two desired activities within a limited amount of time.

Since women still bear the heaviest responsibility for children, they take that burden with them to the workplace. Of the forty-seven families in our sample who had children, we found the following division of responsibilities:

- Wife has main responsibility for children   25 families
- Wife has sole responsibility   13 families
- Shared responsibility between parents   9 families

For not a few women their pride in the job collides with anxiety about their children. Their strong affirmative response on one plane cracks over worry on another plane. Due to early marriages women have come to identify themselves very much with the maternal role. It is a socioculturally esteemed and strongly idealized role, in whose name countless women have been subjugated.

The question of how self is perceived is not solely concerned with how the wife and husband each build up their identities; it is also concerned with the expectations they have for one another. How do they react to their mutual apportionment of parental and breadwinniing responsibilities? How much are they willing to undertake a joint search for good combinations? Those husbands who "let the wife choose," as though her choice did not concern them, have not yet grasped that equality presupposes changes in the man's attitudes and habits.

Practical obstacles

A second kind of obstacle can be created by practical considerations—hours of work, traveling distances and communications, the supply of good child care facilities. For inventive couples, the possible combinations worktimes are virtually unlimited. Our forty-seven families with children, for example, displayed the following work-division patterns:

- Split shifts, spouses relieve each other   5 families
- One works daytime, the other on shift   7 families
- Same working hours for both, shift or daytime   10 families
- One works full time, the other part time[7]   10 families
- Woman is household mother   7 families
- Woman is household mother, but does odd jobs or works at home—for instance, daytime childminding or subcontracted dressmaking   2 families
- Husband home due to illness or unemployment   1 family
- "Solo" parent owing to divorce or separation, or because husband's occupation binds him to another locality   5 families

Despite these variations, however, three kinds of work-family combinations may be singled out: (1) systems where the spouses relieve one another; (2) systems where they do things together, that is, they are at home at the same time and away at the same time; and (3) specialized systems where the spouses are responsible for one area each. The most equal parents, we find, are those who relieve one another: the one spouse is at home when the other is at work.

Obstacles of societal coordination

In addition to the psychological and practical obstacles, however, there are obstacles created by how different societal sectors coordinate with one another—for example, in adjusting the imperatives of production to family obligations. The increasing rationalization in working life has consigned social and psychological needs to private life or put them in the hands of specialized institutions and professional groups. Educating, socializing, and cohering functions have been transferred to other sectors. So pervasive has this change been that, when we asked top management and line-supervision executives in the pilot-project companies about parenthood insurance and child leave for fathers, they were taken by surprise and usually evaded the issue. The fathers themselves expressed much greater positive interest.

Both the personal and the societal solutions needed to overcome all these obstacles are bound up with value judgments and ideologies about female and male spheres, about the relationship between parents and children, and about the family's place in society. The ideologies affect the choice of life style and the weight that people themselves attach to different life areas.

The ways in which the parents share responsibilities between them form a triangular drama, with society's commitment to child care in one corner, the job world's adjustment to the needs of parents and children in a second, and the parent's own willingness in a third. In our families the husbands were debarred from giving more of themselves to their children and from taking over more of the housework by the following reported obstacles: narrow identity as breadwinner; inability to work emotionally with children; the wife's monopolizing the children; the wife's perfectionism and interference with household work; separately pursued leisure interests; work done elsewhere, overtime, extensive moonlighting, housebuilding; physically and mentally strenuous work, where the men are used up by the time they finish working; length and scheduling of working hours; attitudes in the job world which directly inhibit a reappraisal of the male role. Women's opportunities for engaging in paid work outside the home were limited by the following types of obstacles: one-sided perception of self as wife and mother; lack of self-confidence, vacillating and ambivalent attitudes; resistance put up by the husband; heavy constraints and burdens when the husband is away from home; main responsibility for children and housework; shortage of facilities for child care; absence of compelling economic motives (here some women lack arguments with which to persuade their husbands); deterrent features of industrial work (heavy lifting, bad working environment, stress, remuneration systems); length and scheduling of working hours; traditional attitudes in the job world.

CHILDREN AND WORK

These changes in family roles reflect changing conceptions of motherhood and fatherhood as social institutions. But these sweeping redefinitions of being a parent are being made in a society that is by no means prepared to take its own initiatives. Social changes seldom take place simultaneously on a broad front; what happens instead is that individuals, groups, and institutions enter into the process at different paces. Such time lags lead to structural tensions.

To illustrate, the mothers of children under seven have come into the labor market *before* working hours have been adjusted to accommodate parents' and children's needs, *before* the municipalities have expanded their facilities for child care, *before* the attitudes in the job world have adapted themselves to the labor force's responsibility for children, and *before* legislation has built in safeguards to protect the interests of parents and children. Besides, it is not at all unusual for wives to take over partial economic responsibility for the family *before* the husband begins to share in the practical and emotional responsibility for the children.

In 1975, the Family Assistance Committee drew attention to the long hours that many children spend in day nurseries.[8] This investigating body had done a study of stay-in times based on a representative sample of children. The results showed that slightly more than half of all children spend at least nine hours per day in the nursery, and one-fifth spend at least ten hours. And the younger the children, the longer the stay-in time. Over 60 percent of the children of solo parents spend at least nine hours in a day nursery. The very long stay-in times, amounting to ten hours or more, are most common for children of working-class mothers (27 percent of the mothers).

During the first half of the 1970s demands were raised in Sweden to shorten hours of work to a universal six-hour workday. The following arguments were advanced in support of this reform: (1) there would be more contacts between children and parents; (2) the sexes could share the housework more equally (instead of women working part time and men full time); (3) democracy would be vitalized in popular movements, trade unions, and neighborhood communities. Rather than count on such a future solution, however, the Family Assistance Committee proposed immediate implementation of shorter hours for parents of children under three.

The proposal stirred up controversy. The Swedish Confederation of Trade Unions (LO) rejected the idea of a selective cut in working hours, arguing that the reform would not be feasible for their member groups but would lead instead to discriminating against parents of small children in the job world. Since it would not solve the problem of the worst-off groups, opposition to this measure can be seen as an example of the emphasis that Swedish family policy puts on social leveling-out, with its requirement that public measures reach out to the worst-off. But it can also be interpreted to mean a lack of confidence in the solidarity of union members with "odd-ball" groups. Even so, as far as I can see, working life must ultimately be adjusted through selective measures to variations in people's lives and family cycles.

The parental insurance law was updated to accommodate the needs of working parents with young children. Starting with those parents who have children born in 1978 or later, the law allows for a total of nine months of parental leave until the child reaches eight years of age. The law is innovative in what it provides for the final three months of parental leave. First, parents are expected to divide their time off equally. Second, they may take these ninety days as one hundred and eighty half-days, or as six-hour days. Finally, for the first eight months of leave, parents are paid their regular salaries.

Part-time employment for women represents the current "solution" to the conflict between responsibility for children and the demands of the job. Nine out of ten part-time workers are women ("part-time" here means less than thirty-five hours a week). Whereas, as recently as the early 1970s, the majority of those who took part-time work were older women, women between twenty-five and thirty-four now comprise one-fourth of the part-time labor force.[9] The rationale for part-time work stems from various factors, notably problems with child supervision, with the difficulty husbands and wives have in discussing alternative solutions, and with the greater availability of such employment. By shortening their hours of work, women also uphold both asymmetry in the family (phase 3) and their own weaker status on the labor market.

The timing of the workday can also cause problems. In 1974–1975, the Swedish Central Bureau of Statistics mapped out the extent of inconvenient or "unsocial" working hours. Society's "normal rhythm" of motion and rest and nature's diurnal rhythm of day and night run side by side. Hours of work which do not fall between 7 A.M. and 6 P.M. are considered unsocial. The Bureau discovered that 31 percent of all wage-earners put in unsocial hours every workday and that up to 49 percent have unsocial working hours some time during the workweek.

The scheduling of time entails a series of consequences for health, family life, and social life in general. As we have seen, many parents solve their childminding problems by relieving one another. Here the scheduling of worktimes round the clock increases the number of possible combinations. However, the social consequences of unsocial and irregular working hours are mixed. One need only look at the hospitals, where the hours of work cannot possibly be contained inside some "normal rhythm." Mana Martensson has called attention to the effects that parents' worktimes have on the life rhythms of children:

> Children of different ages to a varying extent have a need for the security that a life governed by routines will provide. Routines in the large structure of daily experience probably provide the confidence to dare to try new and unknown things which alter the details of that structure. Repetition and predictability are probably also the basis for the child's development of a concept of time. To [the] extent [that] the preschool child has a long-term stable daily routine, [it] is primarily a matter of the parents' working hours. A distinction can be made between "regular" and "irregular" children. A "regular" child arrives in the group at the same time every day, and thus he always enters at the same phase of the ward's daily program. He recognizes the events and is able to predict what will happen next. This should be important to a small child who cannot tell time by the clock but who longs for particular events at least as intensely as an adult. Thus the sequence of routines divides the day in the same way as the hours and minutes used by the adults.
>
> An "irregular" child does not get the same support from routines. Departure from home takes place at varying phases of the home routine. On different days he joins the child care group at varying phases of its program. It must be difficult for such a child to tell what will happen next, when his parents will return and so on.[10]

A vital question for the future has to do with the way in which working hours might be cut. In a 1972 poll, an overwhelming majority of persons said they would prefer a worktime shortening to take the form of a longer unbroken block of time ("block leisure") around weekends or—alternatively—lengthened vacations, a lower retirement age, or sabbatical leave. Later investigations on a smaller scale indicated that public opinion had shifted somewhat in favor of a shorter workday ("piece leisure").[11]

According to Fryklind and Johansson, who reported the results of these polls, in a society where work and family/leisure are two highly segregated worlds, it seems rational to want long, unbroken leisure "so that you can really relax and rest up, 'be someone else.' "[12] Block leisure affords opportunities for leading another life for awhile, for getting away from the daily round's stress and monotony. By contrast, piece leisure is tightly constrained by necessary social obligations and by everything that is included in the concept of gross worktime: journeys to and from work, fetching of children, visits to post offices and banks.

The researchers press the thesis that it is during their piece leisure that people take part in society-changing activity, social and union struggle, evening studies, and the like and also see to the redistribution of responsibilities for children and homemaking. It is the piece leisure that changes the daily round. Block leisure is by its nature a drawing-back, a way to disengage oneself from society, to devote oneself to private solutions. With these facts in mind, it is interesting that a six-hour workday has been described in Sweden as a reform for women, while men strongly prefer a four-day week. But the whole issue has been put on the shelf for the time being.

DAY NURSERIES

Child care facilities have been unable to keep pace with the ever-growing number of mothers in the labor force. Even so, from the mid-1960s up to the 1970s the number of nursery places nearly tripled. The government has pressed for a vigorous expansion of day nurseries. It agreed with the Swedish Association of Local Authorities to increase the number of places in day nurseries by 100,000 and the number of places in after-school centers by 50,000 during the period 1976–1980. This agreement was reached against a background of severe place shortage. In 1975, provision for child care covered the needs of only about one-third of the preschool children of gainfully employed mothers.

Although national policy can support the expansion of day nurseries by granting state subsidies and providing other stimuli, the decision to expand child care belongs to the municipalities. From all indications the avowed targets will not be reached by 1981, the agreed-upon deadline. Moreover, it is now plainly visible that the plans to build more day nurseries will not meet the demand for places, and for good reason: the number of places in day nurseries is growing fast, but so are the queues of children waiting for admission.

Local authorities say they are hamstrung by the wretched state of their finances, but it is hard to avoid the suspicion that expansion is also being deterred by a traditional view of the family. The shortage of places makes it necessary to assign priorities to admissions. First preference is usually granted to the children of solo parents and to children whose parents are socially disadvantaged, due to nervous complaints, alcoholism, and overcrowding. This procedure is liable to lead in certain locales to a high incidence of children of disturbed families in day nurseries.

Before the decision to build more day nurseries on a large scale, public debate was chiefly concerned with the quantity of day nursery places. Once the expansion plans were officially adopted, however, the focus of concern shifted to quality. (After all, there had been no point in discussing the quality of something that scarcely existed.)

The official commissions of inquiry which published their reports during the 1970s have been instrumental in sensitizing a broad lay public to the effects of social changes on children. The new criticism of day nurseries takes equality between the sexes as given, but seeks new forms for child care. It raises objections to: the artificial quality of screening children off in special child milieus under the supervision of child specialists with child food, child furniture, and special stimulation for children; negative effects attributable to the professionalization of child care and parents' increased uncertainty about their roles; incompatibility of the "wage-earner mentality" with genuine involvement with children; and the defective biographical and social reification of parenting dear to child and developmental psychology, which paints a picture of universal parents bringing up their abstract children in a social and cultural vacuum. In the view of these critics, a search should be mounted for more integrative solutions, work practices in day nurseries which enlist the cooperation of parents, and a revitalization of community spirit. They are searching for a social life scaled to human dimensions and for more despecialization—that is, more diversified milieus.

ATTITUDES IN THE JOB WORLD

In a segmented society, more equality may prevail in one sector than in others—for example, relations in the family look more equal than they do in working life. It is also possible that an individual may favor equality for one life area but not for others. Value judgments on equality may likewise be segmented.

In our study of fifty working-class families, we tried to examine more closely the sex roles of those men who had to support the pilot project which trained women for male jobs. Our interviews with top management and line supervisors started off with questions about conditions at the workplace; only later in the interview did we try to probe into more personal matters. Statements uttered by the same persons a half an hour apart sometimes seemed to come from different people:

> "Equality! Seen from the company's viewpoint I am for the same opportunities at work for men and women."
> "Personally I am old-fashioned and conservative. The equality aspirations violate nature's way. The general witch-hunt after housewives has gone too far."

> "The women come and ask for shorter working hours even though the company has made it perfectly clear that this is a full-time job. First they want to be counted as full-fledged members of the labor force and later on they want half time."
> "My wife works half time. I couldn't imagine any other arrangement. The men prefer part-time jobs for their wives."

"We're pressuring the local authorities to provide more places in day nurseries."

"Nothing can replace a good normal family. . . . The woman must sacrifice some years of her life—in any case my life."

"It's necessary for the community to build child centers."

"But things were better before. My three children never had to go through the child center experience."

"We're making an investment in women. . . . We're looking for healthy specimens with minds of their own."

"My wife wants out in order to work. But I feel she'll have to sacrifice herself for my job—and then she'll reap the benefits of my position. This thing is a problem between her and me. . . . She will probably want to get out, but I'll resist it as long as I can."

We also asked other male members of the adjustment teams what they thought. Several of these men showed a similar tendency to restrict the primary connotation of sex equality to the labor market. In that respect the quotations indicate a fairly high degree of consensus. These responses, then, may be regarded as visible signs of mental cleavage, of a segmentation of value judgments into different compartments, the one reserved for working life, the other for private life.

The differentiation of activities in modern society has taught people generally, and men in particular, to divide their personalities into different segments. Sometimes these segments are poorly coordinated, which makes it possible for one to think and act differently as a politician and as a private person, at work and in the home. Although some specialization according to the purpose of an activity is admittedly necessary, how deeply should the cleavage be allowed to penetrate the personality?

WHAT CRITERIA DO WE USE TO MEASURE SUCCESS?

How far along has the drive towards equality come in present-day Sweden? In what respects has public policy been successful? In the previous sections I identified three sets of obstacles to equality: those associated with personal identity, with practical everyday difficulties, and with lack of coordination between societal sectors. Other obstacles could be regarded as cultural lags in the implementation of necessary reforms related to child care and hours of work. In addition, I have singled out the inconsistent attitudes which restrict the meaning of equality to certain sectors (here working life), and which in effect screen off the fundamental changes necessary to achieve this major policy goal.

The in-depth study of fifty working-class families, entitled *Roles in Transition*, sheds light on the combination of work, family, leisure, and citizen activism. It showed how changes in one life area affect other life areas and how, in turn, rigidly constrained habits in one area prevent changes in others. The line of action that each spouse chooses for his or her self inevitably affects what the other spouse can choose.

The family is a flexible and variable institution. In the course of their lives individuals pass through several different family constellations. Lifestyles are formed by several interacting career lines. (Here the word "career" alludes to the individual's activities/roles within different domains of social relations such as, for example, family life, working life, and public life.) In a differentiated society the individual tries to coordinate his participation within different life areas/domains and to distribute his time, energies, and interests among them. As life unfolds, the individual attaches shifting weights to the different "careers." The family cycle develops continuously or discontinuously in parallel with a work career and participation in civic life. The lifestyles of the family members are interdependent and rest on a synchronization of the members' careers within different life areas.

In common with other industrialized countries Sweden has not given enough careful thought to the issue of synchronizing women's and men's participation within the same life areas. This has led to a botched design of social organization on a large scale. For decades the job world has seen fit to disregard the fact that the labour force has responsibility for the care of children. It is only the fight against sex discrimination that has brought children into the picture. Whereas family policy now strives to put parents on a equal footing in terms of a symmetrical parental and breadwinning responsibility, a massive tradition still forces labor market policy to support a changeover from an asymmetrical family to a family in which the woman has to live with a double work burden, only slightly modified by part-time employment.

In the long run the job world must become more flexible in relation to the family cycle's different phases. It must become feasible for spouses to synchronize their lifestyles so that there will be no discriminating distinctions between women and men, or between families or individuals with children and childless families.

To some extent disparate forces have pushed equality policy into a feminist tradition that goes back to the unmarried women of the nineteenth century and a labor market policy launched after World War II. In the initial alliance of the late 1960s, the emancipatory forces were combined with a situation in which there was a shortage of labor; this opened up opportunities for women. In my opinion, in the late 1970s, we have advanced to a stage where the cleavages may well appear on a new level. The time has come to ask the question: Equality for what?

One of the weaknesses in our political imagination lies in the fact that social science theories as well as political programs are more developed when it comes to production or working life than when it comes to reproduction. By "reproduction" I mean re-creative activities in a broad sense: giving birth; upbringing and care; upholding motivation and a sense of purpose; consumption and recreation; social integration; and the like. To state the case a bit brutally, our social organization seems to have exploited the accessibility and mobility of working-age individuals; but we have created a marginal and second-class citizenry among the young and the aged who do not work and are, therefore, weakly integrated into the life of society.

It is characteristic of male-dominated societies that the reproductive "women's sphere" has been suppressed and rendered invisible. Therefore it does not suffice as a criterion of success to calculate the proportion of women who have taken over male work tasks and come up to equivalent rates of pay. That would be to confuse emancipation with women's "masculinization" on terms laid down by the technocratic male societies.

As in the question of day nurseries, the front lines no longer run only between advocates of upbringing in the home on the one side and advocates of society's child care facilities on the other, but are even more concerned about the quality of child care. By the same token, we say Yes to a symmetric family. But what is to be gained if symmetry amounts to inflicting on fathers the same guilt feelings vis-à-vis their children that the mothers have, or letting women share with men the mental risks in the mad scramble for upgraded pay rates and careers?

These reflections of mine must not be taken to mean that I feel dubious about the idea of equality between men and women or am prepared to set my sights lower. Interpret them rather as signs that we are beginning to gnaw at the nub of the problems: women's liberation as a contributory force and challenge to social changes and as a reappraisal of the way in which we live. We are now traveling more and more along the road that leads to qualitative criteria.

NOTES

1. Michael Young and Peter Wilmott, *The Symmetrical Family* (London: Routledge & Kegan Paul, 1975).
2. Ingemar Lindberg, "Svensk familjepolitik—och her den växt fram" (mimeo., 1978).
3. Robert Eriksson, *Uppväxtförhållanden och social rörlighet* (Låginkomstutredningen; Stockholm: Allmänna Förlaget, 1971).
4. Lindberg, op. cit.

5. As of January 1, 1978, parenthood insurance extended its benefit period to nine months. For the ninth month, a flat rate benefit of 32 kronor a day is payable in line with a uniform guarantee level. The last three months are to be divided between the parents. The benefit period, however, may be easily transferred from one period to the other upon notification.

6. Rita Liljestrom et al., *Roles in Transition* (Stockholm: LiberFörlag/ almänna Förlaget, 1978).

7. Although "part time" may refer to work performed during regular hours, it seems to refer just as often to cleaning work in the evenings, delivering newspapers in the early mornings, or standing night watch in a hospital.

8. Family Assistance Committee, *Förkortad arbetstid för småbarnsföräldrar* (Statens offentliga utreningar, no. 62; Stockholm: Ministry of Health and Social Affairs, 1975).

9. Among men it is chiefly the very young and the older ones who do not work full time (National Labor Market Board, 1978).

10. Solveig Mårtensson, *Childhood Interaction and Temporal Organization* (Research Report for the Department of Cultural Georgraphy; Lund: University of Lund, 1977).

11. Pär Urban Fryklind and Sven Ove Johansson, Arbete och fritid, sekretariatet för framidsstudier, högskolan i karlstad (1978).

12. Ibid.

VI

Policy Goals for the Future

19 *Helen Remick*

BEYOND EQUAL PAY FOR EQUAL WORK: COMPARABLE WORTH IN THE STATE OF WASHINGTON

Equal pay for substantially equal work is a relatively well-established principle for setting salaries. It guarantees that when men and women perform essentially the same tasks in jobs that may or may not have the same title, they will receive equal compensation. For example, janitors and cleaning women must be paid the same wage by a company if their assigned work is substantially the same (but not necessarily identical). But while equal pay for equal work is an important concept, it does not address the question of apparent salary differentials between sex-segregated jobs where assigned tasks are not substantially similar. In fact, many job families (for example, secretarial, crafts and trades, heavy equipment operators, child care or nursing) are segregated in most societies and therefore not covered by equal pay for equal work principles.

The sex segregation of occupations is especially obvious at the level of individual jobs. At a large university with a support staff of more than six thousand persons, and with more than five hundred job classifications, over 40 percent of the job titles with at least six incumbents have 5 percent or fewer males or females in them. If the definition of sex segregation is liberalized to being less than 30 percent of either sex, 82 percent of the classifications are sex-segregated and 99 percent of the employees are in sex-segregated job classifications. Analysis of the workforce clearly shows that jobs held predominantly by women pay salaries substantially below those held predominantly by men; equal pay for equal work concepts are inadequate for understanding these differences.

A fifty-year-old management tool, point factor evaluation systems, provides a means of comparing unlike jobs. These systems arose from industry's desire to quantify salary differentials within job families. Point factor systems break down jobs into factors and assign points to varying degrees of the factors' presence. Though the systems vary in use of terms, the major factors are usually effort, skill, responsibility (the same three that appear in equal pay act legislation in the United States), and sometimes working conditions. The systems assume that jobs with the same total number of points should be compensated more or less equally, at least within job families (e.g., management, clerical, and crafts and trades). The evaluations have two parts: a point system to establish an internal ordering, and the surveying of salaries within the same job families at other firms to establish salary ranges for each family ("prevailing wages"). In a traditional application by management, no attempt is made to adjust wages *between* job families to establish equity. Differences in wages between job families are usually considered to be of little interest since they are assumed to be the result of such "acceptable" forces as supply and demand and union power.

Such job evaluation systems assume that there is an order to existing salary systems and that the factors determining this order can be roughly quantified. I would further suggest that the order of the existing system is intuitively obvious to most workers: many workers would describe themselves as satisfied with their relative salary position; unions, after a point, shift their bargaining focus from salaries to fringe benefits and working conditions.

The point factor systems appear to be reasonably good descriptions of the actual forces at work in our marketplace. The motivation for striving for accuracy of the descriptions is easy to see; the firms developing these systems must sell them to other firms in order to make a profit. The other firms must be pleased with results if they are to make good recommendations and be willing to implement the salary studies. If the resulting salary scales deviate too greatly from the already existing ones—if they indicate, for example, that the secretary to the president should make more than the vice president for sales—the system will not be accepted or implemented, and the consulting firm will have trouble getting more jobs. The payoff to the firms developing these systems has therefore been to imitate as accurately as possible the existing order of salaries. Our analyses as reported below would indicate that at least one firm has done its job reasonably well.

There are limitations to the existing point factor systems. In the United States the systems are based on economic forces as seen from the viewpoint of the private sector; for example, responsibility is assessed in terms of fiscal responsibility only, not the life-death and teaching or counseling responsibilities usually part of public sector jobs. The emphasis on factors found primarily in the private sector is certainly a limitation to be kept in mind and one which needs modification if the systems are to be adequately applied to the public sector. Furthermore, there would appear to be a bias against women in the choice of factors and frequently in application.[1] The above limitations affect the systems in their ability to describe how salaries should be; they do not affect the ability of the systems to reflect what is within related jobs.

This discussion has consistently used qualifiers like "within related jobs" or "within job families." Indeed, present systems have little interest in terms of equal pay within job families. The systems are a tool for making across-family comparisons, however, and it is on this application that this chapter will focus. These systems, with all their limitations, provide a tool for comparing equity of salaries in non-related, sex-segregated jobs; we can answer the question, for example, whether clerical workers are compensated for effort, skill, and responsibility in the same manner as mechanics or the crafts and trades. We can ascertain whether jobs of comparable worth receive comparable pay. The State of Washington conducted such a study on a sample of staff positions specifically to ascertain whether men's jobs and women's jobs were equally compensated. This chapter presents the history and result of this study.

COMPARABLE WORTH IN WASHINGTON STATE

In 1973, persons in management-level government jobs in the State of Washington believed their salaries to be out of line with prevailing wages in the state for jobs of comparable effort, skill, and responsibility. They therefore requested that a job evaluation system be applied to their positions, to establish not so much internal as external equity. The governor approved the expenditure for the study, which was conducted by Norman D. Willis and Associates, a Seattle-based consulting firm. The results were accepted by the legislature with no questions about methodology or the legitimacy of the findings. Though salaries were not raised to fully match prevailing wages in the private sector, increases have been substantial; the salary of the governor, for example, has been increased from $32,500 in 1973 to $55,000 in 1978, based upon Willis results.

At the time the management study was being conducted, the State Women's Council and the Washington Federation of State Employees, AFL-CIO, saw an opportunity to use this same methodology to explore salary differentials between male-dominated and female-dominated jobs in the State Civil Service system. They requested that the governor commission such a study, which he willingly did. Hailed as a national landmark study, it was viewed as the first public sector attempt to use point factor job evaluation technology for the expressed purpose of comparing jobs traditionally held by women with jobs traditionally held by men, and analyzing the potential disparity between them. The Willis Consulting Firm was hired to conduct the study.

Both an advisory and an evaluation committee were appointed to work with Willis on the study, and great care was taken in the process to eliminate possible sex bias in application. The committees represented both the private and public sectors, management and labor, men and women. One hundred twenty-one jobs were selected for evaluation, half traditionally occupied by men, half by women. Female-"dominated" classifications, for study purposes, were those that were 70 percent or more staffed by women; male-"dominated" classes were those occupied 70 percent or more by men.

The results of the study were dramatic. Overall, salaries in female-dominated jobs were only 80 percent of those of male-dominated jobs. In only one case did a male-dominated job pay as little as a female-dominated job of similar worth. Further, the Willis study concluded that "any action to achieve internally equitable salary relationship between women's and men's classifications would involve a significant modification of, or departure from, the present salary setting method."

The legislature did not rise to the challenge of the study, nor did the governor or the unions. Only the State Women's Council continued working for implementation. In 1976 the governor authorized an update of the study, and additional jobs were surveyed. He then included a request for $7 million in his proposed 1977 budget to begin implementation of comparable worth.

The newly elected governor, one of two women governors in the nation, deleted this amount. Questioning the methodology, the new governor said Willis ended up "comparing apples and pumpkins and cans of worms and they are not comparable" and, on another occasion, "I believe that the methods for determining the comparability of jobs needs to be greatly improved over what has been done to date." (Remember that the same methodology was employed by the same consultant in the earlier study of upper-level management jobs in state government, including the governor's position. That study was implemented with no questioning of methodology.)

It may be that Washington, the first state to explore comparable worth, may be one of the last to implement it. In spite of the fact that comparable worth is rapidly gaining support among women's groups, both within the State of Washington and nationally, and public employee unions within the state maintain some level of support, most other unions within the state oppose its implementation. The important political lesson is that job evaluation systems have high acceptability unless they are billed as having more benefit to women than men. It appears important that, even if implementation of systems are proposed for the purpose of establishing sex equity in salaries, the systems must be sold on other bases.

THE WILLIS REPORTS OF COMPARABLE WORTH

In the Willis job evaluation system, an evaluation committee uses responses to a questionnaire on job elements and a sampling of interviews as a basis for assignment of points. The system assigns points to four factors:

Knowledge and skills: This factor encompasses the total amount of understanding, familiarity with facts or information, or dexterity necessary to perform the job in a satisfactory manner. It contains two dimensions: job knowledge and interpersonal skills. Job knowledge is what the position incumbent must know or know how to do to perform satisfactorily. This includes the occupational, specialized, or functional knowledge or skill required of the incumbent. For administrative positions, consideration is given to the need to practice the elements of management. Interpersonal skills are direct-contact skills in relationships with people within and outside the organization—that is, the extent to which the position is required to serve, influence, and/or motivate others.

Mental demands: This is the degree of effort required for analysis and evaluation of alternatives in reaching solutions. It is represented by the latitude permitted for independent judgment, and the extent and nature of the job's decision-making and problem-solving requirements.

Accountability: This is the degree to which the position contributes to overall expected end results. It has two parts: freedom to take action and the nature of the job's impact. Freedom to take action is the extent of restraint under which the job must operate. Limitation can be in the form of necessary supervision or direction or can be inherent in the nature of the position. The nature of the job's impact may be direct, in which principal actions, at the position's organizational level, are taken in achieving results; supportive, in which services are afforded or actions taken that influence rathen than control results; or non-direct, in which services afforded are incidental or collateral in nature.

Working conditions: This includes the physical conditions imposed upon the position incumbent. The dimensions are: physical effort, the amount of physical energy required to be expended in lifting, climbing, or working in tiring positions; hazards, the danger of injury or probability of physical harm associated with the job; and discomfort, the environmental conditions to which the incumbent is exposed while on the job, including, but not limited to, cold, wind, dust, rain or snow, fumes, and dirt. Psychological discomfort is also included within the intent of this last dimension.[2]

Because state salaries are purposely set to correspond to prevailing wages in the State of Washington, a comparison of worth points to state salaries can give insight not only into the public sector but into the private sector as well. We will not attempt here to analyze critically the Willis point factor system. Nor will we discuss the underlying economic assumptions nor what systems might look like with different assumptions. Rather, we will limit ourselves to a discussion of what the existing systems can tell us about economic practices. In our application we will consider the effects of applying a job factor system across job families so that we can compare the actual salaries of jobs of comparable worth. Since, for non-management staff, these jobs were chosen as being representative of jobs held predominantly by women or predominantly by men, we can ascertain whether women's jobs pay less because they require less effort, skill, and responsibility or whether other factors are involved.

The management study

Prior to the study of classified staff positions, a study was conducted to evaluate the top exempt staff of the state. While the classified study specifically set out to study the relationship between men's jobs and women's jobs, the management study had as its objectives to correct internal alignment and to justify increases in state salaries to more closely approximate those in the private sector. This study is briefly summarized here because of the similarities in overall findings and dissimilarities in acceptance and implementation.

The results of the management study were presented in the "State of Washington Comprehensive Salary Study, Project A, Management Evaluation and Salary Recommendations," December 1973. The study reported that the spread of salaries was greater than usually found in industry. Nonetheless, there is a highly significant relationship between salary and points.[3] Figure 19-1 illustrates the relationship. The eight elected officials were clearly underpaid relative to the appointed managers. Eight appointed managers made higher salaries than the governor (a sizable number of administrators and faculty members in higher education also exceeded that salary). The highest paid state manager was the executive director of data processing services; data processing is one area with direct equivalence in the private sector, perhaps making it more susceptible to market factors. The study also revealed that there were obvious disparities between state salaries and those paid in industry.

The classified staff study

The Willis study of classified staff positions included only civil service positions. The evaluated jobs were specifically chosen as representing sex-segregated job classifications. The hypothesis had been that women's jobs would be compensated at a lower rate than men's jobs. The results totally support this hypothesis (see Figure 19-2). There was no overlap in compensation between men's and women's jobs: there was no women's job that paid as much as the lowest men's job in approximately the same range of

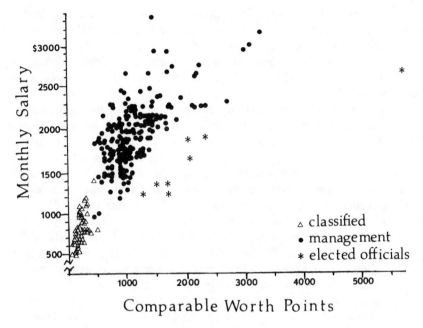

FIGURE 19-1
Combined Willis Data, 1973–1974

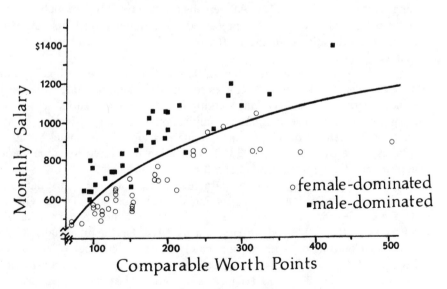

FIGURE 19-2
Willis Data, Classified Staff Only

worth. Only two men's jobs paid as little as the combined curve of best fit[4] and only four women's jobs paid above it. The average female salaries are at best equal to 78.8 percent of those of males at 80 points of value and equal to only 74.1 percent at 500 points; there is increasing discrepancy with increasing worth. (Since 1974 these differences have persisted at the same magnitude.)

Examples can best illustrate the full implications of this application of a point factor system across job families. According to job specifications established for the Higher Education Personnel System in the State of Washington, a Secretary III must be able to type at least fifty words per minute with no more than one error per minute, take shorthand or do machine transcription, manage a small office, supervise other clerical employees, order supplies, keep books, screen mail and phone calls, and perform other clerical duties. A high school diploma and two years' experience are required. Salaries range from $703 to $900 per month. Of the 428 persons holding this title at a large state university, only two are male (0.8%). Secretary III positions are covered in some union agreements, but union membership is not a condition of employment.

In the same system, a Construction Coordinator must inspect construction to ensure adherence to plans and to check for quality of workmanship, prepare progress reports, and review engineering drawings; he may suggest minor changes when field conditions warrant them. Minimum qualifications include two years' related college work or experience. Monthly salaries range from $1,336 to $1,711. All persons holding this title are males. Construction Coordinator is not represented by a union though its salary is based upon those paid in the crafts and trades where membership is required.

Consider a third position, that of Traffic Guide. Someone holding this position must check entering vehicles for valid parking permits, issue daily parking permits and collect daily parking fees, and direct visitors to parking areas and offices. The minimum qualification is a valid driver's license. Seventy-five percent of the persons holding this job title are male. Monthly salaries range from $721 to $923. This position is covered by some union agreements, though membership is not a job requirement.

Table 19-1 summarizes comparable worth points and salary data for the jobs of Secretary III, Construction Coordinator, and Traffic Guide. Traffic Guide, with far fewer points, paid a salary almost equal to that of a Secretary III in 1974 and surpassing it by 1978. On the other hand, Construction Coordinator, with approximately the same number of points as Secretary III, paid more than half again as much in 1974 and almost twice as much in 1978. Secretary III pays substantially less than the expected, or average, salary, while the two male-dominated jobs pay substantially more than expected. Furthermore, during the four years of this study, the

TABLE 19-1

Comparable Worth Points and Expected and Actual Salaries
for Traffic Guide, Secretary III, and Construction Coordinator

		1974			1978			
Job title	Compa-rable worth points	Mid-range salary	Expected salary	Actual salary as % of expected	Mid-range salary	Expected salary	Actual salary as % of expected	% increase 1974–78
Traffic Guide	89	$ 634	$493	129	$ 836	$ 631	132	31.9
Secretary III	210	650	836	78	816	1,073	76	25.5
Construction Coordinator	219	1,092	836	131	1,550	1,073	144	41.9

male-dominated classifications received salary increases far in excess of the total received by the Secretary III classification; by 1978 the salary for Secretary III has lost ground relative to the expected salary, whereas the two male-dominated jobs have increased their salary advantage.

While the above examples represent salary disparities in the extreme, the inequities exist throughout the jobs surveyed. Table 19-2 gives examples from major job families of "women's" and "men's" jobs and shows the wide range of jobs surveyed. Women's jobs include some in clerical work, food service, retail sales, accounting and bookkeeping, nursing, data processing, library work, and various health professions. Men's jobs encompass custodial work, police and security, gardening, technician jobs, crafts and trades, and computer programming. All of the women's jobs and two of the men's jobs would receive salary increases if comparable worth were implemented to bring the salaries of all jobs up to at least the expected average.

The pattern for men's and women's jobs are so different as to constitute separate salary schedules.[5] That is, women's jobs are assigned less compensation for effort, skill, and responsibility than are comparable men's jobs, and increased effort, skill, and responsibility result in smaller salary increases for women's jobs than men's jobs. Salary equity would seem to include compensating men's work and women's work in the same fashion.

CONCLUSIONS

Point factor job evaluations can be valuable tools for correcting salary inequities. The results of the Willis study on classified staff in the State of Washington public sector shows that salaries for women's jobs are substantially lower than those for men's jobs requiring equal effort, skill, and responsibility; women's jobs were paid only 75 percent of the wages of comparable men's jobs. These results would seem to explain a large portion of the difference found between overall men's and women's wages (nationally, women's wages average only 57 percent of those of men). One should keep in mind that existing job evaluation systems are not free of sex bias[6] or bias against the public sector. Much work must be done on existing systems to ensure equity. Were the systems bias-free, the gap between men's and women's jobs would be closed even further.

Implementation will be expensive and politically difficult. Cost of implementation of comparable worth depends upon the method chosen. Because women's jobs often have large numbers of incumbents and men's jobs frequently have smaller numbers of incumbents, the cheapest method for implementation would be to compute an average salary curve for all positions weighted by number of incumbents; all salaries could then be brought up or down to that curve with no overall increase in cost. This option is not feasible politically or legally because of many state laws prohibiting cuts in salary. Cost might be held down by leaving overpaid employees at their present levels, hiring new employees at the average level, and bringing underpaid categories up to the average.

The above procedure could be implemented at a slightly higher cost by computing the curve of best fit with no consideration for the number of incumbents. Overall there are more job titles held predominantly by men but larger numbers of people in the job titles held predominantly by women, so that equal weight to jobs produces a higher average curve. The highest cost would be to use the curve of best fit for male-dominated jobs as the model and to bring all other positions up to it; the political advantage to this model is that no salaries go down, but the disadvantage is the enormous price tag. All such schemes could be implemented all at once or over time.

One of the public employee unions proposed a model of implementation that serves to illustrate the political conflicts of implementation; they suggested that salaries for women's jobs be based upon comparable worth, but that salaries of men's jobs continue to be based upon prevailing wages. They are attempting to solve the conflict of interest of their membership: women wish to be paid fairly, and men do not wish to lose their salary advantage. Perhaps the union suggestion could be translated into a system whereby the benchmarks for across-the-board increases are only male-dominated jobs, with all positions benefiting equally. Any method allowing for differential treatment among job classifications would serve to nullify the basic concept of point factor systems and comparable worth—and no doubt over time would return us to the present situation.

Job segregation will continue as long as such large salary differentials exist between men's work and women's work; comparable worth appears to be a useful tool for equitably reducing salary differentials and then job segregation. There does exist a societal norm for what a fair wage is for given levels of effort, skill, and responsibility. A man violates the rule of optimization of his monetary return if he seeks employment in women's work. He is seen by others as violating this rule and is often labeled as deviant. He can do less and earn more if he stays in men's jobs. Training officers are often faced with a form of this dilemma: to encourage custodians, for example, to return to school to gain additional skills such as typing is to ask them to learn more to move into a job that pays less. Women attempting to gain entry to male-dominated jobs meet with hostility that can in part be explained in comparable worth terms; assuming a finite number of jobs, every male job taken by a female means that some male is being displaced and may have to accept woman's work. And who wants to do more for less? If jobs were compensated equally for equal effort, skill, and responsibility, there would be less impetus for males to seek men's jobs and less hostility toward women entering them. One can be sure that if clerical positions paid $400 more per month, high school counselors and parents

TABLE 19-2
Representative Job Classifications from Comparable Worth Study

Job title	Comparable worth points	1974 Mid-range salary	1974 Expected salary	1974 Actual salary as % of expected	1978 Mid-range salary	1978 Expected salary	1978 Actual salary as % of expected	% of increase 1974–78
Women's jobs								
Office Assistant I	81	$ 472	$ 493	96	$ 563	$ 631	89	19
Food Service Worker	93	472	579	82	637	742	86	35
Telephone Services Operator	116	520	665	73	653	852	77	26
Dental Assistant I	116	533	665	80	721	852	85	35
Retail Clerk I	120	484	665	73	606	852	71	25
Key Punch Operator III	121	604	665	91	703	852	83	16
Accounting Assistant II	132	634	665	95	836	852	98	32
Cook I	139	604	665	91	757	852	89	25
Licensed Practical Nurse I	153	546	751	73	739	963	77	35
Legal Secretary	187	717	836	86	900	1,073	84	26
Library Specialist I	192	773	836	92	946	1,073	88	22
Accountant I	232	832	922	90	1,070	1,184	90	29
Administrative Assistant B	247	853	922	93	1,097	1,184	93	29
Clinical Technician	284	832	1,008	83	1,044	1,295	81	25
Physical Therapist I	328	853	1,008	85	1,044	1,295	81	22
Nurse Practitioner II	385	832	1,094	76	1,097	1,405	78	32
Administrative Services Manager A	506	896	1,180	76	1,211	1,516	80	35

Truck Driver	94	792	578	137	969	742	130	22
Custodian II	97	589	578	102	739	742	100	25
Security Guard	110	683	579	118	796	742	107	17
Stockroom Attendant II	120	700	665	105	816	852	96	17
Gardener II	127	735	665	111	878	852	103	19
Utility Worker II	130	735	664	111	1,070	852	126	46
Mariner II	149	667	751	89	994	963	103	49
Photographer I	162	875	750	117	1,097	963	114	25
Media Maintenance Technician I	175	941	750	125	1,241	963	129	32
Heavy Equipment Operator	181	1,066	836	128	1,272	1,073	119	20
Campus Police Officer	152	896	836	107	1,070	1,073	100	19
Carpenter	197	966	836	116	1,241	1,073	116	28
Electrician	197	1,066	836	128	1,272	1,073	119	20
Drafting Technician II	229	832	922	90	1,097	1,184	92	32
Auditor I	266	966	922	105	1,439	1,184	122	49
Broadcast Technician III	301	1,092	1,008	108	1,370	1,295	106	25
System Analyst III	426	1,397	1,093	128	1,711	1,405	122	22

would be quick to point out the obvious benefits of these jobs to persons with only a high school education—and high school typing classes might rapidly fill with young men. Even if some occupations remained more or less segregated, the importance of job segregation as a problem issue might lessen if it were no longer correlated so highly with wage differentials.

Implementation of comparable worth will be very difficult politically. Implementation of any new system purporting to benefit preferentially any group but white males will be politically opposed by the groups in power. As a union leader said recently, 80 percent of the union members he represented were white males, and there was no reason to expect this 80 percent to sacrifice anything for the remaining 20 percent. Implementation of comparable worth would bring about a major change in the relative salaries of large numbers of jobs. The incumbents in the jobs which will lose relative status will of course oppose such change, just as those who will gain will support the change.

It would appear that implementation is possible only if systems are presented as providing some benefits other than correction of sex inequities in salaries. Job evaluation systems provide a seemingly rational basis for evaluating the relationship among jobs and provides an orderly framework for justifying salary differentials. Especially where past salary setting has been chaotic, employees and management will often embrace a system that promises order.

If the Washington experience is generalizable, it appears that once an evaluation system is touted as eliminating sex bias or benefiting women, it may be impossible to implement it. Other states and private companies which are implementing or considering implementation are encountering less resistance when sex equity is not mentioned; the State of Idaho, for example, has quietly implemented a system very similar to the Willis system during the time since the Washington study.

The final model for implementation will be politically determined as representing either some compromise of the best interests of all concerned groups or possibly the interests only of the most powerful group. At this time in the State of Washington the latter has already occurred; there has been no implementation for classified staff, there has been implementation for management, and both these events represent the optimum economic benefit for white males.

NOTES

1. Helen Remick, "Strategies for Creating Sound, Bias-free Job Evaluation Plans," *Job Evaluation and EEO: The Emerging Issues* (New York: Industrial Relations Counselors, 1974).

2. Norman D. Willis and Associates, State of Washington Comparable Worth Study, 1974.

3. The curve of best fit is salary = \$1,412.88 · log(points) − \$2,333.68. r = 0.62, p < .00001.

4. Salary = \$858.33 · log(points) − \$852.68; r = 0.77, p < .00001.

5. If men's and women's jobs are separated, men's jobs can be described as salary = \$969.51 · log(points) − \$1,275.44, r = 0.88, p < .00001, and women's jobs as salary = \$684.03 · log(points) − \$852.65, r = 0.86, p < .00001.

6. See Remick, "Strategies."

20 *Ronnie Steinberg Ratner*

EQUAL EMPLOYMENT FOR WOMEN: SUMMARY OF THEMES AND ISSUES

The preceding chapters address a wide array of issues and themes that flow from considering the actual institutional means by which equal employment policy for women is implemented. These range from mandating equal employment policy through legislation and collective agreements to implementing it through administrative agency regulations, court decisions, and conciliation and arbitration. They encompass a concern for political action by nongovernmental groups with vested interests in expanding the employment opportunities of women. The chapters explore as well the relationship between equal employment policy and other labor market policies designed both to train workers and to stimulate job creation in the public and private sectors. Finally, they investigate the connection between equal employment policy and other social policies such as day care programs, family allowances, maternal and parental leave policies, social services for the aged, and other family-related incentives implicit in tax policy and social security benefits.

It is impossible to capture and summarize in a few pages the diversity of perspectives on these issues expressed in this book. Instead, this chapter draws on the case material from the preceding chapters and, by moving beyond the detailed attention given to one or two countries, arrives at some general conclusions about five key topics in equal employment policy:[1] the effectiveness of general strategies for achieving equal employment policy (EEP); the improvements gained for women within firms as a result of EEP; the creation of policies to stimulate alternative arrangements in working hours as a complement to EEP; the effect of recession on EEP and methods for dampening its impact; and the limitation of current EEP because of its failure to address the undervaluation of women's work. I will then identify several unresolved issues in EEP. Finally, I will focus on three specific issues that are significant when considering the future direction of EEP, especially for the United States and Canada.

KEY TOPICS IN EQUAL EMPLOYMENT POLICY: GENERAL CONCLUSIONS

Strategies for implementing policy

The chapters in Parts II and III look at the strengths and weaknesses of dominant institutional strategies operating in particular countries—specifically, a legal strategy placing heavy emphasis on the use of litigation in the United States and France; a legal strategy involving administrative enforcement mechanisms in the United States and Great Britain; collective agreements between trade unions and employers in Sweden and West Germany; and general employment and vocational training programs, such as the ones encompassed in the Equality Program of the Swedish Labor Market Board.

To a certain extent, the effectiveness of a strategy or a combination of strategies is country-specific. (Effectiveness of a strategy is defined in terms of the reduction of occupational segregation, the decrease in the wage gap, or both.) For example, we would not expect that using trade union grievance procedures to resolve disputes over equal pay or equal opportunity would be effective if only a minority of employed women fall under collective bargaining agreements, as is currently the case in the United States and Canada. Yet, at the same time, the case material on countries with strikingly different socioeconomic, political, and legal settings suggest a number of general conclusions about the strengths and limitations of various strategies, regardless of the country in which they are carried out.

First, no one policy instrument mandating EEP, whether a law, a government regulation, or a collective agreement, can, by itself, achieve equal employment opportunity for women. Nonetheless, it is important to mandate equality for women in the labor market through a law prohibiting sex discrimination. Past experience suggests that such a law would be of limited effectiveness, especially if it only provides for the investigation of individual complaints about specific employer actions. At the same time, there are certain provisions that, if included in a law, would render it more effective. A law must contain a clear definition of what constitutes discrimination, a set of straightforward enforcement procedures, and strong sanctions for noncompliance. In addition, it must protect individual complainants from the likelihood of retaliation by employers and other employees. Second, a country should draft a law so as not to lose support for its goals from "natural" allies already organized on the labor market, especially trade unions.[2] In Sweden, for example, this would mean including provisions in their proposed anti-discrimination law that would ensure that equality agreements negotiated through collective bargaining would take precedence in all but the most extraordinary of situations. It also would mean that the government could not bring charges of sex discrimination against a union, at least initially, as is now possible in the United States and Canada. Third, mechanisms should be established for monitoring change after an agreement, either through redistributing resources within government agencies, as, for example, the shift by the U.S. Equal Employment Opportunity Commission to targeting to remove systemic discrimination, or through the activities of women's organizations such as the National Action Committee in Canada and trade unions such as the Swedish Confederation of White Collar Employees who currently engage in monitoring change efforts. Individually initiated litigation should be de-emphasized. Instead, other forms of dispute resolution in which decisions would affect whole classes of employees, including class action suits and arbitration and conciliation, should be provided.

Of all the strategies discussed, *litigation* of individual cases is probably the most inefficient and ineffective. Probably more cases on sex discrimination have been brought to the court in the United States than in all the rest of the advanced industrial democracies combined. Certain features of the law in the United States, such as placing the burden of proof on the employer, protecting the employee from dismissal, and allowing for class action suits, can work, under certain conditions, to the benefit of women workers. The impediments to using the courts in the United States, however, remain enormous. Judicial proceedings are an expensive, time-consuming, and painful process; judges vary in their degree of commitment to EEP.[3] This is true for the other countries as well: the record of equal pay and equal opportunity court cases in France and the United Kingdom does not offer much hope to those who regard litigation as the primary strategy for fundamental change. Marguerite Lorée reports that, in France, there were only eighteen complaints lodged under the equal pay law in the first three years of its existence. In twelve of these cases, the findings made by compliance officers proved inconclusive. Only a few complaints were litigated and, while the industrial court has ruled in favor of female employees on a number of occasions, most of these decisions have been a-pealed by the employers. Several cases have taken over five years to litigate. Nancy Seear calculated that, in the United Kingdom, industrial tribunals have settled less than half of the complaints in favor of the employee. Of the 91 cases under the Sex Discrimination Act that reached the industrial tribunal, "only 18, or just under 20 percent, were settled in favor of the applicant."

To be sure, one of the major constraints on the effective use of litigation is the restricted scope of existing equal pay and equal opportunity laws, a shortcoming noted in many of the preceding chapters. Yet, regardless of the content of a law, some features of litigation make it a difficult route to equal employment. This is especially true in the long run, because the U.S. experience suggests that employers (and the lawyers they hire) become more sophisticated in their opposition to the law over time. From the perspective of women workers, U.S. cases that would establish good precedents are increasingly being settled out of court. "Bad" cases move through the judicial system, establishing precedents that constrain future government actions on EEP. These same deterrents to using the courts appear in other countries, including Canada, France, and West Germany.

Litigation must not be abandoned entirely, however. Individuals need and should have the right to a forum in which to redress grievances. In addition, court cases appear to be effective in stimulating political action at the early stages of policy development, especially in countries with an emerging but weak women's movement and with a low or moderate level of unionization. Individual complaints make visible women's subordinate labor market position, "prove" that discrimination is a recurring (if not inherent) feature of the way labor markets operate, and facilitate organization among women around the issue of EEP. Nonetheless, it remains a highly restrictive and inefficient means by which to institute large-scale change in labor market performance.

Laws not only establish the right to EEP; most also provide for some means of government enforcement beyond adjudication. In drafting provisions on enforcement, policy-makers in most of Western Europe investigated the United States' Equal Employment Opportunity Commission (EEOC) and the United Kingdom's Equal Opportunities Commission (EOC) and shaped their own agencies on the basis of this examination. Four aspects of implementing EEP through *administrative agencies* appear to be especially problematic: whether the enforcement of equal pay and equal opportunity should be coordinated or separated; what degree of discretion should be given to the agency to set enforcement priorities; how to deal with "systems overload," such as complaint backlog; and whether models of enforcement agencies from other countries can be transplanted and take root in alien soil.

Peter Robertson offers one answer to the questions on enforcement priorities and systems overload based on a decade of experience in government enforcement. In the United States, the EEOC has come to redefine what discrimination is and how it operates in the labor market. Originally, discrimination was regarded as an intentional and conscious action taken by a specific employer against a specific employee—what is called direct discrimination. Discrimination also was viewed as marginal to the normal procedures for hiring, training, and promoting employees. Thus, the EEOC used conciliation to resolve individual disputes. Moreover, its domain was restricted to equal opportunity, leaving the enforcement of equal pay to another government agency. This limitation stymied early law enforcement efforts, especially where women are discriminated against because their work is undervalued. For example, potential employees often act on the basis of conventional stereotypes about what positions are appropriate to apply for, and never apply for jobs. Or, applicants for jobs or company-run training programs may be required to take a screening test that seems to maintain a consistent pattern of who performs well on the test and bears little relation to the actual requirements for positions. This indirect or systemic discrimination requires a different approach to enforcement. It requires, among other things, that administrative agencies target pre-selected industries and firms and initiate investigations into the patterns of employment. Once these and other companies have agreed to expand employment opportunities for women, administrative agencies need to support company efforts to develop new personnel procedures so that new occupational patterns emerge. Since lack of opportunities and unequal pay are systematically linked, it suggests that the enforcement of these two facets of EEP be coordinated.

Countries currently developing equal opportunity policy can build on the insights gained from U.S. experience: if a country can come up with a definition of discrimination that encompasses indirect (systemic) as well as direct discrimination, administrative enforcement of EEP can yield significantly greater results in a shorter amount of time. This moves concern away from instances in which an employer has acted with prejudice and toward the patterns by which certain groups are treated unequally in the labor market. It also means that enforcement agencies move away from conciliation and dispute resolution and emphasize, instead, systemic discrimination. As the chapters by Dipak Nandy and Jeffrey Jowell observe, the approach to the enforcement of equal opportunity in the United Kingdom builds on this and other lessons from U.S. enforcement efforts. This has led to a number of difficulties in accommodating the U.S. approach to British institutions. Most notably, because British judges traditionally favor a narrow interpretation of statutes, court decisions have tended to go against employees. Moreover, the almost complete separation of complaint resolution and enforcement agency action has meant that enforcement agencies cannot gain needed information through individual complaints. It also has meant that implementation of equal pay and equal opportunity remains uncoordinated, which, according to Dipak Nandy, renders each less effective. Again, the United States will prove the testing ground for the effectiveness of coordinated enforcement because, under President Carter's 1979 reorganization plan, the enforcement of both equal pay and equal opportunity policy has been consolidated under the EEOC.

Some countries, most notably Sweden and Austria, rely on trade unions to implement EEP through collective bargaining, political action, and worker education. (Whether trade unions or government agencies emerge as the dominant institutions for implementing and enforcing EEP is, in large part, a function of the extent and strength of unionization in a country. In Sweden, over 70 percent of employed women belong to unions in contrast to 12 percent in the United States or 20 percent in the Federal Republic of Germany.[4]) Even in countries where most employees are un-ionized, however, there were many problems with *collective bargaining* as a means for implementing EEP, including difficulties in organizing women and moving them into positions of leadership, the likelihood of staunch employer resistance, and the ignorance of workers about equal employment. In addition, during economic downturns, specific demands such as EEP are sacrificed at the bargaining table to the principal objective of maintaining workers' real wages.

In spite of these problems, gains have been made through collective bargaining, especially on equal pay: the wage solidarity policy of the Swedish trade unions discussed by Alice Cook has almost eliminated the gap in wages between men and women. In addition, in several countries, unions have bargained for and won educational leaves, maternity disability benefits, and paid maternity leaves. The example of the Swedish wage solidarity policy is particularly instructive concerning conditions under which trade unions facilitate EEP. First, trade unions are more likely to work on women's issues when they are framed as general issues. Second, a stronger commitment to EEP exists in countries where union bargaining is central-ized rather than decentralized. With decentralized bargaining, decisions on pay and opportunity come to vary as a function of a constellation of fac-tors specific to a company and a local union. At the local level, however, the interests of less powerful workers receive less attention. If women begin to assume leadership positions in their local unions this might facilitate sig-nificant gains in EEP, even with decentralized bargaining.

In Sweden, as Alice Cook has also indicated, equality committees are forming at the local level to ensure that the special concerns of women will be addressed. These committees should be one source of recruiting women into union leadership positions. In other countries, with a low percentage of the female workforce in unions, the first order of priority is to organize women. Once women are in unions, collective bargaining becomes a more viable strategy for achieving EEP for women. As I will argue at greater length below, once women have been organized into unions and have assumed positions of leadership within them, the structure of trade unionism is potentially the best vehicle for achieving labor market equality for women.

Finally, in most countries, the Ministry of Labor, the Ministry of Education, or both have been operating *training programs* for some time. As a matter of course, women are eligible for training, but most enroll in programs oriented toward eventual employment in typically female occupations. Of course, in general, women pursue training in traditionally female fields both because of how they are approached or channeled into programs and because of (realistic) expectations about the types of jobs available to them. The example from the United Kingdom of the Engineering Industries Training Board program to train one hundred women for craft jobs described by Alice Cook in Chapter 9 is especially illuminating in this context. The original advertisement for this program elicited few responses. When the EITB used other, more direct methods of reaching these girls and their parents, and emphasized the benefits to be gained from completing the programs, the number of female applications soared.

With the exception of Sweden, where training programs and other labor market policies are at the center of EEP, most countries are only beginning to incorporate the goals of EEP into their programs. Although experience is limited, it is possible to identify a number of features which would make programs to train women for nontraditional jobs more effective: Special efforts should be made to include re-entry women; past experience suggests that, since late adolescence is a time of heightened awareness of gender identity, it appears to be more difficult to interest high school graduates and dropouts—as opposed to married women with children—to engage in training for typically male jobs.[5] Women should be trained in groups and special sessions should be included on dealing with harassment. Programs should take account of labor market trends so as to train women for jobs in expanding rather than in declining sectors. Finally, some link should be ensured between job training and job placement.

In sum, multiple strategies are needed to achieve equal pay and equal opportunity for women. At the center of a country's policy should be a government agency responsible for identifying patterns of unequal treatment, negotiating agreements to eliminate such patterns, and monitoring agreements. Recent U.S. court decisions establishing consent decrees between employers and women have included provisions for a paid monitor to review implementation.[6] More attention needs to be placed on training as well, so that women can qualify for the skilled positions that will be available to them in the future as a result of the agreements that are made.

Some of the limited government resources currently devoted to litigation and precedent-setting in the United States, for instance, might be better used to underwrite these alternative strategies for equalizing opportunities. I will return to this issue below.

Improvements for women in firms

EEP has been in existence for a long enough time in several countries, and especially in the United States, to make it possible to assess its effect on women's labor market position and on personnel procedures within private firms. Indeed, the results of two major studies of changes that have come about as a result of equal pay and equal opportunity legislation in the United Kingdom and the United States indicate that women's position has become more equal. In her study of the U.S., Ruth Shaeffer found that, while the percentage of women in managerial positions increased in most industries, the greatest gains had been made in female-intensive industries, such as retail trade, textile mill products, and electrical machinery equipment supplies. In addition, she discovered that, while small companies seemed to improve the job opportunities of women differentially, "the greatest improvement in the proportion of women in their upscale jobs" occurred within the very large corporations.[7] Nancy Seear found that the Equal Pay Law in the United Kingdom reduced the gap in wages between men and women by almost 20 percent.

Both Seear and Shaeffer identify several factors that lead to better opportunities for women in firms. Regardless of how a law or other government regulation defines discrimination or specifies procedures for remedying it, the most important stimulus to change within firms appears to be the threat of costly government sanctions for noncompliance.[8] Moreover, beyond the need to disseminate information about the scope and sanctions of the law, the record of improved opportunities for women is better in companies where top managers are committed to the goal of equal employment for women and where, consequently, personnel procedures have been modified to effectuate change.

Once a company has made a commitment to equal opportunity for women, there are, according to Rosabeth Kanter, at least two ways to avoid resistance within companies to programs developed. First, it is important to focus on the structure of the organization as it relates to all employees rather than isolating one particular group. It is then possible to link the goals embedded in affirmative action programs to the expansion of opportunities of all employees, and hence avoid zero-sum situations. Second, it is crucial to stress that the procedures for achieving equal employment opportunity are consistent with sound organizational procedures in general. Affirmative action plans require companies to review the composition, distribution, and use of employees; to compare employees with the available pool of labor; to set goals for changing the composition, distribution, and use of employees; and to establish a plan for meeting these goals. In this sense, proper compliance with equal opportunity policy rationalizes the personnel function within work organizations. Companies that have begun to develop and implement affirmative action plans have concluded that, while the procedures may be painful to initiate, they have resulted in the improved management of all workers in a firm.

Alternative work arrangements

Equal employment policy not only facilitates the development of new personnel procedures; it also stimulates thinking about other changes in the organization of work that would better accommodate the distinctive needs of women workers. Two issues that point to such general changes are the need to remove the link between part-time work and women's unequal labor market position, and the need to change aspects of the work process associated with jobs performed primarily by men. Proposals—in fact, sometimes competing proposals—concerning the issues of part-time work and changing the structure of work are being placed on the public agenda in several countries. Some countries have even enacted policies establishing alternative arrangements of working hours, including flextime; experiments in job sharing; and guaranteed paid leaves.[9]

Flextime encompasses such specific innovations in the reorganization of working hours as compressed and shortened workweeks, staggered hours, and rotating shifts. Although these policies began in Western Europe as a way to attract workers, and especially women workers, during the labor shortage of the late 1960s, they have come to be associated with new demands, emerging from women workers themselves, to make work and family life more compatible. The more flexible arrangement of working hours has been made available to a significant minority of workers in Sweden and in the Federal Republic of Germany. Most other Western European countries have been showing considerable interest in introducing flextime, but trade unions in these countries vary in their support of such proposals.[10]

Job sharing has emerged as one way to enable working couples to divide work and family responsibilities more equally. It has been introduced in Sweden in a number of companies within the cooperative sector and in a number of government offices. In addition, a number of plants in Norway permit married couples to share a job for a certain period of time while retaining their separate fringe benefits.[11]

Worker sabbaticals and other forms of guaranteed paid leaves are under consideration in a number of European countries. Gösta Rehn, a well-known and highly influential Swedish economist, has proposed that every worker be allocated a lifetime "bank of time" during which she or he is guaranteed a leave with pay for a number of purposes of her or his own choosing. This could include a sabbatical to take care of small children as well as a leave to enroll in a training program to shift careers in mid-life. It would be funded through an insurance policy operating along the lines of the unemployment compensation system. While no country has even come close to embracing this proposal, programs for educational leaves without the threat of job loss exist for many employees in France and Sweden, established in the former through national legislation and in the latter through collective agreements.[12]

Women trade unionists, other activists, and even some policy-makers are beginning to press for a number of related political reforms such as shortening the length of the working day to six hours, extending fringe benefits to part-time workers, and reimbursing employers for introducing technological innovations that make it easier for women to perform a job. Of particular interest to Europeans, especially to West Germans and Swedes, is shortening work hours to six per day. (A shortening of work hours appears to be one of the major aims of the European trade unions. Male unionists want to shorten the working week. Female unionists prefer, instead, to shorten the working day.) This demand would contribute to women's labor market equality in several respects. The six-hour day would more closely approximate the part-time workday, decreasing the extent of part-time work and increasing the likelihood that fringe benefits would be extended to all workers. Women and men would have additional time each day to devote to household tasks and leisure activities, increasing the likelihood that leisure and unpaid work would be shared more equally. A decrease in individual working hours would most likely increase the total number of jobs available unless the reduction in working time were accompanied by an increase in the capital-labor ratio. The extra jobs could be filled by those currently unemployed, thus lowering the overall rate of unemployment. A decrease in total unemployment would contribute to a political environment more favorable to EEP.

Recession and equal employment policy

As was mentioned in Chapter 1 and in several other chapters, during the economic downturn of the late 1970s, women suffered a higher rate of unemployment than men in most of the advanced industrial democracies. Despite this fact, public works and training programs to put the unemployed back to work continue to be targeted to unemployed males. Even more disturbing are the proposals surfacing in West Germany, and to a lesser extent in Sweden, to pay mothers "upbringing money" and, in doing so, to remove them from the labor force. As Herta Däubler-Gmelin reports, this reform, as proposed in West Germany by members of the moderate and conservative parties, would extend for one year, would pay a lower stipend than is provided by unemployment compensation, and would not require an employer to rehire an employee. As Däubler-Gmelin concludes, behind such suggestions "stands too clearly a trend toward forcing women more strongly than ever out of the business world. At the very least, those who support equal opportunity for women must oppose these new policies and proposals, and seek to develop new goals."

With the economic downturn creating a policy climate unsympathetic even to maintaining the current level of women's employment, the goal of equal opportunity becomes simultaneously more difficult and more important to sustain. After all, whether or not policy-makers and the general public accept the situation, they must constantly be reminded that one breadwinner will no longer be able to support a family; that married women, including married women with young children, will continue to enter the labor market in ever-increasing numbers, with no evidence of a reversal of this trend; and that the structure of the labor market and the composition of jobs is not static. In short, the problem of integrating women into the labor market will not go away.[13]

Even in this period of low growth, certain sectors of the economy are expanding. New occupations emerge—whether as a result of "impersonal" market forces or through more "conscious" public and private job-creation programs. The projection of labor market trends and the training of women workers to fill emerging positions can do a great deal to reverse the direction of female unemployment and expand their opportunities. This is especially true if such research, planning, and program development include, at each stage, some mechanism to guarantee that women will have access to newly created jobs. Furthermore, in a labor market characterized by occupational segregation, occupations quickly become sex-typed as male or female. The growth of the service sector over the last forty years is only the most recent example of this general phenomenon. Therefore, care must be taken to avoid the creation of new, female job ghettos. Placing women in new jobs that, because they are female, would be low-wage and dead-end, would be a mixed blessing indeed.

Undervaluation of women's work

As the chapters by Remick and Marsden make clear, a new standard of equal value, also referred to as comparable worth, is receiving considerable attention as a way to broaden the scope of equal pay policy. A comparable worth standard would make it possible to compare the wages of women in typically female jobs with the wages of men in typically male jobs. In an occupationally segregated labor market, equal pay for work of equal value carries the potential for improving the collective position of women workers, if not their individual opportunities.

Equal pay for work of equal value requires some method for determining the "worth" of a job independent of the wage rate it commands. It necessitates some exercise in job analysis and job evaluation, which raises a number of technical and political considerations, some of them touched on by Christof Helberger in Appendix B. There are many varities of job analysis; none of them is neutral. Historically, job evaluation has been used to undermine the power position, and the wages, of employees. Because of this, trade unions, and the workers they represent, must be convinced of the progressive potential of job evaluation techniques before this new political goal can receive the type of widespread support that will make it effective. Second, given the subjective nature of job evaluation, women committed to the goal of equal pay for work of equal value always must be included on job evaluation committees. This was the case in the State of Washington, but was not so in West Germany. Finally, job analysis and job evaluation should be treated as tools for assigning relative wages to different jobs in the labor market. This raises considerable difficulties because it must be remembered that, within the market setting, there is unequal power between employers and employees, as well as unequal power between male and female employees. Moreover, the goal of business in capitalist society is to maximize profits. These market features place severe constraints on the likelihood of achieving equal pay for work of equal value.

The political setbacks in the recent attempts to bring women's wages more in line with those paid to men in comparable jobs through the use of job evaluation is sobering. Both in the United States (in Washington state) and in West Germany, studies using job analysis and job evaluation techniques uncovered significant disparities in the wage rates of women and men in comparable jobs. In both situations, the demand to raise the pay scale of women in undervalued work in order to approximate the wages in comparable men's jobs fell on unsympathetic or indifferent ears. Women workers included in these studies continue to be paid the same low wages for performing work assessed to be equivalent in skill, effort, and responsibility to higher-paying male jobs. It is as if the studies had never been conducted and the results never presented. The difficulties were not at the technical stage, but emerged politically in the process of implementation.

In addition, in the United States a number of pending and appealed lawsuits concerning the undervaluation of women's work suggest that the courts are extremely unsympathetic if not hostile to this policy goal.[14] The courts have dismissed a variety of evidence culled from different sources including job evaluations, data on the difficulty of finding men willing to accept jobs at a pay rate typical of women's jobs, and analyses of the historical evolution of jobs. Instead, the courts contended that the women failed to show that they had been barred from men's jobs; that Congress never intended the courts to interfere in the workings of the marketplace; and that Congress never intended that the courts be concerned with the evaluation of jobs.

In summary, what these court cases and the experiences in Washington state and West Germany show has been stated in an editorial by Ellen Goodman on the issue of equal pay for work of equal value:

> If assessing "comparable worth" is hard, getting equal paychecks is going to be even harder. It will take more than the consciousness-raising, more than careful point systems, more than the litigation and the best wishes of the U.S. Equal Employment Opportunity Commission.
>
> It will require increased organization and clout among women workers themselves. If there is one slogan that underlines all the rest, it's the simple one: Equal pay for equal power.[15]

UNRESOLVED ISSUES

Even among those who share a commitment to the development of government policies to further women's labor market equality, many issues remain unresolved. These include differences in what the legitimate focus and scope of equal employment policy should be, which means are most likely to facilitate change, and whether equal pay or equal opportunity policy can bring about greater gains for women in a shorter period of time. One issue involves the conflict between short-run and long-run policy goals. For example, a policy-maker often must decide whether to develop certain policy instruments that take as given the existing unequal division of expectations, roles, and responsibilities between men and women in the household. Alternatively, she or he could choose a more "long-run perspective," in which existing inequalities are ignored or placed to one side and the assumption of equality between women and men is consistently adhered to. In the short run, the policy resulting from this decision in favor of legal equality may be less beneficial to those women with extensive household responsibilities and without sufficient resources to allocate these tasks and obligations to others. Policy-makers who adopt a long-run point of view implicitly act on the assumption that greater equality in the labor market eventually will lead to greater equailty both in the family and in other non–labor market institutions. Therefore, they oppose protective labor laws and prefer parental leave (as opposed to maternity leave) as a policy to cover working parents after the birth of a child. This is typical of equal employment policy in Sweden and in the United States. Other countries, most notably the United Kingdom, incorporate the short-run perspective, preferring instead to take into account and attempt to alleviate the additional burdens that exist for women in lower socioeconomic classes. For example, in the United Kingdom, the Sex Discrimination Act coexists with protective labor laws, the latter being explicitly exempted from the provisions of the former. Similarly, a maternity leave policy is supported through employer contributions, making it costly for employers to hire women of childbearing age.

The issue of quotas also is clearly an unresolved issue. The *Bakke* decision, in which the U.S. Supreme Court upheld the constitutionality of affirmative action programs as a legitimate method for remedying past discrimination but denied the use of inflexible quotas for these purposes, falls midway between the range of positions taken by European and North American countries on the issue of affirmative action, positive discrimination, and quotas. At one extreme are policy-makers who refuse to introduce any programs in their countries where special consideration is given to women in order to place them in positions from which they were formerly excluded. This posture exists regardless of whether their equal opportunity law offers them the option of acting affirmatively. At the other extreme is Sweden; its Labor Market Board requires firms to fulfill sex quotas in order to qualify for regional development support. It has established quotas for the placement of unemployed workers in public service jobs. It is investigating the potential effectiveness of introducing quotas into vocational guidance and training programs and into the hiring of women for nontraditional jobs.

A third set of unresolved issues turns on the choice of policy priorities. Perhaps the most important difference exists over whether equal employment policy should aim at changing women to enable them to conform with the existing labor market norms or aim at changing the labor market and working conditions to conform with the distinctive needs of women. For example, should the labor market continue to "punish" those women who want to stop paid work for several years to be at home with their pre-school children, or who want to work part time as a solution to their dual responsibilities? Can there be labor market equality if women continue to have a more tenuous link to the labor market than men? Or is it necessary to eliminate part-time and discontinuous work in order to attain equality for women in the labor market?

A second difference concerns whether equal pay or equal opportunity policy is the preferred route to labor market equality for women. Where the primary concern is eliminating occupational segregation and equalizing employment opportunities, the policy goal becomes improving women's access to better-paying male jobs. Paying women more money to keep them in the same sex-segregated jobs is not viewed as a meaningful solution to women's labor market integration. In contrast, equal pay for work of comparable worth becomes the goal of those who attach importance to improving the collective position of the majority of women who work at women's jobs. This goal is especially valued because the economic downturn has contracted the opportunities of all employees, regardless of sex. Therefore, rather than allowing all employees to fight over a smaller total number of jobs, redirecting energies toward comparable worth will result in a substantial improvement for women, one that does not come at the expense of male employees.

FUTURE POLICY DIRECTIONS

Three issues touched upon in earlier sections of this chapter seem especially important when considering the direction equal employment policy should take over the next two decades, especially from a North American perspective. One is ensuring that equal employment does not result in multiple responsibilities for women in work and family life. Another is unionizing working women, implementing equal employment policy through trade unions, and strengthening women's organizations. The third is broadening the goals of equal employment policy so that an affirmative action approach dominates equal opportunity policy and so that the standard in equal pay policy is broadened to equal pay for work of comparable worth.

The double burden of working women

In her article on "Changing Sex Roles and Family Structure," sociologist Janet Zollinger Giele reports that "employed American women who have families average a total of 70 hours of work a week. . . . Each week they have a few hours less leisure time than men for sleep or relaxation. . . . Thus, more women have entered employment without having secured the needed adjustments in family life."[16] If this is currently the case, it does not offer much hope that women's double burden of work and family responsibilities will ease when equal employment is achieved unless some adjustments are made.

One set of solutions involves developing family policies and other government services that would facilitate a more equal division of responsibility for the family and household tasks between men and women. Increasing child care facilities, as well as maintaining programs to care for the elderly, would help alleviate some of the more pressing demands made on adults in families. Most countries have been negligent in meeting these needs, however. As Hilary Land points out for the United Kingdom, government social programs have been sharply reduced during the last few years. Those that remain are organized around the assumption that each family has available to it at least one full-time member—namely, the women—who is able to accommodate her schedule to the often rigid timetable of existing facilities. In addition, in many countries, working parents must organize their work and family lives around the school and day care schedules, rather than vice versa.[17] Health care clinics are rarely open on the evenings and weekends, forcing many parents to rely on emergency rooms and other types of discontinuous care.

But the facts indicate that one-earner families in which one adult is available to accomplish all the unpaid family-based work are no longer in the majority in the United Kingdom, nor anywhere else. In the United States, for example, a 1976 study by Hayghe found that "families with both a husband and wife in the labor force now make up 41 percent of all U.S. husband-wife families, a larger single block than any other form; families with husbands only in the labor force account for 34 percent."[18] Consequently, more attention needs to be paid to the conflicting demands placed on the time available to wives, mothers, and adult children. Designing social programs and other service facilities to take into account the needs of two-earner families would constitute an important contribution to equal employment for women.

Second, tax policy, social security laws, and pension programs must be amended to make government incentives to family life consistent with the goals inherent in equal employment policy. Existing policies in the United States are in the process of being modified through court decisions and legislative reform to remove the incentives to the male-earner-only family.[19] By contrast, policies in the United Kingdom continue to embody this traditional model of division of labor within the family. This, Land contends, is an additional factor helping to perpetuate the conflict between women's family responsibilities and equal employment policy.

But obstacles remain even where these biases have been removed, such as in Sweden, where public services have begun to be restructured and where policy is formulated according to an implicit model of family equality. These difficulties take several forms, some of which are more easy to deal with than others. A first set of obstacles is the insufficient number of day care centers and other child care facilities. This could easily be eliminated by creating additional programs and by offering parents a diverse set of child care options. (Of course, the difficult issue behind the easy solution involves finding the funds to pay for these programs.) A second set of obstacles arises out of the lag between women entering the labor market and men assuming responsibility in the home. Because of this asymmetry, family policies and other equality-based social policies may exacerbate tensions within existing families, because the support provided to the husband by the wife has not been replaced by a new relationship predicated on interdependency.[20] This is compounded further by the fact that husbands continue to contribute more to total family income than wives, thereby maintaining their position as primary breadwinner. Although more Swedish men are taking advantage of parental insurance to care for their infants, this difference in income contribution continues to make it beneficial to the family for women to takes leaves from work. These are some of the unintended consequences that emerge along the route to equality and that must be carefully considered when trying to synchronize family policy and equal employment policy.

A final problem raised in Rita Liljeström's chapter is even harder to resolve. This concerns the probability that increased participation by men and women, and eventually even their equality in the labor market as it is currently structured, will come at the expense of their leisure, their hobbies, and their volunteer work. Perhaps even more disturbing is the possibility that increased commitment to work and the concomitant demands such commitment brings will make it more difficult to enter into and sustain intimate relationships in which personal needs are, to a certain extent, satisfied. Any serious discussion of equal employment for women must of necessity confront and think through basic questions of priorities, especially taking into account how individuals want and are able to organize their lives over the life cycle. At the very least, it will raise the issue of whether equality in the work and family spheres is possible in any political economy where the demands of the productive sphere take precedence over the requisite needs in what Liljeström and others call the reproductive sphere. The question then becomes: what changes—as, for example, a radical decrease in the number of hours constituting full-time work—need to be introduced into the way work is organized in order to achieve equal employment for women and still avoid these difficult unintended consequences?[21]

Unionization and women's organizations

It is imperative for employed women to join trade unions in industries where they exist and to organize unions in industries where they do not. Once in unions, they must move into leadership positions, and especially get involved in contract negotiations. First, as women participate in negotiating teams, those teams will come to regard "women's issues" such as equal pay and equal opportunity as a high priority that is not to be lightly compromised away. Second, union grievance procedures potentially offer women a more direct and efficient channel for dispute resolution than do the time-consuming and frustrating methods of litigation and complaining to administrative agencies. Third, unions have direct access to the day-to-day operations within a workplace; hence they can directly monitor the implementation of EEP.

To suggest that unions carry great potential for furthering the priorities of women workers is not to say that it will be easy to get male trade union leadership to give up or even to share their power in existing unions or to offer financial and other support to women organizing in traditionally female sectors. Likewise, it will not be easy to reorient male-dominated institutions to the concerns of women workers. As Barbara Wertheimer points out in Chapter 10, women will be faced with great obstacles as they enter and participate in unions. That is why programs to train women such as the one described by Wertheimer are essential. As Wertheimer remarks, "To incorporate affirmative action plans into collective bargaining agreements will demand all the know-how and energy and skill that we have indicated women need." Nonetheless, the potential gains to be made in organizing women and in implementing equal employment policy through direct action of employees in the workplace far outweigh the initial difficulties associated with changing the power structure, and hence the priorities, of trade unions.

Increasing the extent of unionization among women workers is no substitute, however, for strong women's organizations. Each type of organization has a unique and crucial role to play in building equality for women in the labor market. While, in the United States, most women's organizations are devoting almost all their energies toward getting the required three-quarters of the states to approve the Equal Rights Amendment to the Constitution, several groups of women lawyers are specializing in litigation to establish precedents favorable to women in the area of sex discrimination in employment.[22] Once trade unions assume primary responsibility for settling individual complaints, women's law groups and other political organizations are freed to focus on attaining other, more basic changes. These could range from monitoring consent decrees and other agreements made by private firms (to ensure that employers are instituting the changes specified) to lobbying the legislature to fund the day care and training programs (crucial prerequisites for equal employment opportunity for women). As Lorna Marsden points out for Canada, it was the concerted and coordinated efforts of women working both inside and outside of government that were responsible for including a provision on equal pay for work of equal value in the Human Rights Act. And, of course, equal pay for work of equal value, as Ellen Goodman reminds us, will remain a formal right unless women organize to make it a reality. In summary, then, women must organize both within trade unions and into autonomous organizations in order to create new institutional arenas in which disputes can be resolved, develop educational programs to make women aware of their position in the labor market and of the resources available to them to change that position, exert the political pressure for new governmental and nongovernmental programs and policies, ensure that formal commitments are lived up to, and redistribute power both in the labor market and in society in general.

Broadening policy goals

The scope of government policy on equal employment must simultaneously be broadened and sharpened to confront directly and attack more effectively the sources of female labor market inequality. Specifically, this would mean modifying the goals of both equal opportunity and equal pay policy. Consider equal opportunity policy. In Chapter 1, I described three approaches to equal opportunity: a discrimination approach in which the policy establishes some mechanism for dispute resolution; an expanding opportunities approach in which non–labor market policies that facilitate female labor force participation are stressed; and an affirmative action approach that emphasizes formulating and implementing new personnel procedures within work organizations. While the discrimination approach is likely to remedy specific instances of direct discrimination as well as to make visible the importance of discrimination to the normal functioning of the labor market, it is not a very efficient method for remedying pervasive discrimination. Once systemic discrimination is understood, in other words, it no longer makes sense to rely on individual complaints as the major impetus to enforcement efforts. It follows, then, that the priorities of an equal opportunity policy must be shifted toward modifying the way firms recruit, select, assign, train, or promote employees. This means shifting priorities in enforcement away from a discrimination strategy to an affirmative action strategy.

Policy goals need to be redefined for equal pay policy as well. In a labor market characterized by severe occupational segregation, a law providing for equal pay for equal work is necessarily limited in scope. One need only consider the fact that, since the enactment of the national equal pay law in the United States, the gap in wages between men and women has actually increased. This is true even though federal enforcement efforts of the existing equal pay law have been substantial, as Marcia Greenberger reports. Until equal pay for work of comparable worth is accepted as a legitimate policy goal, equal pay policy will not confront the predominant cause of wage inequality in the labor market.

If a public policy is to be effective, it must incorporate a strategy that meets head on the problem it was established to remedy. As Rosabeth Kanter puts it, "Identifying the causes of inequities and perceived limitations to women's equal opportunity cannot be ignored, for the effectiveness of any intervention strategy is inextricably bound up with how adequately one diagnoses the sources of the problem." While this would appear to be a truism too obvious to mention, I believe that it is a major source of policy ineffectiveness, at least in the United States. The reasons for this lack of fit are beyond the scope of this chapter. But its implications for equal employment policy are extremely relevant.

For equal employment policy, achieving a consistency between problem and policy would mean attacking directly the sources of systemic labor market inequality. Experience with the enforcement of equal opportunity and equal pay policy in the United States has provided an understanding of the sources of female labor market inequality. As Kanter also reasons, "If the problem [of equal opportunity] is analyzed in terms of organizational policies and practices, career paths and access to them, or other features of the design of work systems, then employing organizations themselves should be the target of change efforts." Similarly with equal pay policy: if the gap in wages is a product of the systematic undervaluation of women's work, then the priority of the policy should be to adjust upward the wages paid for women's work.

The development of equal employment policy for women is at a crucial turning point in most of the advanced industrial democracies. Over the next two decades, the parameters of policy in most countries will not only take form, but will also become more difficult to modify.[23] A great deal of work remains to be done: to create programs and policies that will lead to permanent changes in the way women are distributed by industry and occupation, and to make related social and labor market policies consistent with the goal of integrating women workers, to name but a few of the many tasks ahead. If, indeed, efforts to achieve equality for women are successful, one measure of this success will be that enforcement of equal employment policies will, in the long run, render these policies superfluous.

NOTES

1. This chapter is largely based on the report on the Wellesley Conference on Equal Pay and Equal Opportunity Policy for Women: United States, Canada, and Western Europe, May 1979.

2. Preliminary findings of a study of women in blue-collar jobs traditionally held by men suggest that excluding unions from formal equal opportunity procedures has had a negative and divisive effect on implementing these policies (Brigid O'Farrell, principal investigator, "Women, Men and Jobs Project," Wellesley College Center for Research on Women, 1978–1980).

3. Mary C. Dunlap, "The Legal Road to Equal Opportunity: A Critical View," *American Women Workers in a Full Employment Economy: A Compendium of Papers Submitted to the Subcommittee on Economic Growth and Stabilization of the Joint Economic Committee* (Washington, D.C.: GPO, 1977), pp. 61–74.

4. Anne H. Nelson, "The One World of Working Women," Monograph no. 1, Bureau of International Labor Affairs, U.S. Department of Labor, Aug., 1978, p. 6.

5. Rita Liljeström, Gunilla Fürst Mellström, and Gillian Liljeström Svensson, *Roles in Transition: Report of an Investigation Made for the Advisory Council on Equality between Men and Women* (Stockholm: Liber Förlag / Almänna Förlaget, 1978).

6. Sadie Robarts, "Impressions of Affirmative Action in 1978," unpub. report to the German Marshall Fund of the United States, 1979.

7. Ruth Gilbert Shaeffer and Edith F. Lynton, *Corporate Experiences in Improving Women's Job Opportunities* (Conference Board Report no. 755; New York: The Conference Board, 1979).

8. It is interesting to note as well that the U.S. firms studied by Shaeffer reported that they were unable to single out whether Title VII of the Civil Rights Act, which prohibits discrimination, or Executive Orders 11246 and 11375, which require companies doing business with the government to set up goals and timetables for increasing the representation of women and minorities in jobs in which they are currently excluded, was the impetus behind the changes they were undertaking. Most of the major U.S. corporations are government contractors. But even more important is the fact that corporations reported that they found the most effective way to avoid difficulties under Title VII was to adopt the affirmative action approach associated with the Executive Orders.

9. Janet Zollinger Giele and Hilda Kahne, "Meeting Work and Family Responsibilities: Proposals for Flexibility," *Women in Mid-life—Security and Fulfillment: A Compendium of Papers Submitted to the Subcommittee on Retirement Income and Employment, Select Committee on Aging* (Washington, D.C.: GPO, 1978), pp. 158–177.

10. Jeffrey M. Miller, "Innovations in Working Patterns," Report of the U.S. Trade Union Seminar on Alternative Work Patterns in Europe, May 1978.

11. Harriet Holter and Hildur Ve Henriksen, "Social Policy and the Family in Norway," in Jean Lipman-Blumen and Jessie Bernard, eds., *Sex Roles and Social Policy: A Complex Social Science Equation* (Sage Studies in International Sociology no. 14; Beverly Hills, Calif.: Sage Publications, 1979), pp. 199–224.

12. Miller, "Innovations in Working Patterns."

13. This argument is based on the remarks of Alice H. Cook at the wrap-up session of the conference.

14. See, for example, *Lemons* v. *City and County of Denver,* and *Christensen* v. *State of Iowa.*

15. Ellen Goodman, "New Slogan, Same Struggle," *The Boston Globe*, Oct. 10, 1978.

16. Janet Zollinger Giele, "Changing Sex Roles and Family Structure," *Social Policy* 9, no. 4 (Jan./Feb. 1979): 33. See also Jessie Bernard, "Policy and Women's Time," in Lipman-Blumen and Bernard, eds., *Sex Roles and Social Policy*, pp. 303–333.

17. Denise LeCoultre, "L'Aménagement du temps de travail et ses répercussions pour les femmes," paper prepared for the International Symposium on Women and Industrial Relations, Vienna, Austria, Sept. 12–15, 1978; Alice H. Cook, *The Working Mother: A Study of Problems and Programs in Nine Countries*, (Ithaca, N.Y.: School of Industrial and Labor Relations, Cornell University, 1975); Alice H. Cook, "Working Women: European Experience and American Need," *American Women Workers in a Full Employment Economy*, pp. 271–306.

18. Giele, "Changing Sex Roles and Family Structure," p. 36.

19. Grace Ganz Blumberg, "Federal Income Tax and Social Security Law," *American Women Workers in a Full Employment Economy*, pp. 237–248. See also Nancy M. Gordon, "The Treatment of Women in the Public Pension Systems of Five Countries," Urban Institute Working Paper no. 5069-01, March 1978.

20. Liljeström et al., *Roles in Transition*.

21. Annika Baude, "Public Policy and Changing Family Patterns in Sweden, 1930–1977," in Lipman-Blumen and Bernard, eds., *Sex Roles and Social Policy*, pp. 17–38.

22. See, for example, the work of Equal Rights Advocates, the Women's Rights Project of the Center for Law and Social Policy, and the Women's Rights Project of the American Civil Liberties Union, as well as the Center for Law in the Public Interest and the Center for Constitutional Rights.

23. Ronnie Steinberg Ratner, *A Modest Magna Charta: Wage and Hour Standards Laws in the United States, 1900–1973, a Social Indicators Approach* (New Brunswick, N.J.: Rutgers University Press, forthcoming).

APPENDIXES

A *Barbara R. Bergmann*

THE CONTRIBUTION OF LABOR MARKET DATA IN COMBATING EMPLOYMENT DISCRIMINATION

The collection and dissemination of relevant data by the government is of substantial importance in any attempt to reduce discrimination and improve the labor market position of discriminated-against groups. It would not be correct to say that lack of adequate data has been a chief cause of slow progress in any country. However, an improved program of providing useful information might well make a considerable contribution toward a more efficient and more vigorous enforcement effort.

Data which bear on issues relating to employment discrimination are important in two contexts. One set of data is useful in setting national attitudes and broad-brush policies. Another, overlapping, data set is needed so that the situations of individual employers and particular groups of their employees can be diagnosed and dealt with as mandated in the United States under Title VII of the Civil Rights Act. In this appendix, the first part deals with the adequacy and availability of the kinds of data needed for the direction of national policy. The second part deals with data needs for use in connection with individual work establishments.

In all countries, employment discrimination on account of sex occurs, and needs to be monitored. In the United States, as in a number of other countries, racial or ethnic or religious groups have labor market problems in which discrimination plays a part. In the following material, I will be discussing breakdowns of data, and when I suggest a breakdown "race and sex" I mean data tabulated so as to give information separately for each race/sex combination (e.g., for black females) rather than suggesting two tabulations, one broken down by race and a second broken down by sex. If individuals surveyed are characterized by race and sex, no extra cost or space seems required to publish data broken down into race/sex categories, and the gain of information is considerable. It is certainly desirable to know, for example, whether programs designed to help a racial group are benefiting one sex to the exclusion of the other sex.

DATA NEEDS IN SETTING NATIONAL POLICY ON DISCRIMINATION

Probably the most important use of economic data relating to discrimination is their direct use in public discussions of the situation of groups which have been targets of discrimination so as to motivate ameliorative policies on their behalf. Data which are used as ingredients for research may also end up having a policy influence, depending on the relevance of the research and the researcher's flair for exposition and publicity.

The kind of information of most importance for direct use in public policy discussion and in research relating to policy in the discrimination area are: (1) unemployment rates; (2) distribution of employment by occupation; (3) average wage rates or wage income; (4) data on individuals which relate to their labor market "fitness" (such as education, measures of labor market attachment, experience) and their labor market "outcomes" (wage income, employment history); and (5) data relating to labor turnover (separations, accessions, promotions, and vacancies). These data should be broken down into race/sex categories.

The first three kinds of data constitute the prime indicators of a group's success or failure in the labor market. In the United States, concern for the position of blacks in the labor market has been largely fueled by monthly releases of unemployment rates in the Department of Labor's *Employment and Earnings*. Annual income surveys, published in the Census Bureau's *Current Population Surveys*, have also played a prominent part in discussions of the blacks' situation. With respect to women, it is the income survey results and the data on occupational distribution by sex which have had the most influence in arousing women to their situation and educating the public to their labor market problems. On the other hand, it is possible to argue that the lack of monthly unemployment data has allowed the plight of 11.3 million Hispanics to be pushed "under the rug."

The first four kinds of data on our list have been extensively used in the United States in research on the labor market problems of blacks and women. In addressing issues of discrimination, the usual methodology has been to attempt to use data on individuals to measure that portion of the disadvantages suffered by these groups which might be said to be the result of "innocent" causes unrelated to employer discrimination, leaving a residual amount of disadvantage to be explained by employment discrimination.[1] The fifth kind of data—labor turnover data, broadly conceived—is at present used chiefly by researchers, and these data are generally not seen as having direct policy implications. However, as will be discussed below, these kinds of data are of high potential significance in the fight on discrimination.

Having delineated the major kinds of information which are needed in the context of the debate and decision-making over national policies, it is appropriate to ask: What groups of people should be differentiated? How often should each kind of data be made available? What industries and occupations should be broken out? What geographic areas should be distinguished? How do published data cover the needs? What are some of the other problems with published data?

The answers to these questions depend on an assessment of the balance of costs and benefits, and are not going to be the same in all times and places. In Northern Ireland and Canada, a researcher on discrimination would obviously want data relating to employment problems of Protestants and Catholics, while in the United States, such data, although interesting, would not be considered vital in the context of employment discrimination at the present time.

Breaking out particular groups

In the United States, the basic unemployment and occupation data are currently available monthly in a four-way break (white male, black male, white female, black female). For persons of Hispanic origin, who constitute about 5 percent of the population, some of these data are now available quarterly, and more detailed material is available annually. For American Indians (0.4%) and persons of Oriental heritage (1.2%), these kinds of data are available only in the decennial census. As indicated above, frequency of data collection and publication help to keep the publicity spotlight on discriminated-against groups; frequency is also valuable to researchers trying to understand the dynamics of the labor market. Keeping the spotlight on the problem of a group may be a necessary prerequisite to action on the group's behalf by its own members, as well as action on the group's behalf by local, state, or federal governments. In making decisions as to the frequency with which data on the smaller groups should be collected and the form in which it should be published, the size of the group and the seriousness of its problems both need to be taken into account.

Where the decision has been made not to break out particular groups in the monthly data on employment and unemployment (as in the U.S., for all ethnic or racial minorities but blacks and possibly Hispanics), it seems reasonable for the government to compensate partially by making available special funds for support and publication of research designed to make clear the scope and nature of the labor market problems of these groups.

Occupational breakdowns in macro data

Data on sex and race differences in the distribution of employed persons by current occupation are central to all discussions of discrimination. While some employers discriminate by denying equal pay for equal work, the most common form of discrimination is an unwillingness to hire or promote women and minority men into types of jobs from which they have traditionally been absent. Disparities by sex and race in unemployment rates and wage incomes follow from the practice of discrimination in hiring and promotion, but the primary practices themselves are most clearly revealed in the occupational data.

Women and minority men in the United States tend to be excluded from jobs which have a supervisory or management component, or from jobs from which supervisors are chosen. They also tend to be excluded from jobs in which there is a significant and lasting component of learning-by-doing, such as crafts work. Published occupational breakdowns ought to be such as to make these exclusions clear, and also to make it possible to chart progress in breaking down exclusionary practices. The present thirty-one–occupation breakdown by sex and age shown monthly in *Employment and Earnings* is excellent. It would be very desirable if this were published on a race-by-sex-by-age basis (see Table A-1).

Industry breakdowns of employment data

In the past, the employment of women and minority males by a particular industry depended largely on the distribution of the industry's jobs by occupation. If an industry had a great many jobs which were traditionally considered "black jobs" or "female jobs," it would have a high representation of blacks or women. But such a high representation would not necessarily attest to nondiscriminatory behavior. The measure of an industry's progress is not how many blacks and women it employs, but how many it has hired for nontraditional jobs. Thus the industry data most valuable for policy purposes would be data available on an occupation-by-industry-by-race-by-sex basis. The published breakdown giving occupation by industry monthly for all workers (table A-24 of *Employment and Earnings*) would be valuable if broken down monthly by race/sex/occupation/industry categories.

Data on wages or income and on earner's characteristics

Information on basic hourly wage rate paid by race and sex, although it would clearly be useful in many research contexts, including but certainly not limited to studies of discrimination, is most notable by its absence in the United States. Only the Area Wage Surveys of the Bureau of Labor Statistics offer actual wage rates, and these only for a scattering of particular occupations. These data are available by sex but not by race, are for local labor markets, and are obtained from employers. The surveys provide no information on worker characteristics beyond sex. It is perhaps ironic that an astute observer of labor markets believes that the publication of such data actually encourages and aids in employer wage discrimination by sex, since employers allegedly use them in deciding what wages to offer.[2] The Labor Department should perhaps consider the truth to this assertion, and consider discontinuing their publication. Because of their inadequacies, they have been little used in research.[3]

The major source of U.S. government data on wage payments used extensively in research on race and sex bias have been data deriving from the U.S. Census Bureau's *Current Population Reports,* which give wage income. These data are available annually in published form (series P-60), and tapes are made available to researchers which give data on individuals, so that it is possible to relate an individual's wage income to his or her hours, occupation, industry, education, age, family status, and the like.

The surveys of the National Longitudinal Survey sponsored by the U.S. Department of Labor and conducted at Ohio State University provide wage data and are particularly rich in variables relating to the characteristics of the earners, and include information on work history, attitudes, numbers and ages of children, and a host of other topics. They also provide data on individuals at different points in time. Another source of these kinds of data are the surveys done by the Survey Research Center at the University of Michigan.

Geographic breakdown on macro data

For purposes of national policy against discrimination, geographic breakdowns of unemployment statistics by race and sex are important where there is suspected to be significant differences in the degree of discrimination by region. In the case of race, progress for blacks in the South is a continuing issue. In the case of sex discrimination, it is not unlikely that regional differences would develop, although they do not seem of importance now.

Another important use of area statistics on employment and unemployment by race and sex is to justify the local establishment of training programs aimed at discriminated-against groups. While training programs cannot by themselves reduce discrimination, they can be a valuable part of an anti-discrimination program because they negate the argument that there are no qualified women or minorities available.

Since 1970, state and metropolitan area breakdowns of employment and unemployment by race and occupation and by sex and occupation have been available annually in the Bureau of Labor Statistics publication *Geographic Profile of Employment and Unemployment,* which unfortunately gives no race-by-sex break. Naturally, researchers would benefit from monthly or quarterly availability of data on local labor markets, but for purposes of gross monitoring of progress, and for purposes of justifying

TABLE A-1

Employed Persons by Occupation, Sex, and Age (in thousands)

Occupation	TOTAL		MALES, 20 YEARS AND OVER		FEMALES, 20 YEARS AND OVER		MALES, 16–19 YEARS		FEMALES, 16–19 YEARS	
	Oct. 1976	Oct. 1977	Oct. 1976	Oct. 1977	Oct. 1976	Oct. 1977	Oct. 1976	Oct. 1977	Oct. 1976	Oct. 1977
TOTAL	88,697	92,230	49,215	50,610	32,430	34,109	3,756	4,076	3,296	3,436
TOTAL, white-collar workers	44,387	46,332	21,291	21,946	20,871	22,032	611	658	1,614	1,696
Professional and technical	13,612	14,251	7,734	8,069	5,736	6,031	65	70	76	81
Health workers	2,343	2,534	809	876	1,519	1,649	3	3	13	8
Teachers, except college	3,224	3,196	898	905	2,302	2,278	3	5	21	8
Other professional and technical	8,045	8,521	6,027	6,288	1,915	2,104	59	62	42	65
Managers and administrators, except farm	9,463	9,981	7,507	7,715	1,892	2,168	37	58	27	39
Salaried workers	7,757	8,036	6,160	6,218	1,536	1,726	34	56	27	36
Self-employed workers in retail trade	905	957	656	662	247	291	2	2		3
Self-employed workers, except retail	801	988	690	836	110	152	1			
Sales workers	5,592	5,727	2,867	2,966	2,073	2,163	252	247	400	352
Retail trade	3,096	3,093	960	953	1,576	1,604	189	202	371	334
Other industries	2,496	2,634	1,907	2,013	497	558	63	45	29	19
Clerical workers	15,721	16,373	3,183	3,196	11,170	11,670	257	284	1,111	1,223
Stenographers, typists, and secretaries	4,408	4,686	86	75	3,951	4,241	10	7	361	363
Other clerical workers	11,313	11,687	3,097	3,121	7,219	7,429	247	277	750	860
TOTAL, blue-collar workers	29,354	30,536	22,144	22,827	4,779	4,987	2,030	2,260	401	462
Craft and kindred workers	11,486	11,969	10,582	10,932	473	564	393	430	38	44
Carpenters	1,077	1,214	999	1,113	8	7	67	92	4	2
Construction craft, except carpenters	2,393	2,390	2,280	2,278	23	18	92	96		

Mechanics and repairers	3,031	3,243	2,860	3,072	28	52	143	119	2	2
Metal craft	1,200	1,256	1,154	1,200	20	25	24	29	2	1
Blue-collar worker supervisors, not elsewhere classified	1,477	1,549	1,357	1,382	109	155	9	10	3	2
All other	2,307	2,318	1,931	1,887	285	307	59	84	31	39
Operatives, except transport	10,131	10,459	5,567	5,646	3,734	3,849	582	653	248	311
Durable goods manufacturing	4,533	4,801	2,899	3,011	1,381	1,453	178	239	74	99
Nondurable goods manufacturing	3,245	3,328	1,239	1,205	1,776	1,841	115	127	115	155
Other industries	2,353	2,330	1,429	1,430	577	555	289	287	59	57
Transport equipment operatives	3,362	3,499	2,938	3,056	235	257	178	175	11	11
Drivers, motor vehicles	2,843	2,933	2,464	2,553	219	234	149	136	10	10
All other	519	566	474	503	15	22	29	39	1	1
Nonfarm laborers	4,376	4,609	3,057	3,193	337	318	878	1,002	104	96
Construction	751	873	590	693	11	10	144	172	7	
Manufacturing	1,055	1,066	830	814	120	109	100	132	4	12
Other industries	2,570	2,669	1,637	1,687	206	199	634	697	93	86
TOTAL, service workers	12,031	12,485	3,689	3,749	6,284	6,607	823	900	1,235	1,228
Private household workers	1,177	1,191	13	23	890	946	9	21	265	200
Service workers, except private household	10,854	11,294	3,676	3,726	5,394	5,661	814	879	970	1,028
Food service workers	3,975	4,179	730	735	2,066	2,151	509	570	670	723
Protective service workers	1,257	1,291	1,144	1,174	82	101	25	11	7	5
All other	5,622	5,824	1,802	1,817	3,246	3,409	280	298	293	300
TOTAL, farm workers	2,925	2,878	2,091	2,087	496	483	291	257	47	50
Farmers and farm managers	1,550	1,493	1,433	1,373	102	112	14	9	1	
Farm laborers and supervisors	1,375	1,385	658	714	394	371	277	248	46	51
Paid workers	1,015	1,074	630	683	158	161	194	192	33	37
Unpaid family workers	360	311	28	31	236	210	83	56	13	14

SOURCE: U.S. Department of Labor, Bureau of Labor Statistics, *Employment and Earnings* 24, no. 11 (Nov. 1977): 34, table A-21.

of training programs, annual data are adequate.

The anti-discrimination agencies which use geographic differences to allocate resources among regional offices can presumably rely to some extent on establishment-level data the agency should be collecting, as discussed below.

Vacancy data

Vacancies occur when a job is opened up, before a worker is hired to fill it, either because a worker leaves or because the job is newly created. Vacancy data are useful because—when added to employment estimates—they allow estimates of the total stock of job slots. Such information, in conjunction with labor turnover information, is useful in studying the dynamics of the labor market, and in contrasting the workings of a non-discriminatory labor market with a discriminatory one.[4] Vacancy data were published for a number of years in the United States (in *Employment and Earnings*), but they have been discontinued, resulting in lost opportunities for research. To be most helpful, they should be available by occupation and industry.

Labor turnover statistics

Labor turnover statistics have a special place in anti-discrimination efforts. There is very little sentiment for displacing sitting jobholders to take care of members of discriminated-against groups, even if the jobholders are acknowledged to have gotten their jobs through a discriminatory process. The focus of anti-discriminatory efforts is therefore on the hiring and promotion which is now going on or will go on in the future. It is only through affecting the hiring and promotion process (the distribution of the *flows* of employees into particular job categories) that the distribution of *stocks* (the distribution of sitting employees by race/sex/occupation categories) will be affected.[5]

Labor turnover, and in particular accessions to employment or to a different status within a firm, provides the opportunity for change. It is extremely important for policy purposes to know the extent of such opportunities and the extent to which they have been used in a nondiscriminatory way. In a highly segmented labor market, women and minority men are restricted to particular segments of the labor market—that is, those jobs which they have traditionally held. It is through labor turnover information that we can follow the extent to which the discriminatory walls between the segments are being broken down.

In the United States, the information available on labor turnover is totally inadequate for purposes of research which would contribute to national anti-discrimination policy. The Labor Department publishes turn-over data monthly for detailed manufacturing industries and selected non-manufacturing industries from industry sources. For these data to be useful for anti-discrimination purposes, they would have to be broken down by race/sex/major occupation categories.

Data on governmental practices

Researchers on discrimination have made comparatively little use of the potential wealth of information available concerning the operations of government establishments. In the United States, the Civil Service Commission has published some of these data in aggregated form. More would be done by researchers if more data from personnel files (properly sanitized for privacy) could be released to researchers.

Problems with currently published series

A major problem with the published data on unemployment in the United States is that some of the methods of collecting and editing them seem to result in minimizing the gravity of the situation of discriminated-against groups. For women, the most important problem concerns the method of asking about labor force participation, which undoubtedly reduces the reported female unemployment rate. The same question on labor force participation should be asked of persons of both sexes, and interviewer discretion should be minimized.

With respect to race, the notorious undercount of blacks in the decennial census may also work to affect the reported rate of unemployment for blacks in the monthly reports.

DATA NEEDS ON THE FIRM OR ESTABLISHMENT LEVEL AND THE ENFORCEMENT OF ANTI-DISCRIMINATION LAWS

In considering data needs for enforcement purposes we can distinguish the uses to which such data ought to be put: (1) reminding employers of their obligations; (2) reminding employees of their rights; (3) informing the public of progress or the lack thereof; (4) targeting employers for further investigation; (5) deciding which cases to pursue seriously; (6) carrying on lawsuits or disbarment proceedings against employers; (7) allocating the resources of the enforcement agencies by geographic area and industry; and (8) judging the effectiveness of the enforcement agencies' activities.[6] In this list, items 1–3 can be considered educational tasks of the enforcement agencies, 4–5 relate to targeting, 6 to litigation, 7–8 to administration. We shall discuss these topics below, along with some others.

In discussing the information needs with respect to individual firms, it is helpful at the outset to distinguish stocks (the labor force, the applicant pool, the body of employed persons) and flows (the flow of applicants into the applicant pool, hiring, promotions, separations). The relations of the stocks and the flows are shown in Figure A-1, and the possible way in which firm's discriminatory acts can affect the people who make up the flows and stocks are indicated.

The kinds of information which both the firm (or government unit or union) itself and the enforcement authorities need to know relate to what the firm is currently (or has recently been) doing and to what a reasonable standard of nondiscriminatory behavior for this particular firm might be, so that the firm's actual behavior can be compared to that standard.

Information on establishments' behavior

In the United States it has been the practice of the Equal Employment Opportunity Commission to ask firms to supply annually data on stocks of employed persons by race/sex/occupation categories. The EEOC has divided occupations into nine broad groupings. The only other data the firm is asked to give is the number of "formal on-the-job trainees" by race by sex, with "white collar" trainees distinguished from "production" trainees. The information requested on trainees comes near to being information on flows, since the trainees are presumably in transition to being full-fledged occupants of jobs requiring training. However, the present questionnaire obviously stops short of requiring information on all flows on a systematic basis.

Before going on to discuss what changes would be desirable, a short disquisition on the reporting burden seems appropriate. The reporting burden of implementing the suggestions made here is obviously less for those firms which own or employ computers than those which do not, and among those who do have computers is lower for firms with well-developed computerized personnel systems. Therefore, it might be reasonable to require the full range of material only from large firms on the ground that a high proportion of them will be well computerized and that for them the reporting burden will be trivial.

A switch from reporting information on stocks to reporting information on gross flows would be highly desirable. (Gross flows signify all flows in and out of an occupation group, as contrasted with net flows, which are taken by subtracting flow out from flow in.) First of all, getting data on flows would focus both the firms' and the agency's attention on "where the action is." At hiring time, the firm would have to keep a record, and this is when they should be thinking about their EEO obligations. Secondly, a

FIGURE A-1

Occasions of Discrimination on the Part of a Firm

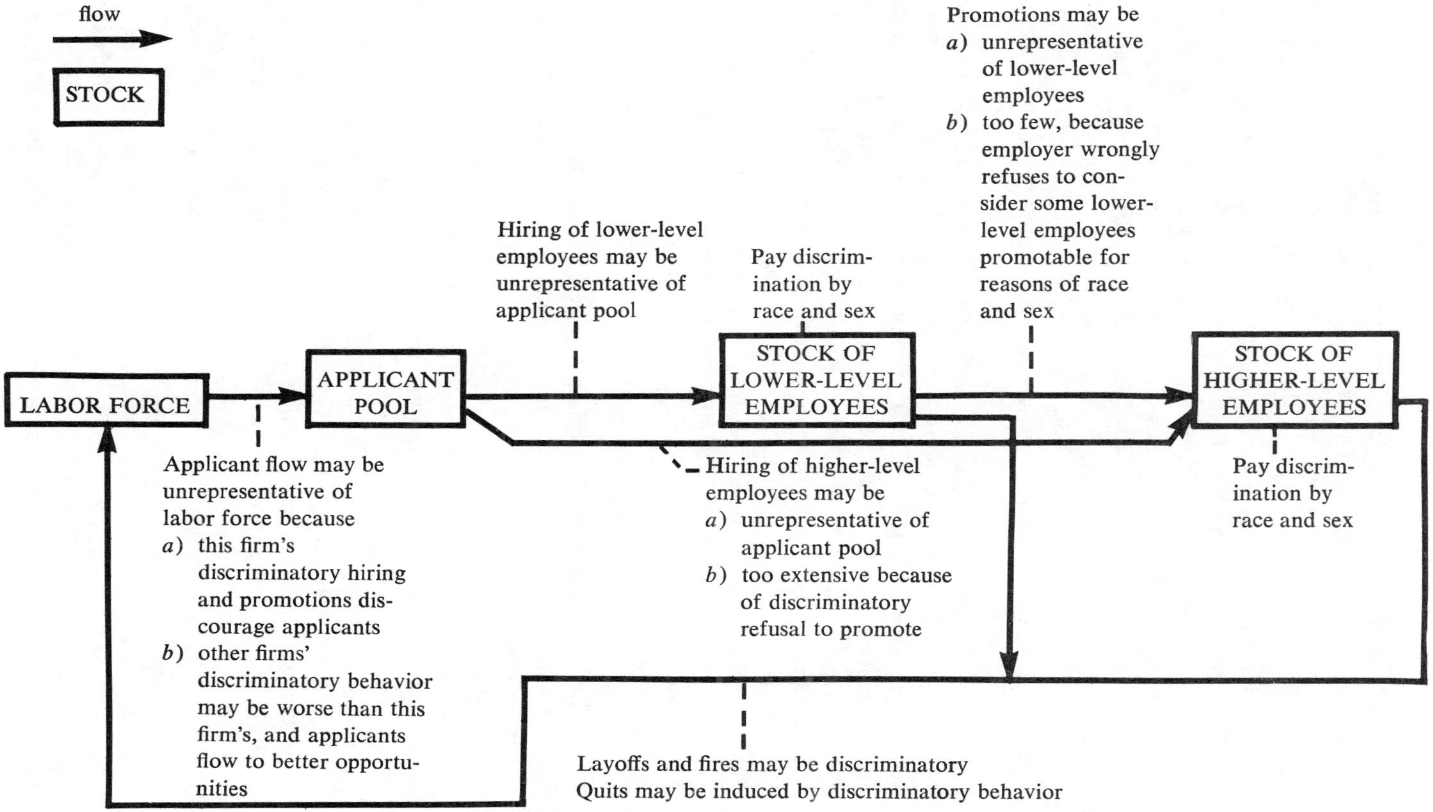

flow →

STOCK

LABOR FORCE

Applicant flow may be
unrepresentative of
labor force because
a) this firm's
discriminatory hiring
and promotions dis-
courage applicants
b) other firms'
discriminatory behavior
may be worse than this
firm's, and applicants
flow to better opportu-
nities

APPLICANT
POOL

Hiring of lower-level
employees may be
unrepresentative of
applicant pool

STOCK OF
LOWER-LEVEL
EMPLOYEES

Pay discrim-
ination by
race and sex

Hiring of higher-level
employees may be
a) unrepresentative of
applicant pool
b) too extensive because
of discriminatory
refusal to promote

Promotions may be
a) unrepresentative
of lower-level
employees
b) too few, because
employer wrongly
refuses to con-
sider some lower-
level employees
promotable for
reasons of race
and sex

STOCK OF
HIGHER-LEVEL
EMPLOYEES

Pay discrim-
ination by
race and sex

Layoffs and fires may be discriminatory
Quits may be induced by discriminatory behavior

firm with static or dropping employment might still be filling vacancies caused by labor turnover. With the present information system, there is no way to see whether a firm which has static or declining employment is failing to improve the race/sex composition of its stock because of discrimination or because it isn't hiring anymore.

Thus, the form on which data are currently collected for stocks should be designed so that from each occupation group the firm would be required to report by race/sex categories all flows in (by hiring, transfer, or promotion) and all flows out (by separation, transfer, promotion). There should be at least one point in time for data on stocks, but subsequent stocks can be deduced from flows. A similar switch from stocks to flows should be made for information collected from government units and unions.

One problem in connection with the present data collection in the United States is that the broadness of the occupational categories may conceal a great deal of discriminatory behavior. In some firms, for example, large numbers of women may be classified as managerial and supervisory, yet be segregated into low-level deadend jobs. Increasing the number of occupations broken out is probably not the way to deal with this problem, because of the reporting burden and increased chance of misclassification. This problem could be dealt with by requiring average compensation by sex/race group for each occupation.

Setting standards of nondiscriminatory behavior

The most important information which is relevant to the determination of what *should,* under a nondiscriminatory regime, be expected to go on in an individual firm concerns the availability of members of each race/sex group who can be deemed competent to fill various jobs. In the United States, information on employment and labor force categorized by race/sex/occupation/county is found in the decennial census. Some of the information for metropolitan areas is available annually.

The most important availability issue relates to "competence." If employers are allowed to take the view that the pool of persons from whom they choose for hiring for a particular occupation need include only those already in the occupation or like occupations, then the pool from which applicants are drawn will have the same race/sex composition as those already in the occupation, and very little progress can be expected. Since discrimination by race and sex in the United States has been pervasive, the current distribution of persons in each occupation by race and sex reflects that history. Unfortunately, some judges, and even some officials of the Equal Employment Opportunity Commission, have been content to hold up as a standard of nondiscrimination the achievement by a firm of a distribution of persons by race or sex which is no more representative of minorities and women than that shown by the industry average.[7]

The key to an understanding of this matter is that there is always recruitment into an occupation of persons who are inexperienced in that occupation; if this were not so, natural processes would reduce the size of the occupation to zero. The first task is to define the pool of inexperienced entrants in a nondiscriminatory way. The second task is to define the employer's obligation to induct inexperienced entrants from that pool, where a sole or major reliance on the pool of persons experienced in that occupation would continue to produce a stock of persons which disproportionately excluded members of certain race/sex groups.

It should be the responsibility of the anti-discrimination agency to issue guidelines as to the race and sex composition of the nondiscriminatory pool of persons who might be eligible to be new inductees into each broad occupational group, and guidelines as to the responsibility to resort to the hiring of inexperienced inductees. These guidelines might take into account valid educational criteria, as well as regional availability of persons by race and by sex.

What would be eminently desirable would be for the agency charged with anti-discrimination efforts to go beyond the issuance of guidelines in this matter and to develop software and data banks which would allow an initial estimate of availability by race/sex groups for most broad occupations in any firm in any labor market. Obviously, those occupations which require specialized off-the-job schooling to establish eligibility (as would be the case in many technical and professional occupations) would have to be treated specially.

The desirability of publishing employment data by name of firm

By U.S. law, individual establishment data are not available to the public, and only summaries by industry or area are published, except in the case of government contractors. It would be highly desirable if information reported by individual establishments (including the information on flows recommended above) were not only available to the public but were also published regularly, so that a firm's workers would know that they could get the information by going down to their public library, or making a routine call to the regional office of the anti-discrimination agency. The knowledge that this information was easily and routinely available might influence firms to structure their personnel activities in such a way as to obey the law.

The rationale for keeping firm and establishment data confidential usually given relates to the harm a firm might suffer if its "trade secrets" were exposed to the eyes of its competitors. The kinds of information that would injure a firm would presumably be those which gave a rival some hint as to new moves the firm was making which would affect its competitive position: a new plant, a new product line, a new technology, a planned change in amounts produced, and so on. It is hard to see that the publication of the kinds of data which would be helpful in matters relating to employment discrimination would adversely affect a firm's competitive position. In any case, the public interest in reducing employment discrimination should be controling here, just as the public interest in regulation of the stock market has mandated the publication of financial data by name of firm. The publication might be in terms of percentage distribution of stocks and flows categorized by race/sex rather than absolute numbers, which would retain the information content necessary for matters relating to discrimination, but reduce the information content with respect to other matters.

Pay information by occupation should also be published by the enforcement agency for firms. This would help to uncover pay discrimination and would also be helpful in showing the extent to which women and blacks were making progress within broad occupational groups. Again, absolute dollar amounts are not essential; all that would be required for anti-discrimination purposes would be the ratio of the wage for each race/sex group to the wage for white males within the major occupation group.

Ideally, for each firm for which the anti-discrimination agency issues a report on its record on hiring, employment, and wages, information on the availability of blacks and women tailored to the establishment's local labor market conditions could be issued, to accompany the information on performance. This would be very useful to the public and in particular to employees of and applicants to each firm in being able to satisfy themselves that they are dealing with an establishment which does not currently discriminate.

Educational activities of enforcement agencies

The anti-discrimination agencies take it as one of their major responsibilities to issue and publicize educational material on the nature and extent of discrimination. In the United States, there is an astounding ignorance on what the law requires. For example, many female complainants, plaintiffs, and even some attorneys think entirely in terms of pay differences, and do not seem aware of the fact that women are entitled by the Civil Rights Act to equal access to managerial and crafts jobs.[8] Appropriate educational material to combat such ignorance, which permits violations of the Act to go unnoticed, would use the data on flows described above and would display the fact that appropriate hiring patterns were being pursued in some firms and not in others.

NOTES

1. See Allan Blinder for a discussion of the methodological problems involved and for a bibliography of such studies: "Wage Discrimination: Reduced Form and Structural Estimates," *Journal of Human Resources,* Fall 1973.

2. Winn Newman, in Martha Blaxall and Barbara Reagan, eds., *Women and the Workplace* (Chicago: University of Chicago Press, 1976).

3. The most notable use has been of the data on office occupations by Francine D. Blau in *Equal Pay in the Office* (Lexington, Mass: Lexington Books, 1977).

4. See Barbara R. Bergmann, "Empirical Work on the Labor Market: Is There Any Alternative to Regression Running?" *Proceedings of the 27th Annual Meeting of the IRRA* (Industrial Relations Research Association) (San Francisco, 1976), pp. 243–251.

5. See Barbara Bergmann and William Krause, "Evaluating and Forecasting Progress in Racial Integration of Employment," *Industrial and Labor Relations Review* 25, no. 3 (April 1972): 399–409.

6. See Andrea H. Beller, "The Impact of Equal Employment Opportunity Laws on the Male/Female Earnings Differential," Institute for Research on Poverty Discussion Papers 436–77 (August 1977, processed), for a discussion of some of these issues and a list of references. I do not believe that a satisfactory way of thinking about these issues has been worked out yet.

7. For references and an extended discussion of this and other relevant issues see Marc Rosenblum, "The External Measures of Labor Supply: Recent Issues and Trends," Conference on Affirmative Action Planning, Cornell University, Oct. 31, 1977.

8. For example, see the pleadings in *Lemons et al.* v. *County of Denver et al.*, where the question of nurses' access to jobs in hospital management, other than "nurse-supervisor," is not hinted at.

B *Christof Helberger*

WORK ANALYSIS AS A MEANS TO ACHIEVE EQUAL PAY FOR WORKING WOMEN: THE FEDERAL REPUBLIC OF GERMANY

WAGE DISCRIMINATION AND EQUAL STATUS POLICY

The labor market discriminates against women in two major ways: by offering unequal pay for equal work, and by providing unequal opportunities despite equal starting conditions. Here, we will examine only the first of these forms of discrimination, with an emphasis on the instrument called "work analysis."

There are different ways to achieve fairness in pay: changing the relative rate of wages in wage-scale contracts, improving wage-bracket definitions in wage agreements, assigning employees to different wage brackets, appealing to law courts in cases of flagrant discrimination, or installing a state supervisory board. In the Federal Republic of Germany legal decisions played an important part in initiating current equal pay policy. In 1955 the Federal Constitutional Court decided that the "principle of equality" enunciated in the West German constitution is also legally binding for wage-scale contracts between employers and trade unions. It declared that the practice of using percentage wage reductions for women in relation to men's wages was in violation of this constitutional principle. Since making that decision, however, the law courts have played only a very subordinate role in the matter of wage discrimination.

In defense of its historical commitment to wage autonomy, the Federal Republic of Germany has not institutionalized a state supervisory board to control wage-paying practices. Only since 1969, when the social-liberal coalition took over the government, have efforts been made at the highest level to accord equal status to women. Among its other efforts, the government commissioned a group of specialists, of which I was a member, to conduct an ergonomic analysis to examine the question whether scientific criteria were available to judge which work activities could be regarded as light or heavy, or as easy or difficult.[1]

This analysis, which we will discuss later, is closely bound up with a question central to German discussions about equity for women: To what wage brackets should jobs done predominantly by women be assigned, and what should be their wages in relation to men's wages? As a rule, open discrimination against women was abolished in the years after 1955, when new wage brackets were added to the tariff contracts. Assigned to the lowest spot, these wage brackets were to stand for physically light or easy work requiring no job training. The fact that women were predominantly, though not exclusively, employed in these jobs gave rise to the suspicion that the brackets were discriminatory.

Although the extent of this discrimination was uncertain, its existence could not be doubted. The heavy work / light work distinction was not the only way discrimination was manifested. It also was the product of tariff contract regulations that discriminated against certain groups of employees (younger employees, part-time employees, persons without professional training) of which women made up an overly large percentage. (See Figure B-1.)

Trade unions took several approaches to the problem. One of the strategies consisted in raising the lowest wage brackets, especially in relation to the others, or possibly eliminating them altogether. Another aimed at improving the wage fact-finding procedure.

In the Federal Republic of Germany two fact-finding procedures are most often employed. In the *summary work evaluation*, several characteristics that define each wage bracket are determined. In the *analytical work evaluation,* a series of requirements is established and each requirement is defined in terms of a measuring scale. Wage brackets are determined by adding together the points attached to each of the requirements. The analytical work evaluation is, as a rule, more comprehensive regarding the determination of requirements and more exact in terms of establishing the requirement level.

Since both procedures are used, with numerous variations, in the different regions and economic sectors, the question of whether the requirements are established with sufficient completeness and exactitude is crucial.[2] In addition, depending on the definitions they use, the various systems of work evaluation may themselves contribute to discrimination against women. Therefore, the strategy of the trade unions aimed at improving both the definition of jobs classified within wage brackets and the procedures by which the requirements of activities were analyzed.

"A SCIENTIFIC INQUIRY PAPER ABOUT ACTIVITY ANALYSIS" (AET) AND WORK ANALYSIS

The summary work evaluation and analytical work evaluation systems employed in the Federal Republic of Germany in order to determine the workload more efficiently and "objectively" are all pragmatic in origin and practical in intent. That is, they were developed by people in the

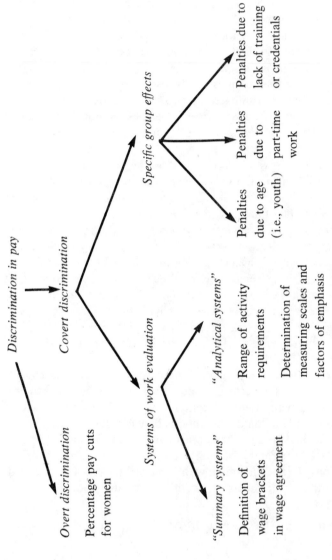

FIGURE B-1

Ways of Discriminating against Women in the Labor Market

SOURCE: Christof Helberger and Hans-Jürger Krupp, *Die Einstufungsgrundsätze der Tätigkeiten hinsichtlich des Grundsatzes des gleichen Arbeitsentgeltes für Männer und Frauen (Art. 119 des EWG-Vertrages)* (Frankfurt: Forschungsbericht im Auftrag der Europ, Gemeinschaften, 1973), p. 20.

field, usually for one branch of the economy only, and mostly for wage and salaried employees separately. They were not subject to scientific standards. If we take the premise that a work evaluation procedure consists of three parts of inquiry—namely (1) a description of activity, (2) an analysis of activity, and (3) an evaluation of activity—then science can contribute to the first two points especially. Classifying the various requirements for the purpose of assigning them to wage brackets, however, requires decisions that cannot be the result of purely scientific analysis. In preparing papers based on the analysis therefore, we confined ourselves to a description and analysis of activities. The questionnaire we developed for this purpose will be referred to hereafter as the AET.[3]

The relevant literature[4] mentions four criteria that any system of work analysis needs to meet: First, it should be based on a *theoretical* (or analytic) model that facilitates a meaningful interpretation of the results in relation to its practical implementation. It is especially important that an analytic framework be complete in its listing of requirements in a work system. A procedure also should be *economical* regarding data compilation, data processing, and data analysis. Third, a procedure should make possible *quantitative* statements that can be standardized across categories and easily communicated. Finally, a procedure should be examined to see if different evaluators of the same activity arrive at the same result (*inter-position reliability*), and if different evaluators judge the same requirements uniformly for different activities (*inter-item reliability*).

Because of their simplicity, existing procedures in the Federal Republic of Germany are economical. They only partially supply quantitative and standardized statements, however. And theoretical reasoning and statements about their dependability are totally absent. Our work analysis procedure and the AET were developed in order to overcome these shortcomings.

Figure B-2 shows schematically the analytic model, called "strain-demand concept," that we employed to do justice to the first criterion: theoretical substantiation. The various difficulties of a job's activities, together with environmental influences, constitute the objective requirements or *demands* of the job, which the individual tries to meet by his or her conduct. In meeting the demands, the individual responds with a wide range of possible behavior, from successfully completing the work to avoiding or rejecting it. Personal attributes play a role in this, including ability, motivation, and concentration. The demands lead to certain *strains*, which vary among people. Therefore, even where the demands of a job are constant, the response to strain can change over time. Positive changes that result with time are processes of adjustment such as learning and habituation; negative ones encompass the diminution of functioning due to fatigue and injury.

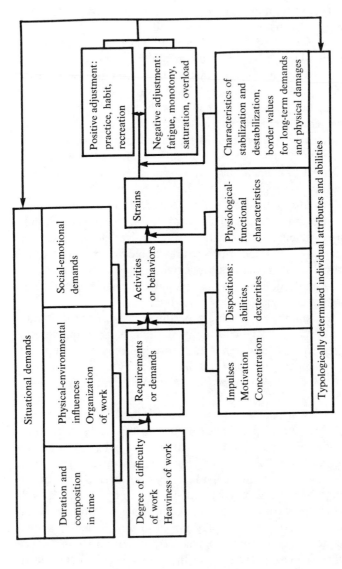

FIGURE B-2

Analytical Model for Work Analysis: Strain-demand Concept for
Human Activities

SOURCE: Walter Rohmert and Joseph Rutenfranz, *Benutzerfreundliche Weiterenwicklung des arbeitswissenschaftlichen Erhebungsbogens zur Tätigkeitanalyse (AET)*
(Bonn: Bundesminister für Arbeit und Sozialordnung, 1975), p. 24.

The analytic framework employed in work analysis consists of defining a set of objective work demands with regard to their effects on the person concerned. The characteristics to be established for the demand analysis are chosen so that all required physical functions are included. In each work analysis exercise, the classification of requirements is to some extent subjective, but at least the procedure permits us to examine objectively the extent to which the listing of physical functions is complete.[5]

Figure B-3 systematizes the kinds of requirements employed. One can proceed from the assumption that "at work a productive contribution can be made by people only in energetics and intellectual areas, that is, people form the various materials with the help of the forces at their disposal and these forces are steered by streams of information, which they are able to assimilate according to their abilities."[6] *Energetics* and *intellectual* demands arise from task-specific functions and environmental influences. The energetics demands can be subdivided into *static* and *dynamic* work, according to the necessary muscle functions, the production and transformation of energy. The intellectual demands can be subdivided into the information-processing functions of reacting (*reflexive* work), transformation of information coming in into information going out (*informational* work), and the production of information in the sense of thinking or deciding (*reflective* work).

Some of these requirements (static and dynamic energetics work as well as informational and reflexive work) can be subdivided even further. This level of analysis is especially important because on this specific level we can define the ergonomic demand thresholds that must be considered by personnel management in determining wage policy. Because of the possible sex-specific differentiation among the requirements at this level, they are also significant for the problem of equal pay for men and women.

The requirement dimensions chosen for measurement constituted 390 questionnaire items. The questionnaire we used was a modified version of the position analysis questionnaire (PAQ) used by McCormick in 1969.[7] The ergonomic questionnaire is of particular interest because of the reliability of the classifications and the validity of the inquiry process. For this purpose, inter-position reliability and inter-item reliability were established. In case of unsatisfactory results the questions were rephrased. Results of a newer application of the AET for activities in the electronic data-processing field can be found in Rohmert and Landau.[8] To obtain the data, we conducted observation-interviews (a lengthy period of observation of the working process, followed by interviews with superiors, the employee, and the work committee). In order to quantify the dimensions, we constructed various types of scales. The definition of the items and the construction of the scales cannot be more closely examined here; for this see the original analysis and the AET. To analyze the data, we

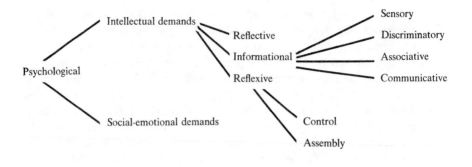

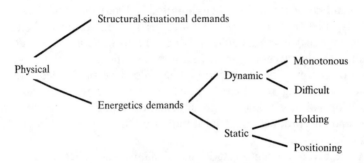

FIGURE B-3
Classification of Work Contents and Kinds of Demands

SOURCE: Walter Rohmert and Joseph Rutenfranz, *Benutzerfreundliche Weiterenwicklung des arbeitswissenschaftlichen Erhebungbogens zur Tätigkeitanalyse (AET)* (Bonn:) Bundesminister für Arbeit und Sozialordnung, 1975), p. 53.

used various techniques, especially tables of frequency, profile analyses, and correlation-, cluster-, and factor-analyses, in order to evaluate and condense the information and eliminate redundant items.

The classification of demand dimensions that we came up with diverges from previously used work evaluation systems because it takes into account psychological stresses as well as physical strains. It turned out, however, that our classification of both physical and psychological dimensions is supported by the results of factor analyses and cluster analyses.

Summing up, one can say that the AET provides the first comprehensive scientific procedure for activity analysis in the Federal Republic of Germany. Because of its analytic framework, it can justifiably claim to encompass the various forms of demand, especially the intellectual strains associated with the processing and production of information. Its comprehensiveness makes the AET largely independent of the economic and technological areas for which it is used, though this does not mean that it could not be expanded for other applications.[9] The listing of different physical activities from different perspectives permits us, to a certain degree, to justify the assumption of additivity of work requirements that underlies almost all procedures of work evaluation inasmuch as the accumulation of different kinds of strain is treated merely as the sum of the single strains.

RESULTS OF THE ERGONOMIC STUDIES CARRIED OUT IN THE ANALYSIS

The analysis was completed in April 1975; a report based on it was published in June 1975.[10] Besides building on the results of ergonomics and industrial medicine then available, it relies on its own theoretical analyses and empirical surveys of 204 chosen activities in industries with a high percentage of female employees. The activities examined were not chosen by chance; rather, we tried to choose positions that are typical for men and women and that are performed by both men and women. In addition, laboratory tests were done for especially interesting activities.

The procedure therefore was employed on a relatively small sample of jobs. The drawing of random samples was not possible because of time constraints. Moreover it proved difficult to find businesses that would cooperate. Consequently, in interpreting the results of the inquiry one must proceed with caution.

In the three years since the completion of the analysis, the ergonomic questionnaire has been used by scientists at the Institute for Ergonomics at the Technical University of Darmstadt, for 616 activities in industry, trade, and public service. Even this choice was not left to chance. It represents a broader and more dependable basis for making general statements about the strains of work, especially for comparing men's and women's activities. Thus, before we examine the conclusions of the original analysis, we should look at these more recent results.

The results are described according to kinds of strain as differentiated by function. The frequency analysis of the sample of activities leads to the findings summarized in Tables B-1 and B-2.

TABLE B-1
Time Quota for Posture and Physical Movement
(as percent of working time)

Postures and physical movements	MEN			WOMEN		
	Free	*Constrained*	*Total*	*Free*	*Constrained*	*Total*
Postures						
Sitting	28	4	32	45	12	57
Standing	18	11	29	16	10	26
Other		11	11		1	1
TOTAL, posture	46	26	72	61	23	84
Physical movements						
Walking/running	16	6	22	12	3	15
Other		6	6		1	1
TOTAL, physical movements	16	12	28	12	4	16
TOTAL quota	62	38	100	73	27	100

SOURCE: Walter Rohmert, H. Luczak, and H. Kugler, *Geschlechtstypische Unterschiede aus de Sicht der Arbeitswissenschaft* (Darmstadt: Techn. Hochschule, Institut für Arbeitswissenschaft, 1978).

Table B-1 addresses the requirements of posture and physical movement. Here we must differentiate between free physical movement without additional exterior strain and constrained standing positions or movements with intense additional strains. On the whole the strains are somewhat greater for men than for women, except for activities requiring a constrained sitting position, which are more frequent among women.

Table B-2 shows the percentage of different forms of energetics work as share of the total work time. The sums can exceed or fall short of 100 percent because of multiple strains or absence of strain. Static work is divided about equally between the sexes. Dynamic work, however, is divided unequally. Heavy dynamic work predominates overwhelmingly

TABLE B-2

Time Quota for Energetic Work Forms (as percent of work time)

Energetic work	Men	Women
Static work	23	24
Highly strained physical movements	28⎫ 47	16⎫ 24
Heavy dynamic work	19⎭	8⎭
One-sided dynamic work	25	60
TOTAL	95	108

SOURCE: Walter Rohmert, H. Luczak, and H. Kugler, *Geschlechtstypische Unterscheide aus der Sicht der Arbeitswissenschaft* (Darmstadt: Techn. Hochschule, Institut für Arbeitswissenschaft, 1978).

among men (47 percent), while women are overproportionally entrusted with monotonous activities (60 percent). The scaling of monotonous dynamic muscle work according to the different kinds of strain proves that for men what we called indicator 1 is the most frequent (expenditure of energy per movement: small to medium; frequency of movement: slight; duration of one-sided strain: short), and for women the most frequent indicator is what we classified as a 3 (expenditure of energy: medium; frequency: slight to medium; duration: long to medium).

For informational work, the sensory-discriminatory strains on the senses can be measured. Only the two highest indicators of the scale (4 and 5) are shown here. They are of primary interest because, since almost every human activity is connected with the assimilation of information, characteristic values above the normal level can be emphasized. For both sexes visual signals are most important (Table B-3). Second, the sensory feedback among women is chiefly tactile; among men it is chiefly acoustic. That is, among women the informational degree of work difficulty lies predominantly in fine motor activity, while for men the exercise of strength and verbal communication predominates.[11]

The associative requirements of work are noted in Table B-4 according to the kind of decision to be made, the level of the decision, and the nature of the activity. Men have a distinctly larger percentage of activities that require combining and analyzing information. On the other hand, examining and transmitting information is more significant among women. The average level of decisions to be made is higher for men than for women.

The communicative components of work differ by sex: among women, movements that require speed and accuracy, and activities requiring less verbal or written communication, are more frequent.

The reflexive requirements are defined by the degree of alertness required and by the rhythmical or repetitive work that the job entails. Repetitive work and a high degree of alertness are prevalent among women.

TABLE B-3
Frequency of Signal in Highly Scaled Sensory and Discriminatory Work

	LEVEL 4 + 5	
Modality	*Men*	*Women*
Visual	73	80
Auditive	28	10
Proprioceptive	9	19
Haptic	5	16
Olfactory	2	2

SOURCE: Walter Rohmert, H. Luczak, and H. Kugler, *Geschlechtstypische Unterscheide aus der Sicht der Arbeitswissenschaft* (Darmstadt: Techn. Hochschule, Institut für Arbeitswissenschaft, 1978).

TABLE B-4
Chosen Associative and Cognitive Processes of Reflexory Work

	% PORTION OF LEVELS 4 + 5	
Group of items	*Men*	*Women*
Combining information	23	9
Analyzing information	22	4
Checking according to fixed norms	21	28
Short-term remembering of information	17	13
Coding/decoding of information	16	17
Transmitting information	11	19
High alertness with monotonous work	6	18
Jobs which lack active work	9	1
Rhythmically defined work	13	12
Repetitive work	10	39
High level of decisions to be made	13	3
Large volume of planning/organizing	17	5

SOURCE: Walter Rohmert, H. Luczak, and H. Kugler, *Geschlechtstypische Unterscheide aus der Sicht der Arbeitswissenschaft* (Darmstadt: Techn. Hochschule, Institut für Arbeitswissenschaft, 1978).

Finally the physical and psychological environmental influence have to be considered. As Table B-5 shows, men work more frequently under negative environmental conditions. Noise strain, however, is very marked for both sexes.

As far as the time schedules in work organizations are concerned (Table B-6), two-shift jobs are distributed indifferently to sex. More men clearly work at three-shift jobs, due primarily to the exclusion of women

TABLE B-5
Highly Scaled Environmental Influences

Type of influence	Components	Scale	% OF ACTIVITIES	
			Men	Women
Lighting	Strength of lighting	Insufficient	18	4
	Effect of lighting	Insufficient	4	1
	Decidedly unfavorable lighting	True/false*	12	3
Noise	Noise level	Loud/very loud	48	38
	Extremely high noise level at times	True/false*	24	15
	Discontinuous noises	Frequent/very frequent	15	14
	Diminished comprehensibility of speech	Frequent/very frequent	26	20
Vibrations	Strength of mechanical vibrations	Slight intensity	16	1
Climate	Unfavorable climatic conditions	Over ⅔ of work time	14	1
	Frequent change of climate	Frequent/very frequent	3	1
Other negative influences	Air pollution through dust	Over ⅔ of work time	24	5
	Annoyance through odor	Over ⅔ of work time	7	5
	Dirty or wet work environment	Over ⅔ of work time	42	8
	Impairment through protective clothing	Over ⅔ of work time	25	0

*Activities calculated as percentage true.
SOURCE: Walter Rohmert, H. Luczak, and H. Kugler, *Geschlechtstypische Unterscheide aus der Sicht der Arbeitswissenschaft* (Darmstadt: Techn. Hochschule, Institut für Arbeitswissenschaft, 1978).

TABLE B-6
Work Organization by Time and Responsibility Required

		% OF ACTIVITIES	
Element of activity	*Scale*	Men	Women
Regular working hours	true/false*	91	88
Part-time work possible	true/false*	21	48
One-shift work	true/false*	47	70
Two-shift work	true/false*	24	22
Three-shift work	true/false*	11	2
Other shift regimes	true/false*	28	8
Line production work	true/false*	20	46
Automatic production	true/false*	16	8
Responsibility for subordinates	1–10 employees/	13	6
	> 10 employees	11	2
Responsibility for the safety of others	substantial/ very substantial	10	2
Responsibility for material assets	more than 300,000 DM	35	9
Responsibility for nonmaterial assets	substantial/very substantial	9	0
Managerial functions (significance)			
Control tasks	high/very high	9	0
Planning tasks	high/very high	5	1
Coordinating tasks	high/very high	3	0
Contacts with direct superiors (significance)	high/very high	27	13

*Activities calculated as percentage of true.
SOURCE: Walter Rohmert, H. Luczak, and H. Kugler, *Geschlechtstypische Unterscheide aus der Sicht der Arbeitswissenschaft* (Darmstadt: Techn. Hochschule, Institut für Arbeitswissenschaft, 1978).

that results from protective legislation. Analysis of managerial functions demonstrates that men more often have jobs with a high degree of responsibility for subordinates, for the safety of others, and for material assets. The same obtains for the authority to give instructions, for supervisory tasks, and for contacts with superiors.

In summary, women's jobs show high values in monotonous dynamic muscle work; tactile sensory feedback; checking and transmitting of information; and receptive work and work with high demands on attentiveness. They have low values especially in combining and analyzing information; the level of decisions to be made; negative physical environmental influences (except noise); night work; and managerial tasks and responsibility for subordinates and for material assets.

On the other hand, men have high classifications in heavy dynamic work; combining and analyzing information; the level of decisions to be made; stressful physical environmental influences; and responsibility for people and material assets. Low values exist for monotonous dynamic work; repetitive work that requires attentiveness; and transmission of information—just those activities that have high classifications in women's jobs. The 1975 analysis came to practically identical conclusions.

As I noted earlier, the controversy over "low wage brackets" as potentially discriminatory was the catalyst that led us, in the analysis, to determine what ergoscientific methods are available to classify activities in today's technical economy as physically or psychologically light or simple. We also had to consider whether practical methods of wage determination could be developed. In our final report we state that "there exist at this time detailed procedures for strain analysis, as well as methods for determining demand, which are appropriate for judging the heaviness and difficulty of work in different places of work."[12] On the basis of this procedure it is possible to classify the activities according to their intellectual strains, and to establish an order of precedence on the continuum "easy–difficult." The same goes for the continuum "light–heavy" regarding the degree of energetics demand—with the restriction that this order of precedence should be additionally defined by physical environmental influences.

Putting the work evaluation procedures into practice, and including them in the wage-findings system, should be approached with caution. We feel that from the ergonomic viewpoint four levels of evaluating human labor can be distinguished: feasibility; tolerability; reasonableness of demands; and work contentment. The feasibility and tolerability of any given working condition depends on how much can be accomplished, or endured, by someone working under that condition. (Both extent of accomplishment and degree of endurance vary from person to person.) Analyzing the degrees of feasibility and tolerability falls within the competency of ergonomics. Wage-determination, however, has to be carried out according to the probable expectations of the people concerned. This kind of leeway among the parties to a wage agreement cannot be removed by ergonomics or by an other scientific procedure.

For these reasons we refrained from a further development of the AET as a work *evaluation* procedure. Likewise no judgment is passed on the way different work evaluation systems assess different work requirements. We must emphasize, however, that the empirical results prove unequivocally that evaluating activities on the basis of energetics strain alone without considering such subjective factors as work contentment is inadequate.

Two other important points must be kept in mind: It has been determined that existing work evaluation procedures are mostly energetically oriented—that is, they neglect, to a certain degree, informational requirements associated witht he psychological dimensions of activities.[13] Second, regarding the wage classification of women, the results of the activity analyses showed that some businesses do pay men and women unequally for equal or equivalent work.[14]

IMPLICATIONS FOR EQUAL PAY POLICY

In order to estimate the policy's prospects for success, we need to look at the reactions of the interest groups concerned. The first reaction came from the minister of labor, when he announced the completion of the analysis. According to his estimate, the analysis contained "new criteria and measuring techniques for the wage policy of the contractual parties." He expected that the utilization of the new criteria would enable contractual parties to develop wage contracts that would ensure a fairer classification and evaluation, especially of the lower wage brackets. The minister appealed to the contractual parties "to examine together the results of the analysis, to develop it, and to incorporate it gradually into the wage practice." He re-emphasized his position that the problem of fair pay be solved by the contractual parties themselves within the framework of wage autonomy, and promised to support such efforts. In recent times this support has manifested itself especially in the organization of meetings of experts of both contractual parties to help clarify the questions and reach some agreement on them. In addition, the minister commissioned the report writers to develop the AET further in order to make it more comprehensible and more manageable in practice. He made it clear, however, that after these studies were completed, he expected further progress to come from the contractual parties and not from more research commissions.

Not everyone agreed with the minister's conclusions. The employers' association[15] wanted further study of the problem of measuring strains and demands, especially for the intellectual-emotional areas and for limits of tolerability for working conditions.[16] The report writers also felt further research into the analysis of activity-specific demands and strains was necessary. In particular, we recommended the use of analysis methods for either a more representative random sample of activities or a thorough investigation in preselected sectors of industry. Obviously, the minister sees no reason to deal with this problem more intensively now, or else he does not see a chance of success.

While the public paid hardly any attention to the analysis, it did receive a great deal of attention from the trade unions and the employers' associations. Fifteen months passed before the trade unions made an official statement, however, and twenty-one months passed before the employers did. This late reaction may reflect the timespan that usually elapses in decision-making processes of this kind, the rather low priority that the organizations give to this problem as well as the difficulties they faced in interpretating the scientific procedure.

The German Trade Union judged the analysis positively:[17] the analysis showed, it said, that the division into difficult and easy work that had been used so far was biased. Above all, it commended the more detailed study of psychological strains. It noted that the report's conclusions support the autonomy of wage policy negotiations and agreed that a mere improvement of the wage contracts is not enough. Tolerable and reasonable work, they agreed, depends on expanding the content of work and establishing minimum regulations for professional training.[18]

The employers also welcomed the analysis, although they denied that equal pay for men and women was still a problem. The existing wage scale systems do not evaluate the individual in relation to his/her sex, they claimed, but only to the work done. For the rest, the terms "light" versus "heavy" physical strain should be understood to mean both muscle strain and strain on the nerves.[19] The principle of "equal pay for equal work," they maintained, has been realized; nothing in the analysis undercut the evaluation systems already employed. They especially pointed out the normative character inherent in any evaluation system and in negotiations over wage policy. Besides, the statement went on to say, contractual parties continually strive to clarify the requirement features and to improve the definition of wage brackets.[20]

Detailed discussions of the analysis by experts among the employers followed in trade journals.[21] These admitted that the criteria for classifying many activities were not sufficiently clear, but only in summary work evaluations.[22] The analytical work evaluation—they say—is a different matter. Here the psychological strains have been explicitly considered for some time.

Because the criticisms by the employers and trade unions are of fundamental significance, we must consider them in more detail. They can be divided into three problem areas: information problems, problems of application, and problems of implementation and prospects of success.

Problems of information

It cannot be denied that the AET is far more costly than the work evaluation procedures already in use: most employees are still classified by summary work evaluations. These procedures use wage-scale definitions that vary in complexity according to the wage contract and contain five to eight wage scales—twelve at most. In the analytical work evaluation, as a rule, ten to twenty, and sometimes thirty, requirements are considered; of these more than half deal with environmental influences only. The AET, however, separates the requirements into approximately 390 items. In addition, detailed time analyses as well as ergonomic and psychological measurements are given, if desired. In the analytical evaluation procedure agreed on by the metal industry of Baden-Württemberg, for example, "strain on the senses and the nerves" is treated as one kind of strain. With this one dimension all perceptions of the different senses, as well as attentiveness, monotony, and time pressure regarding intensity and duration, have to be included and evaluated. In the AET the sensory strains are composed of fifty-one items.

In light of this, two of the employers' arguments are hard to understand. One is that the analysis is not able to prove the measurability of many kinds of strain—for example, psychological strains.[23] The other is that the analysis does not go farther than existing procedures in establishing strains.[24] Furthermore, the trade unions maintained, in a somewhat different sense, that the analysis did not contain any fundamentally new findings. The fact of discrimination and the character of women's work, they said, had already been known. It appears that neither contractual party was fully aware of the conclusions and applications that the analysis and its scientific method offer (or that they did not want to recognize them). This is especially surprising as far as the trade unions are concerned, since, unlike the employers, they agree that the problem of an equitable wage-scale determination is still far from being solved.

In order to tap the wealth of information the AET provides, we reduced the established items to approximately twenty factors per activity by factor analysis. At the same time this analysis produces quantitative information about the factors. By means of cluster analysis, we can match dissimilar activities with similar strain profiles. To the extent that we have relevant information about the wage scale, these results permit comparative analysis of the classification practice.

As far as I know, these data-analysis techniques have been closely examined only by the employers. The factors of the factor analysis gave rise to various misunderstandings, however, insofar as they were equated with the kinds of demands in traditional work evaluation procedures. The demand-strain concept especially proved to be open to misinterpretation. The employers rejected this concept with the argument that only the work itself should be evaluated, and not the individual effort of the employee.

It must be admitted that the terminology of the analysis is not sufficiently clear on this point. The demand-strain concept, as defined in the analysis, has a double function. On the one hand, it should indicate cutting points where the objective limits of the short- or long-term power of endurance are overstepped. In this respect the strain analysis—as has been observed[25]—serves the needs of the work organization and personnel policy of the business, but hardly those of determining wage scales. On the other hand, the strain analysis is (or can be) an informational device for establishing the effect on people of an activity's objective requirements. (It is for this reason, as I mentioned above, that we think more testing is necessary.) This second function could permit significant conclusions about constructing measuring scales (upper- and lower-limit values, direction of scale) by way of strain analysis and about examining item validity.

Problems of application

The AET was consciously constructed as a work analysis procedure and not as a work evaluation procedure; the latter would have gone beyond the scientific framework and violated the autonomy of wage policy that the contractual parties demand. On principle it would not be difficult to develop the AET into a work evaluation procedure. Apart from choice, scaling, and aggregation of requirements, which the AET provides, this would involve evaluating and assigning scale values to wage brackets, which is now done through contract negotiations between employers and employees.

But who is to do it, and by what standards? In view of the potential usefulness of the AET to business personnel policy and personnel planning, and in view of the interest of the business community in efficient evaluation systems, some action in this direction on the part of the employers is to be expected. In view of the problem of women's wages, however, initiatives on the part of the women's departments of the trade unions are also likely. This would require them to abandon their traditional caution in questions of wage policy, but an effective equal pay policy will require this in any case.

The employers especially have pointed out that the methods used in the analysis are too expensive, too complicated, and too difficult to put into practice. It is true that the introduction of the AET made additional expenditures necessary, compared with analytical wage-finding procedures. In our opinion, however, the extra expense is balanced by the widely useable information that accrues. With the proper training, the people who study work conditions in businesses can easily become competent to use the procedure, since a modified version of the AET that facilitates its use has now been completed.

Even if the less refined summary work evaluation is to be retained, the question arises whether wage-scale definitions can be formulated clearly enough to allow a balanced consideration of the work requirements and avoid the kind of free play in the information that can have negative effects on the classification of women. Explicit formulation of the requirements and their gradation would at any rate allow improvements in this direction. Adding indexes of detailed exemplary cases to the wage-scale definitions would also help.

Problems of implementation and prospects of success

The question arises: Which standard is to serve as the basis for determining the equal value of activities—for example, an activity with a certain degree of monotonous dynamic strain (a typical women's activity) and an activity with predominantly heavy dynamic strain (a typical men's activity)? This is the decisive problem in the wage-structure policy, as both sides have emphasized. And it would surely be wrong to declare that employers are solely or primarily responsible for discrimination against women. The traditional attitudes toward wage classification that are responsible for men's activities being more highly classified than women's activities can be found in all trade associations that are dominated by men. They prevail among business management, supervisory personnel, the people making time studies, works committees, trustees, wage commissions, and—last but not least—women themselves.[26] Successful implementation of equal pay policy presupposes a change of these standards. Proper political measures, however, can promote this change.

To what extent can work analysis and work evaluation procedures promote a policy of decreased discrimination in the labor market? Even if the principle of equal pay for equal work were fully realized, the inequities resulting from unequal opportunity would remain unchanged. The role these two factors play in the sex-specific differences of income in the Federal Republic of Germany can hardly be established at this time, because there is no empirical information that allows control of all relevant variables (income, education, job experience, family role, nature of the activity, motivation, and so on). It seems clear, however, that the influence of inequality of opportunity outweighs the influence of wage discrimination.

In the Federal Republic of Germany this results from the extent of sex-segregation in the labor market. Of the 240 activities examined in the report, only 12.7 percent were done by both sexes, and these activities are not a representative sample. Table B-7, which permits an estimate on a different data base, shows that more than half of all jobs (a total of 445) were done by one sex only. In three-quarters of the jobs, 90 percent of the employees were of the same sex. In view of these facts, the principle of equal pay for equal work certainly has only limited utility. What the re-

TABLE B-7

Sex Segregation in the Labor Market

(Federal Republic of Germany, 1969)*

Job characteristic	% of jobs
Occupied by one sex only	53.7
Occupied by one sex in more than 90% of cases	20.4
Occupied by one sex in 80–90% of cases	9.7
Other	16.2
TOTAL (N = 445)	100.0

*Only gainfully employed heads of households, four-digit job classification.

SOURCE: Random sample of income and consumption, 1969 (47,383 household), own analysis.

sult would be for the more complex principle of work of equal value we could tell only by applying the AET or of a similar work analysis procedure to a representative sample and then developing it into a work evaluation procedure. Unequal starting conditions due to unequal educational levels cannot be overcome by a policy of equal wages. Even with equal educational levels, however, men can expect more attractive careers, as Table B-8 shows. (In order to control the variables "job experience" and "motivation," the evaluation was confined to a single age group, and to persons continuously employed between 1960 and 1971.)

As was to be expected, many of the persons are not mobile. With mobile persons, however, differences are evident not only with regard to professional status in 1960 and to level of education, but also with regard to sex. In each starting group more men than women attain a higher position; trained women workers even experience a considerable downward mobility. Typically, women make a relative frequent transition from wage to salaried employee, but even there they stay mostly in lower positions. Thus, an informed assignment of activities is crucial to achieving equal rights. As long as inequality of opportunities exists, women are likely to be displaced from upgraded jobs by men.

And there are other problems. The trade unions can directly influence only the standard rate of wages. Their influence on actual wages is only indirect. For example, the rate of wages of an untrained woman worker between the ages of thirty and forty-five who has worked in the baking industry in the same plant for five to nine years amounted in 1972 on the average to only 71 percent of wages for men with the same features.[27] (This relatively homogeneous group was chosen in order to stabilize other

TABLE B-8
Career Success of Men and Women Continuously Employed between 1960 and 1970

PROFESSIONAL STANDING, 1960					WORKER		
Position	Level of education	Age	Sex	Agri-culture	Un-trained	Trained	Skilled
Worker, untrained	Grade school, no apprenticeship	20–24	M	2	73	17	2
			F	2	82	8	
Worker, trained	Grade school, trade apprenticeship	20–24	M	1	4	65	14
			F	1	18	63	2
Employee, lower level	Grade school, commercial apprenticeship	20–24	M		1	2	3
			F		3	3	4
Employee, lower level	High school, apprenticeship	20–24	M		1		
			F	1			1
Employee, middle level	Professional & technical high schools	20–24	M				
			F				
Employee, middle level	Technical college or university	25–34	M	3			
			F				
Civil servant, upper/middle level	Technical college or university	30–34	M				
			F				

SOURCE: Federal Office of Statistics, *Microcensus: Additional Inquiry, 1971,* "Social Shifts in the Federal Republic of Germany" (486,000 persons), own analysis.

variables.) Only a third of the discrepancy results from different wage brackets. The rest is the result of overtime payments and other bonuses to compensate for negative working conditions (unequal opportunities).

The insights gained through work analysis, then, call for changing wage-bracket definitions. In the Federal Republic of Germany this problem is being dealt with in the basic wage agreements. But while the rates of wages are agreed upon in wage contracts valid for one year, the wage agreements are valid for about four to eight years. This alone makes it obvious that improvements in the basic wage agreements can be carried out much more slowly than improvements in the scale of wage contracts. Moreover, basic wage agreements encounter more resistance from em-

TABLE B-8 (continued)

POSITION 1971

Fore-man	Civil servant, lower/middle	EMPLOYEE Lower	EMPLOYEE Middle	Civil servant, upper/middle	Employee, higher/highest	Civil servant, higher	SELF-EMPLOYED 0–1 Employee	SELF-EMPLOYED More than 1 employee	Total
2	1	2	1				1		100
		6	1				1		100
3	2	3	4		1		2	1	100
1	0	9	5				1	1	100
	3	37	32	1	9		7	5	100
		70	14		1		3	1	100
	1	25	31	4	25		7	6	100
		63	25	1	4		3	2	100
	1		41	3	42		7	5	100
	2	5	84		6		2	1	100
			23	6	53	7	3	6	100
			29	1	33	17	1		100
				63	1	38			100
				88	3	9			100

ployers; employees strike over the agreements less readily since their interests are less obviously touched.

This fact possibly explains why it is easier for the trade unions to attain the principle of wage equality by raising the lowest wage brackets, or abolishing them, than by improving wage-bracket definitions. An analysis of wage contracts shows that in this respect considerable progress has been made in the seventies for female employees in the lower wage brackets. Table B-9 substantiates this. After 1955–1965, when the forced abolition of open sex discrimination caused an obvious decrease of inequality between men and women, few changes occurred until 1970, when the problem was re-opened. The improvements of the seventies are more

TABLE B-9

Income disparity between men and women (income for men = 100)*

	DISPARITY (%)	
Year	*Female wage workers*	*Female salaried workers*
1950	60.5	
1955	59.2	
1960	64.5	62.1
1965	67.5	60.2
1970	68.6	59.9
1975	72.3	63.6
1976	72.4	63.7

*Gross hourly wages.

SOURCE: Statistisches Bundesamt, *Laufende Verdiensterhe bungen*, Fachserie M/15.

distinct among wage than among salaried employees. And the inequality is still considerable. Moreover, the policy of evening out the rates of wages is definitely limited. The more equal the rates of wages, the greater the significance of overtime increases as a factor accounting for unequal pay. In the Federal Republic of Germany, however, this limit has not yet been reached.

Granted that inequality of opportunity is more important than inequality of pay and has to be dealt with by other, political, means, the fact remains that in the Federal Republic of Germany women are disadvantaged by wage-bracket definitions and by assignment to wage brackets. A study by the Ministry of Labor showed that, of the 346 most important wage-scale contracts made in 1974, 104 contracts provided for "low wage brackets."[28] In these contracts the difference between the lowest bracket (i.e., women) and the bracket for untrained workers doing heavy labor (i.e., men) amounted to 1.5–25 percent, with an average of 10 percent. Women who do not belong to low wage brackets are also confronted with the problem of fair classification. For this reason measures which improve the situation are of great long-term importance. The results of scientifically based work analysis procedures, like the results of the analysis, can doubtless be of help here. It appears, however, that employers and trade unions, especially the latter, have not yet perceived the possible range of applications.

One benefit is the capacity to measure the demands and strains of a job and report on them. This information can be broken down by activity for interregional, sectoral, and temporal comparisons, by industry, but also by men's and women's jobs. The present scarcity of such information in the Federal Republic of Germany limits political reform and the control of these change efforts, particularly of the organization of work.

Another benefit is the capacity to measure and check on how much and how often work demands overstep the ergonomic threshold values. So far these functions have been filled primarily by company management, by state legislation, and by factory inspection boards. This area offers a wide field of activity for wage policy and for involvement by factory committees.

Still another is the ability to examine how completely existing wage-finding systems take into account the different kinds of requirements. In particular, strains for monotonous, reflexory work (attentiveness and repetitive work, for example), and some kinds of informational work are not covered in most wage contracts, at least not explicitly.

A fourth benefit is the ability to examine and check the wage-bracket classification of employees within the framework of whatever wage-finding system is being used. All wage-finding systems practiced to date, including analytical work evaluation, allow a wide latitude in interpretation. The dependability and completeness of the listing of the various strains and demands especially need to be checked. Even here it is possible to determine sex-specific differences with the help of precise work-evaluation procedures.

Fifth, the procedure would permit examination of the evaluation scales for determining wage brackets with the help of results arrived at through physiological strain analysis.

Finally, each job makes a certain package of demands on the jobholder. In many cases these demands are lower than the abilities of the worker. A scientific analysis could help determine the degree to which labor potential, including that of women, is underutilized. Such information can be used for job reorganization and assignment of workers to jobs.

Most of these points have already been the object of political efforts. But they all can be tackled more precisely and reliably with the help of findings acquired by ergonomics and related sciences. At the same time, all these points are of special interest for the analysis of women's labor, and for policies to promote equal pay for women. To my knowledge, however, no concrete plans now exist among the trade unions, or their women's divisions, to put even some of these possibilities to practical use.

NOTES

1. Walter Rohmert and Joseph Rutenfranz, *Arbeitswissenschaftliche Beurteilung der Belastung und Beanspruchung an unterschiedlichen industriellen Arbeitsplätzen* (Bonn: Gutachten für den Bundesminister für Arbeit und Sozialordnung, 1975).

2. Christof Helberger and Hans-Jürgen Krupp, *Die Einstufungsgrundsätze der Tätigkeiten hinsichtlich des Grundsatzes des gleichen Arbeitsentgeltes für Männer und Frauen* (Art. 119 des EWG-Vertrages; Frankfurt: Forschungsbericht im Auftrag der Europ, Gemeinschaften, 1973).

3. K. Landau, H. Luczak, and W. Rohmert, "Arbeitswissenschaftlicher Erhebungsbogen zur Tätigkeitsanalyse" (AET), in *Arbeitswissenschaftliche Beurteilung der Belastung und Beanspruchung an unterschiedlichen industriellen Arbeitsplätzen*, ed. Walter Rohmert and Joseph Rutenfranz, (Bonn: Gutachten für den Bundesminister für Arbeitund Sozialordnung, 1975).

4. C. Graf Hoyos, *Arbeitspsychologie* (Stuttgart: Kohlhammer, 1974); Rohmert and Rutenfranz, *Arbeitswissenschaftliche*, pp. 28–29.

5. Rohmert and Rutenfranz, *Arbeitswissenschaftliche*, p. 33 ff; A. T. Welford, "Performance, Biological Mechanism and Age: A Theoretical Sketch," in *Behavior, Aging and the Nervous System*, ed. A. T. Welford and James E. Birren (Springfield, Ill.: Charles C. Thomas, 1965), pp. 3–20.

6. Rohmert and Rutenfranz, *Arbeitswissenschaftliche*, p. 50.

7. E. J. McCormick, P. R. Jeanneret, and P. C. Mecham, *The Development and Background of the Position Analysis Questionnaire (PAQ)* (Lafayette, Ind.: Occupational Research Center, Purdue University, Report No. 5, 1969).

8. Walter Rohmert and Kurt Landau, "Arbeitswissenschaftliche Erhebungen zur Tätigkeitsanalyse im EDV-Bereich," in *Fortschrittl. Betriebsführung und Industrial Engineering* 26 (1977): 153–158.

9. Ibid.

10. Rohmert and Rutenfranz, *Arbeitswissenschaftliche*.

11. W. Rohmert, H. Luczak, and H. Kugler, *Geschlechtstypische Unterschiede aus der Sicht der Arbeitswissenschaft* (Darmstadt: Techn. Hochschule, Institut für Arbeitswissenschaft, 1978), p. 8.

12. Rohmert and Rutenfranz, *Arbeitswissenschaftliche*, p. 10.

13. Ibid., p. 9.

14. Ibid., p. 11.

15. Bundesverband der Deutschen Arbeitgeberverbände (BDA), Feb. 28, 1977, Stellungnahme hinsichtlich der im Gutachten, Rohmert/Rutenfranz und im Forschungsbericht Rohmert/Landau aufgeworfenen Grundsatzfrazen, Köln.

16. A. Hennecke, "Das Gutachten von Rohmert/Rutenfranz aus der Sicht der Arbeitsbewertung," *Mitteilungen des Instituts für angewandte Arbeitswissenschaft (Mitt.d. IfaA)* 65 (1977): 2–36.

17. Deutscher Gewerkschaftsbund (DGB), Sept. 15, 1976, Stellungnahme zum Forschungsbericht und der Gutachterlichen Stellungnahme zum Thema Arbeitswissenschaftliche Beurteilung der Belastung und Beanspruchung an unterschiedlichen industriellen Arbeitsplätzen, Düsseldorf.

18. Ibid.

19. BDA.

20. Ibid.

21. R. Röbke, "Das Gutachten von Rohmert/Rutenfranz, *Mitt. d. IfaA* 62 (1976): 1–51; A. Hennecke, "Neuere Verfahren der Anforderungsermittlung

durch Arbeitsanalyse," *Mitt. d. IfaA* 64 (1977): 3–19; A. Hennecke, "Das Gutachten," pp. 2–36.

22. Hennecke, "Das Gutachten."

23. Ibid., p. 27.

24. BDA, Feb. 28, 1977; Hennecke, "Das Gutachten," p. 27.

25. Röbke, "Das Gutachten"; Hennecke, "Das Gutachen."

26. Claudia Pinl, *Das Arbeitnehmer-Patriarchat: Die Frauenpolitik der Gewerkschaften* (Köln: Kepenheuer & Witsch, 1977).

27. Statistical Office of the European Community, *Structure of Earnings in Industry, Federal Republic of Germany*, Special Series 6B (Luxembourg: Eurostat, 1972).

28. Bundestagsdrucksachen (Lower House Document), 7/3267.

BIBLIOGRAPHY

Aaron, Benjamin, ed. *Labor Courts and Grievance Settlements in Western Europe*. Berkeley and Los Angeles: University of California Press, 1971.

Adams, Arvil A. *Toward Fair Employment and the EEOC: A Study of Compliance Procedures under Title VII of the Civil Rights Act of 1964*. Washington, D.C.: Government Printing Office, 1972.

Agarwal, Naresh C., and Harrish C. Gain. *Pay Discrimination against Women in Canada: Issues and Policies*. Ontario: McMaster University, Faculty of Business, 1978.

Alexandre, Danièle. "The Status of Women—France," *The American Journal of Comparative Law* 20 (fall 1972): 647–659.

Amicht, Monicha. "Women's Leadership Roles in Two Selected Labor Unions in the United States and Belgium: A Comparative Descriptive Study." (unpublished Ph.D. dissertation, University of Cincinnati, 1976.

Armstrong, Pat, and Hugh Armstrong. *The Double Ghetto: Canadian Women and Their Segregated Work*. Toronto: McClelland and Stewart, 1978.

Ashenfelter, Orley. "Discrimination and Trade Unionism." In Orley Ashenfelter and Albert Rees, eds., *Discrimination in Labor Markets*. Princeton, N.J.: Princeton University Press, 1973.

———. "Racial Discrimination and Trade Unionism," *Journal of Political Economy* 80 (May/June 1972): 435–464.

——— and James Heckman. "Measuring the Effect of an Anti-discrimination Program." In Orley Ashenfelter and James Blum, eds., *Evaluating the Labor Market Effects of Social Programs*, pp. 46–84. Princeton, N.J.: Industrial Relations Section, Princeton University Press, 1976.

Aspöck, Ruth, and Brigitte Schramm. "Vocational Training for Girls in the Metal Trade: Pilot Study." Paper presented at the International Symposium on Women and Industrial Relations, International Institute for Labour Studies, Vienna, Sept. 1978.

Aubert, Jacqueline, "La Position des Femmes dans la Gestion des Entreprises et dans les Associations Patronales en France." Paper presented at the International Symposium on Women and Industrial Relations, International Institute for Labour Studies, Vienna, Sept. 1978.

Babcock, Barbara Allen, Ann E. Freedman, Eleanor Holmes Norton, and Susan C. Ross. *Sex Discrimination and the Law: Causes and Remedies*. Boston: Little, Brown, 1975.

Baer, Judith. *The Chains of Protection*. Westport, Conn.: Greenwood Press, 1978.

Bain, Joe S. *International Differences in Industrial Structure*. New Haven: Yale University Press, 1966.

Barrett, Nancy Smith. "Women in Industrial Society: An International Perspective." In Jane Roberts Chapman, ed. *Economic Independence for Women: The Foundation for Equal Rights*, pp. 77–111. Beverly Hills, Calif.: Sage Publications, 1976.

Baude, Annika. "Public Policy and Changing Family Patterns in Sweden, 1930–1977." In Jean Lipman-Blumen and Jessie Bernard, eds., *Sex Roles and Social Policy*, pp. 17–38. Beverly Hills, Calif.: Sage Publications, 1974.

———— and Per Holmberg. "The Positions of Men and Women in the Labour Market." In Edmund Dahlstrom, ed., *The Changing Roles of Men and Women*, pp. 105–134. London: Gerald Duckworth, 1967.

Bécane-Pascaud, Geneviève. "Les Femmes dans la Fonction Publique," *Notes et Etudes Documentaires, la Documentation Française*, no. 4056–4057, Jan. 25, 1974.

Becker, Gary. *The Economics of Discrimination*. 2nd ed. Chicago: University of Chicago Press, 1971.

Bednarzik, Robert W., and Deborah P. Klein. "Labor Force Trends: A Synthesis and Analysis," *Monthly Labor Review* 100 (Oct. 1977): 3–12.

Bell, Derrick, Jr. "Forward: Equal Employment Law and the Continuing Need for Self-Help," *Loyola University Law Journal* (Chicago) 8 (summer 1977): 681–686.

Bell, Duran. "The Economic Basis of Employee Discrimination." In George van Furstenberg, Ann Horowitz, and Bennett Harrison, eds., *Patterns of Racial Discrimination*, pp. 121–135. Lexington, Mass.: D. C. Heath, 1974.

————. "Occupational Discrimination as a Source of Income Differences: Lessons of the 1960's," *American Economic Review* 62 (May 1972): 363–379.

Beller, Andrea. "Aggregate Economic Activity and the Effect of E.E.O. Laws on Earnings." Paper presented at the Econometric Society Meetings, New York City, Dec. 28, 1977.

————. "The Impact of Equal Employment Opportunity Laws on the Male/Female Earnings Differential." Paper presented at the Conference on Women in the Labor Market, Columbia University, Sept. 1977.

Bergmann, Barbara R. "The Effect on White Incomes of Discrimination in Employment," *Journal of Political Economy* 79 (March 1971): 294–313.

————. "Empirical Work on the Labor Market: Is There Any Alternative to Regression Running?" *Proceedings of the 27th Annual Meeting of the Industrial Relations Research Association*, pp. 243–251. San Francisco: The Association, 1976.

————. "Occupational Segregation, Wages and Profits When Employers Discriminate by Race or Sex," *Eastern Economic Journal* 1 (April/July 1974): 103–110.

———— and William Krause. "Evaluating and Forecasting Progress in Racial Integration of Employment," *Industrial and Labor Relations Review* 25 (April 1972): 399–409.

———— and Jerolyn Lyle. "The Occupational Standing of Negroes by Areas and Industries," *Journal of Human Resources* 6 (fall 1971): 411–433.

Bersani, Catherine. "La Femme et La Fonction Publique," *Droit Social* 1 (Jan. 1976): 51–52.

Bibb, Robert, and William Form. "The Effects of Industrial, Occupational and Sex Stratification on Wages in Blue Collar Markets," *Social Forces* 55 (June 1977): 974–996.

Bird, Caroline. *The Two-Paycheck Marriage.* New York: Rawson, Wade, 1979.

Blackstone, William T., and Robert D. Heslep, eds. *Social Justice and Preferential Treatment: Women and Racial Minorities in Education and Business.* Athens, Ga.: University of Georgia, 1977.

Blau, Francine D. "The Data on Women Workers, Past, Present and Future." In Ann H. Stromberg and Shirley Harkness, eds., *Women Working: Theories and Facts in Perspective*, pp. 29–62. Palo Alto, Calif.: Mayfield, 1978.

————. *Equal Pay in the Office.* Lexington, Mass.: D. C. Heath, 1977.

Blau, Peter, et al. "Occupational Choice—A Conceptual Framework," *Industrial and Labor Relations Review* 9 (July 1956): 531–543.

Blaxall, Martha, and Barbara Reagan. *Women and the Workplace.* Chicago: University of Chicago Press, 1976.

Blinder, Allan, "Wage Discrimination: Reduced Form and Structural Estimates," *Journal of Human Resources* 8 (fall 1973): 436–455.

Blumberg, Grace Ganz. "Federal Income Tax and Social Security Law." In *American Workers in a Full Employment Economy: A Compendium of Papers Submitted to the Subcommittee on Economic Growth and Stabilization of the Joint Economic Committee*, pp. 237–248. Washington, D.C.: Government Printing Office, 1977.

Blumrosen, Alfred W. "The Duty of Fair Recruitment under the Civil Rights Act of 1964," *Rutgers Law Review* 22 (spring 1968): 465–527.

————. "Quotas, Common Sense and Law in Labor Relations: Three Dimensions of Equal Opportunity," *Rutgers Law Review* 27 (spring 1974): 675–703.

————. "Strangers in Paradise: *Griggs v. Duke Power Co.* and the Concept of Employment Discrimination," *Michigan Law Review* 71 (Nov. 1972): 59–110.

Borris, Maria. *Die Benachteiligung der Maedchen in Schulen der Bundes-Republik.* Frankfurt-am-Main: Europaeischer Verlangsanstalt, 1972.

Boutellier, Jacques, et al. *Male and Female Wage Differentials in France: Theory and Measurement.* Monograph no. 5, International Institute of Social Economics. Hull: Emmasglen Ltd., 1975.

Bowen, Peter. "White-Collar Jobs and the Unionization of Women." Paper presented at the International Symposium on Women and Industrial Relations, International Institute for Labour Studies, Vienna, Sept. 1978.

Bowen, William G., and T. Aldrich Finegan. *The Economics of Labor Force Participation.* Princeton, N.J.: Princeton University Press, 1969.

British Information Service. *Occupations and Conditions of Work.* London: Her Majesty's Stationery Office, 1975.

Brown, E. H. P. *The Inequality of Pay.* Berkeley: University of California Press, 1978.

Burns, John E., and Catherine G. Burns. "An Analysis of the Equal Pay Act," *Labor Law Journal* 24 (Feb. 1973): 92.

Canadian Broadcasting Corporation. *Women in the CBC.* Ottawa: Canadian Broadcasting Corporation, 1975.

Central Arbitration Committee. *First Annual Report, 1976.* London: Her Majesty's Stationery Office, 1977.

Chiplin, Brian. "The Evaluation of Sex Discrimination: Some Problems and a Suggested Re-orientation." Paper presented at the Conference on Women in the Labor Market, Columbia University, Sept. 1977.

————— and Peter J. Sloane. "Equal Pay in Great Britain." In Barrie O. Pettman, ed., *Equal Pay for Women: Progress and Problems in Seven Countries*, pp. 9–34. Bradford, Eng.: MCB, 1975.

————— and Peter J. Sloane. *Sex Discrimination in the Labour Market (Great Britain).* London: Macmillan, 1976.

Cohen, Malcom S. "Sex Differences in Compensation," *Journal of Human Resources* 6 (fall 1971): 434–447.

Collins, Randall. "A Conflict Theory of Sexual Stratification," *Social Problems* 19 (summer 1971): 3–21.

Comité du Travail Féminin, Ministère du Travail. *Bilan de l'Application de la Loi du 22 Décembre 1972 sur l'Égalité de Rémunération entre Hommes et Femmes.* Paris: Ministère du Travail, Sept. 1976.

—————, assisted by G. Bécane-Pascaud. *Les Femmes aux Postes de Direction de la Fonction Publique.* Paris: Ministère du Travail, 1974.

Commission of the European Communities. *The Employment of Women and the Problems It Raises in the Member States of the European Community.* Abridged version of Mrs. E. Sullerot's report. Brussels: Commission of the European Communities, 1972.

—————. *Men and Women of Europe: Comparative Attitudes to a Number of Problems of our Society.* Brussels: Commission of the European Communities, 1975.

—————. *Report of the Commission to the Council on the Application as at 12 February 1978 of the Principle of Equal Pay for Men and Women.* (Brussels: Commission of the European Communities, 1979.

—————. *Report on the Development of the Social Situation in the Communities in 1976.* Brussels and Luxembourg: European Coal and Steel Community, European Economic Community, European Atomic Energy Community, 1977.

—————. *Vocational Guidance and Training for Women Workers.* Brussels and Luxembourg: European Coal and Steel Community, European Economic Community, European Atomic Energy Community, 1976.

Cook, Alice H. "Equal Pay: A Multinational History and Comparison." Unpubished manuscript, Ithaca, N.Y., Jan. 1, 1975.

(Plate IV) J. M. W. Turner. *Apollo and Python*. Courtesy of the Tate Gallery, London.

Covetousness, or malignity (Phorcys), and Secretness (Ceto), be
the darkening passions, whose hair is always gray; then the sto
merciless passions, brazen-winged (the Gorgons), of whom the d
Medusa, is ice-cold, turning all who look on her to stone. And, l
consuming (poisonous and volcanic) passions—the 'flam
dragon,' uniting the powers of poison, and instant destruction

In books of genesis other than Hesiod's, Ruskin reminds us
image both archetypal authority and resonance, we have
dragon's being busy about an apple tree. Considering that
was, in the Greek mind, descended from the sea, the reader
see a new truth in the biblical verse, "Thou breakest the
dragons in the waters."[55]

Further, in a tradition later than Hesiod, we learn that
child of Typhon and Echidna. Typhon represents "volcan
the evil spirit of Tumult"; while Echidna, the adder, des
Medusa, is "half-maiden, half-serpent" and therefore si
spirit of all the fatallest evil, veiled in gentleness: or, i
treachery;—having dominion over many gentle things;-
over a kiss, given, indeed, in another garden than
Hesperides, yet in relation to keeping of treasure also."[56]
attempts to bring Greek and Christian traditions togeth
force.

Echidna, the woman-serpent, or treachery, had a broth
version, the dragon Geryon, who appears in *The Inferno*
of fraud. And just as Hercules slew Ladon, he also dispatc
a parallel solar episode.

> We find next that Geryon lived in the island of Erytheia (bl
> another kind of blushing than that of the Hesperid Erytheia
> also, a western island, and Geryon kept red oxen in it (said
> red setting sun); Hercules kills him, as he does the Hesperia
> in order to be able to reach him, a golden boat is given to H
> Sun, to cross the sea in.[57]

The parallel shows both sea-born monsters guarding
paradises until slain by Hercules as solar hero. They are
enable Ruskin to fuse the two symbols in a sweepin
which the "complete idea of the Hesperian dragon" ar
from five related accounts.

> The Hesperian dragon . . . is, in fine, the '*Pluto il g*
> Dante; the demon of all evil passions connected with cove
> to say, essentially of fraud, rage, and gloom. Regarded a
> Fraud, he is said to be descended from the viper Echidn
> cunning, in whirl on whirl; as the demon of consum

John Ruskin after Turner. *"Quivi Trovammo"*: his sketch of the dragon in *The Garden of the Hesperides*. An illustration to *Modern Painters*, volume 5, reproduced from *Works* (Library Edition), vol. 7.

J. M. W. Turner. *The Goddess of Discord Choosing the Apple of Contention in the Garden of the Hesperides*. Courtesy of the Tate Gallery, London.

This guardian of earth-wealth, "the demon of covetousness," begins to emerge in Ruskin's mythography as a kind of economic monster. Grasping, breathing fire, and wreathed in serpents of smoke, yet instinct with Medusa's lethal chill, he is the fate that stands between earth-wealth and its unenlightened pursuers.

There remains, however, a shade of meaning in the tone of Turner's picture that he has to interpret for us because it reveals the cast of this landscapist's outlook at this stage and anticipates a crucial change to be illustrated in the following chapter. "The Hesperides in their own character, as the nymphs of domestic joy, are entirely bright (and the garden always bright around them)";[60] therefore, one would expect brightness in this picture. But there is little light there, and the conclusion of Ruskin's analysis is to show that Turner was not yet ready for the Pythian radiance of the Hesperid Aeglé. In this direction, he calls our attention to "the gloom extending, not to the dragon only, but to the fountain and the tree of golden fruit" in the painting. It is "a sad-coloured work, not executed in Angelico's white and gold; nor in Perugino's crimson and azure; but in a sulphurous hue, as relating to a paradise of smoke."[61] The reason for this Turnerian gloom, as he makes clear in the next chapter, is that Turner was not yet able to use the Apolline scarlet to express the Greek tragic human sorrow because he had not yet envisioned Python, the greater spiritual enemy, slain by purifying, redeeming Apollo.

Yet in this, the "sulphurous" painting, he had nonetheless recognized a great enemy who was, as Ruskin later expressed it, "the death which attends the vain pursuit of wealth."[62] This, he thought, was the meaning of Hercules' struggles with Geryon and Ladon: "Geryon is the evil spirit of wealth, as arising from commerce; hence, placed as a guardian of isles in the most distant sea, and reached in a golden boat; while the Hesperian dragon is the evil spirit of wealth, as possessed in households." Hercules, who embodies "manly labor," slays both of these and returns the apples to Juno; the sulphurous gloom, in Ruskin's view, arises in part from the fact that the goddess of discord contrives that "one portion of this household wealth shall be ill bestowed by Paris,"[63] from which issue the sorrows of the *Iliad* and the *Odyssey*. I say "in part" because he tells us that he at first attributed the "sadness of color" in the painting merely to the dark presence of Eris, but that he later found a passage in the *Faerie Queene* that seemed to provide further evidence for the gloom and that in the same line of thought he had been taking. He became convinced that Turner's "diminution of the splendour of the old Greek garden was certainly caused chiefly by Spenser's describing the Hesperides fruit as growing first in the garden of Mammon."[64]

Actually the passage is Spenser's description of the unhealthy richness of the tree of golden fruit as it grew in the Garden of Proserpina:

. . . .

Next thereunto did grow a goodly tree,
With braunches broad dispredd and body great,
Clothed with leaves, that none the wood mote see,
And loaden all with fruit as thick as it might bee.

Their fruit were golden apples glistring bright,
That goodly was their glory to behold;
On earth like never grew, ne living wight
Like ever saw, but they from hence were sold;[65]

. . . .

The Mammon is Ruskin's own; Turner's Ladon has become the Mammon dragon of nineteenth-century materialism, part now of his own bitter personal mythology, a Greco-Christian amalgam. Thus the chapter ends in a swirling jeremiad in which the dragon figures as a private symbol in a web of allusions.

That power, it appears, on the hill-top, is our British Madonna; whom, reverently, the English devotional painter must paint, thus enthroned, with nimbus about the gracious head. Our Madonna,—or our Jupiter on Olympus,—or, perhaps, more accurately still, our unknown god, sea-born, with the cliffs, not of Cyrene, but of England, for his altar; and no chance of any Mars' Hill proclamation concerning him, "whom therefore ye ignorantly worship."

This is no irony. The fact is verily so. The greatest man of our England, in the first half of the nineteenth century, in the strength and hope of his youth, perceives this to be the thing he has to tell us of utmost moment, connected with the spiritual world. In each city and country of past time, the master-minds had to declare the chief worship which lay at the nation's heart; to define it; adorn it; show the range and authority of it. Thus in Athens, we have the triumph of Pallas; and in Venice the Assumption of the Virgin; here, in England, is our great spiritual fact forever interpreted to us—the Assumption of the Dragon.[66]

This, then, through scene, symbol, and tone, is the picture's true message: "the Assumption of the Dragon," the apotheosis of greed. Turner's "first great religious picture" becomes through Ruskin's mythic analysis a true apocalypse of the nineteenth century. It also echoes that ashen vision of death that had consummated the previous discussion of Turner's youthful awareness—the "ball strewn bright with human ashes, glaring in poised sway beneath the sun." This is "the

English death—the European death of the nineteenth century . . . more terrible a thousandfold in its merely physical grasp and grief; more terrible, incalculably, in its mystery and shame."[67] In Turner's vision at this time the Mammon-dragon reigned supreme over a polluted land, and he had no means with which to challenge it, though he was Saint George's child.

> No St. George any more to be heard of; no more dragon-slaying possible: this child, born on St. George's Day, can only make manifest the dragon, not slay him, sea-serpent as he is; whom the English Andromeda, not fearing takes for her lord. The fairy English Queen once thought to command the waves, but it is the sea-dragon now who commands her valleys; of old the Angel of the Sea ministered to them, but now the Serpent of the Sea; where once flowed their clear springs now spreads the black Cocytus pool; and the fair blooming of the Hesperid meadows fades into ashes beneath the Nereid's Guard.[68]

4

But Ruskin would find dragon glory as well as dragon gloom in Turner's myth work. It would not be the last Nereid's dim and sulphurous guard but the roseate brightness of the Hesperid named Aeglé that would become most characteristic of Turner's painting. One can see in Ruskin's earliest essay on the painter, the unpublished "Reply to *Blackwood's* Criticism of Turner," that he intended to build his defense around Turner's peculiarities as a colorist. "All minds move in a peculiar channel," he wrote, "and think and feel in a peculiar manner. Turner thinks and feels in colour; he cannot help but doing so."[69] Yet his main discussions of this subject in the earlier volumes of *Modern Painters*, the chapter "Truth of Colour" in the first volume and that on "Turnerian Light" in the fourth, are primarily technical discussions centered on Turner's achievements in light. His color is shown to be subordinate to his system of chiaroscuro; to be translucent, aerial, subtly graduated and as mimetically true as can be to the more brilliant solar effects in nature. But this does not interpret or defend, from an expressive standpoint, Turner's peculiar intentionality with regard to color; it does not show why he chose this balance of hues and these natural effects and not others. Full defense of Turner as a colorist would depend upon relating his color preferences to other aspects of his meaning. And this phase of the defense is not consummated until now in the penultimate chapter of *Modern Painters*, "The Hesperid Aeglé."

Turner's luminous color may well be like certain aspects of reality, but the meaning of reality is hidden until gathered up in symbol systems. Nature is meaningless without myth. So the defense of the expressive aspects of Turner's color—the meaning of his color—awaited an adequate hermeneutic in Ruskin. This he found in the study of Turner's myth–making; more accurately, he found the central meaning of his color system by reading Turner's main Greek subjects in terms of his own interpretations of Greek myths; but these interpretations, in turn, reflect his own evolving personal myth of social concern.

He has interpreted a solar subject painted in gloom by Turner, the sunset garden of the Hesperides, in order to show by the contrast of subject and tone how, in his early work, Turner could represent this tragic vision only by real dimness. But, since Turner would become the great colorist of his age, Ruskin would have to show how, as the result of some great mental change, Turner could achieve his distinctive brilliance as a colorist and yet retain a deep fidelity to his essential vision, "the labour and sorrow and passing away of men." "He had begun by faithful declaration of the sorrow there was in the world. It is now permitted him to see also its beauty. He becomes, separately and without rival, the painter of the loveliness and the light of the creation."[70]

There would have to be a mythic subject of Turner's that expressed symbolically the revelation that lay behind this great change, a myth that could relate the brightness of Aeglé to the darkness of "the great human truth visible to him." Ruskin finds this in another solar legend of Turner's, *Apollo and Python* (Plate IV).

> Five years after the Hesperides were painted, another great mythological subject appeared by Turner's hand. Another dragon—this time not triumphant, but in death-pang, the Python slain by Apollo.
> Not in a garden, this slaying, but in a hollow among wildest rocks, beside a stagnant pool. Yet instead of the sombre colouring of the Hesperid hills, strange gleams of blue and gold flit around the mountain peaks and colour the clouds above them.[71]

This picture had also been discussed in the *Notes* of 1856 where it is called "one of the noblest pictures in the world"; but now it is this picture, not *Ulysses Deriding Polyphemus*, that assumes a pivotal position in Turner's development.

> The picture is at once the type, and the first expression of a great change which was passing in Turner's mind. A change, which was not clearly manifested in all its results until much later in his life; but in the colouring of this picture are the first signs of it; and in the subject of this picture, its symbol.[72]

In its coloring, then, the painting is an instance and a foretaste of a technical victory; its mythical subject, when properly understood, represents the *meaning* of that victory. Accordingly, Ruskin's first task is to define this technical achievement in color. It consisted simply in

Turner's liberation from the misty yellow conventionalisms by which the classical and Dutch landscapists had represented the sun. "Claude and Cuyp had painted sun*shine*, Turner alone, the sun *colour*."[73] Many colorists had mastered the sweet effect of "softly warm or yellow rays of the sun falling through mist"; thinking that no other but this yellow deception could be given, the respectable colorists refuse the deceptive effect and paint in twilight when the color is full. So, Ruskin asserts, from imperfect colorists we have this deceptive effect of sunshine, and from the great colorists, who will not deceive, we get frankly symbolic representations of sunshine. But Turner, the great naturalist of landscape, will not submit to either the symbol or the deception.

> This was not enough for him. He must paint the sun in his strength, the sun rising *not* through vapour. If you glance at that Apollo slaying the Python, you will see that there is rose colour and blue on the clouds, as well as gold; and if you turn to the Apollo in the Ulysses and Polyphemus—his horses are rising beyond the horizon,—you see he is not "rising through vapour," but above it;—gaining somewhat of a victory over vapour, it appears.[74]

Yet Turner's public would not accept this victory over vapor, could not bear so much solar reality; so they constantly cried " 'Perish Apollo. Bring us back Python.' "[75] So Ruskin must now explain the mythic meaning of this victory—*and* of its rejection by the public. But before he can take up the myth he must explain the archetypal significance of the *color* that was gained by this "victory over vapour of many kinds; Python-slaying in general.[76]

Earlier in this volume, in the chapter "The Cloud-Flocks," Ruskin had eloquently reminded his reader of the fiery glories of cloud color (as he had earlier in the first volume) and had left him with two mysteries concerning these displays: What properties of clouds cause them? ("I never saw crimson or scarlet smoke, nor ultramarine smoke."[77]) What do these colors mean experientially to us? What, as we would say, would be the environmental impact if these skies were denied? Turner's achievement in color raises these old problems because he reveals in his victorious skies truths that no painter before him had acknowledged. Ruskin puts it mythographically: "Hesperid Aeglé, and Erytheia throned there in the west, fade into twilights of four thousand years, unconfessed. Here at last is one who confesses them, but is it well?"[78]

"No man, hitherto, had painted the clouds scarlet." Turner's peculiar achievement is "the perfection of the colour chord by means of *scarlet*"; his "most distinctive innovation as a colourist was his discovery of the scarlet *shadow*,"[79] the shade of the rose.

Here is sunshine which glows even when subdued; it has not cool shade, but fiery shade. This is the glory of sunshine.

Now, this scarlet colour,—or pure red, intensified by expression of light,—is, of all the three primitive colours, that which is most distinctive. Yellow is of the nature of simple light; blue connected with simple shade; but red is an entirely abstract colour. It is red to which the colour-blind are blind, as if to show us that it was not necessary merely for the service or comfort of man, but that there was a special gift or teaching in this colour. Observe, farther, that it is this colour which the sunbeams take in passing through the *earth's atmosphere*. The rose of dawn and sunset is the hue of the rays passing close over the earth. It is also concentrated in the blood of man.[80]

Already Ruskin is beginning to give the scarlet archetypal depth, in which perhaps we see faintly Max Müller's rosy dawn, but he has only begun. To expand upon this idea of a "special gift or teaching" in the red, he takes up the Judeo-Christian connotation of the scarlet: "Chiefly the scarlet, used with the hyssop, in the Levitical law, is the great sanctifying element of visible beauty, inseparably connected with *purity* and *life*."[81] And, digressing into Christian typology of color generally, he derives it from his "sun of righteousness."

And as the sunlight, undivided, is the type of the wisdom and righteousness of God, so divided, and softened into colour by means of the firmamental ministry, fitted to every need of man, as to every delight, and becoming one chief source of human beauty, by being made part of the flesh of man;—thus divided, the sunlight is the type of the wisdom of God, becoming sanctification and *redemption*. Various in work—various in beauty—various in power.[82]

And, gathering meanings broadly in the same vein, he connects color with love, bloom, and death: "Colour is, therefore, in brief terms, the type of love. Hence it is especially connected with the blossoming of the earth; and again, with its fruits; also, with the spring and fall of the leaf, and with the morning and evening of the day, in order to show the waiting of love about the birth and death of man."[83]

Having understood this much of Turner's victory in color and of the symbolic meaning of color, especially of scarlet, the reader is now ready to receive the myth that was Turner's subject in his *Apollo and Python*: "And now, I think, we may understand, even far away in the Greek mind, the meaning of that Contest of Apollo with the Python. It was a far greater contest than that of Hercules with Ladon. Fraud and avarice might be overcome *by frankness and force*; but this Python was a darker enemy, and could not be subdued but by a greater god."[84] I have italicized the "frankness and force" to call attention to the Ruskinian mythologizing in these sentences. This is, of course, the Greek myth, but also and at once it is the Ruskinian "myth" of Turner's progress as a colorist. "Frankness and force" means at once Hercules as "honest labour" and Turner's frank representation of pessimism by visible gloom; in the same way, the "greater god" signifies Apollo, but by the myth–making pun it refers also to Turner's later capacity to represent man's heroic acceptance of his fate by the color of Apolline combat, "the scarlet shade."

Though Apollo emerged victorious from this great struggle, it was not, as Ruskin writes, a "conquest slightly esteemed by the victor deity. He took his great name from it thenceforth—his prophetic and sacred name—the Pythian."[85] Now had Ruskin at this time looked into Karl Otfried Müller's *The Dorians* (there is reason to believe he had read it sometime prior to 1865),[86] he would have found there these among other facts relating to "the Doric worship of Apollo" (Ruskin's phrase of 1869). First, in connection with what has just been said about Ruskin's idea of Apollo's own respect for that combat, we note that K. O. Müller had written, "The battle with the Python being finished, Apollo himself breaks the laurel, to weave a crown of victory. Here too he was said first to have sung the paean, as a strain of triumph." We notice especially that to memorialize his victory Apollo weaves for himself a crown of wild laurel, such a crown as Ruskin took for the symbol of his "religion of Humanity."[87] Then on the meaning of the Python, K. O. Müller had observed:

> The serpent Python is represented as the guardian of the ancient oracle of the Earth, and a son of the Earth itself, sprung from the warm clay that remained after the general deluge, and dwelling in a dark defile near a fountain, which was said to be supplied from the Styx. The serpent, as usual, represents an earthly being, by which is personified the rough shapeless offspring of nature.[88]

Turning to Ruskin we note that Python has become rather a Greco-Christian worm; the interpretation is more etymological.

> Consider the meaning of its name, "THE CORRUPTER." That Hesperid dragon was a treasure-guardian. This is a treasure-destroyer,—where moth and rust doth corrupt—the worm of eternal decay.
>
> Apollo's contest with him is *the strife of purity with pollution*; of life with forgetfulness; of love, with the grave.
>
> I believe this great battle stood, in the Greek mind, for the type of the struggle of youth and manhood with deadly sin—venomous, infectious, irrecoverable sin.[89]

Some of this conception is plain in the Greek epithets that signify the

beneficence of Apollo. K. O. Müller had written, concerning the
different titles of Apollo, that "he was called the Healer at Elis, the
Assister at Phigaleia, the Defender, the Averter of Evil at Athens, and in
many oracles."[90] He also calls attention to the description of the Paean
in Homer, further noticing that the "name clearly betokens a healing
deity, and though the poet indeed speaks of him as a separate individual,
and the physician of Olympus, yet this division appears to have been
merely poetical, without any reference to actual worship."[91] However,
the Homeric epithet was more useful to Ruskin than the historical facts
of worship; and the spell it cast upon him is evident in his description of
Apollo's power:

> In virtue of his victory over this corruption, Apollo becomes
> thenceforward the guide; the witness; the purifying and helpful God [*sic*].
> The gods help waywardly, whom they choose. But Apollo helps always:
> he is by name, not only Pythian, the conqueror of death; but Paean—the
> healer of the people.[92]

Finally, there was an aspect of this legend that Ruskin could not have
found in Homer but that would be particularly helpful to him in
mythologizing about Turner and the Pythian color. This is what one
finds in *The Dorians*: "Although the destruction of the Python is
characterized as a triumph of the higher and divine power of the deity,
yet the victorious god was considered as polluted by the blood of the
monster, and obliged to undergo a series of afflictions and woes.[93]
Turner, we are told, fully understood this dénouement of the myth and
portrays it with "fearful distinctness." This "dragon of decay" has not
the adamantine armor of the Mammon dragon; yet he has his own kind
of permanence: "Wounded, he bursts asunder in the midst, and melts to
pieces, rather than dies, vomiting smoke—a smaller serpent-worm rising out of his blood."[94]

In discussing at length Turner's *Ulysses* in the *Notes* of 1856, Ruskin,
as we noticed, saw the mythic episode as a "type" of the painter's own
experience. Now Apollo the solar purifier, who receives somehow a taint
from the blood of his great enemy who continues to afflict him, becomes
Turner and to some extent Ruskin himself: "Alas, for Turner! This
smaller serpent-worm, it seemed, he could not conceive to be slain. In the
midst of all the power and beauty of nature, he still saw this death-worm
writhing among the weeds."[95] To show this Ruskin invokes three works
of Turner's, *The Bay of Baiae*, *The Golden Bough*, and *The Prayer of
Chryses*, all connected with the help of Apollo yet tinged with sadness.

> You may see it in the foreground of the Bay of Baiae, which has also in it
> the story of Apollo and the Sibyl; Apollo giving love; but not youth, nor

immortality: you may see it again in the foreground of the Lake Avernus—
The Hades Lake—which Turner surrounds with delicatest beauty, the
fates dancing in circle; but in front, is the serpent beneath the thistle and
the wild thorn. The same Sibyl, Deiphobe, holding the golden bough. I
cannot get at the meaning of this legend of the bough; but it was, assured-
ly, still connected, in Turner's mind, with that help from Apollo. He
indicated the strength of his feeling at the time when he painted the
Python contest, by the drawing exhibited the same year, of The Prayer of
Chryses. There the priest is on the beach alone, the sun setting. He prays to
it as it descends; flakes of its sheeted light are borne to him by the
melancholy waves, and cast away with sighs upon the sand.[96]

Ruskin promises to show later how this sadness became persistent in
Turner and gradually overcame him. For the moment we are to
remember that he expressed the Python's contagion both in his subjects
and his color, the scarlet shadow. The reason, Ruskin declares, was that
"he was without hope," alluding perhaps to Turner's poems entitled
The Fallacies of Hope. Therefore, Aeglé's mythic brightness was
shadowed, impure to him, "True daughter of Night, Hesperid Aeglé
was to him; coming between Censure, and Sorrow—and the
Destinies."

Having derived his theme from Turner's mythic subject, Ruskin now
enters upon a conclusive definition of the painter's work: "let not the
real nature of it be misunderstood any more."

He is distinctively, as he rises into his own peculiar strength, separating
himself from all men who had painted forms of the physical world
before,—the painter of the loveliness of nature, with the worm at its root:
Rose and *cankerworm*,—both with his utmost strength; the one *never*
separate from the other.[97]

The rose, then, with its infecting worm is the controlling archetype in
the painter's work, Ruskin declares—as if alluding to Blake's "The Sick
Rose" and predicting a central theme in his own later life. He will take
up these two interinvolved aspects, rose and worm, separately starting
with the rose. He would have preferred to look last at the rose, but, he
says, mythologizing, "that is not the way Atropos will have it, and there
is no pleading with her."[98]

The Turnerian rose is simply the vision he gave "of the loveliness and
kindness of Nature, as distinguished from all visions of her ever received
by other men." The Greeks had distrusted her; the Venetians had dreaded her, and the Flemings had despised her; but Turner had declared the
full beauty of nature, with the help of Apollo. But what was the public
response? Neglect, spiritually of his redemptive vision, physically of his
canvases.

They cried out for Python, and Python came; came literally as well as spiritually; all the perfectest beauty and conquest which Turner wrought is already withered. The cankerworm stood at his right hand, and of all his richest, most precious work, there remains only the shadow. Yet that shadow is more than other men's sunlight; it is the scarlet shade, shade of the Rose. Wrecked, and faded, and defiled, his work still, in what remains of it, or may remain, is the loveliest ever yet done by man, in imagery of the physical world.[99]

Ruskin breaks now into a deep digression, foreshadowing the next phase of his work, in which he appropriates to himself the vision of the worm, though the rose is still his topic. He can no longer speak joyfully about beautiful things with any feeling of being understood, because it is apparent that no one any longer cares for them. The evidence is everywhere about him: "Wherever I look or travel in England or abroad, I see that men, wherever they can reach, destroy all beauty."[100] He would like to take up at this point the proper effect of the beauty of art upon the mind, but the question is so entangled with the problem of the "enervating influence of all luxury" that he now finds himself with "many inquiries to make, many difficult passages of history to examine" before he can determine what hope there is for any labor in the cause of art. *Modern Painters* was written "to show that Turner is the greatest landscape painter who ever lived; and this it has sufficiently accomplished."[101] But the "final use" of this accomplishment remains in doubt.

What he does know at this point is that the world has endured three forms of asceticism: religious, military, and monetary; the last "consisting in the refusal of pleasure and knowledge for the sake of money; seen in the present days of London and Manchester." He knows that all these forms of asceticism are against life; "this is certain—that all men exclusively occupied either in spiritual reverie, mechanical destruction, or mechanical productiveness, fall below the proper standard of their race, and enter into a lower form of being; and that the true perfection of the race, and, therefore, its power and happiness, are only to be attained by a life which is neither speculative nor productive; but essentially contemplative and protective."[102]

In this attack on the modes of asceticism we see the essential tenets of Ruskin's "religion of Humanity" once again and are reminded of its connection with Apollo through the symbol of the wild olive crown. He will reject all paradisaical dreaming, monastic, military or monetary, in favor of the protective enjoyment of the natural lived world. Men must be taught "not how 'to better themselves,' but how to 'satisfy themselves.' ''[103] Such teaching will only be possible, however, after we have studied the art of all arts most in need of present study: the humble life.

> Humble life,—that is to say, proposing to itself no future exaltation, but only a sweet continuance; not excluding the idea of foresight, but wholly of fore sorrow, and taking no troublous thought for coming days; so, also, not excluding the idea of providence, or provision, but wholly of accumulation;—the life of domestic affection and domestic peace, full of sensitiveness to all elements of costless and kind of pleasure;—therefore, chiefly to the loveliness of the natural world.[104]

This educative bond between the humble life and the loveliness of nature is the connection between this digression and the Turnerian rose. His rose, in a sense, symbolizes the natural paradise of the "religion of Humanity," as Dante's white rose symbolizes the paradise of his spiritual vision. In this connection Ruskin concludes his digression on the rose with what is, for him, the ultimate social question: "What is indeed the noblest tone and reach of life for men; and how can the possibility of it be extended to the greatest numbers?"[105] So far, then, is he carried by the significance of the Turnerian rose.

"Last, of the Worm." In the chapter "The Two Boyhoods," comparing the formative world of Turner and Giorgione, he has already indicated that Turner's essential subjects would be the labor, the sorrow, and the death of men. Now, with the distinctive color of his Apolline victory in mind, he can clarify the main symbols of that tragic vision. They are, simply, "ruin, and twilight."

> What was the distinctive effect of light which he introduced, such as no man had painted before? Brightness, indeed, he gave, as we have seen, because it was true and right; but in this he only perfected what other had attempted. His own favourite light is not Aeglé, but Hesperid Aeglé. Fading of the last rays of sunset. Faint breathing of the sorrow of night.
>
> And fading sunset, note also, on ruin. . . . None of the great early painters draw ruins, except compulsorily. The shattered buildings introduced by them are shattered artifically, like models. There is no real sense of decay; whereas Turner only momentarily dwells on anything else than ruin.[106]

This shadow of fatality that hangs over human pursuits, symbolized by twilight and ruin, is the "dark clue" in his work, the "Thread of Atropos" in it. His imagination dwelt particularly on the triumph of the worm over the great cities of Carthage, Rome, and Venice: "Carthage in connection especially with the thoughts and study which led to the painting of the Hesperides' Garden, showing the death which attends the vain pursuit of wealth; Rome showing the death which attends the vain pursuit of power; Venice, the death which attends the vain pursuit of beauty."[107]

These thoughts remind Ruskin of the worm at work on the canvasses on which Turner recorded the twilight of Venice, for these works are but "wrecks of all they were once—twilights of twilight."[108] Similarly, returning to the old comparison, he thinks of the worm's work with Giorgione's frescoes. Their pure brightness is the Venetian counterpart of Turner's rose shadow; but he recalls this sadly, having seen, ten years before, "the last traces of the greatest works of Giorgione yet glowing like a scarlet cloud, on the Fondaco de' Tedeschi."[109] However, though Venice and her art may fade, the light won by her art is ongoing like the voice of Deiphobe the Sibyl, beloved by Apollo. And so Ruskin, in his best mythographic style, ends the chapter with a Hesperidian vision of his own.

> And though that scarlet cloud . . . may, indeed, melt away into paleness of night, and Venice herself waste from her islands as a wreath of wind-driven foam fades from their weedy beach;—that which she won of faithful light and truth shall never pass away. Deiphobe of the sea,—The Sun God measures her immortality to her by its sand. Flushed, above the Avernus of the Adrian lake, her spirit is still holding the golden bough; from the lips of the Sea Sibyl men shall learn for ages yet to come what is most noble and most fair; and, far away, as the whisper in the coils of the shell, withdrawn through the deep hearts of nations, shall sound for ever the enchanted voice of Venice.[110]

5

After such deeply allusive titles as "The Nereid's Guard" and "The Hesperid Aeglé," the title of the last chapter of *Modern Painters,* as if with a promise of relief, is "Peace." Yet I find little of peace in the chapter. Certainly the recently "unconverted" Ruskin, though he had made his peace here with the problem of Turner's greatness, did not close the work in a peaceful state of mind with respect to the visions of the two preceding chapters, the century's worship of the Mammon dragon and the prevalence of ruin in the habitations of those who preferred Python to Apollo. This is evident from the thrust of the digressions in the chapters themselves. There was no question of concluding the work, he observed; there was only the necessity of ending it, since it had led him into "fields of infinite inquiry."[111] So the chapter is stylistically evasive and has more in it of apocalyptic peroration than of sweet benediction. It suggests more the pressure in his mind of darker issues than the calm of achieved truths. Space here permits us only a glance at some of its themes.

The lesson of Turner's life, we are told, is "that all the power of it came of its mercy and sincerity; all the failure of it, from its want of faith."[112] From the sincerity came the rejection of the infidelity that passes for faith in this time of its decline. If one looks, he argues, at the forms and images of faith now valued in England, it will be clear that they are distinguished historically by their radical insincerity. "No nation ever before declared boldly, by print and word of mouth, that its religion was good for show, but 'would not work.' "[113] The English say, "There *is* a Supreme Ruler, no question of it, only He cannot rule." Now, what this singularly perverse form of infidelity reveals is "a precisely *equal unbelief in man*."[114] (Therefore, as we have seen, Ruskin will ground his faith of the middle years in a "religion of Humanity.") The result of this lack of belief in man is the failure to perceive and encourage human genius, to understand the ways of getting a man's proper work from him. We can only imagine what a majestic series of poems Turner might have given us had he received help and not disdain. Yet the sense of alienation he felt is written in the misty obscurities and disordered impressions of his final works. "But few of us yet know how true an image those darkening wrecks of radiance give to the shadow which gained sway at last over his once pure and noble soul." And Turner was not alone in the hopelessness of neglect. "So far as in it lay, this century has caused every one of its great men, whose hearts were kindest, and whose spirits most perceptive of the work of God, to die without hope:— Scott, Keats, Byron, Shelley, Turner."[115] But, though "careful England, in her pure priestly dress" passed these men by on the other side, Ruskin affirms that he has no fear for *them*, "there being one Priest who never passes by," He "Who giveth peace."[116]

"Who *giveth* peace?" Ruskin's emphasis means that this peace is only given to us. We have made many false peace for ourselves, "but the falsest is in that marvelous thought that we, of all generations of the earth, only know the right; and that to us at last,— to us alone,—all the scheme of God, about the salvation of men, has been shown."[117] Again he touches on our lack of faith in humanity, now from a religious rather than artistic perspective. This falsest peace we have made for ourselves enables us merely to reject the faiths by which other nations have lived: "We only have no idolatries—ours are the seeing eyes." He looks for a better peace than this, "though I hear it said of me that I am hopeless."[118] He is not hopeless, though his hope is "dark-veiled." He looks for a peace that will be given to us here, a kingdom that will *come* to humanity.

The chapter, and with it the whole of Ruskin's great work, ends in an involved and prophetic passage, full of Scriptural echoes, but turning on the humanistic meaning of the expressions "light of the world" and "Thy kingdom come." With both tenets his reading is that the light and the kingdom refer to a peace that is distinctly to come, to be given, to us *here*, if we will receive it. Of this kingdom,

> I hear them speak continually of going to it, rather than of its coming to them; which, again, is strange, for in that prayer which they had straight from the lips of the Light of the world, and which He apparently thought sufficient prayer for them, there is not anything about going to another world; only something of another government coming into this; or rather, not another, but the only government,—that government which will constitute it a world indeed. New heavens and new earth."[119]

Then a passage of apocalyptic mythography that catches up some of the storm myths of the volume and points forward obscurely to *The Queen of the Air* and *The Storm Cloud of the Nineteenth Century.*

> Kindreds of the earth, or tribes of it! The "earth-begotten," the Chaos children—children of this present world, with its desolate seas and its Medusa clouds: the Dragon children, merciless: They who dealt as clouds without water: serpent clouds, by whose sight men were turned into stone;—the time must surely come for their wailing.[120]

The kingdom is not for us to bring but to receive. It is come in part already; the question is whether or not we can turn our heads from the worship of the Mammon dragon and receive it. "But it is still at our choice; the simoom-dragon may still be served if we will, in the fiery desert, or else God walking in the garden, at cool of day."[121]

We have noted that in this final chapter of *Modern Painters* Ruskin is able, from the standpoint of his deepening respect for Greek myth, to condemn not only the hypocrisy but the narrowness of English religion. The falsest peace we have made for ourselves, he declares, is our conviction that to us alone of all peoples and times has the whole scheme of salvation been revealed. This far by 1860 he had progressed beyond the Evangelical dogmatism of the first two volumes into the syncretic humanism of his "religion of Humanity." The preface to the new edition of 1873 reveals the extent to which he was embarrassed by the "narrow enthusiasm" of the first two volumes yet convinced of the general soundness of the work's moral aesthetic.

In 1888, for the republication of *Modern Painters*, he wrote a brief epilogue in which he asserts, curiously, that while the whole book is religious (we could say "mythic") in the large sense, it need not be associated with the doctrines of any particular sect, or even with Christianity. "For," he writes, "the divisions of religious tenet and school to which I attached mistaken importance in my youth, do not in the least affect the vital teaching and purpose of this book: the claim, namely, of the Personal relation of God to man as the source of all human, as distinguished from brutal, virtue and art." This simple assertion of the "Personal character of God," he continues, "must be cautiously and clearly distinguished by every reader who wishes to understand either *Modern Painters* or any of my more cautiously written subsequent books, from the statement of any Christian doctrine, as commonly accepted." He goes on to enumerate those aspects of Christian doctrine that are not present in the work: "Nothing is here said of any tradition of Fall, or of any scheme of Redemption; nothing of Eternal Punishment, nothing of Immortal Life. It is assumed only that man can love and obey a living Spirit; and can be happy in the presence and guidance of a Personal Deity, otherwise than a mollusc, a beetle, or a baboon."[122]

This emphasis on the "Personal character of God" represents the mystical turn of Ruskin's religious development after the mid seventies more than it does the mythology of *Modern Painters*. Similarly, though Ruskin insists, from the standpoint of his broader religious humanism, that the Christian schemes of Fall, Redemption, and Eternal Life are not present in the work as *doctrine*, they are clearly part of its diction and its plot. Clearly, as we have seen, Turner has in the work a redemptive role, and Ruskin is his prophet. In *Modern Painters*, Turner comes to redeem the fallen world of post-Reformation art with his naturalism, his mystery, and his direct solar light. He depicts and then dispels, in Ruskin's mythic reading of his development, the sulphurous exhalations of the Hesperides' dragon, the symbol of fatal greed, with his Apolline light, the solemn sunset light that Ruskin sees as present and symbolized mythically in the painter's *Apollo and Python*. But his redemptive light is despised and rejected; he suffers the "isolation of a great spirit . . . disconsolate,"[123] though his luminous color can convey the light of the natural world like that of no other painter. Finally, because Turner's vision *is* of the lived world in its constancy of ruin and decay, he is, like Apollo, tainted by the greater worm, Python, the corrupter. He cannot rise to the pure paradisal light of Giorgione; so his characteristic color remains the "scarlet shadow" that fuses the truths of the rose and of the worm as they are fused in human blood.

CHAPTER 11

Life Against Wealth

Ruskin's long critical labor to disclose the meaning, significance, and value of Turner's art had ended, as he said, without conclusion. The work that had been with him for seventeen years had branched, in its crown, into realms of "infinite inquiry." Little wonder. He had found it necessary to express the "earth," the "world," and the "strife" between them, to borrow Heidegger's terms, that Turner's art had mediated into the light of truth. He had attempted to show literally how this mysterious "earth" sets itself forth, from pebble to peak, from tree twig to thunderhead. Within his dominant idealism he was always aware of the impenetrable stuff of "earth" that juts into the intentional horizon, the "world," of the landscapist's art; this material limitation, present in both subject and medium, he knew the artist must struggle with heroically if there is to be truth in his work. So he had to express his experience of what earth set forth against his historical understanding of what the phases or worlds of landscape art had been morally capable of integrating. That is, in terms closer to his own, he had to convey not only how the aspects of nature appear and how far they had been painted, but also how clearly they had spoken to the painter's soul as cyphers of Being. Further, he had to give his history of the struggle of nature and landscape, earth and world, a mythic plot in order to symbolize Turner's heroic role within that history. Just as, in Ruskin's reading, Turner had been Apolline light against the chthonic monster, Python; so also, in the history of art, there had been Purist innocence, Raphaelesque fall, and Turnerian redemption. Yet he had also to make clear that this redemption of painting meant no release from the continuing struggle with earth; Python's taint and Turner's insistent depiction of "ruin" and "twilight" represented those boundaries, in earth and sky, where cultural man meets his existential self.

He had also to *be* Turner. "Only another Turner could apprehend Turner," he wrote.[1] Though Ruskin's criticism has its analytic mode, his distinctive stylistic strategy is participation. Ruskin's Turner becomes a dramatized character in a kind of critical fiction in which the critic narrates directly the presumed emotions of the painter as he paints.

From the standpoint of modern critical empiricism this is no criticism at all but mere impressionism or intuitionism, though his method has something in common with our criticisms of consciousness or identification. Possibly it is more comfortable to regard *Modern Painters* as a mode of autobiographical fiction that narrates the artistic progress of a subjectivity imagined to be Turner's in a world threatened by various lethal modes of thought such as classicism, scientism, asceticism, which he concentrated symbolically into those two apocalyptic dragons of the final chapters, Ladon and Python.

Such a view might be compatible with the deep disquiet of that final chapter, "Peace." Turner was without hope, Ruskin tells us, and without faith; he never saw the rose without perceiving the worm at its root. Could the "I" of *Modern Painters* participate so sympathetically in that awareness without sharing it? Somewhere between the second and the fifth volumes *Modern Painters* becomes, to use Georg Lukács's famous characterization of the novel, "the epic of a world that has been abandoned by God."[2] At least it has been abandoned by the God of the second volume. Aspects of nature are no longer seen types of divine care. Humanity is left on the darkling Greek plain of the heroic present in the withdrawing light of the Hesperid Aeglé, "true daughter of Night," to decide whether time will bring the kingdom of the Lord or of Ladon. "I am not hopeless," Ruskin protests, "though my hope may be as Veronese's: the dark-veiled."[3] But, against the disquieting tone, this attempt to disclaim the Turnerian despair protests too much.

A final point should be made about these last chapters of *Modern Painters* while we are thinking of them as a kind of critical fiction. They give the feeling of strain or excess. They participate in the fading Hesperidian brilliance in giving one the sense that Ruskin has gone as far as he can now go in this vein of apocalyptic eloquence. He is orchestrating Greek, Biblical, Turnerian, and personal mythology in a prose that is melancholy and richly allusive, to be sure. And there is a foretaste of his central economic thesis in his exposition of the law of help and the assumption of Mammon, yet one has also the feeling that Ruskin's medium has about outrun its message here. Without Turner for a vehicle there is no way in which this level of utterance can be sustained unless a new message, a new system, builds up in Ruskin's mind. Indeed, we have noticed that he confesses within the volume to deep doubts about its utility. Therefore, in the next decade we will see him working out a new message in a new and (for a time) appropriately subdued prose. The new message and its style evolve partly out of his bywork, which consisted mainly of popular lectures on the social functions of art, during the years between the last two volumes of *Modern Painters*. It is necessary to look briefly at the main themes of this secondary or more occasional work before turning to the major writings of the next decade.

1

Ruskin's essential socioeconomic message for the sixties is largely developed through his elaboration of four primary themes in the lesser works of the fifties. All of these themes revolve around his attempts to define the organic without losing it in materialism and at the same time show how its vital laws apply at once to the moral, social, and artistic spheres. What he intuits but cannot say directly at this point is that these formative principles he perceives as common to nature, art, and ethics must be grounded in some believed myth of a "forming power," as he will later call it, or else the whole organic scheme of existence is simply a vast "intentional fallacy." Hence the necessity for the "Spiritual Invention" in landscape discussed in volume 5 of *Modern Painters*. At this point, however, he appears to be attempting to make the organic itself into a kind of myth that will have greater critical utility than the rigid natural theology of volume 2 of *Modern Painters* with its "types" of divine attributes. This mythologizing of the organic is, like his deepening interest in Greek belief, an attempt to fill the spiritual vacuum left by the gradual failure of his Evangelical faith.

The secondary works of this period—the public lectures on art, design, and manufacturing; the *Times* letters on Pre-Raphaelitism; the reviews of current exhibits at the academy; the catalogues of Turner's work; the introduction to Giotto's work at Padua; the letters on the Oxford Museum; the manuals of drawing and perspective—represent efforts so diverse and yet particular that it would be impossible to gather them up in a brief account here and at the same time glance through them toward the sixties. It must simply be remarked, for the reader's own testing, that stylistically, especially in the lectures he delivered in the manufacturing towns, we see Ruskin working in a more lucid, aphoristic, and synoptic prose, a style that is less pictorial and allusive and more suited to platform impact; thematically he is increasingly engaged with social concerns and, more explicitly, with the development of the following four themes.

While bearing witness to the gradual triumph in the Academy of the Pre-Raphaelite principles he has advocated, he becomes aware that these principles (naturalism), mechanically applied, lead to a kind of materialism in art in which nature becomes dead and demythologized.

The record of this Pre-Raphaelite victory, and of his partial disillusionment with it, is in his *Academy Notes*, the selective reviews of paintings he prepared for the annual exhibitions of 1855 through 1859 and for 1875. This experience with naturalism in painting is analogous to his disillusionment with the spiritless and superficial application of Gothic design in contemporary architecture, attempts to use Gothic as if it were a code of conventions rather than a coherent system of organic forms rooted in certain conditions of labor and ultimately in myth. These are distinctions Ruskin attempts to clarify, in his two letters to Acland (1858, 1859) on the Gothic design of the Oxford Museum.

In the case of Pre-Raphaelitism, Ruskin had been a contributing influence in the formation of the school through his advocacy of direct painting from nature ("having one thought but to penetrate *her meaning*; rejecting nothing, selecting nothing, scorning nothing")[4] in *Modern Painters*, volume 1, and his praise of medieval purist painting in *Modern Painters*, volume 2. He had expounded their principles in his pamphlet *Pre-Raphaelitism* (1851), where he argued that Turner and the Pre-Raphaelites shared an "intense sense of *fact*."[5] He defended them in four letters to the *Times* (1851, 1854), helping to turn the critical tide in their favor. In his letter of 5 May 1854, which lauded and interpreted Holman Hunt's *The Light of the World*, a theme close to his own archetypal interests, he felt it necessary to distinguish between true and false Pre-Raphaelite work: "The true work represents all objects exactly as they would appear in nature in the position and at the distances which the arrangement of the picture supposes. The false work represents them with all their details, as if seen through a microscope."[6] That is, true Pre-Raphaelite work contains the element of mystery; it gives the natural details yet suggests more than one can see.

In the Edinburgh *Lectures on Architecture and Painting* (1853) he schematized the development of naturalism in European art and placed Pre-Raphaelitism in that tradition. In his overview, there were four phases of assault on conventionalism in the representation of nature. First, there were the Giottesque, Leonardesque, and the Titianesque rebellions; these were followed by a relapse into the conventional in classical pastoralism, but the naturalistic tradition was redeemed by Turner and passed to the Pre-Raphaelites. These painters attacked conventionalism by going back to the religious innocence of the painters before Raphael and to nature to paint directly from her with innocent eyes. Sincerity, Ruskin argues, is the essence of their work; it is a return to *honest*, not archaic art.

The same general theme is taken up in the introduction to *Giotto and*

His Works in Padua (1853, 1854, 1860), where Ruskin places Giotto in the tradition of the struggle against conventionalism as the originator of that struggle. Like his master, Cimabue, Giotto began with a healthy respect for the conventions of his Byzantine models, but he innovated through the introduction "A. of gayer or lighter colors; B. of broader masses; and C. of more careful imitation of nature than existed in the works of his predecessors."[7] He was "a daring naturalist, in defiance of tradition, idealism, and formalism." The movement he began, "the Giottesque movement in the fourteenth, and the Pre-Raphaelite movement in the nineteenth centuries, are precisely similar in bearing and meaning: both being the protests of *vitality* against *mortality*, of spirit against the letter, and of truth against tradition."[8]

But in the *Academy Notes* there is a detectable crisis in this tradition as the naturalism that had been pitted against convention was itself becoming a convention. The thematic thread of these *Notes* is the triumph (at least in the pictures chosen for review) of Pre-Raphaelitism over the "old art of trick and tradition." Consequently, by 1856 Ruskin can announce that the gallery patron "will find that he can no longer distinguish the Pre-Raphaelite works as a separate class, but that between them and the comparatively few pictures remaining quite of the old school, there is a perfectly unbroken gradation, formed by the works of painters in various stages of progress, struggling forward out of their conventionalism to the Pre-Raphaelite standard." This means simply, he continues, "that the battle is completely and confessedly won by the latter party; that animosity has changed to emulation, astonishment into sympathy, and that a true and consistent school of art is at last established in the Royal Academy of England."[9]

Yet this full bloom of naturalism was bound to fade. The triumph of the "real" in art can never be permanent, because its "reality" is an interpretation of what is, translated into conventions which are not static but historical. Furthermore, such syntheses of "earth" and "world" cannot be standardized for any great artist but must be his unique resolution of the struggle of those forces in his work. More particularly, great landscape is, for Ruskin, what nature says to a great soul; ultimately it is the expression of an interior by means of an exterior. Great landscape painting reflects, not mere objectivity, but, within and controlling that, the synthesizing and visionary powers of a great imagination. As such it invokes the holy. Ruskin does not say this much here, but he does explain that even the standardization of Pre-Raphaelite principles will not guarantee superior work from every painter who applies them. "Distinction, if it is justly won, can of course be won only by superior intellect; a change in the methods or objects of a school does not raise the capacities of the scholars to one level, nor render it more possible than it has been hitherto to be illustrious in large companies."[10] Ruskin forgets that the methods in question were not, for him, those of a school, but of *the* school, of nature herself.

Painters, he continues in the *Notes* of 1857, fall into three classes: "first, the large class who are more or less affected or false in all their work, and whose productions, however dexterous, are of no value whatever; secondly the literally true painters, who copy with various feeling, but unanimously honest purpose, the actualities of Nature, but can only paint them as they see them, without selection or arrangement; whose works are therefore of a moderate but sterling value, varying according to the interest of the subject; lastly, the inventive painters, who are not only true in all they do, but compose and relieve the truths they paint, so as to give each the utmost possible value; [they are the] great Imaginative group of Masters."[11] Ruskin says that this division is "implied a hundred times" in his work, but that mysterious means by which the greatest masters "relieve the truths they paint" suggests a standard beyond the aesthetic of truth to nature. The fact is that his aesthetic is being driven back from naturalism, which he is now beginning to see as a mode of nineteenth-century materialism, toward the more difficult concepts of organic composition and mythic invention.

This shift is obvious in the *Notes* for 1859. There, for instance, he sees in J. F. Brett's photographically naturalistic *Val d'Aosta* the dead end of the naturalist aesthetic. It is simply a minute but mythless work. "I never saw the mirror so held up to Nature; but it is Mirror's work, not Man's. This absence of sentiment is peculiarly indicated by the feeble anger of the sky. . . . There is no majesty in the clouds, nor any grand encumbency of them on the hills; they are but a dash of mist, gusty and disagreeable enough—in no otherwise to be dreaded; highly un-divine clouds—incognizant of Olympus."[12] The fate of Pre-Raphaelite naturalism that Ruskin implies here is that it has come to reflect the century's disbelief in either deity or humanity. Great art needs mythopoeic awe: "I do not say, observe, influence of 'religion,' but merely of a belief in some invisible power—god or goddess, fury or fate, saint or demon. Where such belief existed, however sunk or distorted, progressive art has been possible, otherwise impossible."[13] Even the art produced by warped belief is preferable to that which lacks all mystery: "The distortion of the belief, its contraction or its incoherence, contract or compress the resultant art; still the art is evermore of another and mightier race than the art of materialism."[14]

Another theme of these byworks of the later fifties is Ruskin's gradual refinement of his view of nature into a more versatile organic model, that is, into a model of order based on the mutual implication of infinitely varied parts in living form. We are speaking of minor works but of a major theme. In fact, the metaphorical transference of certain qualities of natural form into creative, moral, and social aspects of experience is the central thrust of Ruskin's teaching. His uses of myth and poetic apocalypse both serve this fundamental purpose. As he wrote in his first preface to *The Two Paths*, "the dependence of all noble design, in any kind, on the sculpture or painting of Organic Form" is the "vital law," the law "lying at the root of all I have ever tried to teach respecting architecture or any other art."[15] His letters on the Oxford Museum at this time reiterate the multifold dependence of the Gothic on the organic; his theoretical Gothic building would be nearly a visible myth of organic form that could be built only by an organic society, if it could be built at all. A difficulty, however, is that he did not formulate his organic model in an orderly philosophic way, as Coleridge did, for instance, in following Schlegel; it emerged here and there, explicitly and implicitly through the work of this period. We have already referred to it in connection with the chapters on vegetation in volume 5 of *Modern Painters*. Also, while Ruskin emphasizes the unity of the whole and its priority over the part, as do other organic theorists, he differs from them in his incorporation of liberty and infinity or mystery into his model. The organic, for Ruskin, is not simply a model of perfection, but of perfect imperfection. This may be because the organic entity he generally has in mind as an image is not the cell or the shell or the plant, but the tree, at least, or the whole of a natural scene on the verge of composing itself into landscape. Finally, the conjunction of unity, liberty, and mystery in Ruskin's organic model allows it to serve two valuable functions in his thought. It is antithetical to all forces of mechanism, formalism, or materialism. And it can be applied to society as well as to art. Much of this will be obvious if we look briefly at his manual of drawing, which is the chief presentation of his organicism in these secondary works. (*The Elements of Perspective* [1859], incidentally, is a technical exposition with little of any implicit meaning; it therefore has no literary interest, though it illustrates the diversity of Ruskin's mind.)

In *The Elements of Drawing* (1857) the student is confronted by successively higher levels of the nearly inimitable in nature, from the difficulties of representing the subtleties of gradated light on natural forms (a task at least partly within his grasp) through the problems posed by the intersensitivities of color, to the incredible gifts involved in composing a whole landscape. This last is presented as a harmony of harmonies that the student, left far behind, can merely admire. At the outset he is urged to recover his childlike *"innocence of the eye,"*[16] to surrender himself in a presuppositionless way to nature as she reveals herself. In this attitude he will come to see everything in nature as given in delicacies of gradation. Every visible form is an intricate organism of gradated light; even the single leaf has its own complex system of shadow. "No natural object exists which does not involve in some part or parts of it this inimitableness, this mystery of quantity, which needs peculiarity of handling and trick of touch to express it completely."[17]

From the problems of gradation the student is led onward to the problems of line; he learns that a great master's work is an organism of line in which no line is superfluous, and that all mere outline work is bad because true artists see masses, not edges, in nature. These problems of delicacy and unity in gradation and line are further multiplied when the painter attempts to capture a scene as opposed to an isolated form; the features of the scene will change constantly with the slanting of the light as he draws, thereby limiting the degree to which the whole can be imitated. However, in this task he is aided by learning to perceive higher laws of coherence—now seen as quasi-moral—in nature. He must learn to seize the "leading lines" of grace and vital truth in organic forms. "Try always, whenever you look at a form, to see the lines in it which have had power over its past fate and will have power over its futurity. Those are its *awful* lines; see that you seize on those, whatever else you miss."[18] At the higher level, within the natural scene as a whole, there are three primary laws which all good landscape drawing must express: "There is first, the organic unity; the law, whether of radiation, or parallelism, or concurrent action, which rules the masses of herbs and trees, of rocks, and clouds, and waves; secondly, the individual liberty of the members subjected to these laws of unity; and, lastly, the mystery under which the separate character of each is more or less concealed."[19]

Ruskin makes the point that these laws governing the "beautiful arrangement of visible things" are the same as hold for the moral and social spheres. A society without a "ruling principle, and associated by no common affection" would be a sorry thing, but a worse thing would be a society "of men so oppressed into assimilation as to have no more any individual hope or character." This is why "perpetual difference, play, and change of form are more essential to them than their being subdued by some great gathering law: the law is needful to them for their perfection and their power, but the difference is needful to them for their life."[20]

The student is now able to see that drawing is at root an ethical study, for "there is no moral vice, no moral virtue, which has not its *precise* prototype in the art of painting; so that you may at your will illustrate the moral habit by the art, or the art by the moral habit."[21] Take the "law of mystery," which means that "nothing is ever seen perfectly, but only by fragments, and under various conditions of obscurity." This law, Ruskin explains, makes the system complete as a metaphor of human nature: "We have, observe, first, Subordination; secondly, Individuality; lastly, and this is not the least essential character, Incomprehensibility; a perpetual lesson, in every serrated point and shining vein which escapes or deceives our sight among the forest leaves."[22]

Ruskin has initiated his student into the moral and social secrets of organic form, but his education in drawing and perception is by no means complete. To the already complex unities of gradation, line, and related forms in a scene, two other sets of variables are added, those of color and composition. Here the task recedes from the student's grasp. He may in time produce dutiful drawings in light and shade. "But to colour well requires your life,"[23] he warns. This is because the complexities of line and gradation already introduced are "multiplied almost to infinity by this great fact, that, while form is absolute . . . colour is wholly *relative*."[24] That is, it is a perfect model of organic unity, with every touch of color that goes into a work being altered by every other touch. This follows particularly from Ruskin's insistence on translucent, subtly gradated color instead of solid or "dead colour."

But color with all its interactive sensitivities is not the ultimate problem for the artist; that is composition. Here he must impose, according to certain laws, a unity upon all the other unities "so as to make *one* thing out of them."[25] Composition as the organism of organisms is "the type, in the arts of mankind, of the Providential government of the world."[26] It is the ultimate ethical and ideological statement of the world of the work. Every kind of mind, Ruskin insists, is sensitive to the act of composition. "It seems to be appointed in order to remind us, in all we do, of the great laws of Divine government and human polity, that composition in the arts should strongly affect every order of mind."[27] He proceeds to set forth for the student eight primary laws of composition and to suggest some of their moral analogues. "Radiation," for instance, "typically expresses that healthy human actions should spring radiantly (like rays) from some single heart-motive,"[28] preferably that at the root of life. The principle belongs ultimately to the solar archetype; ray comes straight from the "Sun Himself."[29] The work ends, with a kind of final orchestration of all these harmonies to which the student has been introduced, in moving analyses of Turner's *Lancaster Sands* and especially of his *Heysham*. In the latter, Ruskin evokes scene and a social order coherent with each other, a "wild, yet gentle, country life, monotonous as the succession of noiseless waves, patient and enduring as the rocks."[30] This kind of composition, with depths of consistency that can never be rendered by convention but only by a great synthesizing imagination, is for Ruskin an apocalypse of Being as the forming power.

Another primary theme in these shorter works of the late fifties, and the most forward looking of all, is Ruskin's attempt to apply the principles of his organicism to the social household. In the *Political Economy of Art*, two lectures delivered (significantly) at Manchester in 1857, he developed something in the direction of a unified socioeconomic theory in which to place the creation and use of art. He was evidently pleased with the work at the time. "Of all the books I have written," he wrote to a friend, "it's the only one I'm proud of."[31] And in the preface he prepared for its reissue in 1880 (as "*A Joy for Ever*" *and its Price in the Market*) he declared that "the exposition of these truths, to which I have given the chief energy of my life, will be found in the following pages first undertaken systematically and in logical sequence."[32]

The essential purpose of *The Political Economy of Art* is to outline a socioeconomic order in which art can be properly nurtured and shared: developed out of the whole community for the whole community. This would be a society in which the political economy of the society and the inherent economy of art are coherent, not at odds. Ruskin has two tasks then, to outline a social system as a whole and to show how art would be developed and distributed within it. He does not, of course, see his social scheme as a utopian formulation; he is merely setting forth the laws that must operate, as he sees it, in any coherent social order; naturally they reflect the principles of form (unity, liberty, and mystery) declared that year in *The Elements of Drawing*, because these laws are common to the social, as well as to the natural and aesthetic realms.

In his first preface to the lectures Ruskin takes the basic stance of his social theory by opposing the notion that the principles of political economy are the preserve of professional theoreticians. Political economy means simply "citizen's economy" and therefore household economy. The necessary first principles of it, apparently, are organic and will reveal themselves to any receptive mind, much as will the "leading lines" of natural form disclose themselves to any painter who gives himself to nature with an innocent eye. His criticism of academic economics parallels his assults on formalistic aesthetics. Both are essentially analytic and mechanistic, whereas his primary relation to experience is phenomenological and organicist.

The first lecture, with a touch of irony directed at his Manchester audience, is entitled "The Discovery and Application of Art." It is concerned ostensibly with art, but Ruskin's essential interest is in the social system that will generate it. His model of the state is the familial household, particularly the farm, because the state's main function is to produce sustenance. It is an organic complex directed by a paternal authority (who reflects the will of the mythic Father) and unified by bonds of brotherhood. "The real type of well-organized nation must be presented, not by a farm cultivated by servants who wrought for hire, and might be turned away if they refused to labour, but by a farm in which the master was a father, and in which all the servants were sons," a farm regulated, moreover, not by "the order of expediency, but the bonds of affection and responsibilities of relationship."[33] Ruskin's nascent system here is organic because it is familial, and it is mythic in its biblical implications; as a model it is opposed to the dehumanized, demythologized Manchester system, the market mechanism of supply and demand energized by divisive competition. Here also, at the level of a social scheme, we can see an equivalent of that fusion of unity and liberty that Ruskin perceived in the arrangement of natural forms. He imagines free brothers linked by life, not wealth. In his "Addenda" to the published lectures he used another metaphor for what could be the "Law of Help" in *Modern Painters*, volume 5: "The whole nation is in fact bound together, as men are by ropes on a glacier."[34] Still later, in *The Ethics of the Dust*, he will use molecules in a crystal to make the same point.

Within this organic system economics consists primarily in the wise management of labor. Primary wealth consists in the vital energy and creative capacity of the laborer, his true life. Each person's labor properly directed, Ruskin argues, is sufficient to supply the necessities of his existence; there is enough vital energy in the system to sustain the health and happiness of all. Happiness involves the creative as well as the useful application of labor. But if this vital wealth is misused either in the overproduction of luxuries (things that do not sustain life) or in the unnecessary production of things that degrade the laborer (things that do not sustain his creative being) lethal, alienating forces are set in motion. Since it is the competitive drive to wealth (in the ordinary sense) that tends to disrupt the unity and liberty of the system, there is a constant conflict between vital wealth, creative productive life, and wealth in the lethal sense, the object of greed. Good "housewifery" (ultimately a feminine function?) in the state, as in the household, consists in keeping a proportionate balance between objects of utility and of splendor. But the controlling question will always concern sustenance: How much activity distributed in what way will be necessary to keep "this great farm of ours running"? The chief function of the paternal government of the social farm "is to discipline the masses" to the "toils of peace," to organize "soldiers of the ploughshare" as well as of the sword.[35]

The essence of Ruskin's familial-organic model of the state is its opposition to the alienating competitiveness that characterized the market mechanism, a model in which individuals were perceived as discrete, self-interested entities, and government held to be essentially irrelevant to the self-regulation of the mechanism. Hence Ruskin's need to deliver this attack on Manchester economics on its home ground and at its very heart. His is a government of total interference. "The notion of Discipline and Interference," he insists, "lies at the very root of all human progress or power; . . . the 'Let-alone' principle is, in all things which man has to do with, the principle of death. . . . It is only in the concession of some great principle of restraint and interference in national action that he can ever hope to find the secret of protection against national degradation."[36] His emphasis is equally upon paternal discipline and paternal help. He sums this up in one of the "Addenda": "Every so named soul of man claims from every other such soul, protection and education in childhood,—help or punishment in middle life,— reward or relief, if needed, in old age; all of these should be completely and unstintingly given; and they can only be given by the organization of such a system as I have described."[37]

The avowed purpose of Ruskin's lectures, however, was to deal with the economics of art; the social system is described, one would suppose, mainly to show how art would be generated and distributed in it. His announced topic in the first lecture, again, concerned the "Discovery and Application" of art and in the second lecture its "Accumulation and Distribution." But these are obviously not his most intense concerns here, and there is no need to follow him in detail in them. I have suggested that the system just sketched reflects the organic-ethical principles of unity and liberty in natural form he explained that year in the *Elements of Drawing*. But the function of the third principle, mystery, is not apparent until he takes up artistic labor. Presumably, the ordinary craftsman in his state would be properly encouraged by a social unity from which he derived a decent wage and by liberty to vary his designs.

But this would not produce art, though it might produce useful things and happy laborers. The appearance of artistic genius is a mystery; it cannot be educated into existence, only discovered by such state agencies as "trial schools" and fostered by the provision of materials standardized by the state and by models of art made available to all. The part of mystery or incomprehensibility in Ruskin's social organism is, as I interpret it, played by the vast inequities in creative capacity among men, the ever-receding outlines of imaginative vision, which the state can neither create nor alleviate. "No state of society, nor stage of knowledge, ever does away with the natural pre-eminence of one man over another," Ruskin notes in his "Addenda," "and it is that pre-eminence, and that only, which will give work high value in the market, or which ought to do so. . . . Noble art is nothing less than the expression of a great soul; and great souls are not common things."[38]

Expressions of such souls in works can and must be made a part of the enduring communal wealth; "the beauty," he would say, "which is indeed to be a joy for ever, must be a joy for all."[39] Works of the past must be preserved and made available to everyone; they cannot, however, be "restored." Because a work is organic, coherent in itself and with the hand, mind, and culture from which it emerged, no alien hand can ever hope to reproduce the precise complex of unity, liberty, and mystery that went into it. The work, Ruskin might have said, will reject restoration as a body rejects alien tissue.

The aim of Ruskin's ideal political economy will be the maintenance of life at the highest common level of health and joy, including in life the natural environment in which it is physically and spiritually rooted, and the forms of art in which it flowers. Years later, in *Fors Clavigera*, he will assert that any political economy that truly has become a science will supply the six material and immaterial necessities of life: "Pure Air, Water and Earth"; "Admiration, Hope, and Love."[40] It will be necessary, therefore, for his life-oriented economics to delineate and oppose, as impurities, the forms of wealth that are destructive to life. This aspect of his analysis had begun to appear in his discussion of deadly labor in "The Nature of Gothic." The analysis is furthered now in the addenda to *The Political Economy of Art* as Ruskin divides "property" into "that which produces life, and that which produces the objects of life" and then reclassifies all property into five kinds: (1) "Property necessary to life, but not producible by labour, and therefore belonging of right, in a due measure, to every human being as soon as he is born, and morally inalienable." (2) "Property necessary to life, but only producible by labour, and of which the possession is morally connected with labour." (3) "That which conduces to bodily pleasures and conveniences, without directly tending to sustain life; perhaps sometimes indirectly tending to destroy it." (4) "That which bestows intellectual or emotional pleasure, consisting of land set apart for purposes of delight more than for agriculture, of books, works of art, and objects of natural history." This fourth type of property, he continues, "is the only kind which a man can truly be said to 'possess.' " (5) "Representative property," consisting of documentary claims against things of real value.[41] We will return, as Ruskin does, to this theme of true and false wealth, but for the moment we must touch on another issue that engaged him at this time.

As Ruskin considers the social problem of teaching art and design, especially to industrial designers and craftsmen, he takes a position based on his idea of the intrinsic unity of the arts, and this is the last theme in the shorter works of the late fifties that must be mentioned before we move forward. Not only is art unified with organic form, and the work an organic composition within itself, but the arts are bonded to each other. There is really no such thing as a lower form of art, such as decorative art; all art is one; something either is or is not art. There is only one "complete and right way" of doing any given thing in art, though there may be a thousand wrong ways; similarly there is only one way of seeing things in art, "and that is seeing the whole of them, without any choice or more intense perception of one point than another."[42] To Ruskin, the unity of art means that art in manufacture and design cannot be achieved by training part of the man, that is, by teaching the artisan to apply certain codes of convention in design in a mechanical way. If a society is to have art it must educate the whole being of its artists; the range of art cannot be extended beyond the reach of such education. This education, of course, is primarily an education in sight. Sight, as he said in his "Inaugural Address at the Cambridge School of Art" (1858), is the forgotten basis of all our metaphors of intellectual and religious illumination. And what is to be seen are essentially the vital lines, the "awful lines," the controlling lines of organic forms; and, since these are also moral and mythic lines, true sight is essentially a moral state: "The perception of nature, is never given but under certain moral conditions."[43] So the education of the sight, its surrender to nature, can become a means of social regeneration as it is communicated through the unified system of the various forms of the arts, since this system is a second "nature," always illustrative or interpretive of organic nature.

These, broadly stated, are the essential positions Ruskin takes in *The*

Two Paths (1859), five lectures entitled "Art and its Application to Decoration and Manufacture." The two paths, characteristically, are the way of convention and the way of nature in the study of art. They are really mechanical as opposed to organic models. On the path of convention the artist is the tool of rules formulated by the tradition; there is no mystery in them; on the path of nature his whole being is educated, through innocent sight, into harmony with nature. The one path deadens his moral perception; the other opens it. Of course, decorative art must be conventional to a certain extent, but there are only three necessary causes of conventionalism: "Conventionalism by cause of inefficiency of material"; "Conventionalism by cause of inferiority of place"; "Conventionalism by cause of inferiority of office."[44]

None of these limitations, however, prevents the great workman from introducing organic form. "Inferiority of office," for instance, in ornament may cause him to reject the use of higher organisms in his design, but he will at least introduce those "infinite curves"[45] Ruskin had discussed in volume 4 of *Modern Painters*. This thought leads him into a brief but significant clarification of his position on Greek art. He notes that he has been wrongly accused of hostility to Greek work. Indeed, he admits, he has attacked Palladian work and modern imitations of Greek design. But of original Greek work he has "never spoken but with a reverence quite infinite"; in fact, he continues, since the second volume of *Modern Painters* his "effort has not been less continually to make the heart of Greek work known than the heart of Gothic."[46] England, however, has no good design at present; to get it there is but one primary dictum to be followed: "You must raise your workman up to life, or you will never get from him one line of well-imagined conventionalism."[47] Beautiful design proceeds only from those who have the beautiful forms of nature about them.

2

Out of Ruskin's major and minor work of the late fifties, three major themes carry him forward because they have come to dominate that work: mythic or archetypal consciousness, the organic model, and the direct mandate of his social concern. This, broadly speaking, is what has happened to his thought in the period just reviewed, insofar as it has established the main thrust of his thought for the sixties: first, his sectarian narrowness has been supplanted by an interest in religion in the larger, archetypal sense. He is now interested in the religions of humanity, at least whatever is sincere in them. This syncretic outlook comes down in practice primarily to an interest in Greek belief. Hence he can write sympathetically of Greek myth in the great chapters on spiritual invention that conclude *Modern Painters,* and at the end of the sixties he will produce his own "myth book," *The Queen of the Air.* He has left the religion of England for the "religion of Humanity." Within myth, his particular interest continues to be in the symbology of cloud and storm and in the solar archetype. This last is deeply coherent with his lust for natural light (his critical hatred of all excesses of shading, all flash and sparkle) in art and life. It also engages his preference for the *"coeli enarrent"* theme in biblical mythology, with the frequent emphasis he places on such symbolism as "The Light of The World" and the "Sun of Justice."

Second, for Ruskin, nature has now become something more than the infinity of visible forms, or the Neo-Platonic natural theology of "types" of Divine attributes, or the poetry of revelational "experience" in the presence of particular scenic effects, especially sky effects. Nature has become the organic model that borrows to some extent from all three modes. Chiefly it is the controlling image of a living whole characterized by inherent "laws" of unity, liberty, and mystery. This group of qualities, hence the model itself, applies in a general way to all the modes of life: natural, aesthetic, and social. Since the organism implies an organizer it is both grounded in myth and used *as* a myth by Ruskin.

Third, he has received a new mandate in his work based on the interaction of these truths with his direct observation of social and environmental degeneration. Art is rooted in the social order and its controlling ethic; to regenerate art and taste one must regenerate the social organism. Life in the social organism is centered in the law of help, but this life is threatened by one great enemy, the lust for wealth (in our ordinary sense, riches), which invokes the fatal law of competition and death. Its sacred scripture is mechanistic laissez-faire economics. If the social organism, life, is to survive its conflict with lethal wealth, wealth must be redefined in terms of the organic model, and the cohesive moral and social laws must be delineated and their practical implications projected.

This, briefly stated, is the direction that Ruskin's public mind was taking at the turn of the decade. There are other peripheral concerns, such as his interests in etymology, spiritualism, and biblical fortune-telling that might be mentioned; but each of these will be found to relate to the same mystical leaning in him, to the search for a quintessential language in things that underlies his communions with mythical truths and organic laws.

His private mind, conscious and unconscious, as revealed by his letters, diaries, actions, and dreams, is another subject that is not ours here. It would require much space merely to summarize biographical details and retrace the related lines of speculation developed by other students of Ruskin. But a few factors of his personal life in the sixties must be touched on because of their inescapable bearing on his work.

One point is that he looked on the turn of the decade as a distinct watershed in his life. He kept no diary for 1860, but a comment under that year in *Praeterita* indicates the attitude with which he put aside volume 5 of *Modern Painters*: "On the strength of this piece of filial duty, I am cruel enough to go away to St. Martin's again, by myself, to meditate what is to be done next. Thence I go up to Chamouni,—where a new epoch of my life and death begins."[48] Another comment on this transition refers also to the writing of *Unto This Last* and his retrospective attitude toward the consequences of that act. "I got the bound volume of *Modern Painters* in the valley of St. Martin's in that summer of 1860, and in the valley of Chamouni I gave up my art work and wrote this little book—the beginning of my days of reprobation."[49] Perhaps the character of this moment in Ruskin's life is gathered up well enough in the ideas *redirection, rededication,* and *reprobation.* The redirection is the simplest idea; he is turning away from a primary emphasis on the study of art. Rededication is implicit in the reference to Chamouni, for this is the sacred place in Ruskin's private mythology; it was there, in gazing on the cloudless peace of the high snows, that he had first consecrated his life to the study of nature and art; and to this place he will return, at the end of the decade, in hope of spiritual regeneration.

"Days of reprobation" refers more broadly, it may be supposed, than to the generally hostile public reception of his writings on political economy. Alienation might be a better word for what he would experience during this period. It must be remembered that Ruskin was making a multifold break with his past self here, all aspects of the break coming at virtually the same moment. He was leaving for a time the study of art, where he had established identity and critical authority. He had left the sheepfold of religious truth in which he was reared, which had formed his style and the moral core of his aesthetic, and which remained the professed religion of his family and his class. He was attacking the other great faith of his class, the *laissez-faire* market system and the belief in progress founded on it. He was at odds, then, with the two primary faiths of his class in his perception that those faiths were at odds with each other. At the more personal level, he was in rebellion against the wishes of his father, who, while he supported his son against his attackers, had always made plain that he felt his son's gifts should be used in the study of art. There was even a partial repudiation of his own earlier style; for a time his works, especially on economic matters, showed the effects of a deliberate effort to chasten and subdue the poetic impressionistic excesses of his earlier writing in an effort, based on his platform work, to reach the people he desired most to help.

Ruskin's retrospective characterization of this period as "a new epoch of my life and death" might, in terms of his writing, be taken simply as a reference to the redirection of his interests, or even to the new "being toward death," in Heidegger's phrase, of a man who has lost or has set aside hope of another life (a view he associated with the Greek religion). In his diary of 1857 he calculated the number of days he might reasonably expect to live and began a daily countdown. But there is another more private meaning in this phrase, for he echoed it in another reference, left in manuscript, to the self he was at this period: "The year 1860 the 'new epoch of life' . . . began for me in this wise, that my father and mother could travel with me no more, but Rose, in heart, was with me always, and all I did was for her sake."[50]

He had met Rose La Touche in 1858 when her mother invited him to instruct her and her sister Emily in drawing. Ruskin was immediately attracted to Rose. He was then nearly forty and she was ten, but they began an exchange of letters, he in the role of "St. Crumpet" and she as "Rosie pet, and Rosie, puss." One wonders whether this nascent involvement with Rose influenced his emphasis on the Turnerian tragic "shade of the rose" in the last chapters of *Modern Painters*. This would have been prophetic indeed, for so began one of the most prolonged agonies in the annals of Eros. The adorations and degradations of Mann's Gustave Aschenbach seem a thin contrivance by comparison with this true and central tragedy of Ruskin's life.

The intricacies of this labyrinth of suffering, the twists and deadwalls of hope and despair, ecstasy and humiliation into which Ruskin pursued his fatal woman have been ably traced by Derrick Leon, Van Akin Burd, and Joan Abse. We must return to some of these details later on. For the moment, we merely take note of the fact that this private agony was operative behind his public work in the sixties. Ruskin was not even released from his thraldom by her death in 1875, but only from the hope of mortal union with his epipsyche. It was a seventeen-year quest (just the length of his earlier involvement with *Modern Painters*, and, as we have noted, concurrent with his "religion of Humanity") for love that becomes virtually a mythic quest, in the written record that we have of it, through its burden of spiritual projection and symbolism. It was a doomed quest, partly because his was a sick Rose; her illness, Joan Abse

John Ruskin. *Portrait of Miss Rose La Touche*, 1874. Reproduced from *Works* (Library Edition), vol. 35.

suggests, was anorexia nervosa. Her condition made him a Dante in pursuit of a divided Beatrice. As Leon points out, two women occupied Rose, "and her personality became more perilously divided as her mysterious malaise increased. Rose well, wrote Ruskin letters of spontaneous and beguiling beauty, full of affection, intelligence and humour: Rose ill—tormented by the resistance of those around her, became harsh and alien, withdrawing herself completely, or else cruelly accusing him of nameless sins."[51]

The pursuit that he had looked upon as the beginning of a new life gradually drained that life. To Mrs. Cowper he complained that Rose had "become the patient murderess day by day of the creature who had loved her more than all creatures living,"[52] and later, "My heart is dead within me."[53] So his quest for Rose is in a sense, an epoch of his life and death. It also gives a different meaning to his "days of reprobation." His religious condition ("How could one love you if you were a pagan?" his pious Rose queried in 1863),[54] his capacity to arouse and return genuine affection, even his potency, all came into question and were obstacles, apart from Rose's self-division. But perhaps the most succinct reprobation of his life came not from hostile critics but in the poisoned words he never read that summed up his former wife's reply to Mrs. La Touche's second inquiry about him: "He is quite unnatural."[55]

Unnatural? What did she mean? We have seen that Ruskin, thinking mainly of the public reaction to his work, speaks of the days of reprobation as having begun in 1860. But he must have felt some sense of condemnation in 1854 from the circumstances surrounding the dissolution of his marriage, particularly since these events were bruited into something of a scandal, in the midst of which he kept silence. Having endured all she could of his "perpetual neglect," annoyed at the interferences of his mother, her affections perhaps already transferred, Effie left him abruptly in April. With her father's help she immediately began her suit for nullity. Ruskin submitted without defense to the annulment of their marriage by the ecclesiastical court on grounds of his impotence. The decree of nullity was issued in July, and, the following June, Effie was married to their close friend, the rising painter John Everett Millais. The embarrassment or other pain in this for Ruskin was softened by the relief he felt in being released from the six-year burden of his incompatible and unconsummated marriage. Yet relief would be temporary, since the rest of his emotional life would be shadowed by the mysterious failure of his wedding night. The fact that his wife had been examined by two doctors and found by a jury of matrons to be *virgo intacta* provided, apparently, sufficient grounds for a judgment of "incurable impotence,"since Ruskin did not contest it. Derrick Leon finds it "extremely doubtful whether there was any truth in the verdict of the court," there being, in his view, no other evidence that Ruskin was organically, or even functionally, impotent.[56] And Mary Lutyens concludes that "the reason why John did not consummate the marriage can only be conjectured."[57] Indeed, Ruskin himself may not have known; at least, the record of his reasons contains contradictions.

Ruskin's statement of the facts of his marriage, prepared for his Proctor before he decided not to contest his wife's suit, has been published by J. H. Whitehouse, who regarded it as a "vindication" of the author from the false judgment that would thwart so much he later hoped for. To the student of his writings, the question of Ruskin's impotence may be irrelevant, but the fact that he was forced by circumstances, partly of his own making, to bear an identity that he *believed* to be false, can be read as contributing to the tragic or embittered tone of much of his work after the mid fifties. Furthermore, in his statement about his relations with his wife we have another "text" to correlate with the symbolism we have been tracing in his work.

"Impotence," Rollo May writes, "is the failure not of intention, but of intentionality."[58] Intention he associates with conscious will; intentionality with imagination, fantasy, and love. Ruskin's statement makes clear that while his intention may have been to consummate his marriage, his intentionality recoiled from it. In the portion of the statement devoted to "general facts" he asserts that they "agreed" immediately in consideration of her health, to a brief postponement of consummation, and then to a four-year delay until she was twenty-five. Meanwhile, he states, he became aware "of points in her character which caused [him] to regard with excessive pain any idea of having children by her"; and, though he never "pressed or forced" consummation, he "offered it again and again," always to be refused. Effie, we may surmise, wanted attention (intentionality) rather than intention.

In an appended section of "details" relating to the general statement, he begins, in a confusing passage, by blaming the first failures of his marriage on psychological factors rooted in the financial anxieties of the Grays. Because these intimations of ruined fortune, the details of which were concealed from him, created the general anxiety which led to the first fatal postponement of intercourse, he claims that these conditions, financial shadows, "entirely destroyed the immediate happiness of [his] marriage." Yet in touching on the wedding night he mentions other factors, belonging to intentionality rather than intention, that contradict his previous statements. He speaks of her anxiety and his fear of "subjecting her nervous system to any new trials," but then he admits that his "own passion was also much subdued by anxiety," so that he had "no difficulty in abstaining that first night." Later on, however, he assigns a different cause; he explains that he "*could* abstain" because "though her face was beautiful, her person was not formed to excite passion. On the contrary there were certain circumstances in her person which completely checked it." In tracing the "progress of alienation" that followed, he cites other circumstances: that he had married her "to have a companion—not for passion's sake"; that she constantly attempted to withdraw him from the influence of his parents and was particularly antagonistic toward his mother; and that she was "always thinking that I ought to attend *her*, instead of *herself* attending me." His "virility" he could prove "at once" by medical examination, but he no longer wishes to have back the woman who has made such a charge against him.[59]

These, then, are the facts of the relationship from Ruskin's side; they center on an intended but deferred consummation resisted by various feelings amounting to a failure of intentionality on his part. Something of Effie's version appears in a letter written to her father on 7 March 1854, six weeks before she left Ruskin, in which she confides that, though he had from time to time "alleged various reasons" for nonperformance, he had finally, after five years, "told me his true reason (and that to me is as villainous as all the rest) that he had imagined women were quite different to what he saw I was and that the reason why he did not make me his wife was because he was disgusted with my person the first evening 10th April."[60] Her tone suggests disbelief in all these "reasons" as such, and her letter to Mrs. La Touche in 1870 is decisive in pointing to an incapacity in Ruskin: "From his peculiar nature he is utterly incapable of making a woman happy."[61]

But whether would not or could not—his plans or his image of woman—was primary in Ruskin's inaction, his hopes, and to some extent his works, were to be caught in the tragic web of its consequences. The La Touches would be concerned not only for their daughter's direct happiness but also with the legal possibility that, if Ruskin were to marry her, the annulment would be void and the marriage bigamous. And, Effie, it can be supposed, was anxious to prevent such a marriage for the same reason and because its success could call her motives for leaving Ruskin into question. Only by the strongest assertion of his literal need could he hope to escape the entrapment in lovelessness that would poison his self-world relationship, yet he continued to Platonize his love. "I will take her," he said of Rose, "for Wife—for Child,—for

Queen—for any Shape of fellow-spirit that her soul can wear, if only she will be loyal to me with her love."[62] In this very expression of his love is also the problem of intentionality that beset him; he wanted a spirit that was a projection of his own, not a woman. Yet it is not unnatural to idealize the beloved; he had written to Effie in such terms prior to their marriage. What prevented (and might prevent) his transmuting the ideality into sexuality? Mary Lutyens conjectured that when Ruskin, who presumably knew all he knew of a woman's nakedness from art, confronted the reality in his wife, his sexuality was traumatized; furthermore, he could only believe that what he saw represented a unique disfigurement in her. That is, as Richard Jenkyns puts it, "It appears that the great critic, who had seen countless sculpted and painted nudes, did not know that women had pubic hair."[63]

Possibly, but I suggest that Ruskin was too acute an observer of nature not to have formed a more realistic image of female nudity; and, even if we assume he had not, we have still to wonder why his passion did not recover from the shock in a day or two. It seems more likely that his sexuality was fully sublimated or inhibited in the first place, that his eros was ruled by the never-to-be-assimilated anima, arising from his domination by his mother, and only momentarily projected, before marriage, upon Effie. Joan Abse has stressed also his domination by his father. Yet there is no accounting for Ruskin's condition without recourse to some form of psychoanalytic interpretation; hence, I have been suggesting that the Jungian analysis will best relate what we know of his private experience to the recurrent symbols of his work. The projections of the anima would leave him loveless (his life, "one succession of Love-sorrow,"[64] he told Norton); yet she had to be obeyed, could not be assimilated, because the dragon of impurity (the repressed), like the Nereid's Guard, watched over the treasure of sensual love. And there were other modes of isolation in store for him.

In 1861 Ruskin complained to Norton of the solitude he felt in his own home, where parental love included no sympathy for his religious or economic views. He spoke his bitterness plainly in a letter to his father on 16 December 1863, where he charged that parental protectiveness had thwarted all true passion and life in him. Thus, at his father's death in 1864 he had to face both the finality of their estrangement and the futility of his own sacrifices. He had to accept, he told Acland, the loss of a father who would have sacrificed his life for his son, yet had exacted the actual—and vain—sacrifice of his son's. John James's death also thrust upon him the necessity of managing both the wealth he had inherited (over £130,000) and his mother. Both the money and the mother involved aspects of alienation. The capital brought with it responsibilities of its prudent use for life under the law of help, and help meant more than gift. This complex moral sign attached to his wealth remained a source of anxiety for Ruskin. However, at this point, in the sixties, he found a partial outlet for it in financing the slum improvement, fixed-rent projects of Octavia Hill, though he eventually came into some conflict with her over the amount of "gift" involved in her scheme.

He was left with the security of wealth, then, plus the moral and prudential weights of it, pulling in different directions. At the same time he was left, in a way, homeless. His mother, always a dogmatic and astringent power to be reckoned with, now became the solitary despot of Denmark Hill. "And the older she grew," writes Derrick Leon, "the more disagreeable life at Denmark Hill became."[65] Though he spent considerable periods of time there in the years immediately following his father's death, he and his guests were under the duress of constant respectful deference to her conservative and tenaciously expressed opinions and to her household regimen. The "unconverted" Ruskin could hardly have felt at home, for instance, with a Sabbatarian observance so strict that it required his pictures to be covered by special screens on Sundays. Again, the theme of reprobation. Household tensions were eased somewhat by the ministrations of Joan Agnew, a distant cousin and a sweet-natured girl of seventeen who came to the house for a visit and, entering Margaret Ruskin's good graces, stayed on as her companion. Eventually "Joanna" (later Mrs. Arthur Severn) would become the center of Ruskin's familial affection and the surrogate mother of his declining years.

Given Ruskin's essential homelessness in the sixties, his interests in education, and his delight in the innocence and beauty of young girls, one can understand the pleasure he found in stays at Miss Bell's School at Winnington Hall, Cheshire. There, from time to time during this period, he enjoyed serving as educational advisor, lecturer, benefactor, and general uncle-in-residence. This idyllic situation became the stage for *The Ethics of the Dust,* and the relative peace he found there is apparent in the sweetness of that book.

From friends as from his father, his protected upbringing led him to expect more understanding than he could give. At the time of Millais' marriage to Effie, Ruskin was developing a new protege in Rossetti, to whom he confided at the time (1855) that he had "no friendships, and no loves."[66] Theirs was a friendship that would last nearly a decade. In this period Rossetti loved, married, and lost by her suicide, his hauntingly beautiful model Elizabeth Siddal, whom Ruskin also admired and whose modest artistic talents he had tried to encourage. Though their lives would be ridden by the anima in similar ways, Ruskin, whom Rossetti nicknamed The Great Prohibited, condemned the painter's sexual meanderings, and, characteristically, he came to see moral faults in his work also. So the two fell out in 1864, with Rossetti resenting the criticism and Ruskin complaining that he had never gotten from his friend what he most needed, not love but "understanding." Despite a brief quarrel in 1867, his friendship with Carlyle deepened during this period, and the "master" continued until his death to champion the "divine rage" of his disciple. In the dimension of friendship that involved Ruskin's quest for intimacy rather than critical sympathy, he acquired very important new bonds in the complex of relationships that centered on his involvement with the La Touches. These were persons (particularly the novelist George MacDonald and Mrs. Cowper-Temple) who were primarily linked to him as confidants in that episode.

Mrs. La Touche introduced Ruskin to MacDonald in 1863. She seems to have had a genuine concern for Ruskin's well-being at that point; their estrangement, with its element of submerged triangularity, did not set in until it became apparent that his affection was directed primarily at her daughter and that he intended to wed her. Shortly after the introduction she wrote to thank MacDonald "for loving and helping and letting yourself be loved by that poor St. C." She continued, "nothing will ever get *me* right, save getting *him* right."[67] She went so far as to urge him to let Ruskin unpack his heart with talk about Rose, if he would. "You will talk to him, and let him talk—about his pet Rosie if he pleases," she said. Ruskin and MacDonald quickly became close; they shared a number of attitudes, it seems, including a love of Turner and a distrust of sectarian narrowness in religion. The extent to which Ruskin was able to take MacDonald into his confidence is indicated by his letters, especially by the famous "mouse-pet" letter of 1865: "I can't love anybody," he confessed, "except my mouse-pet, in Ireland, who nibbles me to the very sick death with weariness to see her—and sends me bits of mignonette, for sooth—as if they were just as good as her own self, and makes me hate everybody else."[68]

We are unlikely ever to know just what dimension of desire Ruskin meant by love here. In 1866 he proposed marriage to Rose. But would this marriage have meant gratification of his desire or merely its disillusionment and re-projection? This is perhaps the central psychological question in Ruskin's life. Rose, it appears, wished to maintain the illusion, for she bade him wait three more years for her answer. Apparently we must think of the erotic, if we are to understand this affair, in the Greek mythic or archetypal sense of Eros, which, as Rollo

May suggests, is "distinguished by the function of giving the spirit of life, in contrast to the function of sex as the release of tension."[69] I suggest that Ruskin yearned to recover by way of Rose the union with Being—with nature, with others and with his own potentials—that he had once derived primarily from a religio-erotic communion with nature. ("I wish Vesuvius could love me, like a living thing," he told his diary in 1841). This desire for Rose could have contained but could never have been gratified by the sexual, one suspects. It was, in short, an urge to overcome alienation, and its frustration was felt as a darkening of nature against him and a generalized sense of being unable to be intimate with anyone. In losing Rose he would be losing the world. However, he plainly did not "hate everybody else." Surely not Joan Severn or Mrs. Cowper-Temple.

Ruskin's friendship with Mrs. Cowper (who became Mrs. Cowper-Temple and later Lady Mount-Temple) developed in the late fifties out of their mutual interest in spiritualism. Later she became his primary confidant and intermediary in the La Touche affair, and her husband, Lord Mount-Temple, assisted Ruskin in various practical and legal ways in the seventies and later became one of the first trustees of Saint George's guild. The letters Ruskin wrote to Mrs. Cowper in the sixties and seventies are the major documents we have concerning this central tragedy of his life, since this episode is present in his public writing only as occasional allusion and in symbolic transformations. The letters have been heavily relied upon by Derrick Leon and have recently been edited with great care by John Bradley. A quotation from them will reveal not only the extent to which Ruskin confided in Mrs. Cowper but also something of the peaks of private agony he was enduring behind the public writings we are about to consider. There are more poignant passages in the letters, but in the following section from a letter dated 1868 he summarizes the developing enthrallment that has led to his present state of anguished desire touched with antipathy.

> I had loved Rosie since she was ten years old—saw her first in 1858 (autumn)—I have had no thought within me—ever since—but was in some part of it hers. For months of solitude among the hills—I have had *no other* thought. Well—at last I had my dream changed into hope—Then into certainty. I entirely trusted in her love—and in this joy I had dwelt— binding my whole soul upon it with cords of love—as to an altar—In an instant—wholly without warning came this stern—final—fearful word of death—and only resting on this strange sentence—unexplained. "There is nothing, but this frail *cannot* to separate our life and love."[70]

But this was not the exit, it was merely a deceptive turn in the mirrored maze of their relationship, which had other turns to take before its end more than six years later.

The frustration Ruskin met here in his quest for Eros was paralleled, we should note, by frustration and discouragement in the public aspects of his work during the same period. Society would not heed his law of help. Like Rose it was divided against itself; its practical economic values were at odds with its professed religious beliefs. This aspect of his despair he occasionally spoke of aloud in his works themselves. He wrote this, for instance, midway through *Time and Tide*: "I mean these very letters to close my political work for many a day; and I write them, not in any hope of being at present listened to, but to disburthen my heart of the witness I have to bear, that I may be free to go back to my garden lawns, and paint birds and flowers there."[71]

Given this hydra-headed frustration one can understand the noticeable sickening of nature in his diaries during the period. "Lake not clear—made me sad," he noted in 1866. "Nature herself not right."[72] 1866: "Such a black day of hopeless fog as I have seldom known."[73] 1867: "Bitter frost, black sky, wild east wind. Rose ill."[74] 21 April 1867, Easter Sunday: "Today violent wind again—fierce and like evil spirits."[75] Next day: "Black rain in evening."[76] April 1868: "All the blossoms destroyed."[77] 1868: "All life disconsolate, in midst of loveliest possibilities."[78] Interspersed with entries such as these (and others with less evidence of depression) are allusions to storm dreams and especially to fearful serpent dreams. "I cannot understand why my dreams are not nobler, more consistent," he recorded in 1867, "must watch this."[79] In a dream he recorded in March 1868, he had made Joanna feel the serpent's scales.[80] In November 1869, he noted "the most horrible serpent-dream I ever had yet in my life. . . . The deadliest came out into the room under a door. It rose up like a Cobra—with horrible round eyes and had a woman's, or at least Medusa's, breasts."[81]

Of course at this time he had just finished the *Queen of the Air* and had Athena on his mind. And she, like Rose, had two personalities, as we shall see, one of which was Medusa's. "My head," he had written Mrs. Cowper in 1864, "is full of misshapen Gods, & worse misshapen inter-pretations of them—but it is all so interesting—and will bear at last on what interests you—."[82] What interested her was spiritualism, and the "misshapen Gods" were the Egyptian powers he was about to interpret in *The Ethics of the Dust*. It is little wonder, finally, that, given the worldly discouragements he encountered, Ruskin should withdraw more deeply at the end of the sixties into myth-work and the style of prophetic or enigmatic utterance; for these, like dreams, are modes of wish-fulfillment.

3

In discussing Ruskin's major works of the sixties it will be convenient to place them loosely in three categories. There are works primarily economic or political in concern, works in which virtually no reference is made to the uses of art: *Unto This Last* (1862), *Munera Pulveris* (1862–63, 1872), *Time and Tide* (1867). With these are to be included several dozen letters to the *Times* and other newspapers on such subjects as the price of gold, the operations of supply and demand, work and wages, domestic service, the expenditures of the rich, and similar socio-economic topics. The most interesting of these peripheral works is his pamphlet "The General Principle of Employment for the Destitute Poor and Criminal Classes" (1868).

The second category consists of works more broadly concerned with the arts and their relation to society. They are closer to the established lines of Ruskin's thought and are marked by more emotive uses of prose, yet as theoretical statements they are less significant than the first group. These are *Sesame and Lilies* (1865), *The Cestus of Aglaia* (1865–66), and *The Crown of Wild Olive* (1866). Linked to this group are two important shorter works, a paper read before the Royal Institute of Architects entitled "The Study of Architecture in Our Schools" (1865) and his Rede lecture at Cambridge, "The Relation of National Ethics to National Arts" (1867).

Finally, though it will be our purpose to trace the thread of mythic thinking in most of these books, two works of this period are so deeply dependent on myth that they must be placed in a third category. I mean *The Ethics of the Dust* (1866) and *The Queen of the Air* (1869). These, along with the more closely related art studies of the second group, must be reserved for discussion in the next chapter, while the subject immediately before us is the body of socio-economic thought represented by the first group.

Now the cardinal points of Ruskin's political economy are these: first, he thinks of his system as existential and organic, though he does not use these terms. He assumes that people actually live (or need to live) in social structures quite unlike those assumed by the theoretical economists of his time. Life means not individual survival, but the existence of communities in which people are united more fundamentally by bonds of affection and care than they are divided by competition and self-interest. His system is organic because it emphasizes the life of the whole over that of the individual and because its primary law is help, not competition; therefore, he tends to measure local concentrations of riches against reciprocal losses in other parts of the social organism. The "art of getting rich" discussed by the theoreticians is also, he reminds us, the art of keeping someone else poor. His scheme is existential in intent because it tries to deal with the lived reality of care against the theoretical premise of the self-interested "economic man" and the market mechanism that operates him.

Second, Ruskin's system invokes a concept of intrinsic or life-support value of things. As opposed to the exchange value of commodities in the flux of opinion, their life-support value in nature is fixed, he supposes, and relatively determinable. This view ties his organic political economy (the economy of maintenance of the social organism) to the intrinsic economy of the organic globe and gives his economy an ecological bias. Third, his is a scheme of total governmental interference. However, he thinks of government interference as ethical rather than fiscal. These two can never be totally separated, but he supposes that *true* wealth for all (physical abundance and spiritual satisfaction) can be based only on certain ethical conditions, epitomized in the terms honesty and grace. The role of government is primarily to inculcate and enforce these principles through its educational and judicial systems. Fourth, Ruskin's scheme does not involve social leveling. He explicitly distinguishes it from socialism. He would limit but not abolish private property. His government would fuse paternal monarchy with pastoral theocracy. Everyone would be known and helped by the system, but the recognition of "necessary inequality" among men is as important to him as their necessary unity and (within these limits) their necessary liberty.

It may seem strange that a discussion of Ruskin's political economic thought should have a significant place in a study devoted to the uses of myth and apocalypse in his writing. But the works of this group are involved with myth in a number of ways which it will be well to point to as we begin to discuss them. First, in its fundamental direction toward a simpler, preindustrial state characterized by tribal unity and harmony with nature, Ruskin's ideal community participates in the archetypal theme of return to origins, a primary theme in primitive mythology and in the literary mythology of Romanticism. Again, in its fundamental organicism his political thought leans heavily on the mythic intuition of the solidarity of all living things. He constantly employs the word *law* in the scriptural or mythic sense, and he sees himself less as the theorist or formulator of a personal system than as the interpreter of the final or guiding laws of the only system that is, as a reader of its primordial language.

Most important, Ruskin sees the laws of which he is the voice—the system that he insists is not his[83]—as being in conflict with an antagonistic system, of which the immediate temporal form is the "dismal science" of Mill and other economists. However, he does not see this simply as an ideological conflict. In his vision it is partly represented as a mythic conflict. Beneath the "dismal science" of the economists is the abysmal science of Mammon. Consequently, Ruskin's economic writing resonates with classical and scriptural allusions and interpretations that express the depth of this archetypal conflict. The Christian "Sun of Justice" opposed to the archenemy Mammon, the Greek Apollo in conflict with Python the corrupter, his own humanist vital-wealth system against the death-wealth laissez faire system: all, as he sees it, are one archetypal conflict—the solar hero with cloudy impurity—that I express by the phrase *life against wealth*. Therefore, mythic references have, for Ruskin, a natural place in his political discussions; the same is true for his strange recourse to etymology in the midst of economy. Like his references to myth and his analogies with organic forms, etymology is a prophetic device for getting back to truths of primordial language; all involve his fundamental role as prophet-interpreter. Finally, in *Time and Tide* there is an apocalyptic element that becomes more pronounced in *Fors Clavigera*. The archetypal struggle has reached a climactic stage; contemporary events reveal this when they are properly interpreted. The prophet's moment is always crisis; to Ruskin as apocalyptist and prophet, a momentary instance of popular taste can be interpreted as a symbol revealing the deployment of mythic forces in climactic conflict.

The first publication, in *Cornhill Magazine* for August through November 1860, of the essays collected in *Unto This Last* (1862) aroused such a furor of reader indignation that the editors were forced to halt the series with the fourth installment. "Even a theological heresy hunt could not have been more fast and furious,"[84] Cook observes; and indeed it *was* a heresy hunt, for Ruskin was attacking the received socio-economic mythology of his time. More antagonistically, he was, in his use of scriptural references, attacking the confessed religion of his age in the terms of its professed belief. He was picking at the primary schizoid character of his period. As G. M. Young has noted, "English society was poised on a double paradox which its critics, within and without, called hypocrisy. Its practical ideals were at odds with its religious professions, and its religious belief was at issue with its intelligence."[85] Ruskin's way of undercutting the second paradox is to carry his political economy back not merely to a Biblical but to a mythic and organic base. Over against the "science" of the political economists he puts the "science" of the organic model and etymological mythology. Since the essays were stopped they do not represent the fulfillment of his intentions, although he was allowed to lengthen the final essay. He gave the work a concluding passage, but the work remains a fragment, and in the final essay he indicated the titles of three planned chapters: "Thirty Pieces," a chapter on price; "Demeter," on production, and "The Law of the House," on economy.

In the collected version the essays were reprinted without significant change. In his preface to this edition Ruskin observes that the essays were "reprobated in a violent manner . . . by most of the readers they met with," yet he considers them "the truest, rightest-worded, and most serviceable" of his writings, particularly the last essay, which, he declares, is "probably the best I shall ever write."[86] He regrets that the most radical of all statements in them, proposing the organization of labor and fixed wages, should have appeared in the first essay because it is the least important of his principles. The primary purpose of these essays, he explains, is to give "a logical definition of WEALTH," as the necessary "basis of economical science," and then to show what follows from this: that wealth properly defined could only be attained "under certain moral conditions of society, of which quite the first was a belief in the existence, and even, for practical purposes, in the attainability of honesty."[87] That is, he will show that the "veins of wealth" and the living "roots of honour" belong to one and the same organism.

Since Ruskin's wealth is "life," and since life means that of the social whole, he does not begin with a definition of wealth but with what he considers to be its roots in a cohesive social ethic. His first essay, "The Roots of Honour," is essentially (or rather, existentially) an attack on the hero of the antimyth, the "economic man" of the so-called science of political economy. The "dismal science" has created this abstract entity of calculable impulses as an alienated projection of man's selfish and competitive impulses that function predictably within the market mechanism. Over against this figment of the economists' imagination Ruskin offers existential and organic man, rooted in the social whole and linked to others by bonds of affection and ideals of justice. A proper economic theory, he argues, must be founded on concern not competition. His is an organic-existential economics of care. The life of society, like that of any other coherent organization such as the fighting brigade or the crew of a ship at sea is the spirit of the whole, *esprit de corps.* Of course laborers, if they are to enter this spirit, must be freed from contingencies of employment and competitive wages. All workmen are to be paid alike, or else bad labor will drive out good; and labor is to organize itself to secure constant employment. Social roles are conceived in terms of care; the true function of the merchant is to provide for the whole, even to die for it. And the manufacturer's duties are, first, "to produce what he sells, in the purest and cheapest forms," and, second to make the employment he offers "most beneficial to the men employed."[88] Like the captain of a ship, he is primarily a governor of *men*, not a producer of things; his is a paternal authority and responsibility.

In his second essay, "The Veins of Wealth," Ruskin considers the meaning of wealth and the nature of its flow within the social organism. He begins to distinguish two different senses of wealth in terms of two meanings of *economy. Political* economy has to do with the maintenance of a state; it is the production of useful or pleasurable things. It generates wealth in a sense yet to be defined. *Mercantile* economy, the economy of "merces," or "pay," is the accumulation in private hands of claims upon labor. This mercantile wealth, representing a debt of labor, he sometimes distinguishes as "riches." Riches is always a relative term, bearing the same relation to poverty as north to south. Since this wealth is power over men, it is greater or less in direct proportion to their relative poverty. The art of becoming rich is that of establishing maximum inequality in our favor. The benefits of the accumulation of this power over lives depends upon how it is spent. The circulation of wealth is like the circulation of blood in the body. This analogy holds, "down even to minute particulars." In general, "all morbid local action of riches"[89] is detrimental to the body politic. Since the wealth of an individual may or may not contribute to the life of the social whole, the actual life value of any wealth (riches) depends on the "moral sign" attached to it. Hence the futility of attempting to give any rules for the accumulation of true wealth (as opposed to mere riches) apart from consideration of questions of social justice. What is accumulated is power over people, in them flow the true veins of wealth.

Ruskin has argued that mercantile economy is the accumulation of relative power over the lives of others. If, as its proponents say, political economy is the science of getting rich, it is equally and necessarily the science of keeping someone else poor. So riches and poverty, wealth (in this sense) and the life it commands are locked in eternal struggle that can be mitigated only by ideals of justice. This is the subject of the third essay of the series, "*Qui Judicatis Terram.*" In it Ruskin's thought takes a mythic turn. In the encounter of rich and poor "there is no other light than this by which they can see each other's faces, and live;—light, which is called . . . 'the sun of justice' . . . of which it is promised that it shall rise at last with 'healing' (health-giving or helping, making whole or setting at one) in its wings."[90] Thus we meet the solar archetype again at the center of Ruskin's economics. Theorists argue that the streams of wealth, like those of the earth, flow whither they will; but, like those streams also, they can be directed by human forethought to become the water of life to parched regions; the unguided flow of these wealth-streams is "the last and deadliest of national plagues."[91] In sum, political economy must mean "getting rich by legal or just means."[92] But the addition of that little word *just* will alter the whole cast of the science; for "jurisprudence" rests ultimately on divine, not human, laws. So Ruskin comes back again to myth and explains that in Dante the souls who have excelled in jurisprudence in life form eternally the eye of an eagle in heaven, "having been in life discerners of light from darkness," they are the light of the social body as the eye is of the human body. The souls who form the wings of the eagle, "trace also in light the inscription in heaven: "DILIGITE JUSTITIAM QUI JUDICATIS TERRAM. 'Ye who judge the earth give' (not, observe, merely love, but) 'diligent love to justice': the love which seeks diligently, that is to say, choosingly, and by preference to all things else."[93]

But what, in practice, are the laws of justice regarding payment of labor? They are simply, Ruskin insists, that the laborer must receive as much labor (life) as he gave, and that this equity of payment must be independent of the supply of labor. He traces the effects of the just and the unjust systems of payment of labor. Under the unjust system the power of wealth becomes increasingly concentrated as two men are hired for the just wages of one and so forth. Under the just system, however, the first laborer is paid enough to hire a second, "and so on down or up" until an organic "chain of men is created," and in this way the wealth and its moral influence are distributed rather than concentrated. Ruskin insists that his just system has nothing to do with socialism; it does nothing to alter the necessary inequality among men. It is essentially, he explains, an extension of the law of help set forth in volume 5 of *Modern Painters.* The poor, he concludes, have no right to the property of the rich, nor have the rich any right to the property of the poor.

A central law of his system, then, is that just payment of labor must be an amount of money that would enable the laborér to command equivalent labor at some future time. The problem of equivalency leads him to the definition of the terms *value, wealth, price* and *produce*, which are the subjects of the last essay in the group, *"Ad Valorum."* Value, for the economists, is simply "exchange value," and as such is dependent on opinion and supply. But in Ruskin's system *value*, which he derives from *valere* and *valor*, "to be well or strong (ὑγιαίνω);— strong, *in* life (if a man), or valiant; strong *for* life (if a thing), or valuable," is the intrinsic life-sustaining capability of a thing: "to be 'valuable,' therefore, is to 'avail towards life.' "[94] Here the mythic and organic elements combine, for value is independent of human opinion; it is the absolute life-sustaining power in certain things, fatefully fixed in them by their creator. True political economy is, then, a moral "science," for it "teaches nations to desire and labour for things that lead to life," and to scorn the things that lead toward death; it teaches them "what is vanity, and what substance; and how the service of Death, the Lord of Waste, and of eternal emptiness, differs from the service of Wisdom, the Lady of Saving, and of eternal fulness." The mythic "Lady of Saving" is "Madonna della Salute,—Lady of Health."[95]

His definition of value clears the way for a definition of wealth. Wealth is not, as the economists say, the possession of "useful articles"; it is "the possession of useful articles, *which we can use.*"[96] Accumulation is inescapably linked to capacity. True wealth, vital wealth, is "THE POSSESSION OF THE VALUABLE BY THE VALIANT."[97] Wealth beyond the capacity for its use acts as an impediment to life; it wants a separate name embodying this negative capacity; so Ruskin calls this impedimentary wealth "illth."[98] It follows from these definitions that "profit," authentic material gain, can be realized only by discovery or construction which adds new life-support value to the system. Whatever "gain" there is by mere exchange is simply a loss to someone else in the system.

Ruskin's view of the value of labor is peculiar and also mythic. Bad labor, he argues, "cannot be valued; it is like gold of uncertain alloy, or flawed iron."[99] It is the contest of life with an opposite, but it does not avail toward life in any necessary way. A note of his explains that the Greeks regarded true labor as a divine thing, to be honored with the kind of honor reserved for the gods; "whereas the *price* of false labour, or of that which led away from life, was to be, not honour, but vengeance," and they attributed the exaction of this particular price to Tisiphone, "with whom accounts current have been opened also in modern days."[100] However, the value, in availing toward life, of a given quality and kind of labor, he says, "like that of all other valuable things, is invariable."[101] He means, it appears, that the life-value of something produced, an ear of corn, say, does not vary with the labor needed to produce it. But all labor may be divided into positive and negative; "positive, that which produces life; negative, that which produces death."[102]

Capital has the same signs attached to it. It is only capital proper when it is producing something different from itself. The question always to be asked of capital is: "What substance will it furnish, good for life?" But capital that is merely reproducing itself is useless and may be worse than useless, "for capital may destroy life as well as support it," in which case it is only "an advance from Tisiphone, on mortgage—not a profit by any means."[103] The danger inherent in useless capital Ruskin documents with the myth of Ixion, which he interprets as a cloud myth. (As such it has a distinct bearing on his own plague-cloud myth.) The Greeks, he tells us, saw rightly that "capital is the head, or fountainhead of *wealth*—the 'well-head' of wealth, as the clouds are well-heads of rain: but when the clouds are without water, and only beget clouds, they issue in wrath at last, instead of rain, and in lightning instead of harvest." Ixion desired Juno, but embraced a cloud or phantasm instead ("the power of mere wealth being, in itself, as the embrace of a shadow,— comfortless"); this comfortless union begat the Centaurs, who were "a mingling of the brutal with the human nature: human in sagacity— using both intellect and arrow; but brutal in its body and hoof, for consuming, and trampling down." For his sin, Ixion is bound to a wheel, "fiery and toothed, and rolling perpetually in the air;—the type of human labour when selfish and fruitless."[104]

Consumption, life, is the right end of production; money reproducing itself is shadow; "consumption is the crown of production; and the wealth of a nation is only to be estimated by what it consumes."[105] But the fruit of consumption is life; and so Ruskin arrives at the famous aphorism that summarizes his organic economy and implies the contest of his definition of wealth with that of the economists: "THERE IS NO WEALTH BUT LIFE. Life, including all its power of love, of joy, and of admiration. That country is the richest which nourishes the greatest number of noble and happy human beings; that man is richest who, having perfected the functions of his own life to the utmost, has also the widest helpful influence, both personal, and by means of his possessions, over the lives of others."[106] Emile Durkheim, whose theories of organic solidarity in society have certain analogies with Ruskin's, pointed out in *Division of Labor in Society* that societies are integrated by diversification of labor and that this allows the broadest individuality. Like Ruskin, he argued that real social enrichment depends upon increased density, life, in the social organism, since only this leads to the increased diversity of interaction from which the higher "psychic life" of society, its true wealth, can emerge.

4

Ruskin's second major economic work, *Munera Pulveris* (1872), was, like *Unto This Last*, begun as a series of magazine essays, this time for *Fraser's* (1862, 1863), and was likewise suspended after the fourth install-ment because the pressure of hostile readers was brought to bear upon the magazine. In collecting the essays for book publication in 1872 he made a number of significant changes and numerous minor ones. (In the following discussion references are, of course, to the collected edition.) There the generic title "Essays in Political Economy," applied to the separate essays, became the more cryptic collective title *Munera Pulveris*. The four essays were divided into six chapters with separate titles; and in the text, most significantly, a long mythic passage interpreting the Sirens in Homer and Dante that had been a note in the first version, was integrated into the text of the third chapter of the book. The title, drawn from Horace, means "gifts of the dust" and parallels the earlier *Ethics of the Dust*, but its force is ironic. It points to the choice between vital and fatal conceptions of wealth, which is the central theme of the work; either we are to take "dust for deity," as received political economy does, or accept the "religion of Humanity," where wealth is life and its only reward is the crown of wild olive. But the title, like *Fors Clavigera*, has multiple meanings and refers also to the mythic Persephone, who, as earth mother, judges as she gives the gifts of the dust. He would explore this meaning in *Proserpina* (1875-86).

Munera Pulveris, while it is in general more carefully planned and closely reasoned than *Unto This Last*, is a far more tortuous work than its predecessor. Ruskin attributed its "affected concentration of language" to the meditative solitude in which it was composed, par-ticularly during his retreat at Mornex in 1862-63. During this period he plunged deeply into economic and narrative work by classical authors, glossed, as usual for him, by Dante. The power of their "strange enigmas" tugged at his thoughts. He found, for instance, new depths in the *Odyssey* and expressed this discovery to his father: "This which I used to think a poet's fairy tale, I perceive to be a great enigma—the Apocalypse, in a sort, of the Greeks." Calypso, he proposes, should be understood as an apocalyptic spirit; "She is the Patmos spirit of the Greeks (Calypse, Apo-Calypse), the goddess of wild nature."[107] The result of such meditations is that the style of *Munera* itself leans toward the cryptic, allusive, and enigmatic. The thread of his argument frequently disappears in a tangle of mythic symbolism and etymological derivations, making it, surely, the most syncretic of all studies in political economy.

In the preface to the collection Ruskin refers to his particular qualifications as a political economist. His studies in art have made him the only economist able to deal with the question of *intrinsic* value. His study is therefore founded on the delineation of intrinsic value and intrinsic *dis*value. This is the essential work of the *political* economist, not the disinterested observation of the operation of supply and demand. For all wise political economy is a moral system, a "system of conduct, founded on sciences," which is meant to *interfere* with the laws of supply and demand in favor of intrinsic value and life. He sees the book as essentially prefatory to further work in the subject. However, this prefatory study, though incomplete, is a "body of definitions" to which he must refer in the letters he is writing to English workmen. These letters, *Fors Clavigera*, he intends, will accomplish in a less formal way the "chief purpose of *Munera Pulveris*," which is "to examine the moral results and possible rectifications of the laws of distribution of wealth, which have prevailed hitherto without debate among men."[108]

Accordingly, the first chapter, called "Definitions," deals with certain crucial terms to which Ruskin assigns, in abbreviated form, the definitions he had worked out in a more discursive way in *Unto This Last*. Chiefly his task is to redefine wealth in terms of life; this is necessary in order to point up the lethal elements in what is conventionally called wealth. That is, the false or fatal definition of wealth is always implicit in his vital definition. The work of the political economist "is to determine what are in reality useful or life-giving things, and by what degrees and kinds of labour they are attainable and distributable." This study leads the economist directly into certain foundational distinctions of wealth, value, cost, price, money, and riches; and Ruskin lays down his definitions briskly and with prophetic, perhaps arrogant, self-confidence. " 'Wealth' consists of things in themselves valuable." Its study is therefore "a province of natural science."[109] "*Value is the life-giving power of anything; cost, the quantity of labour required to produce it; price the quantity of labour which its possessor will take in exchange for it.* Cost and price are commercial conditions, to be studied under the head of money."[110] Value is "intrinsic" and "effectual." Intrinsic value is the absolute life-support capacity of anything; it is fixed by the Creator, but measurable. Effectual value couples the production of useful things with the production of the capacity for their use.

Money consists of "documentary claims" to the possession of things of value. Riches and poverty are contrary and interactive terms like *warmth* and *chill* and are used to express relative degrees of possession of useful things. To clarify the meaning of valuable things, Ruskin introduces a scale of categories of things according to value. They are (1) land; (2) buildings, furniture, and instruments; (3) food, medicine, and articles of luxury; (4) books; and (5) works of art.

Having established what a national store should be, what value means, and what things are of value, Ruskin now proceeds in the following two chapters, called "Store-Keeping" and "Coin-Keeping" respectively, to raise fundamental questions about the relationship between the distribution of the national store and the distribution of the national currency. When we remember that "possession is in use only, which for each man is sternly limited,"[111] we are led to ask certain questions about the character of any national store and of its holders. These fall chiefly under three categories: (1) "What is the nature of the store? Has the nation hitherto worked for and gathered the right thing or the wrong? On that issue rest the possibilities of its life."[112] (2) "What quantity of each article composing the store exists in proportion to the real need of it by the population?"[113] (3) "What is the quantity of the store in relation to the Currency?"[114] National property is divided between the holders of the store and the holders of the currency, "and whatever the claiming value of the currency is at any moment, that value is to be deducted from the riches of the store-holders."[115] The relationship between the two in the social body is that of creditors and debtors. The nature of that relationship or bond is revealed by the etymology of the words "duty" and "creed" or "faith" which embody the central ideas. This leads to a discussion of the characters of these two holders, for the interaction of their natures is of the greatest importance to the nation. In fact it is "of incomparably greater importance to the nation in *whose* hands the thing is put, than how much of it is got." The character of the store-holders is fundamental, then, and it "may be conjectured by the quality of the store."[116] The holders of currency, on the other hand, "always increase in number and influence in proportion to the bluntness of nature and clumsiness of the store-holders; for the less use people can make of things, the more they want of them, and the sooner weary of them. . . . . The large currency-holder himself is essentially a person who never has been able to make up his mind what he will have."[117]

This discussion of the character of the holders leads Ruskin to a general "political law" governing the danger of wealth, in the ordinary sense, to life: "What is unreasonably gathered is also unreasonably spent by the persons into whose hands it finally falls."[118] This law, governing the generation of "illth," Ruskin connects with Dante's judgment of the prodigal and avaricious: "That ill they gave, and ill they kept, hath deprived them of the beauteous world."[119] By the action of this enigmatic law "the circulation of wealth [sic], which ought to be soft, steady, strong, far-sweeping, and full of warmth, like the Gulf stream . . . changes into the alternate suction and surrender of Charybdis."[120] This fanciful interpretation of Charybdis leads Ruskin into a long digression on mythic economics meant to document archetypally the fatal lure of accumulation.

He begins by remarking the "strange habit of wise humanity to speak in enigmas only, so that the highest truths and usefullest laws must be hunted for through whole picture-galleries of dreams, which to the vulgar seem dreams only."[121] So it is with Dante and Homer, and he will sketch here "the first broad intentions of their symbols" relating to the phantasms of wealth. In the *Inferno*, for instance, those avaricious and prodigal ones whose souls are beyond redemption, "meet in contrary currents, *as the waves of Charybdis*, casting weights at each other from opposite sides." This means that is not mere greed but *contention* for riches, leading to rash gathering and rash spending, which is the unredeemable sin. Their place of punishment is guarded by Plutus, "the great enemy," who, in Dante as distinct from the Greeks, is "definitely the Spirit of Contention and Competition" which " 'makes all men strangers.' "[122]

At the entrance to the same place Dante encounters another evil spirit, a feminine spirit he calls a Siren. She stands, Ruskin asserts, for the "phantasm or deceitfulness of riches," she is Dante's "Wealth Siren," the same as Spenser's Philotimé, daughter of Mammon. Dante followed Homer, Ruskin continues, in understanding the mythic Sirens to mean *desires*, not pleasures. In the *Odyssey* they are "phantoms of vain desire." (Is Ruskin touching on his personal agony here?) As such their power is to be distinguished from Circe's, which is "pure animal life; transforming—or degrading—but always wonderful." But the Sirens (like Rose La Touche?) "promise pleasure, but never give it. They nourish in no wise; but slay by slow death. And whereas they corrupt the heart and the head, instead of merely betraying the senses, there is no recovery from their power." Hence "the Siren's field is covered, not merely with the bones, but with the *skins*, of those who have been consumed there."[123]

Ruskin's mythic digression concludes with an interpretation of Ulysses' passage between the rocks of Scylla and Charybdis. The *rocks*, as distinct from the monsters, represent the choice of Labor or Idleness, getting or spending, and each choice has its "attendant monster, or betraying demon."[124] His interpretive descriptions of these rocks and their monsters are interesting, but enough of this long digression has already been given to show that Ruskin continued to have myth on his mind during this political work. To him, of course, myth was by no means incompatible with political economy, because he thought of the latter not as a "science" but as a "system of conduct" for the maintenance of the social organism. Therefore, he concludes his essay with the remark that when this "rambling note"[125] appeared in *Fraser's Magazine* he received a compliment on it from the editor. He was "very proud" of the compliment and still thinks "a great deal" of the note, hence he is elevating it to large print in the present (1872) edition. It is, of course, just possible that a private meaning in the myth of the Sirens was operative behind this decision.

The fourth essay, "Commerce," is closely related to the preceding two. Currency conveys the right to choose from many things in exchange for one, but commerce conveys the power to do so. In Ruskin's conception, commerce is not a means of profit ("trader" and "traitor" have the same root, he notes) but is true and faithful exchange as between friends or members of a family. Commerce is the circulatory system of the social body. "For as, taking the body natural for symbol of the body politic, the governing and forming powers may be likened to the brain, and the labouring to the limbs, the mercantile, presiding over circulation and communication of things in changed utilities, is symbolized by the heart; and, if that hardens, all is lost."[126]

Opposing this hardening of the social heart is the idea of "grace" in language and myth. So, using his customary tools, speculative etymology and classical allusion, Ruskin devotes the rest of his chapter to the meanings of grace in the consciousness of the West. Our great benediction "Grace, mercy, and peace," he begins, contains a deep truth, for there can be no peace "without triplicity of graciousness"; therefore, the Greeks, "who began that with one Grace, had to open their scheme into three before they had done."[127] This leads him to an interpretation of the mythic Graces that, in a way, balances with his interpretation of the Sirens in the preceding chapter; however in Athenian worship the Graces balanced with the Fates. His essential subject is twofold: the meaning of the evolution of the Greek Graces from one person to three, and the inescapable continuity of these ideas into our own consciousness through the evolution of words. His emphasis on etymology has a double purpose, then; it reveals the ancient meaning through the modern usage (sometimes an ironic revelation), and it shows how myth continues to operate through language. We have already considered the possible influence of Max Müller on this etymological bias of his thought.

We think of the Graces (or Charities), he continues, "as if they only gave loveliness to gesture; whereas their true function is to give graciousness to deed, the other loveliness arising naturally out of that."[128] His discussion of the Graces is more allusive than analytic and is therefore confusing, as is the actual history of the Greek worship of their powers, differing accounts of them being given in Homer, Hesiod, and Pausanius. In the *Iliad* Charis is the wife of Hephaestus; in the *Theogony*, Aglaia is his wife. Adding to the confusion is Ruskin's tendency to mix mythology and etymology freely; the derivation of three Graces from Charis and of various words from her name are confluent ideas in his account.

"Charis becomes Charitas," and a whole river of modern words springs from that source. ("The derivation of words," he notes in an appendix to this section, "is like that of rivers; there is one real source, usually small, unlikely, and difficult to find, far up among the hills; then, as the word flows on and comes into service, it takes in the force of other words from other sources.")[129] So from Charis we have, he points out, such words as *cher* for "dear" (as opposed to *cheap*) and "charity," in which Charis has become confused with the Latin *carus* and loses "the essential sense of contentment" and becomes mere alms-giving. But the Greek Charis "is in her countenance always gladdening (Aglaia), and in her service instant and humble; and the true wife of Vulcan, or Labour."[130] (As Aglaia she becomes the tutelary symbol of his papers on the laws of art, *The Cestus of Aglaia*.) "As Charis becomes Charitas on the one side, she becomes—better still—Chara, Joy, on the other"; and her influence descends into our words "choir" and "choral." Finally, "as Grace passes into freedom of action, Charis becomes Eleutheria, or Liberality." But this is a form of liberty "intensely different" from our usual meaning of liberty, because it derives from the original meaning of the word, a meaning many of us would equate with slavery, "for a Greek always understood, primarily, by liberty, deliverance from the law of his own passions."[131]

This third form of Charis brings him to the discussion of the general principles of government, particularly the government of the poor by the rich, which are the subjects of his last two essays, "Government" and "Mastership." There it will be discovered how "the Graciousness joined with the Greatness, or Love with Majestas, is the true Dei Gratia, or Divine Right, of every form and manner of King."[132] Ruskin is aware of the fusion of any economic system with a political system, yet a central difficulty is that his scheme is ultimately mythic as well as organic. It assumes not only a social organism unified by familial bonds of care but one that is also governed by a paternal authority both gracious and great. Such authority can never be assured by any temporal form of government; therefore, it is ultimately mythic or religious at its apex. For this reason after having analyzed the various modes of government within a state (customs, laws, councils) he is driven back upon a simple principle, but one that is as elusive as true grace: "All forms of government are good just so far as they attain this one vital necessity of policy—*that the wise and kind, few or many, shall govern the unwise and unkind.*"[133]

With "Mastership," the economic government of the poor by the rich, he must also fall back on a utopian precept: honorable government of the poor by the rich involves "the collection of the profits of labour from those who would have misused them, and the administration of those profits for the service either of the same persons in future, or of others." The dishonorable government "consists in the collection of the profits of labor from those who would have rightly used them, and their appropriation to the service of the collector himself."[134] In the employment of any poor person there are three points to consider. It is not enough, first, merely to employ him. He must be employed to produce useful things. Then, second, of the useful things he could produce equally as well, "you must set him to make that which will cause him to lead the healthiest life," and third, of the things he produces "it remains a question of wisdom and conscience how much you are to take yourself, and how much to leave to others."[135] In this final question of wisdom and conscience, however, there is one guiding law governing the struggle of life with wealth and reducing it to harmony: "die, not as rich, but as poor, as possible, calculating the ebb tide of possession in true and calm proportion to the ebb tide of life."[136]

5

Ruskin's third major socio-economic statement, *Time and Tide* (1867), represents an important departure in form and style, though not in theoretical content, from the two works just discussed. We recall that the two earlier series of essays had both encountered so much hostility from readers that the magazines in which they first appeared were forced to suspend publication of them. By publishing through such monthly vehicles as *Cornhill* and *Fraser's*, Ruskin was aiming at readers who largely represented the very economic establishment he was attacking. In *Time and Tide* he directed his remarks at an audience closer to the heart of his system, the skilled and thoughtful working man; and at the same time he chose a mode of publication less sensitive to radical opinion and more proletarian. Here we do not have systematic essays at all but rather a collection, to quote the subtitle, of "Twenty-Five Letters to a Working Man of Sunderland on the Laws of Work." The complete series appeared in 1867 in two newspapers, the *Leeds Mercury* and the *Manchester Daily Examiner and Times* (two were published in the *Scotsman* and one in the *Pall Mall Gazette*), and they were collected and published in volume form that year. The working man to whom they were addressed was Thomas Dixon, a cork cutter by trade, who had written to Ruskin asking for copies of his writings on political economy. The economist responded willingly, not only with this course of letters on the subject but with his warm friendship. Dixon a sober, competent, self-educated, and quietly philanthropic man of business was, as Cook puts it, "a man after Ruskin's heart." He could serve as Ruskin's archetypal workman, the perfect sounding board for his ideas.

These, of course, were not his first letters on economic issues, throughout the decade he continued to address such letters to the *Times* and other newspapers; but as a discursive series of letters to workmen on what he thought should be their concerns, this project is the prototype of *Fors Clavigera*, though in content it was intended to supplement *Munera Pulveris*. Like that of the brief *Academy Notes* in art, the particular format of this political work, a series of letters written as chance directed yet loosely connected to a central subject, nicely suited the working of Ruskin's mind and style. It might even be called a therapeutic form for him. *Munera Pulveris* had been distorted by the inclusion of disparate materials. Brisk sequences of definitions and patterns of systematic economic reasoning were interrupted by densely allusive digressions and probings into mythology and etymology; they were materials of interest to two quite different audiences.

Time and Tide is ostensibly about the "laws of work," but few "laws" in the ordinary economist's sense are set down, though some precepts for an ideal social order are given. In general, however, the "laws" referred to are the laws of things a prophet discerns, not an inductive or deductive code of controlling principles, but revealed moral operations and their consequences, apocalyptic laws. The epistolary sequence allows Ruskin to avoid the demands of sequential or systematic thought and follow the demands of an incidental digression or a revelational experience. The loose linkage of subjects permits him to take a personal moment, an incident, and peer through it as a symbol into vast moral and mythic operations and their fateful consequences. The form also fitted a time of social crisis. England in 1867 was troubled by considerable and ominous labor agitation for Parliamentary reform, but Ruskin saw himself as writing to a society verging on anarchy and desperate for any credible voice of leadership. Not only did he perceive an "imminent danger" brought about by the "gradually accelerated fall of our aristocracy," the "correspondingly imminent prevalence of mob violence here, as in America," and the "continually increasing chances of insane war, founded on popular passion," but further, "the monstrous forms of vice and selfishness which the *appliances* of recent wealth, and of vulgar mechanical art, make possible to the million,—will soon bring us to a condition in which men will be glad to listen to almost any words but those of a demagogue, and seek any means of safety rather than those in which they have lately trusted. So, with your leave, I will say my say to the end, mock at it who may."[137] What he has to say, to the end of these letters at least, is so diverse and agitated, such a mixture of revelation, moral law, and utopian particulars, that these letters defy any brief summary. One can only indicate some of the thematic patterns in them.

In his preface (1867) Ruskin explains that these letters were primarily intended to tell English workmen that their parliamentary influence would be useless or worse to them until they could agree on what they wanted, and that once they had made up their minds they could accomplish this on their own, without Parliament. These letters were to help them make up their minds, especially with regard to the ethics of labor.

The first three letters, accordingly, have some direct bearing on this subject. They speak, for instance, of the organic meaning of "cooperation," which is "opposed not to masterhood but to *competition*,"[138] and ought to lead to regular and fixed wages, retirement provisions, and so forth, in a kind of corporate state in which the master is *"held, responsible, as a minor king or governor, for the conduct as well as the comfort of all those under his rule."*[139] In any "healthful system of social economy," furthermore, the incomes and properties of the upper classes would be restrained within certain fixed limits. Laborers, he observes, can immediately organize into any kind of cooperative system they want (provided it does not infringe upon the "liberties and properties" of others); they can elect their own parliament and pass their own laws, but they will not find the present order of things easy to change. If they passed economic laws solely to their advantage, neglecting the deep meaning of cooperation, "the only result would be that the riches of the country would at once leave it, and you would perish in riot and famine." Great change for the better does not come easily or quickly, yet it is still a question of whether we will reach our social goals (if we do) "through a chain of involuntary miseries, many of them useless, and all of them ignoble; or whether we will know the worst at once, and deal with it by the wisely sharp methods of Godsped courage."[140]

Knowing the "worst at once" seems to be the controlling theme of the next series of letters. This group of eight letters, numbers 4 through 11, sets forth no economic or social principles; its method is subjective, prophetic, and apocalyptic. The section is a kind of harrowing of hell in which, using impressions of current tastes as symbolic revelations, Ruskin illuminates the infernal condition of modern sensibility, places it in mythic perspective, and, by this, declares the need for (and the inevitability of) some kind of social deluge and new order. In this way he clears the ground, prophetically and cathartically, for the principles of a new community that are to be given in the calmer sequence of letters that follows. The method of this middle group of letters is essentially that of *Fors Clavigera*, his major work of the seventies.

The series opens with a brief letter describing the absurd disproportion between what his society spends for art and what it spends for war; more and more is being spent to guard less and less. In the next letter Ruskin comments on the format of this string of personal letters; chance (Fate, *Fors*) directs what will go into them from day to day. (This means that they drift with and participate in the innate tendencies of things, become involved organically with the movement of the whole.) What chance brings on this occasion, as he lets the culture speak him, is a revelational encounter with a pantomime at Covent Garden. The subject of the pantomime was "Ali Baba and the Forty Thieves"; in it the forty thieves were forty girls. In the audience the author of *Sesame and Lilies* (1865) had two contrasting revelational moments. In one scene a lovely little girl danced a graceful and innocent *pas de deux* with a donkey, and not a single hand was raised in applause except his. But then: "Presently after this, came on the forty thieves, who, as I told you were girls; and, their being no thieving to be presently done, and time hanging heavy on their hands, arms, and legs, the forty thief-girls proceeded to light forty cigars. Whereupon the British public gave them a round of applause. Whereupon I fell a thinking; and saw little more of the piece, except as an ugly and disturbing dream."[141]

The next letter also concerns "The Corruption of Modern Pleasure." Ruskin has attended an exhibition of Japanese jugglers, and there something is revealed to him by the "demoniacal" character of Japanese masks, as opposed to mere loathsome ugliness of English masks. What is revealed is "a nation, afflicted by an evil spirit, and driven by it to recreate themselves in achieving, or beholding the achievement, through years of patience, of a certain correspondence with the nature of the lower animals."[142] In the next letter, concerned with "Various Expressions of National Festivity," the demonic again appears in two distinct experiences. The first is an account of another number from the Ali Baba pantomime in which a girl's dance becomes a dance of death to a serpent's rattle.

> It was also a dance by a little girl—though one older than Ali Baba's daughter, (I suppose a girl of twelve or fourteen). A dance, so-called, which consisted only in a series of short, sharp contractions and jerks of the body and limbs, resulting in attitudes of distorted and quaint ugliness, such as might be produced in a puppet by sharp twitching of strings at its joints; these movements being made to the sound of two instruments, which between them accomplished a quick vibratory beating and strumming, in nearly the time of a hearth-cricket's song, but much harsher . . . in the monotony and aimless construction of it, reminding one of various other insect and reptile cries or warnings; partly of the cicada's hiss; partly of the little melancholy German frog which says "Mu, mu, mu," all summer-day long, with its nose out of the pools by Dresden or Leipsic; and partly of the deadened quivering and intense continuousness of the alarm of the rattlesnake.[143]

The second revelation of the possessed condition of modern sensibility comes in the form of Gustave Doré's illustrations of Balzac's *Contes Drôlatiques*, for which Ruskin conceived a near-pathological detestation.

> The text is full of blasphemies, subtle, tremendous, hideous in shamelessness, some put into the mouths of priests; the illustrations are, in a word, one continuous revelry in the most loathsome and monstrous aspects of death and sin, enlarged into fantastic ghastliness of caricature, as if seen through the distortion and trembling of the hot smoke of the mouth of hell. Take the following for a general type of what they seek in death: one of the most laboured designs is of a man cut in two, downwards, by the sweep of a sword—one half of him falls toward the spectator; the other half is elaborately drawn in its section—giving the profile of the divided nose and lips; cleft jaw—breast—and entrails; and this done with farther pollution and horror of intent in the circumstances, which I do not choose to describe.[144]

Both instances, the girl's puppet dance and the accurate human section, are violations of the organic, as is the smoking of the forty thief-girls (and, of course, animal vivisection, which Ruskin actively opposed). It is a further ironic "sign of the times" that this detested Doré has been chosen by the "British Evangelical Public . . . to adorn their hitherto unadorned Bible."[145]

This point leads him into a letter on the four possible theories respecting the authority of the Bible. This letter (number 8) is interesting because in it he discusses his own position on the illustration of organic laws by Scripture. Honesty is not, he begins, to be based *on* religion or social policy; rather these are based on honesty, which "must be based, as the sun is, in vacant heaven." The four theories of Biblical authority are (1) literalist: "every syllable of it His 'Word' "; (2) inspirationalist: it was "furnished to man by Divine inspiration of the speakers and writers of it" and is therefore absolutely true; (3) existentialist: its sayings were not collected by any Divine guidance which protected them from error; there is truth and error in it as in life, but it is an attempt to "relate, on the whole, faithfully, the dealings of the one God with the first races of man, and His dealings in aftertime through Christ"; (4) archetypalist or mythicist: "that the mass of religious Scripture contains merely the best efforts which we hitherto know to have been made by any of the races of men towards the discovery of some relations with the spiritual world; that they are only trustworthy as expressions of the enthusiastic visions or beliefs of earnest men oppressed by the world's darkness, and have no more authoritative claim on our faith than the religious speculations and histories of the Egyptians, Greeks, Persians and Indians; but they are, in common with these, to be reverently studied."[146]

This last, of course, would be the humanist position of Ruskin's "religion of Humanity"; however, he does not identify with this position directly. He says: "I . . . always imagine myself speaking to the fourth class of theorists. If I can persuade or influence *them*, I am logically sure of the others."[147] He goes on to say, interestingly, that in his political thought he uses organic theory to get at the archetypalists and them to get at the fundamentalists. That is, in "deducing principles of action first from the laws and facts of nature, I nevertheless fortify them also by the appliance of precepts, or suggestive and probable teachings of this Book, of which the authority is over many around you, more distinctly than over you [fourth group], and which, confessing to be divine, *they*, at least can only disobey at their mortal peril."[148]

The discussion of Scriptural authority concludes with a text concerning the music of Miriam the prophetess ("which haunted me through the jugglery") and this becomes his text for a letter on the religious significance of music, "The Use of Music and Dancing under the Jewish Theocracy, compared with their Use by the Modern French." This letter involves another of his revelations in modern pleasure, a kind of culminating vision of the modern sensibility, climaxing the theme of demonic possession we have seen developing in this series of letters. In Paris, "following, for once, the lead of my countrymen," Ruskin had gone to see the *Lanterne Magique*, which was the rage among the English there. The show concluded with "the representation of the characteristic dancing of all ages of the world; and the dance given as characteristic of modern time was the Cancan."[149] Ruskin had described his impression of it in a note to *Sesame and Lilies*, and he refers his reader to it.

> "The ball terminated with a Devilish Chain and a cancan of Hell, at seven in the morning." It was led by four principal dancers . . . and it is many years since I have seen such perfect dancing, as far as finish and accuracy of art and fullness of animal power and fire are concerned. Nothing could be better done, in its own evil way; the object of the dance throughout being to express, in every gesture, the wildest fury of insolence and vicious passions possible to human creatures. So that you see, though, for the present, we find ourselves utterly incapable of a rapture of gladness or thanksgiving [as danced in the Jewish Theocracy], the dance which is presented as characteristic of modern civilization is still rapturous enough—but it is with rapture of blasphemy.[150]

This dance of modern times, the devilish chain or cancan of hell, Ruskin takes as a symbol of the corrupted or possessed condition of the modern feeling. The last two letters of this series (numbers 10 and 11), both concerning the operation of "Satanic or Demoniacal Influence," serve to put this condition in mythic perspective, Christian and Greek.

In the first of these two letters on the demoniacal power Ruskin asserts the real and effective power of the archetype of the archenemy over human life. Hell is real. "I do not merely *believe* there is such a place as hell. I *know* there is such a place; and I know also that when men have got to the point of believing virtue impossible but through the dread of it, they have got *into* it."[151] We can get there and be here. As for the evil spirit, his presence is equally real, and his work is *here* among us, and it is to be dreaded that we should not recognize him among us when we see him. "In fearful truth, the Presence and Power of Him *is* here; in the world, with us, and within us, mock as you may; and the fight with him, for the time, sore, and widely unprosperous."[152] However, his view of that presence is not sectarian but archetypal or syncretic.

> I do not care what you call it,—whose history you believe of it,—nor what you yourself may imagine about it; the origin, or nature, or name may be as you will, but the deadly reality of the thing is with us, and warring against us, and on our true war with it depends whatever life we can win. Deadly reality, I say. The puff-adder or horned asp is not more real. Unbelievable,—*those*,—unless you had seen them; no fable could have been coined out of any human brain so dreadful, within its own poor

material sphere, as that blue-lipped serpent—working its way side long in the sand.[153]

What, then, is that venomous power, as real as this living myth, the asp, and with whom we are in decisive conflict? It is, of course the power of Mammon, false wealth, whose kingdom is the sterile "Valley of Diamonds" in *The Ethics of the Dust*. The second of these two letters on demoniacal power identifies him: "This thing, or power, opposed to God's power, and specifically called 'Mammon' in The Sermon on the Mount, is, in deed and in truth, a continually present and active enemy, properly called '*Arch*-enemy,' that is to say, 'Beginning and Prince of Enemies,' and daily we have to record our vote for, or against him."[154]

He is always recognizable by his two main agencies in human existence: he is the "Lord of *Lies*" and the "Lord of *Pain*." The primary fight against him is by way of education; the aim of education should be, Ruskin asserts, to "make yourselves and your children *capable of Honesty* and *capable of Delight*; and to rescue yourselves from iniquity and agony." This great enemy attacks the unity and harmony of the social organism; his presence is seen in the failure of personal integrity and in the corruption of the musical ear and bodily rhythm. This is the apocalyptic meaning, it appears, that Ruskin perceived in the spasmodic dance of the thief-girl in the pantomime or in the devilish chain and cancan of hell. Finally, we learn that the Greeks understood all this. With them, music was "quite the first means of education." And in their mythology, Apollo, their god of life and light, is the power also of righteousness and music. As such he is "the God who purges and avenges iniquity, and contends with their Satan as represented under the form of Python, 'the corrupter.' "[155]

In this apocalyptic and mythic unit of eight letters Ruskin has identified the conflict of social life with its final enemy. In an earlier letter he remarks to Dixon that even though he is writing everything in a straightforward way, leaving his alterations visible, he nonetheless does not consider these letters to be a trivial utterance. "This only I know," he writes, "that what I tell you is true, and written more earnestly than anything I ever wrote with my best literary care."[156] And now, having identified the inherent crisis in this long prophetic digression, he must come back to the original plan of the letters and lay down some of the social principles, the "necessary laws," by which the enemy of life may be controlled. This code is the subject of the remaining fourteen letters of the series. However, since many of these principles are adapted from *Unto This Last* and *Munera Pulveris*, we may briefly notice a few laws or structures that he has not previously advocated.

One such principle is the suggestion that in his ideal commonwealth there would be appointed, for every 500 families, "an overseer or bishop" whose duty it would be to render an account to the state of every individual in those families, so that no person, however humble, would be allowed "to suffer from unknown want or live in unrecognized crime." This is to be the foundational law of his state. "All men ought to be in this sense 'noble'; known of each other, and desiring to be known. The first law which a nation, desiring to conquer all the devices of the Father of Lies, should establish among its people, is that they *shall* be so known."[157] It would be an attempt to legislate community in the social "open boat," a law of help and light.

But another basic feature of Ruskin's social scheme is the emphasis he places on education. Crime, he argues, cannot be effectively legislated against; it must be educated against. The education he advocates, however, would not be of the intellect only, nor would it be used for "getting on in the world," rather it would be "a means for staying pleasantly in one's place there."[158] State education would involve (1) perfecting the body as far as is possible with each individual; (2) development of the major innate graces, reverence and compassion; (3) education in truth, "truth of spirit and word, of thought and sight"; (4) urban-oriented or rural-oriented vocational education, dependent upon individual needs.

The idea that "manual occupations *are* degrading" is constant with Ruskin, and one of the primary aims of his society is to keep the dirty work and its moral effects to a minimum. This would be accomplished in part by combining moral and vocational education and in part by the inculcation of consumer ethics. "It is the duty," he asserts, "of all persons in higher stations of life, by every means in their power, to diminish their demand for work of such kind, *and to live with as little aid from the lower trades,* as they can possibly contrive."[159] This principle of minimization or conservation of wants ("living with as few wants as possible") is crucial to Ruskin's organic scheme, is perhaps its central ethic. On the one hand, it reduces the oppression of others: a want, he notes "does not cost money only. It costs degradation. You do not merely employ these people. You also *tread* upon them."[160] But the precept involves not only the conservation of human or inner nature by minimizing its degradation; it also involves the preservation of outer nature and its moral influences. For if we demand what we do *not* need of nature, she will eventually plague us with what we do not want. "Demand what you deserve, and you shall be supplied with it, for your good. Demand what you do *not* deserve, and you shall be supplied with something which you have not demanded, and which Nature perceives that you deserve, quite to the contrary of your good. That is the law of your existence, and if you do not make it the law of your resolved acts, so much, precisely, the worse for you and all connected with you."[161]

Two other important aspects of Ruskin's scheme have to do with family planning and land tenure. As a governor of Christ's Hospital he was particularly sensitive to the problem of unwanted or under-privileged children. He proposes to deal with this problem in his ideal state through the regulation of marriage, thinking, perhaps naively, that this would control sexuality and conception. "You leave your marriages to be settled by 'supply and demand,' " he notes, "instead of some wholesome law."[162] His law is that marriage should be a privilege conferred by the state and made contingent upon satisfactory preparation for life; "it should be granted as the national attestation that the first portion of their lives had been rightly fulfilled."[163] There would be two annual festivals, in May and at harvest time, at which "maidens" who had received permission to marry (not before the age of seventeen) would be crowned by "the old French title of *Rosières*" and the eligible men (not before their twenty-first year) by the also significant title "bachelor," meaning "*laurel* fruit." Finally, "every bachelor and rosière should be entitled to claim, if they needed it, according to their position in life, a fixed income from the State, for seven years from the day of their marriage."[164]

Ruskin does not favor what is ordinarily called land reform, that is, the redistribution of land to the poor. He argues that this would, in affect, amount simply to a small increase in their incomes, and "they would multiply into as much extra personality as the extra pence would sustain, and at that point be checked by starvation, exactly as they are now."[165] Land reform will not answer the ultimate population questions. These are, "first, by what methods of land distribution you can maintain the greatest number of healthy persons; and secondly, whether, if, by any other mode of distribution and relative ethical laws, you can raise their character, while you diminish their numbers, such sacrifice should be made, and to what extent?"[166]

These are unanswerable questions, of course, and Ruskin has no detailed solutions, but he does lay down a few distinct precepts regarding land tenure. One organic principle is central: land must not be considered personal property, to be sold or rented. This is because he considers the land as an extension of the human being, and it may not be sold any more than the souls it is lent us to support. "Bodies of men, or women, then (and much more, as I said before, their souls) must not be bought or sold. Neither must land, nor water, nor air, these being the necessary sustenance of men's bodies and souls."[167] The state may lend to a man as much land as is needful for his life, in much the same sense as it secures his wife to him, without his owning her. Far from being profitable to own, land would be an expense, as Ruskin sees it; for the holder should be under obligation to maintain what he does not cultivate in a state of natural coherence and grace. Agriculture and other energy-intensive work must be done, insofar as possible, without machinery. His principle of energy conservation requires that energy sources that do not violate the organic unity of nature (manpower, wind power, waterpower) must be fully utilized before the expedients which involve the disunion of elements and the expenditure of resources.

There are many other details of Ruskin's scheme as it appears in this last series of fourteen letters that cannot be discussed here, such as the various officers of his hypothesized government and their functions. One final point, however, leads in the direction we have yet to go. From the paternal monarch and "Supreme Judges" on down, his is a system involving helpful, watchful, and wise inequality and submission to authority. This interdependent inequality of parts is a characteristic of organic form, as we noted in his discussion of tree growth in volume 5 of *Modern Painters*. This inevitable inequality in rank and capacity is not rectified by education; rather it is intensified by true education. It is only false education that is the great leveler; true education gains all it gains "at compound interest"; so that every hour of progress in it is a felt loss against the great men with whom we started out as equals. There is a law and its mythic symbol by which we may distinguish true education from false. "False education is a delightful thing, and warms you, and makes you every day think more of yourself. And true education is a deadly cold thing, with a Gorgon's head on her shield, and makes you every day think worse of yourself."[168]

In his last letter to Dixon, Ruskin returns to that mythic struggle which occupied the earlier, prophetic sequence of these letters. He reminds his reader that "all Christ's main teachings, by direct order, by earnest parable, and by His own permanent emotion, regard the use and misuse of *money*."[169] With the Prodigal Son, it was not his sensuality that was his main fault, but his *wastefulness*. And if any readers, he concludes, are alarmed by the stress he has placed on Christ's teachings about the struggle with wealth, they must only remember the centrality of Mammon among the mythic powers of evil. "Let them be assured that it is with no fortuitous choice among the attributes or powers of evil, that 'Mammon' is assigned for the direct adversary of the Master whom they are bound to serve. You cannot, by any artifice of reconciliation, be God's soldier, and his."[170]

CHAPTER 12

In the Midst of Judgment

Ruskin's main efforts in the fifties belonged to aesthetics. He evolved a theory of the diverse arts that stressed their dependence on organic form, the mysteries of subtly gradated light, and myth (or "spiritual invention"). But there were strong undercurrents too of social criticism in this first phase. He related the vitality of the work to the life of the workman and the life of the workman to the health of the social organism. In fact these themes forecast his later social doctrines clearly enough to permit one to say that his message is largely complete with the publication of the last volume of *Modern Painters* and *The Political Economy of Art*. However, the early currents of social criticism became a kind of undertow in his life by the turn of the decade, drawing his work of the early sixties entirely down from the higher mysteries of art to the murky struggle of life with greed. And in the works just discussed (*Unto This Last, Munera Pulveris* and *Time and Tide*) we observed the foliation of his early social theory into an organic economics meant to oppose what he regarded as the fatally divisive economics of the autonomous market system. Thus by the mid sixties he had formulated an aesthetics and an economics, both founded primarily on the organic model.

But there is an even more profound and continuous pull in Ruskin's work than either aesthetics or economics; this might be called *prophetics*. The prophetic bent, implying a sense of mission conferred by mythic authority and leading to visionary utterance, is simply the distinctive characteristic of his way of being—the essential quality of his mind, his style, his sense of his role. This quality is present from the beginnings of his work, of course; but now, from the mid sixties on, prophecy becomes its dominant feature. This final phase of his work must be called a prophetic phase, though in the end it will often fall beneath this level into arrogant and truculent denunciation.

In this period the theoretical content of his message does not advance greatly, and the medium that bears it takes precedence. The causes of this increased reliance upon prophetic devices might be sought in a number of directions in his personal life: frustration and disillusionment with the failure of his rational schemes to win general approval, the need for a plurisignative discourse in which he could express at once his public message and private agony, the dependence of his platform success upon rhetorical extravagance.

These and other causes could be considered, but there is a final all-important qualification to be made about this prophetic phase: it is an advance in a different dimension. Prophecy in the literary sense (not mere prediction) is impossible without myth and apocalypse. It depends upon symbolic referents binding a transcendent order of arrangements to moments of experience in which those arrangements are revealed. For his prophecy Ruskin needed, in effect, an integrating "spiritual invention" such as he found in a great landscape like Turner's *Apollo and Python*. The organic model, while it is mythic in a sense, is too abstract to have prophetic value unless it could be seen as reflecting the intentions of a personal "Forming Power," much as his view of the market mechanism became prophetic only as he could reveal in it the intentions of a deforming power, Mammon. Therefore, in the secondary works of the sixties, which we are about to examine, we can observe the fragmentary formation of a "prophetics" in Ruskin's work. Out of a gradual study of Greek symbol that culminates in *The Queen of the Air* he formulates a mythic core for the organic model and makes himself its prophet.

These noneconomic works of the sixties can be placed in two categories already mentioned. One group consists of works concerned with the problem of finding moral guides or outlines for the social body without depending on a supernatural system of reward and punishment and with the thesis that art inevitably reflects the moral condition of the society out of which it grows. Under this heading we place *Sesame and Lilies, The Crown of Wild Olive, The Cestus of Aglaia* and a related group of lectures on art and ethics. To a separate category belong *The Ethics of the Dust* and *The Queen of the Air*, because these works return to the precepts of the organic model itself and its guardian mythic powers. The mythology of Athena, which links these two works and emerges also in works of the first group, will carry us beyond this chapter into the next. However, in both chapters we will be concerned with Ruskin's attempt to construct a prophetic system of symbols, speech of the judgment we are in the midst of, and with the meaning and sources of this system.

1

Sesame and Lilies (1865) shows the resurgence of the prophetic in his writing of the sixties, but in a calmer, less embittered and ironic mode than other works of the period. His thought proceeds in a more direct and unified way here; his arguments are eloquent and high-toned but less entangled in digression and allusion. The relative purity and peaceful concentration of its style have made this one of Ruskin's most popular books. But the two original lectures show little in the way of theoretical advance. Unlike the three socioeconomic works just discussed, it is not concerned with social organization and sustenance but with the problem of ethical authority in the lived world. This is its prophetic direction. The work consists of two, then three, then two lectures, depending on which edition one speaks of. The version of 1865 consisted of the two lectures delivered at Manchester in 1864, "Of Kings' Treasuries" and "Of Queens' Gardens." The first, the *Sesame*, speaks of the moral influence of books that are true books, works in the great literary humanistic tradition; the second, the *Lilies*, concerns the guiding influence of good (he says "pure") women in the gardens of human life.

With these lectures a third, "The Mystery of Life and Its Arts" (1868), was collected in the edition of 1871. This lecture raises again "that old Greek question" of the transience and obscured meaning of human life, the problem of human ends. While its view is generally more pessimistic than that of the accompanying lectures, its uplifting denouement speaks of the possible illumination of life's mystery in hand work and helpful action, though not in contemplation. It is one of the central expressions of his "religion of Humanity." "I put into it all that I knew," he told a friend.[1] The lecture was delivered at The Royal College of Science, Dublin, and his preface of 1871 makes plain that this lecture in particular was addressed *to* Rose, while the whole of *Sesame and Lilies* was written *for* her. In the edition of 1882 this relatively existential essay was withdrawn because Ruskin had passed into a new phase of quasi-Catholic religious mysticism.

The three prefaces Ruskin wrote for the book are an interesting little history of his development from the mid sixties on. The preface of 1865 (to the second edition) is the least self-conscious of the three. News of an Alpine climbing accident provides him with a metaphoric text for reflections on the divisive effects of greed on life, that is, on the natural linkages among men and between man and nature. Were the Swiss guides bribed into danger? Well, this could be expected, for the British at home are not entirely innocent of buying the lives of their fellow creatures. The ghosts of greed are everywhere. "They do not, perhaps, often calculate how many souls flit annually, choked in fire-damp and sea-sand, from economically watched shafts, and economically manned ships; nor see the fiery ghosts writhe up out of every scuttlefull of cheap coals."[2] Alpinists' ropes must not break, and in an organic society "*nothing* should break; banks,—words,—nor dredging tackle."[3] The effect of English tourism in Switzerland has been a violation of the organic unity of its people and its environment.

Ruskin prepared the 1871 edition of *Sesame and Lilies* to be the first volume in his projected "Works Series"; consequently, the second preface is both subjective and interpretive where the first preface was neither. He assesses broadly the value of his past work (even, in effect, retracting portions of it) and provides an analytic commentary on these lectures (now including "The Mystery of Life and Its Arts") so that the reader may understand their significance. Surveying his past work, he points out that his earliest writing shows the effect of his having been "educated in the doctrines of a narrow sect," and is therefore "wholly mistaken" in religious outlook; it is also "disfigured by affected language," owing to the influence on him of his "then favourite, in prose, Richard Hooker."[4] Though his opinions on art, policy, and morality (but not religion) hold true from his earliest work, because of their religious narrowness and stylistic inauthenticity he would reprint scarcely anything out of volumes 1 and 2 of *Modern Painters* and omit much of the *Seven Lamps* and *Stones*. But all his books since 1856 would be reprinted without change.

Turning to the three lectures, he finds the first two "fragmentary and ill-arranged"; although there is much in them that is "accurately and energetically said, there is scarcely anything put in a form to be generally convincing, or even easily intelligible."[5] The whole gist of them, he continues, is in the injunction of helpful work and wasteless living that concludes the third lecture. These six paragraphs (135 to the end) contain, he declares, "the best expression I have yet been able to put in words of what, so far as is within my power, I mean henceforward both to do myself, and to plead with all over whom I have any influence, to do also according to their means."[6] He explains that the *Fors Clavigera* letters to the workmen of England, begun on 1 January of that year (1871), have the purpose of originating "this movement among them." He urges the reader also to look again "by the fiery light of recent events" at certain paragraphs (117-18, 129-31) on economics and famine and to take note of the fact that at least five hundred thousand persons have died of starvation in British dominions, "the best possible illustration of modern political economy in true practice, and of the relations it has accomplished between Supply and Demand."[7]

From these portents of world famine Ruskin shifts the reader back to his second lecture, the *Lilies* ("Of Queens' Gardens"), and what he would now say "to any girl who had confidence enough in me to believe what I told her, or do what I asked her." What he would say he says at length in the following ten paragraphs of the preface. They are essentially an attack on sectarian narrowness and consequent neglect of the needs of this life—a characteristic statement of his humanist creed. These remarks have also a private significance for him in being directed at the morbidly pious Rose, who was putting her religion between them. First, he tells English girls, don't think that you have been singled out by your Maker from all the world of girls "to be specially informed respecting His own nature and character."[8] Don't think that you have been born on a luminous point of the globe where you alone might be nurtured in a perfect theology. Again, the "religion of Humanity": "Of all the insolent, all the foolish persuasions that by any chance could enter and hold your empty little heart, this is the proudest and foolishest,—that you have been so much the darling of the Heavens, and favourite of the Fates, as to be born in the very nick of time, and in the punctual place, when and where pure Divine truth had been sifted from the errors of the Nations."[9]

He would further tell English girls that whatever faults they may think they have, the only ones of real consequence are idleness and cruelty. " 'Work while you have light,' " he enjoins, "especially while you have the light of morning. . . . There is no solemnity so deep, to a rightly-thinking creature, as that of dawn."[10] Their work must be useful before all things, including daily work that is "useful in the vulgar sense." And of cruelty, there is cruelty through want of imagination (imagination, Ruskin supposes, is a rarer and weaker faculty in women than in men), but a worse kind of cruelty is "the subtle encouragement of your selfishness by the religious doctrine that all which we now suppose to be evil will be brought to a good end." Modern education, he trusts, will encourage a more organic view of salvation and will not "permit young people to grow up in the persuasion that, in any danger or distress, they may expect to be themselves saved by the Providence of God, while those around them are lost by His improvidence." However religious, persons may be "yet long restrained from rightly kind action. . . . by misconception of the eternal and incurable nature of evil."[11] (Perhaps we should read a special message to Rose in a remark he makes at this point: "Let heart-sickness pass beyond a certain bitter point, and the heart loses its life forever.")[12] It is a tenet of his "religion of Humanity" that the theological notion of evil, in which it is by definition irremediable, ought not to prevent action against evil in our natural, organic sense of it in the daily world. "Believe me," he continues, "the only right principle of action here is to consider good and evil as defined by our natural sense of both; and to strive to promote the one, and to conquer the other, with as hearty endeavour as if there were, indeed, no other world than this."[13] A final injunction to English girls is again an expression of organic humanism: "Joy in nothing that separates you, as by any strange favour, from your fellow-creatures, that exalts you through their degradation—exempts you from their toil—or indulges you in time of their distress."[14]

Ruskin concludes this important preface with a strikingly personal reference, especially if we remember that his private romantic agony in pursuit of Rose reached a crisis between the composition of *Lilies* (1864) and that of the preface. "I wrote the *Lilies*," he declares, "to please one girl; and were it not for what I remember of her, and of few besides, should now perhaps recast some of the sentences in the *Lilies* in a very different tone: for as years have gone by, it has chanced to me . . . to see the utmost evil that is in women, while I have had but to believe the utmost good." He explains further that the "weak picturesqueness" of his early style of writing brought him into contact with the "emptiest enthusiasm" of women, while "the chances of later life gave me opportunities of watching women in states of degradation and vindictiveness which opened to me the gloomiest secrets of Greek and Syrian tragedy."[15] But despite this bitter knowledge about the nature of women he leaves the words of *Lilies* unchanged and dedicates the work to the help of one woman (Mrs. Cowper-Temple) but for whom "the day would probably have come before now, when I should have written and thought no more." He remains convinced that "no man ever lived a right life who had not been chastened by a woman's love, strengthened by her courage, and guided by her discretion."[16]

In 1882, having been urged to do so by his friend Susan Beever, Ruskin reissued *Sesame and Lilies*. On this occasion he had the two original lectures reprinted without additional material. In the "Preface to the Small Edition of 1881" he explains that the first preface, with its sweeping political moral drawn from Alpine tourism, is being dropped as irrelevant. The revealing antisectarian preface of 1871 he calls "gossiping" while explaining that it and the third lecture, "The Mystery of Life and Its Arts," are being dropped "not as irrelevant, but as following the subject too far" and disturbing the simplicity of the original lectures.[17] Having taken all the bite out of the book he can correctly observe that what is left is a work "wholly of the old school" that ignores the "ferment of surrounding elements" including "positivism with its religion of humanity, and negativism with its religion of Chaos,—and the like, . . . together with a mass of realistic, or materialistic, literature and art, founded mainly on the theory of nobody's having any will, or needing any master."[18]

Such, then, are the three prefaces with their three different moods: prefaces of the political radical, the confessional humanist, and the pious conservative. Turning now to the *Sesame* ("Of Kings' Treasuries"), the first lecture of the volume, we find Ruskin explaining that the lecture is "about the treasures hidden in books; and about the way we find them, and the way we lose them."[19] It typifies works of the group we are observing in their movement toward his last or prophetic phase because here an aspect of culture (depth of reading) is used to reveal its spiritual state, and the concern is not for a system of social organization but for its moral inspiration. As for the first aspect of his present subject, the treasures *hidden* in books, the main point is a fundamental distinction between two kinds of books. There are, he says, "books of the hour" and "books of all time." This is a difference in species, he asserts, not a qualitative one; there are good and bad books in each category. The book of the hour is "simply useful or pleasant *talk*" of a person you cannot meet; it is merely a medium for multiplying that person's voice. The true book, however, is "not a talking thing, but a written thing"; it is meant "not to multiply the voice merely . . . but to perpetuate it."[20] The distinction is not entirely clear, of course, but it is apparent from what follows that Ruskin is thinking of the concentrated, enigmatic, and plurisignative quality of the written thing, its intensity and density of meaning. Yet even a true book will not be all truth; this is "mixed always with evil fragments—ill-done, redundant, affected work. But if you read rightly, you will easily discover the true bits, and those *are* the book."[21]

Coming to the second part of his subject, the way we find the treasures hidden in books, Ruskin emphasizes self-annihilation and surrender to the thoughts and hearts of those written beings who are the "court of the past." First, the thoughts; we must enter *their* thoughts, to find *their* meanings, not merely to find our own meanings in the books. These thoughts may be hidden in parables (he notes again the "puzzling reticence," the enigmatic quality of great writers) or hidden deep in the roots of their words. "I tell you earnestly and authoritatively . . . you must get into the habit of looking intensely at words."[22] This assertion leads him into a discussion of etymology; his emphasis on the roots, stems, and branchings of words I take to be a kind of verbal organicism, analogous to his readings of nature and myth. Words, myths, natural forms, and great works of art are all modes of a primordial organic language to which a prophet like Ruskin must attune his ear. Words have descended into English through the family of language from Greek, he observes (strangely unaware of the Aryan hypothesis); yet they retain "a deep vital meaning, which all good scholars feel in employing them, even at this day."[23] In contrast, there are also "masked" political words "droning and skulking" abroad, words which, no one caring to unmask them, have a talismanic power over men's actions. In connection with this need for deep study of words, as part of the sesame of self-discipline that can open the "kings' treasuries" of moral power, he alludes to Max Müller's *Lectures on the Science of Language* (1861, 1864) as a valuable guide. We have already considered the possible influence of the famous Oxford philologist on the mythology of volume 5 of *Modern Painters*; here in *Sesame* Müller's influence is again suggested as Ruskin advises his audience to "read Max Müller's lectures thoroughly, to begin with; and, after that, never let a word escape you that looks suspicious."[24]

To illustrate this sort penetrative reading he proceeds to explicate, etymologically, lines 108–129 of *Lycidas*. We need not follow him in this; however, it should be noted that Milton's "The hungry sheep look up, and are not fed, / But, swoln with wind, and the rank mist they draw, / Rot inwardly, and foul contagion spread" is a description of particular significance to Ruskin. It provides him with the opportunity to elaborate on the etymology of "spirit" in a way that forecasts some of the meaning in his myth of Athena as the Queen of the Air and his "plague-wind" of the nineteenth century, and at the same time looks back at the cloud myths in the last volume of *Modern Painters*. "Spirit," he explains,

> is only a contraction of the Latin word "breath," and an indistinct translation of the Greek word for "wind." The same word is used in writing, "The wind bloweth where it listeth"; and in writing, "So is every one that is born of the Spirit"; born of the *breath*, that is; for it means the breath of God, in soul and body. We have the true sense of it in our words "inspiration" and "expire." Now, there are two kinds of breath with which the flock may be filled,—God's breath, and man's. The breath of God is health, and life, and peace to them, as the air of heaven is to the flocks on the hills; but man's breath—the word which *he* calls spiritual—is disease and contagion to them, as the fog of the fen. They rot inwardly with it; they are puffed up by it, as a dead body by the vapours of its own decomposition."[25]

But who are these that are puffed up with the gas of their own decomposition? They are the sudden converts who fancy themselves now God's special messengers; also they are "your sectarians of every species, small and great, Catholic or Protestant, of high church or low, in so far as they think themselves exclusively right and others wrong"; but preeminently they are those who believe they can be saved "by thinking rightly instead of doing rightly"—those who have, that is, no "religion of Humanity," of care, in them—"these are the true fog children—clouds, these, without water; bodies these, of putrescent vapour and skin, without blood or flesh."[26] These rainless clouds we have met before in volume 5 of *Modern Painters* and *Unto This Last*. As the cloud is a source and symbol of life to Ruskin, so the dry cloud signifies the various modes of life that violate the law of help: heaven-bent pietism, fruitless accumulation of capital, the pursuit of dissective, and inorganic knowledge.

Suggestions arising from Milton's "swoln with wind, and the rank mist they draw" not only provide him with an example of deep reading in the spirit of words, they also lead toward the second division of his discussion of book-treasures: "how we lose them." He had said that to commune with the court of the past we have not only to enter their thoughts but also their hearts. This can be done only by disciplined sympathy. The vulgar person cannot enter there. This thought leads Ruskin to consider the true meaning of "vulgarity," which is not "an untrained or undeveloped bluntness of body and mind," rather it is a "dreadful callousness, which, in extremity, becomes capable of every sort of bestial habit and crime, without fear, without pleasure, without horror, and without pity. It is in the blunt hand and the dead heart, in the diseased habit, in the hardened conscience, that men become vulgar." We enter the "great concourse of the Dead" to learn from them what is true and to share their feeling for the just, but we must be like them to feel with them. Just as "true knowledge is disciplined and tested knowledge,—not the first thought that comes, so the true passion is disciplined and tested passion,—not the first passion that comes."[27]

Ruskin has now cleared the way for what appears to have been the true purpose of his lecture (which, we remember, was originally delivered at Manchester). In a style that becomes increasingly the central characteristic of the last phase of his work, he enters a sweeping diatribe on the deadly conditions of greed that are hardening the English heart into final vulgarity and self-division. There is a parallel here with the attack on the "fog children" of introverted piety that concludes the previous section on entering the thoughts of the great. Vulgarity and religious narrowness are making the nation incapable of cultivating the spirit, the sesame, that opens the treasures of the kings of the past through submission to their passion as well as their thoughts. The signs of vulgarity are everywhere, signs of the lost struggle of life with greed, for instance, in that failure of compassion by which the nation allows "the lives of its innocent poor to be parched out of them by fog fever, and rotted out of them by dung hill plague, for the sake of sixpence a life extra per week to its land-lords,"[28] or in the hypocritical self-division that permits it to "mock Heaven and its Powers, by pretending belief in a revelation which asserts the love of money to be the root of *all* evil, and declaring, at the same time, that it is actuated, and intends to be actuated, in all chief national deeds and measures, by no other love."[29]

No deep or sympathetic reading is possible, Ruskin continues, to a nation in this state of mind. Therefore, the life source of spiritual guidance in books is lost to English society, "so incapable of thought has it become in its insanity of avarice." Yet this "disease" is only incapacity of thought, it has not yet corrupted the "inner nature" of the English; they still have the capacity for sympathy: "we ring true still, when anything strikes home to us." But this "instinctive, reckless virtue cannot last" unless it is disciplined: "No nation can last, which has made a mob of itself, however generous at heart. It must discipline its passions, and direct them, or they will discipline *it*, one day, with scorpion whips. Above all, a nation cannot last as a money-making mob: it cannot with impunity,—it cannot with existence,—go on despising literature, despising science, despising art, despising nature, despising compassion, and concentrating its soul on Pence."[30]

Ruskin concludes his lecture with categorical proof of the veracity of these seemingly "wild words" as he attempts to show, clause by clause, how English society has (by its choosing wealth) despised the five life sources mentioned: literature, science, art, nature, and compassion. For instance, he attempts to show that the nation has despised science by exploitation and has despised nature by desecration: "The French revolutionists made stables of the cathedrals of France; you have made race-courses of the cathedrals of the earth. Your *one* conception of pleasure is to drive in railroad carriages round their aisles, and eat off their altars."[31]

To illustrate how compassion is being despised, Ruskin prints in red a revelational newspaper clipping from his collection. This one describes the conditions of life and death of a boot restorer whose hard labor could provide so little support for himself and his family that he died of exhaustion and malnutrition. " 'For four months he had had nothing but bread to eat. There was not a particle of fat on the body.' "[32] Such persons as these would rather die than accept our relief, Ruskin declares, because we make it so insulting and painful to them. Further, he concludes that we are able to commit such crimes of neglect because the theatrical Christianity we practice disguises the nature of the true religion of care; "it is our imaginary Christianity that helps us to commit these crimes, for we revel and luxuriate in our faith, for the lewd sensation of it; dressing *it* up, like everything else, in fiction."[33] By our ceremonial "gas-lighted, and gas-inspired" Christianity we shut out the fact that there "is a true Church wherever one hand meets another helpfully, and that is the only holy or Mother Church which ever was, or ever shall be."[34]

The second lecture of the volume, *Lilies* ("Of Queens' Gardens"), is a sequel to the first. Delivered also at Manchester, a week later, it takes up in a roughly parallel way another source of moral guidance. Sesame stood for the capacity—through self-surrender, root reading of words, and disciplined passion—by which one might enter the minds and hearts of the great writers and thus gain access to the "kings' treasuries" of moral power there; these are kings' treasuries because there is but one kingship, that "which consists in a stronger moral state, and a truer thoughtful state, than that of others; enabling you, therefore, to guide or to raise them."[35] We noted that the lecture emphasized vain and narrow piety, along with greed and vulgarity, as one of the chief "inhibitors of the power of sesame." *Lilies,* on the other hand, deals with the complimentary queenly power, and the lily, emblematic of purity, is the scepter of the woman's rule. He divides his topic into three basic questions: What is the archetypal testimony concerning the moral power of women within the family? What kind of education will best fit her for her rule? What is her power with respect to the larger family, the state?

Under the first question he considers three sources of testimony as to the queenly power; these are literature, myth, and the social history of love. As literary testimony, Ruskin takes up Shakespeare, Scott, and Dante. Shakespeare, he argues, "has no heroes;—he has only heroines. . . . In his laboured and perfect plays you have no hero. . . . The catastrophe of every play is caused always by the folly or fault of a man; the redemption, if there be any, is by the wisdom and virtue of a woman."[36] In Scott, "it is the woman who watches over, teaches, and guides the youth," never vice versa; and Dante's great poem "is a love-poem to his dead lady; a song of praise for her watch over his soul. Stooping only to pity, never to love, she yet saves him from destruction—saves him from hell."[37] Coming to the example of Homer and Greek myth, Ruskin briefly ties the theme of woman's guiding power to the major myth-symbol complex of his work of the sixties: Neith-Athena and her associated emblems, especially the wild olive crown and the Gorgoneum. Neith (who will appear more fully as a character in *The Ethics of the Dust*) is here the "spirit of Wisdom" that "the great Egyptian people, wisest then of nations," gave a woman's shape; and later "the name and the form of that spirit, adopted, believed, and obeyed by the Greeks, became that Athena of the olive-helm, and cloudy shield, to faith in whom you owe, down to this date, whatever you hold most precious in art, in literature, or in types of national virtue."[38] Athena, we will learn from *The Queen of the Air* as from the introduction to *The Crown of Wild Olive*, is the presiding spirit of Ruskin's "religion of Humanity"; as the guardian goddess of the pure air, of wisdom, of passionate and helpful life, she is the antithesis of that "rank mist" and plague breath of religious introversion he invoked in his discussion of *Lycidas* in the previous lecture.

Having looked into literature and myth for testimony respecting the queenly power, he has yet another source of archetypes to draw upon: historical patterns of love, especially courtly love. Here his point is simply that "in all Christian ages which have been remarkable for their purity or progress, there has been an absolute yielding of obedient devotion, by the lover, to his mistress. . . . Where that true faith and captivity are not, all wayward and wicked passion must be; and . . . in this rapturous obedience to the single love of his youth, is the sanctification of all man's strength, and the continuance of all his purposes."[39] Marriage, he observes, is meant to mark the continuance of this "temporary into untiring service, and of fitful into eternal love."[40] Two points: in the personal dimension one may perhaps read here an address to Rose; he has told us that he wrote this lecture "to please one girl." Second, it is curious that Ruskin does not draw upon the testimony of art along with that of literature and myth in this discussion of what Jung would call the anima as archetype. But we do know that his art criticism continues a number of guiding feminine symbols that have announced turning points in his life to him, as Fors will do (one thinks of Ilaria di Caretto, Veronese's Queen of Sheba, Giorgione's Hesperid Aeglé, Giotto's Lady Poverty, and Carpaccio's Saint Ursula).

As for the vexed question of sexual "superiority," his position is that the whole argument is absurd, for each sex "completes the other." It is an organicist's argument, as is his emphasis on one final and fateful love. He therefore supposes that the idea of "true wifely subjection" can be reconciled with the idea of woman's rule through the notion hers is "a *guiding*, not a determining, function."[41] The woman's guiding power, however, is based on her purity; home is wherever the true wife is, but, since she must be perfect in order to rule it, her rule is the soul's rule.[42]

This thought leads naturally to the second question, concerning the kind of education that will fit her for queenly rule in the gardens of human life. First, he observes, quoting Wordsworth, she must be reared by nature in *"vital* feelings of delight," not in deadly ones. "Do not think you can make a girl lovely, if you do not make her happy."[43] Her function especially seems to be as a link between the organic language of nature and the human community. But she must be educated for this; "she should understand the meaning, the inevitableness, and the loveliness of natural laws; and follow at least some one path of scientific attainment, as far as the threshold of that bitter Valley of Humiliation, into which only the wisest and bravest men [and women?] can descend." She must have religious training in the broad humanistic sense; "it is for her to trace the hidden equities of divine reward, and catch sight, through the darkness, of the fateful threads of woven fire that connect error with retribution."[44] But there is the subject that is forbidden to her, says Ruskin (perhaps thinking of his mother or of Rose); this is theology. The danger is "that they dare to turn the Household Gods of Christianity into ugly idols of their own;—spiritual dolls for them to dress according to their caprice; and from which their husbands must turn away in grieved contempt, lest they should be shrieked at for breaking them."[45] Yet a girl's education, both in content and spirit, should be as serious as a boy's. This means that we must ourselves respect the teachers we choose for them. The necessity of reverencing teachers leads Ruskin into a diatribe on the disrespect the English obviously have for the girl's primary teacher, nature. You cannot educate pure lilies in a polluted landscape; hence this source of moral guidance is threatened at the root. This thought leads also to an ironic contrast between the pagan reverence for nature and its desecration by professed Christians: "Waters which a Pagan would have worshipped in their purity . . . you worship only with pollution. You cannot lead your children faithfully to those narrow axe-hewn church altars of yours, while the dark azure altars in heaven—the mountains that sustain your island throne,—mountains on which a Pagan would have seen the powers of heaven rest in every wreathed cloud—remain for you without inscription; altars built, not to, but by an Unknown God."[46]

Ruskin's final topic in the lecture is the relation of the woman's queenly power to that of the state. Working from the family-state analogy he had used in the *Political Economy of Art*, he argues that her function in the state may be discovered by extending analogically her function in the home. The man's duty in the home is "to secure its maintenance, progress and defense"; likewise in the commonwealth, his function is to "assist in the maintenance, in the advance, and in the defence of the state." Similarly the woman's home duty is "to secure its order, comfort, and loveliness," and her state duty is to assist in "the ordering, in the comforting, and in the beautiful adornment of the state."[47] *Lady*, he reminds his audience, means at root "loaf-giver," as *lord* means "warden of the laws." He concludes by charging women with a global task of compassion and healing in the gardens of humanity. "There is no suffering, no injustice, no misery, in the earth but the guilt of it lies with you. Men can bear the sight of it, but you should not be able to bear it."[48]

"The Mystery of Life and Its Arts," which Ruskin published as a third part of *Sesame and Lilies* in 1871, was delivered in 1868, four years after the other two, and it shows a striking advance in prophetic pessimism over them. One can understand why in 1882, eight years after his period of apostasy had ended, he chose not to reprint it with these calmer lectures. There is also the fact that its essential message is more succinctly stated in the introduction to *The Crown of Wild Olive*; nevertheless it has generally been regarded as one of Ruskin's least affected and most moving works. It is essentially a statement of his faith at this period, his "religion of Humanity."

We have already discussed its central symbol: clouds as symbols of human life in their transience, their mystery, and their power. Life shares the evanescence and indeterminateness of the cloud; "its avenues are wreathed in darkness, and its forms and courses no less fantastic, than spectral and obscure," but it shares also the storm power of the cloud, for "in the cloud of the human soul there is a fire stronger than lightning, and a grace more precious than the rain."[49] We will see how, in the following year, he goes on in prophetic depth to unite all these powers under the mythic dominion of Athena, the Queen of the Air; furthermore, he will argue that this mythic truth, the Greek vision of organic unity as revealed to him, still holds, for his use of myth is not the scholar's but the prophet's.

Here he begins on the subjective level by referring first to the cloud of his own life, which has been darkened by deepening disappointment. He makes his personal discouragement apocalyptic, as a prophet will. His response to the cataclysmic external "changes which are, hour by hour in accelerating catastrophe, manifesting themselves in the laws, the arts, and the creeds of men" is, he admits, "much deepened in my own mind by the disappointment, which, by chance, has attended the greater number of my cherished purposes."[50] He touches briefly on some of the causes of his personal discouragement (though not on the all-important private cause) and then turns to the "results" in terms of his present attitude toward the mystery of his own life, projecting his life out before him as an ominous cloud: "The more that my life disappointed me, the more solemn and wonderful it became to me. . . . It became to me not a painted cloud, but a terrible and impenetrable one: not a mirage, which vanished as I drew near, but a pillar of darkness, to which I was forbidden to draw near."[51] The passage is remarkable not only for its candor but for its grasp of the psychological sources of the *Storm-Cloud*, the monster cloud already beginning to form in the dark weathers of his diaries.

This forbidden darkness of his life loomed, he explains, as he saw that all his own failure, and petty successes worse than failure, "came from the want of sufficiently earnest effort to understand the whole law and meaning of existence, and to bring it to noble and due end," coupled with his realization that all rightness in art and life come from a true comprehension of ends.[52] This paradoxical situation, the dependence of any great work upon ultimate answers yet our "intense apathy" with respect to the final questions, is, to him, the first great mystery of life. "That the occupations or pastimes of life should have no motive, is understandable; but—That life itself should have no motive—that we neither care to find out what it may lead to, nor to guard against its being for ever taken away from us—here is a mystery indeed."[53]

Ruskin insists that his audience take note of this mysterious apathy about ends. "Can you answer," he asks, "a single bold question unflinchingly about that other world?—Are you sure there is a heaven? Sure there is a hell?"[54] If we are not sure, do we at all care to make sure? And if we do not care about ultimate ends, how can any of our immediate ends be wise? The prophet has given himself the central hermeneutic paradox of existence to explore. His next step is to consider what kinds of answers or resolutions have been given.

First, he charges the great artists of the past with assenting to the conspiracy of apathy about ends. "I saw also that . . . poetry, and sculpture, and painting, though only great when they strove to teach us something about the gods, never had taught us anything trustworthy about the gods, but had always betrayed their trust in the crisis of it."[55] To illustrate this he undertakes a brief rhetorical survey of the wisest religious and contemplative minds of our literary tradition to see what they have to offer in the way of dependable truths about our existence. Among the wise religious men, with their visions of the other world, Milton and Dante are the highest representatives, yet Milton's account is largely "picturesque drama," full of artifice and invention, but "not a single fact being, for an instant, conceived as tenable by any living faith"; and Dante's scheme, while "more intense, and, by himself, for the time, not to be escaped from . . . is indeed a vision, but a vision only, and that one of the wildest that ever entranced a soul."[56] Of the wise contemplative men, men of worldly faith, Homer and Shakespeare are preeminent. Yet there is no sadder image of human fate than that of the *Iliad*, where Achilles, "though aided continually by the wisest of the gods, and burning with the desire of justice in his heart, becomes yet, through ill-governed passion, the most unjust of men: and, full of the deepest tenderness in his heart, becomes yet, through ill-governed passion, the most cruel of men." And Shakespeare? Are his words on human fate more cheerful than the heathen's? "Ah, no! He differs from the Heathen poet chiefly in this—that he recognizes, for deliverence, no gods nigh at hand; and that, by petty chance—by momentary folly—by broken message—by fool's tyranny—or traitor's snare, the strongest and most righteous are brought to their ruin, and perish without a word of hope."[57] So it is, then, that about the ends of present life and their relation to the life beyond, neither the wise religious men nor the wise contemplative men tell us any dependable truths. But Ruskin has two other types of men to question.

He suggests applying to the men of business, for, though they have no visions of heaven, they can surely tell us how to live in this world and what to gather here. To express their answer Ruskin tells a dream of his: "For though I am no poet, I have dreams sometimes."[58] The dream parable is of a children's birthday party in a great house surrounded by lovely gardens and filled with every conceivable toy and the instruments of every pastime: music, books, shells, microscopes, lathes, kaleidoscopes, and so forth. The children play happily with these until two or three begin to dig the brass nailheads out of the furniture, and soon all other toys and delights are forgotten and the whole party becomes a competition for brass nailheads. This is the lecturer's dream, and the answer of the practical men to the question of life's ends.

However, there is a final group of men to whom this question may be put, and the purpose of the lecture is to bring the question around to them, for these are the competent workmen, the people who do useful work. "Yes; from these, at last, we do receive a lesson." But their lesson "can only be received by joining them—not by thinking about them." Their answer is organic; it is in their living skills and cannot be abstracted. "The moment a man can really do his work he becomes speechless about it."[59]

This thought leads him to a comparison of two works of art, a "corrigible" Lombardic Eve and an "incorrigible Angel," which turns out to be an "Irish Angel" (the lecture, we remember, was delivered at Dublin, not far from Rose's home). The fatal difference between these two works, he concludes, is this: in both examples there was an equal falling short of the demands of fact; "but the Lombardic Eve knew she was in the wrong, and the Irish Angel thought himself all right."[60] This comparison leads to two primary lessons about the mystery of life taught by wise workmen. First, "the more beautiful the art, the more it is essentially the work of people who *feel themselves wrong*"; and second, "whenever the arts and labours of life are fulfilled in this spirit of striving against misrule, and doing whatever we have to do, honourably and perfectly, they invariably bring happiness, as much as seems possible to the nature of man."[61] All other paths by which happiness is pursued lead to disappointment; even "the loftiest and purest love," he notes, as if addressing Rose, "too often does but inflame the cloud of life with endless fire of pain."[62]

There is yet a third lesson that the useful men have to teach, but this they teach only with their tombs. It is a lesson in futility. "Do it with thy might," is the scriptural injunction to labor.[63] Yet in six millenia of the application of human might to the arts of agriculture, weaving, and building we have not achieved anything like universal abundance; millions remain in desperate want, their number seems even to be increasing. "On the near coast of Africa, once the Garden of the Hesperides, an Arab woman, but a few sunsets since, ate her child, for famine."[64] Organic nature teaches better provision: "The ant and the moth have cells for each of their young, but our little ones lie in festering heaps, in homes that consume them like graves."[65]

Contemplation of this world of want leads Ruskin to conclude his sermon with an assertion of the essential ethic of his "religion of Humanity." Is our life ever to be without profit or possession until it vanishes, as the vapor? *Does* it really vanish so? We have seen how unreliable the information is. There are those who believe it does simply vanish. "Be it so: will you not, then, make as sure of the Life that now is, as you are of the Death that is to come?" Since you of this persuasion have no belief in immortality, since "your hearts are wholly in this world—will you not give them to it wisely, as well as perfectly?" The ethic of humanity is simply "let us do the work of men while we bear the form of them . . . though our lives *be* as a vapour, that appeareth for a little time, and then vanisheth."[66]

But there are also those who do *not* believe life has the transience of vapor, those who look for a Day of Judgment when every eye shall see God. For these also Ruskin's organic religion of the lived world has a message. There is not merely one Day of Judgment. For us here "every-day is a day of judgment—every day a Dies Irae, and writes its irrevocable verdict in the flame of its West . . . we are in the midst of judgment— the insects that we crush are our judges—the moments that we fret away are our judges—the elements that feed us, judge, as they minister—and the pleasures that deceive us, judge, as they indulge."[67] Here Ruskin's prophetic style is at a high pitch made possible, at one level, by the fusion of the organic and the mythic senses of judgment and, at another level, by the mixture of Johnsonian and Biblical cadences. But what, finally, *is* the work of men "while we bear the form of them"? It is essentially obedience to the law of help; and such a regimen has two dimensions "at this crisis." First, "to live on as little as we can" and second, to do all the useful work we can "in feeding people, then in dressing people, then in lodging people, and lastly in rightly pleasing people, with arts, or sciences, or any other subject of thought."[68]

2

The Crown of Wild Olive (1866) is, like *Sesame and Lilies*, a collection of popular lectures mixing social, aesthetic, and religious themes. Although it leans more toward economic concerns than does the previous collection, it is also more prophetic and dogmatic than systematic or theoretical in its cast. We have already had occasion to speak at length of its famous introduction, or preface, as it was called in the three editions prior to 1873. This introduction has two related functions; it states, in an illustrative way, his economic position on the crucial matter of intrinsic value, and it contains a moving declaration of his religious position at the time. This creed, a "religion of Humanity," as he explained later in *Fors*, was built, as he said then, on his belief that "human probity and virtue must be independent of any hope of futuri-ty." We have considered this portion of the preface and its creed in connection with the religious change that Ruskin underwent in 1858. It should now be clear that the symbol of the wild olive crown has two meanings in the light of the whole preface; it stands for both intrinsic wealth and existential honor. In a note of 1873 commenting on the change of title from preface to introduction in that year Ruskin observes that one of his bad habits is "to put half my book into preface," and that the book mainly represents themes expressed more fully in earlier volumes but now put into popular form, "all but this Introduction, which was written very carefully to be read, not spoken."[69] The introduction is, in fact, as important as anything in the collection both for its thought and style. So we must begin with a glance at the first half of it, the part not yet considered.

Ruskin opens his introduction with two direct revelational experiences that are interactively related through the idea of misused or misconceived wealth. Both are instances of violation of the organic. There was once, he begins, no sweeter seat of human life than that of the village bordering the sources of the Wandel. His terms for it are paradisaical: "No clearer or diviner waters ever sang with constant lips of the hand which 'giveth rain from heaven'; no pastures ever lightened in spring-time with more passionate blossoming; no sweeter homes ever hallowed the heart of the passer-by with their pride of peaceful gladness,—fain hidden—yet full-confessed."[70] In its larger outlines the place, which is also recollected in the first chapter of *Praeterita*, remains unchanged. Yet there is one feature of it that is genuinely apocalyptic of hell: "I have never seen anything," he explains, "so ghastly in its inner tragic meaning,—not in Pisan Maremma,—not by Campagna tomb—not by the sand isles of the Torcellan shore,—as the slow stealing of aspects of reckless, indolent, animal neglect over the delicate sweetness of that English scene." He describes this vision of the pollution of vital wealth in an affecting sentence:

> Just where the welling of stainless water, trembling and pure, like a body of light, enters the pool of Carshalton, cutting itself a radiant channel down to the gravel, through warp of feathery weeds, all waving, which it traverses with its deep threads of clearness, like the chalcedony in moss-agate, starred here and there with the white grenouillette; just in the very rush and murmur of the first spreading currents, the human wretches of the place cast their street and house foulness; heaps of dust and slime, and broken shreds of old metal, and rags of putrid clothes; which, having neither energy to cart away, nor decency enough to dig into the ground, they thus shed into the stream, to diffuse what venom of it will float and melt, far away, in all places where God meant those waters to bring joy and health.[71]

A few hours of useful work would save this source of intrinsic wealth. But this scene does not exist in isolation; he perceives it in subtle organic relation to another encounter in the neighboring village of Croydon, this time with the effects of useless labor and lethal, self-accumulating wealth. When last he visited these waters, he continues, he walked from them up through the back streets of Croydon. At one point in his walk he passed a new pub where the owner had attempted to add dignity to his establishment by fencing it from the sidewalk with a new iron rail-and-spear fence. "And by this stately arrangement, the little piece of dead ground within, between wall and street, became a protective receptacle of refuse; cigar ends, and oyster shells, and the like, such as an open-handed English street-populace habitually scatters; and was thus left, unsweepable by any ordinary methods."[72]

Having presented these two revelational instances of pollution Ruskin proceeds to examine some of the underlying economic implications; indeed, it is the fateful conflict beneath the level of detail that makes the experiences revelational, apocalyptic. The iron bars enclosing the publican's piece of ground represent negative value in several senses. First, they have turned a bit of clean earth into a pestilent receptacle. Second, the work by which this disvalue was produced was necessarily dangerous and degrading to those who had to do it, "work, partly cramped and perilous, in the mine; partly grievous and horrible, at the furnace: partly foolish and sedentary, of ill-taught students making bad designs: work from the beginning to the last fruits of it, and in all the branches of it, venomous, deathful, and miserable."[73] Finally, of course, the publican's railings represent useful work not done, such as the cleaning of the Carshalton pools.

How does it happen that the one work was done and not the other? The conclusive reason, Ruskin argues, is "that the capitalist can charge a percentage on the work in one case and cannot on the other."[74] Hence these black iron railings, by which the publicans are induced to "out-rail" each other, are a form of "black mail," by cozening, of the poor by the rich. And the effect of this negative work on the social-natural organism is that it is the poorer by the capitalist's private gain. The organic laws of the social system have been violated, much as the health (the life-support value) of the environment, including quality of life, has been violated by the choice of work that, in Ruskin's view, the capitalist's greed has enforced. The problem is that laborers, like capitalists, naturally look at the short-run effect of the uses of capital on their immediate interests. They are unaware of the fatal conflict implicit in the fact that, though capital can appoint the immediate object of labor, it cannot control that labor's ultimate life-support value, which is intrinsic and fixed.

> It matters little, ultimately, how much a labourer is paid for making anything; but it matters fearfully what the thing is, which he is compelled to make. If his labour is so ordered as to produce food, and fresh air, and fresh water, no matter that his wages are low;—the food and fresh air and water will be at last there; and he will at last get them. But if he is paid to *destroy* food and fresh air, or to produce iron bars instead of them,—the food and air will finally *not* be there, and he will *not* get them, to his great and final inconvenience.[75]

Here in the first part of his fine introduction, then, Ruskin attacks one system that is destructive of the organism of the lived world, its social and natural unity, and that is the accumulation of capital as an end. In the second part of it, as we have seen, he criticizes, more indirectly, another powerful system, which, often in secret collusion with the first, he sees as also destructive of the lived world. This is the system of spiritual capitalism under which, through faith alone, without need of helpful work, one can accumulate capital in the heaven. And the crown of wild olive, organic reward of worldly honor (associated with both Christ and Athena), signifies defiance of both of these life-neglecting systems of asceticism. In opposing his religion of worldly care to these two devotions by which men separate themselves from life, Ruskin makes this introduction a definitive and poetic statement of his spiritual position in mid life.

In the first piece in the collection itself, the lecture "Work," which he delivered before the Working Men's Institute at Camberwell in 1865, Ruskin asserts that "the first of all English games is making money." Like any other game, this effort is "absolutely without purpose," in terms of the real ends of life. For these players there is no use in the money but to gain more of it. That it is a lethal game, an antiorganic game, is obvious, he maintains with prophetic extravagence, from the fact that the whole doomed city of London is its field of play. "So all that great foul city of London there,—rattling, growling, smoking, stinking,—a ghastly heap of fermenting brickwork, pouring out poison at every pore,—you fancy it is a city of work? Not a street of it! It is a great city of play; very nasty play, and very hard play, but still play. It is only Lord's cricket-ground without turf:—a huge billiard table without the cloth, and with pockets as deep as the bottomless pit."[76] There are other games that amuse the idle classes: hunting, riding, dressing up, and "the great gentleman's game of war—which ladies like best to play at,"[77] but all such games have in common the fact that they are paid for by the deadly *work* of someone who does not play.

Another of Ruskin's points in this lecture to working men is that work is for life, for its use *as* work, not for fee. The service of fee is fatal. "If your work is first with you, and your fee second, work is your master, and the lord of work, who is God. But if your fee is first with you, and your work second, fee is your master, and the lord of fee, who is the Devil; and not only the Devil, but the lowest of the devils—the 'least erected fiend that fell.' "[78]

He is troubled, as usual when he speaks of work, by the problem of the degrading, even degenerative, nature of certain kinds of necessary work;

he will hear no nonsense about the "dignity of labor." The question is: who is to do the dirty work for the rest, and for what reward? The only force that can mitigate the harsh realities of dirty work and its distribution is the ideal of social justice. We cannot salve our consciences by referring the problem to supramundane justice. The question, for the present world, about those who must do our dirty work for us, is still "Did Providence put them in that position—or did you?" Relating to Providence, Ruskin again, as in the last chapter of *Modern Painters*, makes his point that God's kingdom "is to come to us—we don't go to it." This apparent promise of the Lord's Prayer enables him to tie the Christian kingdom (which "is not to be of the dead, but of the living") to his religion of the present world with its olive crown. The wise work that will prepare us for this kingdom, which is within, has three characteristics: it is honest, useful, and cheerful. The greatest of all wastes is the waste of labor. To waste men's labor is to kill them with many deaths, *daily* deaths.

He closes the lecture with his customary prophetic device of apocalyptic peroration. In this passage he alludes to the archetypal emblem (used earlier in the essay and in many other places, as he does also the image of the sun of justice) of the sun who, as the cheerful worker, "rejoiceth as a strong man to run his course." I quote a portion of the passage to illustrate the tone of acerbity he will use with increasing frequency.

> There is death in the thoughts of men: the world is one wide riddle to them, darker and darker as it draws to a close. . . . Yes, and there is death—infinitude of death—in the principalities and powers of men. As far as the east is from the west, so far our sins are—*not* set from us, but multiplied around us: the Sun himself, think you be *now* "rejoices" to run his course, when he plunges westward to the horizon, so widely red, not with clouds, but blood? And it will be red more widely yet. Whatever drought of the early and latter rain may be, there will be none of that red rain.[79]

The second lecture in the collection is the famous "Traffic," which Ruskin delivered at the town hall of Bradford in 1864. His hosts expected him to offer an appropriate Gothic design for the commodities exchange they intended to build there; what they received was a scathing denunciation of the effect of Mammonism on the life of taste. Taste was for Ruskin not a peripheral indulgence, but the outward, visible manifestation of a person's or a nation's spiritual condition. "Taste," he declares, "is not only a part and an index of morality;—it is the ONLY morality."[80] It is organically continuous with every other aspect of personal and national character. "Tell me what you like, and I'll tell you what you are.''[81] As a vital force in the social organism, taste is not merely a passive expression but an active agent in the formation of character; it refers to what people enjoy *doing* as well as to what they possess. It follows from the organic continuity of taste with every other national choice, that every nation's condition of vice or virtue is written in its arts—an old argument of Ruskin's but a central one to this group of noneconomic writings of the sixties.

Take, as a symptomatic expression of taste, he continues, the fact that the English reserve their Gothic architecture for churches. That is, they have a specialized architecture for religion that is not used elsewhere in life. What is revealed by this particular manifestation of taste? "It signifies neither more nor less than that you have separated your religion from your life.''[82] However, this schizoid condition of national character reveals a deeper violation of the organic unity of the earth. Certain places, identified by Gothic architecture and called churches, are set aside from the rest of the earth to be sacred; but, Ruskin insists, it is not merely the church place that is sacred, "the whole Earth is.''[83]

At this point he shifts his attention to the presumed question in the minds of his audience: What should be the style of the Bradford Exchange? He answers with the assertion that the whole endeavor of his past work on architecture has been to show that, while all good architecture is religious in the large sense, it is "not *ecclesiastical.*" Every great architectural mode has been organically continuous with a great national faith, and, as its "result and exponent," has found its way into every aspect of national life; it has not merely been set aside for ecclesiastical uses. There have been three great architectures of Europe, each vitalized by a great religion. The Greeks worshiped a "God of Wisdom and Power," and their architecture grew out of this worship; medieval man revered a "God of Judgment and Consolation"; and the Renaissance a "God of Pride and Beauty.''[84] The modern English also have a deity of their own whom he will mention after he has looked more closely at these old religions.

This digression gives Ruskin the chance to make the kind of synoptic sweep of Western religious development that was necessary to the perspective of his humanistic creed; by it he establishes a kind of prophetic elevation from which he can look down scornfully upon the English faith as an insular perversion. He also finds an opportunity, once again, to introduce Athena, who has made her appearance in *Sesame and Lilies* and in the introduction to this work by way of her sacred olive crown, and who will appear again in *The Ethics of the Dust* and *The Queen of the Air* as his central prophetic symbol in the works of the sixties. Here he reminds his audience that the Greeks' first idea of deity was "that expressed in the word, of which we keep the remnant in our words '*Di*-urnal' and '*Di*-vine'—the god of *Day*, Jupiter." (His source for this etymology, as Cook's note explains, was Max Müller's *Lectures on the Science of Language*.)[85] Athena, springing armed from his head, stands for vital wisdom, for "perfect knowledge" or organic knowledge, while the Gorgon on her shield stands mainly for "the chilling horror and sadness . . . of the outmost and superficial spheres of knowledge—that knowledge which separates, in bitterness, hardness, and sorrow, the heart of the full-grown man from the heart of the child. For out of imperfect knowledge spring terror, dissention, danger, and disdain; but from perfect knowledge, given by the full-revealed Athena, strength and peace, in sign of which she is crowned with the olive spray, and bears the resistless spear."[86] We note that no mention is made of Athena as the queen of the air, of life as well as wisdom, at this point.

Ruskin continues briefly in this view with summaries of medieval and Renaissance mythologies to arrive at this rhetorical summation and question, the climax of his lecture: "Your Greek worshipped Wisdom, and built you the Parthenon—the Virgin's temple. The Mediaeval worshipped Consolation, and built you Virgin temples also—but to our Lady of Salvation. Then the Revivalist worshipped beauty, of a sort, and built you Versailles and the Vatican. Now, lastly, will you tell me what *we* worship, and what *we* build?"[87] His answer, of course, allows him to close with his essential antagonist, the national pursuit of wealth at the expense of life. What is England's national worship? Her real as opposed to her nominal faith? This English deity is obviously the "Goddess of Getting-on," or "Britannia of the Market" (in perverse parallel with "Athena Agoraria," who was "but a subordinate type of their goddess.") Her temples are everywhere already, there is no need for him to tell them how to build another temple to her.

> Your railroad mounds, vaster than the walls of Babylon; your railroad stations, vaster than the temple of Ephesus, and innumerable; your chimneys, how much more mighty and costly than cathedral spires! your harbour-piers; your warehouses; your exchanges!—all these are built to your great Goddess of "Getting-on"; and she has formed and will continue to form, your architecture, as long as you worship her; and it is quite vain to ask me to tell you how to build to *her*; you know far better than I.[88]

His parallel points set, Ruskin drives them home. "The Greek Goddess of Wisdom gave continual increase of wisdom, as the Christian Spirit of Comfort (or Comforter) continual increase of comfort." But what does the worship of getting-on bring? "Getting on—but where to?

Gathering together—but how much? Do you mean to gather always— never to spend?''[89] If there is to be any joy in this goddess there must be spending in life as well as accumulation; if we do not spend somebody else must. This, he explains, is why his attack on the so-called science of political economy has centered on this point, because "it has omitted the study of exactly the most important branch of the business—the study of *spending.*''[90]

From this broad review of his lecture "Traffic" we can see that Ruskin has brought organicism, myth, and political economy together again but now with a notable increase in prophetic irony and historical vision. His peroration, as usual, brings in the apocalyptic elements of vision and crisis. Here is his final warning against the English idol of ac- cumulation:

> This idol of yours; this golden image, high by measureless cubits, set up where your green fields of England are furnace-burnt into the likeness of the plain of Dura: this idol, forbidden to us, first of all idols, by our own Master and faith; forbidden to us also by every human lip that has ever, in any age or people, been accounted of as able to speak according to the purposes of God. Continue to make that forbidden deity your principal one, and soon no more art, no more science, no more pleasure will be possible. Catastrophe will come; or, worse than catastrophe, slow mouldering and withering into Hades.[91]

The third of these lectures, "War," was delivered at the Royal Military Academy, Woolwich, in 1865. Here Ruskin's organicism permits him to praise a kind of historical ideal of war while condemning modern warfare. His argument, of course, is that war lends organic coherence, esprit de corps, to the nation, fusing it into productive unity of purpose. "War is the foundation of all the arts," because "it is the foundation of all the high virtues and faculties of men."[92] Hence among the Greeks Athena and Apollo were warrior deities; and one can read in K. O. Müller's *The Dorians* what a high ideal the Spartans had of war and of how they sacrificed to the muses (for regularity and order) and to the god of love (as the confirmer of mutual esteem and shame) before going into battle. This represents Ruskin's ideal of war; but for modern warfare, war waged against civilians, also "scientific war,—chemical and mechanic war," he has no use. Nor can he idealize imperialist war; a nation's true territory is its coherence. There would be few territorial wars if leaders understood the spirit of human loyalty by which a ship's captain chooses to die with his remaining passengers. "He does not do it from any religious motive,—from any hope of reward, or any fear of punishment; he does it because he is a man."[93] Yet Ruskin finds the notion that peace and civic virtue flourish together untenable. "Peace and the *vices* of civil liberty flourish together."[94] Therefore he finds it "the Law of Nature and life, that *a nation once utterly corrupt can only be redeemed by a military despotism*—never by talking, nor by its free effort. And the health of any state consists simply in this; that in it, those who are wisest shall also be strongest; its rulers should be also its soldiers; or, rather, by force of intellect more than of sword, its soldiers also its rulers."[95]

The first three editions of *The Crown of Wild Olive* consisted of the three lectures just discussed. But in 1873, when he re-edited the book as the fourth volume in his "Works Series," Ruskin added a fourth lecture and an appendix, "Notes on the Political Economy of Prussia," drawn from Carlyle's *Friedrich* and intended as a supplement to the lecture on war. The added lecture, "The Future of England" was also delivered at Woolwich, but four years after the war lecture, in 1869. It is not about war but is, in fact, the most strictly "political" lecture of the group.

The coming "political crisis," which he takes for a text, will, he maintains, consist of a double struggle: a conflict between rising democracy and the fading feudalism of the established order, and a struggle between poverty and wealth. These two conflicts, he explains, have generally been thought of as one and the same, but they are not, and he will attempt to distinguish between them. For the causes of wealth and of nobility are not the same; neither has poverty anything in common with "anarchy," which is the forerunner of poverty as obedience is the forerunner of prosperity. Ruskin shifts his term here from "democracy" to "anarchy," suggesting his view of the former.

Turning his attention to the prior problem of the struggle of the oppressed with the established order, he considers this conflict justified, because over the past millenium by and large "the people *have* been misgoverned";[96] they have done the dirty work and have lost the wages of it. In the past "fifty years" they have begun to suspect this, and as a consequence the populace of Europe "has lost even the power and conception of reverence."[97] But all social progress (and therefore the outcome of the other struggle, of poverty with wealth) depends upon a society's having something to reverence—a principle of organic coherence. "It is a crisis, gentlemen; and time to think of it. I have roughly and broadly put it before you in its darkness. Let us look at what we may find of light."[98]

The source of the light and of the cohesive principle he has in mind is "education." But, for Ruskin, education has a special etymological meaning. To educate and to govern mean the same. "Education does not mean teaching people to know what they do not know. It means teaching them to behave as they do not behave."[99] Fundamentally this education is "to make the best of every creature," which means to give him self-developing, nonalienating work. And the only way such mass education can be extended to all is through universal employment of hand labor. "For the continual education of the whole people, and for their future happiness, they must have such consistent employment as shall develop all the powers of the fingers and the limbs, and the brain: and that development is only to be obtained by hand-labour . . . hand labour on the earth, hand-labour on the sea, hand-labour in art, hand-labour in war."[100] Closely connected with the idea of the redemption of labor through the extension of hand work is the redemption of *land* through the same means: "All land that is waste and ugly, you must redeem into ordered fruitfulness; all ruin, desolateness, imperfectness of hut or habitation, you must do away with; and throughout every village and city of your English dominion, there must not be a hand that cannot find a helper, nor a heart that cannot find a comforter."[101] There in brief statement is Ruskin's utopia. Finally, this redemption of the land must not be accomplished by machines, because if we put, say, a steam-plow on the land it is (apart from being an ugly, inorganic incoherence— probably Ruskin's basic instinct about it) likely to force the men who maintained the land either into starvation or into useless (nonlife-sustaining) work and at the same time concentrate the wealth of the owner. Suppose you have a hundred and fifty men healthfully working the land: "Without machines, you have a hundred and fifty yeomen ready to join for defence of the land. You get your machine, starve fifty of them, make diamond-cutters or footmen of as many more, and for your national defence against an enemy, you have now, and *can* have, only fifty men, instead of a hundred and fifty; these also now with minds much *alienated* from you as their chief, and the rest, lapidaries, or footmen;—and a steam-plough."[102]

3

The two collections of lectures just discussed, *Sesame and Lilies* and *The Crown of Wild Olive*, touch on a wide variety of topics from the aegis of Athena to women's education, and from the mystery of life to the steam-plow; but recurrent in them is the prophet's problem of pointing to principles of coherence for the social organism. Their primary subjects, moral power in books, moral guidance in women, life's mystery and its ends, the meanings of work, worship, and war, are aspects of this question of unifying principles; and behind them all stands the basic tenet of Ruskin's religious position at the time (symbolized by the crown of wild olive): that these principles of coherence cannot be based on the expectation of another life. Faith without works is, for Ruskin at this point, as dangerous as self-multiplying pools of capital.

The small group of works we must now consider, Ruskin's aesthetic studies of the sixties, are more exclusively concerned with art and its social implications than any others of the period. They show little advance in thought, and in them Ruskin expresses several times a weariness with art topics and a determination to give them up for good, which, of course, he cannot do. Their recurrent thesis is that art cannot be taught by abstraction and rule; it is the organic outgrowth of certain moral conditions in society, and as such a natural and inevitable growth it represents (as does taste) those moral conditions infallibly. To those who can read them, works of art produced in a nation or valued by it are the nation's ethical fingerprint. Thus works of art may be, to the prophetic imagination, an apocalypse, a moment of revelation of demonic forces operative in the national character, as are helpless individuals, scarred landscapes, and blatant vulgarities in taste.

In 1865 Ruskin read a paper called "The Study of Architecture in Our Schools" to the Royal Institute of Architects. In it he urges students to put human or animal life into every form, as the Egyptian or Greek architects did. An architect, he maintains, should always be "taught to look at the organic, actions and masses, not at the textures or accidental effects of shade; meantime his sentiment respecting all these things should be cultivated by close and constant inquiry into their mythological significance and associated traditions."[103]

He realizes that his plea for architectural organicism has little chance against the prevailing effects of mechanism in modern urban life. Structures built primarily to house machines are so choked with soot that any sculpture they had would quickly be obscured; streets are mere drains to conduct the unobservant mob; human existence is mere mechanical transition; and "every creature is only one atom in a drift of human dust, and current of interchanging particles, circulating here by tunnels underground, and there by tubes in the air; for a city, or cities, such as this no architecture is possible—nay, no desire of it is possible to their inhabitants."[104] Nothing but a religion can cause these human particles to begin to cohere and pursue the ethics of the dust rather than the gifts of the dust. Religion, however, is to be distinguished from superstition. Superstition is fear of a spirit whose passions are human and whose presence is limited to certain places, making those particular places sacred; religion is reverence of a spirit whose presence is everywhere and whose action is helpful. While superstition must be overcome, worship of *some* kind is essential to social life. "I would say to every youth who entered our schools—Be a Mahometan, a Diana-worshipper, a Fire-worshipper, a Root-worshipper, if you will; but at least be so much a man as to know what worship means."[105] The prophet concludes with an apology for speaking "despondingly" about the prospects for architecture; but he has personally come to think that the study of art is of little use in the midst of judgment. "For my own part, I feel the force of mechanism and the fury of avaricious commerce to be at present so irresistible, that I have seceded from the study not only of architecture, but nearly of all art; and have given myself, as I would in a beseiged city, to seek the best modes of getting bread and water for its multitudes, there remaining no question, it seems, to me, of other than such grave business for the time."[106]

But he did not, while he continued to work, cease to speak about art. His Rede Lecture at Cambridge in 1867 dealt with "The Relation of National Ethics to National Art." There he said he had to stress one great practical truth, the most vital he had to declare after thirty years of art study. This was the organic thesis that "we cannot teach art as an abstract skill or power. It is the result of a certain ethical state in the nation, and at a full period of the natural growth that efflorescence of its ethical state will infallibly be produced: be it bad or good, we can no more teach nor shape it than we can streak our orchard blossom with strange colours or infuse into its fruit a juice it has not drawn out of the sap."[107] The seeds of art we sow we must also reap. Bad art begets bad art; bad art drives out the good. The failure of beauty is a sure sign of national depravity. As the arts spring from the whole of humanity, their objects must be for the whole of humanity. The artist "must always feel that the whole, out of which he has chosen, could he have rendered it, was greater and more beautiful than the part he chose, and that the free fact was greater than his formalism. And therefore it is necessary that the living men round him should be in an ethical state harmonious with his own,"[108] and that he himself should be in harmony with the external organism he mediates. In a discussion summarizing his organic aesthetic it is appropriate that Ruskin should conclude, in his customary apocalyptic tones, by denouncing what he considers to be a distinct sign of national putrescence; "the fatallest sign among the evidences of our present state of declining virtue [is] our increasing habit of jesting with circumstances of horror and death."[109]

A month later in a lecture at the British Institution, "On the Present State of Modern Art," he used the same organic thesis for his point of departure. "The art of a nation much resembles the corolla of a flower; its brightness of colour is dependent on the general health of the plant, and you can only command the hue, or modify the form of the blossom, by medicine or nourishment applied patiently to the root, not by manipulation of the petals."[110] The chief characteristics of modern art are, he finds, its compassionateness (disproportionate emphasis on the humble life), domesticity (little interest in public life), consequent shallowness and narrowness, selfishness, eccentricity, and the desire for dramatic excitement (emphasis on what its subjects are doing rather than on what they *are*.) All of these characteristics are violations of the organic mandate that art should be about and for the whole of humanity. Again he decries the most fatal sign of organic violation, the tendency of modern art to dwell on death; he has in mind especially Rembrandt's *The Anatomy Lesson*, Géricault's *The Raft of Medusa*, and, of course, Doré's illustrations of Balzac and the Bible. "I think it is the strangest form of curse and corruption which attends humanity, but it is a quite inevitable one, that whenever there is a ruthless pursuit of sensational pleasure it always ends in an insane and wolflike gloating over the garbage of Death."[111] He concludes ("my last words on art") with his central aesthetic assertion that the "beginning of art is religion"[112] and with a revelational glance at the holy temple of getting-on, the Crystal Palace. There enshrined he sees a symbol of the present national reverence for mechanism:

> As you know this Crystal Palace of ours is always held up to us—superannuated disciples of the old school of work in brick or in marble—as an entirely glorious and exalted novelty superseding everything done yet. So one has a natural tendency to look also to the apse of this cathedral of modern faith to see the symbol of it, as one used to look to the concha of the Cathedral of Pisa for the face of Christ, or to the apse of Torcello for the figure of the Madonna. Well, do you recollect what occupied the place of these—in the apse of the Crystal Palace? The head of a Pantomime clown, some twelve feet broad, with a mouth opening from ear to ear, opening and shutting by machinery, its eyes squinting alternately, and collapsing by machinery, its humor in general provided for by machinery, with the recognized utterance of English Wisdom inscribed above—"Here we are again."[113]

"The Flamboyant Architecture of the Valley of the Somme," a blazing lecture Ruskin delivered at the Royal Institution in 1869, is his most eloquent elaboration of the thesis that has occupied him in the three lectures just discussed: that art is an inevitable outgrowth of the spiritual condition of a people and that this state can be read through the art like the meaning through a myth. He will read the moral truths concerning the death of Gothic that are implicit in its flamboyant excesses. It is an art of disclosing the inner language of art, a hermeneutic act that is analogous to his readings in myth, etymology, and organic forms. It is also a prophetic task of revelation that he performs on this fallen architecture, and the word "flamboyant" has an infernal as well as an architectural meaning.

His essential point is that flamboyant Gothic reveals a religious basis that (unlike that of Florentine art) was too weak to take the "pagan graft" of cursive, ideal form that fastened upon it with the classical revival. Therefore, it fell into feverish linear excesses. Flamboyant architecture, epitomized in that of Abbeville, he depicts as revealing a doomed skeletal quality in its deeply cut chalky stone. "But, broadly;— here is the final corruption:—that it becomes a design of lace in white, on a black ground; not a true or intelligent rendering of organic form."[114] Its sculptors show a preference for copying dead instead of living form. Not merely this, there are also intellectual excesses of ingenuity in construction, the builders preferring mechanism to human passion, as if their minds were full of theology and philosophy. The effect of mechanistic over organic meaning in the architect's mind is that "the shaft and the arch rib became everything and the wall nothing,—until it was found that, in fact, a building might be constructed by nothing but ribs, a mere osseous thorax of a building instead of a living body."[115]

The "disease" that proved fatal to Gothic architecture, Ruskin insists, as he had in *The Stones of Venice*, was the serpentine temptation to subtitute line for mass in decoration. This style is to be distinguished from the fibrously rigid yet elastic linearity of true organic Gothic; flamboyant Gothic became "flexibly linear, twisted and wreathed so as to make the stone look ductile";[116] it was thereby in defiance of the limits of its materials. Ruskin concludes his lecture, therefore, with apocalyptic passages suggesting the weaving, languid, yet licentious death dance of the flamboyant linearity. Everywhere in this weakening Gothic, as in the Renaissance style that was superseding it, "loose lines of fillets, ribands, and weakly or wildly undulatory drapery, were beginning to be chosen in preference to the elastic lines of organic form; and thus, to the smallest particular, the forms of art echoed the temper of their age; the fluttered line announced the feeble will, and the unbound robe, the licentious temper."[117] In the North, however, in response to the hardship of life there, this licentiousness became mixed with melancholy fear and eventually revealed a fevered and frantic tendency towards the contemplation of death. We see it, for instance, in the "fantasy and fever of Dürer's 'Apocalypse,' " and in the "mixed mockery and despair of Holbein's

'Dance of Death,' " and in the interwoven stone of this enervated Gothic: "The very threads of the now thin and nervous stone work catch the ague of mixed wantonness and terror, and—weak with unwholesome and ominous fire—flamboyant with a fatal glow—tremble in their ascent as if they were seen through troubled and heated air over a desert horizon;— and lose themselves at last in the likeness,—no more as the ancient marbles, of the snows of Olympus,—but of the fires of condemnation."[118]

"I cannot get to my work in this paper, somehow; the web of these old enigmas entangles me again and again."[119] Ruskin is speaking here of a specific paper and a specific web of "grey" enigmas (to be glanced at in a moment), but the remark will serve to bring into focus the obsessional undertow that becomes an increasingly insistent feature of his style after 1865. One might speak of symptoms of derangement in prose, but prose cannot go mad; it is better to speak of the tendency for "structure," the process of analysis, or exposition, to become entangled and dissipated in local textures of meaning, that is, in obsessive webs of allusion, suggestive etymologies and ambiguities, images, symbols, and jeremiads. The onset of this cryptic and obsessively allusive element, which culminates in *Fors Clavigera*, could be documented out of nearly any of the first six of the nine chapters of *The Cestus of Aglaia*, the book in which the remark just quoted appears.

This book is unique among the longer works of the sixties because it is the only one devoted, at least ostensibly, to matters of art. The linking intention of the eight papers that make up the work (each a separate contribution to the *Art Journal* for 1865–66) was to set forth an "art creed" for modern England, to formulate "some laws for present practice of Art in our schools, which may be admitted, if not with absolute, at least with sufficient consent, by leading artists."[120] But by "laws" of practice Ruskin does not, of course, mean technical procedures but the root of these in such conditions of the artistic character as modesty, patience, liberty, and haste. Their unity and binding influence is signified symbolically by "the girdle of the Grace," Aglaia. In this theme, the "relation of social character to the possible supply of good art," lies the relevance of the work to his social program and the rationale of its style.

His method in the work, insofar as any is apparent, is to take some image, symbol, or verbal enigma and explore its anagogic possibilities in two interrelated dimensions, in the moral life and in the practice of art. Art in this work means particularly techniques of engraving, an art that is especially significant to Ruskin for its fusion of the social and individual uses of talent.

But, as usual in Ruskin, even questions of technique are made emblematic of moral values. Thus, for instance, in several places, but especially in the paper "Liberty," the circle of Giotto is invoked to stand for the complex fusion of moral and muscular control in art. Giotto had declared that his mastery might be judged by his ability to draw unerring circles "free hand." Yet here is the paradox of artistic freedom: Giotto's hand was only made sufficiently "free," serene, unhesitating, precise, by immense self-discipline. In a similar way the first paper plays on the meaning of "The Black Outline." Superficially it is directed toward the basic practical question of the quantitiy of shading that a student ought to introduce in outlining any form having a varied contour. But it is plain from the context of the question (it is posed only at the end of the paper, after divagations on mechanism, myth, and the silence of the masters) that the problem of whether to shade or not to shade, the division of lights from darks, is really a metaphor for larger questions of being. At any rate, "The Black Outline" problem appears to be the closest thing to a girdling theme that could bind up the whole range of mythic, literary, artistic, historical, etymological, incidental, and private associations with which Ruskin plays.

It may be that some more arcane principle of coherence governs the texture of wordplay, image, and allusion that makes *The Cestus of Aglaia* seem an "esoteric" book, but this is not the place to attempt to decode it. And yet, because of its weave, the book will not yield to summary. Perhaps the best that can be given here is a brief sampling of its rhetorical materials.

There are three patches of memorably purple rhetoric that might serve to represent the fusion of image, message, and obsession in *Cestus*. For convenience of reference they might be given these titles: The Fury of Turin, Locomotive and Pantheon, and Rembrandt's Rushlight. In each case some reference is made to the implicit presence of serpent symbolism interfused with the primary image. This ambiguity is coherent with the ambiguity present in the word *Graces*. On the one hand the Graces meant the sisters Aglaia (brightness), Euphrosyne (joy), and Thalia (bloom); but on the other hand *Graces* was used in euphemistic irony to refer to the Furies Alecto, Tisiphone, and Megaera whose distinguishing characteristic was the serpents entwined in their hair. Thus, by implication, behind each grace (in life and art) stood its alter ego, a fury, suggested by the serpent; the girdle of Aglaia might be confused with that of Alecto; "Patience," for instance, could belong to the girdle of the Grace or of the Fury depending on its use. Consider for a moment how Ruskin explores this paradox of patience by means of the explicit and biographically notorious image of the Fury of Turin with which he begins his paper "Patience."

He has been thinking, he says, of Chaucer's vision (in the *Parlement of Foules*) of Dame Patience with a pale face seated on a hill of sand, but the image will not come into focus for him because it keeps merging with a scene he remembers so explicitly that the memory cannot be refused. He reconstructs the remembered image, but as he does so the whole event takes on a kind of archetypal translucence. He recalls an Italian girl of perhaps ten or twelve, a pale child upon whom poverty had enforced the lessons of patience. Fatigued in play, she had thrown herself down upon a heap of dirt to rest, "full in the sun, like a lizard."[121] She looms there in his memory like a mythic image in chiaroscuro. "The sand was mixed with the draggled locks of her black hair, and some of it sprinkled over her face and body, in an 'ashes to ashes' kind of way; a few black rags about her loins, but her limbs nearly bare, and her little breasts, scarce dimpled yet,—white—marble-like—but, as wasted marble, thin with the scorching and the rains of Time."[122] Lying so, a study in black and white in the solemn afternoon light, she suggests a Niobid slain by the sungod, angered by Italy's neglect of her children. "Black and white she lay, all breathless, in a sufficiently pictorial manner." But suddenly there is a furious metamorphosis. Taunted by a playmate, the girl rises "with a single spring, like a snake" and with a cry so sharp that the watcher tries to stop his ears, and thus goes on his way, thinking of the metamorphosis of Alecto in the *Aeneid* and reflecting on the meaning of the "asp-like Passion, following the sorrowful Patience."[123]

Possibly the psychoanalytic reader would overhear a quite different message in this revelational event which had lingered in Ruskin's memory for a decade: the girl of Turin as an anima-projection, or perhaps as the furious patience of repressed libido. It is interesting to observe that he returns from the girl in the dust to Chaucer's Patience on her hill of sand, reminding us that she and her companion figures "Beheste" and "Art" stand for "Long-suffering," "promise," and "cunning" in the courts of love. From there the process of association carries him to Griselda, "the stone lady" (so different from that "Rosetta stone," he had been trying to decipher) and thence into a cathartic burst of puns on the first syllable (*gris*-grey) of her name. This is the particular entangling web of "old enigmas" alluded to above. From this knot of allusions grey (dust color) emerges as the color of patience; being between the archetypal light and dark (Aglaia and Alecto), grey expressed the ambivalence of patient human dust, kneadable, as he had said earlier, into the "spiced-bread" of noble life, but also into the explosive social gunpowder of the "Grey slavery" which Englishmen seemed to endure willingly even as they vociferated against Black slavery. But the grey threads deeply into Ruskin's private and public symbolism: Effie's name (Gray), the color that Rose's eyes became, and his hair with the chilling of his patient heart.[124] Athena's owl eyes were sky grey, and grey was the color of the wild olive crown.

This archetypal grey is obscurely tied to moral and aesthetic questions of shading that Ruskin approaches so obliquely in the first paper of *Cestus*, "The Black Outline," and that figures importantly in nearly all his aesthetic judgments, most notoriously in outburst against Whistler. Near the beginning of "The Black Outline" is a famous piece of eloquence, hymning the locomotive as a symbol of mechanistic art:

> What assemblage of accurate and mighty faculties in them; more than fleshly power over melting crag and coiling fire, fettered and finessed at last into the precision of watchmaking; Titianian hammer-strokes beating, out of lava, these glittering cylinders and timely-respondent valves, and fine ribbed rods, which touch each other as a serpent writhes, in noiseless gliding, and omnipotence of grasp; infinitely complex anatomy of active steel, compared with which the skeleton of a living creature would seem, to a careless observor, clumsy and vile—a mere morbid secretion and phosphatous prop of flesh![125]

The submerged serpent image, signifying Python's deadly presence, and the ironic comparison of mechanism to organism are both recurrent in his work as symbol and message, tied to his spinal theme of the vital against the lethal. But Ruskin has a more intricate comparison working at this point. The locomotive image leads him to the question of whether there is any "entirely human Art, with spiritual motive power" that is inherently distinct from "mechanical Art, with its mechanical motive force."[126] The enigma of the interdependence of the mechanical and the spiritual in art, signified by the circles of Giotto, is deepened by the fact that, as Ruskin understands it, the great masters tend to be secretive about their techniques in direct proportion to their power.

However, with the Greek and Egyptian masters, he continues, we have something else to go on; having "no conception of what modern men of science call the 'conservation of forces'," they projected mythic representations of the forces they felt in themselves, and in myth those forces may still be read. Thus in this first paper the locomotive and the pantheon are juxtaposed as representing the mechanical and the spiritual dynamics of art. There follows an interesting catalog of archetypal figures rationalized as projections of the spiritual energies that governed Egyptian and Greek art. The list is too long to reproduce at this point, but Neith-Athena is there, of course, described as "The Spirit of Wisdom in *Conduct*, bearing, in sign of conquest over troublous and disturbing evil, the skin of the wild goat, and the head of the slain Spirit of physical storm. In her hand a weaver's shuttle, or a spear." And the list is headed (after Max Müller, perhaps) by the solar deity, the "Spirit of Light, moral and physical, by name 'Physician—Destroyer.' . . . Physically, Lord of the Sun; and a mountain Spirit, because the sun seems first to rise and set upon the hills."[127]

What all this, the sun god and the locomotive, has to do with the special technical question, to shade or not to shade in outline, which the essay arrives at in its penultimate paragraph, is not apparent from its discursive structure. But from the texture of details and implications it is apparent that the technical question of shading is only a metaphor for the moral question of shading, that the black outline is the moral outline, the question of distribution of light and shade a question of the vital and the deadly in art and life.

The tenor of the "black outline" metaphor is clarified in the fifth paper, "Rembrandt and Strong Waters," a paper for which its author apologizes as not really belonging to the girdle of Aglaia (brightness) but rather to "the cestus of Scylla." In Rembrandtean tenebrism Ruskin saw the palpable image of spiritual death in art, the antitype of Turnerian luminism. In Rembrandt technical mastery (the locomotive) seemed coupled with utter moral negation, ultimate "evasiveness" in black outline. Hence the "strong waters" of the title is a burst of apocalyptic condemnation of Rembrandt and his "rushlight" (with special weight on the implications of that word). This passage conveys not merely the essential message but also the fusion of esoteric and apocalyptic features that will become increasingly characteristic of Ruskin's style. His allusions are to Rembrandt's *Flight into Egypt*, *The Good Samaritan*, *The Angel Appearing to the Shepherds*, and the particularly detested *Anatomy Lesson*.

> By rushlight, observe: material and spiritual. As the sun for the outer world; so in the inner world of man, that which "ερευνᾷ ταμεῖα κοιλίας" —"the candle of God, searching the inmost parts." If that light within become but a more active kind of darkness;—if, abdicating the measuring reed of modesty for sceptre, and ceasing to measure with it, we dip it in such unctuous and inflammable refuse as we can find, and make our soul's light into a *tallow* candle, and thenceforward take our guttering, sputtering, ill-smelling illumination about with us, holding it out in fetid fingers—encumbered with its lurid warmth of fungous wick, and drip of stalactitic grease—that we may see, when another man would have seen, or dreamed he saw, the flight of a divine Virgin—only the lamp-light

Rembrandt. *Doctor Nicolaes Tulp Demonstrating the Anatomy of the Arm*, 1632. [*The Anatomy Lesson*] Courtesy of the Mauritshuis, The Hague.

upon the hair of a costermonger's ass;—that, having to paint the good Samaritan, we may see only in distance the back of the good Samaritan, and in nearness the back of the good Samaritan's dog;—that having to paint the Annunciation to the Shepherds, we may turn the announcement of peace to men, into an announcement of mere panic to beasts; and, in an unsightly firework of unsightlier angels, see, as we see always, the feet instead of the head, and the shame instead of the honour;—and finally concentrate and rest the sum of our fame, as Titian on the Assumption of a spirit, so we on the dissection of a carcase,—perhaps by such fatuous fire, the less we walk, and by such phosphoric glow, the less we shine, the better it may be for us, and for all who would follow us.[128]

The serpent symbol, submerged in the images of both the girl and the locomotive, does not appear at this point. But toward the end of the chapter Ruskin shifts his attention to Doré's illustrations for Balzac's *Contes Drôlatiques*, also a dark and infected work in his view. They were taught, he says, by that fatal woman, Paristown, who was "for ever letting fall her silken raiment so far as that one may 'behold her bosom and half her side.' "[129] His allusion, of course, is to the partially scaled body of Geraldine, the lamia of Coleridge's *Christabel*.

In connection with this last point we might note that Ruskin's name for Mrs. La Touche was Lacerta, Latin for "lizard" (also a constellation); in a letter of 1868 he refers to her as being "a horror of iniquity— like a lamia."[130] The presence of the serpent archetype in Ruskin's consciousness, private and literary, is immense. In the later diaries he complains occasionally of serpent dreams and all the antagonists of his purifying heroes are serpent types: Hercules and Ladon, Apollo and Python, Christ and Mammon, Athena and Medusa, Saint George and the Dragon. At this point, in the late sixties, Python especially became the symbol of all forces antagonistic to his life. In Jungian theory the anima, the soul as she lures us into life, is closely associated with the serpent, representing either her amoral power (for she is not the soul in the dogmatic sense, but the creative, life-giving energy in man) or (as serpent-dragon) those instincts which hold her hostage.

4

We have seen that Ruskin's works in the sixties are of two primary kinds, works on political economy in his special sense of maintenance of the whole body politic, and works on the continuity of national ethics into natural art. Both aspects of this work, we have observed, depend upon the organic model. This often implicit metaphor of living form based on the active unity, limited liberty, and infinity or mystery of natural wholes is developed most explicitly in his chapters on vegetation in *Modern Painters*, volume 5, and in the discussion of the "laws" of organic form in *The Elements of Drawing*; but its origins are in the organic conceptions of architecture in *The Poetry of Architecture*, and this organic metaphor underlies his theories of unity in landscape and the Gothic. Organic form, emphasizing purposive self-unification of parts, is simply the controlling metaphor in Ruskin's work. He sees society as an organism unified, like all living things, under the law of help, and wealth or value is what can sustain its life; whatever causes violations of organic coherence, of help, is deadly. Art is an inevitable efflorescence of the social organism and, as such, infallibly reflects the moral nourishment it has received. The state of the organism, its health or coherence, can be diagnosed from specimens of its art.

As these theories, extensions of the organic model, have become decisively formulated, we have noted a tendency on Ruskin's part to lean away from systematic statement toward prophetic devices such as mythography, revelational moment, etymology, intertwined nets of allusions; though some of these techniques, as we have seen, are present in his earliest work and are the foundations of his style. However, at this moment we come to two works that represent the farthest reach, in the sixties, of that prophetic tendency: *The Ethics of the Dust* and *The Queen of the Air*. In these two closely related works Ruskin attempts to face some ultimate questions about the nature of the organic model itself. He examines the connection of life with form, and of form with ideas of a forming power, which, in turn, leads him to consider the nature of mythopoesis and the basis of the organic model in myth. Correlatively, he comes to his fullest recognition of a third force threatening the organic model: physical science, dissecting knowledge. We have been following his skirmishes with two other antiorganic forces: narrow, otherworldly religion and the worship of Mammon, deadly wealth. All three are fatal powers because they are forms of asceticism, denying the immediate experience of the world considered as nature or as the human field of care. Of course, science in the general sense of rationalism and materialism has been an antagonistic force in his work before this. Renaissance science is the forbidden knowledge that brings about our expulsion from the Gothic Eden; Pre-Raphaelite art fails as it becomes a science; the science of political economy exhibits a fatal neglect of the organic bonds of the human community; and science as technology is implicit (along with competition) in the worship of getting-on. But what is attacked is rationalistic or mechanistic codes, not the method of physical science itself. In fact down to this point Ruskin considers himself a scientist of sorts, a scientist of aspects, in botany and geology. And it is this very interest that leads him into increased distress over the attack by science on the mythic core of the organic model. "Ah, masters of modern science," he exclaims in his preface to *The Queen of the Air*, "give me back my Athena out of your vials."

His method of counterattack, however, is not primarily the philosopher's but the prophet's. What he does is to use the techniques of what his age considered to be scientific mythological research in order to interpret and invoke a myth against the forces of antimyth. We have already noticed that Athena makes some kind of appearance in most of his other works of the sixties, especially in *The Crown of Wild Olive*, where she stands for the Greek worship of existential wisdom and is ironically juxtaposed with the British worship of the goddess of getting-on, Britannia Agoraria. Now in *The Ethics of the Dust* and *The Queen of the Air* she emerges as a fully formed archetypal power, the queen of the air and consequently of organic form, the goddess of life and its wisdom. I say an archetypal power because in *The Ethics of the Dust* she appears also in her *ur*-form as the Egyptian Neith, who inspires the forming of crystals as well as of pyramids, and is connected obscurely with Saints Sophie and Barbara, and, even more obscurely, with his private deity, Rose La Touche.

The Ethics of the Dust (1866) consists of ten dialogues involving an "Old Lecturer" and his class of "little housewives." The subject, the subtitle declares, is "The Elements of Crystallization." The various properties of crystals are used, as the organic model is used, to symbolize various truths or laws of social behavior; the book is partly allegorical crystallography. Yet allegory is not an accurate description because the same laws are seen as applying to crystals and to higher forms of organization, and facts about crystals become the occasion for simple and direct discussions of the elements of existence: life, form, self, and so forth. Most important, however, is the fact that Ruskin not only moralizes crystallography, he mythologizes it as well (though it may be argued that the latter is always implicit in any attempt at the former). And the work becomes also an introduction to the nature of myth and to the tradition of Athena in particular. Several of the "little housewives," especially Egypt and Sibyl, have names which the Old Lecturer can draw upon symbolically from time to time. One of the girls is named Lily; none is named Rose, though there are a number of remarks that could be read as private allusions. The general setting and content of the dialogues derive from Ruskin's conversations with the girls at Winnington Hall. The preface to the first edition explains that these little lectures "were really given, in substance, at a girls' school (far in the country)." In the same place he also indicates that the work was "not intended for an introduction to mineralogy," but then, he concludes cryptically, "the less we speak of our intentions, the more chance there is of our realizing them."[131]

The preface to the second edition (1877) finds him more committed to the value of the work and more explicit as to his intentions there. He explains that the dialogues contain summaries, intended for young people, of all he has written on the same topics in his larger books. On rereading them he finds that they satisfy him better than anything else he has done of the kind. He goes on to recommend particular passages for close study. Heading this list are two passages on the forming power and on myth that he considers to have definitive value as statements, not as simplifications for the young. Both are found in the final lecture. The first passage, which begins with the words "you may at least earnestly believe," he calls "the clearest exposition I have ever yet given of the general conditions under which the Personal Creative Power manifests itself in the forms of matter." The other is an "analysis of the heathen conceptions of Deity" which, he continues, "not only prefaces, but very nearly supersedes, all that in more lengthy terms I have since asserted, or pleaded for, in *Aratra Pentelici* and the *Queen of the Air*."[132] This study demands that we follow Ruskin's recommendation and look closely at these passages, but it will also be necessary to give some sense of the tendencies of the other lectures that are climaxed by these passages.

The first lecture, called "The Valley of Diamonds" (from the "Second Voyage of Sindbad" in the *Arabian Nights*) is distinct from the others in not being about the ethics of the dust but the ethics of the dust-gatherers. The valley is an infernal place, a "metaphorical description of the kingdom of Mammon,"[133] he explains, in which the worldly function of gold and diamonds is shown to be "the multiplied destruction of souls . . . and the paralysis of wholesome human effort."[134] The "dust" we meet here is the dead dust of *Munera Pulveris*. The features of the valley are a lexicon of Ruskin's private symbols. There are forests with crimson-crested serpents singing like cicadas in the trees,[135] dark fields full of deceptive fireflies that look like the stars of heaven but burn like real sparks, labyrinthine cliffs and glaciers of fused gold and ice, and wreathing among the passes is a fatal cloud: "a mixed dust of snow and gold, ponderous, yet which the mountain whirlwinds are able to lift and drive in wreaths and pillars, hiding the paths with a *burial cloud*, fatal at once with wintry chill, and weight of golden ashes."[136]

The second and third dialogues draw heavily upon the Lecturer's account of his own mythic dream of "The Pyramid Builders," with special emphasis being given to the dream image of the god named Lower Pthah and to his "beetle-gospel." The dreamer finds himself standing at sunset beside the unfinished brick "Pyramid of Asychis." This brick pyramid, Ruskin's notes explain, is a symbol, like the Tower of Babel, of great labor expended on a shoddy and pretentious project. As the dreamer looks toward the sunset two vast forms approach him: first a shadowy pillar that gradually assumes a man's form as it glides toward him, and then a silver cloud from within the aura of the sun, which first darts its energy at the dark pillar and then approaches the dreamer, but as a lovely woman with calm blue eyes and robed to the feet in sunlit cloud. (There is a slight resemblance here to the action of the two clouds in "Harry and Lucy," the tale Ruskin wrote when he was seven and cited in *Praeterita* as a paradigm of his mind.'[137] The dreamer now understands that the pillared darkness is the Egyptian "Lord of Truth" (objective exactness), called Greater Pthah, and that the cloud-clad woman is his sister, Neith.

He understands also that Pthah has been building the brick pyramid and that Neith is displeased with it because she sees "only pieces of dark clay" there unrelieved by any fair stone fit to receive the images of the gods. She takes her brother to task for the degraded work he has forced upon his slaves (mankind). But Pthah argues that men have no need to work in noble stone, for they have no true love for the gods: "Let them make their clay four-square; and labour; and perish." Neith's answer: "Brother, wilt thou also make league with Death, because Death is true?" (Why should the Lord of Truth mock the children of men if the Lady of Wisdom does not? And Pthah: "They sought to bind me; and they shall be bound. They shall labour in the fire for vanity.") Then Neith asks how long it will take to build Pthah's pyramid, and when the Lord of Truth declares that it will take ten years, the Lady of Wisdom derides his teaching, offering to put her winged shoulders to work and build the pyramid before nightfall. This she does in the rosy light. At her command the stones fly up in swarms from the four quadrants and settle into form like seabirds blanketing a ledge. "I closed my eyes for an instant," says the dreamer, "and when I looked again, the pyramid stood on its rocks, perfect; and purple with the light from the edge of the sinking sun." Finally, the dreamer is plunged into desolation as the god images recede, leaving him alone with the desert.

But the dream has a sequel.[138] As the purple pyramid darkens in the twilight, the dreamer becomes conscious of a heavy whirring in the air, and a huge horned beetle with frightful claws thumps into the sand at his feet. To his amazement the huge insect begins its transformation into a bandy-legged laborer. "Its four claws became strong arms, and hands; one grasping real iron pincers, and the other a huge hammer; and it had a helmet on its head, without any eyelet holes." The figure announces itself as the Egyptian beetle-headed Pthah, the god in his lesser function ("His presence in the first elements of life," Ruskin's notes say, "the most painful of all their types of any beneficent powers"). Beetle-Pthah, it appears, is able to transform Thou's into It's by his command of force, for he announces that he has come to make Neith's pyramid small. And indeed it happens; beneath the touch of his iron pincers Lady Wisdom's pyramid becomes first deep purple, then blood red, then glowing with pale roselike fire from within, until finally it sinks down to the size of a gem. "Everything that is great I can make like this pyramid," the beetle-god explains, "and give into men's hands to destroy." With this he offers to drop Neith's belittled pyramid into the dreamer's hands, who at first starts back for fear of the thing's heat, but, receiving it, finds its burning cold and gemlike. The god laughs, becomes a beetle again, and burrows away fiercely into the sand.

The girls, of course, especially Little Egypt, want to know what Neith's pyramid was when Pthah placed it in the dreamer's hand; and so, explaining that it is "a little rosy transparent pyramid, built of more courses of bricks than I can count, it being made so small," the Old Lecturer places in Egypt's hands a crystal of rose fluor. There are murmurs of disappointment from the girls; however, the lecturer goes on to explain that when Neith forms snow crystals she needs to marshal atoms more rigorously than in making this one, and she must do it in a moment. But does he actually mean to imply that Neith is a *real* spirit? Egypt asks. The Lecturer is evasive: "What I mean is of little consequence," he continues. "What the Egyptians meant, who called her 'Neith,'—or Homer, who called her 'Athena'—or Solomon who called her by a word which the Greeks render as 'Sophia,' you must judge for yourselves." But having identified the crystal of rose fluor with the idea of numinous form, the Lecturer's final injunction can be simply, "Take that rose crystal away with you and think."

Ruskin's involved notes to this section explain, among many other mythic things, that Egypt of the dialogue is addressed as having once been Queen Nitocris, " 'the greatest heroine and beauty' of Egyptian story. The Egyptians called her 'Neith the Victorious' and the Greeks, '*Face* of the Rose,' (Rodope)."[139] Egyptian deities, he notes farther on, "are related to each other in mysterious triads; uniting always symbolism of physical phenomena with real spiritual power."[140] Neith, as he had explained in *Sesame and Lilies,* is the Egyptian spirit of divine wisdom, whose powers are essentially those of the Greek Athena. Though Athena's attributes are too complex to explain briefly, he observes that Neith's vulture wings in Egyptian sculpture mark her relation to Athena as the goddess of the air, representing both its "beneficent calm and necessary tempest."[141]

In the third lecture the "little housewives" are given further thoughts about the meaning of life, of self, and of the Egyptian beetle-god. They have been working at playground exercises in social crystallography in which they play the parts of atoms and attempt to form themselves suddenly into crystals, remembering their relative places and trying not to splinter egos. This raises the problem of how real atoms can know their places, and the Lecturer points out that one cannot imagine any single physical "law of attraction" among the particles that could arrange them in such complex structures: "One would need," as Mary (who is twenty) points out, to assume "all kinds of attractions. But you do not mean that the atoms are alive?" "What is to be alive?" the Lecturer throws back. A modern scientist, John Tyndall, speaks of life as a "mode of motion." The problem, the Lecturer suggests, taking the organicist position, "is not so much to say what makes a thing alive, as what makes it a Self. As soon as you are shut off from the rest of the universe into a Self, you begin to be alive." Life, then, is to be identified with unified form, not force or motion. "I do not think we should use the word 'life' of any energy which does not belong to a given form."[142] He recognizes that organic form, as opposed to crystalline, appears to be characterized by more definite internal determinateness and periodicity, but, he concludes, "If you choose to think the crystals alive, do, and be welcome."[143]

He will return more decisively to the relations of life and form in the final lecture, but at the moment the girls have been reading about the lower Pthah in J. Gardner Wilkinson's *The Manners and Customs of the Ancient Egyptians* and want to know why they gave him such an ugly shape. The symbol of the beetle-god fits Ruskin's political economy so he expands on it here, adding touches of topical satire. The Egyptians, he explains, concentrated into the beetle-god their sense of the degrading effects of manual labor, especially labor done near fire; the lame Hephaestus is the Greek type of the same spiritual meaning. But in the lower Pthah's power to diminish everything great and aggrandize everything small he had, he admits, a little of his "own separate meaning" with reference to modern times. Pthah's eyelessness ("having no eyes—he can see only himself") represents "the character of pure and eyeless manual labor to conceive everything as subjected to it: and, in reality, to disgrace and diminish all that is so subjected; aggrandising itself, and the thought of itself, at the expense of all noble things."[144] The temple of modern beetle worshippers is the temple of technology, the Crystal Palace, where people are taught "nothing but the lowest of the lower Pthah's work."[145] Finally, the scarab is not as true an emblem of him as is the northern dung beetle. "It is beautiful to see it at work, gathering its treasures (such as they are) into little round balls; and pushing them home with the strong wrong end of it—head downmost all the way,—like a modern political economist with his ball of capital, declaring that a nation can stand on its vices better than on its virtues. But away with you, children, now, for I'm getting cross."[146]

Ruskin does not again take up questions of life and myth until the final lecture; the intervening lectures generally stay closer to the "ethics" of crystallization. The fourth lecture, "The Crystal Orders," speaks of the tendency of crystals to divide into three great classes: needle crystals; leaf crystals, made of interwoven needles, and crystals in "heaps or knots, or masses."[147] And, in fulfilling as best they can the conditions of their "adopted form under given circumstances," crystals exhibit "conditions entirely resembling those of human virtue."[148] This observation leads into the fifth lecture, "Crystal Virtues," where the "little housewives" learn that crystals are governed by "a limited, though a stern, code of morals; and their essential virtues are but two;—the first is to be pure, and the second is to be well shaped."[149] Virtue in a crystal, as in a person, is to be "bright with coherent energy."[150] This idea of vital virtue is an important subtheme in the *Ethics* and allows Ruskin to restate some of the tenets of his "religion of Humanity." Virtue is in the healthy and courageous outgoing action of help and self-fulfillment, not in the introspective search for sin, in self-effacing sacrifice for others, or in yearning toward another life. "An immense quantity of modern confession of sin, even when honest, is merely a sickly egotism; which will rather gloat over its own evil, than lose the centralisation of its interest in itself."[151] Know thyself, which is "Apollo's proverb, and the sun's," is "the proverb of proverbs," but we can only know ourselves by looking out of ourselves, measuring ourselves in relation to others. Deeds are the seeds of destiny.

The sixth lecture, "The Crystal Quarrels," returns to the theme of vital virtue as the girls are told that (as with the constant yielding of quartz to other crystals) "self-sacrifice of a human being is not a lovely thing. . . . It is often a necessary and noble thing; but no form nor degree of suicide can ever be lovely."[152] For, as the Old Lecturer-prophet sees it, "the will of God respecting us is that we shall live by each other's

happiness, and life; not by each other's misery, or death."[153] This theme
of vital virtue is consummated in the seventh lecture, "Home Virtues,"
as the lecturer sends his pupils to Max Müller's *Lectures on the Science
of Language* to discover that the root meaning of the first syllable *vir-*
"really means 'nerve' " and that the "essential idea of real virtue is that of
a vital human strength, which instinctively, constantly, and without
motive, does what is right."[154] That is, virtue is organic and does not
depend upon the corrective of religion or the expectation of eternal
reward. "It is the blackest sign of putrescence in a national religion,
when men speak as if it were the only safeguard of conduct; and assume
that, but for the fear of being burned, or for the hope of being rewarded,
everybody would pass their lives in lying, stealing, and murdering."[155]

A piece of "wild crystallization" serves as the visible text for the eighth
lecture, "Crystal Caprice," in which the teacher discusses strange
varieties of crystalline form that appear to be owing to no antagonistic
force but simply to the "variable humor and caprice of the crystals
themselves." This he suggests, with jocular chauvinism, appears to be
"a part of the crystal mind which must be particularly interesting to a
feminine audience."[156] Actually the lecture is something like a
children's introduction to the death of Gothic described in "The
Flamboyant Architecture of the Valley of the Somme," for the type of
capriciousness in architecture is flamboyant Gothic. To illustrate this
Ruskin tells an allegorical fable of a building contest between Neith,
whose builders create a massive pyramid, and Saint Barbara (another
patroness of architecture and a variant of Neith-Athena), whose Gothic
"imps" throw up an overwrought and spidery tower with great speed,
until the sand runs away at the corners of it, and the tower leans, and
then, as he tells it, "the Gothic imps rose out of it like a flight of puffins,
in a single cloud; but screaming worse than any puffins you ever heard;
and down came the tower, all in a piece, like a falling poplar." Such was
the fall of Gothic, for "no architecture was ever corrupted more
miserably . . . by the accomplishment of its own follies."[157]

The last two lectures of the book, "Crystal Sorrows" and "Crystal
Rest," are far more profound and powerful than the other eight; they
could hardly have been intended for children. The very situation of the
dialogues, the Lecturer ("of incalculable age") and his audience of
"little housewives," allows Ruskin to don the prophetic mantle for
youthful minds, but in these he takes up the prophetic role for all who
care to listen. The "Crystal Sorrows" stems out of his intense interest in
"Banded and Brecciated Concretions." "I began to examine them
thoughtfully," he explains, "and perceived, in the end, that they were,

one and all, knots, of as rich mystery as my poor little human brain was ever lost in."[158] He went on to publish seven chapters on these forms in various issues of the *Geological Magazine* between 1867 and 1870. This lecture is a curious fusion of visual and visionary data, another illustration of the peculiar mixture of the phenomenological and the prophetic in Ruskin's makeup. The subject is crystals that have had a particularly hard life of it, crystals of crisis. The stone that is his text for this lecture is "brecciated agate," of which marble is a type. It is a stone in which one can read the primordial language of continental stress. This geological scar tissue formed at the points of incalculable strain and massive shifts in the earth's crust becomes in the prophet's mind an apocalyptic emblem of vast global forces at work, geologically and socially, in the midst of oppression and upheaval. Even in these stones we can see ourselves in the midst of judgment: "You see the broad shadow and deadly force of inevitable fate, above all this; you see the multitudes of crystals whose time has come; not a set time, as with us, but yet a time, sooner or later, when they all must give up their crystal ghosts:—when the strength by which they grew, and the strength given them to breathe, pass away from them; and they fail, and are consumed, and vanish away: and another generation is brought to life, framed out of their ashes."[159]

This vision leads towards the last lecture, "The Crystal Rest," with its questions of crystal life and death and of the ultimate destination of geological change. One of the pupils remarks that the Old Lecturer is in the habit of speaking of these crystals as if they were alive, and he in turn throws back the question left unanswered in the third lecture: "What is it to be alive?" Scientists "seem to have been getting some of it into and out of bottles, in their 'ozone' and 'antizone' lately: but they still know little of it; and, certainly, I know less." But he does recognize a particular danger in their speculations, against which "we artists can stand literally as 'Life Guards' at bay . . . however hard the philosophers push. And you may stand with us, if once you learn to draw nicely." However, the girls are confused about what their stand is to be, so the Lecturer puts his position into an aphorism, which is to be explained later in *The Queen of the Air*: "You may always stand by Form, against Force."[160] Yet the girls are still in doubt, and one of them, Mary, declares, "I don't think we shall any of us like having only form to depend on." To which the Lecturer replies, "It was not neglected in the making of Eve, my dear." But Mary insists that it is the "breathing of the life" which they want to understand. The Lecturer agrees, but he urges that form must be distinguished first from the "mere transition of forces.

Discern the moulding hand of the potter commanding the clay, from his merely beating foot as it turns the wheel." Even with such a difficult mode of force as light, we must remember "how far the existence of it depends on the putting of certain vitreous and nervous substances into the formal arrangement which we call an eye."[161]

Sibyl, at least, is still dissatisfied, and declares that she cares less about defying the philosophers than about getting a clear idea of life or soul for herself. With this, however, the Lecturer falls into a particularly riddling mood. He had meant, he says, to quiz Sibyl herself about "inspiration, and the golden bough, and the like," but he will settle instead for such an easy question as this: "At least, tell us whether the ideas of Life, as the power of putting things together, or 'making' them; and of Death, as the power of pushing things separate, or 'unmaking' them, may not be very simply held in balance against each other?"[162] Little Sibyl has no answer because, as she says, she is not in her cave at the moment.

But the Lecturer's answer to his own question is sufficiently sibylline. Life and death may well be held in balance, but "Modern Philosophy is a great separator"; that is, presumably, science disturbs the organic balance of existence by separating subject from object in dispassionate observation. There was once a unifying mode of awareness (now all but discredited) that projected feeling into things, composed purposive worlds wherever it looked, and thus helped to sustain the vital balance against unmaking. "When you used to be in your cave, Sibyl, and to be inspired, there was, (and there remains still in some small measure) beyond the merely formative and sustaining power, another, which we painters call 'passion' . . . the most truly 'poetic' or 'making' force of all, creating a world of its own out of a glance, or a sigh: and the want of passion is perhaps the truest death, or 'unmaking' of everything;—even of stones."[163] He is thus bringing into the balance of life and death, the organic balance, two modes of awareness: the analytic and the relational, the worlds of "I-It" and "I-Thou," numinous nature against neutral nature.

To illustrate his meaning the Lecturer contrasts a remark made by a recent climber of the Aiguille Verte ("Oh, Aiguille Verte, vous êtes morte, vous êtes morte!"—an example of "Real philosophic joy.") with a passage from Virgil in which "pater Apenninus" is brought to life by personification. These lines "full of a passionate sense of the Apennine fatherhood, or protecting power" illustrate that fusion of reverence and rhetoric that Ruskin had identified as the *true* pathetic fallacy in his earliest discussion of mythopoesis.[164] But the girls will not be put off by a pathetic fallacy; they want an outright answer: *Are* the mountains alive? This question leads the Lecturer to the passage that Ruskin identified in the preface of 1877 as his clearest exposition of the "general conditions under which the Personal Creative Power manifests itself in the forms of matter" and this, in turn, leads to the analysis of myth, which he also recommended for special attention.

"You may at least earnestly believe," he continues, "that the presence of the spirit which culminates in your own life, shows itself in dawning, wherever the dust of the earth begins to assume any orderly and lovely state." Life begins with the presence of an organizing power; this is the presence of help, or the holy, he had explained in volume 5 of *Modern Painters*, and to which he will return at the conclusion of the lecture. But now, having identified the presence of the vital spirit with the assumption of form, he moves on to a theory of the "gradation of life" in which ideas of organicism, animism, and the great chain of being appear to be mixed. It will not be easy, he explains, to separate the idea of degrees of organization ("gradated manifestation") from the idea of the vital power itself. "Things are not either wholly alive, or wholly dead. They are less or more alive."[165] Life seems to mean merely that things manifest subtly gradated intensities of organization. (One thinks of light as a life symbol here and of the constant emphasis Ruskin places on delicacy of gradation in expressing the mysteries of form.) This theory of life, like the chain of being, leads toward a discussion of myth, for, the Lecturer continues, "there seems to me this great good in the idea of gradation of life—it admits the idea of a life above us, in other creatures, as much nobler than ours, as ours is nobler than that of the dust."[166]

This is an appropriate point for Mary, the oldest, to ask why the Lecturer is always speaking about the heathen deities as if he "half believed in them," and why he represents them as good. What can he mean by this? So, with the warning that "this is indeed the longest, and the most wildly confused question that reason can deal with," the Lecturer sets out to give his pupils "a few clear ideas about the heathen gods."[167] This is the second passage that is given special praise in the preface of 1877. This attention is appropriate because Ruskin sets down the principles of mythological interpretation he will later use in *The Queen of the Air* and *Aratra Pentelici*.

Every mythic deity has three levels of meaning. (1) "It has a physical character." It signifies some natural power or object, and the mythic narrative represents "figuratively, the action of the natural power." (2) "It has an ethical character, and represents, in its history, the moral dealings of God with man." (3) "It has, at last, a personal character . . . realized in the minds of its worshippers as a living spirit with whom men may speak face to face." This emphasis on the "personal character" of the deity, we will see, causes Ruskin to differentiate his interest in myth from the theoretical position, common in his day, that reads myths as nature allegories. He also distinguishes himself from theorists whose primary interest is in the origins of a myth; he is interested in the myth at its highest stage of imaginative development. "For the question is not at all what a mythological figure meant in its origin; but what it became in each subsequent mental development of the nation inheriting the thought."[168] He is not a mythological scientist probing the savage roots of myth, but a humanist studying its poetic efflorescence.

To illustrate this idea of mythic growth the Lecturer returns to the ideas of Neith-Athena he had opened in the second lecture, and now he summarizes.

> The Neith, of Egypt, meant, physically, little more than the blue of the air; but the Greek, in a climate of alternate storm and calm, represented the wild fringes of the storm-cloud by the serpents of her aegis; and the lightning and cold of the highest thunder-clouds, by the Gorgon on her shield: while morally, the same types represented to him the mystery and changeful terror of knowledge, as her spear and helm its ruling and defensive power. And no study can be more interesting, or more useful to you, than that of the different meanings which have been created by great nations, and great poets, out of mythological figures given them, at first, in utter simplicity.[169]

Here in the tradition of Athena, and the "passionate" awareness it is summoned to illustrate, is the germ of the *Queen* and ultimately of *The Storm-Cloud of the Nineteenth Century*; but here Ruskin puts the mythic belief in the past tense: Athena *was* the queen of the air. He has not yet "discovered" that she *is* the queen of the air; here the connection with immediate belief is made by a different route. The Lecturer supposes his pupils want to ask such questions as: Were these figures "idly imagined to be real beings? And did they usurp the place of the true God?" What, in short, does he mean by their "personal" character?

Here he advises them to look into their own beliefs for the answer, for it "will much depend upon the clearness of your faith in the personality of the spirits which are described in the book of your own religion;— their *personality*, observe, as distinguished from merely symbolical visions."[170] For instance, it might be, he suggests, that when you think of the four horsemen of the Apocalypse, "a distinct sense of personality begins to force itself upon you. And though you might, in a dull temper, think that (for one instance of all) the fourth rider on the pale horse was merely a symbol of the power of death,—in your stronger more earnest moods you will rather conceive of him as a real and living angel."[171] If such literal belief in the "personality" of angels is the essence of our own religious experience, is there any impiety in believing that Greek seers, to whom our humanistic tradition owes so much, may have had similarly authentic visions? If we can believe in an Hebraic Apocalypse why not also a Greek counterpart? This device of devotional transference is characteristic of Ruskin's remarks on "Greek religion"; by analogy he hoped to convey the earnestness of their belief and at the same time open sectarian minds to a sense of the "religion of Humanity." Here he observes, tellingly, that "our scorn of Greek tradition depends, not on our belief, but our disbelief, of our own traditions."[172]

The Lecturer has a final point to emphasize concerning the "personality" of Greek angels, and this is important because it comes back to their defensive power, rooted in "passion," against the separations and pollutions of modern science. "The whole heart of Greek mythology is in that; the idea of a personal being in the elemental power;—of its being moved by prayer; and of its presence everywhere, making the broken diffusion of the element sacred."[173] A question logically following from this explanation would be whether the intensity of the Lecturer's own faith permits *him* to see any sacred or organizing power in the elements. The girls do not ask this, but he appears to be answering such a question in the optimistic vision of Crystal Rest, under the law of help, with which the lecture concludes.

Once, he explains, he had remarked (in *Modern Painters*, volume 4,) that the "earth seemed to have passed through its highest state"; he believed he saw evidence of final geological degeneration everywhere, "unaccompanied, as it seemed, by redeeming or compensatory agencies."[174] But now he perceives a happier, more cohesive law far more deeply interfused with the dust.

> I am still under the same impression respecting the existing phenomena; but I feel more strongly, every day, that no evidence to be collected within historical periods can be accepted as any clue to the great tendencies of geological change; but that the great laws which never fail, and to which all change is subordinate, appear such as to accomplish a gradual advance to lovelier order, and more calmly, yet more deeply, animated Rest. . . . For, through all the phases of [the dust's] transition and dissolution, there seems to be a continual effort to raise itself into a higher state; and a measured gain, through the fierce revulsion and slow renewal of the earth's frame, in beauty, and order, and permanence.[175]

This mythopoesis of his own illustrates the profound inworking of the law of help, the "holy" law of organized form which he had annunciated in volume 5 of *Modern Painters*. And so the lecturer concludes by asking Mary to read aloud the lovely passage from that volume (beginning with "A pure or holy state of anything . . . is that in which all its parts are helpful or consistent"), in which a handful "of the blackest slime of a beaten foot path, on a rainy day, near a manufacturing town" undergoes geological self-purification through the secret ministry of the ethics of the dust.[176]

CHAPTER 13

The Goddess in the Vial

Even when allowances are made for his frequent inconsistencies and for what Carlyle termed his "flightiness," there is a residue of strangeness about the significance Ruskin attached to *The Queen of the Air* (1869). It is as if the very quality of the things attempted there had enshrined the work in his regard. He described the book in its preface as consisting merely of "desultory memoranda on a most noble subject" that he would publish "as they stand" because "no time nor labour would be enough to complete them to my contentment."[1] But there must have been something in these "desultory memoranda" that was a settled perfection with him. For, in the first place, he had been quite unreceptive to the revisions suggested by Norton, to whom he had entrusted the task of seeing them through the press, nor would he ever revise them himself; yet he spoke of the volume as "beginning the series of my corrected works."[2] And five years after it appeared we find him confiding to Susan Beever that he thought the book "the best I ever wrote . . . the last which I took thorough loving pains with, and the first which I did with full knowledge of sorrow";[3] then later to the same correspondent: "It is the most useful and careful piece I have done. . . . Did it not shock you to have a heathen goddess so much believed in?"[4]

"Believed in" by whom? we ask. By the heathen or by the author? Perhaps this very ambiguity contains a hint of an explanation for his attitude toward that fragmentary and discursive book: imperfect and incomplete as it may have been in form, he thought it much more nearly perfect in faith: the goddess "so much believed in," the discovery made "with full knowledge of sorrow." An entry in his diary for that same year (1874) in which he had corresponded with Miss Beever about his "best" book also suggests the presence, for him, of some precious intuition in it. "Plan a little preface for *Queen of Air*," he wrote. "The discovery of it. I knew ten times less Latin and Greek than the philologists; a thousand fold more about the morning and its breeze. Also, I knew something of Greek art, and had a little, in my own mind, of actual Greek Faith."[5]

In a different way, a rebuke he had addressed in 1871 to one of the book's reviewers also asserted both the "faith" and the "discovery" in it. Though generally respectful, the reviewer (for the *Asiatic*) had boldly opined that "mythology is useful as a storehouse for poets, and for literary men in want of some simile or metaphor to produce a striking effect."[6] But the slip of "actual Greek Faith" that had taken root in Ruskin's own nature worship had made such a view of myth intolerable to him. *"The Queen of the Air,"* he replied, "was written to show, not what could be fancied, but what was felt and meant in the myth of Athena." And the "discovery" in the book was, he said, "the first clear and connected approximate proof . . . yet rendered by scientific mythology" that "Athena is the goddess of the air."[7] The use of "is" here, as will be seen, conveys, perhaps by intuition, something basic in Ruskin's attitude toward his Athena: for her appearance in his work is not as myth allegorized but as a charged vision, no less vital than Blake's "Antediluvians" or Yeats's *anima mundi.* "Playing with thunder" he called his myth-work in a letter to J. P. Faunthorpe in 1881, reconfirming after twelve years *The Queen*'s precedence in his affections:

> It is a great joy to me that you like *The Queen of the Air.* I shall be so thankful for your revise of it. *In the point of original power of thought it leads all my books.* My political economy is all in Xenophon and Marmontel; my principles of art were the boy's alphabet in Florence; but the Greeks themselves scarcely knew all their imaginations taught them of eternal truth, and the discovery of the function of Athena as the Goddess of the Air is, among moderns, absolutely I believe my own. I *meant* to have written a mythology for both girls and boys, but it is playing with thunder, and after being twice struck mad—whether for reward or punishment I cannot tell—I must venture no more.[8]

Carlyle, it seems, felt some of the book's mystical voltage. To Froude he wrote, "Passages of that last book *Queen of the Air* went into my heart like arrows."[9] And to the author he allowed that, though he "remained here and there a little uncertain" about "the natural history of those old Myths," he had few misgivings about the interpretations Ruskin had put upon them. "No such Book have I met with for long years past," he declared. Here, in fact, was "the one soul now in the world who seems to feel as I do on the highest matters, and speaks *mir aus dem Herzen* exactly what I wanted to Hear!"[10]

Indeed, with the glowing image of Athena to help him disarm the noisy company of his adversaries, Ruskin's prophetic bow was here, perhaps, most nearly at full draw. However, few modern readers have been as much troubled by those arrows as Carlyle was. Though movingly paeanic in many passages, the book repels by its matted allusiveness and discursiveness. But such judgments as R. H. Wilenski's that *The Queen of the Air* consists merely of "fantastic interpretations of Greek myths" worked up by Ruskin because he "had to learn to talk about the Greeks in preparation for a University appointment" and in this way "relieved his boredom" with Greek subjects,[11] must, if *The Queen* is to be understood, be opposed by such points as the following, several of which Cook has presented in his critical introduction to the work.

First, of course, there is the point just considered, that the work was, in Cook's phrase, "a favourite book with its author." We know also that Ruskin's interest in Greek mythology was, in fact, a long-standing one, extending back at least to his work on the chapter entitled "Of Classical Landscape" in *Modern Painters*, volume 3, and forward through *Fors Clavigera*. He assessed this interest himself in 1880: "I believe no interpretations of Greek religion have ever been so affectionate, none of the Roman religion so reverent, as those which will be found at the base of my art teaching, and current through the entire body of my works."[12] Furthermore, as we have seen, in 1862, during the period of his nominal apostasy, his enthusiasm for Greek belief led him to call himself a "Pagan" and to speak of his religion as being the "old Greek."[13] Indeed, as Richard Jenkyns asserts, "though Ruskin's passionate adherence to Christianity was at times shaken to its foundations, his love and admiration for Greek beliefs never wavered."[14] We have also noticed that his work suggests a familiarity with the most advanced tendencies of mythological scholarship, both English and Continental, in its time; and we have speculated that his avowed respect for the philological studies of Max Müller, later his acquaintance and colleague at Oxford, may have been catalytic in this area. Finally, we have seen that the theoretical core of *The Queen of the Air* is specifically anticipated in *The Ethics of the Dust*, where Athena makes important appearances in her own form and as the Egyptian Neith.

In sum, these considerations have been adduced in support of that idea which Ruskin's peculiar respect for the book suggests, namely, that *The Queen* is not the mythological droodle it is often considered to be; on the contrary, we will see that within the tangle of allusion, digression, and doxology there is to be found one of Ruskin's major prophecies.

John D. Rosenberg has given the book more nearly its due. As Carlyle had, he calls attention to the mystique of the prose, which he regards as "a prose not of statement but of *prayer*," having "the magic of an incantation." And though he justly observes that the work is hardly to be reckoned a contribution to scholarly mythology, he evinces a respect for the book that resembles Ruskin's own when he calls it "an extraordinary recreation of the Greek sense of the gods and their ruling presence throughout nature.''[15] Richard Jenkyns takes the position that Ruskin's thoughts about myths are more to be valued than his imitations of them. He allows that in *Modern Painters* Ruskin shrewdly distinguished between Greek animistic belief and Romantic pantheism and explored the complexities of particular myths with ''subtlety and lucidity.'' But he dismisses *The Queen of the Air* as ''one of his maddest works,'' because Ruskin's eloquent efforts to ''moralize'' the natural world led him into patent absurdities of detail. Yet he does perceive that the work is not about dead myths but asserts a living and personal faith; ''the strange feature of Ruskin's exposition, he notes, ''is the apparent implication that Greek beliefs were in some respects truer than those of the nineteenth century. The theories of the scientists 'fail'; Christian beliefs in transcendence and monotheism seem inadequate.''[16] More relevantly, Harold Bloom has reminded us that ''Ruskin's Athena is finally a goddess of his own creation, and as such she is one of the major mythmakings of the Victorian age.''[17]

Indeed, *The Queen of the Air* is less interesting as Greek mythology than as Ruskinian. The first two of these three ''lectures'' are discursive invocations of the ''mnemonic deposit'' surrounding certain mythic themes that he took to be heiroglyphs of the physical and spiritual significance of the air. In the midst of this, Athena emerges as his supreme attempt to connect mythographically the sensual and the moral perceptions; her complex image amounts to a statement of the dependence of the spiritual upon the physical landscape, given in a prophetic vision of the goddess of the air as the armed avenger of his century's joint pollution of air and inspiration. Her wisdom is that unless man's spirit, as opposed to his science, teaches him his place in nature she soon will not support his life at all.

1

The Ethics of the Dust is, as we have seen, partly an earth myth for the century's children in which Ruskin declares the priority of form over force as the meaning of life; asserts the correlative importance of passionate, relational responses to things in which they are seen as expressions of a forming power; and identifies the working of the purifying ''law of help'' deep down in geological change. In a parallel way *The Queen of the Air* is an air myth for the century, in which a purifying mythic power, centered in the Athena symbol, is extended to everything the air enters into, the entire organic model, and includes also the inspiration by which her formative influence is perceived, and the storm power by which insolent, inorganic knowledge is punished. But *The Queen* is a more comprehensive and quasi-scholarly piece of interpretive myth-making than *The Ethics*, though it expands upon the general theory of myth and the brief analysis of Athena set forth in the earlier book and draws also upon the cloud myths interpreted in volume 5 of *Modern Painters*.

Broadly speaking we have four areas of concern with respect of this book. First, and most significant, is the place *The Queen* occupies in the development of his own mythology, in his thought and faith. This I indicate by calling her the queen of the organic model; she is also the major symbol of the syncretic religious phase (the "religion of Humanity") through which he was passing. There may also be a private significance in Athena's (the rosy dawn's) relation to Rose and to all the other symbols in his feminine pantheon. Second, there is the actual interpretive content of the book: his "discovery" concerning Greek myth. Third, since the book is more scholarly than most of his works, there is a natural question concerning his particular sources on the meaning of Athena in her cult epithets. Finally, there is a more general source question about the involvement of the book with certain intellectual developments in its time. The preface (1869) alone suggests *The Queen*'s response to the problem of scientific knowledge, to advances in the study of language and myth, and to the effects of progress on the environment. The remainder of this section will be concerned mainly with his fourth point, the preface and the intellectual setting to which it refers.

"My days and strength have lately been much broken"; his preface begins, "and I never more felt the insufficiency of both than in preparing for the press the following desultory memoranda on a most noble subject."[18] The book is indeed fragmentary and discursive; however, since his aim is prophetic utterance rather than systematic interpretation, his purposes would not be served by turning his notes on myth into definitive analysis. Perhaps this is why he says, "I leave them as they stand, for no time nor labour would complete them to my contentment." Yet he does believe they contain suggestions that may be safely followed by any one "beginning to take interest in aspects of mythology, which only recent investigation has removed from the region of conjecture into that of rational inquiry." That he has benefitted from these researches (which, as Cook's note informs us, were in the philological rather than the later anthropological method of mythology), is implied in his next statement. "I have some advantage, also, from my field work, in the interpretation of myths relating to natural phenomena."[19] He acknowledges the guidance of his long-time friend Charles Newton, the archeologist, and then goes on to emphasize a final compensating qualification of his for the interpretation of myth: a special sympathy with the ancient mind. "But I knew that there was no hope of my being able to enter with advantage on the fields of history opened by the splendid investigation of recent philologists; though I could qualify myself by attention and sympathy, to understand, here and there, a verse of Homer's or Hesiod's as the simple people did for whom they sang."[20]

In contrast to this Homeric feeling, the mythopoeic awareness with which he is in sympathy, the next several paragraphs bring in the scientific mode of knowing. They contain an ironic allusion to Professor John Tyndall's current experiments on the chemistry of the sky and Ruskin's assertion that these experiments merely verify the truth of the mythic conception of Athena. We must return to these passages in a moment. The preface ends with a moving plea for the release of Athena from the vials of the scientists, the great separators. But in coming to this plea Ruskin enters another theme. This is the apocalyptic darkening and degeneration of nature through the defilement taught by science, concerning the progress of which he bears prophetic witness.

> This first day of May, 1869, I am writing where my work was begun thirty-five years ago, within sight of the snows of the higher Alps. In that half of the permitted life of man, I have seen strange evil brought upon every scene that I best loved, or tried to make beloved by others. The light which once flushed those pale summits with its rose at dawn, and purple at sunset, is now umbered and faint; the air which once inlaid the clefts of all their golden crags with azure is now defiled with languid coils of smoke, belched from worse than volcanic fires; their very glacier waves are ebbing, and their snows fading, as if Hell had breathed on them; the waters that once sank at their feet into crystalline rest are now dimmed and foul, from deep to deep, and shore to shore.[21]

Going back a bit we notice that the primary claim Ruskin makes to authority in the interpretation of myth (and the basis of his prophecy against antimyth, or science) is his ability to participate, at least at moments, in mythopoeic awareness. He could understand bits of Homer or Hesiod as a Greek would have; he had a little in his "own mind, of actual Greek Faith." Of course participation in mythopoeic awareness was a common Romantic claim or aim; the poet's mind overcomes, or hopes to overcome, the subject-object separation induced by Western rationalism and re-wed his mind to nature; when he does he is likely either to participate in the transcendental unity of one life or, more mundanely, to recover the primitive sense of presences in nature. Ruskin had long ago, in volume 3 of *Modern Painters*, condemned the mere poetic diction by which modern poets animated natural forms with presences in which they, being moderns, could not believe though they might wish to; however, he contrasted this stylistic fashion with the restrained and true pathos of a mythic poet's matter-of-fact awareness of presences in natural powers. In *The Ethics of the Dust* he emphasized a law of spiritual life, "passion" by which artists see things as animated by indwelling power and as whole, and he went on to conclude, after an analysis of Greek belief, that the heart of that belief (in which he thought he participated to some extent) was "the idea of a personal being in the elemental power . . . making the broken diffusion of the element sacred."[22] This particular law or stage of spiritual development was important to Ruskin because it referred to a state of the human mind, perhaps a necessary state, when it was still a part of the organic model, that is, before it fell into separation from nature into the subject-object dichotomy and the "Fallacy of Misplaced Concreteness" (Whitehead's term)[23] contingent upon this separation. This vital law of spiritual life was about to come into technical discussion in Ruskin's time under the term *animism*.

Ruskin, however, does not use the word. It was introduced into modern currency several years later by E. B. Tylor in his famous *Primitive Culture* (1871), where we find him applying the term to principles of belief that are central to the arguments of *The Ethics* and *The Queen*. He reminds us, as Ruskin had, that "first and foremost among the causes which transfigure into myth the facts of daily experience, is the belief in the animation of all nature, rising at its highest pitch to personification. This, no occasional or hypothetical action of the mind, is inextricably bound in with that primitive mental state where man recognizes in every detail of his work the operation of a personal life and will."[24] In fact, it will be plain that the *raison d'etre* of *The Queen of the Air* is the recreation of that animistic sense, which Tylor was soon to call "the deep-lying doctrine of Spiritual Beings, which embodies the very essence of Spiritualistic as opposed to Materialistic philosophy."[25]

The point, of course, is this: though the official introduction of the term *animism* into mythological theory came two years after the publication of Ruskin's "myth-book," both the concept of "universal animation" and even the term itself had appeared earlier. For instance, in March 1867 Tylor had delivered at the Royal Institution a lecture entitled "Traces of the Early Mental Condition of Man," in which he had sponsored the term *animism* as appropriate for "the state of mind which . . . sees in all nature the action of animated life and the presence of innumerable spiritual beings."[26] And there is even a reasonable possibility that Ruskin, as an active member of the institution at that time, may have heard this lecture or perused the abstract of it.[27]

But it is more important, if the matter of Ruskin's source is to be considered, to notice first that Tylor actually uses the term *animism* in two basic senses in the passages just quoted: as signifying belief in the "universal animation of all nature" but also the "deep lying doctrine of Spiritual Beings." It is the first of these senses that most nearly squares with Ruskin's notion of a personal power at work in the dust. But this vitalistic sense of animism (properly called animatism) had appeared in the writings of the philological nature mythologists several decades before Tylor applied his famous term. Indeed, this concept of *animatism* as a stage of belief is implicit in Tylor's own early *Researches into the Early History of Mankind* (1865), where one finds him acknowledging a debt to earlier theories concerning the origin of myth that had been set forth by Adelbert Kuhn and Max Müller.[28]

The allusion in *The Queen*'s preface to "the splendid investigations of recent philologists" is, as Cook observes, very likely a reference to the work of Max Müller in particular. In discussing the interpretations of Turner's solar myths that Ruskin constructs in the last section of *Modern Painters,* I noted that he might, in writing these, have felt the influence of Müller's solarist theories of myth through his popular essay "Comparative Mythology," which had been published in *Oxford Essays* for 1856. Yet there was nothing to connect the two discussions but a comparable interest in myths of sky phenomena. There were no references on Ruskin's part to Vedic sources, or to the primacy of the solar journey in mythic narratives; there were only the beginnings of his tendency to build arguments around the roots of words. In the meantime, however, we have seen that *Sesame and Lilies* and *The Ethics of the Dust* both contain etymologies drawn from Müller and distinct recommendations of his *Lectures on the Science of Language* (delivered at the Royal Institution in 1863 and published in the following year) as a work worthy of careful study. Therefore, it seems reasonable to assume that Ruskin took his own advice and was familiar with these lectures at least, if not with the "Comparative Mythology." With this assumption in mind, then, we should notice a few points of particular relevance to his work that he would have found in Müller's lectures.

For instance, in his eleventh lecture Müller is at some pains, as indeed he had been in "Comparative Mythology," to sketch in the theoretical position of Adelbert Kuhn, a contemporary German comparative mythologist whose work was then virtually unknown in England. The professor is careful to clarify the point that, though he is himself strictly a *solar* mythologist, Kuhn and "the most eminent mythologians in Germany" adhere to the "meteorological theory," looking "upon clouds and storms and other convulsive aspects of nature as causing the deepest and most lasting impression on the minds of those early observers who had ceased to wonder at the regular movements of the heavenly bodies."[29] It is attractive to speculate on the interest Müller's brief accounts of the meteorological mythologists might have had for Ruskin, considering that he had already written on the Pegasean and Gorgonian storm legends in volume 5 of *Modern Painters* and planned to make a book of these,[30] and that in *The Queen of the Air* he was to identify Athena with "the ambient air, which included all cloud, and rain, and dew, and darkness, and peace, and wrath of heaven."[31] Could the eventual interpreter of the *Storm-Cloud of the Nineteenth Century* have responded, for instance, to Müller's remark that Kuhn identified the Greek Gorgons and Erinnys with the Vedic *Saranyu* and these, in turn, with "the fleet, impetuous, dark, storm-cloud (Sturm-wölke), which in the beginning of all things soared in space"?[32] We know at least that Ruskin was to connect the Gorgons with Athena's serpent-fringed "robe of indignation," signifying chastisement by storm.

But although Ruskin was evidently impressed with the "splendid investigation" of the philologists and perhaps willing to have their support where he could claim it, there is an important difference to be noted between his approach to myth and theirs. For Ruskin "the real meaning of any myth is that which it has at the noblest age of the nation among whom it is current";[33] for Müller the real meaning of a myth is to be found at its roots in the history of language, and for him there was no doubt that "the more we go back, the more we examine the earliest germs of every religion, the purer . . . we shall find the conceptions of the Deity."[34] He sought the state of greatest spiritual ingenuousness in myth at the point where *nomina* of external nature tended to become *numina* in the Aryan mind. But the bloodless Aryan deities who emerged from the equations of the philologists could serve no prophetic purpose for Ruskin except by way of documentation. What interested him was the myth in its highest imaginative state, when deities were perceived as personal and even companionable powers.

Where the philologists were concerned to trace myths backwards historically, Ruskin wished to look forward through them toward the present; this was not merely because, as he said in the preface, he could not hope "to enter with advantage on the fields of history" the philologists had opened, but because it would not serve his prophetic purpose to do so. It was crucial for Ruskin to hold that even later mythic expressions (like Dante's or his own) might partake of the same involuntary animistic vision that the philologists had discerned in the nascent religious expressions of man. To him the real "language" of myth was not in its linguistic vehicle but in the enigmatic cyphers of involuntary communion between the poet or seer and the animating or forming power in things, organic form speaking through the spirit of man.

Ruskin's theory of myth was a personal hybrid; he was interested in the philological evidence and willing to use etymology where he could as a tool with which to open, or appear to open, what he took to be the organic meaning of a mythic epithet or symbol. One can suppose that he would have been interested in Müller's assertion that "mythology, in the highest sense, is the power exercised by language on thought in every possible sphere of mental activity"[35] and in his view that myths still form around metaphors and we still believe in them and can be used by them. Yet for Ruskin myths do not originate in a "disease of language" but in worship, in the communal bond of mind and nature; hence they are the authentic "voice" of the organic model. That is, in his view, myths can speak without language in Müller's sense; they can speak through art, and, most important, they can speak directly through natural form; there are such things as "living myths." And the vital powers still speak to us and judge us through nature whether we listen or not, but they can never be synthesized in the vials of the scientists because that awareness is dead to them and they to it. It is our passions we murder as we dissect.

Perhaps the whole antivitalistic attitude of science, which was, to Ruskin, simply one way of death, is best epitomized by Huxley's famous lecture "On the Physical Basis of Life." In this discourse, delivered in 1868 and published in the *Fortnightly Review* for 1 February 1869 (*The Queen* was begun in that month), Huxley discussed protoplasm as the "physical basis," the "potter's clay" of all forms of life. This was harmless enough in itself, but Huxley went on to a provocative mechanistic desecration of the vital essence itself: "What justification is there, then, for the assumption of the existence in the living matter of something which has no representative, or correlative, in the not-living matter which gave rise to it? What better philosophical status has 'vitality' than 'aquosity'? And why should 'vitality' hope for a better fate than any other 'itys'?" Perhaps, he proposed, "all vital action may be said to be the result of the molecular *forces* of the protoplasm which displays it."[36] When, in the second Athena lecture ("Athena Keramitis," where Athena is the formative energy in the clay), Ruskin identified her with the *"forming* power" and vital energy in material organism, he meant to counter mythically the chilling omination in such views as Huxley's.

Huxley's remarks, again, are merely representative. Ruskin need never have seen them to know the tendency. In a general way, it could be said that to understand properly *The Queen of the Air* and *The Ethics of the Dust* one ought to examine not only the cloud myths of volume 5 of *Modern Painters*, the darkening weathers and serpent dreams of the diaries, and the philological and mythological studies of Max Müller, but in addition the first five volumes (1851–1869) of the *Proceedings of The Royal Institution*. For, in a complex way, there are matters here that *The Queen* and *The Ethics* are about.

In 1853, for instance, John Tyndall had delivered a famous lecture, "The Influence of Material Aggregation upon the Manifestations of Force," in which he had made these remarks on the relationship between force and matter: "There are no two words with which we are more familiar than matter and force. The system of the universe embraces two things,—an object acted upon, and an agent by which it is acted upon;— the object we call matter, and the agent we call force; thus the luminiferous *ether* is the vehicle or medium by which the pulsations of the sun are transmitted to our organs of vision."[37] In 1859 N. S. Maskelyne had spoken of "the ultimate units of material consistence, which form the centres of chemical force."[38] W. S. Savory, in 1861, had said "chemistry draws no line of demarcation between the organized and inorganic kingdom," going on to point out that "even in the vital functions may be recognized the operation of forces, some of which, at least, are common to both kingdoms of nature; while, between these and others, which appear to be peculiar to living tissues, it is probable that a relation may exist like that which prevails between chemical and physical forces."[39]

We are representing here a central impulse of nineteenth-century science: the tendency to explain natural phenomena in terms only of matter and energy and their laws. We have already examined Ruskin's reply in *The Ethics*: there is not merely *matter* and *force* in things but also *form*. And to concentrate upon the forms of existence is to be able to "discern the hand of the potter . . . from his merely beating foot," a discernment that, he was certain, had characterized the happiest ages of man. So much had been said in *The Ethics of the Dust*. But the attack on mechanism had to be taken up again in *The Queen of the Air*, the immediate provocation, it appears, having been one particular experiment which, to judge from the bitterness with which he refers to it in his preface, must have seemed a crowning insolence of science.

On 15 January 1869 (*The Queen* was written in February, March, and April of that year) Professor Tyndall delivered an address at a meeting of the Royal Institution entitled "Chemical Rays, and the Light of the Sky." His lecture, like Huxley's, is a distillate of those views that Ruskin was bound to oppose. Apropos of "aether waves," for instance, Tyndall observed that, "though we are speaking of things which lie entirely beyond the range of the senses, the conceptions are as truly *mechanical* as they would be if we were dealing with ordinary masses of matter, and with waves of sensible magnitude."[40] Tyndall's real purpose in the lecture was to demonstrate "that sky-blue may be produced by such particles,"[41] but the concrete insult was that the lecturer offered to reproduce within his "experimental tube" a vaporous blue "which shall rival, if it does not transcend, that of the deepest and purest Italian sky."[42] And then before the eyes of the assembly he concocted a test-tube sky the blueness of which was, in his description, "as deep and dark as the sky seen from the highest Alpine peaks, and for the same reason."[43]

In such activities as these Ruskin's organicism found its ultimate antagonist. This was the Gorgon face of knowledge, "the cloudy coldness of knowledge, and its venomous character"[44] as he called it. The hieroglyphs of it are first the ragged, hissing Gorgon cloud, then Athena's serpent-fringed aegis, and finally a sooty cloud, the sound of which was "a hiss instead of a wail."[45]

We have already noticed the first elements of this obsessive and confluent symbolism for impurities, the enemies of life (or help), those images of swift, dark, malevolent clouds confounded strangely with worms or serpents of physical and moral decay, in his discussion of the Graiae, the Medusa, and those steamy serpents Ladon and Python, all appearing in volume 5 of *Modern Painters*. And one can detect even from the tone of Ruskin's treatment of them there that these are never merely Greek or Turnerian images objectively considered. We have seen that faint but legible indications of black, unwholesome weathers, together with descriptions of polluted or disconsolate landscapes and references to serpent dreams, begin to appear in his diaries of sixties. Considering this, we are not surprised to learn in the preface to *The Queen* that even the crags of the highest Alps were being defiled by (notice the choice of words) "languid coils of smoke belched from worse than volcanic fires."[46]

What fires were those? One might argue, of course, that Ruskin has merely the fires of the Coketowns in mind here and that he is thinking of all the careless and divisive acts of industrialism, the "burning grasp" of avarice and materialism. But why, if this is so, should the evocation of those "worse than volcanic fires" follow abruptly upon that embittered reference to Professor Tyndall's experimental sky?

Simply because within the coils of smoke, the "dense manufacturing mist," behind the obvious blights of "Getting-on," Ruskin now saw that more formidable enemy moving: the tendency to reduce every form productive of human awe, the god-stuff itself, to a complex of forces. The mechanists seemed quite confident of turning the substance of all myths into algebraic abstractions, of profaning by their equations the very possibility of companionable and ministering deities. Whatever the elements and forms of nature said to the Tyndalls, they hoped to translate it into formulae. The myth-stuff once secured in flasks and on slides, they were not disposed to reverence it. Everything plainly was energy: consuming, consumable, burning.

With, perhaps, such thoughts as these in his mind, Ruskin concluded his preface to *The Queen of the Air* with this plea:

> Ah, masters of modern science, give me back my Athena out of your vials, and seal, if it may be, once more, Asmodeus therein. You have divided the elements, and united them; enslaved them upon the earth, and discerned them in the stars. Teach us, now, but this of them, which is all that man need know,—that the Air is given to him for his life; and the Rain to his thirst, and for his baptism; and the Fire for warmth; and the Sun for sight; and the Earth for his meat—and his Rest.[47]

And, in the same sense, his plain and central task in those lectures was to rescue the myth-stuff (typified first by the air) from the vials of the analysts. To do so it would be necessary to show that myths participated in a continuum of instinctive truth that anticipated and transcended scientific discoveries. He would explain, for example, that the results of recent modern investigation concerning the relationship between the air and the life force, the color of the sky, or the prevalence of ether had been anticipated symbolically by the Greeks in the attributes and visible image of Athena. But his higher purpose would always be to show that, by the same reasoning, there might be other equally verifiable truths (or warnings) embodied in the worship of Athena that have yet to be rediscovered or are being perilously ignored.

> Even while I correct these sheets for press, a lecture by Professor Tyndall has been put into my hands . . . which, I now find, completes, in two important particulars, the evidence of an instinctive truth in ancient symbolism; showing, first, that the Greek conception of an ethereal ele-

ment pervading space is justified by the closest reasoning of modern physicists; and, secondly, that the blue of the sky, hitherto thought to be caused by watery vapour, is, indeed, reflected from the divided air itself; so that the bright blue of the eyes of Athena, and the deep blue of her aegis, prove to be accurate mythic expressions of natural phenomena which it is an uttermost triumph of recent science to have revealed.

Indeed, it would be difficult to imagine triumph more complete. To form, "within an experimental tube, a bit of more perfect sky than the sky itself!" here is magic of the finest sort! singularly reversed from that of old time, which only asserted its competency to enclose in bottles elementary forces that were—not of the sky.[48]

If the significance of her flashing eyes and glowing helmet had only lately been reconfirmed by the ether concept, what might wait to be relearned about the meaning of her serpent-fringed "robe of indignation," the "thunderous purple" of her aegis?

2

The dominant conceptual stance of mythological scholarship in Ruskin's day was that myths and mythic figures are the products of an unconscious personification of the elements and powers of nature. This conception amounted to a defense of the ultimate dependence of the spiritual (and hence the moral) life upon visible landscape. Ruskin found it possible to adapt the viewpoint and procedure of the nature mythologist to the support of his most pervasive teaching: the sanctity of living forms.

The technique of the nature mythologist, briefly stated, involved an etymological or philological examination of the cult epithets associated with a deity in the hope of deducing the aspect of nature which that deity had first personified. Of course, as we have seen, Ruskin recognized some relevant limitations in himself and in the theory. He knew that he was unable to stalk the various god names back to their Aryan roots; however, he also knew that a Sanskrit root meaning *sky* or *bright*, or some such, really did not go far toward explaining the solid, companionable images of the later Greek deities. Further, his purpose with myths is never explanation, *per se*. Indeed, Ruskin wishes to make a myth out of his explanation of one. The etymologists and philologists had attempted certain epithets of Athena back to early personification; Ruskin accepts the "physical root," but his primary concern is to show what the mythic image of Athena meant to Hesiod, Homer, and later artists. He knows that these seers perceived in the myth an eternal bond of mind and nature, an organic harmony, that the modern dualistic and analytic intellect (represented by Professor Tyndall and his synthetic "sky") was ignoring at its peril. He was not interested in showing what Athena had meant before the Greeks, but in showing that the Greeks had known what Athena would always *have* to mean.

His likely debts to nature mythology as represented by Max Müller's "Comparative Mythology" and *Lectures* have already been adduced. More specifically, Müller's well-known equations connecting Athena with Sanskrit *Ahana*, "the dawn,"[49] and (through the Latin Minerva) with "*mens*, the Greek *menos*, the Sanskrit *manas*, mind"[50] might have served to establish in his thought a general identification of Athena with wisdom and light. But this very consideration leads to a significant problem. For, whereas Ruskin's treatment generally follows Müller's in making her spiritual meaning wisdom, he goes his own way, apparently, in calling her the air, since Müller's famous analysis had traced her physical significance to the dawn.

In fact, though Max Müller may have had a good deal to say to Ruskin on the broader subject of mythogenesis, his discussions of Athena myths in particular are very brief (in the two relevant works), and we are left with the plain fact that most of the specific attributes of Ruskin's Athena are not to be found in anything Müller had published by that time. Consider, for instance, that the three epithets *Chalinitis*, *Keramitis*, and *Ergane*, which are the titles and, nominally, the themes for the three separate divisions of *The Queen*, are not discussed by Müller, nor does he give any indications that the ancients thought of Athena as the air.

Of course we have heard Ruskin speaking of this connection between Athena and the air as his "discovery"; hence it looks at first as though he were convinced he had been first to derive her air meaning, and this directly from the classics and the skies without any help from the scholars. But two observations militate against this view. First, though this could not have been widely known in England then, Ruskin's basic equation of Athena with "Myths of Cloud and Storm" is smack in the mainstream of German scholarly opinion on Athena laid down by F. G. Welcker, and others.[51] In fact, Max Müller's Vedic roots for Athena and Minerva actually represented a new philological departure from an older continental tradition of etymological nature mythology that had already made Athena goddess of various sky phenomena. Further, the German researches were not entirely unrepresented in England, and a sketchy recipe for Athena as an air goddess was even available in English, had Ruskin wished to make use of it.

I have illustrated in another work the useful suggestions Ruskin might have found for his interpretations of Athena and the lesser meteorological deities in Thomas Keightley's *Mythology*, which, as its author noted, "unnoticed by reviewers and unaided by favour or influence," had reached a third edition in 1854.[52] Keightley, who frequently cites such scholars as K. O. Müller, Welcker, Voss, and Buttmann, must have been one of the very few Victorians who had at this time any real familiarity with the German mythologists. His work, though not widely known, was the most advanced general survey of classical mythology then available in English.

G. W. Cox's *Mythology of the Aryan Nations*, an up-to-date and readily accessible source on Greek myth, did not appear until 1870, a year after *The Queen of the Air*. But we should glance briefly at it because this work clearly illustrates the tone and technique of the interpretations to which Ruskin's "Study of the Greek Myths of Cloud and Storm" is related. Here is Cox, who acknowledges Max Müller and most of the important German mythologists as his sources, exfoliating myths of the Graiae and the Gorgons. Notice first a passage from a section devoted to the story of Perseus, in which Cox is working out what both he and Ruskin would have called the "physical meaning" of that myth.

> But he [Perseus] cannot reach the Gorgon's den until he has first passed the home of the Graiai, the land of the gloaming, whose solitary eye and tooth he refuses to restore until they have pointed out the road which shall bring him to his journey's end. In other words, the sun must go through the twilight-land before he can pierce the regions of utter darkness and reappear in the beautiful gardens of the Hyperboreans, the asphodel meadows of the tinted heavens of morning. When at length his task is done, and he turns to go to the upper world, the Gorgon sisters (the clouds of darkness) start up in fury, and their brazen talons almost seize him as he reaches the clear blue heaven, which is called the land of the brilliant Etheopians. Here, again, the same war is going on in which he has already been the conqueror. The storm-cloud is seeking to devour the dawn and to blot out its tender light.[53]

This then is the style of a fellow mythologist, in this case of the solarist persuasion,[54] writing in England at the time when Ruskin was working up these same subjects for *The Queen*.

As a nature mythologist Cox is, of course, talking about *myths* in terms of nature. But the reader can see how easy it would be for a writer of Ruskin's faith to shift the emphasis of the allegory, his purpose being to talk about *nature* in the afterglow of myth. Returning, however, to the subject of the natural significance of the Gorgons and the associated Graiae as this was understood when Ruskin wrote about them, we open Cox again.

> These sisters [the Graiae] are either always youthful and radiant, or they are from time to time restored to their former beauty. But we may think

also of clouds as dwelling for ever far away in the doubtful gloaming, not wholly dark, but faintly visible in a weird and dismal twilight. These clouds, which are never kindled into beauty by the rays of the sun, are the Graiai, the daughter of Phorkys, whose hair was grey from their birth, like the white streamers which move in ghastly lines across the sky, as evening dies into night.[55]

And, concerning Medusa,

It is, of course, possible or even likely, that the writhing snakes which, by the doom passed on her, take the place of her beautiful locks may represent the hideous storm vapours streaming across the heaven at night, and still more likely that the wings and claws given to her fearful sisters attest their cloud nature.[56]

Finally:

The remaining feature of the story is the early loveliness of Medousa, which tempts her into rivalry with the dawn goddess Athena herself, a rivalry which they who know the moonlit nights of the Mediterranean can well understand. But let the storm-clouds pass across the sky, and the maiden's beauty is at once marred. She is no longer the darling of Poseidon, sporting on the grassy shore. The unseemly vapours stream like serpents across her once beautiful face, hissing with the breath of the night-breeze, and a look of agony unutterable comes over her countenance, chilling and freezing the heart's blood of those who gaze on the brow of the storm-tormented night. This agony can pass away only with her life; in other words, where the sword of Phoibus smites and scatters the murky mists. But although Medousa may die, the source from which the storm-clouds come cannot be choked, and thus the Gorgons who seek to avenge on Perseus their sister's death are themselves immortal.[57]

These passages of storm mythology, composed almost simultaneously with Ruskin's *Queen,* have been introduced to show at once how ready to Ruskin's hand the technique of the allegorical mythologist was; that is, how readily nature mythology could be made to bear nature mysticism, and also to illustrate the prevailing doctrine on Athena and the Medusa. This, in sum, was that the Gorgon was the "hostile Pallas," and that she, like an aegis on which the Gorgoneum appears, stood for the storm cloud or for hissing, tormenting mists.

The fact that Athena's relation to the air had been part of a long-standing scholarly doctrine of which Ruskin need not have been ignorant makes us wonder if he really meant that she was his "discovery" in the scholarly sense. And thus one is brought to a second consideration which makes it seem somewhat less likely that he was really claiming priority for a scholarly discovery. The reader will recall that Ruskin said he had rendered proof in his book that Athena *"is* the goddess of the air." In the light of what has been said about the preface in the preceding section, this could be taken as his prophetic assertion that the "discovery" was not merely what Athena had meant to the Greeks but what her ministry continued to mean. That is, *The Queen of the Air* was important to Ruskin, not because he really thought the book a definitive contribution to Athena scholarship, but because he was sure his contribution came from the same vein of vision as the Greek original. This is why he called it "playing with thunder." His real "discovery," though he could hardly say so, was a sense for how the mythologists might be remythologized, *their* comparatively dry discoveries orchestrated into new myths for modern admonition.

Ruskin, of course, had already written in this vein on the Gorgons and the Graiae in cloud myths of *Modern Painters*, volume 5. At the same time he had also mythologized upon the opposition of Apollo's purifying light to Python's corruptiveness and smoke, the struggle symbolized by the rose light of the Hesperid Aeglé. But, as we have seen, the significance of torment by storm and mist seemed to grow in Ruskin's mind as his life became shadowed by disappointment and the weathers of his diaries darkened. The Gorgon days became the other face of Athena: spiritual death in the tormenting mists of unwise knowledge expressed physically by the pollution of the form-and life-giving stuff of the air, its desecration by the two great separating forces of analysis and competition. In its public meaning at least, (not as a representation of the anima,[58] or of Rose) Ruskin's storm myth was meant to defend the forming mystery, life, against two sorts of adversaries: primarily against the pursuers of fatal wealth in commerce and science, secondarily and implicitly against the tendency of scientific mythology to impoverish sacred symbols by its disinterested research, reducing them to dead allegory.

3

Of the three sections that make up *The Queen of the Air*, only the first, "Athena Chalinitis" ("Athena the Restrainer") was actually delivered as a lecture. Ruskin's descriptive heading indicates that this "Lecture on Greek Myths of Storm" was partly given at University College, London, in 1869. The other two sections of the volume are treated as collections of materials supplementary to the lecture yet dealing with separate aspects of Athena. We will consider their titles as we proceed, noting here only that Athena is considered as a *trinity* of powers, uniting in herself every sense of life. It is Ruskin's attempt to set forth the myth of Athena in a way that is at once scholarly and comprehensive yet poetically and prophetically true that causes the work to break down into discursive and fragmentary assertions; the system will not hold together because he is trying to unite different dimensions of discourse in it, the rational and systematic, the apocalyptic and plurisignative. So the work remains incomplete as system yet complete for the purposes of prophecy.

The fifty paragraphs of "Athena Chalinitis" (hardly a manageable lecture when one considers the allusive density of these paragraphs) can be subdivided into four units of exposition; however, these are not fully integrated, possibly because this first section represents a further elaboration, for publication, of the original lecture. In the first eighteen paragraphs Ruskin gives a statement of his theoretical position with respect to myth and a survey of the major powers in the Greek pantheon. This discussion borrows heavily from the analysis of myth in *The Ethics of the Dust* and the breakdown of Greek mythic "forces" in *The Cestus of Aglaia*. This general discussion is followed by twelve interpretive and allusive paragraphs on "inferior deities of storm"; not all of these symbols are clearly linked to Athena, though several are. This section partly incorporates the cloud myths he had interpreted in volume 5 of *Modern Painters*. Then there are fourteen paragraphs relating directly to the various aspects of the Greek conception of Athena as an air and storm power. Here Ruskin attempts to systematize and elaborate the meaning of Athena that he has brought to bear in some way in nearly all his works of the sixties. Finally, there is a unit of six paragraphs dealing with the question of intensity or literalness of belief in these myths among the various social levels of the Greek populace.

In fairness to Ruskin's achievement and purposes, nothing could be more important than realization of the fact that these theories of Athena are not to him momentary impressions or a pastiche of derivative ideas but represent efforts toward the definitive assertion of a mythic system that has been developing for more than a decade in his work and is intimately related to his religious position and his primary hypothesis of experience, the organic model. We have been reading Ruskin with constant reference to three themes, the model of organic form, the "religion of Humanity," and Greek myths, particularly of sky phenomena; we must now look at *The Queen of the Air* as an attempt, in part, to integrate these themes into a comprehensive myth, of which he would be the prophet.

He opens the first section of the lecture with an apology that immediately links it to the "religion of Humanity" theme. Myth is to be treated here in "a temper differing from that in which it is frequently treated."[59] It will not be possible to understand the religion of a people unless our minds are open enough to admit that we as well as they are liable to errors in matters of faith, and to admit also what follows from this, that there may even be some particulars of faith in which they are right and we are wrong. Hence his apology: "You must forgive me, therefore, for not always distinctively calling the creeds of the past 'superstition,' and the creeds of the present day, 'religion'; as well as for assuming that a faith now confessed may sometimes be superficial, and that a faith long forgotten may once have been sincere."[60] There is a prouder and deeper folly than the assertion that there is no God, and this is the declaration that there is no God but mine. He will assume, then, not only the sincerity, but even, in some matters, the continuing truth of Greek belief.

His next step is a definition of myth. In simplest terms, we learn, a myth is "a story with a meaning attached to it, other than it seems to have at first" and the presence of such a meaning is marked by some "singular circumstance," which in ordinary use of the word we call "unnatural."[61] As an example he points to the myth of Hercules and the Hydra (meaning that Hercules, the type of heroic worldly help, "purified the stagnation of many streams from deadly miasmata") and, by analogy, to the legend of Saint George and the dragon. But he pointedly reminds his audience that to make this analogy is to "deeply degrade the position which such a myth . . . occupied in the Greek mind," and that the analogy, while "perfect in minor respects" utterly "fails to give you any notion of the vitally religious earnestness of Greek faith." The first steps in interpretation of a myth involve not only the recognition of it as such but realization of the intensity of belief it implies. To the Greek mind "in its best days" Hercules and the Hydra was a tale about reality, "about a real hero and a real monster."[62]

Moving toward consideration of the structure of myth, Ruskin explains that myths owe their shape to one or the other of "two sources—either to actual historical events, represented by the *fancy* under figures personifying them; or else to natural phenomena similarly endowed with life by *imaginative power*, usually more or less under the influence of terror."[63] Though Ruskin recognizes a historical source of myth, he shows no interest in it and the operations he assigns to fancy; instead he moves directly to myths deriving from nature through "imaginative power." Nature myths, he continues, spring from two primary roots, "from the real sun, rising and setting;—from the real atmosphere, calm in its dominion of unfading blue, and fierce in its descent of tempest,— the Greek forms, first, the idea of two entirely personal and corporeal gods." And then, "collaterally with these corporeal images, and never for one instant separated from them, he conceives two omnipresent spiritual influences, of which one illuminates, as the sun, with a constant fire, whatever in humanity is skillful and wise; and the other, like the living air, breathes the calm of heavenly fortitude, and strength of righteous anger, into every human breast that is pure and brave."[64] Here, for Ruskin, are the two primordial archetypal powers in the religions of humanity. He intended, as he explained elsewhere, to define fully the Greek conception of Apollo relative to their Athena.[65] But he never managed to write his study of Apolline myths. Possibly this is because, although his aesthetics leans heavily on the solar archetype, the virgin goddess and storm power better served the more urgent demands of his private symbolism and social prophecy.

Moving further into the theory of myths, Ruskin assigns them the tripartite structure he had analyzed in *The Ethics of the Dust*, only now he makes use of an organic metaphor. Myths have a "root and . . . two branches:—the root, in physical existence, sun, or sky, or cloud, or sea; then the personal incarnation of that; becoming a trusted and companionable deity, with whom you may walk hand in hand . . . ; and, lastly, the moral significance of the image, which is in all the great myths eternally and beneficently true."[66]

This idea of the eternal and beneficent truth of myth leads him to the most important topic of this introductory portion of "Athena Chalinitis," the matter of his own authority as interpreter of myth. Here he must defend intuitive over scholarly mythology and argue that there is a continuity of mythic vision in which modern visionaries may participate by "answering sympathy." This sympathetic participation is far more important to the right reading of a myth than any amount of cold, objective scholarship, which is by its nature antimythic. There are two modes by which the modern reader can enter the spirit of myth: by a shared sense of spiritual presences in natural form and by an ability to respond with imaginative sympathy to the symbols in a myth as one would to those in a work of art.

Ruskin grounds his argument for interpretive authority in the view, expressed earlier in *The Ethics of the Dust*, that "the real meaning of any myth is that which it has at the noblest age of the nation among whom it is current."[67] As he would say later in *Fors*, Letter 71, "a great myth can only be written in the central time of a nation's power."[68] He tends to confuse the myth with its embodiment in art. But, as with works of art, right reading of myths is founded on awe of natural powers and intuitive perception of the operation of organic laws. "Through whatever changes it may pass . . . our right reading of it is wholly dependent on the materials we have in our own minds for an intelligent answering sympathy. . . . We shall be able to follow them into this last circle of their faith only in the degree in which the better parts of our own beings have been also stirred by the aspects of nature, or strengthened by her laws. It may be easy to prove that the ascent of Apollo in his chariot signifies nothing but the rising sun. But what does the sunrise itself signify to us?" If the sunrise signifies to us nothing but "languid return to frivolous amusement, or fruitless labour" we are unlikely to rise to any conception of power in the name Apollo, but "if the sun itself is an influence, to us also, of spiritual good—and becomes thus in reality, not in imagination, to us also, a spiritual power,—we may then soon overpass the narrow limit of conception which kept that power impersonal, and rise with the Greek to the thought of an angel who rejoiced as a strong man to run his course, whose voice, calling to life and labour, rang round the earth, and whose going forth was to the ends of heaven."[69]

We have from this some idea of the direction his intended analysis of Apolline myths would have taken. He includes also, still for introductory purposes, a brief summary of the major powers worshipped at the "culminating period of the Greek religion." Ranged "under one governing Lord of all things" are "four subordinate elemental forces, and four spiritual powers living in them and commanding them." Demeter, Poseidon, Apollo, and Athena are each "descended from, or changed from, more ancient and therefore more mystic deities of earth and heaven, and of a finer element of aether supposed to be beyond the heavens."[70] There are no mere forces, as in modern science; each reflects the intentions of an indwelling yet personal power; together these powers command every aspect of organic and spiritual life. Demeter, for instance, as earth mother is "first, . . . the origin of all life—the dust from whence we were taken: secondly, . . . the receiver of all things back at last into silence." Her daughter, Persephone, represents "the most tender image of this appearing and fading life, in the birth and fall of flowers"; as she plays in the fields of Sicily, she is "torn away into darkness, and becomes the Queen of Fate—not merely of death, but of the gloom which closes over and ends, not beauty only, but sin; and chiefly of sins, the sin against the life she gave: so that she is, in her highest power Persephone, the avenger and purifier of blood."[71]

There are many other details in his preliminary survey of the Greek powers, but the most important are in the interpretive description of Athena that Ruskin draws chiefly from representations of her in sculpture. Spiritually she represents moral wisdom, wisdom of the heart as opposed to that of the imagination or intellect; as such she commands the four "cardinal" virtues of the Greek religion, which men receive as if from the four quarters of the wind. These are prudence, temperence, justice ("righteous bestowal of favor and indignation"), and fortitude ("patience under trial by pain"), the last two being the two main ones; they are the powers she breathed respectively into Achilles and Odysseus, and that Ruskin himself must have prayed for. Each of these four virtues is signified by some feature of her image.

> In her prudence, or sight in darkness, she is "Glaukopis," owl-eyed. In her justice, which is the dominant virtue, she wears two robes, one of light and one of darkness; the robe of light, saffron colour, or the colour of daybreak, falls to her feet, covering her wholly with favour and love,—the calm sky in blessing; it is embroidered along its edge with her victory over the giants, (the troublous powers of the earth). . . . Then her robe of indignation is worn on her breast and left arm only, fringed with fatal serpents, and fastened with Gorgonian cold, turning men to stone; physically the lightning and the hail of chastizement by storm. Then in her fortitude she wears the crested and unstooping helmet; and lastly, in her temperence, she is the queen of maidenhood—stainless as the air of heaven.[72]

In concluding this introductory section of "Athena Chalinitis" Ruskin returns to the matter of authority in the making and reading of myths; again the basis of his argument is the analogy with imaginative mythic vision in art, though he does not speak of analogy. He declares, in the words he had used of painters' visions in *Modern Painters*, volume 3, that "all the greatest myths have been seen, by the men who tell them, involuntarily and passively"; such true visions are seen with the distinctness of "a dream sent to any of us by night when we dream clearest," and they are sent with "a veracity of vision that could not be refused," there is no deliberate fallacy about them. This veracity of vision is a point about myth "which in modern historical inquiry has been left wholly out of account," because it is a capacity that belongs wholly to "the creative or artistic group of men" and therefore "can only be interpreted by those of their race, who themselves in some measure also see visions and dream dreams." For this reason one may "obtain a more truthful idea of the nature of Greek religion and legend from the poems of Keats, and the nearly as beautiful, and, in general grasp of subject, far more powerful, recent work of Morris, than from frigid scholarship, however extensive."[73]

Therefore, the first requirement for the right reading of myth is not historical or linguistic knowledge but "the understanding of the nature of all true vision by noble persons; namely, that it is founded on constant

Athena: From a statue from Herculaneum. Reproduced from *Works* (Library Edition), vol. 19.

laws common to all human nature; that it perceives, however darkly, things which are for all ages true;—that we can only understand it so far as we have some perception of the same truth;—and that its fullness is developed and manifested more and more by reverberation of it from minds of the same mirror-temper, in succeeding ages."[74] Thus within his theory of myth Ruskin has an argument for the continuity and transmission of prophetic authority. He is thinking specifically here of the communication of mythic truth from Homer to Dante, but there is nothing to suggest that he is not including himself in the line of visionaries.

He is about to approach, in this light, his essential subject, which is to show "how much, in the Homeric vision of Athena, has been made clearer by the advance of time, being thus essentially and eternally true,"[75] when he plunges off into a tangled digression of twelve paragraphs on "the inferior deities of storm." This web of mete-orological myths is complex and confusing, but two facts about it are apparent from the start: first, it is an effort to elaborate and incorporate into the controlling concept of Athena the storm powers he had first interpreted in the chapter entitled "The Angel of the Sea" in *Modern Painters*, volume 5; second, the title of this chapter, "Athena the Restrainer" (or bridler), indicates that the tie will be made most clearly with the Perseus-Medusa-Pegasus-Bellerophon myth group.

In these paragraphs Ruskin organizes the secondary weather divinities into two groups, wind gods and cloud gods. One confusing feature of his analysis is the appearance of an Aeolus in both groups, until we realize that the Aeolus who heads the list of wind divinities is that amiable personage who gives the winds to Odysseus, while the Aeolus who appears among the cloud deities (whom Ruskin calls the "historic Aeolus") is treated mythically as one of the legendary trunks of the Greek race who reigned in Thessaly and sired the Aeolid lines, from which Bellerophon is descended.

The Homeric Aeolus, then, is the first of the wind gods Ruskin takes up. He is a beneficent power, whom Milton perceptively calls "sage Hippotades." To the system of *The Queen* this wise "steward" of the winds contributes simply the primordial "idea of the gifts and preciousness of the winds of heaven";[76] his myth is a parable of intrinsic value and the necessity of its wise management. Boreas is mentioned as another "beneficent storm power," and then the Harpies, who are by no means beneficent powers.

With the Harpies, his interpretation turns intriguingly psy-chological; it is as if these particular mythic symbols are being used as vehicles through which he can express his own emotional state. Physically, they mean "the short, violent, spiral gusts that lift the dust before coming rain: the Harpies get identified first with these, and then with more violent whirlwinds, and so they are called 'Harpies,' 'the Snatchers,' and are thought of as entirely destructive; their manner of destroying being twofold—by snatching away, and by defiling and polluting."[77] Their "mental" meaning he expresses at length and seizes this meaning with a greater intensity of feeling than with any other expressed thus far in his lecture. "Devouring, and desolating, merciless. . . . They are the gusts of vexatious, fretful, lawless passion, vain and overshadowing, discontented and lamenting, meagre and insane,—spirits of wasted energy, and wandering disease, and unappeased famine, and unsatisfied hope."[78]

The winds have thus been divided into two subgroups, those of "prosperity and health" and those of "ruin of sickness." He has a particular interest in the latter for the psychological truths they convey. Again we hear the more intimately subjective note: "Understand that, once, deeply—any who have ever known the weariness of vain desires; the pitiful, unconquerable, coiling and recoiling, and self-involved returns of some sickening famine and thirst of heart:—and you will know what was in the sound of the Harpy Celaeno's shriek from her rock; and why, in the seventh circle of the *Inferno*, the Harpies make their nests in the warped branches of the trees that are the souls of suicides."[79] Further, if the Greek myths appear to intertwine into arabesques of connected symbols, this is further proof of their veracity, "because the truths of emotion they represent are interwoven in the same way." Such is the case with the obscure connection between the Harpies, representing "vain desire" and the Sirens, "who are the spirits of constant desire"; both are represented as birds with women's heads, so it is difficult to distinguish them. But the Sirens are "great constant desires— the infinite sickness of heart—which, rightly placed, give life," while the desire signified by the Harpies is always fatal.[80] Hence the Harpies are curiously involved with the group of myths surrounding Tantalus.

This suggestion leads Ruskin into a subdigression on Tantalus and other Harpy connections. We need not follow him in this except to note one further point he makes about the nature of myth. Discussing the dog as mythic symbol (apropos of Pandareos' dog, the stealing of which was one of Tantalus' sins), he observes that the mythic meaning of the dog is "confused between its serviceable fidelity, its watchfulness, its foul voracity, shamelessness, and deadly madness," and further that this paradoxical quality, this "curious reversal or recoil of the meaning which attaches itself to nearly every great myth,"[81] is especially to be noted, later, in the relation of the serpent to Athena.

But he is now ready to take up the second, more important, division of meteorological powers, the deities of cloud. These are headed by Hermes, who is lord of cloud and also "the god of lying, as he is of mist"; also with this function of making things vanish is connected "his grand Egyptian authority of leading away souls in the cloud of death."[82] By assuming that the name *Hermes* mean "Impulse" (apparently deriving Ερμης from ορμή) Ruskin manages to make him not merely the director of cloud movement but the very "spirit of the movement of the sky or firmament," in which capacity "he corresponds to the 'primo mobile' of the later Italian philosophy." Because of the diversity of his functions and the dispersion of clouds in a variety of forms through a host of minor storm myths, the Greek conception of Hermes is, he concludes, "more mystic and ideal than that of any other deity."[83]

This reference to the diversity of minor storm-cloud myths in the Greek tradition leads Ruskin into a densely allusive section in which he attempts to suggest at once the range of these storm images, their significances to him, and, obscurely, their relation to Athena. There is, for instance, a series of storm myths connected with the family of Aeolus, all of them "concentrating themselves darkly into the legend of Bellerophon and the Chimaera" in which, he observes (also darkly and prophetically of his own life), "there is an under story about the vain subduing of passion and treachery, and the end of life in fading melancholy,—which, I hope, not many of you could understand even were I to show it you." The connection of the myth of Bellerophon and the Chimera with Athena (left unexpressed here, though discussed earlier in volume 5 of *Modern Painters*) is that Athena, as Chalinitis, "the Restrainer," enabled Bellerophon to bridle Pegasus (wild fountains, the passions) and slay the Chimera, a storm-being of peculiarly noxious character. The Chimera, in its physical meaning "the cloud of volcanic lightning, connected wholly with earth-fire, but resembling the heavenly cloud in its height and its thunder,"[84] is a Greek mythic prototype of Ruskin's own "storm-cloud" of the nineteenth century. This may be why these storm myths are spoken of as "concentrating themselves darkly into the legend of Bellerophon." Another reason for this dark concentration in Bellerophon is that he is the link between the Aeolic storm myths and the Pegasean-Gorgonian group, which he will take up in a moment.

But first, still in connection with the Aeolic storm myths, he must mention the myth of Sisyphus, which he intends one day to work out thoroughly by itself. Sisyphus' link to Athena is in his connection with Corinth, the Isthmian location of that city, and its consequent focal power over Greek trade. The Corinthian Acropolis, he explains, was "two thousand feet high, being the center of the crossing currents of the winds, and of the commerce of Greece. Therefore, Athena, and the fountain cloud Pegasus, are more closely connected with Corinth than even with Athens in their material, though not in their moral power." Sisyphus, founder of the Isthmian games, "becomes the type of transit, transfer, or trade, as such; and of the apparent gain from it, which is not gain; and this is the real meaning of his punishment in hell—eternal toil and recoil (the modern idol of capital being, indeed, the stone of Sisyphus with a vengeance, *crushing* in its recoil)."[85] Throughout these myths of cloud power there is the moral reference to vain and illusory pursuits, "the dreams of avarice and injustice, until this notion of atheism and insolent blindness becomes principal," as in the *Clouds* of Aristophanes, where "the personified 'just' and 'unjust' sayings in the latter part of the play, foreshadow, almost feature by feature, in all that they were meant to mock and to chastize, the worst elements of the impious 'δῖνος' ["whirling"] and tumult in men's thoughts, which have followed on their avarice in the present day."[86]

Apart from this Aeolic group of storm myths there is also at least one other important tradition to which Ruskin must allude; this is the Danaides-Perseus-Gorgons-Graiae group that he had already interpreted in "The Angel of the Sea." Here he touches on these only briefly but with the promise (unfulfilled) to "collect afterwards and complete" what he has already written about these myths. We recall from volume 5 of *Modern Painters* that Danae in her brazen tower (which Ruskin interpreted as meaning the altocumulus clouds lighted by the sun) was approached by Zeus in the form of a golden shower. Perseus was the fruit of this affair; and he, with Athena's help, was able to deprive Medusa of her head. In that discussion Medusa emerged as a particularly significant image for Ruskin; he identified her with "the true clouds of thunderous and ruinous tempest," also with the "cloudy coldness of knowledge, and its venomous character." As her chief enemy, she is also the alter ego of Athena. From Medusa's blood sprang Chrysaor ("Angel of Lightning") and the flying steed, Pegasus, "the Angel of the 'Wild Fountains,' that is to say, the fastest flying or lower rain-cloud," and also, we note, "the source of evils, or of passions."[87] To these earlier interpretations, which he does not repeat, Ruskin adds only the assertion that the sickle with which Perseus decapitates Medusa is "another image of the whirling harpy vortex." It is an apocalyptic image, he supposes; for it "belongs especially to the sword of destruction or annihilation; whence it is given to the two angels who gather for destruction the evil harvest and evil vintage of the earth (Rev. xiv, 15)."[88]

Having dealt with the problem of authority in the interpretation and transmission of mythic truth and with the "inferior deities of storm," Ruskin is now ready, after thirty paragraphs, for his essential subject: "the central myth of Athena herself, who represents the ambient air, which included all cloud, and rain, and dew, and darkness, and peace, and wrath of heaven."[89] Why, one may ask, has he delayed so long in coming to his central interpretation, the agencies of Athena that have been on his mind throughout the decade? One obvious reply is that Athena's powers, reduced to analytic terms, can be simply stated, and he does so in this way at paragraph thirty-one; however, his more fundamental problem is to secure belief in this unity of powers, and this involves acceptance of his authority to teach these things. Therefore, the argument for the inviolate transmission of mythic truth from age to age in men of vision—the archetypal theory—and the scholarly tangle of allusions to minor deities have the functions of defining and presenting his credentials as a seer of truth in myth.

Another point is that this deep involvement with the minor symbols serves to place Athena at the head of something vaguely resembling a hierarchy of mythic powers, or, perhaps more accurately, to place her at the center of a web of symbols that extends into every aspect of organic and psychic life. Further, these minor deities of wind and cloud, at least those which most interest him, represent transient or illusory careerings of the mind that must be restrained by the deeper forces of life: gusts of futile passion and vain desire, clouds of chimerical wealth and chilling abstract knowledge. Most important, though most difficult to express, is the final point that this thicket of mythic connections is but another version of Ruskin's organic perception of experience. Within all of its details the basic strategy of *The Queen of the Air* is to create that sense of "entwined prehensive unities," to use Whitehead's phrase again, which is the essence of Ruskin's vision. His method is to invoke assent to Athena's continued rule through the revelation of a vast coherence of elemental powers, all deriving from verbal associations stemming out of the breath-spirit etymology. *The Queen* is thus a kind of Gothic cathedral, an organic structure, with the thunderous image of Athena (described earlier) in its apse, her primary agencies (to be set forth) as the arches of its nave, and the minor storm myths as its secondary chapels and sepulchral recesses.

He interprets the *physical* agencies of Athena as being simply five global functions of the air, a pentagon of powers. "First, and chiefly, she is the air as the spirit of life, giving vitality to the blood. Her psychic relation to the vital force in matter lies deeper," he explains, and he will examine this in the second division of his book.[90] This requires separate treatment because it refers to the all-important matter of her queenship of organic form. "Secondly—Athena is the air giving vegetative impulse to the earth. She is the wind and the rain—and yet more the pure air itself, getting at the earth fresh turned by spade or plough."[91] The Christian symbol of the olive, representing the "chief Agonia of humanity," is sacred to her, and also the "rose tribe." Her virginity is remembered to this day in our *vir*-words, which mean "nerve" and are connected, also, he had noted in *The Ethics of the Dust*, with " 'virga'—a 'rod'; the green rod, or springing bough of a tree, being the type of perfect human strength."[92] In her third function "Athena is the air in its power over the sea."[93] "Fourthly—Athena is the air nourishing artificial light—unconsuming fire."[94] Her function here is opposed to that of the sun, on one hand, and to consuming fire on the other. "Lastly—Athena is the air conveying vibration of sound." The sun is "master of time and rhythm" and of "the composing and inventive discovery of melody," but the air is the "prolonging and sustaining power" of the living voice "and the symbol of its moral passion."[95] One can easily imagine what use Ruskin might have made of the idea of Athena as the protective "ozone layer" that we now fear is being dissipated by fluorocarbons, a current skirmish between life and wealth.

Such, then, are the physical powers of Athena. Her spiritual powers are in two dimensions: "first, she is the Spirit of Life in material organism; not strength in the blood only, but formative energy in the clay: and, secondly, she is inspired and impulsive wisdom in human conduct and human art, giving the instinct of infallible decision, and of faultless invention."[96]

We have noticed that Ruskin has limited the physical agencies of Athena to five. It may be that he intended to tap the symbolic implications of that number: the pentangle as mystic symbol of perfection and purity; the five fingers, senses, Joys, Wounds, Virtues, or even the Pentecost. At any rate, he does hint at a crucial analogy between Athena and the Holy Ghost. "You would, perhaps, hardly bear with me if I endeavoured farther to show you—what is nevertheless perfectly true—the analogy between the spiritual power of Athena in her gentle ministry, yet irresistible anger, with the ministry of another Spirit whom we also, believing in as the universal power of life, are forbidden, at our worst peril, to quench or to grieve."[97] By this he would be saying, if we follow out his mythic system, that the atmosphere desecrated in Dr. Tyndall's experimental tubes, is the "Spirit of Life in material organism" that the great mythologies of the West have successively represented as Neith, Athena, and the Holy Ghost. But the anima is also here, another feminine spirit of life, with a hostile side; a representation of Ruskin's own soul was in that goddess in the vial.

4

The second and third sections of *The Queen* cannot be described as either lectures or essays; they are rather appendixes of argumentative materials, discursive, yet important, and intended to extend the myth of Athena into vast areas of experience, into organic form, and into the moral core of fine art and useful industry. The second section, "Athena Keramitis" ("Athena in the Earth") is the more coherent of the two; consequently Ruskin's subtitle refers to it as a "study" of the "relations of Athena to the vital force in material organism."[98] The third section, "Athena Ergane" ("Athena in the Heart") is more fragmentary and is vaguely subtitled "Various Notes" having to do with the idea of Athena as "Directress of Imagination and Will," as the vital force in art and industry. "Athena Keramitis" is by far the more important, for us, of the two, since it deals with Athena's rule over the organic model; and it will be our main concern in the next few pages. But first we should glance briefly at "Athena Ergane."

Here Ruskin's line of argument is familiar to us from earlier things, especially his Rede Lecture "The Relation of National Ethics to National Arts" and the lecture "War" in *The Crown of Wild Olive*. It is again essentially an organic argument. The faults and virtues of a work of art are a direct and inevitable outgrowth of those in the artist. "If the work is a cobweb, you know it was made by a spider; if a honeycomb, by a bee; a worm-cast is thrown up by a worm."[99] The key truth to be known about art is simply that "while manufacture is the work of hands only, art is the work of the whole *spirit* of man; and as that spirit is, so is the deed of it: and by whatever power of vice or virtue any art is produced, the same vice or virtue it reproduces and teaches. . . . All art is either infection or education. It *must* be one or the other of these."[100] But the organic filaments of art go deeper than the individual spirit of the artist; his gift is rooted in the moral character of the people from whom he springs; this condition of character in a people is the slow growth of generations, and, more than by anything else, this vital growth is nourished by *war* as a principle of cohesion, integrity, and vitality in a people. This is the meaning of the Greek vision of Athena as warrior and maiden.

"The first sign . . . of Athena's presence with any people, is that they become warriors." National interests of every other sort, "wealth, and pleasure, and even love, are all, under Athena's orders, sacrificed to this duty of standing fast in the rank of war." National vitality has gone when a people loses its "power of noble anger."[101] The mythic idea of Athena's own noble anger (against a nation, say, that attempts to defend itself with "money and machinery," a nation content to "dig coals and sit in the cinders") gives Ruskin the prophet the opportunity to rise to apocalyptic tones.

> In this war of hers she is wholly implacable. She has little notion of converting criminals. There is no faculty of mercy in her when she has been resisted. Her word is only, "I will mock when your fear cometh." Note the words that follow: "when your fear cometh as desolation, and your destruction as a whirlwind;" for her wrath is of irresistible tempest: once roused, it is blind and deaf,—rabies—madness of anger—darkness of the Dies Irae.
>   . . . Wisdom never forgives. Whatever resistance we have offered to her law, she avenges for ever;—the lost hour can never be redeemed, and the accomplished wrong never atoned for.[102]

This is the essential argument of "Athena Ergane." A remark about the goddess's rule also over industry, particularly over women's industry (her command: "Fight and weave"),[103] ends his discussion of Athena.

To fill out this section Ruskin appends some miscellaneous and tangential work. There are, for instance, some passages "written long ago" that briefly summarize his political economy; their presence suggests that he may have had plans to draw both art and economics under the myth of Athena.[104] But since these arguments are not integrated with the myth and have been examined earlier, we may now turn back to the second section, "Athena Keramitis," where the arguments are largely new to his work, though they were opened in *The Ethics of the Dust*. The epithet *Keramitis*, Athena "fit for being made into pottery," is a coinage of Ruskin's; that is, it is not an historical cult epithet for Athena, though Grote, in the first volume of his *History* mentions her particular sacredness to Athenian potters. But the real reference of the epithet is not to the scholarship but to his admonition in the *Ethics* that we should distinguish the hand of the potter on the clay of creation from the mere beating of his foot as he kicks the wheel.

In thinking about "Athena in the Earth," which deals with Athena's rule over "life" or the organic model, we should remember simply that this part of his myth was written against those "masters of modern science" alluded to in the last paragraph of the preface, where Ruskin urges them to release Athena from their vials and seal the pollutants of progress back up in them. We have already spoken of their work on the theory of life as being typified by Huxley's famous essay "On The Physical Basis of Life." To contemporary science, as Ruskin saw it, the essence of life was force or a composition of forces; to him the essence of life is form. His model of life is a purposive or "helpful" coherence of parts; this model is characterized in various ways in his work, but primarily its features are cohesive unity, variation or liberty, and mystery or infinity of extension (having no simple location). This model is present in every natural form: trees, clouds, crystals, landscapes, communities, and in works of art based on a true intuition of the model in these forms.

In one sense it can be said that Ruskin never examines this model closely, perhaps because he realizes that as soon as it is analyzed into a structure it ceases to be organic form; that its nature is always to be involved with other unities. In another sense he is always examining this model because it is at the center of his thought; his aesthetics, his economics, his prophetics, all depend upon it. Unlike the force concept, his model has a qualitative as well as a quantitative dimension; and this aspect, the quality or purity of the life in anything, is always his concern. Finally, life as form implies a forming power, the hand of the ultimate potter; and in elaborating the idea of Athena as the air into Athena as the forming power, Ruskin arrives at a controlling myth for all his work. This is the public significance of *The Queen of the Air*.

He begins this central section with the observation that it is easy enough for us to decipher the Greek meaning of Athena's physical power over the clouds and the sky because we ourselves know what they are. But it is not as easy for us to trace her corresponding power "in giving life, because we do not ourselves know clearly what life is, or in what way the air is necessary to it, or what there is, besides the air, shaping the forms that it is put into." It is of little consequence, he continues, to ponder what the Greeks may have meant, "until we have determined what we ourselves think, or mean, when we translate the Greek word for 'breathing' into the Latin-English word 'spirit.' "[105]

What, then, do we mean by "spirit" and what is signified by its root in "breath"? There is, Ruskin argues, a "certain and practical sense of this word 'spirit,' " a sense we must hold "against the baseness of mere materialism on the one hand, and against the fallacies of controversial speculation on the other." This is the sense of its real existence "as the power which shaped you into your shape, and by which you love, and hate, when you have received that shape." There is no danger of this, "the sculpturing or the loving power," ever being "beaten down by the philosophers into a metal or evolved by them into a gas"; but beyond this there is the danger of losing the word in theological or philological abstraction: "Take care that you yourselves, in trying to elevate your conception of it, do not lose its truth in a dream, or even in a word." There are many related derivatives of the Greek *"pneuma,"* but "in Greek and in English, and in Saxon and in Hebrew, and in every articulate tongue of humanity, the 'spirit of man,' truly means his passion and virtue." Further, the central meaning of the idea of spirit is endurance or patience, a burning "constancy against the cold agony of death"; therefore, just as Athena means physically the burning power of the air that sustains the flesh, so she is spiritually, "the queen of all glowing virtue, the unconsuming fire and inner lamp of life." And as an antithetical symbol of this meaning she "bears always on her breast the deadly face of her chief enemy slain, the Gorgonian cold, and venomous agony, that turns living men to stone."[106]

Ruskin's purpose here is not to write a homily on the general value of passion but to show Athena's hostility to one specific Gorgonian enemy, scientific or dispassionate analysis. In this sense his attack here parallels his earlier assault on economic science for its neglect of human affections in reducing political economy to the operation of the market mechanism. This antiscientific meaning emerges in the following paragraphs as he observes that "so long as you have that fire of the heart within you, and you know the reality of it, you need be under no alarm as to the possibility of its chemical or mechanical analysis." These modes of analysis tell us little about the quality and mystery of immediate experience in the mind. "It is quite true that the tympanum of the ear vibrates under sound, and that the surface of the water in a ditch vibrates too: but the ditch hears nothing for all that; and my hearing is still to me as blessed a mystery as ever." There has been much speculation, he notes, about "brain waves"; however, "the consciousness itself is not a wave."[107]

His point is that between objectivity and consciousness there is feeling or passion (the qualitative aspect of experience) which enters into knowledge because it preselects and shapes our awareness. This passionate aspect of ordinary or immediate experience is under the rule of Athena and with her aid can lead to wise knowledge. But passionate awareness can be chilled by deliberate detachment, by invoking the subjective-objective separation and the process of abstraction from the lived world. This mode of knowing is under the power of Medusa. Athena's knowledge, passionate awareness, is thus organic knowledge because it derives from immediate experience of the lived world, participates in it by feeling, and receives messages of feeling from the world. This mode of knowing does not strive to separate itself from its world and the mysterious unities of that world, nor does it strive to objectify the world in cold abstractions or, in fallacies of misplaced concreteness.

So it is Ruskin's concern here to present what passionate or immediate experience knows about the "vital force in material organism." This awareness reveals "two plain facts" about the nature of life: "first, that there is a power which gives their several shapes to things, or capacities of shape; and, secondly, a power which gives them their several feelings or capacities of feeling; and that we can increase or destroy both of these at our will."[108] He has dealt with the primordial connection, as revealed by etymology, between breath and spirit or passion. Now, disregarding half-formed theories of the chemical and mechanical connections between the air and organism, he will attempt to explain "what, at least, remains to us after science has done its worst;—what the myth of Athena, as a Formative and Decisive power—a Spirit of Creation and Volition,—must eternally mean for all of us."[109]

Science, he continues, has shown us that life is inseparably dependent on heat and force and also "on a form of substance, which the philosophers call 'protoplasm.' " But what is this "protoplasm" but Greek for "first stuck together"? The vital fact appears to be that this cellular plastic differs from potters' clay by being dependent on a measurable degree of heat, developed by respiration in higher forms of life, "which it borrows from the rest of the universe while it lives, and which it as certainly returns to the rest of the universe, when it dies." This heat is, therefore, connected with "certain assimilative powers . . . which the tendency of recent discovery is to simplify more and more into modes of one force; or finally into mere motion, communicable in various states, but not destructible." Assuming that "science has done its utmost . . . that every chemical or animal force is demonstrably resolved into heat or motion, reciprocally changing into each other," we are still left with a question about the nature of this primal force. "It is by definition something different from matter, and we may call it as we choose—'first cause,' or 'first light,' or 'first heat'; but we can show no scientific proof of its not being personal, and coinciding with the ordinary conception of a supporting spirit in all things."[110]

Yet we do not use the word "spirit" of this primal force until the breath is involved; that is, in the atmosphere, under the joint influences of air and solar light, this primal force enters a unique phase of organization that we call life. "It does not now merely crystallize indefinite masses, but it gives to limited portions of matter the power of gathering, selectively, other elements proper to them, and binding these elements into their own peculiar and adopted form." It is this self-forming and particularizing power, involved with the atmosphere, that may properly be called life or spirit, and that is "continually creating its own shells of definite shape out of the wreck around it."[111] This is why he had said, in *The Ethics of the Dust*, "you may always stand by form against force."[112] Because "the mere force of junction is not spirit; but the power that catches out of chaos charcoal, water, lime, or what not, and fastens them down into a given form, is properly called 'spirit'; and we shall not diminish, but strengthen our conception of this creative energy by recognizing its presence in lower states of matter than our own."[113]

With this last sentence Ruskin's argument enters a new and far-ranging phase. He has identified Athena with two correlative forces in the organic model as it appears to ordinary observation. She is spirit in the sense of passion (thus far related only to human life), and she is spirit or power by which matter decisively forms itself into particular organizations. For him, these are modes of the same power; hence, as he has said, she is a "Formative and Decisive power—a Spirit of Creation and Volition." Of course, she is also the operation of the law of help, defined in volume 5 of *Modern Painters*; also, in the same context, he had identified the helpful with the holy; therefore, by this connection we perceive another identification of Athena with the Holy Spirit. Finally, this identification of the organizing principle with spirit or passion leads him to the position that there must be evidences of this spirit and its varying intensities written on organic forms themselves, lineaments of their vital spirit that may be read by those in whom the correspondent passion has not been chilled by analytic knowledge. Therefore, his next point is that direct evidence of the quality or purity of life or spirit in organic forms is their message to passionate perception in man. This truth is most obvious in the case of blossoming plants. "The Spirit in the plant—that is to say, its power of gathering dead matter out of the wreck round it, and shaping it into its own chosen shape,—is of course strongest at the moment of its flowering, for it then not only gathers, but forms, with the greatest energy."[114]

This line of argument connects neatly with the vitalistic aesthetic of *Modern Painters*, volume 2; evidence that this communication between the spirit in the organism and passion in man is somehow intended and necessary is given, in Ruskin's view, by the fact that life is strongest in those moments of organic form that are most delightful to us. "Where this Life is in it at full power, its form becomes invested with aspects that are chiefly delightful to our own human passions; namely, first, with the loveliest outlines of shape; and, secondly, with the most brilliant phases of the primary colours, blue, yellow, and red or white, the unison of all; and, to make it all the more strange, this time of peculiar and perfect glory is associated with relations of the plants or blossoms to each other, correspondent to the joy of love in human creatures, and having the same object in the continuance of the race." But with plants as with us, the primary object of life is its quality, not its mere continuity. "The flower is the end or proper object of the seed, not the seed of the flower. The reason for seeds is that flowers may be; not the reason of flowers that seeds may be."[115]

The idea that the various qualitative states of the "spirit" (or selecting, self-unifying power like Coleridge's "esemplastic power") recorded in organic forms is a mode of communication between the forming spirit and our own passion leads Ruskin to another important point and brings him back also to the subject of myth and Athena. He perceives a link between myth and natural theology. The various species of plants and animals are, in fact, living myths to be interpreted by the human spirit into religion. "It is perfectly possible, and ultimately conceivable," for instance, "that the crocodile and lamb may have descended from the same ancestral atom of protoplasm"; however, they represent totally opposed states of the forming spirit, "the one repellant to the spirit of man, the other attractive to it, in a quite inevitable way, representing to him states of moral evil and good, and becoming *myths* to him of destruction or redemption, and, in the most literal sense, 'Words' of God."[116]

This notion of living myths brings Ruskin into his own expertise as an interpreter of myths and gives him a case against the scholars. "It seems to me," he continues,

> that the scholars who are at present occupied in interpretation of human myths have most of them forgotten that there are any such things as natural myths; and that the dark sayings of men may be both difficult to read, and not always worth reading; but the dark savings of nature will probably become clearer for the looking into, and will very certainly be worth reading. And, indeed, all guidance to the right sense of the human and variable myths will probably depend on our first getting at the sense of natural and invariable ones. The dead hieroglyph may have meant this or that—the living hieroglyph means always the same; but remember, it is just as much a hieroglyph as the other; nay, more,—a "sacred or reserved sculpture," a thing with an inner language."[117]

In accordance with the theory of living myths he has just outlined he is now ready to undertake the interpretation of a number of living hieroglyphs of the "forming power," especially those connected with the worship of Athena. What these "natural" myths are intended to document in that "human" myth is simply that the air *is* the vital power in organic forms and that the species which were sacred to Athena articulate this. And thus his next step is to show that the meaning of the air as the "sculpturing power" is symbolized in the mythology and iconography of the serpent and the bird. For both were sacred to Athena, "the serpent, in which the breath, or spirit, is less than in any other creature, and the earth-power greatest:—the bird, in which the breath, or spirit, is more full than in any other creature, and the earth-power least."[118]

His point is simply that man's instinctive but accurate understanding of vital ministry of the air has been expressed throughout the ages in mythic deposit that has accumulated about these two forms, and, indeed, that one may still sense this in the living creatures. In the bird, "the Spirit of the Air is put into, and upon, [in color] this created form; and it becomes, through twenty centuries, the symbol of Divine help." Particularly, "in the type of the dove with the olive branch, the conception of the spirit of Athena in renewed life prevailing over ruin, is embodied for the whole of futurity."[119] The serpent, on the other hand, associated with the alter Athena, "is a divine hieroglyph of the demoniac power of the earth,—of the entire earthly nature. As the bird is clothed with the power of the air, so this is the clothed power of the dust; as the bird is the symbol of the spirit of life, so this of the grasp and sting of death." In sum, "it is the very omnipotence of the earth."[120]

The meaning of that Judeo-Hellenic serpent to Ruskin's own mythology defies easy statement. There is something of the "maggot's might" in the image, a composite suggestion of virulence and virility. Rosenberg is certainly correct in pointing out the "phallic and diabolic" qualities of the serpents in his dreams,[121] but in his works they are subtly bound up with smoke, storm, and pollution of all sorts. One recalls the images of Ladon, Python, and the Gorgon there, the "assumption of the Dragon" in a "paradise of smoke"; "disgusting snake dreams" of his diaries appearing concurrently with intimations of polluted landscapes; the Medusae as "cloudy" and "venomous" knowledge; and the coming plague cloud, whose sound would be distinctly "a hiss instead of a wail." Here, the *The Queen*, the allusions to serpent mythology suggest the venomousness of some modern environments: "There is more poison in an ill-kept drain,—in a pool of dish-washings at a cottage door,—than in the deadliest asp of the Nile"; or, "All the walls of those ghastly suburbs are enclosures of tank temples for serpent worship."[122] And the whole interlude on the serpent hieroglyph is climaxed in a strange jeremiad on the deformities of his race, in which the clouds of mythology part for a moment exposing that spiritual malaise, of which the air myth and the storm delusion were sequelae.

> There is yet the clearest evidence of a disease, plague, or cretinous imperfection of development, hitherto allowed to prevail against the greater part of the races of men. . . . And truly, it seems to me, as I gather in my mind the evidences of insane religion, degraded art, merciless war, sullen toil, detestable pleasure, and vain or vile hope, in which the nations of the world have lived since first they could bear record of themselves—it seems to me, I say, as if the race itself were still half-serpent, not extricated yet from its clay; a lacertine breed of bitterness—the glory of it emaciate with cruel hunger, and blotted with venomous stain: and the track of it, on the leaf a glittering slime, and in the sand a useless furrow.[123]

Not only the serpent and the bird but also certain plant forms, particularly the olive, were sacred to Athena; and thus (at paragraph 74) we leave the relatively coherent discussion of those natural myths and enter a slough of Ruskinian ethical botany.

He had already sketched faint outlines of his natural mythology of plants in *The Ethics of the Dust* when he instanced flowers to illustrate the ideas of the gradation of life: "Notice what a different degree and kind of life there is in the calyx and the corolla."[124] But this flower myth section of *The Queen* still means little unless one recalls that he had said more about the flower and the gradation of life earlier in this lecture. The principle enunciated in paragraph 61 is simply that the "inner rapture" of vital force in flowers "is usually marked for us by the flush of one or more of the primary colours." Whatever the color may be or wherever within the flower it may appear, we are to know as a general truth that "in all cases, the presence of the strongest life is asserted by characters in which the human sight takes pleasure, and which seem prepared with distinct reference to us."[125] In sum, the "ethical signs of good and evil" have been set upon plants as well as upon animals, and we may take these as "among the most notable indications of volition of the animating power."[126]

The air influence that served as the point of contrast between the serpent and the bird is submerged momentarily in the discussion, but now with plants Ruskin moves his general argument ahead to include the idea of volition in the "sculpturing power." The reasoning, observed within the tangle of allusions and half-pursued suggestions, seems to have some such pattern as this: since even science cannot practically distinguish the "spirit of life" from the joint influences of air and solar warmth, it is natural that this vital power should, in human thought, have been substantiated primarily in those energies and secondarily in the living shells into which those energies have been cast. However, because these forms have tended to impress the mind as having a particular relevance to human needs and fears, they suggest that the form-giving power is a volitional power. This seems to be Ruskin's argument for the essential verity in the Greek conception of Athena.

So now, in reading certain plant forms that were connected with Athena (we are never entirely sure just *what* plants were sacred to her) as "living Hieroglyphs" of the "animating power," he undertakes to show that the "signs of good and evil" in the floral world are "indications of volition" in that power; again we are to understand, apparently, that the Greeks had not misread the everlasting gospel of physical life. We may take his remarks on the nightshades as illustrating the way in which the sentence of the "forming power" is manifested in plants: "The nightshades are, in fact, primroses with a curse upon them; and a sign set in their petals, by which the deadly and condemned flowers may always be known from the innocent ones,—that the stamens of the nightshades are between the lobes, and of the primulas, opposite the lobes, of the corolla."[127]

Apparently his argument would have been best served by his showing somehow that those plants particularly informed by the air are marked as beneficent, but the reader will find himself hard pressed to discover just what Ruskin's loquacious plants are saying about Athena or the air. We are left simply with the principle that the myriad plant forms are, in their color, a litmus of life, and that they have suggested to men by their designs, pleasing or displeasing, and their utility, healthful or destructive, the purposive working of a "forming power," and that men have for ages articulated these intimations in their various plant myths.

> We always come at last to a formative cause, which directs the circumstance, and mode of meeting it. If you ask an ordinary botanist the reason of the form of a leaf, he will tell you it is a "developed tubercle," and that its ultimate form "is owing to the direction of its vascular threads." But what directs its vascular threads? "They are seeking something they want," he will probably answer. What made them want that? What made them seek for it thus? Seek for it, in five fibers or in three? Seek for it, in serration, or in sweeping curves? Seek for it, in servile tendrils, or in impetuous spray? Seek for it, in woolen wrinkles rough with strings, or in glossy surfaces, green with pure strength, and winterless delight?

Following this, in what is probably the central passage of *The Queen*, Ruskin sums up his whole vitalistic synthesis from entity to deity.

> But the sum of all is, that over the entire surface of the earth and its waters, as influenced by the power of the air under solar light, there is developed a series of changing forms . . . all of which have reference in their action, or nature, to the human intelligence that perceives them; and on which, in their aspects of horror and beauty, and their qualities of good and evil, there is engraved a series of myths, or words of the forming power, which, according to the true passion and energy of the human race, they have been enabled to read into religion. And this forming power has been by all nations partly confused with the breath or air through which it acts, and partly understood as a creative wisdom, proceeding from the Supreme Deity.

He delivers his supreme admonition to the devotees of antimyth: "And whatever intellectual results may be in modern days obtained by regarding this effluence only as a motion or vibration, every formative human art hitherto, and the best states of human happiness and order, have depended on the apprehension of its mystery (which is certain), and of its personality (which is probable)."[128]

The whole morphology of physical existence, then, evidences design with respect to our immediate perceptions and thus has suggested to men the presence of an analogous, personal creative power at work in the nourishing elements and in every form they shape. This is what Ruskin had asserted in *The Ethics* when he said that the "Personal Creative Power" shows itself "whenever the dust of the earth begins to assume any orderly and lovely state."[129]

Throughout much of his spiritual history, man rested content in his inability to distinguish between the vital force and the natural elements through which it acts and so projected upon these elements the personality and volition he seemed to discover in the forms of life, rendering those elements sacred. Recently, however, enamored of Medusa, the "cloudy coldness of knowledge," man has attempted to reduce the action of the vital power to modes of force. But by doing so he has unwittingly imperiled his spiritual and physical wellbeing. In his apotheosis of abstractions, the core of man's sympathy with physical existence has been turned to stone; he has become an imperfect creature, a half-man.

But for those who can still heed it the Greek conception of Athena contains a spiritual truth written in living hieroglyphs and hence engraved upon the mind of man. What the Greeks knew was that "the blue, clear air *is* the sculpturing power upon the earth and sea. Where the surface of the earth is reached by that, . . . organic form becomes possible. You must indeed have the sun, also, and moisture; the kingdom of Apollo risen out of the sea: but the sculpturing of living things, shape by shape, is Athena's, so that under the brooding spirit of the air, what was without form, and void, brings forth the moving creature that hath life.[130] In sum, "The deep of air that surrounds the earth enters into union at its surface, and with its waters; so as to be the apparent cause of their ascending into life."[131]

Finally, to those who, with unwise knowledge, would prefer "the mere force of junction" to the pure, living, and sculpturing air, the Greek representation of Athena in art contained an ominous storm warning in the deep blue of her aegis. When they are angered both Apollo and Athena take toward men, "*the form of evil which is their opposite*—Apollo slaying by poisoned arrow, by pestilence; Athena by cold, the black aegis on her breast."[132] (In his *Storm-Cloud* Ruskin would stress the darkening, chilling, and pestilential qualities of that scourge.) On her aegis Athena bore the Gorgoneum, symbolic, as we know, of the "passionate folly of storm," the "ruinous tempest" in the souls of those given over to knowledge in its venomous character. But her "dark blue" aegis itself suggests, in Ruskin's thought, utter hostility between the spirit of man and the vital power in living things. The "thunderous purple" of this, Athena's "robe of indignation," he compares first with "the colour of heavy thundercloud" and then with "the gloom of Erebus, or of our evening," as if her judgments were to come in both storm and smoke.

> Her aegis was dark blue, because the Greeks thought of this tint more as shade than colour . . . it was . . . in their minds as distinctly representative of darkness as scarlet was of light, and, therefore, anything dark, but especially the colour of heavy thundercloud, was described by the same term. . . . Its spiritual power is chiefly expressed by a word signifying deeper shadow;—the gloom of Erebus, or of our evening, which, when spoken of the aegis, signifies not merely the indignation of Athena, but the entire hiding or withdrawal of her help, and beyond even this, her deadliest of all hostility—the darkness by which she herself deceives and beguiles to final ruin those to whom she is wholly adverse.[133]

It should now be plain why we have held throughout this discussion that the primary importance of *The Queen* is that it utters the prophecy that the "storm-cloud" came to fulfill. Indeed, there is a passage in the second of the *Storm-Cloud* lectures that contains a hint of this connection.

> I remember both these blights well; they were entirely terrific; but only sudden maxima of the constant morbific power of this wind . . . and the actual effect of it upon my thoughts and work has been precisely that which would have resulted from the visible phantom of an evil spirit, the absolute opponent of the Queen of the Air,—Typhon against Athena,—in

a sense of which I had neither the experience nor the conception when I wrote the illustrations of the myth of Perseus in *Modern Painters*.[134]

When we regard the prophecy of "thunderous purple" as a premonitory of the black plague-wind, the "gloom of Erebus, or of our evening" or foreshadowing "the ashes of the Antipodes" that "glare through the night," we arrive at an answer to the question with which this chapter was begun: why Ruskin spoke of this as his "best" book and the first he had written with "true knowledge of sorrow." And we may now conclude that, disordered and fanciful as they may seem, these first two lectures of *The Queen* are at once the culmination of a decade of deep interest in Greek myths and the supreme prophetic utterance in all his work. *The Queen of the Air* augurs spiritually the infection of the very stuff of praise by mechanistic or materialistic knowledge and physically the occlusion of the nourishing sky by smoke, a prophecy that seems curiously appropriate as we in the present consider the threats of air-pollution and depletion of the ozone layer.

Taking the clear, sunlit air (already manifesting to him dark visible symptoms of the age's spiritual disease) as the type of god-stuff (there were plans for work also on Apollo), Ruskin theorizes, through what purports to be a reconstruction of the later Greek's conception of Athena, the dependence of spiritual upon natural perceptions. The forms life assumes, he argues, suggest the presence of a forming and volitional power in them, if the passionate eye dwells upon the forms themselves. But what form has that power? What name shall it be given? All we really know is that the vital power is dependent upon some influence in the sunlit air; yet if we stand by the evidences of volition apparent in living forms, "stand by form against force," that is, then we are under the same necessity as the Greek was: that of speaking of this sun-warmed air as a "personal Creative power" (and considering the element sacred). But suppose, as is the tendency of science, we refuse the Greek wisdom? What if we determine to look for forces and not form in nature, refuse to grant the god-stuff any existence but as a mode or quantity of energy? ("What consolation, through plague, danger, or darkness, you can find in the conviction that you are nothing more than brute beasts driven by *brute forces*, your other tutors can tell you—not I.")[135] Indeed, it was to appear to the author of the *Storm-Cloud* that we had lost our "inspiration," that Medusa had taken our breath away, that we had all been turned to stone ("The universal instinct of blasphemy in the modern vulgar scientific mind is above all manifested in its love of what is ugly, and natural enthralment by the abominable"),[136] and that we must perish in our own soot or ashes. For the luminous blue of the clear air was being turned to "thunderous purple." The "sacred fume of modern devotion," a "poisonous smoke" that was "full of blight and damnation in every breath," had obscured god-stuff in one raging pall of black, making it plain to one who had loved it more than most, that the sky was becoming deadly.

CHAPTER 14

My Message Is Not Mine

Having looked rather carefully at *The Queen of the Air*, we might pause to consider one final question about it, a question that will lead toward the last topics of this study. How should we place this book generically? The superficial answer is easy enough. It is a group of three studies, in varying degrees discursive and fragmentary, in allegorical nature mythology. The perversity of this view, however, is that it accounts for nothing in the book that really matters, suggests none of its considerable range of implicit meanings. But to summarize at least a few of the ways in which *The Queen* defies this superficial classification is to stress the work's uniqueness and to indicate the set of Ruskin's prophetic mind as he enters the final stage of his work.

There is, for instance, the paeanic quality of Ruskin's prose. One would not expect the scholarly analyst of the Athenaic cult epithets to take up the tone of personal reverence for her. Then there is the fact that he invokes special visionary authority as an interpreter of myth; he claims to participate in the mythopoeic awareness on which the myth was based and in the continuum of vision by which it was elaborated, rather than to possess historical or linguistic expertise. He spoke of the *involuntariness* of true vision, coming with an immediate veracity that could not be refused, as dreams come, and there is the implication that his own discovery of Athena's meaning shared this quality. Perhaps this is why he held the fragmentary work in such high regard and why he would not revise it or accept Norton's suggestions for revision.

Another quality of *The Queen* that distinguishes it from the scholarly essay is its inclusiveness. This has both public and private dimensions. On the one hand Athena belongs to his personal mythology of the woman as spiritual guide that includes such tutelary figures (fixations of his anima) as Quercia's Ilaria, Veronese's Queen of Sheba, Giorgione's "Hesperid Aeglé," Rose, Saint Ursula, and Fors-Atropos. On the other hand, the book continues the interpretations of storm myths he had begun in volume 5 of *Modern Painters* and points toward his own storm myth in *The Storm-Cloud of the Nineteenth Century*. At the same time it is also related to the symbolic theme of the cloud as representing life's transience, mystery, and menace he had worked out in the chapter entitled "The Firmament" in volume 4 of *Modern Painters* and his lecture "The Mystery of Life and Its Arts." United with his interpretation of the Greek myths of Athena are several other idea complexes in his work that might be called "mythic": the existential "religion of Humanity" he symbolized by Athena's wild olive crown, the recurrent model of organic form as the controlling life image in his work, and the Evangelical themes of natural theology and scriptural eschatology. Taking Athena to mean the atmosphere and organic knowledge and spirit in the double sense of passion and the shaping spirit of life in organic form (analogous to the Holy Spirit and his own law of help), Ruskin can connect her with nearly every aspect of experience: with the vital environment, the moral inspiration of art and industry, and the spirit of social coherence developed, in his view, chiefly by war. In fact the burden of implications is so great that *The Queen* simply breaks down under the load into discursive and fragmentary pronouncements. Ruskin was apparently attempting to bind everything in his public thought (and perhaps certain private imagery as well) into one coherent archetypal vision of the Holy Spirit, its manifold operations and those of its deadly, serpentine antagonist. Thus, in her opposition to Medusa, who is also her hostile face, Athena largely assimilates the powers of the other purifying heroes of his work: Hercules, Apollo, Turner, Saint George.

This adversarial element brings us to one final point of difference between *The Queen* and scholarly mythology. Athena, as we have seen, is not simply interpreted but brought into the present; she *is* the air, the spirit of organic form, and the answering spirit of passionate knowing. But her chief antagonist, her antiself, also continues to exist as the chilling knowledge that can turn living men to stone. In the book itself this Gorgonian knowledge is chiefly science, but elsewhere in Ruskin's writings of the sixties the enemies of Athena have included worldly materialism (the pursuit of deadly wealth) and otherworldly or sectarian theology. The important point, however, is that in his myth Ruskin represents a continuing conflict (in the preface it figures as a critical conflict) between two ways of knowing (the passionate and organic, the dispassionate and dualistic) with the further implication that the warrior goddess stands ready to bring thunderous punishment upon her antagonists.

From these points it should be apparent that *The Queen of the Air* is not simply an exercise in allegorical nature mythology but is essentially an apocalypse. Generically it is a revelation concerning ultimate things; in particular it is a mythic vision of the forming (holy-helping) spirit in the organic model and of the storm punishment that follows upon chilling or separating knowledge. It is Ruskin's most profound and comprehensive "spiritual invention" or vision, and in this respect it can lay claim to being the most significant work of his final phase, though it is less interesting than the more diverse and topical *Fors Clavigera*.

This third phase that begins to take control of his work after 1865 we have loosely characterized as "prophetic" to differentiate its impulse from the primarily aesthetic and economic motives of earlier stages of his work. The term was also meant to indicate the increased reliance of his writing upon webs of allusions,scornful or castigating rhetoric, and apocalyptic perorations. Yet to assert the primacy of the prophetic mode in the remainder of his work is not to deny that the other two motives (criticism of art and the social order) persist or to deny the presence of this prophetic urge in his work from the beginning. Indeed, the prophetic tendency is coeval with the Romantic and Evangelical influences upon him and is the basic undercurrent of his mind. However, while his earlier aesthetic and socioeconomic ideas continued to serve as the substance of his prophecy in this final stage, it was his manner not his message that underwent the most significant changes after 1870. Various internal and external stresses combined to drive him increasingly into the stance and style we must call prophetic, oracular, until this, in aspects to be considered, became the dominant feature of the rest of his writing.

1

Two decades of work remained to Ruskin between the publication of *The Queen* and the final descent of nescience on him in 1889. Of course this period encompassed the gradual deterioration of his mind; yet it would be a subtle critical problem to determine just when the features of style we have been referring to as prophetic become pathological. As a problem deeply involved with imagination and spiritual invention it is one that had long attracted Ruskin himself. He addressed it vaguely as early as his discussion of imagination in volume 2 of *Modern Painters*. Although he holds that all true vision is involuntarily given and is literally "seen" and believed, as a deep dream is, he is as yet apparently untroubled by the difficulty of distinguishing the healthy from the morbid products of visionary experience. But he makes no clear distinctions. He is certain, for instance, that "some vital chord" snaps in Turner in 1845,[1] but he is vague about the effects of this in his work, alluding merely to impurity of color and uncertainty of purpose and handling.

The dangerous fascination this problem of fevered vision had for Ruskin is evident from the fierceness with which he dogmatized on the subject and from the care with which he recorded his own private experiences of this very sort. Much of his criticism is devoted to attacking, often in hyperbolic language, what he considers to be evidence of morbid mentality in an artist or his society: disordered imagination, forced pathetic fallacy; the unnatural; the grotesque; all tendency to dwell on death or decay in painting and fiction; anything dissected, excessively shadowed, glittering, or serpentine. But the repressed returned on him, and both his dreams and his writing manifest some of the very disorders his criticism had deplored. It is as if this were yet another meaning of the doubleness of Athena and Medusa.

The essential criterion he uses to distinguish between prophetic and pathological visions is the ultimate control of the former by a conscious mind that knows "dream for dream, truth for truth,"[2] Yet he has allowed that imaginative vision is ungovernable, involuntary, and often associated with derangement.[3] Consequently, his assessment of Blake's poetry, in *The Eagle's Nest* (1872), is confusing, but it seems to assert the presence of a Blake who is ultimately in control of his delusions, who is not, at least, deceived by them: "His poems have much more than merit; they are written with absolute sincerity, with infinite tenderness, and, though in the manner of them diseased and wild, are in verity the words of a great and wise mind, disturbed, but not deceived, by its sickness; nay, partly exalted by it, and sometimes giving forth in fiery aphorism some of the most precious words of existing literature."[4] Similarly, when Ruskin's own mind begins to give way his primary effort is not to be deceived by it, to make the effects of his sickness part of his message, and thereby be in control of it though disturbed by it.[5] We find him sifting his dreams and delusions, recording them in his diaries, corresponding about them, and letting them spill over into his public work, as if to find a higher truth in them and to be himself exalted by his sickness. We find him, for instance, with frank admission, including three dreams from his first illness in the series of Oxford lectures entitled *Ariadne Florentina* (1872).

This illness overtook him at Matlock in July 1871; the complaint seems to have been in large measure physical, but it was also partly mental, premonitory of the three distinctly mental attacks he was to suffer. He wrote to his friend Henry Acland emphasizing the seriousness of its physical side only. "I knew very thoroughly how ill I was," he declared, "I have not been so near the dark gates since I was a child."[6] In a letter to another friend, Mrs. Cowper-Temple, he hinted, while insisting on his rational control, at the mental side of the illness: "*Was* I so very ill, really? when you saw me first? Everybody thought I was acting in mad or foolish whims of sickness, but I could have written a medical statement of the case, when I was too weak to raise myself; and I was acting all along with as fixed purpose as in painting a picture."[7] Perhaps another indication of his mental condition in 1871 is the fact that at Oxford that spring he had first detected and recorded the plague cloud or storm cloud, the malignant, hissing wind of modern times. The phenomenon was also evident to him at Matlock in July. He had noted that to Turner as to the Greeks storm clouds seemed messengers of fate; this particular cloud formation troubled his sight recurrently from this year onward until he confronted it and described it in mythic and meteorological terms in his *Storm-Cloud* lectures (1884).

This plague cloud is one of several basic psychomythic themes, which, to judge mainly from his letters and diaries, tend to take obsessional control of Ruskin's mind during this period. It may not be a useful effort to search for meanings in his madness, yet these major psychic themes do seem to bear a close relationship to some of the overt mythic elements we have been tracing in his books down through *The Queen of the Air*. The difference is that now these themes become subjective and tend to drift beyond rational control; they are often now expressed in terms of struggle within and for his psyche as well as for nature. The term *psychomythic* seems appropriate for these themes because often in expressing them Ruskin projects his anxieties or needs into mythological or hagiological figures, as when, for instance, he personifies the "reality principle" in his life as Fors-Atropos, which is a figure comparable to Freud's Ananke, necessity. In a way he agrees, unknowingly, with Freud and Jung in using quasi-mythic terms for the semantics of psychic energy or in connecting the private with the racial dream. Only, for Ruskin, these figures are now often there in person, in communication or conflict with him or confused with the real persons of his recollection. Some might say that this tendency is evident in his myth work before any evident illness overtakes him; that we should look for the receptive side of Rose in Athena (who is passion as well as breath) and for the hostile, theological Rose (or her mother, whom he called "Lacerta," the serpent) in the Gorgon side of Athena.

However, the essential point is that from the tangles and snares of allusions and associations in his private writings during this distressed period, four primary themes emerge that connect, as one would expect, with the mythology of his earlier public writing and will have significant influence on that which is to follow. The themes to be stated, of course, represent generalizations based on an intricate text, and the reader must be left to test them for himself or herself. In doing so he or she will find that Derrick Leon's detailed biographical account and Helen Gill Viljoen's copious introductions and annotations to the *Brantwood Diary* are especially useful guides.

The first of these psychomythic themes is his personal confrontation with the demonic Adversary. We have already seen this figure looming up in a dangerously subjective and entangling way in the *Time and Tide* letters, and we have noticed this adversarial pattern in the mythic materials he had interpreted: Hercules and Ladon, Apollo and Python, Christ and Mammon, Athena and Medusa. But now the archetypal enemy is confronted in person; in his delusions the Adversary is no archetypal image to be consciously explored, but a presence. The figure is archetypally the Devil, Mammon, the Prince of Darkness, et cetera, but it is subconsciously the dark side of his own psyche, Jung's "the Shadow." His most notable encounter with this fiendish presence occurred on the crucial "Good Friday" of 22 February 1878, when he kept a naked, night-long vigil against the appearance of the Evil One until, at dawn, as he approached his window "to make sure that the feeble blue light really was the heralding of the gray dawn," a black cat sprang suddenly from behind his mirror. By his own account he knew the creature for the "foul fiend" and seized it and hurled it with "all my might and main against the floor. . . . A dull thud—nothing more. . . . I had triumphed! Then, worn out with bodily fatigue, with walking and waiting and watching, my mind racked with ecstacy and anguish, my body benumbed with bitter cold of a freezing February night, I threw myself upon the bed, all unconscious."[8]

Not only did the Adversary appear, or threaten to appear, to him directly as a presence, it bedeviled him also as an infection of nature (of the organic model) particularly manifested in the skies. Here, in this second major theme, the multiple and quasi-prophetic implications of his demonic vision are most in evidence. For his "Storm-Cloud" and "Plague-Wind," the "Ghastly cloud-spirits of evil"[9] stand for a complex of antagonistic forces. In one meaning they work particularly against *him*. "Devils try hard to put me off good work," he said in the diary of 1877.[10] But the "devil's skies"[11] can refer also to pollution, signifying the worship of Mammon (or the pursuit of fatal wealth) and the clouds of dead lives sacrificed to him. Similarly, the chill, hissing plague wind that accompanies the storm cloud can be connected with the hostile, Gorgon face of Pallas: the plague of fact and cloudy, cold, analytic knowledge attacking the bond of human passion to the forming spirit in nature. Finally, the storm cloud may, like the demonic presence, be a projection of Ruskin's psychic shadow, repressed thoughts, upon the world.[12] Accordingly, his storm watch seems to reach a crisis in 1878, with the manifestations decreasing somewhat in virulence and frequency after that until it was largely exorcised by his public prophecy of storm in 1884.

These apocalyptic storm, plague, and demon symbols, then, represent at once the lethal or antiorganic forces in his world and the repressed or unassimilated forces in his psyche. Where, one might ask, went the power of Athena (and his other guiding feminine spirits) to oppose these menaces? In one sense that power died with Rose in 1875 or with the death of heart he said he had suffered before this in the desperate swings of hope and despair that held him to the end; in the psychoanalytic sense she assumed, in repression and denial, her demonic face to him, much as his Athena became Medusa to her adversaries and her pure air became the storm cloud. But gradually after Rose's death he combatted the demonic power by mythologizing and beatifying Rose into another version of the spirit of life, the archetype of psychic energy he had represented by Athena. He connected her with Saint Ursula and Proserpina (whose meaning as the Queen of Fate and of the ebb and flow of life in flowers he had mentioned in *The Queen of the Air*.) This, then, is the third psychomythic theme of this period; in the subconscious dimension these appear to be projections of anima, or "Lady Soul," as do Athena, Ilaria, and other such figures in his work.

It has been suggested that "Ruskin's woman ultimately is a Christ-figure,"[13] but as much can be said for his conception of himself, his storm-demon antagonists gathering into the archetype of the Antichrist. Christ, Jung observes, "exemplifies the archetype of the self";[14] however, in the Christian conception "the Christ symbol lacks wholeness in the modern psychological sense, since it does not include the dark side of things, but specifically excludes it in the form of a Luciferian opponent." Therefore, "if we see the traditional figure of Christ as a parallel to the psychic manifestation of the self, then the Antichrist would correspond to the shadow of the self, namely, the dark half of the human totality which ought not to be judged too optimistically."[15] Ruskin's tutelary women, who represent a complex of ideas centering on purity and peace, might be regarded as complements of the bright Redeemer aspects of his psyche, or Athena to his Apollo; but he was also aware of a lacertine antagonist among women. The difficulty is that these symbolic women combine several aspects of meaning for him apart from his practical relation to them: the psychic, relating to the health and wholeness of the light side of his psyche; Greek mythic, in the sense that they are involved symbolically with the "living myths" of nature, the organic model; and Christian-mythic in that they are, in this period, associated with ideas of sainthood, redemption, and the "eternal morning." This complexity of symbolism is evident in his relation to Rose-Ursula.

In 1884, with Rose, Proserpina, and Carpaccio's *St. Ursula's Dream* on his mind, he summarized the nature and extent of Ursula's mythic influence: "You will never see such hair, nor such peace beneath it on the brow—*Pax Vobiscum*—the peace of heaven, of infancy, and of death. No one knows who she is or where she lived. She is Persephone at rest below the earth; she is Proserpina at play above the ground. She is Ursula, the gentlest and rudest of little bears; a type in that, perhaps, of the moss rose, or of the rose *spinosissima*, with its rough little buds. She is in England, in Cologne, in Venice, in Rome, in eternity, living everywhere, dying everywhere."[16] Although in this late passage she appears as a mythic symbol like his Athena, his interest in the "myth" of Ursula was more intimate and mystical. To Norton, in 1878, he confessed that he "went crazy about" her and other saints, "chiefly young-lady saints."[17] In an earlier *Fors* (Letter 72, 1876) he had announced that he would attempt nothing thenceforward without Ursula's "counsel,"[18] and in the agonized diaries of the late seventies there are frequent references to Ursula's "help,"[19] as opposed to *Fors'* "order."

There are also passages in his diaries and in *Fors* that show that he felt he had received personal messages from Rose-Ursula-Proserpina, messages he felt he could decode as the result of his careful study of Ursula's myth and the living mythology of plants. Thus in *Fors* 74 (1877) he announced, "Last night St. Ursula sent me her dianthus 'out of her bedroom window with her love.' . . . She sent me the living dianthus (with a little personal message besides, of great importance to *me*, but of none to the matter at hand) by the hands of an Irish friend now staying here: but she had sent me also, in the morning from England, a dried sprig of the other flower in her window, the sacred vervain."[20] The vervain, like the dianthus, had been sent by a living friend;[21] but Ruskin recorded in his diary that it had been a command, from the dead Rose by way of Ursula, to "forgive poor L[acerta]"—"a direct command from St. Ursula, with her leaf: a command given by *her*, with the mythic power of her nature-origin used to make me understand that Rosie had asked her."[22] In the *Fors* account Ruskin went on to explain that mythically the vervain was sacred to "domestic purity" and that the dianthus, by its name, celebrated the god of day, Jupiter.

It is clear that the myth of Ursula had a Christian-mystical as well as a personal meaning and a Greek nature-meaning for him: "The one great meaning," he said, "is the victory of her faith over all fears of death."[23] His allusion (in the first Ursula passage quoted above) to the paradisal peace he saw depicted on the girl-saint's brow in Carpaccio's *St. Ursula's Dream* (a picture he read with intense, even pathological, care),[24] "the peace of heaven, of infancy, of death," brings us to the fourth major psychomythic theme of his mental trial. This theme is the recovery of innocence; it is the unfallen world to which his guiding feminine angels now summon his spirit.

Not all of his diary entries of the seventies and eighties record demonic dreams or days marked by the "curse on the sky."[25] There are entries interspersed that speak of relatively calm work and of moments in which his spirit and that of nature appear jointly redeemed. "Y[esterday] a soft, gradually purifying, at last clear afternoon, with clear though little beautiful sunset. But I saw some blessed purple walls against sunshine among the farms, and seemed to find my life again on the green banks. To-day crashing rain and all black."[26] This was in 1876, two years before the first of his mental attacks, but it typifies the redemptive moments that one finds recorded here and there among the devilish days. The diaries of the seventies and eighties are, before all other meanings they may have, a fearful daily record of the struggle of antagonistic powers for control of Ruskin's skies and his mind. The miasmic power has by far the upper hand, but occasionally a redemptive power manifests itself against the "hell-sky."[27] Sunday, 25 February 1885, for instance, was such a day. "Entirely cloudless, with warm sweet quiet light, which came full glow at sunrise, and made me—to my great wonder, deeply melancholy, with the strange sense of the dream of return of departed youth and a departed world."[28] In 1887, while he was attempting to recover that departed world in the writing of *Praeterita*, he remarked in a letter to Mrs. La Touche that work on the book seemed to renew the light of nature for him. "It will all come out, if I live, with whatever I have in me of the best, at least—a little expressed so that it may explain what I have done or tried to do, and writing it seems to lift the smoke from the hills and bring sunshine on the sea."[29]

Throughout Ruskin's writings, from the Alpine ecstasies of his better poems, through his studies of landscape, architecture, and political economy, there is a continuous thread of a quest for a kind of earthly paradise. He sought this quasi-mythical source first directly in nature, for instance in the unspoiled Alpine valleys watched over by stainless snows. (Though, as communities, even these places were threatened by the demonic "Mountain Gloom.") In painting he sought the spiritual source in the idea of Turnerian landscape, icons of organic form, to him, that caught its interfusion of unity, liberty, and mystery in majestic syntheses of apprehension, worlds within world. Concurrently he sought the place also in the historical and aesthetic idea of the Gothic, suggesting an architecture and a source of community characterized by the same organic coherence. (But the organic paradises of landscape and the Gothic were constantly threatened by a fall into the forbidden knowledge represented by the mere mechanical application of rules and systems.) Even in his religious development—the break with sectarian narrowness, the "religion of Humanity" culminating in his poetic reconstruction of Athena as the Queen of Life—there is this same interest in a return to the unfallen, pre-analytic source. Finally, he sought the place also in his social thought in the idea of a community in which the laws of life would take precedence over the lethal, fallen laws of the market as taught by economic "science." His thought points to a redeemed world characterized by purity (spiritual and environmental), abundance, organic harmony, and community, sustained by the ethic of care and monitored by wise and benevolent authority.

This redeemed world that is the essential, ever-threatened goal of Ruskin's criticism and prophecy has affinities with archetypal and mythic themes of loss and recovery of paradise, of origins. It is linked also to the major Romantic *topos*, recently surveyed by M. H. Abrams,[30] of the redemption of the world in the recovery (through imagination) of that childlike innocence of eye in which the alienating subject-object dichotomy of the rationalistic tradition is overcome. Then nature becomes "ours" and the god-stuff again, the human mind rewedded to it in innocence and joy. Psychologically this state of universal health involves the reassimilation into the psyche of aspects of the self (the materials of dreams, visions, imagination, et cetera) that have been exiled from consciousness dominated by reason.

In a way, Ruskin the critic-prophet had been engaged in this process of reintegration of the self all along, always reminding us that there are mysterious unities at the periphery of consciousness that have been accessible only to the great visionary and artistic minds of the past. What we have been calling the organic model in his work, with its emphasis on prehensive and mysterious unities, is somewhat analogous to the Jungian self[31] (an entity more comprehensive than conscious personali-

ty); and its opposite, rationalistic mechanism, seems analogous to the
ego that extends only to consciousness. The total self, in Jung's conception, "is a God-image, or at least cannot be distinguished from one,"[32]
and includes, therefore, what in mythic language are referred to as the
designs, intentions, or acts of God.

Now in this phase of mental crisis and breakdown, the practical
achievement of the redeemed world, his essential "work," recedes from
Ruskin's hope; though that work goes forward in a diffusive and
fragmentary way. (Perhaps it is the frustration of this drive, and of the
personal drive to some sort of completion with Rose, that brings on the
disastrous displacement of psychic energy in dream and delusion.) His
own consciousness and its environing world is now threatened by
formless upheavals from the depths of the self that consciousness must
attempt to assimilate, to interpret. The struggle is now most urgently an
inward one, and Ruskin, the practical Romantic, is forced into the more
common Romantic recourse of world redemption through the theodicy
of the self.[33] The way forward was still primarily the way back, but in
this phase the redeemed world was most nearly achieved through the
regressive exploration of his own sources. The calm sweetness of
Praeterita testifies to the success of this process. A remark with which he
concluded *Notes on His Own Handiwork Illustrative of Turner* (1878),
indicates the admonition he felt he received from his first definite mental
attack and the direction he was meant to take: "Unable therefore now to
carry forward my political work, I yet pray my friends to understand that
I do not quit it as doubting anything that I have said, or willingly
ceasing from anything that I proposed: but because the warning I have
received amounts to a direct message from the Fates that the time has
come for me to think no more of any Masterhood; but only of the Second
Childhood that has to learn its way towards the other world."[34]

Ruskin suffered his first attack of insanity in 1878. His diary entries
after 18 February of that year show the "Long Dream" gradually taking
control of his consciousness. Webs of dangerous associations entangle
him; his language becomes a cryptic yet often dramatic mixture of
interfused personal and literary allusions, sometimes taken up in
dialogic address. At moments, and this is the most striking feature of
these entries, he actually projects himself into delusory scenes. Thus, for
instance, as Hamlet, Rose having been identified as Ophelia ("Oh
Devil—cunning Devil—do you think I want to provoke Beata Vigri and
Little Ophelia then—?"), he confronts Laertes: "And Bishop Laertes,—
you had as lief take your fingers from my throat—the Devil will not take
my soul, yet a while—Also—look you—and also looking other [things

may be at YOUR throat before long.] (Thou pray'st not well—even by your own account and the Devil will not answer you therefore[)]] and least said is soonest mended—for—if up when the scuffle comes—the foils should be sheffield whettles—it is dangerous work—Laertes—'very'—as Mr. Jingle said, even the public press & Mr. Jingle will advise you of that."[35]

Helen Gill Viljoen, who has annotated these passages, points out that even Ruskin's script at points "reveals the receding intellectual control."[36] There are messages from his guiding saint-spirits intermixed, of course, and interesting confessional remarks: "February 16. Saturday.—Such a bewilderment as Santa Vigri sent me yesterday! and horrible fog, and all the devils doing their best against her! . . . And what else!—should I expect? because I've never practiced patience or prudence before—little wicked lamb that I've been—and now setting—sticking—taking—myself up for a knight!"[37] In another entry, part of that for "February 22. *Good* Friday," in which Ruskin's mind is possessed by an overwhelming mass of associations, Rose is Proserpina and there is a passing nod of sympathy to Blake among the pressing crowd: "To Joseph Severn—Keats—Endymion—quenched in the Chaste beams—yes—oh yes—Proserpina mine. I have not looked back, nor took my hand from the Jason plough. And when Gold and Gems adorn the plough! Oh—you dear Blake—and so mad too—" And, curiously, his last remark in the entry for that desperate night remembers Athena: "I couldn't find the key and then remembered I had not thanked the dear Greek Princess—nor Athena of the Dew—and Athena κεραμῖτις." He was found demented on the morning of the twenty-third. His next entry, heading a blank page, says simply, "February,—to April—the Dream."[38]

Our interest here is not in the causes of Ruskin's dementia but in his attempt to assimilate and interpret the materials overwhelming his consciousness into a "theodicy of the self," a personal allegory of passion and redemption in which the struggle to reintegrate the self, the struggle for health and wholeness, is involved with the salvation of the world and the recovery of paradise. This theodicy is implicit in the four psychomythic themes just discussed. Of course this integrative process is private and therapeutic rather than literary, as we trace it here in his letters and diary entries. But this subjective theodicy, the rudiments of self-analysis, is projected into his public work to such an extent that it becomes the major drive of his prophecy in the final phase, and his failure of self-integration is reflected in his work as fragmentation and loss of control.

This effort to assimilate the volcanic materials of his delusions is evident in a letter he wrote to George Richmond shortly after his first recovery. "The dream itself," he wrote, "though full of *merest* fantasy and madness in many respects, was on the while a sifting examination of me, by myself, on all the dark sides and in all the dark places; coupled with some passages of proud conceit enough; and others of great beauty and bright jest."[39] At a greater remove, in the diary for 1880, he saw the dream in a more visionary and theological way: "I lying awake since five, thinking over the great dream, which I am ashamed to find is beginning to pass from me—and that too, in one of its most wonderful parts—the great contest between the Devil and—Georgie! (who represented throughout the adverse queenly or even angelic power), for the Kingdom of the world."[40] We will consider in a moment what more comprehensive interpretation he would put upon the "great dream" as he looked back on it after five years; in the meantime, however, he had two other major mental attacks to endure.

The second assault came in 1881, in a "month of terrible delirium" between 20 February and 22 March. Unlike the breakdown of 1878, this one was not preluded in the diaries by gradual surrender to dangerous currents of association. The entries remain under rational control until they stop abruptly on 10 February, not to be resumed until 8 April. The point to be noticed about this crisis is that it seems to have been less jolting to him. Perhaps this is because he was more resigned to his illness by this time or because the process of self-purgation and prophetic assimilation of his dream work was underway.

Whatever the case, he clearly speaks of these dreams as being somehow more profitable to him than the last. To his friend, Dr. John Brown, he wrote, shortly afterward: "I've been wool-gathering a bit again, that's all, and have come round all right, with more handfuls of golden fleece than on my last voyage to Medea's land."

> The illness was much more definite in its dreaming than the last one, and not nearly so frightful. It taught me much, as these serious dreams do always; and I hope to manage myself better, and not go Argonauting any more. But *both* these illnesses have been part of one and the same system of constant thought, far out of sight to the people about me, and of course, getting more and more separated from them as *they* go on in the ways of the modern world, and *I* go *back* to live with my Father and my Mother and my Nurse, and one more,—all waiting for me in the Land of the Leal.[41]

To Norton he wrote in much the same vein, speaking of the dreams as part of a purgative and educative process, though not mentioning the paradisal journey back in time.

I went wild again for three weeks or so, and have only just come to myself—if this be myself, and not the one that lives in dream.

The two fits of whatever you like to call them are both part of the same course of trial and teaching, and I've been more gently whipped this time and have learned more; but I must be very cautious in using my brains yet awhile. . . .

I shall have some strange passages of dream to tell you of as soon as I am strong again. The result of them, however, is mainly my throwing myself now into the mere fulfilment of Carlyle's work.[42]

The theme of ego annihilation suggested by this last sentence might be tied to that same theme in *Sartor Resartus* where the theodicy of self points to redemption of the world through annihilation of the ego (which, in Jungian terms, would mean the integration of the suprapersonal self). The *Sartor* connection is further suggested by Ruskin's later reference to a "terrible fire-dream in the streets of London," as if a psychic allusion to Teufelsdröckh's fire baptism in the Rue St. Thomas d'Enfer and Carlyle's own on Leith Walk, Edinburgh. Carlyle's death on 5 February of that year may have been among the precipitating causes of his 1881 illness. He had come to speak of Carlyle as "Father" or "Papa Carlyle"; and, as with his own father, he felt some guilt for not having loved this father enough while the man lived. "My remorse," he told Mary Gladstone, "every day he lived, for not having enough loved him in the days gone by, is not greater now, but less, in the hope that he knows what I am feeling about him at this—and all other—moments."[43]

The third mental assault came at Herne Hill in March 1882. He seems to have felt considerably restored after this session, if one judges from his note to Susan Beever written a few days after his recovery: "I have had a happy Easter morning, entirely bright in its sun and clear in sky; and with renewed strength enough to begin again the piece of St. Benedict's life where I broke off, to lose these four weeks in London,—weeks not wholly lost neither, for I have learned more and more of what I should have known without lessoning; but I *have* learnt it, from these repeated dreams and fantasies, that we walk in a vain shadow and disquiet ourselves in vain."[44] To Mrs. La Touche, a few days earlier, he expressed the feeling that this illness completed a cycle associated with Rose and would be his last. "These fits of illness are all *accidents* (what an Accident is—God knows—not I) not in the least consequences of my general work: and I rather fancy the three of them are all I'm meant to have. They were all part of a piece, and, Ireland and *her* 'Rest' has had much more to do with them than my English work."[45]

There were more attacks to come, of course, in 1885, 1886, and 1888, but these are largely lost to us in silence. The diaries and letters of his last five articulate years continued to record his moods, dreams, and weathers, but there was no attempt to find a message in his madness. His self-integrative energies were going into *Praeterita*; the effort was to recover the sources of his consciousness, not in the interpretation of his dreams and delusions, but in the remembrance of the epiphanies of his past. However, in the *Brantwood Diary* for 1883, nearly a year after that third illness (which he took to be the last he was "meant to have"), there is a fascinating series of entries (for 2, 3, and 4 February) in which we find him attempting to interpret the messages of his three dream phases into something like the rudiments of a personal theodicy. This effort brings us back to his remark about Blake as a "great and wise mind, disturbed, but not deceived by its illness."

There are more prophetic filaments connecting this series of entries to others near it than we can pause to trace here. On 31 January, for instance, he refers to the "strange floods of sudden teaching" he found in the random opening of his diary at 2 November 1877 with its allusion to Titus II that begins "But speak thou the things which become sound doctrine." And then to the "contrary warnings" he found in the entry for 1 November, where the reference is to I Timothy, particularly: "Neglect not the gift that is in thee. . . . *Take heed unto thyself, and unto the doctrine* . . . for in doing this thou shalt save thyself, and them that hear thee."[46] We note here simply the joint command to prophecy and self-analysis and also the fact that Ruskin, plunging into his personal myths, is using his own diary for *sortes Biblicae*.

"And now—" he tells himself on 2 February, "how am I even forgetting the lessons of my three illnesses, of contention between good and evil! I will try to fasten some, here—." This statement of his intention is followed by a text (Rom. 8:13) described as the "proper head of all to be taught or learned by me"; that is, "if ye through the Spirit do mortify the deeds of the body, ye shall live." Then there is a brief summary of the three "visions": "Well—the first thing to be noted of those three illnesses, that in the first there was the great definite Vision of the contention with the Devil, and all the terror and horror of Hell—& physical death. In the second, there was quite narrowed demoniacal vision in my room, with the terrible fire-dream in the streets of London; in the third, the vision was mostly very sad & personal, all connected with my Father. Enough, for 'to day.' " Of course much of Ruskin's meaning is obscure, even to him, but there appear to be shadowy stages of self-purgation and redemption represented here (perhaps even an allusion to the three mystical stages in *Sartor*). There is a trial by confrontation with the full power of the shadow-self or Adversary indicated in the first vision, a purgative or baptismal theme arises in the second phase with its "meaner visions of dragons and spectres" and its "terrible fire-dream," and finally there is a hint of meek reunion or reconciliation in the reference to the third vision as "mostly very sad & personal, all connected with my Father." At the climax of his second illness, he explains in the following entry, came the "Madaleine part" which was "I suppose, the period of highest exaltation, showing the exact connection of pride with insanity—I thought I had a kind of crucifixion to go through—and to found a farther phase of Christianity and that Rose was as the Magdalen to me."[47]

This crucifixion phantasy epitomizes the last of the four psychomythic themes of his illness that we have been discussing in an attempt to get at the major private involvements of his final or "prophetic" phase. This redemption theme, by which his inner torments and the outer plagues are "justified" in a private theodicy, is the one that is most dangerously intertwined with his "general work" in this final phase. Outwardly he is the priest of Athena, or the Redeemer, or the Master, or Saint George, struggling against the multitudinous effects of the Adversary, in nature, art, and society: "The unconscious personality merges with our environment."[48] Psychologically the struggle is to integrate the self, to assimilate the autonomous materials from the depths that are threatening to overwhelm and control the ego. The crucifixion image, a Jungian might argue, represents the paradoxical sacrifice of the part of the psyche that would be pure for the redemption of that which would be whole or complete.

In Jung's interpretation the symbolic meaning of the crucifixion is "that the progressive development and differentiation of consciousness leads to an ever more menacing awareness of the conflict and involves nothing less than a crucifixion of the ego, its agonizing suspension between irreconcilable opposites."[49] A psychic analogue of the organic model with its coherent imperfection. Ruskin, ominously, repudiates the image as a phantasy of pride. Rose, who figures in the dream as Mary Magdalen, the woman Christ healed of evil spirits and who provided for Him and accompanied Him to the crucifixion, would, in the Jungian line of interpretation, represent Ruskin's consciousness striving to assimilate the projections of his anima. As for the psychodynamic implications of the third vision, the sad and personal dreams, "all connected with my Father," we might simply note Jung's observation that "the relation of the ego to the self is like that of the son to the father."[50]

A more elemental version of this quest for psychic wholeness through integration and transformation of unconscious forces is represented symbolically, for Jungians, by the hero-dragon contest and particularly, for us, by the legend of Saint George. Ruskin was drawn to the symbolism (especially as represented by Carpaccio) and incorporated it into his personal mythology of serpent fighters along with his Hercules and Ladon, Apollo and Python, Athena and Medusa. The fact that he was drawn by the archetype but unaware, consciously, of its full significance could be read as an indication of his psychological condition; the legend represented an ungratified urge to integration. Dragons, a modern psychoanalytic commentator explains, represent "the mother depths" or "the nonpersonal forces in the depths of the human psyche that nourish and aid or devour and destroy man's feeble and naked consciousness."[51] We have noted (p. 16) that the dragon-contest may represent the deep hostilities that must arise if the hero is to overcome the "devouring, terrible mother" and achieve a potent and independent ego. Further, "the attempt to appease the dragon by the gift of a beautiful maiden means that man's soul, his anima, the feminine component, is the first value to be swallowed by the aroused powers of the unconscious."[52] Saint George, we are told, was "believed to have peculiar powers—in particular, power to heal lunatics."[53]

The hero's birth was miraculous; he was predestined to be a dragon slayer, marked with the stigmata of the cross and the dragon. He was reared by a foster mother, a sorceress with invincible powers, and his first heroic task was to overcome her, for she attempted to prevent him from fulfillment his destiny by entombing him in a rock cave. "This is always the first task of the potential hero, who must free himself from the mother before he can set out to enlarge the field of human endeavor."[54] The hero's primary task, of course, is to redeem his anima from the dark psychic forces that hold her captive; in this he is a "champion of light," a solar hero. So much of the legend's meaning Ruskin very likely perceived; what he does not recognize consciously is the suggestion of "essential kinship between the dragon and the dragon slayer."[55] The hero's conquering energies are derived from the same source as the dragon, a psychological truth indicated by the fact that "in some of the legends the hero has to taste of the dragon's blood before he is strong enough to give the *coupe de grace*, to his daemonic antagonist."[56] In Ruskin's conscious symbolism the serpent power, though it fascinates (he noted that both Apollo and Athena, when angered, take the forms of their serpent-opponents), is vigorously repudiated, only to recur with equivalent insistence in his serpent dreams, as if it represented a power in the self that his consciousness could not assimilate. His self-identification with Saint George appears to represent its final rejection.

This complex theme of the failed integration of the self (an inner failure of the organic model) is reflected in many disintegrative features of Ruskin's public work in this phase. On the one hand he takes roads that suggest ego annihilation: the squandering of his energies in hopeless, self-sacrificing work; the frequent allusions to the control of his efforts by powers (like *Fors*) which, in effect, speak him; the recovery of innocence in autobiography; his attempt to record, with an innocent eye, the phenomenology of the life-spirit in birds and plants; his conversion to a quasi-mystical Christianity. On the other hand, there are constant regressions from peaceful unity. His message is dispersed, discursive, often fragmentary. He strives for comprehensiveness, but the center will not hold. His syntax is often overtaxed. His language frequently shifts into the hyperbolic and vituperative, though there are moments of painfully deliberate control. This study will make no effort to trace this final despersion of Ruskin's thought in detail. Our interest is in the development, mainly, of two related themes: the mythology of the organic model and the theodicy of the self. In considering these themes it will be useful to divide his work biographically at 1878, the year of his first breakdown.

2

The multifarious events and projects that, apart from his writing, are also Ruskin's life during this stressful period between the publication of *The Queen* and his first attack of insanity would themselves take many pages to survey in detail, as they do in Derrick Leon's absorbing account. Since the biographical details have been set forth by others, and since their relevance to the writing is a separate problem, we here need only to outline briefly the major occurrences and schemes that were shaping Ruskin's destiny at this time.

In 1870 he assumed duties as the first Slade Professor of Art at Oxford, where Greek art, its Italian continuities, and the destructive effects of "science," particularly anatomy, on art would be his major themes. On 5 December 1870 his mother died at the age of ninety; and in that year, following his illness at Matlock, he purchased Brantwood on Coniston Water and began the renovation of it for his home.

The details of his relationship with Rose have been traced by Van Akin Burd in his scholarly introduction to her diaries and in Joan Abse's recent biography of Ruskin. The intricacies of its final phases can only be suggested here. In January and February 1869, while he was at work on *The Queen*, Rose reached her majority and the three years she had told him to wait before renewing his proposal had expired; yet the two were prevented from meeting during this period. After Effie's reply to Mrs. La Touche's first inquiry in 1868, even Rose's occasional letters of encouragement were silenced, and Ruskin ceased recording in his diary the number of days until she should come of age. However, an accidental encounter in January 1870, their first meeting in four years, fired a new cycle of hope and despair. Though she were still forbidden to correspond, a letter from her reached him in February, clearly professing her love for him. This and other less direct communications gave Ruskin hope that, despite her general silence, she had returned to him. Through the intermediation of the Cowper-Temples, Ruskin began again to assert his fitness for marriage. Alarmed once more, Mrs. La Touche again applied to Effie, and this produced her famous declaration of Ruskin's unnaturalness, the letter of 1870, already mentioned, in which she asserts that he could have no communion with a woman except by way of artistic subjects. This letter was shown to Rose, and it effectively cancelled this revival of their relationship.

Yet in 1872 she would again tease him out of reason with vain hopes of reconciliation. By late spring of that year she had given their intermediaries, the MacDonalds and the Cowper-Temples, reason to believe that she had had a change of heart toward Ruskin and that her deteriorating mental and physical health might benefit from a meeting with him. Despite the fact that she had been severely shocked at seeing, while visiting the Cowper-Temples, certain letters in which Ruskin had confessed to the "sin" of auto-erotism in his youth (and, therefore, could no longer be thought of as a "saint"), she agreed to see him. Accordingly, in late June 1872, MacDonald wrote to Ruskin, who was then in Venice, informing him of Rose's state and urging his return. After some hesitation he returned at the end of July to meet with her. The two had some peaceful days together in August, and the hopes that he had struggled to extinguish over the past half-decade were rekindled. But these were hopes against fate, for Ruskin also realized that she was seriously ill. A letter he wrote to MacDonald at this time indicates the effect of these August meetings upon him.

> I thought before I saw her, that she could never undo the evil she has done—but she brought me back into life, and put the past away as if it had not been—with the first full look of her eyes. What she has done now, she has no power to help—it is natural—human pain, and not deadly—but think what it was to have her taught daily horror of me—for years and years, in silence. I had prepared myself to hear that she was dead—and had

died in indignation with me. I know that she is ill—but she is at peace with me, and I may help to save her. I think you may be *very* happy in having done all this, for us both. It is of no use trying to tell you anything that I think or feel about the possible future. Her illness is very grave—*her entire soul and being have been paralysed by the poisoned air*. What I can or may be allowed to do for her, I will—whatever she does to me. She is still happy to be with me, if she will let herself be happy; and she can't forbid my loving her, though she fain would; how infinitely better this is for me than if I had never found the creature. Better all the pain, than to have gone on—as I might twelve years ago—with nothing to love—through life.[57]

But this comparative peace was not to last. Rose suffered yet another relapse and turned her Gorgon face to him again in September. "She is mad," he wrote to MacDonald on 8 September, "—and it is an experience for me of what 'possession' means, which I could not have had otherwise, nor have I any cause to be angry with her, but only to be grieved for us both—and angry with the people who have driven her to this."[58] Hence it was in a mood, as Carlyle put it, of "thick quiet despair again on the personal question"[59] that he took possession of Brantwood in September 1872 to make a home for his remaining years.

In 1873 his cousin Joan Agnew Severn and her husband Arthur came to live with him at Brantwood, where their company and care would become increasingly important to his survival. He began to find also a renewed source of consolation in the testimony of religious art. Travelling abroad in a heavy mood in 1874 he spent a disquieting month at Assisi living in the "Sacristan's cell" at the convent and studying the frescos of the upper and lower churches. "My life here," says the diary for 18 June, "on the whole, is very miserable; the desire to save things, and the perpetual misery of the people, mingle my drink with weeping. I really ought to do something good for the world after being so tormented."[60] And on the nineteenth: "Little sleep last night; many crowding thoughts. Chanced on Jeremiah IV. 23. The uncreation by folly of what had been created by wisdom. Or—by God's anger. The earth becomes void again; the word goes forth: 'Let there be no light.' There is no man, but only dust; and the birds of heaven are fled."[61] But the entry for the following day records an important revelation: "Yesterday discovered Cimabue in lower church, altering my thoughts of all early Italian art."[62] Evidences he found, especially in Giotto and Cimabue, of vital mythic continuity in early Italian art reversed the opinion he had held of it since 1858, involved a personal religious recovery, and provided a central theme for his ongoing Oxford lectures.

In 1874 Rose again encouraged Ruskin to resume their relationship, and this time her parents permitted the exchange of letters as a possible benefit to her health. Ruskin's hopes were revived once more. The La Touches agreed to further meetings between the two, though they still opposed a marriage; and Mrs. La Touche wrote to him, breaking a silence of eight years. Ruskin and Rose spent a number of pleasant social evenings together in the late fall while she was staying in London under a doctor's care. But when she left for her home at Harristown in mid December, Ruskin realized not only that she was dying but that she would be delivered finally into the tyranny of her father, which he now took to be the root cause of her insanity. In January he announced to readers of *Fors* that the woman he had hoped would be his wife was dying. In that month, her health still failing, she was sent again to London for medical care; by mid February, when Ruskin saw her for the last time, her derangement was such that only he could calm her. She returned to Ireland; tormented Ruskin shuttled back and forth that spring, between professorial duties at Oxford, and London, where the Severns might have news of Rose. Her death in May 1875 ended the temporal crises of that tragic enthrallment, leaving him free, in a way, to complete the mythologizing of Rose that he had long since begun.

In 1877 (*Fors*, Letter 79) came his acerbic attack on Whistler's work, a reaction triggered by the painter's "night pieces" exhibited that year at the Grosvenor Gallery, and in particular by the *Nocturne in Black and Gold: The Falling Rocket*. Ruskin's response to this work was predictable. He had attacked Whistler four year earlier for displaying "daub" and "rubbish";[63] furthermore, his neurotic detestation of all excesses of shadow and glitter is evident in his assault on Rembrandt in *Cestus*. The outburst against Whistler, however, while consistent with his standards, was pure indignation, not criticism: "I have seen, and heard, much of Cockney impudence before now; but never expected to hear a coxcomb ask two hundred guineas for flinging a pot of paint in the public's face."[64] It resulted, appropriately, in Whistler's suit for libel and in the celebrated trial of 1878, at which time Ruskin was prevented from testifying by the mental breakdown which the attack on Whistler in its way portended. In that year also came the death of "Papa" Carlyle, and in the following year his first resignation from the Slade Professorship, an action necessitated, he thought, by the decision against him in Whistler v. Ruskin.

His social projects during this period, though they reveal the curious mixture of the practical and quixotic in Ruskin's nature, were tangential to his literary work and can be mentioned only in passing here. Most important among these, of course, was his attempt to form a "body of companions pledged to devote a fixed portion of their belongings to public service and *primarily* to the reclamation, on monastic principles, or cultivation of, food producing land, on which as many persons as possible may live in comfort and refinement."[65] This Christian company for the production and enjoyment of intrinsic wealth, his practical utopia, was conceived by Ruskin as early as 1855. In 1871 he established Saint George's Fund with a "tithe" of his property, 7000 pounds. There were a few additional subscribers, mostly from among Ruskin's friends. In 1878 the company was incorporated as The Guild of Saint George, with Ruskin as its first "Master," a position he retained until his death. The duties of the Master, involving management of the Guild's extant property and designs for its projected utopia (organization, coinage, schools, dress) absorbed much of Ruskin's effort during this period, though little would come of it.

Similarly hopeful but languishing experiments were Mr. Ruskin's Tea Shop in Paddington Street, meant to demonstrate the possibility of selling pure tea in portions and at prices the poor could afford; his street-sweeping experiment, meant to exhibit "an ideally clean street pavement, in the centre of London, in the pleasant environs of Church Lane, St. Giles's";[66] and the Hincksey road-building effort by which he involved his Oxford students in the manual labor of building an ideal stretch of rural road. His publishing venture, by which he eventually became the publisher of all his own books at fixed prices, circumventing the competitive discounting practices of the trade, was more successful; it provided him with a substantial income from his works and pioneered the modern net book system. Meanwhile he was also engaged in endowing and arranging demonstrational art collections at Oxford and in the Guild's educational museum at Walkley. Despite the practical success of a few of these projects, and some happiness also from the people and places in his life, the essential dynamics of this phase are feverish dispersion and fragmentation of effort (driven perhaps by emotional deprivation, self-doubt, and guilt) leading inevitably to frustration and depression.

Some of these mental conditions are suggested also by the form and range of Ruskin's writing during this period between his assumption of the Slade Professorship and his breakdown in 1878. His books at this time consist entirely of lectures, letters, other collections of brief detachable units, and edited works, all forms giving vent to the discursiveness of his mind. We have, first in importance, eighty-seven of the total of ninety-six *Fors Clavigera* letters, "Letters to the Workmen and Labourers of Great Britain," begun in 1871 and published monthly (with notes, correspondence, and Guild Master's reports) until interrupted by his illness in 1878. Then there are ten series of lectures delivered at Oxford during this period (two other series were given in his second tenure, 1883-84): four *Lectures on Art* (1870); *Aratra Pentelici*, six lectures on "The Elements of Sculpture" (delivered in 1870), followed by a seventh entitled *Michael Angelo and Tintoret* (1871); three *Lectures on Landscape* (1871); *The Eagle's Nest: Ten Lectures on the Relation of Natural Science to Art* (1872); *Love's Meinie: Lectures on Greek and English Birds* (1873-81); *Ariadne Florentina*, six lectures on engraving delivered in 1872; *Val d'Arno: Ten Lectures on the Tuscan Art Directly Antecedent to the Florentine Year of Victories* (delivered in 1873); eight lectures entitled *The Aesthetic and Mathematic Schools of Art in Florence* (1874); a series of lectures on glaciers (1874) eventually collected with other geological studies into *Deucalion: Collected Studies on the Lapse of Waves, and the Life of Stones* (1875-83); and, finally, a series of twelve lectures called "Readings in *Modern Painters*" (1877).

We do not wonder that Ruskin's mind was strained at the end of this period, given the quantity and scope of his output. But there were other works. Four collections could be called guidebooks: *Mornings in Florence* (1875, 1876, 1877); his *Guide to the Principal Pictures in the Academy at Venice* (1877), *St. Mark's Rest* (1877, and the *Notes on His Drawings by Turner* (1878). There is *The Laws of Fésole* (1877), a fragmentary and quasi-mythic collection of drawing exercises, and *Proserpina* (1875-82), an attempt to reclassify familiar wildflowers in terms of their mythic associations and the direct description of their visible aspects in ordinary language. As such this work is related to similar phenomenological descriptions of birds and "stones" in *Love's Meinie* and *Deucalion*. Finally, there are his introductions to the first two volumes of his projected *Bibliotheca Pastorum* or "Shepherd's Library": volume 1, *The Economist of Xenophon* (1876) and volume 2, *Rock Honeycomb*, part 1 (1877), which is an edition of the *Psalter* of Sir Philip Sidney.

Although it is difficult to generalize with any accuracy about such a massive and diffuse body of work, a few features stand out and have already been touched on in the foregoing discussion. There is, for instance, an obvious drive toward catholicity of vision here, in both synchronic and diachronic dimensions, as Ruskin struggles to interpret everything by his light: from the current of public and personal events in *Fors* to the generative "grammar" and evolution of the arts in his Oxford lectures, to the forms of nature as living myths or "words of the forming power" in *Proserpina* and other studies in natural history. A familiar passage in *The Bible of Amiens* declares that the "fragmentary expressions of feeling or statements of doctrine" found here and there in his works "bind themselves into a general system of interpretation of Sacred Literature,—both classic and Christian."[67] In fact, his works in this period strive toward a general system for the interpretation of the sacred everywhere: in the biosphere, in the development of the arts, in history and the social order. As such, his system, in this period especially, becomes more and more distinctly opposed to that of the natural sciences; science, as the chilling and dissective mode of knowing, appears to take precedence now over his other enemies: the teaching of art by rule, the "asceticisms" of dead wealth and otherworldly theology. "I am gradually rising to greater indignation against the baseness and conceit of the modern scientific mob," he admitted in a note to *Fors*, Letter 62 (1876), "than even against the mere money-seekers."[68]

Other pervasive characteristics of these works have also been mentioned. There is an increasing tendency to involve the system of his prophecy with the mythologized events of his personal life; this theodicy of the self is particularly evident in *Fors*, where he objectifies, apocalyptically, the actions of the "Forses" upon his personal history. To this feature is tied also that surrender of control which is part of the intricate bond of madness and mysticism. There is the "divine rage" of one crying unheard in a wilderness of hostile values; there is the tendency to relinquish his usual stylistic control to ever more insistent trains of allusive associations; and there is the urgent implication that the message he conveys is not wholly his own but is somehow the vehicle of a tragic conflict of powers at the global or cosmic level.

In this respect, his prophecy as apocalyptic vehicle, these works merely exhibit in a more intense form the polarity that is the basic infrastructure of Ruskin's awareness. He has consistently tended to organize his experience in terms of the oppositions of various forces that are all versions of the symbolism of good and evil that must have been part of his earliest religious training. These opponent forces include light against dark, vital against lethal, organism against mechanism, purity against pollution, benevolent against malevolent powers of storm. It might be shown that this same polarity controls not only his prevalent syntactic structures but also the most common organizational schemes of his books. In this study we have noticed simply that Ruskin's interest in myth centered on certain antagonistic pairs: Hercules and Ladon, Apollo and Python, Christ and Mammon, Athena and the Gorgon, and now, Saint George and the dragon. This adversarial pattern culminates in his annunciation of the coming of the demonic storm cloud to a presumptive final struggle for the sky. Within this adversarial mythology the light-darkness archetype is primary: a hero of light or bright air is characteristically opposed to a serpentine antagonist whose breath or coils signify the light's defilement. This solar conflict is equated also, particularly in *The Queen of the Air*, with the struggle of formative power with the clay. Therefore, as we might expect, the meaning of solar light as the giver of life, health, form, and sight continues to be a central theme in the work of this period as it is in Ruskin's earlier writing. "All up and down my later books," he declares in *Fors*, Letter 66, "from *Unto This Last* to *Eagle's Nest*, and again and again throughout *Fors*, you will find references to the practical connection between physical and spiritual light—of which now I would fain state, in the most unmistakable terms, this sum: That you cannot love the real sun, that is to say physical light and colour, rightly, unless you love the spiritual sun, that is to say justice and truth, rightly."[69]

"Purifying, literally, purging, and cleansing." This, he explains in *The Eagle's Nest*, is the power of light; it is the "meaning of Apollo's war with the Python—of your own St. George's war with the dragon." It is also the meaning of those central Christian metaphors "Giver of Light," "Light of the World," and partly the meaning of the "Sun of Justice," which "is said to rise with health in its wings." The letting in of light is thus "the first 'sacred art' all men have to learn." Therefore, the one piece of advice he would give to the world's well-meaning people is, " 'For Heaven's sake—literally for Heaven's sake—let the place alone and clean it.' "[70]

Further, "the 'fiat lux' of creation is . . . in the deep sense of it, 'fiat anima.' " This is because "even the power of the eye itself, as such, is *in* its animation. You do not see *with* the lens of the eye. You see *through* that, and by means of that, but you see with the soul of the eye." Therefore, "sight is an absolutely spiritual phenomenon; accurately, and only, to be so defined; and 'let there be light,' is as much, when you understand it, the ordering of intelligence, as the ordering of vision."[71] Given the spiritual power of light and sight, it will be, of course, the "lowest national atheism to drive out the sun with smoke."[72]

But Ruskin has a more complicated point to make about light, sight, and the ordering of intelligence. There is an organic, hence spiritual, relationship between our natural capacity of sight and the objects we were meant to see: "we are as we see." This is the deeper meaning of the metaphor that makes the eye the "light" of the body. "Literally, if the eye be pure, the body is pure; but if the light of the body be but darkness, how great is that darkness!"[73] But what is purity of sight? What are we meant to see? The crux of Ruskin's argument is that organic or pure sight, in art at least, "has nothing to do with structures, causes, or absolute facts; but only with appearances."[74] Therefore the "artist has no concern with invisible *structures,* organic or inorganic." Though the artist "has much concern with invisible *things,*"[75] as in mythic painting, he is concerned only with the visible aspects of what he imagines, as they show themselves to him. Pure sight, then, appears to be essentially phenomenological, not concerned with analysis or anatomy but with what reveals itself to plain sight and in the manner in which it reveals itself.

This is the basis of Ruskin's present hostility to science; scientific awareness is dissective and analytic; it is opposed to purity of sight. Therefore, in *Michael Angelo and Tintoret* he argues that the anatomical science of Michelangelo represented a destructive impulse in art. Finally, to this doctrine of the natural bond of sight to its object under solar light, we must add his view—expressed particularly in *The Queen of the Air* and *Aratra Pentelici*—that the proper objects of the artist's sight (under Athena's wisdom) are those organic forms that reveal the contest of life with clay. "Sophia," as he declares in *The Eagle's Nest,* "is the faculty which recognizes in all things their bearing upon life."[76] If we take his view that there is a natural unity of light, sight, and vital form, which he expresses mythologically in the joint powers of his Athena and Apollo, and remember also that for him this unity was threatened by antiorganic powers (science, mechanism, competitive greed) that he associated symbolically with the chilling storm-serpent-plague complex, we have the thematic core of his diverse writings during this period. His prophetic task was to read the "words of the forming power" (and its opponent power) everywhere and to justify these words to his age; in a sense his writings are now a massive, though discursive, theodicy of the unitary pre-objective world (Husserl's *lebenswelt*), our precarious paradise. But, since this threatened world is also a projection of his own psychic struggle with ominous powers, it is at the same time a theodicy of the self. Both theodicies are entwined in *Fors Clavigera.*

His deliberately antiscientific effort to read and reclassify natural forms as "living myths," begun in second lecture of *The Queen,* is carried forward fragmentarily in this period in *Proserpina, Love's Meinie* and *Deucalion.* His emphasis in these works is on pure description of the visible external form of the thing as opposed to an analysis of its structure. The natural object is intentionally viewed as the exponent of formative energy. It is likely to be perceived also in relational awareness of its life to ours; Ruskin tends to name or classify the object in terms of its mythological associations, because the mythic name epitomizes the form's relation to human life. "Mythology of the bird," he declares in *Love's Meinie,* "would always be for us the most important part of its natural history."[77] Perhaps the essence of his approach to these "living myths" is expressed in a remark he makes about the being of a pebble in *Deucalion*: that the fortune of Sheffield would be made if it could tell what the pebble is—"what it *is,* . . . not merely what *it is made of.* . . . To know what it is, we must know what it can do and suffer."[78] Just as these works tend toward the reading of natural forms as mythic expression of the life struggle in their clay, as a language of the "forming power," so *Fors Clavigera* is an apocalyptic reading of intentions of the Fates in the social tendencies of his age, and the Oxford lectures, in their central theme, trace the impact of the Greek mythic "school" of line and light on later art. The whole body of his work in this phase can thus be viewed as fragments of a sacred scheme or theodicy centered symbolically on the light-darkness archetypal conflict and pivoting, biographically, on his conversion to Christian mysticism in 1874 as the result of his discoveries of Greek mythic continuities in Christian art.

3

Fors Clavigera, like *Aratra Pentelici* and *Proserpina,* has some important conceptual links with Greek myth, and there are many allusions to mythic figures scattered throughout the sequence of letters. Structurally and stylistically its antecedents in his work are the impulsive *Time and Tide* letters and the freely associative style (his "third way of writing") that first appears in *The Cestus of Aglaia.* The basic conception of the work derives from a design he had seen many years before on a bronze mirror case, a design representing "the figure of the death-goddess Atropos, who is on the point of driving a nail fast home with a hammer, the symbol of unalterably determined, or fixed, fate." The work's final title stands, plurisignatively, for his conception of the three determining lines of being, the three "Forses": Force, Fortitude, and Fortune. *Clavigera* means that Fors, in her separate aspects, bears either the club, the key, or the nail. The principle signification, however, is simply "Fortune, the Nail-Bearer," indicating that the work's controlling subject is the mystery and finality of fate. "The current and continual purpose of *Fors Clavigera,*" he declares in Letter 43 (1874), "is to explain the powers of Chance, or Fortune (Fors), as she offers to men the conditions of prosperity; and as these conditions are accepted or refused, nails down and fastens their fate for ever, being thus 'Clavigera,'—'nail-bearing.' "[79] As the letters proceed Ruskin tends increasingly to associate the three "Forses" directly with the Greek Fates; he emphasizes particularly the association of the third Fors with Atropos, "the death goddess." She is also identified with Jael. Each aspect of Fors is also identified with a particular Greek hero such as Force with Hercules, Fortitude with Ulysses, and Fortune (Necessity) with Lycurgus.

Fors is not, of course, a systematic work, any more than is the work of fate. Yet, like the concurrent and equally unsystematic series of Oxford lectures and the miscellaneous studies in natural history, its concern is with the mysterious shaping laws of life; here, in society and its work; there, in natural form and the progress of art. Ruskin's aim is to reveal, as time tells, the action of the three "Forses," especially Fors-Atropos, in his "world"—his whole sphere of awareness, subjective and objective (excepting only the unconfessed), including his environment, the quality of social life, major and minor events that catch his attention, movements, policies, schools of art, and the growth of his own mind. The style of the work is as shifting as its contents; portions of it are variously theoretical or analytic, confessional, ruminative, riddling, vituperative, gossipy, scholarly, aphoristic, or freely associative. One might argue that in Julia Kristeva's sense it is an *avant-garde* or revolutionary text, representing a subjectivity in process, the predominance of struggle over structure. "The gesture of the moment," Ruskin said, "must be as the humour takes me."[80]

Yet a mystical fervor makes itself felt in the letters written after the epiphany of 1874. A passage in Letter 86 (1878) reviews his mission of study among the "seers" of history and hints at some new plane of comprehension (or self-integration) to which he also has risen. The "Spiritual lesson" of history, he concludes, is "that in the ages of faith, conditions of prophecy and seer-ship exist, among the faithful nations, in painting and scripture, which are also immortal and divine;—of which it has been my own special mission to speak for the most part of my life; but only of late have I understood completely the meaning of what had been taught me."[81]

Composed of ninety-six letters, some 650,000 words, written over a span of fifteen years, *Fors* is in one sense planless, then dictated by moment, mood, and event. By its wind-formed drifts of utterance Ruskin gives partly the impression that its message is not his, but is sibylline, written by the Fates through him. "Nay, I am wrong," he notes in Letter 49, "even in speaking of it [his object in *Fors*] as a plan or scheme at all. It is only a method of uniting the force of all good plans and wise schemes: it is a principle and tendency, like the Law of form in a crystal; not a plan."[82] Yet within these apparently fortuitous etchings of fate, three thematic elements are fundamental, and they are typical of Ruskin's thought during this period. These recurrent and unifying elements might be called the apocalyptic, the organic, and the eschatological.

Four other primary motifs are closely interwoven with these; they are: the recurrent storm-cloud theme; frequent attacks on the inorganic, antimythic world view, including science, "mechanism," and economism; autobiographical or confessional references; constant allusions to scripture, myth, and the visionary in art. There are other materials in the work, of course; Ruskin appears there not only as critic, prophet, and exemplary sufferer but as the organizer of Saint George's Guild and other social schemes. Finally, while the seven features just mentioned are interdependent qualities of the structure and texture of *Fors*, we must speak of them as if they were separable units, our primary interest here being simply to indicate the function of one element: myth.

Fors is apocalyptic, essentially, as a revelation of the destiny of contemporary England, suggesting the fate of modern industrial societies in general; that fate is suggested primarily by references to the onset of strange meteorological effects and by patterns of events that reveal ominous rents in the social fabric and are thus intimations of alienation or revolution. The intentions of Fors, he declared in Letter 13, while indecipherable, follow "certain laws of storm, which are in the last degree wonderful and majestic."[83] Much later, in Letter 81, he insisted that *Fors Clavigera* was not "intended as counsel adapted to the present state of the public mind, but is the assertion of the code of Eternal Laws which the public mind *must* eventually submit to or die"; its purpose was to reveal the inevitable, not to correct the mere "manners, customs, feelings, or modified conditions of piety in the modern England which I have to warn of the accelerated approach either of Revolution or Destruction."[84]

The work concerns the organic in at least three senses: in its attempt to reveal the ultimate laws of cohesion in things ("like the laws of form in a crystal"), the "Forses" that "bind us to others in life and death"; in the fact that Ruskin lets the work take the shape of experience itself ("the gesture of the moment"), using in it both the immediate and the archetypal; and, most clearly, it concerns the organic model in the sense that the messages of "the forming power" transmitted through him point ultimately to the fate of the biosphere. *Fors*, he said, is "a system not mine, nor Kant's, nor Comte's—but that which Heaven has taught every true man's heart." And further, "I use the word 'Heaven' here in the absolutely literal sense, meaning the blue sky, and the light and air of it."[85]

But the storm laws that Ruskin cannot help but reveal are not an ongoing system but a terminal one; our fate is nailed down forever in every act. The central message of the work is simply "that on disobedience always follows darkness, the forerunner of death." And we, of course, have been disobedient. In this sense *Fors* is eschatological; doom is imminent in it. And Ruskin announces it *"Ex Cathedra Pestilentiae."*[86]

The primary messengers of the coming judgment are strange effects of weather, storm cloud and plague wind, obscuring and chilling the light. Of course practically everything discussed in *Fors*, even Whistler's "night pieces," is seen as a manifestation of the fatal infection in the quality of modern life; but the storm symbolism unites the mythology of *The Queen of the Air* with the theme of judgment in Scripture: "The ungodly were scourged with strange storms." Ruskin, significantly, had begun to observe these phenomena in 1871, the year *Fors* was begun, and there are recurrent allusions to these "strange storms" throughout the work. Thus, for instance, in Letter 8, he notes, being now fifty and a careful observer of skies since he was five, the new appearance of a "dry black veil" covering the sky. It is simply "poisonous smoke," but it "looks to me as if it were made of dead men's souls," the souls of "murdered men" in the ground of the world.[87]

In Letter 60, the prophet complains that, whereas the order of creation is *Fiat Lux*, "the United Grand Steam Percussion and Corrosion Company, Limited (Offices, London, Paris, and New York), issues its counter-order, Let there be darkness; and that the Master of Creation not only at once submits to this order, by fulfilling the constant laws He had ordained concerning smoke,—but farther, supernaturally or miraculously, enforces the order by sending a poisonous black wind, also from the east, of an entirely corrosive, deadly, and horrible quality, with which, from him that hath not, He takes away also that light he hath; and changes the sky during what remains of the day,—on the average now three days out of five,—into a mere dome of ashes, differing only by their enduring frown and slow pestilence from the passing darkness and showering death of Pompeii."[88] And in Letter 61, this storm turns inward in its effects, becoming linked to spreading insanity and spiritual plague: "In times of more ignorant sinning, they were punished by plagues of the body; but now, by plagues of the soul, and widely infectious insanities, making every true physician of souls helpless and every false effort triumphant. Nor are we without great and terrible signs of supernatural calamity, no less in grievous changes and deterioration of climate, than in forms of mental disease."[89]

Ruskin's chief antagonist in *Fors*, and the essential disobedience for which the storm-plague infection is a punishment, is the value complex represented by science, mechanism, and laissez faire economics. He has no satisfactory word for this complex of fatal values; hence the utility of the old dragon. However, the prime mover of the whole antagonistic system is obviously a false conception of wealth that sets it against the only true wealth, life. Life, for Ruskin, now means the mysterious unity and harmony of the organic model, coupled with a new religious emphasis on recognition of an obedience to its divine ordinance. Thus in Letter 75 (1877) we are told that the only way to wealth "so far as in your present power, is this: first, acknowledgement of the mystery of divine life, kindly and dreadful, throughout creation; then the taking up your own part as the Lord of this life; to protect, assist, or extinguish, as it is commanded you."[90]

Science, as the neutralizer of all mythologies but its own, is the great antagonist of all vital mystery in the intellectual sphere; therefore, its achievements are frequently attacked in *Fors*. The result of the progress of science, Ruskin points out, has been the disappearance of any sacred *telos* of hierarchic order of things, "both of any 'arche,' beginning, or princedom of things, and of any holy or hieratic end of things . . . except in eggs of vermin and embryos of apes."[91] Along with the disappearance of all sacred order goes the loss of the distinctively human position, the disappearance of man: "Now in exactly the sense that modern Science declares there is no such thing as a Flower, it has declared there is no such thing as a Man, but only a transitional form of Ascidians and apes."[92] Along with the disappearance of man goes his sense of ordained curatorship over the lower forms of nature, and with it the sense of any such power over him: "When men rule the earth rightly, and feel the power of their own souls over it, and its creatures, as a beneficent and authoritative one, they recognize the power of higher spirits also; and the Name of God becomes 'hallowed' to them, admirable and wonderful."[93]

In "mechanism" Ruskin recognizes a dangerous intermediate power between science and economics. Its effects are the pollution and destruction of nature, the disappearance of the vital human touch from art and artifact, and the transformation of man into the tool of his tools: "Day after day your souls will become more mechanical, more servile."[94] To mechanism he opposes the significance of instinct in all art: "Nor has ever any great work been accomplished by human creatures, in which instinct was not the principal mental agent, or in which the methods of design could be defined by rule, or apprehended by reason. It is therefore that agency through mechanism destroys the powers of art, and sentiments of religion, together."[95] As for the industrial uses of mechanism his rules are simple: "You are to do good work, whether you live or die. . . . And be sure of this, literally: *you must simply rather die than make any destroying mechanism or compound.* You are to be *literally* employed in cultivating the ground, or making useful things, and carrying them where they are wanted. . . . In your powder and petroleum manufactory, we work no more."[96]

E. T. Cook has pointed out that *Fors* is, among other things, "a book of Personal Confessions" and a "Confession of Faith."[97] We have already referred in an earlier chapter to Ruskin's accounts of his religious crises in the work, particularly in Letter 96 (1877). What must be said here is simply that by means of the autobiographical and confessional elements in *Fors*, Ruskin makes himself the hero of it, that is, he establishes his fitness to prophecy. He declares, in effect, as the work proceeds, that he is one who has had and is having the lived *experience* (as opposed to mere learning) that qualifies him to interpret life. This experience is of three kinds (apart from long intimacy with nature and the arts): the suffering of personal losses and the frustration of cherished purposes, making the prophet an exemplary sufferer at the hands of Atropos; the religious crises that mark the prophet as man of faith; and, in the letters after 1877, nearness to madness, by which the prophet links himself with visionaries of the past.

In Letter 88, for instance, he comments frankly on his recent illness, marking, however, "the precise and sharp distinction between the state of morbid inflammation of brain which gave rise to false visions . . . and the not morbid, however dangerous, states of more or less excited temper, and too much quickened thought which gradually led up to the illness." His point is that, up to the "transitional moment" when his vision became unhealthy, "this more or less inflamed, yet still perfectly healthy, condition of mental power, *may be traced by any watchful reader, in 'Fors,' nearly from its beginning,*—that manner of mental ignition or irritation being for the time a great additional force, enabling me to discern more clearly, and say more vividly, what for long years it had been in my heart to say." His madness, therefore, is simply visionary power which has passed through some "transitional edges."[98]

Coming to the uses of myth in *Fors*, apart from the "Forses" themselves and their messengers of storm cloud and plague wind, one can find the main outlines of the work's mythic symbolism in his earlier writing; so also with the cloud-fate connection. In general his mythwork here differs from his earlier studies in that Greek-Christian archetypal continuities are more likely to be stressed; further, there is an element of personal or "mystical" involvement as he receives direct messages from his mythic Saint Ursula; and finally, in the same vein, one has the feeling that the whole mythic scheme of the work is obscurely linked to his, the hero's, personal epiphany that becomes something like the peripety of its tragic advance, or the redemptive crisis of its personal theodicy. There is something analogous to overreaching tragic purpose in his determination to delineate the laws of fate for his world; there is tragic passion as the fates descend on him in the loss of his earthly hope of love and the frustration of his world-redemptive schemes, and tragic perception and identification as he rediscovers the faith of the "purist" painters through the Assisi frescoes of the life of Saint Francis, especially since this "reconversion" is tied aesthetically to his discovery of the Greek "school" of solemn or tragic chiaroscuro.

Apollo as purifying light and the power of sight, associated with the "Sun of Justice," is frequently alluded to here, of course, as is Athena in her capacities as the air, inspiration, and especially as the spirit of life in contest with clay. We learn that the chthonic "earth-giants" were her first enemies, before Medusa. Saint George and the dragon are linked to these Greek symbols. Saint George's adversary was descended, Ruskin supposes, from those of Apollo and Perseus: "The representation of all his spiritual enemies under the form of the Dragon was simply the natural habit of the Greek mind: the stories of Apollo delivering Latona from the Python, and of Perseus delivering Andromeda from the sea monster, had been as familiar as the pitcher and wine-cups they had been painted on.[99] All these figures have serpent antagonists, earth creatures to Ruskin, in which the ascendency of the life spirit over the clay is minimal. Further, "the Dragon is too true a creature," he notes. "That it is an indisputably living and venomous creature, materially, has been the marvel of the world, innocent and guilty, not knowing what to think of the terrible worm; nor whether to worship it, as the Rod of their lawgiver, or to abhor it as the visible symbol of everlasting Disobedience."[100] This same ambivalence appears to be present in the relation of Athena to Medusa, who is, in Ruskin's conception, at once her chief enemy slain and her antithetical self. These points verge on the problem of the hidden kinship of the hero and his dragon adversary that Ruskin does not perceive, though his student J. R. Anderson suggests, in *Saint Mark's Rest*, that "George" and "Gorgon" may be descended from the same root.[101] Ruskin, however, derives George from the Greek spirit of agriculture who had harnessed the dragon for labor.[102]

Another group of mythic symbols of particular use to him in *Fors* is that connected with Theseus and the Minotaur. Daedalus the labyrinth builder appears as the master of "mechanical as opposed to imaginative art."[103] The labyrinth itself is a symbol of soulless work and its entanglements; its spiral form is reproduced in Dante's hell, with Minos, who stands for retributive justice, assigning evildoers their places in the infernal labyrinth. Ruskin is fascinated by a Florentine conception of the labyrinth in which it looks like a low chimney; thus an intuitive link between the labyrinth and the storm cloud is established for him.[104] Theseus is the "setter to rights . . . the exterminator of every bestial and savage element, the type of human, or humane, power."[105] He enters the web of soulless, mechanical work and slays the monster that inhabits it, the Minotaur, who stands for anger, and lust for wealth,[106] and who is also "the type of the English nation today: man-bull."[107] Ariadne's clue, her thread, "implied that even victory over the monster would be vain unless you could disentangle yourself from his web also,"[108] by love.

But the most personal thread of mythic symbolism for Ruskin in *Fors* is that involving Persephone, Saint Ursula, and (in his private thought) Rose. Here his thought shifts from the public and prophetic use of the mythic image (which is nevertheless "believed in" as Athena was) to the private and mystical communion with the mythic figure. Some of his readers were evidently alarmed when, in speaking of the "Eastern Question" in *Fors*, Letter 74, he announced that the girl-goddess-saint had sent him "her dianthus out of her bedroom window with her love." That is, it was the naturalistic yet mythic figure realized in his mind from Carpaccio's *St. Ursula's Dream* who, as he said, "sent me the flower of the dawn in her window, to put me in mind of,—the religious meanings of the matter [The Eastern Question]."[109] Thus a fortuitous but ordinary event, the gift of a dianthus to him by a friend at Venice in 1877, is transmuted by the weave of *Fors* into a major mythic event, an Ariadne's clue for its hero. Dianthus, Ruskin explained means "flower of God," especially of "the Greek Father of the Gods," the god of day (Max Müller's *dyaus-pitar*, "Jupiter"). Ruskin would also have been aware of the association, in the solar mythologists, of the rosy dawn with Athena; however, he does not make any explicit connection between Ursula and the Queen of the Air, rather he associates her with Persephone, who appears briefly in *The Queen* as the goddess of the bloom and fading of flowers and of fate, subjects that were then weighing heavily on his mind.

John Ruskin after Vittore Carpaccio. *The Dream of Saint Ursula*. Reproduced from *Works* (Library Edition), vol. 27.

In his study of Carpaccio's paintings of Saint Ursula's life, and of the "old myth," her legend, which he presents in *Fors* Letter 71 (1876), Ruskin found three primary links with his own life end thought. First he found a private spiritual and emotional significance in Carpaccio's vision of the virgin rest and "rising in the eternal morning" of this girl who preferred death to a loveless marriage. "For this is the first lesson which Carpaccio wrote in his Venetian words for the creatures of this restless world,—that Death is better than *their* life; and that not bridegroom rejoices over bride as they rejoice who marry not, nor are given in marriage, but are as the angels of God, in Heaven."[110]

Secondly, Ruskin perceived that not only did Carpaccio truly visualize the beauty and peace of the saint's virgin rest but also by the plants he placed in her room (olive, vervain, and dianthus) he expressed her connection with the Greek Persephone (and possibly also Athena). So Ruskin, following the painter as he understands him, comes to think of the girl as at once a personal and a mythic figure. He had always argued that the Greeks regarded their deities as "personal" powers. Therefore, to those of his readers of *Fors* who were disturbed by the idea of his receiving messages from her, those who "do not believe in Ursula's personality," he explained that "all great myths are conditions of slow manifestation to human imperfect intelligence; . . . [spiritual personalities] can only be revealed, in their reality, by the gradual confirmation in the matured soul of what were at first only its instinctive desires and figurative perceptions."[111] However, in a later *Fors* letter (88) he seemed to stress her archetypal as opposed to her personal significance to him. "When I say that 'St. Ursula sent me a flower with her love' it means that I myself am in the habit of thinking of the Greek Persephone, the Latin Proserpina, and the Gothic St. Ursula, as of the same living spirit."[112]

The third element of answering sympathy that Ruskin found in Carpaccio's paintings of Ursula will bring us to the essence of his art teaching during this period and to the point of intersection between the aesthetics of his Oxford lectures and the personal theodicy of *Fors*, which occurs in the moment of religio-aesthetic conversion he describes in Letter 76, 1877. He had begun the serious study of Carpaccio's work in 1869, shortly after finishing *The Queen of the Air*. During the seventies he became convinced that here was a great Christian "naturalist" painter, with "purist" leanings like his own, who was at the same time thoroughly versed in the symbolism of the Greek religion. Carpaccio, in brief, was a painter who participated in that continuum of mythic vision he had discussed at the beginning of "Athena Chalinitis," a tradition to which he (and Turner) also belonged. Carpaccio, he felt, was at once a naturalist, a mystic, and a master of iconology. This viewpoint is the essential thesis of the discussions of Carpaccio's works, especially the Saint George series, in *Saint Mark's Rest*.

But this assertion of Carpaccio's place in the mythic and visionary tradition is simply a confirmation of the main line of reasoning in his Oxford lectures. His Oxford teaching begins (following, as it does, immediately upon his Greek studies for *The Queen*) in his discovery of the true significance and greatness of Greek art, which he had largely neglected in his earlier aesthetic studies. More accurately, he extends his mythology of the light-darkness archetype and the organic model, the powers of Apollo and Athena, to include Greek aesthetics. He finds (in the *Lectures on Art*) that the Greek artists are the founders of all great tragic chiaroscuro, the "school of solemn light." Not only this, they are the true masters of organic form in sculpture (*Aratra Pentelici*), representing the strength of life in its contest with matter, opposing the grotesque, the momentary, and the anatomical in the rendering of living form. However, the final point to be made here is that this discovery of the roots of light and life in Greek art leads in later lectures to a rediscovery of these elements in the Christian "purist" painters from whose work he had been "un-converted" concurrently with the loss of his own faith in 1858.

To judge from the retrospective account of it in *Fors* Letter 76, the conversion of 1874 was a relatively rational yet instantaneous aesthetic enlightenment. That is, while living in the sacristan's cell at Saint Francis's church in Assisi, he had been allowed "to have scaffolding erected above the high altar, and therefore above the body of St. Francis which lies in the lower chapel beneath it; and thence to draw what I could of the great fresco of Giotto, 'The Marriage of Poverty and Francis.' "[113] And there, while making this drawing, he discovered the great fallacy of his previous art teaching. He found, simply, that

> all Giotto's "weaknesses" (so called) were merely absences of material science. He did not know, and could not, in his day, so much of perspective as Titian,—so much of the laws of light and shade, or so much of technical composition. But I found he was in the make of him, and contents, a very much stronger and greater man than Titian; that the things I had fancied easy in his work, because they were so unpretending and simple, were nevertheless entirely inimitable; that the Religion in him, instead of weakening, had solemnized and developed every faculty of his heart and hand: and finally that his work, in all the innocence of it, was yet a human achievement and possession, quite above everything that Titian had ever done![114]

School of Giotto. Detail from *The Marriage of Poverty and Saint Francis* (formerly attributed to Giotto). Lower Church of S. Francesco, Assisi. (Alinari Editorial Photocolor Archives)

However, as the phrase "and therefore above the body of St. Francis" suggests, this change was not simply an aesthetic oversight discovered. It was, as Cook has pointed out, bound up with his state of mind: respite from despair in his pursuit of Rose, response to the roses above Lady Poverty in the fresco, spiritual identification with St. Francis.

> Ruskin had been living at the home of St. Francis, drawing the pictures of his life and passion, writing in the cell of his convent, handling the relics of the saint, and feeling ever more and more in sympathy with him who "in his Catholic wholeness used to call the very flowers sisters, brothers," and who "took the doves out of the fowler's hand." His mood was one of spiritual exaltation, and "he dreamt that they had made him a brother of the third degree of the order of St. Francis—a fancy that took strong hold of his mind."[115]

Whatever may have been the private emotional bases of this experience with the fresco, then attributed to Giotto, Ruskin chose to explain it publicly in religio-aesthetic terms, merely connecting for us the aesthetic discovery with some sort of spiritual condition involving his "religion of Humanity." But when we recall that it was from the Greek religion as he understood it in the late 1850's that Ruskin had derived his particular "religion of Humanity," and then that Titian had been valued as its standard-bearer in art, we begin to suspect that the elevation of Giotto over him, coming at the end of a period of intensive study of Greek art, will be linked to these Greek studies in much the same way as his apotheosis of Titian and his followers in 1870 is tied to his conclusion that their greatness depended upon the fusion in them of Gothic color and solemn Greek chiaroscuro.

4

His final theory of color, that of the Oxford lectures, depends primarily upon two earlier observations of his which are obscurely connected by the symbolic rose. The first, and prior, is his doctrine of scarlet shadow, built on his observation that there is no shadow in the rose except what is composed of color. We noticed in Chapter 10 that in *Modern Painters*, volume 5, the rose shadow, represented by analogy the highest condition of the colorist's art, and in actual color, Turner's distinctive hue. The second basis of his advanced color theory was the observation that the primary object of the Greek worship was a god of wisdom and light, really "light" in two senses. But this solarist notion is itself bound to the rose because its hue is symbolic of Apollo's purifying combat with Python. For Ruskin the rose concentrates symbolically the effects of light in giving vital form, color, and purity:

The rose is the most beautiful organism existing in matter not vital, expressive of the direct action of light on the earth, giving lovely form and colour at once, (compare the use of it by Dante, as the form of the sainted crowd in highest heaven); and . . . therefore, the rose is, in the Greek mind, essentially a Doric flower, expressing the worship of Light, as the Iris or Ion is an Ionic one, expressing the worship of the Winds and Dew.[116]

In the fifth of his *Lectures on Art* (1870), the lecture on "Line," his doctrine of colored shade brought to completeness. First, we are reminded that

every light is a shadow compared to higher lights, till we reach the brightness of the sun; and every shadow is a light, compared to lower shadows, till we reach the darkness of night.

Every colour used in painting, except pure white and black, is therefore a light and shade at the same time. It is a light with reference to all below it, and a shade with reference to all above it.[117]

And therefore

every *colour* in painting must be a shadow to some brighter colour, and a light to some darker one—all the while being a positive colour itself. And the great splendour of the Venetian school arises from their having seen and held from the beginning this great fact—that shadow is as much colour as light, often much more.[118]

This perception of colored shade—the highest naturalism in terms of color—Ruskin thought the Venetians owed, like their worldly humanism, indirectly to Greek belief. And he was concerned in these *Lectures* to trace Venetian (hence Turnerian) color backward from school to school to its source in the Hellenic worship of light. Toward this purpose the Greeks are introduced a few pages further on as founders of what he will shortly call the "School of Light." As worshippers of "bright, serene, resistless wisdom," sprung from the head of Dyaus-Zeus, "the god of *Day*." Their spiritual propensity (like Turner's) was to seek light in art:

The Greeks look upon all colour first as light; they are, as compared with other races, insensitive to hue, exquisitely sensitive to phenomena of light. And their linear school passes into one of flat masses of light and darkness, represented in the main by four tints,—white, black, and two reds, one brick colour, more or less vivid, the other dark purple; these two standing mentally [for] their favourite πορφύρεος colour, in its light and dark powers.[119]

In contrast with the Greeks, however, the nations of Northern Europe are "at first entirely insensible to light and shade, but exquisitely sensitive to colour, and their linear decoration is filled with flat tints, infinitely varied, but with no expression of light and shade.''[120]

From these racial traits it follows, as Ruskin sees it, that the earliest forms of painting—the "School of Line"—must have developed into "Greek, Line with Light" on the one hand and "Gothic, Line with Colour" on the other. And these divisions in turn produced "the two vast medieval schools": the School of "Mass and Light," characterized by "exquisite drawing of solid form, and little perception of colour: sometimes as little of sentiment" and the School of "Mass and Colour," from which we have "flat and infinitely varied colour, with exquisite character and sentiment added, in the forms represented; but little perception of shadow.''[121]

Ruskin will not talk long about the color or about light and shade without beginning to use them as metaphors for the artist's perception. And so here when he speaks of the Gothic colorists as having "little perception of shadow" as against the descendents of the Greek school, we sense that a spiritual distinction is about to be made; and we are prepared for the following lecture, "Light," in which the purist-naturalist dichotomy is correlated with the colorist-chiaroscurist one, all in terms of the organizing light metaphor, and all profoundly rooted for us in Greek belief.

He begins with the assertion that the two great paths of advance in art—the way by color and the way by light and shade—have been taken by types of minds as entirely different as their chosen departments of tone. The colorists have been, by and large, "men of cheerful, natural, and entirely sane disposition in body and mind," On the other hand, the chiaroscurists—with whom, incidentally, Ruskin linked his own work—have been "men of the highest powers of thought, and most earnest desire for truth," men who "long for light and knowledge of all that light can show. But seeking for light, they perceive also darkness; seeking for truth and substance they find vanity. They look for form in the earth,—for dawn in the sky; and seeking these, they find formlessness in the earth and night in the sky.''[122] In sum, as to their desire for "light,"

> you have then these two great divisions of human mind: one, content with the colours of things, whether they are dark or light; the other seeking light pure, as such, and dreading darkness as such. One, also, content with the coloured aspects and visionary shapes of things; the other seeking their form and substance. And, as I said, the school of knowledge, seeking light, perceives, and has to accept and deal with obscurity: and seeking form, it has to accept and deal with formlessness, or death.[123]

This is the spiritual division for which that of tone has become a metaphor. It is also plain that Ruskin is bringing together two essential qualities which he has now traced to Greek art—light and naturalism. Therefore, as we might expect, the early schools of color are to be generally identified with what has elsewhere been called Purist art. For we are meant to understand that "the school of colour in Europe . . . is essentially Gothic *Christian*: and full of comfort and peace. Again, the school of light is essentially Greek, and full of sorrow."[124]

Ruskin's main purpose here in his lecture on "Light" (the sixth of his *Lectures on Art*) is to clarify the spiritual origins of this school of light, which he will now also call variously the Greek, naturalistic, or chiaroscurist school. "You, cannot but wonder why," he begins, "this being the melancholy temper of the great Greek or naturalistic school, I should have called it the school of light." The reason, of course, is to be sought in the knowledge and dread of darkness consequent upon its love of light. It must be remembered that this school's "first development and all its final power, depend on Greek sorrow, and Greek religion."[125] And here we will find the source of all true understanding of the dread of psycho-physical darkness. It is to be found, Ruskin believes, in two particular aspects of the Greek faith. In the first place,

> the school of light is founded in the Doric worship of Apollo, and the Ionic worship of Athena, as the spirits of life in the light, and of life in the air, opposed each to their own contrary deity of death—Apollo to the Python, Athena to the Gorgon—Apollo as life in light, to the earth spirit of corruption in darkness;—Athena, as life by motion, to the Gorgon spirit of death by pause, freezing or turning to stone . . . both of them, when angry, taking to men the form of evil which is their opposite—Apollo slaying by poisoned arrow, by pestilence; Athena by cold, the black aegis on her breast.[126]

But lying still deeper

> there is the Greek conception of *spiritual* darkness; of the anger of fate, whether foredoomed or avenging; the root and theme of all Greek tragedy; the anger of the Erinnyes, and Demeter Erinnys, compared to which the anger either of Apollo or Athena is temporary and partial;—and also, while Apollo or Athena only slay, the power of Demeter and the Eumenides is over the whole life; so that in the stories of Bellerophon, of Hippolytus, of Orestes, or Oedipus, you have an incomparably deeper shadow than any that was possible to the thought of later ages, when the hope of the Resurrection had become definite.[127]

Having thus traced the school of light back to the Greek conception of inward darkness, Ruskin devotes much of the rest of his lecture on light to examining evidences of their impressions of the power of light as recorded in vase paintings. Then, as the lecture is drawn towards its conclusion, he looks away from the Greeks toward modern schools again. First, he redefines the "Greek school" in such a way as to remind us that it had continuity in the history of art, at least down into the work of Turner.

> Remember that in future, when I briefly speak of the Greek school of art with reference to questions of delineation, I mean the entire range of the schools, from Homer's days to our own, which concern themselves with material form—beginning practically for us with these Greek vase paintings, and closing practically for us with Turner's sunset on the *Téméraire*; being throughout a school of captivity and sadness, but of intense power; and which in its technical method of shadow on material form, as well as in its essential temper, is centrally represented to you by Dürer's two great engravings of the "Melancolia" and the "Knight and Death."[128]

He then redefines the "Gothic school" in such a way as to indicate that it generally remained primitive and incomplete without some sort of union with the "Greek school," though work resulting from this union is greater than that of either progenitor.

> When I briefly speak to you of the Gothic school . . . I mean the entire and much more extensive range of schools extending from the earliest art in Central Asia and Egypt down to our own day in India and China:— schools which have been content to obtain beautiful harmonies of colour without any representation of light; and which have, many of them, rested in such imperfect expressions of form as could be so obtained; schools usually in some measure childish, or restricted in intellect, and similarly childish or restricted in their philosophies or faiths; but contented in the restriction; and in the more powerful races, capable of advance to nobler development than the Greek schools, though the consummate art of Europe has only been accomplished by the union of both.[129]

This great union of schools occurred, of course, at Venice; and it is plain in Ruskin's next lecture—Lecture 7, "Colour"—that the whole purpose of this spiritual genealogy of schools has been to exalt by elaborate rationale what had already been exalted in the 4th and 5th volumes of *Modern Painters*, Venetian colored shade. The doctrine for which he has been so carefully supplying spiritual roots is, it will be remembered, simply that the Venetians and all the greatest colorists have seen that shadows are as much colors as lights are. In *Modern Painters* this Venetian achievement appears simply as truth to natural observation, but now, in *Lectures on Art*, the Venetians are thought of as having learned a solar lesson from the Greeks.

His argument is simply that in the earliest days of Venetian colorists, before the sixteenth century, their work was marked by an unworldly, crystalline light; paradisaical light, not solar. "None of their lights are flashing or blinding; they are soft, winning, precious; lights of pearl, not of lime: only, you know, on this condition they cannot have sunshine: their day is the day of Paradise; they need no candle, neither light of the sun, in their cities; everything is seen clear, as through crystal, far or near."[130] But eventually solar light is introduced, and with it, of course, mortal shadows.

> Then they begin to see that this, beautiful as it may be, is still a make-believe light; that we do not live in the inside of a pearl; but in an atmosphere through which a burning sun shines thwartedly, and over which a sorrowful night must far prevail. And then the chiaroscurists succeed in persuading them of the fact that there is a mystery in the day as in the night, and show them how constantly to see truly, is to see dimly. And also they teach them the brilliancy of light, and the degree in which it is raised from the darkness; and instead of their sweet and pearly peace, tempt them to look for the strength of flame and coruscation of lightning, and flash of sunshine on armour and on points of spears.[131]

This, in Ruskin's mind, was the Greek lesson of solemn light. The greatest men—Titian, Tintoretto, Correggio—learn it nobly; the base men,—especially the Dutch tenebrists—learn it basely. "The great men rise from colour to sunlight. The base ones fall from colour to candlelight."[132] But in this way the "complete painters" brought worldly "dimness and mystery into their method of colouring. That means that the world all round them has resolved to dream, or to believe, no more; but to know, and to see."[133] This, in sum, is the spiritual meaning of the great transition to Greek naturalism in color:

> In the sweet crystalline time of colour, the painters, whether on glass or canvas, employed intricate patterns in order to mingle hues beautifully with each other, and make one perfect melody of them all. But in the great naturalist school, they like their patterns to come in the Greek way, dashed dark on light,—gleaming light out of dark. That means also that the world around them has again returned to the Greek conviction, that all nature, especially human nature, is not entirely melodious nor luminous; but a barred and broken thing: that saints have their foibles, sinners' their forces; that the most luminous virtue is often only a flash, and the blackest-looking fault is sometimes only a stain: and, without confusing in the least black with white, they can forgive, or even take delight in things that are like the νεβρίς, dappled.
> You have then—first, mystery. Secondly, opposition of dark and light. Then, lastly, whatever truth of form the dark and light can show.
> That is to say, truth altogether, and resignation to it, and quiet resolve to make the best of it. And therefore portraiture of living men, women, and children,—no more of saints, cherubs, or demons.[134]

So far does Ruskin go, then, in his first series of Oxford lectures, the *Lectures on Art*, to connect the great Venetian (and Turnerian) color with Greek belief and the school of solemn light he derives therefrom. There is little here that could signal a return of his interest in purist art.

The line of thought that leads Ruskin toward mystical art again begins when he joins his notion of the Greek belief in Athena as the "forming power" in material life to the techniques of sculpture and thence to all highest kinds of work in art. This application is worked out in considerable detail in the lectures "Imagination" and "Likeness," published as parts of *Aratra Pentelici*. There, the reader may find, for instance, the whole pattern of thought that we are to trace represented enigmatically by such a passage as this: "Thus, briefly, the entire material of Art, under Athena's hand, is the contest of life with clay; and all my task in explaining to you the early thought of both the Athenian and Tuscan schools will only be the tracing of this battle of the giants into its full heroic form."[135] Notice that Ruskin looks toward Tuscan art here, not Venetian.

The meaning of this "contest of life with clay" in art is important to Ruskin but not easy to convey. It looks backward, of course, to his notion of the Greek worship of "Athena Keramitis," the formative energy in the clay, and back through that, as he reminds us in "Imagination," to that central dictum of *The Ethics of the Dust*: "You may always stand by Form against Force." The relationship between Athena and the artist is defined by his observation that "to a painter, the essential character of anything is the form of it, and the philosophers cannot touch that."[136] But the reference to "philosophers" suggests the real distinction that Ruskin is getting at between the worshippers of Athena, who see a spiritual power in the forms of life, and the servants of Medusa, who see only forces there. Hence he defines the ultimate object of art, particularly of sculpture, as "exclusively the representation of form as the exponent of life." Among moderns, of course, the art of sculpture has become degraded because "we have absolutely ceased from the exercise of faithful imagination; and the only remnants of the desire of truth which remain in us have been corrupted into a prurient itch to discover the origin of life in the nature of the dust, and prove that the source of the order of the universe is the accidental concurrence of its atoms."[137]

From these conditions Ruskin draws out his essential laws of sculpture. The first law is that "you must see Pallas as the Lady of Life; the second is, you must see her as the Lady of Wisdom." That is, one must "carve nothing but what has life," bearing in mind that "proper subject of sculpture . . . is the spiritual power seen in the form of any living thing."[138] These are the central vitalistic truths of Greek design. There will be, of course, a number of more specific corollaries, and much of the *Aratra* material is devoted to their definition and illustration. Observe again Ruskin's crucial points: from their worship of Athena as wisdom and life the Greeks learned the humanity and veracity of their sculpture, meaning their distrust of the grotesque and of the merely elaborate in design: "From all vain and mean decoration—all weak and monstrous error, the Greeks rescue the forms of man and beast, and sculpture them in the nakedness of their true flesh, and with the fire of their living soul." So it was the legacy of their sculpture "to give health to what was diseased, and chastisement to what was untrue. So far as this is found in any other school, hereafter, it belongs to them by inheritance from the Greeks, or invests them with the brotherhood of the Greek."[139] And we must still learn from the Greek "his disdain of mechanism:—of all work which he felt to be monstrous and inhuman in its imprudent dexterities."[140]

Such, then, is the first stage of Ruskin's return to the Christian painters; truth in art is understood to be a vision of Pallas, a revelation to the artist of the spirit of life in living forms, leading to the wisdom which informs him that this truth is never to be approached in art by dissective literalism or "imprudent dexterities" in lifeless scrimshaw. This amounts to the reintegration of art and belief on a new mystical basis for Ruskin, the worship of Pallas, of vitalism, in the face of all mechanism whether in art or in philosophy. The sum of this, with the love of light, is the Greek truth in art as he understood it at the end of 1870.

Now the next stage in this mystical drift is climaxed in the year before his reconversion (1874) by the introduction into his thought of a new Greek school, the "Etruscan Greek School" of Florence. Conceived, as a sort of coordinate spiritual alternative to his other Greek schools (the Academic and the Venetian), this span of influence is supported by two main ideas: that of the historical transfusion of Greek into Tuscan art, and of the consequent harmonizing of Christian and pagan ideals as accounting for the greatness of Botticelli. Ruskin makes a beginning in this direction in the fifth and sixth lectures of *Aratra Pentelici*, intended to contrast "The School of Athens" with "The School of Florence." What we learn in these two lectures, essentially, is that "the Greeks found Phoenician and Etruscan art monstrous, and had to make them human."[141] We are shown, in the seventh lecture, a Lombardic griffin representing the "true Gothic or Northern spirit" of barbaric horror. Then we are reminded that "in the thirteenth and fourteenth centuries the Greek school meets this at Pisa, and the great Tuscan art instantly develops itself." But "this is not the adoption of Greek forms; it is the vital naturalistic and sincere element, poured into the breasts now ready to receive it." Particularly, we learn, "Niccolo Pisano is taught by the veracity and humanity of Paganism, and the phantom of the Lombard [typified by the Griffin of Verona] is in his hands to become true, and his cruelty to become gentle."[142]

Then in his next series of lectures, the *Lectures on Landscape*, primarily a tribute to Venetian color, Botticelli first appears as a representative of the pagan spirit in Florence. His *Nativity* is recommended as "a quite perfect example of what the masters of the pure Greek school did in Florence."[143] But Ruskin has not yet worked out the deeper meaning of this master's Grecism, and Botticelli's painting is introduced here simply as a fine example of Greek chiaroscuro. "It is impossible for you ever to see a more noble work of passionate Greek chiaroscuro—rejoicing in light."[144]

The historical influence of Greek art upon the Tuscan, and the Christian paganism of Botticelli are two vectors of his interest that must be drawn out more fully, but there is also another that must be kept in mind if Ruskin's return to the Christian aesthetic is to be understood as a resultant. Acting constantly upon these two new interests is his notion of the vanity of science as a deformative factor in art, an influence he associated particularly with Michelangelo in Italy and with Holbein and Dürer in the "German schools." We have already observed how this doctrine became the basis for the central distinction in *Michael Angelo and Tintoret*, and now, in a particularly interesting passage in *The Eagle's Nest*, Ruskin lays before us his broader intention in this area. Not only does he promise to prove that the study of anatomy "will not help us to draw the true appearances of things," but we are also given to understand that this proof will somehow be relevant to his discussion of Florentine art:

> I must reserve for my lectures on the school of Florence any analysis of the effect of anatomical study on European art and character; you will find some notice of it in my lecture on Michael Angelo; and in the course of that analysis, it will be necessary for me to withdraw the statement made in the *Stones of Venice*, that anatomical science was helpful to great men, though harmful to mean ones.[145]

The "lectures on the school of Florence" referred to were published as *Ariadne Florentina* (1873–76), but they were delivered in 1872 and announced then as "Sandro Botticelli and the Florentine Schools of Engraving." And in fact what is important in these lectures is the elaborate contrast between Botticelli's paganism in its effect upon his "design" and the influence of "science" in several senses, especially "Medicine, and Physical Science" and "Reformation, and Religious

Science," upon the forms of imagination in the "Northern Schools" of engraving. Ruskin's main effort is to set the art of Botticelli before us, "especially as exhibiting the modesty of great imagination trained in reverence, which characterized the southern Reformers; and as opposed to the immodesty of narrow imagination, trained in self-trust, which characterized the northern Reformers."[146] This is accomplished particularly in the two successive lectures entitled "Design in the German Schools" and "Design in the Florentine Schools." In these two lectures Botticelli emerges, paradoxically, as at once a "Greek reanimate,"[147] and the first evangel of Ruskin's reconversion to Christian art.

The art of engraving, Ruskin explains, was nurtured by three Renaissance "sciences": "1. Classicism, and Literary Science. 2. Medicine, and Physical Science. 3. Reformation, and Religious Science."[148] With these divisions of the new learning before him, he proceeds to contrast certain Northern engravers, chiefly Holbein and Durer, with Botticelli in order to show the comparative purity with which the Greek tradition of vitalistic truth is continued in him.

Both Holbein and the Florentine, we learn, were in contact with "Classicism." The German found it "foreign to his nature, useless at the best, probably cumbrous." "But Botticelli receives it as a child in later years recovers the forgotten dearness of a nursery tale; and is more himself, and again and again himself, as he breathes the air of Greece, and hears, in his own Italy, the lost voice of the Sibyl murmur again by the Avernus Lake." The result is that "Holbein is a civilized boor: Botticelli a reanimate Greek."[149]

To illustrate his point Ruskin selects a solar image, Botticelli's *Sun in Leo*, which he finds "more purely Greek in spirit than the Apollo Belvidere." This is because the power of Apollo was not a genteel fable to the Florentine but at once his natural philosophy and his theology, while

> the Apollo Belvidere is the work of a sculptor to whom Apollonism is merely an elegant idea on which to exhibit his own skill. He does not himself feel for an instant that the handsome man in the unintelligible attitude, with drapery hung over his left arm, as it would be hung to dry over a clothes-line, is the Power of the Sun. But the Florentine believes in Apollo with his whole mind, and is trying to explain his strength in every touch.[150]

The effect of this faith of Botticelli's is

> natural philosophy, and also natural art, for in this *the Greek reanimate was a nobler creature than the Greek who had died.* His art had a wider force and warmer glow. I have told you that the first Greeks were dis-

tinguished from the barbarians by their simple humanity; the second Greeks—these Florentine Greeks reanimate—are human more strongly, more deeply, leaping from the Byzantine death at the call of Christ, "Loose him, and let him go." And there is upon them at once the joy of resurrection, and the solemnity of the grave.[151]

This infusion of Greek influence in Florence Ruskin refers to again as the "resurrection of the Greek," and his metaphor is an apt expression of what he understood to be the true communion of Greek and Christian impulses in the art of Botticelli. In this way the *Sun in Leo* becomes a kind of solar emblem of his recovered Christianity much as Turner's *Apollo and Python*, a dozen years earlier, had marked the onset of his "religion of Humanity."

But what of the Germans, Holbein and Dürer, and the meaning of their work in the light of Botticelli's? These comparisons are important because Ruskin intends the Northern schools, dominated by the joint influences of science and the Reformation, to stand for much of modern art. He insists first that "Botticelli and Holbein together fought foremost in the ranks of Reformation"; both were "Reformers."

> Reformers, I mean, in the full and, accurately, the only, sense. Not preachers of new doctrines; but witnesses against the betrayal of the old ones, which were on the lips of all men, and in the lives of none. Nay, the painters are indeed more pure reformers than the priests. They rebuked the manifest vices of men, while they realized whatever was loveliest in their faith.[152]

However, the chilling effects of knowledge marked out a darker path for Holbein in art and belief. He represents "the *Rationalist* spirit of reform, preaching the new Gospel of Death,"[153] while Botticelli "represents the *Faithful* and *Catholic* temper of reform."[154] Now, considering Ruskin's own tendencies at this time, it is important to understand his argument that Botticelli's faithful reform was actually made possible by his Grecism. This was because

> for Botticelli, the grand gods are old, are immortal. The priests may have taught falsely the story of the Virgin;—did they not also lie, in the name of Artemis, at Ephesus;—in the name of Aphrodite, at Cyprus?—but shall, therefore, Chastity or Love be dead, or the full moon paler over Arno? Saints of Heaven and Gods of Earth!—shall *these* perish because vain men speak evil of them! Let *us* speak good for ever, and grave, as on the rock, for ages to come, the glory of Beauty, and the triumph of Faith.[155]

But Holbein had no Greek faith to secure his Christianity; therefore,

> when the work of the Catholic Church proved false, and its deeds bloody; when he saw it selling permission of sin in his native Augsburg, and

strewing the ashes of its enemies on the pure Alpine waters of Constance, what refuge was there for *him* in more ancient religion? Shall he worship Thor again, and mourn over the death of Balder? He reads Nature in her desolate and narrow truth, and she teaches him the Triumph of Death.[156]

Unable to see Pallas, the forming spirit in the clay, and thus left to read "Nature in her desolate and narrow truth," Holbein became "par excellence the draughtsman of skeletons."[157]

Thus, while Botticelli could hear "the Sibyl murmur again by the Avernus Lake," the voice of Holbein's reason drowned her out, but not "death's ironic scraping." The voice of reason, note, not of science. For Holbein "refused the venomous science of his day."[158] He is on the side of Botticelli at least in his refusal to study anatomy. "He draws skeleton after skeleton, in every possible gesture; but never so much as counts their ribs!"[159] But Dürer, on the other hand, marks the farthest remove from the Florentines, for Dürer would study anatomy, "would, and did:—went hotly into it—wrote books upon it, and upon 'proportions of the human body,' etc., etc., and all your modern recipes for painting flesh."[160] And what is the effect of all this science on Dürer's art? "You have only three portraits, by Dürer, of the great men of his time, and those bad ones; while he toils his soul out to draw the hoofs of satyrs, the bristles of swine, and the distorted aspects of base women and vicious men."[161]

It was their Greek faith, then, that saved the Christianity and the art of Botticelli and his followers, making these vital and human, just as reason and science in Holbein, Dürer, and especially in Michelangelo poisoned their imaginations and infused their work with death or deformity. For, and here Ruskin seems to be justifying his own position as well as Botticelli's, while the "learned men of his age in general brought back the Greek mythology as anti-Christian"; Botticelli and Perugino receive it "as pre-Christian; nor only as pre-Christian, but as the foundation of Christianity. But chiefly Botticelli, with perfect grasp of the Mosaic and classic theology, thought over and seized the harmonies of both."[162]

But to Michelangelo, in his immodesty of knowledge, "all Christian and heathen mythology alike become . . . only a vehicle for the display of his own powers of drawing limbs and trunks."[163] And it is, finally, a supreme irony to Ruskin that Michelangelo should represent his Cumaean sibyl, "the poor nymph beloved of Apollo,—the clearest and queenliest in prophecy and command of all the sibyls,—as an ugly crone, with arms of Goliath, poring down upon a single book."[164] Thus, at the end of *Ariadne Florentina* he is left with "the old superstitious art represented *finally* by Perugino, and the modern, scientific and anatomical art represented *primarily* by Michael Angelo."[165]

As the contrast between Botticelli's faithful Apollonism in *The Sun in Leo* and the ironic ugliness of Michelangelo's sibyl ("the nymph belov- ed of Apollo") suggests, the mythological aesthetic of light is profound- ly interfused with all this material on engraving, so much so that only a separate study could properly define its meaning there. Generally, all excessive shading is made to stand for the petrifaction of faithful im- agination by unwise science or imprudent technical dexterities. This is carried even into social philosophy when Ruskin attacks the wanton use of cross-hatching among modern artists, arguing that such "free" work in shade signifies the literal enslavement of those who must engrave it: "Now calculate—or think enough to feel the impossibility of calculating—the number of woodcuts used daily for our popular prints, and how many men are night and day cutting 1050 square holes to the square inch, as the occupation of their manly life. And Mrs. Beecher Stowe and the North Americans fancy they have abolished slavery!"[166]

At the aesthetic level this overuse of shading means vain facility, because the greatest engraving does not dabble in gratuitious gradations; form is brought forth insofar as possible as a vision in light only; great engraving "expresses only form, and *dark local colour*."[167] This follows from his observation that "Nature herself draws with diffused light and concentrated dark;—never, except in storms or twilight, with diffused dark, and concentrated light."[168] But he has in mind also that "the eye is not in the least offended by quantity of white, but is, or ought to be, greatly saddened and offended by quantity of black."[169]

This matter of excessive shading is confusing because, while Ruskin sees it as standing literally for Daedal vanity in the execution of a work, he takes it also as a symbol for the shadows that must confound all vain pursuit of knowledge, a particular threat, acknowledged or un- acknowledged, to the chiaroscurist, whose work as opposed to the colorist's is understood to be concerned with knowing rather than feeling. For "light and shade imply the understanding of things— Colour, the imagination and sentiment of them."[170] But on each side, chiaroscuro or color, light is the sign of vital truth or devout imagina- tion. Holbein and Dürer are both chiaroscurists. Dürer practiced science and lost himself in intricacies of light and shade, but Holbein divided his lights from his darks frankly, and "Holbein is right, not because he draws more generally, but more truly, than Dürer. Dürer draws what he knows is there; but Holbein, only what he sees. And, as I have told you often before, the really scientific artist is he who not only asserts bravely what he *does* see, but confesses honestly what he does *not*."[171]

Supreme in the opposite realm, color, we now have Perugino, for whom Apollo is always in his heaven. Turner, of course, struggles reverently, heroically for light; in his "distinctive work, colour is scarcely acknowledged unless under the influence of sunshine . . . nothing is cheerful but sunshine; wherever the sun is not, there is melancholy or evil. Apollo is God; and all forms of death and sorrow exist in opposition to him."[172] But in Perugino's work "there is simply *no* darkness, *no* wrong. Every colour is lovely, and every space is light. The world, the universe, is divine: all sadness is a part of harmony; and all gloom, a part of peace."[173]

This conception of Botticelli and Perugino as "reanimate" Greeks handing down the believing tradition in art toward Tintoretto, and the final extinction of that tradition by pride of science in Michelangelo and his followers, is central to the lectures of 1872 and represents, the penultimate stage in the process of his aesthetic reconversion. The rest is accomplished in the next three series of lectures, *Val D'Arno* (1873), *The Aesthetic and Mathematic Schools of Art in Florence* (1874), and *Mornings in Florence* (1875-77); it is significant that this last is subtitled *Simple Studies of Christian Art for English Travelers.*

Read in the light of the foregoing, these lectures make it plain that Ruskin's rediscovery of supreme power in Christian art was no instantaneous reaction to *The Marriage of Poverty and St. Francis*, as he explained it, but at most the final, glad acceptance of an aesthetic position toward which he had been reasoning his way since the completion of *The Queen of the Air*. Reconsideration of the threat of mechanism to all vitalistic reverence in life and art had forced him to the position that asceticism was by far the lesser enemy. From there it was no great step to the view that pious men like Giotto or Carpaccio were actually closer to the true Greek vitalistic spirit, as defined in *The Queen* and *Aratra*, than those worldly Venetians who were the true Greeks of his earlier conception. This religio-aesthetic shift from a "pagan" to a Christian conception of the Greek influence could be attractively rationalized into ethnic considerations by which the pious Florentines could be shown to have had prior historical intimacy with the Greek spirit, and Giotto, (to whom he attributed the particular Assisi fresco that now most influenced him) could be shown to have been the *first* of the distinctly great recipients of Greek aesthetic truth in Italian art, where Titian and Tintoretto had been among the last.

By 1872 Ruskin had completed the courses of lectures in which he had, among many other things, described the perfection of Venetian color as deriving from the admixture of Greek solemn worldly light with Gothic crystalline color; differentiated the Greek desire for truth in art (the desire to reveal the spiritual power in living forms, which therefore rejoices in light and life) from the "prurient itch" of science leading to desolate dexterities; and undertaken a careful reexamination of Florentine art that had led him directly to Botticelli as "the only one . . . who understood the thoughts of Heathens and Christians equally, and could in a measure paint both Aphrodite and the Madonna. So that he is, on the whole, the most universal of painters; and, take him all in all, the greatest Florentine workman."[174]

But this analysis of Greek impulses in both Venetian and Florentine art was gradually disclosing a gap in Ruskin's critical system for Italian art that demanded to be filled. These Greek impulses had first been understood as essentially naturalistic, then as humanistic, finally as vitalistic, believing in a spirit of life. This last marks Ruskin's ultimate dissociation of artistic *truth* and *knowledge*. But notice that this reasoning must force him backward historically. In 1870 he had learned that the true clue to the death of Italian art lay in "Il disegno di Michael Agnolo," which, it seemed, had "killed Tintoret."[175] There was obviously, then, no going forward chronologically from his great Venetians; Italian art had looked on Medusa. But working backward presented equal problems, for Ruskin was still in his Greek faith. In a sense he was hemmed in aesthetically by scientism in one direction and purism in the other, and both were hostile to vitalistic art. In the instance of Botticelli he could safely make a slight but significant move backward historically and toward purism without damage to his Greek ideals by viewing that painter as balancing Greek and Christian aesthetic values, a position strikingly analogous to his own at that very moment.

From there, however, any real critical movement would be difficult to reconcile with Greek ideals. Yet critical activity was a necessity of Ruskin's life; it was spiritual bread and therapy. From Botticelli there was really only one obvious direction to take, and that was back toward the origins of Italian art to Niccola Pisano, Cimabue, and Giotto. He had to go this way, I judge, because Botticelli came relatively late on the chronological scale, his life overlapping Tintoretto's and ground already Atticized, and especially because in the way ahead through Michelangelo there had recently been disclosed to him a more vigorous enemy to art than purism. His studies in the Northern engravers and Michelangelo had meant that the way to truth in art could not lie through the study of anatomy or any other science, and, in contradistinction, that this truth had been instinctive in earlier, less analytic men who could revere a power in the forms of things. Plainly, he was poised to turn again and seek for greatness in the simpler, pious times of Italian art, but there was still that old problem of reconciling Greek vitalism and Christian asceticism.

The rational key to this problem lay in finding some deeper Greek strain in the pious painters of the thirteenth century. And Ruskin found it, simply enough, in a conception of the Etruscan-Greek descent of these painters. The Venetians and Turner he had found Greek by temperament; Botticelli and Perugino, Greek by respectful classicism; but Cimabue and his pupil Giotto he finds Greek by birth. This is the essence of Ruskin's rediscovery of Florentine Christian art; he found it Etruscan-Greek, with all the meaning of truth in form and color that this might convey.

This Etruscan recognition forms the thematic warp of the Florentine lectures he delivered in 1873, 1874, and 1875. The details of its demonstration in various artists are too diffuse for presentation here, but Ruskin has summarized their effect for us in a note to *Mornings in Florence* (1875).

> Etruscan art remains in its own Italian valleys, of the Arno and upper Tiber, in one unbroken series of work, from the seventh century before Christ, to this hour, when the country whitewasher still scratches his plaster in Etruscan patterns. All Florentine work of the finest kind—Luca della Robbia's, Ghiberti's, Donatello's, Filippo Lippi's, Botticelli's, Fra Angelico's—is absolutely pure Etruscan, merely changing its subjects, and representing the Virgin instead of Athena, and Christ instead of Jupiter. Every line of the Florentine chisel in the fifteenth century is based on national principles of art which existed in the seventh century before Christ; and Angelico, in his convent of St. Dominic at the root of the hill of Fésole, is as true an Etruscan as the builder who laid the rude stones on the wall along its crest—of which modern civilization has used the only arch that remained for cheap building stone.[176]

Earlier, in a lecture on Cimabue, he had established his essential line of reasoning. The school of sculpture in the Val d'Arno descends from Niccola Pisano, who, "finding Greek Byzantine sculpture degraded, learns how to reform and restore it from Graeco-Roman sarcophagi, and treats Scripture history as a Greek Naturalist."[177] The school of painting there descends from Cimabue, whom Ruskin calls the "Florentine Tintoret."

> He is the Florentine spirit itself—the Etrurian lover of religion and mystery returning to its strength as the nation recovers its glory, ex-

pressing itself in the genius of one great man as that of Venice in Tintoret. Parallels are never exact in these wide things. The greatest man in Venice comes last; in Florence, first. Step by step, Carpaccio, Bellini, Giorgione create the Venetian power, culminating in Tintoret. The Florentine Tintoret is sent where all around is dark; he breaks through the darkness, forms the greatness of Giotto, and there is nothing greater afterwards.[178]

But the ultimate question for Ruskin in all this concerns the source of Cimabue's power: "There is reason for Niccola's newly-born power: he sees the masters of the perfect time. But what reason is there for Cimabue's newly-born power, who ignores?"[179] The reason, of course, is ethnological.

> My own belief is that these men [Cimabue and Giotto] are both absolutely of Graeco-Etruscan race, as opposed to the Norman; that they represent the new budding of an underground stem which has its root partly in Greece proper, partly in Egypt, and that the spirit-life which invented the forms of the throned gods and kings of Thebes is in the veins of Cimabue; and that the domestic truth and tenderness which gave us the tales of Nausicaa and Penelope, again lives in Giotto. They are at once Greek of the Greeks, and Christian of the Christians—the flower and purest force of both.[180]

Again, on one of his "Mornings" he observed that "painting a Gothic chapel rightly is just the same thing as painting a Greek vase rightly"[181] and then promised to demonstrate "that Giotto was a pure Etruscan-Greek of the thirteenth century: converted indeed to worship St. Francis instead of Heracles; but as far as vase-painting goes, precisely the Etruscan he was before."[182]

To understand the significance of this Etruscanizing of Giotto and the Florentines one must refer to all that has been said about the Greek aesthetic in Ruskin's criticism. Participating in Greek veracity, for instance, Giotto had the habit of seeing things as they were, and so "finding out that a red thing was red, and a brown thing brown, and a white thing white—all over." Thus "he simply founded the schools of colour in Italy—Venetian and all."[183] But we have also learned that a Greek, like Turner, rejoices in light and his color speaks through an ancient symbolism. So too with Giotto: "All the other great Italian colourists see only the beauty of colour, but Giotto also its brightness. And none of the others, except Tintoret, understood to the full its symbolic power; but with those—Giotto and Tintoret—there is always, not only a colour harmony, but a colour secret."[184] But, above all, the Greek is a vitalist; the gesture he paints is, before all things, a living gesture, studied living to express life, and never to be captured in death or dissection. In this also he found Giotto a true Greek. The Assisi

frescoes on which his praise is centered are attributed today to pupils of
Giotto; but, just as Ruskin read a private truth in the roses of the *Poverty*, a woman's gesture in one of the *Miracles* may have meant more to
him than the proof of mastery he describes.

> Thus in Giotto's fresco of St. Francis restoring the boy to life who had
> fallen from an upper story of his house into the street, as the child rises, one
> of the women standing by throws up her arms to Heaven, clasping her
> hands with the perfect expression of an instantaneous cry of thankfulness.
> No "science" whatever is shown in drawing the muscles of the arms. The
> science is in seizing the exact angles of them with the body, the exact bend
> at the elbows, and the precise degree of pressure in the clasped fingers,
> which express sudden thankfulness. The number of observations which
> must have been made on human gestures and of accurately mathematic
> comparisons of the angles, taken by the arms in different degrees and kinds
> of passions (as, for a rough instance, despair would have thrown them up,
> not forward; and joy, without thankfulness, closer to the breasts), before
> the painter could strike his line so finely as to express even the difference
> between sudden thanks and sudden prayer, are indeed a scientific opera-
> tion far more prolonged and delicate than the analysis of a mineral, but
> requiring for its success a gift of sympathy which not one man in a million
> would be found to possess, while science, commonly so called, consists
> only in the collection of observations which it is in the power of everybody
> to make. Any hospital demonstrator could have marked the muscles of the
> woman's arms, and any apothecary's apprentice analysed the fluid which
> lubricated their joints, but science at that universally communicable level
> does not make a painter.[185]

In "Giotto's Pet Puppy" (1874) he insisted that even a sculptural
detail like the shepherd's "puppy vigilant" in the "Jabal"[186] (of the
Campanile) will show us "pure Greek work of the highest style."[187] But
from it we are to understand that life must be shown by something more
than mere action; in Giotto's puppy life is perfected in repose. For this is
"the law of Phidias—life in perfect power, but in repose." True, "a vile
modern sculptor—nay, a vulgar ancient one—would have made the dog
in action." But "no, say Phidias and Giotto; brightness, strength, and
cheerfulness and peace—these are what great art has to contemplate."[188]
The sum of all is that "from the Greeks, Giotto learned the spirit of
Nature," this being opposed to "her physical conditions and practical
laws."[189]

As this remark suggests, Florentine Grecism has significant spiritual
implications. Indeed, what Ruskin seems to be saying is that the Greek
religion continued to reign in Florence, though it expressed itself
through Christian images, and this made possible Florentine artistic
greatness. Notice again his saying that "all Florentine work of the finest
kind—Luca della Robbia's, Ghiberti's, Donatello's, Filippo Lippi's,

Botticelli's, Fra Angelico's—is absolutely pure Etruscan, merely changing its subjects, and representing the Virgin instead of Athena, and Christ instead of Jupiter."[190] And perhaps no better indication of the nature of his "reconversion" to religious art could be given than by the following passage in which Botticelli's *Zipporah* is seen as a transformed Pallas.

> His Zipporah is simply the Etruscan Athena, becoming queen of a household in Christian humility. Her spear is changed to a reed and becomes then her sceptre, cloven at the top into the outline of Florentine Fleur-de-lys, and in the cleft she fastens her spindle. Her χιτών falls short of the feet, that it may not check her motion, and is lightly embroidered; above, the πέπλος unites with its own character that of the aegis. Where Athena's had the wars of the giants, it is embroidered with mystic letters, golden on blue, but it becomes the αἰγὶς θυσσανόεσσα at its edge, where what are only light tassels in the πέπλος become this waving fringe, typical of sacrificial fire, for you know she is a priest's daughter; but when the peplus falls in Greek statues into its κόλπος,, sinus, gulph, or lap, the aegis is here replaced by a goatskin satchel, in which the maiden holds lightly with her left hand apples, here taking the character of the Etruscan Pomona, and oak for the strength of life. Her hair is precisely that of the Phidian Athena, only unhelmed, and with three leaves of myrtle in its wreaths.[191]

Six months before this passage was written, while copying *The Marriage of Poverty and St. Francis,* which he assumed to be Giotto's, Ruskin had discovered, as he said, the fallacy that had underlain sixteen years of his art teaching, "the fallacy that Religious artists were weaker than Irreligious." We have seen that this fallacy had rested on the notion that there was a strain of fearless Greek naturalism in the great Venetian colorists that set them above the Florentine purists. But as Ruskin pondered Greek belief and the threats of modern antimythic science, he concluded, correlatively, that the essence of the Greek aesthetic was the intuitive vitalism that could make its forms the exponents of life, not of mere empirical veracity. This became for him the new Greek truth in art, a truth more to be approached by simplicity and faith than by any amount of technical facility or dissective observation. Under this condition of mind he began to reexamine the early Christian painters. And the nature of his "re-conversion" was simply this: that he found certain Christian painters (especially Carpaccio, Botticelli, and Giotto) were better Greeks than his painters of "worldly harmony," Titian, Tintoretto, Correggio, et cetera, a truth that, he said, had been masked by the apparent lack of technical facility in some of the earlier painters.

Two points must, finally, be borne in mind. First, notice that, because he made these Christian painters Greek, this reconciliation with pious

John Ruskin after Botticelli. *Zipporah*. Reproduced from *Works* (Library Edition), vol. 23.

art represents an extension rather than a contraction in his mind of the domain of Greek aesthetic and spiritual influence. He made this plain in his "Editor's Preface" to the *Economist of Xenophon*.

> Any reader acquainted with my former statements on this subject (as for instance in page 107, vol. iii. *Stones of Venice*) will understand now why I do not republish those earlier books without very important modifications. I imagined, at that time, it had been the honour given to classical tradition which had destroyed the schools of Italy. But it was, on the contrary, the disbelief of it. She [Venice] fell, not by reverence for the Gods of the Heathen, but by infidelity alike to them, and to her own.[192]

In sum:

> the general ideals of the twelve great Gods of the Fates, Furies, Sibyls, and Muses, remain commandant of all action of human intellect in the spiritual world, down to the day when Michael Angelo, painting the Delphic and Cumaean sibyls in equal vaults with Zechariah and Isaiah on the roof of the Sistine Chapel; and Raphael, painting the Parnassus and the Theology on equal walls of the same chamber of the Vatican, so wrote, under the Throne of the Apostolic power, the harmony of the angelic teaching from the rocks of Sinai and Delphi.[193]

Secondly, this "re-conversion," as it has been called here for the sake of convenience, no more represents for Ruskin a true return to Christian belief than to Christian art. He found no permanent solace in Christianity, though the figures of his faith, like Botticelli's, came out in Christian dress. Athena became the Madonna or Saint Ursula; Apollo, Saint George; the Chimera, a "Devil Cloud"; but the "Greek Sorrow" remained with him to the end, which was, like his Bellerophon's, "in fading melancholy."[194]

5

I have been considering Ruskin's thought mainly in terms of the pervasiveness in it of the organic model. If there is any one unifying concern in the massive body of his work it is his effort to elucidate this obscure "system" of "eternal laws." It is this vital but mysterious code, the transcendent laws of form and fate, that he seeks to discern in nature, art, and history; it is this model of creation also that he attempts to supernaturalize through mythic symbolism and the tactics of apocalyptic revelation. This model is as elusive as the mind's capacity for prehensive unification, and Ruskin can never perceive it steadily and whole. It is simply an intuition of sacred unity (partly indebted to the Platonic tradition) that is opposed to all fallacies of simple location and concreteness.

Although the sacred model is ultimately mysterious, there are three important emanations from it: the visible aspects of natural form; the visionary sympathy or imaginative power that enables certain men to transfuse these qualities of organic form into art; and the continuum of symbolic language, including myth, by which the truths of vision are passed on in answering minds from age to age. For Ruskin, the primary symbol of the ultimate mystery of the organic model, the mystery of life, the holy or helping spirit, is the lighted cloud. The laws of form and fate are also, to him, laws of storm. Therefore, a major theme in his work is the progressive mythology of sky phenomena that culminates in *The Queen of the Air*.

However, as I have observed, Ruskin's vision is also consistently adversative; the conflict of intended good with permitted evil, ingrained by his nursery Puritanism, is the infrastructure of his thought, underlying the organic model in all its manifestations and associated symbolism. Therefore, the sacred unity, pure integration, is continuously threatened by increasingly malignant and disintegrating antagonists; the organic model in art is opposed by mechanistic rule systems; the organic model in society is threatened by mechanistic economics and by otherworldly theology; the whole idea of man's place in any order is threatened by the progress of his science. At the level of social motives, behind all of those forces that separate consciousness from the perception of that mysterious unity that is life, lies the divisive pursuit of dead wealth.

Just as the vital mystery of the organic model has its sky mythology of cloud and light, so its opponent forces in Ruskin's thought have their own archetypal symbols: darkness and shadow, the chthonic serpent dragon, and smoking coils of storm. Of course, as I have noted in discussing his periods of delirium, this recurrent and developing conflict could be regarded from the psychological standpoint as nothing more than a symbolic projection of the increasingly desperate struggle of Ruskin's ego with the repressed. One might give a Jungian interpretation to his constant interest in the struggle of the solar hero with the serpent. However, though such considerations might yield something like a diagnosis of Ruskin's personal illness, none of this would, of itself, deny the power of his prose or the truth of his vision.

In the seventies Ruskin's effort to "reform the world" in accordance with the organic model foundered in rejection and gloom; the rose queen of his affectional life was lost to him in death, along with the many other tutelary figures: his mother, his old nurse, and his master in prophecy, Carlyle. Enemies of the sacred model gained darkly against him in every failure and loss; his consciousness was assailed increasingly by morbid and involuntary spectra. It was natural that he should dwell on the thread of Atropos in the weave of things. In *Fors Clavigera* he sought to project his sense of fate prophetically and apocalyptically in a processional verbal web into which he could weave nearly every aspect of his experience. It was to be expected also, given the history of cloud mythology in his earlier work, that woven into the fabric of *Fors* should be the progressive account of the plague cloud that he had first observed shortly before his illness at Matlock in 1871, the year *Fors* was begun. These urgent reports of adverse skies warn of more than pollution; they symbolize the ending, the final infection of the organic model (his "myth" of life) by lethal ideas of wealth and knowledge. They project also the blighting of his private hopes for wholeness in love and appear to signal the dangerous return of repressed hostility or desire. But, as a counterforce, his idea of the continuity of Greek mythic vision into early Christian art by way of Etruscan served to orient the art theory of his Oxford lectures and became the version of the organic model that meant most to him in this period. We have seen how this discovery of the continuity of mythic vision in art was instrumental in the conversion to a kind of medieval, mystical Christianity that he underwent in 1874.

As one might expect from this line of development, the work of Ruskin's final decade of productivity (1879-89), while becoming increasingly arcane, discursive, and agitated, is dominated by two main themes: first, the idea of a continuum of mythic vision or sacred system of mythology and hagiology, of which the mystical elect, himself included, are interpreters; and second, the signs of fatal infection in the organic model, manifested chiefly by the prophetic meteorology of the plague cloud. The peaceful *Praeterita* is the main exception to this generalization, but it could be argued that even here the youthful Ruskin's discovery of these two realities is the essential message of that work. Further, these two themes are related in the sense that the continuum of vision, the sacred system in which he could participate because his mind possessed the same "mirror temper" as the seers of other ages, is the source of his prophetic authority as an interpreter of the auguries of storm. Of course these themes are by no means the only topics of Ruskin's thought at this time, nor are they set forth in any fully articulated scheme, rather they are the primary poles of concern to which his meandering thoughts are drawn. Since there is no theoretical advance and much repetition of his earlier thought in this final phase, in the following paragraphs I shall merely indicate some of the ways in which these two concerns are expressed in the last works.

The first of these two themes, the organic model taking the form of mythic continuum, but not the second theme, appears in *The Bible of Amiens* (1880-85). In this peacefully historical, descriptive, and interpretive study Ruskin retreats from the modern world almost entirely; bitterness and blighting wind are forgotten as he dwells in the historical, mythic, and artistic forces that have gathered themselves into the Cathedral of Amiens. He reads this "Parthenon . . . of Gothic architecture"[195] mainly as a text in the sacred continuum rather than as a structure of organic forms. The building is organic now, not merely because its forms are rooted in nature and display the touch of the living hand, but because the mythic tradition speaks through it directly (along with history), untainted by separating knowledge: "Who built it, shall we ask? God, and Man,—is the first and most true answer. The stars in their courses built it, and the Nations. Greek Athena labours here—and Roman Father Jove, and Guardian Mars. The Gaul labours here, and the Frank: knightly Norman,—mighty Ostrogoth,—and wasted anchorite of Idumea."[196]

It is in this book also, we should remember, that Ruskin speaks of his own writings as, like the text of Amiens itself, to be seen "by an attentive reader to bind themselves together into a general system of interpretation of Sacred literature,—both classic and Christian, which will enable him without injustice to sympathize in the faiths of candid and generous souls, of every age and every clime." He continues with the assertion, typical of this first theme, that "there *is* a Sacred classic literature, running parallel with that of the Hebrews, and coalescing in the symbolic legends of mediaeval Christendom." Further, "the teaching of every master trained in the Eastern schools was necessarily grafted on the wisdom of the Greek mythology; and thus the story of the Nemean Lion, with the aid of Athena in its conquest, is the ideal root-stock of St. Jerome's companion, conquered by the healing gentleness of the Spirit of Life."[197] Again in his lecture "Mending the Sieve" (1882) on the life of Saint Benedict, he asserted the same continuity: "We said that the first five hundred years after Christ saw the extinction of Paganism. In the deeper sense, nothing that once enters the human soul is afterwards extinct in it. Every great symbol and oracle of Paganism is still understood in the Middle Ages."[198]

In one sense Ruskin's incomplete autobiography *Praeterita* (1885-90) belongs with *The Bible of Amiens* and *Valle Crucis*, parts of an intended series on the sacred legends and locales of Christendom called *Our Fathers Have Told Us*. They connect because, in recounting the mythology and hagiology of medieval Christianity and in the selective remembrance of his own life (his own legend, as it were), Ruskin could escape the stresses of his immediate life into a relatively coherent and unfallen world of his own devising. Yet, as I have shown in the introduction to this discussion, adversarial forces are present in *Praeterita*. On the one hand it recalls the bright, coherent, and sacred world of his childhood, the growth of the poetic mind in him that enabled him to see what Homer saw and become a reader in the mythic continuum, and it documents his discovery of the organic model: "I then saw, in their [trees sketched at Fontainbleau in 1844] beauty, the same laws which guided the clouds, divided the light, and balanced the wave."[199] But the work also recounts the disappearance of his childhood faith and, before this, the first Cumaean intimations to him of a real demonic presence in the world: "When I saw the birdless lake; for me also the voice of it had a teaching which was to be practically a warning law of future life:—'Nec te/ Nequidquam lucis Hecate praefecit Avernis.' The legends became true,—*began* to come true, I should have said,—trains of thought now first rising which did not take clear current till forty years afterwards."[200] Both themes are important to *Praeterita*, then, the continuity of mythic truth which Ruskin receives and, with this, the earliest warnings of plague.

In the other significant works of this final period, in *Fiction, Fair and Foul* (1880); in the Oxford lectures of his second tenure, collected as *The Art of England* (1883); in *The Pleasures of England* (1884); and in *The Storm-Cloud of the Nineteenth Century* (1884); his concern is more completely with the fallen present, though it is judged in terms of the religio-aesthetic continuities of the past. We have fallen into selfish isolation and discontinuity, lacking all sense of a cohesive value system, of purposes not our own yet working through us. "In every thing you now do or seek," he told his Oxford students in *The Pleasures of England*, the lectures in which he attempted to trace, out of their continuity with Christian history, the "pleasures" or spiritual values of early England, "you expose yourselves to countless miseries of shame and disappointment, because in your own doing you depend on nothing but your own powers, and in seeking choose only your own gratification. You cannot for the most part conceive of any work but for your own interests, or the interests of others about whom you are anxious in the same faithless way."[201] To recover the sense of organic purposiveness and consequent peace, simply

> set to any work you have in hand with the sifted and purified resolution
> that ambition shall not mix with it, nor love of gain, nor desire of pleasure
> more than is appointed you; and that no anxiety shall touch you as to its
> issue, or any impatience or regret if it fail. Imagine that the thing is being

done through you, not by you; that the good of it may never be known, but that at least, unless by your rebellion or foolishness, there can come no evil into it, nor wrong chance to it."[202]

Although Ruskin appears to have intended that his message should be that of the mythic continuum, the spiritual tradition that built Amiens speaking through him, it did not give him the peaceful control the passages just quoted promise, and there are signs of distress and discontinuity of purpose in these last works. They are frequently marred by excesses of acrimony and dogmatic scorn, obscure allusions and discursive trivia, overburdened syntax, strained analogies, and other indications of loss of control. The Oxford lectures, we are told, were heavily patronized by those who enjoyed his excesses; some, however, felt his last lectures had become "an academic farce"[203] and he was persuaded, much against his will, to cancel his intended lectures on science ("The Pleasures of Sense") and atheism ("The Pleasures of Nonsense"). The attempt to retrace here Ruskin's associative links in these last articles and lectures would not repay the reader's attention, since there is no real advance in his thought or symbolism. However, it is clear that the same two poles of conern, the continuity of mythic truth and the opponent signs of infection in the organic model, are again dominant. Broadly speaking, Ruskin's final theme is the signs of plague in the social values, the fiction, the fine art, and the skies of his century.

In the collection of five meandering essays entitled *Fiction, Fair and Foul* the fiction (prose or poetic) of the cohesive, organic, primarily agrarian community (typified by the best novels of Scott) is placed over against the fiction generated by the anomie of urban life. *Bleak House* and *The Hunchback of Notre Dame*, among other works, exemplify the fiction decomposition. The first essay, the most coherent and trenchant of the series, opens with a powerful description of the failure of the organic model. Croxted Lane of his youth with its tangled banks and crystalline brook, full of visual delight for the exploring boy, is contrasted with Croxted Lane as it appears in the present, a study in incoherence.

> Half a dozen handfuls of new cottages, with Doric doors, are dropped about here and there among the gashed ground: the lane itself, now entirely grassless, is a deep-rutted, heavy-hillocked cart-road, diverging gatelessly into various brickfields or pieces of waste; and bordered on each side by heaps of—Hades knows what!—mixed dust of every unclean thing that can crumble in drought, and mildew of every unclean thing that can rot or rust in damp: ashes and rags, beer-bottles and old shoes, battered pans, smashed crockery, shreds of nameless clothes, door-sweepings, floor-sweepings, kitchen garbage, backgarden sewage, old iron, rotten timber,

jagged with out-torn nails, cigar ends, pipe-bowls, cinders, bones, and ordure, indescribable; and, variously kneaded into, sticking to, or fluttering foully here and there over all these, remnants, broadcast, of every manner of newspaper, advertisement or big-lettered bill, festering and flaunting out their last publicity in the pits of stinking dust and mortal slime.[204]

In effect this is Ruskin's vision of hell, the place to which the wild pursuit of throwaway goods at the expense of the living environment must bring us. We know such places.

But what, he asks, will be the educative effect of this polluted world upon minds growing up in it? "One result of such elementary education," he has concluded, is already clearly indicated: "the pleasure which we may conceive taken by children of the coming time in the analysis of physical corruption" is already evident in modern literature, where "the reactions of moral disease upon itself, and the conditions of languidly monstrous character developed in an atmosphere of low vitality, have become the most valued material of modern fiction, and the most eagerly discussed texts of modern philosophy."[205]

He goes on to outline at length five reasons for this, as he considers it, morbid bias of modern fiction: (1) is the "hot fermentation and unwholesome secrecy" characteristic of urban centers, where people become "oppressive and infectious, each to his neighbor, in the smoking mass of decay";[206] (2) further "the disgrace of grief resulting from the mere trampling pressure and electric friction of town life" acquire quasi-mythological authority of their own and "become to the sufferers peculiarly mysterious in their undeservedness and frightful in their inevitableness," thus creating "an elaborate and ingenious scholasticism in what may be called the Divinity of Decomposition."[207]

(3) The monotony of urban life is relieved, Ruskin argues, only by mischief; and this need, unless there happens to be some "more than ordinary godsend of fatality," must be gratified by the daily violence of the streets. One would expect that these urban "laws of inanation" would provoke some reactionary desire in which "the dreariness of the street would have been guilded by dreams of pastoral felicity." In fact the Londoner insists on fiction based on the kind of excitement to which he has become accustomed, "but asks for *that* in continually more ardent or more virulent concentration; and the ultimate power of fiction to entertain him is by varying to his fancy the modes, and defining for his dullness the horrors, of Death."[208] *Bleak House*, illustrating nine modes of death, "all grotesquely violent or miserable," which happen with one exception to generally respectable and inoffensive persons, is Ruskin's chief instance of the fiction of the plague here.[209]

(4) The exposure of urban man to the joint conditions of vice and gloom apparently fosters in him a particular sympathy with the guilt and misery of those confined in prisons. "The specialty of the plague is a delight in the exposition of the relations between guilt and decrepitude; and I call the results of it literature 'of the prison-house,' because the thwarted habits of body and mind, which are the punishment of reckless crowding in cities, become, in the issue of that punishment, frightful subjects of exclusive interest to themselves; and the art of fiction in which they finally delight is only the more studied arrangement and illustration, by coloured firelights, of the daily bulletins of their own wretchedness, in the prison calendar, the police news, and the hospital report."[210] (5) Finally, a vast field for modern fiction is opened up by the "dice-cast or card-dealt calamity which opens itself in the ignorance, money-interest, and mean passion, of city marriage."[211]

As we would expect, Ruskin is more interested at this point in tracing the symptoms of plague in "foul" fiction than in defining the limits of "fair" fiction; just as it is foul weather that dominates the skies of his diaries in these years. Therefore, these forceful passages on the fiction of decomposition in the first essay are followed by many pages of knotted allusions and tortuous sentences as, in the following essays, he spins out lines of prophetic association from passages in Scott, Byron, and Wordsworth before bringing us to his definition of "fair" fiction. However, in the third essay he sets forth, with surprising specificity for this period of his work, his six tests of literary style in prose or verse. These tests are: (1) "Absolute command over all passion, however intense." (2) "Choice of the fewest and simplest words that can be found in the compass of the language, to express the thing meant." (3) "Perfectly emphatic and clear utterance of the chosen words; slowly in the degree of their importance, with omission, however, of every word not absolutely required." (4) "Absolute spontaneity in doing all this, easily and necessarily as the heart beats." (5) "Melody in the words, changeable with their passion, fitted to it exactly, and the utmost of which language is capable." (6) "Utmost spiritual contents in the words; so that each carries not only its instant meaning, but a cloudy companionship of higher darker meaning according to the passion—nearly always indicated by metaphor."[212] Obviously Ruskin wished for an organic style characterized by simplicity, intensity, rhythm, and restraint, a style of which he himself was no longer capable, though he had achieved something close to it in *Unto This Last* and *Sesame and Lilies*.

It is not until the last essay that Ruskin comes around to his definition of "fair" fiction, and here the element of mythic continuity and organic coherence reappears in counterposition to the plague pattern in modern fiction. His image of fiction has an Attic shape and a fair attitude. "The best type of it being the most practically fictile—a Greek vase." "Fair" fiction is to be "planned rigorously . . . as ever Memphian labyrinth or Norman fortress. . . . Intricacy full of delicate surprise; . . . not a stone useless, nor a word or an incident thrown away." Further, it is to be "rounded smoothly—the wheel of Fortune revolving with it in unfelt swiftness." Like the vase, it will be "balanced symmetrically . . . its figures moving in majestic law of light and shade" and "handled handily . . . comprehensible . . . tenable, not a confused heap of which you can only lift one pebble at a time." Lastly, it is to be "lipped softly—full of kindness and comfort." This is his essential distinction, the gentle feminine curvature of fair fiction; it is to be beautiful in the sense of a woman's beauty, and helpful: "All beautiful fiction is of the Madonna, whether the Virgin of Athens or of Judah—Pan-Athenaic always."[213]

Within the diverse topics of the last two series of Oxford lectures (*The Art of England, The Pleasures of England*) one may detect the same underlying polarity of concern: the veracity and continuity of mythic vision; the prophecy of plague. In his lecture "The Mythic Schools of Painting" in *The Art of England* his friend Burne-Jones is praised as a true mythic painter among moderns. But this assertion really serves as the occasion for a defense of mythic truth. "Never confuse a Myth with a lie," he warns, "—nay, you must even be cautious how far you even permit it to be called a fable."[214] Hence, because this school has made a careful study of mythic symbols, its truth is assured by the truth of those symbols.

> Truth is the vital power of the entire school,—truth its armour—Truth its war-word; and the grotesque and wild forms of imagination which, at first sight, seem to be the reaction of a desperate fancy, and a terrified faith, against the incisive scepticism of recent science, so far from being so, are a part of that science itself: they are the results of infinitely more accurate scholarship, of infinitely more detective examination, of infinitely more just and scrupulous integrity of thought, than was possible to any artist during the two preceding centuries.[215]

Through archeological science, their work has been the authentic continuance of myth.

However, before this school's achievement can have the significance Ruskin wishes to give it, he must clear up two mistaken ideas modern "archeologists" have about myth. The first notion is "that mythology is a temporary form of human folly, from which they are about in their own perfect wisdom to achieve our final deliverence"; the second is that the nature of myths may be ascertained from the "types which early art presents of them." He had disposed of the "first supercilious theory" in *The Queen of the Air*, his essential point then being that "the thoughts of all the greatest and wisest men hitherto, since the world was made, have been expressed through mythology."[216] In answer to the second error his argument—one of the most important perceptions of this final phase of his thought—is that we must distinguish the essential truth of a given myth from the technical capacity of the early artist in his representation of it. The function of modern mythic painters is—through scholarship, empathy, and advanced technical competence—to continue the mythic truth in modern technique: "to place, at the service of former imagination, the art which it had not—and to realize for us, with a truth then impossible, the visions described by the wisest of men as embodying their most pious thoughts and their most exalted doctrines."[217]

Ruskin is suggesting here what is probably an untenable distinction between the form and content of mythic truth; he would presumably not insist that the truth could be carried by technique alone, without participation in the believed vision. His basic argument, however, is that a careful study (like his own) of the continuity of myth has been, as he now sees it, a major contribution of the Pre-Raphaelites: "The transition of Athenian mythology, through Byzantine, into Christian, has been first felt, and then traced and proved, by the penetrative scholarship of the men belonging to this Pre-Raphaelite school, chiefly Mr. Burne-Jones and Mr. William Morris."[218]

By contrast, as we might expect, the work of the so-called classic schools of painting, headed by Alma Tadema has been marked by dismal failure. Here he sees signs of plague. Characteristically, in discussing this school he quotes a passage from the *Iliad* to "assure you of the association of light and cloud in their terrible mystery, with the truth and majesty of the human form, in the Greek conception. . . . In all ancient heroic subjects, you will find these two ideas of light and mystery [cloud] combined."[219] This has been the core of Ruskin's aesthetic doctrine in this period, and it points to what, for him, is the primary fallacy of Tadema's classical idealism. Despite this painter's great "technical accuracy," his pictures are "always in twilight." With this gloom Ruskin associates a cretinism in his human forms, joint failure of light and life by the powers of Apollo and Athena; therefore, Tadema's *Pyrrhic Dance* is, in his view, clearly infected by "fuliginous and cantharoid disfigurement and disgrace."[220]

In the final lecture of *The Art of England*, Ruskin returns with sweeping prophetic indignation to the larger infection of the organic model. All veracity and joy in the sense of color, he asserts, are dependent "first on vigour of health, and secondly on the steady looking for and acceptance of the truth of nature as *she* gives it you, not as you like to have it—to inflate your own pride, or satisfy your own passion. If pursued in that insolence, or in that concupiscence, the phenomena of all the universe become first gloomy, and then spectral; the sunset becomes demoniac fire to you, and the clouds of heaven as the smoke of Acheron."[221] I requote this passage because there is no more forceful statement in Ruskin's work of his position on the self-giveness of nature's truths and the dangers of ignoring them. But the truths of life, as he understands them, have been consistently ignored in the interests of false wealth; the consequent judgment is written in our infected skies and the states of mind these breed: "It has been my fate to live and work in direct antagonism to the instincts, and yet more to the interests, of the age; since I wrote that chapter ["The Open Sky," *Modern Painters*, volume 1] on the pure traceries of the vault of morning, the fury of useless traffic has shut the sight, whether of morning or evening, from more than the third part of England; and the foulness of sensual fantasy has infected the bright beneficence of the life-giving sky with the dull horrors of disease, and the feeble falsehoods of insanity."[222]

In the second lecture of *The Pleasures of England*, "The Pleasures of Faith," Ruskin reasserts the existence of an organic bond of truth between myth and nature in the minds of early men whose experience of nature was immediate and passionate. "I must farther advise you," he instructs,

> that the legends of these passionate times are in no wise, and in no sense fictions at all; but the true record of impressions made on the minds of persons in a state of excitement, brought into bright focus by acting steadily and frankly, under its impulses. I could tell you a great deal more about such things than you would believe, and therefore a great deal more than it would do you the least good to hear. . . . But don't accuse your roughly bred and fed fathers of telling lies about the aspect the earth and sky bore to *them*, till you have trodden the earth as they, barefoot, and seen the heavens as they, face to face.[223]

This conception of a vital harmony between the innocent eye and the self-given aspects of nature, a harmony testified to by the continuum of mythic vision, is at the center of Ruskin's prophecy. With the two lectures entitled *The Storm-Cloud of the Nineteenth Century* we arrive at the point from which we started, perhaps to know the place for the first time. The *Storm-Cloud*, though comparatively weak in literary value, is

Ruskin's final and most deliberate contribution to the continuum of vision, the ultimate testimony of a life-long adoration of the sky, face to face. This prophecy is prepared for as far back as the Alpine ecstacies of his poems and *Modern Painters*; it is deepened by his studies in Greek mythology and shadowed by his analysis of the social motives of his age. We have already noted that it is a scientistic apocalypse, fusing mythic and meteorological discourse. The chilling and hissing qualities he ascribes to the plague wind can be connected with his Athena's Gorgon face, the face she assumes for the punishment of unwise knowledge, and with the anger of his Apollo, whose scourge is Python's pestilence. The final point to be made is simply that this cloud symbolizes in Ruskin the fatal infection of the organic model by analytic detachment, while referring at the same time to the ominous increase in airborne pollutants (or, as we might see it, the threatened destruction of the ozone layer). The harmony of mind and nature, the bond of innocent eye and phenomenological truth, an ideal that plays such an important role in Romantic mythology, has been broken; the plague cloud announces this broken harmony and is a manifestation of it. It is a portent of our fall from the paradise Ruskin had known as a child and had declared in *Modern Painters*:

> Every argument, and every sentiment in that book, was founded on the personal experience of the beauty and blessing of nature, all spring and summer long; and on the then demonstrable fact that over a great portion of the world's surface the air and earth were fitted to the education of the spirit of man as closely as a schoolboy's primer is to his labour, and as gloriously as a lover's mistress is to his eyes.
>
> That harmony is now broken, and broken the world round: fragments, indeed, of what existed still exist, and hours of what is past return; but month by month the darkness gains upon the day, and the ashes of the Antipodes glare through the night.[224]

NOTES

Introduction

1. Harold Bloom, "Ruskin as Literary Critic," in *The Ringers in the Tower* (Chicago: University of Chicago Press, 1971), p. 183.

2. Ruskin to John James Ruskin, 13 May 1845, *Works*, 36:45. Unless otherwise specified all quotations from Ruskin are from the Library Edition of *The Works of John Ruskin*, ed. E. T. Cook and Alexander Wedderburn (London: George Allen, 1903–12) and will be cited in the manner just indicated. (A group of closely related passages occurring on the same page or on contiguous pages in a particular work will frequently be cited in one note.)

3. "Traffic" (1864), second lecture of *The Crown of Wild Olive* (1866), *Works*, 18:458. Compare the tone of the peroration of the first lecture in this collection, "Work" (1865): "Yes, and there is death—infinitude of death—in the principalities and powers of men. As far as the east is from the west, so far our sins are—*not* set from us, but multiplied around us: the Sun himself, think you he *now* 'rejoices' to run his course, when he plunges westward to the horizon, so widely red, not with clouds, but blood? And it will be red more widely yet. Whatever drought of the early and latter rain may be, there will be none of that red rain," (*Works*, 18:432).

4. *Works*, 34:9.

5. Ibid., p. 42, (italics mine).

6. As quoted by Ruskin, ibid., p. 13.

7. Ibid., p. 46.

8. Ibid., pp. 7–8.

9. *The Diaries of John Ruskin*, ed. Joan Evans and J. H. Whitehouse (Oxford: Clarendon Press, 1956–59), 1:220, December 1841 (hereafter cited as *Diaries*).

10. *Modern Painters*, 1, in *Works*, 3:373.

11. Ibid., 34:24.

12. Ibid., pp. 23-4, n. 3. Cf. *The Brantwood Diary of John Ruskin*, ed. Helen Gill Viljoen (New Haven: Yale University Press, 1971), pp. 248–49.

13. *Fors Clavigera*, Letter 8, August 1871, *Works*, 27:132.

14. *Works*, 34:33-34. The details of the plague wind summarized in this paragraph are quoted from paragraphs 30-38 of "Lecture I" (ibid., pp. 33–41) where they are divided into six characteristic features of the phenomenon.

15. Ibid., pp. 34-39.

16. Ibid., pp. 40-41.

17. Ibid., p. 59, Cf. ibid., 7:184–85.

18. Ibid., p. 34:68 (italics mine).

19. Ibid., p. 27.

20. Ibid., pp. 61–62.

21. Ruskin to George MacDonald, 11 August 1872, as quoted in Derrick Leon, *Ruskin: The Great Victorian* (London: Routledge and Kegan Paul, 1949), p. 495.

22. *Works*, 34:38. Ruskin quotes from his diary entry for 17 August 1879.

23. John D. Rosenberg, *The Darkening Glass* (New York: Columbia University Press, 1961), pp. 185–86.

24. *Daily News*, 6 February 1884. This report was noted by Ruskin in the second lecture and quoted by E. T. Cook. *Works*, 34:77 and n.1; 28:488.

25. *Works*, 34:78 and n. Ruskin uses the reference to "the ashes of the Antipodes" for its apocalyptic implications; however, as naturalist he took note of the possibility that the "unnatural" sunsets of the preceding autumn (and other climatic aberrations) were caused by the ash cloud from the Krakatoa eruption.

26. M. H. Abrams, *Natural Supernaturalism* (New York: Norton, 1971), p. 41.

27. E. H. Gombrich, *Art and Illusion: A Study in the Psychology of Pictorial Representation* (Princeton: Princeton University Press, 1961), p. 363.

28. Walter A. Davis, *The Act of Interpretation: A Critique of Literary Reason* (Chicago: University of Chicago Press, 1978), p. 66.

29. C. G. Jung, *Aion. Collected Works*, Vol. 9, Part II, tr. R. F. C. Hull (New York: Bollingen Foundation, 1958), in *Psyche and Symbol*, ed. Violet S. de Lazlo (Garden City, N.Y.: Doubleday, 1958), p. 8 (hereafter cited as *Psyche and Symbol*).

30. *The Archetypes and the Collective Unconscious*, 2nd ed. *Collected Works*, Vol. 9, Part I, tr. R. F. C. Hull, Bollingen Series XX (Princeton: Princeton University Press, 1968), p. 28.

31. Jolande Jacobi, *The Way of Individuation*, tr. R. F. C. Hull (New York: Harcourt, Brace and World, 1967), p. 64.

32. *Works*, 29:54.

33. Van Akin Burd, *John Ruskin and Rose La Touche: Her Unpublished Diaries of 1861 and 1867* (Oxford: Clarendon Press, 1979), p. 140.

34. From the ms. of the intended preface for *Proserpina* in *Works*, 35:628.

35. *Diaries*, 1:364.

36. Ibid., 2:389-90.

37. Ibid., p. 400.

38. These passages are from the entries in *Diaries*, 3:773-871. Locations are indicated by dates.

39. Jung, in *Psyche and Symbol*, p. 20.

40. Ibid., p. 26.

41. Ibid., p. 8.

42. Ibid., p. 9.

43. *Works*, 33:387.

44. Ibid., p. 388.

45. Bk. 2, ll. 829-51.

46. *Pall Mall Gazette*, 19 November 1883, as quoted in *Works*, 33:389, n.3.

47. Quoted by Eliseo Vivas in *Creation and Discovery* (New York: Noonday Press, 1955), p. viii.

48. Serge Doubrovsky, *The New Criticism in France*, tr. Derek Coleman (Chicago: University of Chicago Press, 1973), Ch. 11.

49. *Works*, 35:314-15.

50. Ibid, and Eccles. 3:11.

51. Alfred North Whitehead, *Science and the Modern World* (New York: Macmillan, 1925), reprinted. (New York: New American Library, 1948), p. 87.

52. *Works*, 35:315.

53. Patrick Conner, *Savage Ruskin* (Detroit: Wayne State University Press, 1979), pp. 56-8, 105-10.

54. *Athenaeum* (11 July, 1857) as quoted ibid., p. 117.

55. *Modern Painters*, Vol. 5, *Works*, 7:262.

56. *Sesame and Lilies*, "Lecture III," *Works*, 18:180.

57. Samuel Taylor Coleridge, *Biographia Literaria*, ed. J. Shawcross (London: Oxford University Press, 1907), 1:202.

58. *Modern Painters*, Vol. 2, *Works*, 4:250-1.

59. Ibid., p. 225, 226 n.

60. Ibid., p. 239.

61. Ibid., p. 251.

62. Ibid.

63. Ibid., p. 308.

64. Philip Wheelwright, *Metaphor and Reality* (Bloomington: Indiana University Press, 1962), p. 158.

65. Van Akin Burd, in "Another Light on the Writing of *Modern Painters*," *PMLA* 68

(1953), 755–63, has compared Ruskin's account of his Fontainebleau epiphany given in *Praeterita* (quoted in part above, pp. 25–26) with that in his diary for 1842 which he was unable to consult when he integrated this moment into his autobiography. The evidence is that the later Ruskin gave the event a more mystical cast than it originally had. As we shall see, Ruskin did record other more distinctly mystical experiences after the mid seventies when his consciousness and his religion underwent a crucial change. Obviously this later mystical change would affect the developmental shape he gave to his life in *Praeterita* and color much of the evidence derived from that work.

66.   *Works*, 26:99, and cf. p. 336. Ruskin's immediate concern in these passages is to defend the enduring truth of "the myths of betrayal and redemption," which speak of the contest of good and evil spirits for the body and soul of man, the victory in the present world of the deceiving spirit, and the "promised final victory of the creating and true Spirit," against the Darwinian view of human development.

67.   Coleridge, "On Poesy or Art," *Biographia*, 2:259.

68.   Ernst Cassirer, *The Philosophy of Symbolic Forms*, vol. 2, *Mythical Thought* (New Haven: Yale University Press, 1955), p. 175.

69.   *Works*, 35:51.

70.   Ibid., pp. 15–16.

71.   Ibid., p. 67.

72.   Ibid., p. 56. The excerpt from "Harry and Lucy" appears on pp. 52–55.

73.   Ibid., p. 115.

74.   Thomas Carlyle *Sartor Resartus*, Bk. 2, Ch. 6, *The Works of Thomas Carlyle*, Centenary Edition, 30 vols. (London: Chapman and Hall, 1897; reprinted, New York: AMS Press, 1969), 1:123 (hereafter cited as Centenary Ed.).

75.   *Works*, 35:218.

76.   Ibid., p. 219n.

77.   Ibid., p. 219.

78.   Ibid., p. 220.

79.   *Diaries*, 3:869, and Matt. 13:28.

80.   *Time and Tide*, letter 11, "The Golden Bough", in *Works*, 17:368.

81.   Ruskin to Lady Mount-Temple, 4 May 1869, *The Letters of John Ruskin to Lord and Lady Mount-Temple*, ed. John Lewis Bradley (Columbus: Ohio State University Press, 1964), p. 200 (hereafter cited as *Letters*, ed. Bradley).

82.   *Diaries*, 2:685.

83.   Ruskin to Lady Mount-Temple, 19 March 1867, *Letters*, ed. Bradley, p. 112.

84.   *Works*, 33:104.

85.   *Diaries*, 2:498.

86.   *Works*, 4:250–1.

87.   Ibid., 7:408.

88.   Ibid., pp. 387–88.

89.   Ibid., p. 207.

90.   Ruskin to Lady Mount-Temple, 1869 17 April, *Letters*, ed. Bradley, p. 197.

91.   Ruskin to Lady Mount-Temple, September 1873, Ibid., p. 351.

92.   Fredric Harrison, *John Ruskin* (London, 1902), pp. 182–84 quoted by E. T. Cook in *Works*, 27:xxiii–iv.

93.   *Works*, 25:463.

94.   Ibid., p. 436.

95.   Ibid., p. 466. In a note to "Spirit" Ruskin refers the reader to paragraph 52 of *The Queen of the Air* for the sense in which this word is used "throughout" his writings: "the power which shaped you into your shape, and by which you love, and hate, when you have received that shape."

96.   Carlyle, *On Heroes, Hero-Worship, and the Heroic in History*, Lecture 1, Centenary Ed., 5:30.

97.   *Works*, 35:428.

98. Ibid., p. 344.
99. Ibid., p. 288.
100. Ibid., pp. 288–89.
101. Ibid., p. 289.
102. Bloom, *The Ringers in the Tower*, p. 181.
103. G. M. Young, *Victorian England: Portrait of an Age*, 2nd ed. (London: Oxford University Press, 1953), p. 112.
104. *Works*, 19:408. "I have always had three different ways of writing: one, with the single view of making myself understood, in which I necessarily omit a great deal of what comes into my head; another, in which I say what I think ought to be said, in what I suppose to be the best words I can find for it; (which is in reality an affected style—be it good or bad;) and my third way of writing is to say all that comes into my head for my own pleasure, in the first words that come, retouching them afterwards into (approximate) grammar."
105. Ibid., 33:390.
106. *Diaries*, 3:851.
107. *Works*, 20:33, 144, 246.
108. Richard Jenkyns, *The Victorians and Ancient Greece* (Cambridge: Harvard University Press, 1980), p. 179.
109. Ibid., pp. 183–185.
110. James Kissane, "Victorian Mythology," *VS* 6 (1962): 11.
111. Albert S. Gérard, *English Romantic Poetry* (Berkeley and Los Angeles: University of California Press, 1968), p. 8.
112. E. F. Schumacher, *Small is Beautiful: Economics as if People Mattered* (London: Blond and Briggs, 1973; reprint ed. New York: Harper and Row, 1973). Schumaker acknowledges the influence of Gandhi, who was influenced by Ruskin. This influence of Ruskin on Gandhi has recently been assessed by Elizabeth McLaughlin in *Ruskin and Gandhi* (Lewisburg, Pa.: Bucknell University Press, 1974).
113. James Clark Sherburne, *John Ruskin, or the Ambiguities of Abundance: A Study in Social and Economic Criticism* (Cambridge: Harvard University Press, 1972), p. 296.
114. R. G. Collingwood, "Ruskin's Philosophy" in *Essays in the Philosophy of Art*, ed. Alan Donagan (Bloomington: Indiana University Press, 1964), pp. 17–24, 30–37.
115. Robert Tucker, *Philosophy and Myth in Karl Marx*, 2nd ed. (Cambridge: Cambridge University Press, 1972), pp. 218–32.
116. *Works*, 24:371.
117. Ibid., 22:505.
118. Robert Hewison, *John Ruskin: The Argument of the Eye* (Princeton: Princeton University Press, 1976), pp. 65, 69–70, 117, 207–8.
119. W. S. Johnson, "Style in Ruskin and Ruskin on Style," *VN* 59 (1981): 5.
120. Maurice Merleau-Ponty, *The Phenomenology of Perception*, tr. Colin Smith (New York: Humanities Press, 1962), xvi–xvii.

Chapter 1: Apocalyptic Landscape

1. Ursula Bridge, ed., *W. B. Yeats and T. Sturge Moore: Their Correspondence, 1901-1937* (New York: Oxford University Press, 1953), pp. 63-114.
2. Ibid., pp. 99-100.
3. During his mental breakdown of 1878 Ruskin did have a hallucinatory encounter with the "Evil One" in the form of a cat as the climax of a night-long vigil he maintained on Friday, 22 February; at this time he grappled with the presence and hurled it to the floor: "A dull thud—nothing more." Years later he described the experience publicly in "Mr. Ruskin's Illness Described by Himself" (*British Medical Journal, 1900*, reprinted in

Works, 38:172-73). Ruskin's state of mind at the time is discussed below in ch. 14. See also Helen Gill Viljoen, ed., *The Brantwood Diary of John Ruskin* (New Haven: Yale University Press, 1971), "1878 Introduction," pp. 61-79.

4. W. B. Yeats, *Autobiography* (New York: Macmillan, 1965), p. 226.

5. *Works*, 1:313-14.

6. Ibid., p. 327.

7. Ibid., p. 331.

8. John Rosenburg has noted the recurrence of "juxtaposed elements" balanced in his prose, a "polarization of reality in Ruskin's writing." "Almost invariably," he observes, "the greatest passages in Ruskin's prose are structured around two opposing visions, one of felicity and the other of some form of hell" ("Style and Sensibility in Ruskin's Prose," in *The Art of Victorian Prose*, ed. G. Levine and W. Madden [New York: Oxford University Press, 1968], pp. 177-200).

9. The passage alluded to is from "The Everlasting Yea." " 'Often also could I see the black Tempest marching in anger through the Distance: round some Schreckhorn, as yet grim-blue, would the eddying vapour gather, and there tumultuously eddy, and flow down like a mad witch's hair; till, after a space, it vanished, and, in the clear sunbeam, your Schreckhorn stood smiling grim-white, for the vapour had held snow. How thou fermentest and elaboratest in thy great fermenting-vat and laboratory of an Atmosphere, of a World, O Nature!—Or what is Nature? Ha! why do I not name thee GOD. Art thou not the "Living Garment of God"? O Heavens, is it, in very deed, HE, then, that ever speaks through thee; that lives and loves in thee, that lives and loves in me?' " Thomas Carlyle, *Sartor Resartus*, Bk. 2, ch. 9 *The Works of Thomas Carlyle*, Centenary Edition, 30 vols. (London: Chapman and Hall, 1897; reprint ed., New York: AMS Press, 1969), 1:150. Hereafter cited as Centenary Ed.

10. *Works*, 1:335.

11. Ibid., p. 336.

12. Ibid., p. 337.

13. Ibid., p. 338.

14. Ibid., p. 341.

15. Ibid., pp. 341-42.

16. Ibid., p. 342.

17. *Sartor Resartus*, Bk. 1, ch. 8, "The World Out of Clothes," Centenary Ed., 1:41.

18. *Works*, 3:616.

19. Ibid., p. 611.

20. Ibid., pp. 630-31.

21. Ruskin does not use this phrase, but his view resembles Coleridge's position, after Schelling, that "the old definition of painting will in fact be the true and best definition of the Fine Arts in general, that is, *muta poesis*, mute poesy, and so of course poesy" ("On Poesy on Art," in, ed. J. Shawcross *Biographia Literaria* [Oxford: Oxford University Press, 1907], 2:255). Ruskin has assumed, in a vague way, the "poetry" of plastic art in "The Poetry of Architecture" (1837-38), and he will consider the analogy between poetry and painting more closely in *Modern Painters*, vol. 3 (1856). See ch. 5 of this study. Ruskin's indebtedness to the *ut pictura poesis* tradition has been carefully traced by George Landow in his *Aesthetic and Critical Theories of John Ruskin* (Princeton: Princeton University Press, 1971).

22. *Works*, 3:92.

23. Ibid., pp. 51-52.

24. Ibid., p. 104.

25. Ibid., p. 108.

26. Ibid., p. 147.

27. Ibid., p. 148. Coleridge had followed a similar line of reasoning. "The artist," he wrote, "must imitate that which is within the thing, that which is active through form and figure, and discourses to us through symbols—the *Natur-geist*, or spirit of nature." He also

used the example of the portrait. "Each thing that lives has its moment of self-exposition." It is the business of the painter to catch this moment in the features. "Hence a good portrait is the abstract of the personal; it is not the likeness for actual comparison, but for recollection. This explains why the likeness of a very good portrait is not always recognized" ("On Poesy or Art," in *Biographia Literaria*, ed. Shawcross, 2:259).

28.   *Works*, 3:148.
29.   Ibid., p. 387.
30.   Ibid., p. 27.
31.   Coleridge, "On Poesy or Art," *Biographia Literaria*, 2:257. This essay, which closely resembles Schelling's oration *On The Relation of the Formative Arts to Nature*, was first printed in vol. 1 of *Literary Remains*, 1836.
32.   From ms. sheets related to *The Stones of Venice* as quoted in *Works*, 11:xvii-xxi.
33.   *Works*, 3:156.
34.   Ibid., p. 164.
35.   Ibid., p. 169.
36.   Ibid., p. 188.
37.   Ibid., p. 217.
38.   Ibid., p. 177.
39.   Ibid., p. 246.
40.   Ibid., p. 252.
41.   From the conclusion to the chapter as it appeared in the first and second editions. As reprinted in *Works*, 3:253-58. (italics mine).
42.   *Works*, 3:308.
43.   Ibid., p. 284.
44.   Ibid., p. 261.
45.   Ibid., pp. 262-63.
46.   Ibid., p. 274.
47.   Ibid., p. 275.
48.   Ibid., p. 292.
49.   Ibid., p. 293.
50.   Ibid., p. 299.
51.   Ibid., p. 314.
52.   Ibid., p. 381.
53.   Ibid., pp. 285-86.
54.   Ibid., p. 344.
55.   Ibid., p. 373 (italics mine).
56.   Ibid., p. 363. (Ruskin had referred to the same passage of *The Excursion*, bk. 9, 11. 592-608, earlier on p. 353.)
57.   Ibid., p. 363.
58.   Ibid., pp. 418-19.
59.   Ibid., p. 413.
60.   Ibid., pp. 571-72.
61.   *The Diaries of John Ruskin*, ed. Joan Evans and J. H. Whitehouse (Oxford: The Clarendon Press, 1958), 1:273.
62.   *Science and the Modern World* (New York: Macmillan, 1925 rpt. New American Library, 1948), p. 85.
63.   *Works*, 3:483.
64.   Ibid., 4:xiiv.
65.   Ibid., 35:41.
66.   Ibid., 4:348-50.
67.   In "The Dabchicks," published in 1881 as pt. 3 of *Love's Meinie* (1873-1881), *Works*, 25:122.
68.   *Works*, 4:35, and fn.
69.   Ibid., 25:122.

70.   Ibid., 35:288.

71.   Ibid., pp. 314-15. Ruskin's retrospective account of this epiphany is important for its expression of an illumination that was central to his thought and because it is analogous with more generalized romantic accounts of the coalescence of mind and nature. His experience, characteristically grounded in the visual, becomes nonetheless encounter with Coleridge's "the essence, the *natura naturans*, which presupposes a bond between nature in the higher sense and the soul of man" (see above note 31). It is also reminiscent of the "high argument" of Wordsworth's poetry, "The discerning intellect of Man / When wedded to this goodly universe / In love and holy passion" or "my voice proclaims / How exquisitely the individual Mind / . . . to the external world is fitted." These lines from the "Prospectus" to the *The Recluse*, as M. H. Abrams has shown, announce a central theme of romantic myth-making, the apocalyptic marriage of mind and nature (see *Natural Supernaturalism* [New York: Norton, 1971], pp. 21-32).

72.   *Works*, 1:465.

73.   Ibid., 35:344.

74.   Ibid., pp. 218-19.

75.   Ibid., p. 414.

76.   A.-F. Rio, *De la Poésie Chrétienne dans son principe, dans sa matière, et dans ses formes* (Paris, 1836).

77.   *Works*, 28:146. The spell of this image upon him is in some ways comparable that cast upon him by the expression of the sleeping Ursula (in Carpaccio's *The Dream of Saint Ursula*) as he "studied" it with quasi-mystical intensity in 1876 after the death of Rose La Touche.

78.   Ibid., 4:347.

79.   Ibid., 35:350.

80.   Ibid., p. 360.

81.   Ibid., 4:354. Cf. ibid., 35:371-2.

82.   See *The Relation between Michael Angelo and Tintoret* (1872). Ibid., 22:82.

83.   Ibid., 35:371-2.

84.   Ibid., p. 413.

85.   Ibid., 26:334.

86.   Ibid., 4:49.

87.   Ibid., p. 64.

88.   Ibid., p. 72.

89.   Ibid., p. 87.

90.   Ibid., p. 128.

91.   Ibid., p. 130.

92.   Henry Ladd, *The Victorian Morality of Art: An Analysis of Ruskin's Aesthetic* (New York: Long and Smith, 1932) p. 186. For a more recent and also illuminating analysis of the significance of the concept of purity in Ruskin, see James Clark Sherburne, *John Ruskin, or the Ambiguities of Abundance: A Study in Social and Economic Criticism* (Cambridge: Harvard Univ. Press, 1972), Ch. 1, "Purity."

93.   *Works*, 4:148.

94.   Ibid., p. 153.

95.   Ibid., p. 187.

96.   Ibid., p. 191.

97.   Ibid., p. 148, n.

98.   Ibid., p. 241.

99.   "It dissolves, diffuses, dissipates, in order to recreate; or where this process is rendered impossible, yet still at all events it struggles to idealize and to unify. It is essentially *vital*, even as all objects (*as* objects) are essentially fixed and dead." Further: "Imagination . . . reveals itself in the balance or reconciliation of opposite or discordant qualities: of sameness with, difference; of the general with the concrete; the idea, with the image; the individual, with the representative; the sense of novelty and of freshness, with

old and familiar objects; a more than unusual state of emotion, with more than usual order; judgment over awake and steady self-possession, with enthusiasm and feeling profound or vehement; and while it blends and harmonizes the natural and the artificial, still subordinates art to nature; the manner to the matter; and our admiration of the poet to our sympathy with the poetry." (Coleridge, *Biographia Literaria*, ed. Shawcross, 1:202; 2:12). Harold Bloom asserts that "Ruskin's own theory of imagination is clearly derived from Coleridge's, "but of the three modes that Ruskin assigns to the imagination this Associative or integrative function seems to echo Coleridge most closely. Bloom adds that Ruskin possessed more confidence in the autonomy of the imagination than Coleridge, and this seems true in the light of his later emphasis on great imagination as "involuntary" vision ("Ruskin as Literary Critic," in The *Ringers in the Tower: Studies in Romantic Tradition* [Chicago: University of Chicago Press, 1971], pp. 169–83).

100. *Works*, 4:289, Ruskin's marginal gloss.
101. Ibid., p. 226, n.
102. Ibid., p. 284.
103. Ibid., p. 251.
104. Ibid., p. 250.
105. Ibid., p. 252.
106. Ibid., p. 253.
107. Ibid., p. 247.
108. Ibid., p. 257.
109. Ibid., p. 298.
110. Ibid., pp. 221-22.
111. Ibid., pp. 276-77.
112. Ibid., p. 288.
113. Ibid., p. 314.
114. Ibid., p. 315.
115. Ibid., pp. 315-316.
116. Ibid., p. 329, note to the original edition.
117. Ibid., p. 329.
118. Ibid., p. 308.
119. Ibid., p. 330, n.

Chapter 2: Life and Death in Architecture

1. Robert Tucker, *Philosophy and Myth in Karl Marx* (London: Cambridge University Press, 1961), pp. 21-22, 228-30.
2. Kristine Ottesen Garrigan has discussed this narrowness of Ruskin's architectural interests—his concern with surfaces and ornamental parts, his use of Italian Gothic as a standard—in her *Ruskin on Architecture* (Madison: University of Wisconsin Press, 1973). If one considers Ruskin's views on architecture or architectural history apart from the larger implications of his writing such as his myth-making and his social prophecy, they do indeed seem limited and impractical.
3. *Works*, 35:224.
4. Ibid., p. 225.
5. Ibid., 1:5.
6. Ibid., p. 8.
7. Ibid., p. 167, n.
8. Ibid., 3:347; 28:146; and cf. 34:xxxii, 170-74.
9. Ibid., 35:350.
10. See above, ch. 2, pp. 104-5 and *Works*, 35:371-72.

11. Diaries, 1:245.
12. Joan Evans, *John Ruskin* (New York: Oxford University Press, 1954), p. 147.
13. *Diaries,* 2:367.
14. Ibid., p. 370.
15. Ibid., p. 371.
16. Ibid.
17. Ibid.
18. *Works,* 4:151.
19. Ibid., p. 153.
20. *Diaries,* 1:352.
21. Ibid., p. 346.
22. *The Crown of Wild Olive,* "Lecture 2," *Works,* 18:434-35.
23. *Works,* 35:409.
24. Ibid., 8:xxxiii.
25. J. A. Froude, *Carlyle's Life in London,* 1:468, as quoted in Derrick Leon, *Ruskin: The Great Victorian* (London: Routledge and Kegan Paul, 1949), p. 116.
26. Elie Halévy, *A History of the English People in the Nineteenth Century,* vol. 4, *The Victorian Years: 1841-1895* (New York: Peter Smith, 1951), p. 246.
27. Thomas Carlyle, *Past and Present,* ed. R. D. Altic (Boston: Houghton Mifflin, 1965), p. 148.
28. Ibid., p. 261.
29. G. M. Young, *Victorian England: Portrait of an Age* (London: Oxford University Press, 1936), p. 55n.
30. Ibid., p. 52.
31. Ibid., p. 54.
32. D. C. Somervell, *English Thought in the Nineteenth Century* (London: Methuen, 1929), pp. 95-96.
33. *Works,* 8:194, n.
34. Preface to the edition of 1880. *Works,* 8:15.
35. Ibid.
36. *Works,* 35:378.
37. Ibid., p. 422.
38. Ibid., p. 422.
39. *Diaries,* 1:364.
40. Evans, *John Ruskin,* p. 134.
41. Quoted by Cook in *Works,* 8:xxxiv.
42. *Sheepfolds* (1851), was originally an appendix to volume 1 of *Stones.* Ruskin's purpose was to define the visible church as a religious community. He differentiated it from the invisible or mystical church, insisting that its authority was not doctrinal but disciplinary and that it was therefore necessarily inseparable from the state. While *Sheepfolds* was actually meant to suggest a scheme for the reconstruction of the Protestant church, it was, Cook tells us, now and then mistakenly purchased by farmers looking for a practical manual on fold construction.
43. *Works,* 8:22.
44. Ibid., p. 28, n.
45. Ibid., pp. 39-40.
46. Ibid., p. 53.
47. Ibid., p. 54.
48. Ibid., p. 58, n.
49. Ibid., p. 59.
50. Ibid., p. 67. However Ruskin, does allow, in the same place, that "the time is probably near when a new system of architectural laws will be developed, adapted entirely to metallic construction."
51. Ibid., p. 68.
52. Ibid., p. 73.

53. Ibid., pp. 87-88.
54. Ibid., p. 89.
55. *The Flamboyant Architecture of the Valley of the Somme* in *Works*, 19:240–275. See below pp. 509–11.
56. *Works*, 8:101.
57. Ibid., p. 102.
58. Ibid., p. 109.
59. Ibid., p. 116.
60. Ibid., p. 117.
61. Ibid., p. 120.
62. Ibid., p. 121, n.
63. Ibid., p. 143, n.
64. Ibid., pp. 176–7.
65. Ibid., p. 183.
66. Ibid., p. 189.
67. Ibid., p. 189.
68. Ibid., p. 190.
69. Ibid., p. 191.
70. Ibid., p. 191.
71. Ibid., p. 192.
72. Ibid., p. 192 and n.
73. Ibid., p. 193.
74. Ibid., p. 195.
75. Ibid., p. 197.
76. Ibid., p. 198.
77. Ibid., p. 199.
78. Ibid., p. 204.
79. Ibid., p. 209.
80. Ibid., p. 214.
81. Ibid., p. 215.
82. Ibid., p. 218.
83. Ibid., p. 219–20.
84. Ibid., pp. 226–27.
85. Ibid., p. 233.
86. Ibid., p. 242.
87. Ibid., p. 242.
88. Ibid., p. 256, n.
89. Ibid., pp. 265–66.
90. Sir Kenneth Clark sums up Ruskin's reaction to the Gothic revival in this way: "Ruskin . . . found that very few Gothic Revival buildings satisfied his hunger for beauty, and the greater number were positively distasteful to him. Of course the forms they used appealed to him strongly; the tune they played was his tune, but they played it very badly" (*The Gothic Revival*, 1928; rpt. New York: Holt, Rinehart and Winston, 1962, p. 198).
91. Frank Lloyd Wright, *An Organic Architecture: The Architecture of Democracy* (London: Lund Humphries, 1941), p. 40.
92. Ibid., p. 47.

Chapter 3: Venetian Approaches

1. Ruskin to Mary A. Mitford, 15 April 1849, quoted by Derrick Leon in *Ruskin: The Great Victorian* (London: Routledge and Kegan Paul, 1949), p. 131.

2. *Works,* 35:451.
3. Ibid., pp. 288–89.
4. *Diaries,* 2:408.
5. *Works,* 35:34–35.
6. *Diaries,* 2:389–90.
7. Ibid., pp. 388–89.
8. *Works,* 35:453 and n.
9. Letter of 1852, quoted in *Works,* 9:xxxvi.
10. Quoted in *Works,* 9:xxviii.
11. Ruskin's letters from Venice are, on the whole, disappointing in their relative paucity of direct visual impressions of the city or comments on the argument of *Stones;* they do, however, contain many interesting social observations and important religious ruminations. See *Ruskin's Letters from Venice: 1851–1852,* ed. John L. Bradley (New Haven: Yale University Press, 1955) and cf. *Young Mrs. Ruskin in Venice: Unpublished Letters . . . 1849–1852,* ed. Mary Lutyens (New York: Vanguard Press, 1965).
12. Ruskin to Norton, May 1859, quoted in *Works,* 9:xxvii–xxix.
13. *Diaries,* 2:454.
14. Ibid., pp. 455–56.
15. Ibid., p. 458.
16. Ibid., pp. 462–63.
17. Ibid., p. 463.
18. Ibid., pp. 474–75.
19. Ibid., pp. 475–76.
20. Ibid., p. 476.
21. *Works,* 35:483.
22. *Diaries,* 2:465.
23. Ibid., pp. 465–66.
24. *Works,* 36:127.
25. Quoted in *Works,* 10: xxxviii–xxxix.
26. *Works,* 36:137–38.
27. *Works,* 35:481.
28. *Works,* 10: p. 66.
29. Ibid., p. 67.
30. Works, 9:4.
31. Ibid., p. 9.
32. Ibid., pp. 11–12.
33. Ibid., pp. 12–13.
34. Ibid., p. 14.
35. Ibid.
36. Ibid., pp. 14–15.
37. *The Builder,* 13 August 1853; quoted by Ruskin in *Works,* 11:356.
38. Ibid., p. 356.
39. Ibid.
40. Ibid., p. 357.
41. *Works,* 9:27.
42. Ibid., p. 32.
43. Ibid., p. 36.
44. Ibid., p. 36, n.
45. Ibid., p. 37.
46. Ibid., p. 38.
47. Ibid., p. 44.
48. Ibid., p. 45.
49. Ibid., pp. 46–47.
50. Ibid., p. 55.

51. Ibid., p. 70.
52. Ibid., p. 79.
53. Ibid., p. 152.
54. Ibid., p. 226.
55. Ibid., p. 287.
56. Ibid., p. 290.
57. Ibid., p. 293.
58. Ibid., p. 301 (italics mine).
59. Ibid., pp. 306–307.
60. Ibid., p. 337.
61. Ibid., p. 369.
62. Ibid.
63. Ibid., p. 371.
64. Ibid., p. 406.
65. Ibid., p. 410.
66. Ibid., p. 411.
67. Ibid., pp. 411–12.
68. Ibid., p. 412.
69. Ibid., p. 414.
70. Ibid., p. 415.

Chapter 4: The Judgment of Venice

1. *Works*, 10:9.
2. Ibid., pp. 14–15.
3. Ibid., p. 14.
4. Ibid., p. 13.
5. See p. 136.
6. *Works*, 8:130 and n.
7. Ibid., 10:24.
8. Ibid., p. 26.
9. Ibid., p. 36.
10. Ibid., p. 65.
11. Ibid., pp. 78–79.
12. Ibid., p. 79.
13. Ibid., p. 81.
14. Ibid.
15. Ibid., p. 82.
16. Ibid.
17. Ibid., pp. 82–83.
18. Ibid., p. 84.
19. Ibid., pp. 84–85.
20. Ibid., p. 85.
21. Ibid., p. 86.
22. Ibid., pp. 87–88.
23. Ibid., p. 90.
24. Ibid., p. 98.
25. Ibid., p. 109.
26. Ibid. p. 115.
27. Ibid., p. 123.

28.   Ibid., p. 124.

29.   Ibid., p. 127.

30.   Ibid., p. 129.

31.   Ibid., p. 140. This consideration of the cathedral as a kind of visible myth is developed further in *The Bible of Amiens* (1880–85). It should be noticed that in this concept Ruskin points not only to the iconographic significance of the church's scriptural imagery but also to the iconological significance of the whole building as a cultural myth: "the Redeemed Church of God." It is interesting to observe that while Ruskin, as religious Romantic, would need to stress the mythic significance of the cathedral, a modern authority, speaking of the Gothic cathedral (not of the Byzantine Saint Mark's) makes his analogy with science: "Designed in an attempt to reproduce the structure of the universe, not unlike the great scientific experiments of the modern age in this respect, the cathedral is perhaps best understood as a 'model' of the medieval universe. That may give us a better idea of the speculative significance of these great edifices, a significance that transcends their beauty and practical purpose as a place of public worship." (Otto von Simson, *The Gothic Cathedral*, Bollingen Series 48 [New York: Pantheon Books, 1956], p. 35).

32.   *Works*, 10:160.

33.   Ibid., p. 161.

34.   Ibid., p. 163.

35.   Ibid., p. 173.

36.   Ibid., p. 174.

37.   Ibid., p. 176.

38.   Ibid., pp. 178–79 (italics mine).

39.   Preface to the Kelmscott edition (1892) of ch. 6 of *The Stones of Venice*, in *Works*, vol. 10, Appendix 14, pp. 460–62.

40.   Ibid., p. 182. If we look back at his observation in *The Seven Lamps of Architecture* that Gothic climax came "at the instant when the light had expanded to its fullest, and yet not lost its radiant energy, principality, and visible first causing of the whole" and tie this to the organic concept of forms composed so as "to have life," and other implications of vitality in the features of Gothic described in the succeeding paragraphs, it will appear that, for Ruskin, the governing characteristics of Gothic *structure* are light and life. It is interesting to compare his view with that of Otto von Simson, who observes that "Gothic may be described as transparent, diaphanous architecture. During the first century after its emergence, this aesthetic principle was developed with complete consistency and to its ultimate consequences. The gradual enlargement of the windows as such is not the most important manifestation of this process. No segment of inner space was allowed to remain in darkness, undefined by light." He also points to a vital unity of form and function in Gothic: "We cannot enter a Gothic church without feeling that every visible member of the great system has a job to do. There are no walls but only supports; the bulk and weight of the vault seem to have contracted into the sinewy web of the ribs. There is no inert matter, only active energy. However, this cosmos of forces is not the naked manifestation of tectonic functions, but their translation into a basically graphic system." We can assume that Ruskin would have agreed with von Simson on these two defining characteristics of the Gothic building, but from here their analyses diverge. Von Simson goes on, following the language of early dedication rituals, to relate the aesthetic and geometric principles of Gothic structure to the controlling idea that "the church is, mystically and liturgically, an image of heaven." Ruskin, however, turns away from structure to sculpture and ties his church firmly to earth in terms of representation of natural form and its integration of labor. Quotations are from Otto von Simson, *The Gothic Cathedral*, pp. 4, 7–8.

41.   *Works*, 10:188.

42.   Ibid., p. 190.

43.   Ibid.

44.   Ibid., pp. 192–93.

45.   Ibid., p. 193.

46. Ibid., p. 194.
47. Ibid., p. 199.
48. Ibid., p. 202.
49. Ibid.
50. Ibid., p. 203.
51. Ibid., p. 204.
52. Ibid., p. 205.
53. Ibid., p. 214.
54. Ibid., p. 217.
55. Ibid., p. 220.
56. Ibid., pp. 221–22.
57. Ibid., pp. 222–23.
58. Ibid., p. 222 (italics mine).
59. Ibid., p. 224.
60. Ibid., p. 231.
61. Ibid., p. 239.
62. Ibid., p. 240.
63. Ibid., p. 244.
64. Ibid., p. 247.
65. Ibid., p. 260.
66. Ibid., p. 265.
67. Ibid., pp. 271–72.
68. Ibid., p. 306.
69. Ibid., p. 340.
70. Ibid., p. 357.
71. Ibid., p. 352.
72. Ibid., p. 359.
73. Ibid., p. 360.
74. Ibid., p. 363.
75. Ibid., p. 370.
76. Ibid., pp. 371–72.
77. Ibid., p. 370.
78. Ibid., pp. 372–73.
79. Ibid., pp. 374–75.
80. Ibid., pp. 376–77.
81. Ibid., p. 403.
82. Ibid., p. 404.
83. Ibid., p. 432.
84. Ibid., pp. 432–33.
85. Ibid., 11:6.
86. Ibid., p. 9.
87. Ibid., p. 11.
88. Ibid., p. 22.
89. Ibid., p. 25.
90. Ibid., pp. 46–47.
91. Ibid., p. 47.
92. Ibid., p. 49.
93. Ibid., pp. 47–48.
94. Ibid., p. 48, n.
95. Ibid., p. 51.
96. Ibid., pp. 66–67.
97. Ibid., p. 70.
98. Ibid., pp. 81–82.
99. Ibid., p. 115.
100. Ibid., p. 117, and 2 Cor. 3:6.

101. *Works,* 11:109.
102. Ibid., p. 122.
103. Ibid., p. 129.
104. Ibid., p. 130.
105. Ibid., p. 131.
106. Ibid., p. 132.
107. Ibid., pp. 133–34.
108. Ibid., p. 135.
109. Ibid., p. 145.
110. Ibid., p. 150.
111. Ibid., p. 161.
112. Ibid., p. 163.
113. Ibid., pp. 163–64.
114. Ibid., p. 165.
115. Ibid., p. 166.
116. Ibid., p. 172.
117. Ibid., p. 180.
118. Ibid., 6:437.
119. Ibid., 11:180, and 1 Cor. 13:12.
120. *Works,* 11:181.
121. Ibid., p. 182.
122. Ibid., p. 185.
123. Ibid., pp. 185–86.
124. Ibid., p. 187.
125. Ibid., p. 195.
126. Ibid., p. 198, and n.2.
127. Ibid., p. 200.
128. Ibid., p. 201.
129. Ibid., p. 205 (italics mine).
130. Ibid., p. 212.
131. Ibid., p. 221.
132. Ibid., p. 226.
133. Ibid., p. 230.
134. Ibid., 12:521.
135. Ibid., p. 530.
136. Ibid., p. 533.
137. Ibid., p. 534. Ruskin continues with a characteristic metaphor: "There may be light *in* it, but the light is not of it; and it diminishes the light that it gets; and lets less of it through than it receives, Christ being its sun."
138. Ibid., p. 537.
139. Ibid., p. 540.
140. Ibid., p. 541.
141. Ibid., p. 545.
142. Ibid., p. 551.
143. Ibid., pp. 553–54.
144. Ibid., p. 557.
145. Ibid., p. 558.
146. Ibid., 23:154.
147. Compare the summary passage from Lindsay quoted by Ruskin in his review (*Works,* 12:181–82).
148. *Works,* 12:177.
149. Ibid., p. 182.
150. Ibid., p. 187.
151. Ibid., pp. 172–73.
152. Ibid., p. 255.
153. Ibid., p. 283.

154. Ibid., pp. 284–85.
155. Ibid., p. 282.
156. Ibid., p. 287.
157. Ibid., pp. 287–88.
158. Ibid., p. 298.
159. Portions of this review are quoted in *Works*, 12:319, n.
160. Ibid., p. 319.
161. Ibid., p. 322.
162. Ibid., p. 324.
163. Ibid., p. 330.
164. Ibid., p. 331.
165. Ibid., p. 334.
166. Ibid., p. 357, n.
167. Ibid., p. 358, n.
168. Ibid., p. 385.
169. Ibid., p. 68.
170. Ibid., pp. 81–82.
171. Ibid., p. 102.
172. Ibid., p. 104.
173. Ibid., p. 107.
174. Ibid., p. 116.
175. Ibid., p. 123.
176. Ibid., p. 135.
177. Ibid., p. 142.
178. Ibid., p. 145.
179. Ibid., p. 158.
180. Ibid., pp. 157–58.
181. Ibid., p. 159.
182. Ibid., p. 161.

Chapter 5: Pathetic Fallacy and Mythopoesis

1. George P. Landow, *The Aesthetic and Critical Theories of John Ruskin* (Princeton: Princeton University Press, 1971), ch. 5, "Ruskin and Allegory."
2. Samuel Taylor Coleridge, *The Statesman's Manual in Biographia Literaria*, Bohn's Standard (London, 1905), p. 322.
3. M. H. Abrams, in *Natural Supernaturalism* (New York: Norton, 1971).
4. Ibid., p. 29.
5. Ibid., p. 151.
6. *Works*, 4:308.
7. Harold Bloom, *The Ringers in the Tower* (Chicago: University of Chicago Press, 1971), p. 180.
8. Works, 3:138.
9. Ibid., 5:17.
10. E. T. Cook in *Works*, 4:xliv.
11. *Works*, 10:202.
12. Ibid., 8:139.
13. Ibid., 10:156.
14. Ibid., 11:xvii and 201.
15. Ibid., 11:xxi.
16. Ibid., 8:197.
17. Ibid., 5:liii.

18. "Inaugural Address at the Cambridge School of Art," in *Works*, 16:187. XVI, p. 187.
19. *Works*, 5:4.
20. Ibid., p. 24, Ruskin's rephrasing of a sentence in a passage from *Idler* no. 79 he has just quoted. Reynolds, who had been contrasting Dutch "historical" painting with Italian "poetical" painting (which "attends only to the invariable, the great and general ideas . . . fixed and inherent in universal Nature"), praised Michaelangelo (where Ruskin demurred) as representative of this greater "poetical" style: "His works may be said to be all genius and soul; and why should they be loaded with heavy matter, which can only counteract his purpose by retarding the progress of the imagination?"
21. *Works*, 5:30.
22. Ibid., p. 31.
23. Landow, *Aesthetic and Critical Theories*, ch. 1.
24. *Works*, 5:28.
25. Ibid., p. 33.
26. Ibid., p. 42.
27. Ibid., p. 40.
28. Ibid., p. 48.
29. Ibid., p. 52.
30. Ibid., p. 60.
31. Ibid., p. 65.
32. Ibid., p. 70.
33. Ibid., p. 72.
34. Ibid., p. 73.
35. Ibid., p. 76.
36. Ibid., p. 77.
37. Ibid., p. 92.
38. Ibid., p. 102.
39. Ibid., p. 104.
40. Ibid., p. 107.
41. Ibid., p. 109, n.
42. Ibid., p. 111.
43. Ibid., p. 113.
44. Ibid., p. 114 (second set of italics mine).
45. Martin Heidegger, *An Introduction to Metaphysics*, tr. R. Manheim (New York: Doubleday, 1961), p. 86.
46. *Works*, 5:118.
47. Ibid., p. 119.
48. Heidegger, *Introduction to Metaphysics*, p. 134.
49. *Works*, 5:125.
50. Ibid., p. 127.
51. Ibid., p. 130.
52. Ibid., p. 134.
53. Ibid., p. 141.
54. Ibid., p. 137.
55. Ibid., p. 150.
56. Ibid., p. 169.
57. Ibid., p. 172.
58. Ibid., p. 173.
59. Ibid., p. 177 and 4:251.
60. Ibid., p. 178 (italics mine).
61. Ibid., p. 179.
62. Ibid., p. 181.
63. Ibid., pp. 184–85.
64. Ibid., p. 185.
65. Ibid., p. 186.
66. Ibid., p. 187.

67. Ibid.
68. Ibid., p. 188.
69. Ibid., p. 192.
70. Ibid., p. 196.
71. Ibid., p. 205.
72. Ibid., p. 204–5.
73. Ibid., p. 205.
74. Ibid., p. 208.
75. Ibid., p. 209 (italics mine).
76. Geoffrey Hartman, "Romantic Poetry and the *Genius Loci*," in *Beyond Formalism*: *Literary Essays*, 1958–1970 (New Haven: Yale University Press, 1970).
77. *Works*, 5:211.
78. Homer, *Iliad* 3. 243, quoted in *Works*, 5:213.
79. *Works*, 5:213.
80. Alain Robbe-Grillet, *For a New Novel: Essays on Fiction*, tr. Richard Howard (New York: Grove Press, 1965), p. 73.
81. Bloom, *The Ringers in the Tower*, p. 181.
82. Ibid., p. 183.
83. *Works*, 5:210.
84. Ibid., p. 216.
85. George Grote, *History of Greece* (New York, 1865–67), 1:340.
86. Isaiah 55:12; *Works*, 5:215–16.
87. *Works*, 5:218.
88. Ibid., p. 220.
89. Ibid., p. 221.
90. Ibid., p. 222.
91. Ibid., pp. 222–23.
92. Ibid., p. 223 (italics mine).
93. Fitch, "The Golden Furrow: John Ruskin and the Greek Religion" (Ph.D. diss., University of Pennsylvania, 1965).
94. Grote, *History of Greece*, 1:367–68.
95. Ernst Cassirer, *Language and Myth*, tr. Susanne K. Langer (New York: Harper, 1946), p. 10.
96. *Works*, 5:224.
97. Ibid., p. 225.
98. Ibid., p. 226.
99. Ibid.
100. Ibid., p. 227.
101. Ibid., p. 229.
102. Ibid., p. 230.
103. Ibid., p. 231.
104. Ibid., p. 232.
105. Ibid., 4:328.
106. Ibid., 5:232.
107. Ibid., p. 234 (italics mine).
108. Ibid., p. 259.
109. Ibid., p. 252.
110. Ibid., p. 257.
111. Ibid., p. 290.
112. Ibid., p. 279.
113. Ibid., p. 280.
114. Ibid., p. 281.
115. Ibid., p. 285.
116. Ibid., p. 301.
117. Ibid., p. 311.

118.   Ibid., pp. 313–14.
119.   Ibid., p. 317.
120.   Ibid., pp. 317–18.
121.   Ibid., pp. 318–19.
122.   Ibid., p. 319.
123.   Eric Heller, *The Artist's Interior Journey* (New York: Random House, 1959), p. 133.
124.   *Works*, 5:320.
125.   Ibid., p. 321.
126.   Ibid.
127.   Ibid., p. 323, and n.
128.   Ibid., p. 324.
129.   Ibid., p. 329.
130.   Ibid., p. 331.
131.   Ibid., p. 333.
132.   Ibid., p. 334.
133.   Ibid., p. 340.
134.   Ibid., p. 341.
135.   Ibid., p. 350.
136.   Ibid., p. 358.
137.   Ibid., p. 359.
138.   Ibid., p. 367.
139.   Ibid., p. 376.
140.   Ibid., p. 378.
141.   Ibid., p. 382.
142.   Ibid., p. 385.
143.   Ibid., p. 386.
144.   Ibid., p. 387.
145.   Ibid., p. 391.
146.   Ibid., p. 396.
147.   Ibid., p. 398.
148.   Ibid., p. 399.
149.   Ibid., p. 400.
150.   Ibid., p. 406.
151.   Ibid., p. 408.
152.   Ibid., p. 409.

Chapter 6: The Sun as God

1.   Thomas Carlyle, *On Heroes, Hero-Worship, and the Heroic in History*, Lecture 3, "The Hero as Poet" in *The Works of Thomas Carlyle*, Centenary Edition, 30 vols. (London: Chapman and Hall, 1897 reprint ed., New York: AMS Press, 1969), 5:80, 105. Hereafter cited as Centenary Ed.
2.   Francis Townsend, *Ruskin and the Landscape Feeling*, Illinois Studies in Language and Literature, vol. 35, no. 3 (Urbana, Illinois, 1951).
3.   Ibid., p. 69.
4.   Ibid., p. 59.
5.   In *Past and Present* Carlyle was interested in nature primarily as "organic process by which the self reawakens its full possibilities and those of society," and in which the self participates primarily by means of "Work" (Albert J. LaValley, *Carlyle and the Idea of the Modern* [New Haven: Yale University Press, 1968], pp. 194, 206–7). In his own later social thought Ruskin would often echo Carlyle's attack on the "Gospel of Mammonism," and

he too would rely heavily on the organic model; however, Ruskin's organicism is fundamentally more structural than processional; the vital, "formative" energy he senses in nature moves toward the patterns of organization, unity, or coherence he perceives within the intricate textures of natural forms; whereas for Carlyle the organic is open-ended process, obscure becoming.

6. Patricia Ball, *The Science of Aspects*, (London: The Athlone Press, 1971).
7. Ibid., p. 57.
8. Ibid., p. 56.
9. Ibid., p. 71.
10. Ibid., p. 65.
11. Alfred North Whitehead, *Science and The Modern World* (New York: Macmillan, 1926), ch. 5, "The Romantic Reaction."
12. Ball, *Science of Aspects*, p. 98.
13. *Works*, 35:157, n.
14. Kristine O. Garrigan, *Ruskin on Architecture* (Madison: University of Wisconsin Press, 1973), p. 177.
15. *Diaries* 1:245 (February 1843).
16. *Works* 3:252.
17. Ball, *Science of Aspects*, p. 100.
18. Ibid., pp. 100–101.
19. Martin Foss, *Symbol and Metaphor in Human Experience* (1949; reprinted, Lincoln: University of Nebraska Press, 1964), p. 65.
20. Ball, *Science of Aspects*, p. 101.
21. *Works*, 35:315.
22. Albert Gérard, *English Romantic Poetry* (Berkeley and Los Angeles: University of California Press, 1968), pp. 98–99.
23. *Works*, 5:172.
24. Martin Heidegger, "The Origin of The Work of Art," in *Philosophies of Art and Beauty*, ed. A. Hofstadter and R. Kuhns (New York: Modern Library, 1964), p. 672.
25. Thomas Carlyle, *Sartor Resartus*, Bk. 3, Ch. 3 ("Symbols"), Centenary Ed., 1:177.
26. W. M. Zucker, "In the Light of Being," *Journal of Aesthetics and Art Criticism*, vol. 27, no. 2, p. 156.
27. *Works*, 5:333.
28. Mircea Eliade, *Myth and Reality* (New York: Harper and Row, 1963), p. 142.
29. Ernst Cassirer, *An Essay on Man* (1944; reprint ed., New York: Bantam Books, 1970), pp. 103–4.
30. Ernst Cassirer, *The Philosophy of Symbolic Forms*, (New Haven: Yale University Press, 1955), vol. 2, *Mythical Thought*, tr. R. Manheim, pp. 49–50.
31. Karl Jaspers, *Truth and Symbol* (New York: Twayne, 1959), p. 55.
32. Ibid., p. 56.
33. Ibid., p. 61.
34. Ibid., p. 63.
35. *Works*, 6: xxii.
36. Ibid., 8: 236.
37. Ibid., 6:11.
38. Ibid.
39. Ibid., p. 14.
40. Ibid., p. 15 (italics mine).
41. Ibid., pp. 25–26.
42. Ibid., p. 27.
43. Ibid., p. 28 (italics mine).
44. Ibid., p. 29 (italics mine).
45. Ibid., p. 31.
46. Ibid., p. 30.

47.   Ibid., p. 32.
48.   Ibid., p. 35.
49.   Ibid., p. 36.
50.   Ibid., p. 41.
51.   Ibid., p. 42.
52.   Ibid., p. 44.
53.   Ibid., pp. 44–45.
54.   M. H. Abrams, *The Mirror and the Lamp* (1953; reprint ed., New York: Norton, 1958), pp. 58–59.
55.   *Works* 6:55.
56.   Ibid., p. 56.
57.   Ibid., p. 58.
58.   Ibid., p. 63.
59.   Ibid., p. 64.
60.   Ibid., p. 67.
61.   Ibid., p. 71.
62.   Ibid., p. 69.
63.   Ibid., pp. 71–72.
64.   Ibid., p. 73.
65.   Ibid., 5:318.
66.   Ibid., 6:73.
67.   Ibid., p. 75.
68.   Ibid., p. 79.
69.   Ibid., p. 81.
70.   Ibid., p. 80, Cf. ibid., 12:159.
71.   Ibid., p. 86.
72.   Ibid.
73.   Ibid.
74.   Ibid., p. 94.
75.   Ibid., pp. 103–4.
76.   Ibid., p. 104.
77.   Ibid., p. 106.
78.   Ibid., p. 110.
79.   Ibid., pp. 111–12.
80.   Ibid., pp. 112–13.
81.   Ibid., p. 113.
82.   Ibid., p. 117.
83.   Garrigan, *Ruskin on Architecture*, p. 200.
84.   *Works*, 6:214 n.
85.   Ibid., p. 292.
86.   Ibid., p. 289.
87.   Ibid., pp. 345–46.
88.   Ibid., p. 353.
89.   Ibid., p. 380.
90.   Ibid., p. 381.
91.   Ibid.
92.   Ibid., pp. 382–83.
93.   Ibid., p. 388.
94.   Ibid., p. 389.
95.   Ibid., p. 389–90.
96.   Ibid., p. 394.
97.   Ibid., p. 395.
98.   Ibid.
99.   Ibid., p. 396.

100. Ibid., pp. 400–1.
101. Ibid., pp. 402–3.
102. Ibid., p. 406.
103. Ibid., p. 411.
104. Ibid., pp. 412–13.
105. Ibid., p. 428.
106. Ibid., p. 429.
107. Ibid., p. 441.
108. Ibid., p. 449.
109. Ibid., p. 456.
110. Ibid., p. 459.
111. Ibid., p. 463.
112. Ibid., p. 465.
113. Ibid., p. 466.

Chapter 7: A Religion of Humanity: 1858–1874

1. *Praeterita*, vol. 2, ch. 3, "Cumae," *Works*, 35:289.
2. *Works*, 35:288.
3. Ibid., p. 289.
4. Ibid., p. 435.
5. *Diaries*, 2:498.
6. *Works*, 35:475.
7. *Diaries*, 2:374–75.
8. *Works*, 35:475.
9. Ibid., p. 476.
10. Ibid., p. 477.
11. Ibid., p. 478.
12. Ibid., p. 481.
13. Ibid., p. 482.
14. Ibid., p. 490.
15. Ibid., p. 492.
16. Ibid.
17. Ibid.
18. Ibid., p. 494.
19. Ibid., p. 495.
20. Ibid., p. 496.
21. Ibid., p. 497.
22. D. H. Lawrence, *The Plumed Serpent* (New York: Knopf, 1926), p. 61.
23. *Works*, 36:115.
24. Ibid., pp. 137–38.
25. Ruskin to Mrs. Hewitt, *Works*, 38: 384. In the same year Ruskin also alluded to his "heathen" phase in a letter to Norton: "I've become a pagan, too; and I am trying hard to get some substantial hope of seeing Diana in the pure glades; or Mercury in the clouds (Hermes, I mean, not that rascally Jew-god of the Latins). Only I can't understand what they want one to sacrifice to them for" (*Works*, 36:427). Similarly, he wrote to his father that "Rosie's mightily vexed about my heathenism, (her mother has let her see some bits of letters I never meant her to see), and that Rose had written him to say that he " 'must not give the one true good—containing all others—God—up.' " But, he told his father, archly, he could "set her little wits at rest on that matter at any rate, and tell her that being a heathen is not so bad as all that" (*Works*, 36:429).

26. *Works,* 36: 465.
27. Ruskin to F. Charteris: "I think the error of blind credence is error on the right side, but it *is* an error for all that." *Letters to a College Friend* (1840–45), *Works,* 1:465.
28. *Works,* 25:415.
29. *Diaries,* 3:810.
30. *The Bible of Amiens,* in *Works,* 33:118.
31. *Works,* 29:90.
32. Ibid., p. 90.
33. Ibid., pp. 88–90.
34. Ibid., p. 86.
35. Ibid., p. 91.
36. Ibid., pp. 88–89.
37. Ibid., pp. 89–90.
38. Ibid., p. 335.
39. Ibid., pp. 335–36.
40. Ibid., 18:lxxvi.
41. Ibid., pp. 394–99.
42. Letter to Susan Beever, written in 1874, five years after the publication of *The Queen of the Air,* in *Works,* 38:86.
43. *Works,* 11:207.
44. Ibid., 18: 398–99 and n.
45. Ibid., 19:336.
46. Ibid., p. 337.
47. Ibid., 35:641.
48. Ibid., 25:245.
49. Ibid., 7: 274–75.
50. Ibid., pp. 275–76. Ruskin put the essentials of this position bluntly and without mythic supports in a letter to his father written five years earlier, in December 1861: "You know in that matter of universal salvation, there are but three ways of putting it. 1. Either 'people *do* go to the devil for not believing.' 2. Or 'they—don't.' 3. Or—'We know nothing about it.' Which last is the real Fact, and the sooner it is generally acknowledged to be the Fact, the better, and no more said about Gospel, or Salvation, or Damnation." Ibid., 36:400.
51. *Works,* 7:263.
52. A recent and useful survey of this movement will be found in W. M. Simon, *European Positivism in the Nineteenth Century* (Ithaca, New York: Cornell University Press, 1963).
53. Frederic Harrison, *The Creed of a Layman : Apologia pro Fide Mea* (New York, 1907), p. 341.
54. Ibid., p. 289.
55. Frederic Harrison, *John Ruskin* (New York, 1903), p. 100.
56. *Works,* 28:615.
57. *Fors Clavigera,* Letter 67, *Notes and Correspondence, Works,* 28:662.
58. *Fors Clavigera,* Letter 66, *Works,* 28:619, n.
59. *Fors Clavigera,* Letter 67, *Notes and Correspondence: Works,* 28:662.
60. Ruskin's four questions to Harrison were: "(1) What is 'Usury' as defined by existing law? (2) Is Usury, as defined by existing law, an absolute term, such as Theft, or Adultery? and is a man therefore a Usurer, who only commits Usury a little, as a man is an Adulterer who only commits Adultery a little? (3) Or is it a sin incapable of strict definition, or strictly retributive punishment; like 'Cruelty'? and is a man a criminal in proportion to the quantity he commits? (4) if criminal in proportion to the quantity he commits, is the proper legal punishment in the direct ratio of the quantity, or inverse ratio of the quantity, as it is in the case of theft?" (*Fors Clavigera,* Letter 66, *Works,* 28:624).
61. *Works,* 28:625.

62. Frederic Harrison, "Past and Present: A Letter to Professor Ruskin, in Reply to One Addressed to the Writer by Mr. Ruskin in *Fors Clavigera* for June, 1876," *Fortnightly Review* 26 (July, 1876), p. 94. (Passage reprinted in *Works*, 28:625, n.).
63. *Fors Clavigera*, Letter 67, "Notes and Correspondence," *Works*, 28:663–64.
64. *Works*, 28: p. 662.
65. *Fors Clavigera*, Letter 66, *Works*, 28:623.
66. *Fors Clavigera*, Letter 76, *Works*, 29:88.
67. *Works*, 29:88, n.
68. Harrison, *John Ruskin*, p. 97.
69. For the passage quoted in this paragraph see *Fors Clavigera*, Letter 76, *Works*, 29: 86–89 and above p. 310.
70. *Works*, 7:279.
71. Ibid., pp. 279–80.
72. Ibid., p. 281.
73. Ibid.
74. Ibid., p. 282.
75. Ibid.
76. Ibid., p. 283.
77. Ibid., pp. 283–84.
78. Ibid., p. 284.
79. Ibid., p. 289.
80. Ibid., p. 296.
81. Ibid., p. 297.
82. Ibid., 8:121, n.
83. Ibid., *Works*, 20:142.
84. Ibid., pp. 140–42.
85. Ibid., p. 153.
86. Ibid., p. 154.
87. Ibid., p. 170.
88. *Modern Painters*, vol. 2, in *Works*, 4:197, n.
89. *Lectures on Art*, in *Works*, 20:170.
90. *Works*, 7:456.
91. Ibid., p. 458.
92. Ibid., p. 455.

Chapter 8: The Medusa Cloud

1. *Works*, 26:99, 336.
2. I have attempted to do this in "The Golden Furrow: John Ruskin and the Greek Religion," (Diss., University of Pennsylvania, 1965).
3. Quoted by Cook in *Works*, 7:lv.
4. *Works*, 7:262.
5. Ibid., p. 7.
6. Quoted by Cook in *Works*, 7:lix.
7. Ibid., lviii.
8. My phrase to suggest Ruskin's view, fully formulated a decade later in *The Queen of the Air*, that an organic form, reverently read, becomes a "living hieroglyph" or "natural and invariable" myth, "a thing with an inner language." That is, on natural forms "in their aspects of horror and beauty, and their qualities of good and evil, there is engraved a series of myths, or words of the forming power, which, according to the true passion and

energy of the human race, they have been enabled to read into religion." See *Works,* 19:361, 378.

9.   *Works,* 7:14–15.
10.   Ibid., p. 16.
11.   Ibid., p. 19.
12.   Ibid., p. 21.
13.   Ibid., p. 25.
14.   Ibid., p. 26.
15.   Ibid., p. 28.
16.   Ibid., p. 41.
17.   Ibid., p. 42.
18.   Ibid., p. 47.
19.   Ibid., p. 48.
20.   Ibid., p. 49.
21.   Ibid., p. 52.
22.   Ibid., p. 54.
23.   Ibid., pp. 55–56 and 3:339.
24.   Ibid., p. 56.
25.   Ibid., p. 105 and 3:236.
26.   Ibid., p. 58.
27.   Ibid., pp. 71–72.
28.   Ibid. p. 73.
29.   Ibid.
30.   Ibid., p. 74.
31.   Ibid., p. 74–75.
32.   Ibid., p. 98.
33.   Ibid., pp. 85–86.
34.   Ibid., p. 86.
35.   Ibid., pp. 92–93.
36.   Ibid., p. 96.
37.   Ibid., p. 98.
38.   Ibid., p. 102.
39.   Ibid., p. 119.
40.   Ibid., p. 106.
41.   Ibid., p. 119.
42.   Ibid., p. 129.
43.   Ibid., p. 114.
44.   Ibid., p. 133.
45.   Ibid., p. 135.
46.   Ibid., p. 140.
47.   Ibid., p. 135.
48.   Ibid., p. 141, Ruskin's note, and Carlyle, *Sartor Resartus,* bk. 2, ch. 2. In his original note Ruskin went on to observe that this passage in *Sartor* on the clouds as a Hebrew scroll "signifies in a word or two nearly all that is to be said about the clouds." In 1884, when he reprinted this chapter as the second chapter of *Coeli Enarrent* (in the same year as *The Storm-Cloud of the Nineteenth Century*), he qualified his note with a further remark: "Not quite."
49.   Martin Heidegger, "Remembrance of the Poet," tr. Douglas Scott, in *Existence and Being* (Chicago: Regnery, 1949), p. 259.
50.   *Works,* 7:146.
51.   Ibid., p. 147.
52.   Ibid., p. 150.
53.   Ibid., p. 156.
54.   Ibid., p. 159.

55.   Ibid., p. 162.

56.   Ibid., p. 163.

57.   Ibid., p. 166.

58.   He takes up the subject of the "helmet cloud" phenomenon again in *The Storm-Cloud*, lecture 2 (1884), paragraphs 52 and 53, in *Works*, 34:49–51.

59.   *Works*, 7:175.

60.   Ibid., p. 177.

61.   Ibid.

62.   Ibid., p. 178 (italics mine).

63.   Ibid., pp. 178–79.

64.   Ibid., p. 179 (italics mine).

65.   Ibid., p. 181.

66.   Ibid.

67.   Ibid.

68.   Ernst Cassirer, *An Essay on Man*, (1944; reprint ed., New York: Bantam Books, 1970), p. 90. Cassirer observes that mythical thought is characterized by "the deep conviction of a fundamental and indelible *solidarity of life* that bridges over the multiplicity and variety of single forms."

69.   *Works*, 7:182.

70.   Ibid., pp. 182–83.

71.   Ibid., pp. 183–84.

72.   Ibid., p. 184.

73.   Psalms 147:17.

74.   *Works*, 7:184.

75.   Ibid. Ruskin clarifies this connection later in par. 30 of *The Queen of the Air*, in *Works*, 19:327.

76.   *Works*, 7: 185.

77.   Ibid., p. 185 and Gen. 7:11.

78.   Ibid., p. 186.

79.   See his preface to *The Queen of the Air*. *Works*, 19:292.

80.   *Works*, 7:186–87.

81.   Ibid., p. 188.

82.   Ibid.

83.   Ibid. For the meaning of the "sanguine rain" Ruskin's note refers us to part 9, Chap. 2, "The Hesperid Aeglé."

84.   "Venga Medusa, si lo farem di smalto," *Inferno* 9. 52 et seq. Cf. *Works*, 5:285; 11:169; 27:427.

85.   *Works*, 7:188–89.

86.   Ibid., p. 189.

87.   Ibid., p. 190.

88.   Ibid., pp. 190–91 (italics mine).

89.   Ibid., p. 193.

90.   Ibid.

91.   Ibid., p. 195.

92.   Ibid., p. 196.

93.   Ibid., p. 197 (italics mine).

94.   Ibid., p. 198.

Chapter 9: That Old Greek Question

1.   *Works*, 7:203.

2.   Ibid., 3:313.

3. Ibid., 7:204 (italics mine).
4. Ibid., p. 204.
5. Ibid., p. 205-6.
6. Ibid., p. 206.
7. Ibid., p. 206, n.
8. Ibid., p. 207.
9. Coleridge, *Biographia Literaria*, chapters 10 and 13.
10. Works, 7:207-8.
11. Ibid.
12. Ibid., p. 209.
13. Ibid., p. 210.
14. Ibid., p. 215.
15. Ibid.
16. Ibid., p. 217.
17. Ibid., p. 224.
18. Ibid., 6:30.
19. Ibid., 7:233.
20. Ibid., p. 234.
21. Ibid., p. 249.
22. Ibid., p. 250.
23. Ibid., p. 255.
24. Ibid., p. 257 (italics mine).
25. Ibid.
26. Ibid., p. 258.
27. Ibid.
28. Ibid., pp. 258-59.
29. Ibid., p. 259.
30. Ibid.
31. Ibid. p. 260. Cf. 1 Cor. 13:12: "For now we see in a mirror, darkly; but then face to face."
32. *Works*, 7:262.
33. Ibid. (italics mine).
34. Ibid.
35. Ibid., p. 263. Ruskin's word is "delight" here, but his meaning is close to that of "joy" in romantic thought. " 'Joy,' " as M. H. Abrams points out, "is a central and recurrent term in the Romantic vocabulary which often has a specialized meaning. In Coleridge's philosophy of the one and the many, in which a central concern is reconciliation of subject and object in the act of perception, 'joy' signifies the conscious accompaniment of the fully, living and integrative mind." Abrams reminds us that in Coleridge's *Dejection* joy is an apocalyptic and redemptive power that in a recurrent romantic metaphor unites self and nature in a sacred marriage in which, all subjective isolation lost, earth and heaven are renewed. "Joy, Lady! is the spirit and the power, / Which, wedding Nature to us, gives in dower / A new Earth and new Heaven." Ruskin's image for this renewed attunement is life-giving solar light; although the idea of a redemptive bond is important to him, he never uses the romantic spousal metaphor (M. H. Abrams, *Natural Supernaturalism* (New York: Norton, 1971), pp. 276-77).
36. *Works*, 7:263.
37. Ibid.
38. Ibid., p. 264.
39. Ibid., p. 265.
40. Ibid., p. 266.
41. Ibid.
42. Northrop Frye, *The Critical Path* (Bloomington: Indiana University Press, 1971), p. 36.

43. *Works,* 7:267.
44. Ibid., p. 271.
45. Ibid.
46. Ibid., p. 273.
47. Ibid.
48. Ibid., p. 274.
49. Ibid.
50. Ibid., p. 275.
51. Mircea Eliade, *Myth and Reality,* (New York: Harper and Row, 1963), pp. 18-19, 145.
52. *Works,* 7:275.
53. Ibid., p. 276.
54. Ibid. Cf. 1 *Cor.* 15:54.
55. Ibid., pp. 276-67.
56. Ibid., p. 279.
57. Ibid.
58. Ibid., p. 280.
59. Ibid., p. 281.
60. Ibid., p. 283.
61. Ibid., p. 284. CF. *Rev.* 6:14.
62. Ibid., pp. 285-86.
63. Ibid., p. 286.
64. Ibid., pp. 289-90.
65. Ibid., p. 290.
66. Ibid., p. 294.
67. Ibid., p. 295.
68. Ibid., pp. 295-96.
69. Ibid., p. 296.
70. Ibid., p. 297.
71. Ibid., p. 298.
72. Ibid.
73. Ibid., p. 299.
74. Ibid., p. 300.
75. Ibid.
76. Ibid., pp. 300-1.
77. Ibid.
78. Ibid., p. 302.
79. Ibid.
80. Ibid., p. 310.
81. Ibid.
82. Ibid., p. 312.
83. Ibid., p. 311.
84. Ibid., p. 313.
85. Ibid., pp. 312-13.
86. Ibid., pp. 313-14.
87. Ibid., p. 314.
88. Ibid., p. 302.
89. Ibid., p. 307.
90. Ibid., p. 308.
91. Ibid.
92. Ibid., pp. 309-10.
93. Ibid., p. 315.
94. Ibid., p. 316.
95. Ibid., p. 317.
96. Ibid.

97. Ibid., p. 318.
98. Ibid., p. 320.
99. Ibid., p. 323.
100. Ibid., p. 331.
101. Ibid., p. 332.
102. Ibid., p. 342.
103. Ibid., p. 344.
104. Ibid., p. 359.
105. Ibid., p. 362.
106. Ibid., p. 363.
107. Ibid., p. 373.

Chapter 10: The Assumption of the Dragon

1. *Works*, 7:374.
2. Ibid., p. 375.
3. Ibid.
4. Ibid., p. 377.
5. Ibid.,
6. Ibid., p. 378.
7. Ibid., p. 379.
8. Ibid., 13:42.
9. Ibid., 7:380.
10. Ibid., pp. 381-82.
11. Ibid., p. 382.
12. Ibid., pp. 382-83.
13. Ibid., p. 384.
14. Ibid., p. 385.
15. Ibid., pp. 385-86.
16. Ibid., p. 386 (italics mine). (Cf. p. 275: "And beyond that mortality, what hope have we?")
17. Ibid., p. 386.
18. Ibid., pp. 386-87.
19. Ibid., p. 387.
20. Ibid., pp. 387-88.
21. Ibid., p. 386.
22. Ibid., 1:484.
23. Ibid., 13:137, 160.
24. Ibid., p. 171.
25. Ibid., p. 118.
26. Ibid., p. 119.
27. Ibid., p. 122.
28. Ibid., p. 133.
29. Ibid., p. 150.
30. Ibid., p. 136.
31. Ibid., pp. 136-37.
32. Ibid., p. 137.
33. "The real meaning of any myth is that which it has at the noblest age of the nation among whom it is current" (*The Queen of the Air*, lecture I, in *Works*, 19:301).
34. See ch. 8, n. 8.
35. *Works*, 7:215.

36. F. Max Müller, "The Philosophy of Mythology" (1871) quoted by Ernst Cassirer in *Language and Myth*, tr. S. K. Langer (New York: Harper, 1946), p. 5.
37. F. Max Müller, *Oxford Essays* (London, 1856), p. 65.
38. Ibid.
39. Ibid.
40. Ibid., p. 66.
41. Ibid., p. 62.
42. *Works*, 7:390 and *Paradise Lost*, bk. 5, lines 185-88.
43. Ibid., 7:390-91.
44. Ibid., p. 407 (italics mine).
45. Ibid., p. 392.
46. Ibid., Fig. 78, opposite p. 402.
47. Ibid., p. 393.
48. Ibid., p. 394.
49. Ibid., p. 393.
50. Ibid., p. 395.
51. Ibid., p. 396.
52. Ibid.
53. Ibid., p. 397.
54. Ibid., pp. 397-98.
55. Ibid., p. 398 and Psalm 74:13-15.
56. Ibid., 7:399.
57. Ibid., p. 400.
58. Ibid., pp. 400-401 (italics mine).
59. Ibid., p. 402.
60. Ibid., p. 406.
61. Ibid., pp. 407-8.
62. Ibid., p. 457.
63. Ibid., p. 403.
64. Ibid., pp. 406-7.
65. Ibid., p. 407. Part of the section quoted by Ruskin from *The Faerie Queene*, bk. 2, canto 7, stanzas 52-55.
66. *Works*, 7:408.
67. Ibid., pp. 386-87.
68. Ibid., p. 408.
69. Ibid., 3:640.
70. Ibid., 7:410.
71. Ibid., p. 409.
72. Ibid.
73. Ibid., p. 410.
74. Ibid., p. 411.
75. Ibid., p. 412.
76. Ibid., p. 411.
77. Ibid., p. 160.
78. Ibid., pp. 412-13.
79. Ibid., p. 413.
80. Ibid., pp. 413-14.
81. Ibid., pp. 414-15 (italics mine).
82. Ibid., p. 418 (italics mine).
83. Ibid., p. 419.
84. Ibid.
85. Ibid.
86. He read from the work in his lecture "War," the second lecture of *The Crown of Wild Olive*, and referred to it at that point as "a book which probably most of you know well and ought to know" (*Works*, 18:472).

87. K. O. Müller, *The History and Antiquities of the Doric Race*, tr. H. Tufnell and G. C. Lewis, 2 vols. (Oxford, 1830). 1:325.
88. K. O. Müller, *History and Antiquities*, 1:324. For Ruskin's remarks on the laurel crown as being, like that of wild olive, the purest reward for service to humanity see *Works*, 7:475 and 35:641.
89. *Works*, 7:420 (italics mine).
90. Müller, *History and Antiquities*, I: 307–8.
91. Ibid., 1:308.
92. *Works*, 7:420.
93. Müller, *History and Antiquities*, I:326.
94. *Works*, 7:420.
95. Ibid.
96. Ibid., p. 421.
97. Ibid., pp. 421–22.
98. Ibid., p. 422.
99. Ibid.
100. Ibid., pp. 422–23.
101. Ibid., p. 423.
102. Ibid., pp. 424–25.
103. Ibid., p. 426.
104. Ibid., p. 427.
105. Ibid., p. 430.
106. Ibid., p. 432.
107. Ibid., pp. 436–37.
108. Ibid., p. 438.
109. Ibid., pp. 438–39.
110. Ibid., p. 439.
111. Ibid., p. 441.
112. Ibid., p. 442.
113. Ibid., pp. 445–46.
114. Ibid., p. 448 (italics mine).
115. Ibid., p. 455.
116. Ibid., p. 456.
117. Ibid.
118. Ibid., p. 457.
119. Ibid., p. 458.
120. Ibid., pp. 458–59.
121. Ibid., p. 459.
122. Ibid., p. 462.
123. Ibid., p. 452.

Chapter 11: Life Against Wealth

1. *Modern Painters*, vol. 5, in *Works*, 7:453.
2. Georg Lukács, *The Theory of the Novel*, tr. Anna Bostock (Cambridge: M. I. T. Press), p. 88.
3. *Works*, 7:457.
4. Ibid., 3:624 and n. I have italicized *"her meaning"* in this important passage in order to stress again the apocalyptic and hermeneutic as opposed to the mimetic aspect of Ruskin's theory of truth in landscape art. His doctrine seems phenomenological insofar as it demands from the painter a strict record of what appears to his sight in the presence of

nature, not in painting "from" nature. If the painter goes to nature directly with studious innocence of eye—in "utter forgetfulness of self," of science (apart from knowledge of the species character of forms), and of aesthetic rules—she will reveal *"her meaning"* to him: her "system," the organic model.

5. Ibid., 12:385 (italics mine).
6. Ibid., p. 331.
7. Ibid., 24:25.
8. Ibid., p. 27 (italics mine).
9. Ibid., 14:47.
10. *Academy Notes*, 1857, ibid., p. 14:92.
11. Ibid., p. 14:106–7.
12. Ibid., p. 237.
13. Ibid., p. 243–44.
14. Ibid., p. 244.
15. Ibid., 16:251.
16. Ibid., 15:27, n. and cf. p. 67.
17. Ibid., p. 74.
18. Ibid., p. 91.
19. Ibid., pp. 115–16.
20. Ibid., p. 117.
21. Ibid., p. 118.
22. Ibid., p. 120.
23. Ibid., p. 133.
24. Ibid., p. 134.
25. Ibid., p. 161.
26. Ibid., p. 162.
27. Ibid., p. 163.
28. Ibid., p. 187.
29. Ibid., p. 188 n.
30. Ibid., p. 210.
31. Ibid., 16:xxii.
32. Ibid., p. 12.
33. Ibid., p. 25.
34. Ibid., p. 110.
35. Ibid., p. 26.
36. Ibid.
37. Ibid., p. 115.
38. Ibid., pp. 121–22.
39. Ibid., 20:212.
40. *Fors Clavigera*, Letter 5 (1871), in *Works*, 27:90–91.
41. *Works*, 16:129–36.
42. Lecture 2, "The Unity of Art" in *The Two Paths*, ibid., pp. 296–97.
43. Ibid., p. 310.
44. Lecture 3, "Modern Manufacture and Design," ibid., pp. 324–25.
45. Ibid., p. 325 and *Works*, 6:323–30.
46. Ibid., pp. 325–26.
47. Ibid., p. 329.
48. Ibid., 35:485.
49. "Readings in *Modern Painters*," as quoted in *Works*, 17:xxi.
50. *Works*, 35: p. 533.
51. Derrick Leon, *Ruskin: The Great Victorian* (London: Routledge and Kegan Paul, 1949) p. 399.
52. Ruskin to Lady Mount-Temple, 4 March 1868, in *Letters of John Ruskin to Lord and Lady Mount-Temple*, ed. J. L. Bradley (Columbus: Ohio State University Press, 1964), pp. 128–29 (hereafter cited as *Letters*, ed. Bradley).

53. Ruskin to Lady Mount-Temple, March 1868, in *Letters*, ed. Bradley pp. 138–39.

54. Quoted by Ruskin in a letter to Norton, 10 March 1863, in *Works*, 36:436.

55. Effie's letter of 1870 quoted by Leon, in *Ruskin*, p. 405 from *The Order of Release*, ed. Admiral Sir William James (London: John Murray, 1947), pp. 254–56.

56. Leon, *Ruskin*, pp. 198, 403.

57. Mary Lutyens, *Young Mrs. Ruskin in Venice* (New York: Vanguard Press, 1965), p. 20.

58. Rollo May, *Love and Will* (New York: Norton, 1969; reprinted ed., New York: Dell, 1974), p. 277.

59. "Ruskin's Statement to his Proctor in the Nullity Suit," in J. H. Whitehouse, *Vindication of Ruskin* (London: George Allen and Unwin, 1950), pp. 12–16. The statement also appears in Mary Lutyens, *Millais and the Ruskins* (London: John Murray, 1967), pp. 188–92. Lutyens points out that Ruskin apparently thought proof of his general virility would have been sufficient defense, but Effie had only to prove his impotence with respect to her.

60. Effie to her father, 7 March 1854, in Lutyens, *Millais and the Ruskins*, p. 156.

61. Effie to Mrs. La Touche, 10 October 1870, in W. James, *The Order of Release*, p. 255.

62. Ruskin to Lady Mount-Temple, March 1868, in *Letters*, ed. Bradley, p. 139.

63. Richard Jenkyns, *The Victorians and Ancient Greece* (Cambridge: Harvard University Press, 1980), p. 137.

64. Ruskin to Charles Eliot Norton, 11 September 1868, quoted in Van Akin Burd, *John Ruskin and Rose La Touche* (Oxford: Clarendon Press), p. 116.

65. Leon, *Ruskin*, p. 343.

66. Ruskin to Rossetti, quoted ibid., p. 215.

67. Mrs. La Touche to George MacDonald, May 1863, quoted in Greville MacDonald, *Reminiscences of a Specialist* (London: George Allen and Unwin, 1932), p. 107. "St. Crumpet," or "St. C.," was Rose's nickname for Ruskin. See *Works*, 35:528.

68. Ruskin to George MacDonald 8 February 1865, quoted in G. MacDonald, *Reminiscences*, p. 109.

69. May, *Love and Will*, p. 71.

70. Letter of March 1868, in *Letters*, ed. Bradley, p. 133.

71. *Works*, 17:377.

72. *Diaries*, 2:590.

73. Ibid., p. 605.

74. Ibid., p. 613.

75. Ibid., p. 616.

76. Ibid., p. 616.

77. Ibid., p. 647.

78. Ibid., p. 655.

79. Ibid., p. 628.

80. Ibid., p. 644.

81. Ibid., p. 685.

82. Ruskin to Lady Mount-Temple, in 26 September 1864, *Letters*, ed. Bradley, p. 41.

83. See pp. 604–5 below, and *Works*, 28:107; 29:138, 192, 342; 33:273.

84. *Works*, 17:xxvii.

85. G. M. Young, *Victorian England: Portrait of an Age*, 2nd ed. (London: Oxford University Press, 1853), p. 16.

86. *Works*, 17:17.

87. Ibid., pp. 18–19.

88. Ibid., p. 41.

89. Ibid., p. 48.

90. Ibid., pp. 59–60.

91. Ibid., p. 61.

92. Ibid., p. 62.

93. Ibid., pp. 62–63.
94. Ibid., p. 84.
95. Ibid., p. 85.
96. Ibid., p. 87.
97. Ibid., p. 88.
98. Ibid., p. 89.
99. Ibid., p. 95.
100. Ibid., p. 95, n.
101. Ibid., p. 95.
102. Ibid., p. 97.
103. Ibid., p. 99.
104. Ibid., pp. 100–101 (italics mine).
105. Ibid., p. 101.
106. Ibid., p. 105.
107. Ruskin to father, 23 October 1862, as quoted in *Works*, 17:lxiii–iv.
108. *Works*, 17:144.
109. Ibid., p. 152.
110. Ibid., p. 153.
111. Ibid., p. 168.
112. Ibid., p. 174.
113. Ibid., p. 178.
114. Ibid., p. 181.
115. Ibid., p. 204.
116. Ibid., p. 206 (italics mine).
117. Ibid., pp. 206–7.
118. Ibid., p. 207.
119. *Inferno* 7, 1. 58, translated in *Works*, 17:208, n. 1.
120. *Works*, 17:208.
121. Ibid., 208.
122. Ibid., 209–10.
123. Ibid., pp. 213–14.
124. Ibid., p. 215.
125. Ibid., p. 216. This note is continued in appendix 5, pp. 290–91, where Ruskin observes that "all Greek myths . . . have many opposite lights and shades; they are as changeful as opal, and like opal, usually have one colour by reflected, and another by transmitted light."
126. Ibid., p. 222.
127. Ibid., p. 224.
128. Ibid., p. 225.
129. Ibid., p. 292.
130. Ibid., p. 226.
131. Ibid., p. 227.
132. Ibid., p. 229.
133. Ibid., p. 248.
134. Ibid., p. 269.
135. Ibid., p. 275.
136. Ibid., pp. 276–77.
137. *Time and Tide*, in *Works*, 17:381 (italics mine).
138. *Works*, 17:317.
139. Ibid., pp. 319–20.
140. Ibid., p. 328.
141. Ibid., p. 338.
142. Ibid., pp. 341–42.
143. Ibid., p. 343.

144. Ibid., pp. 345–46.
145. Ibid., p. 346.
146. Ibid., pp. 348–49.
147. Ibid., p. 350.
148. Ibid., p. 351.
149. Ibid., p. 357.
150. Ibid., p. 358.
151. Ibid., pp. 360–61.
152. Ibid., p. 361.
153. Ibid., p. 365.
154. Ibid., p. 367.
155. Ibid., p. 368.
156. Ibid., p. 354.
157. Ibid., p. 378.
158. Ibid., p. 397.
159. Ibid., p. 423.
160. Ibid., p. 424.
161. Ibid., pp. 424–25.
162. Ibid., p. 419.
163. Ibid., p. 420.
164. Ibid., p. 421.
165. Ibid., p. 434.
166. Ibid., p. 435.
167. Ibid., p. 438.
168. Ibid., p. 458.
169. Ibid.
170. Ibid., p. 463.

Chapter 12: In the Midst of Judgment

1. *Works*, 18:lviii; cf. p. 34.
2. Ibid., p. 22.
3. Ibid., p. 24.
4. Ibid., pp. 31-32.
5. Ibid., p. 33.
6. Ibid., p. 34.
7. Ibid., p. 35.
8. Ibid.
9. Ibid., p. 36.
10. Ibid., p. 37.
11. Ibid., p. 41.
12. Ibid., p. 42.
13. Ibid.
14. Ibid., p. 44.
15. Ibid., p. 47.
16. Ibid., p. 48.
17. Ibid., p. 49.
18. Ibid., pp. 50-51.
19. Ibid., p. 54.
20. Ibid., pp. 60-61.
21. Ibid., p. 61.

22. Ibid., p. 64.
23. Ibid., p. 68.
24. Ibid., p. 69. With *Modern Painters*, volume 5, as we have noted, Ruskin began to stress the significance of root meanings of words; thereafter he frequently refers to Max Müller's *Lectures* and to the revelation to be found in the origins of words. Obviously etymology became for him a source of vital truth comparable to that which he found in nature, Scripture, great art, and myth. The source of a word would reveal its organic or instinctive meaning; further, the investigations of Müller and other philologists appeared to be disclosing that even myth was rooted in metaphor. There are allusions to Müller's *Lectures* or borrowings from them in *The Crown of Wild Olive*, *The Ethics of the Dust*, *The Queen of the Air*, *The Eagle's Nest*, *Fors Clavigera*, *Proserpina*, and *The Pleasures of England*. Most of these will be considered as we proceed. (See, ed. note to page 69 and *Works*, 19:340.)
25. *Works*, 18:73–74.
26. Ibid., p. 74.
27. Ibid., p. 80.
28. Ibid., p. 82.
29. Ibid., p. 83.
30. Ibid., p. 84.
31. Ibid., p. 89.
32. Ibid., p. 93. From the paragraph quoted by Ruskin from the *Morning Post*, 13 February, 1865. See *Works*, 18:90, ed. n. 5.
33. *Works*, 18:95.
34. Ibid., p. 96.
35. Ibid., p. 110.
36. Ibid., pp. 112–113.
37. Ibid., p. 116.
38. Ibid., p. 118.
39. Ibid., p. 119.
40. Ibid., p. 121.
41. Ibid.
42. "So far as she rules, all must be right, or nothing is. She must be enduringly, incorruptibly good; instinctively, infallibly wise—wise, not for self-development, but for self-renunciation: wise, not that she may set herself above her husband, but that she may never fail from his side: wise, not with the narrowness of insolent and loveless pride, but with the passionate gentleness of an infinitely variable, because infinitely applicable, modesty of service—the true changefulness of woman" (*Works*, 18:123) In this definition of the household goddess, and in his eulogy of the home as "the place of Peace . . . a sacred place, a vestal temple, a temple of the hearth watched over by Household Gods" (ibid.), Ruskin is, of course, participating in the Victorian mythology of the home typified by such works as Coventry Patmore's *The Angel in the House* (1854-60), which he has approvingly quoted earlier in the lecture. For a discussion of the Victorian idealization of the home and the woman's place in it see Walter E. Houghton, *The Victorian Frame of Mind* (New Haven: Yale University Press, 1957), pp. 341-348. He notes that for Victorian agnostics the home "was the foundation for the Religion of Humanity" (p. 347).
43. *Works*, 18:124.
44. Ibid., p. 126.
45. Ibid., p. 128.
46. Ibid., p. 136.
47. Ibid.
48. Ibid., p. 140.
49. Ibid., pp. 146–47.
50. Ibid., p. 147.
51. Ibid., p. 151.
52. Ibid., p. 152.

53. Ibid., pp. 153–54.
54. Ibid., p. 155.
55. Ibid., p. 153.
56. Ibid., pp. 157–58.
57. Ibid., p. 161.
58. Ibid., p. 163.
59. Ibid., p. 166–67.
60. Ibid., p. 173.
61. Ibid., p. 174.
62. Ibid., pp. 174–75.
63. Ibid., p. 174, and Eccles. 9:10.
64. *Works*, 18:176.
65. Ibid., p. 178.
66. Ibid., pp. 179–80.
67. Ibid., p. 180.
68. Ibid., p. 182.
69. Ibid., p. 385, note to the edition of 1873.
70. Ibid.
71. Ibid., p. 386.
72. Ibid., p. 387.
73. Ibid., pp. 387–88.
74. Ibid., p. 388.
75. Ibid., p. 391.
76. Ibid., p. 406.
77. Ibid., p. 408.
78. Ibid., p. 413.
79. Ibid., p. 432.
80. Ibid., p. 434.
81. Ibid., pp. 434–35.
82. Ibid., p. 440.
83. Ibid., p. 442.
84. Ibid., pp. 443–45.
85. Ibid., p. 445 and note.
86. Ibid., pp. 445–46. Ruskin goes on here to remind his audience of the existential implications of Greek belief: that human work had to be done, "not with any ardent affection or ultimate hope; but with a resolute and continent energy of will, as knowing that for failure there was no consolation, and for sin there was no remission." And in a note to the same page he observes that it is an error to suppose that the Greek religion was centered on the worship of beauty. "It was essentially [a religion] of rightness and strength, founded on Forethought: the principal character of Greek art is not beauty, but design: and the Dorian Apollo-Worship and Athenian Virgin-worship are both expressions of adoration of divine wisdom and purity." This note of 1871 shows how Ruskin's earlier interest in Greek belief led to the reassessment of Greek art that he was then expressing in *Aratra Pentelici*.
87. *Works*, 18:447.
88. Ibid., p. 448.
89. Ibid., p. 451.
90. Ibid., pp. 451–52.
91. Ibid., pp. 457–58.
92. Ibid., p. 464.
93. Ibid., pp. 474–75.
94. Ibid., p. 464.
95. Ibid., p. 484 (italics mine).
96. Ibid., p. 496.

97. Ibid., p. 497.
98. Ibid., p. 498.
99. Ibid., p. 502.
100. Ibid., p. 508.
101. Ibid., p. 512.
102. Ibid., p. 510 (italics mine).
103. Ibid., 19:37.
104. Ibid., p. 24.
105. Ibid., p. 32.
106. Ibid., p. 38.
107. Ibid., p. 166.
108. Ibid., p. 184.
109. Ibid., p. 190.
110. Ibid., p. 197–98.
111. Ibid., p. 212.
112. Ibid., p. 215.
113. Ibid., p. 217.
114. Ibid., p. 252.
115. Ibid., p. 257.
116. Ibid., p. 258.
117. Ibid., p. 260.
118. Ibid., p. 261.
119. Ibid., p. 87.
120. Ibid., p. 135.
121. Ibid., p. 82.
122. Ibid., pp. 82–83.
123. Ibid., p. 83.
124. Ruskin to Lady Mount-Temple, 20 October, 1866 and 4 September, 1873, *The Letters of John Ruskin to Lord and Lady Mount-Temple*, ed. John Lewis Bradley (Columbus: Ohio State University Press, 1964), pp. 99, 349. Hereafter cited as *Letters*, ed. Bradley.
125. *Works*, 19:61.
126. Ibid., p. 62.
127. Ibid., p. 64.
128. Ibid., pp. 109–10.
129. Ibid., p. 115.
130. Ruskin to Lady Mount-Temple, 1868, *Letters*, ed. Bradley, p. 182.
131. *Works*, 18:202.
132. Ibid., pp. 203–4.
133. Ibid., p. 206.
134. Ibid., p. 218.
135. "I meant the serpents," Ruskin told his pupils, "for the souls of those who had lived carelessly and wantonly in their riches; and who have all their sins forgiven by the world, because they are rich; and therefore they have seven crimson-crested heads, for the seven mortal sins; of which they are proud" (ibid., p. 367).
136. Ibid., pp. 214–15 (italics mine).
137. *Praeterita*, vol. 1. in *Works*, 35:52–55. The "dream" from which the following passages are quoted is told in *Works*, 18: 224–29.
138. Ibid., pp. 229–32.
139. Ibid., p. 361.
140. Ibid., p. 362.
141. Ibid., p. 364.
142. Ibid., p. 238.
143. Ibid., p. 239.

144. Ibid., p. 242.
145. Ibid., p. 244.
146. Ibid., p. 245.
147. Ibid., p. 256.
148. Ibid., p. 259.
149. Ibid., p. 261.
150. Ibid., p. 263.
151. Ibid., p. 273.
152. Ibid., p. 283.
153. Ibid., p. 286.
154. Ibid., p. 301. Cf. p. 288.
155. Ibid., p. 302.
156. Ibid., p. 311.
157. Ibid., p. 323.
158. Ibid., p. 327.
159. Ibid., p. 335.
160. Ibid., p. 341.
161. Ibid., p. 343.
162. Ibid., p. 344.
163. Ibid., pp. 344–45.
164. Ibid., p. 345.
165. Ibid., p. 346.
166. Ibid., p. 347.
167. Ibid.
168. Ibid., p. 348.
169. Ibid., pp. 348–49.
170. Ibid., p. 349 (italics mine).
171. Ibid., pp. 349–50.
172. Ibid., p. 352.
173. Ibid., p. 353.
174. Ibid., p. 357. Cf. *Modern Painters*, vol. 4, in *Works*, 6:177.
175. *Works*, 18: 357–58.
176. Ibid., 7:207.

Chapter 13: The Goddess in the Vial

1. *Works*, 19:291.
2. Ibid., pp. lxvii, lxxi, and 283–84.
3. Ibid., 37: 86–87.
4. Ibid., p. 87.
5. *Diaries*, 3:810.
6. "Aryan Mythology: Second Notice," *Asiatic*, 23 May 1871. Reprinted by Ruskin in *Arrows of the Chace* (1800), 2:248–49. Ruskin quotes this passage from the review in his reply (*Works*, 34:505).
7. *Works*, 34:504.
8. *Works*, 37:380–81 (italics in the third sentence mine).
9. J. A. Froude, *Carlyle's Life in London*, 2:383, quoted by Cook in *Works*, 19:lviii.
10. Ruskin to J. A. Froude, 17 August 1869, printed in *Works*, 19: lxx–lxxi.
11. R. H. Wilenski, *John Ruskin* (London, 1933), p. 193, n.
12. *Works*, 19:lxxi.
13. Ibid., 33:118.

14. Richard Jenkyns, *The Victorians and Ancient Greece* (Cambridge: Harvard University Press, 1980), p. 185.

15. John D. Rosenberg, *The Darkening Glass* (New York: Columbia University Press, 1961), pp. 171–73.

16. Jenkyns, *The Victorians and Ancient Greece*, pp. 183–85.

17. Harold Bloom, "Ruskin as Literary Critic," in *Ringers in the Tower* (Chicago: University of Chicago Press, 1971), p. 181.

18. *Works*, 19:291.

19. Ibid.

20. Ibid., p. 292.

21. Ibid., p. 293.

22. Ibid., 18:353.

23. Alfred North Whitehead, *Science and the Modern World*, (1925, reprint ed. New York: New American Library, 1952) pp. 52, 59.

24. E. B. Tylor, *Primitive Culture*, 2 vols. (London, 1871), 1:258.

25. Ibid., p. 384.

26. E. B. Tylor, "Traces of the Early Mental Condition of Man," *Proceedings of the Royal Institution* 5 (1866–69): 87. For Tylor's remarks on earlier uses of "animism" see *Primitive Culture*, 1:384, n.

27. His own address, "On the Present State of Modern Art with Reference to the Advisable Arrangements of a National Gallery," was delivered at the meeting on 7 June of that year (*Proceedings* V: 187).

28. E. B. Tylor, *Researches into the Early History of Mankind* (London, 1865), p. 326.

29. F. Max Müller, *Lectures on the Science of Language*, (London, 1864) 2: 538–39.

30. *Works*, 19:327.

31. Ibid.

32. *Lectures*, 2:503.

33. *Works*, 19:301.

34. *Lectures*, 2:443.

35. "The Philosophy of Mythology" appended to his *Introduction to the Science of Religion* (London, 1873), pp. 353–55.

36. *The Fortnightly Review*, n. 5. 5 (February 1869): 140.

37. *Proceedings of the Royal Institution*, 1 (1854): 254.

38. "On the Insight Hitherto Obtained into the Nature of the Crystal Molecule by the Instrumentality of Light," *Proceedings*, 3 (1862):95.

39. "On the Relation of the Vegetable and the Animal to the Inorganic Kingdom," *Proceedings*, 3 (1862):368–69.

40. *Proceedings* 5 (1869):432.

41. Ibid., p. 444.

42. Ibid., p. 440.

43. Ibid., p. 445.

44. *Works*, 7:184.

45. Ibid., 34:34.

46. *Works*, 19:293.

47. Ibid., p. 294.

48. Ibid., pp. 292–93.

49. Max Müller, *Lectures*, 2:521–22.

50. Ibid., p. 524.

51. For instance, the Arcadian worship of Athena *Alea* had been supposed by K. O. Müller (*Introduction to a Scientific System of Mythology*, tr. John Leitch [London, 1845], 51), Friedrich Creuzer (*Symbolic und Mythologie der alten Völker besonders der ⌐   ⌐ vols. [Liepzig and Darmstadt, 1836–42], 3:308–477 and 505 ff.), Edward G⌐.   *Griechische Mythologie*, 2 vols. [Berlin, 1854–55], 1:224 ff.), Friedrich G. Welcker, (*Griechisc   ⌐ötterlehre* [Göttingen, 1857–62], 1:309–10), and L. Preller

(*Griechische Mythologie*, 2 vols. [Berlin, 1860], 1:156; 2:241–43) to identify her as the warm and nourishing ether. For Welcker she is "der weiblich personifizierte Aether" (*Griechische Götterlehre*, 1:301); for Preller, "der milde gedsihlich Wärme des atherischen Himmels" (*Griechische Mythologie*, 1:156). The nearness of this ether tradition in Athena scholarship to Ruskin's second *Queen* lecture ("Athena Keramitis—Athena, fit for being made into pottery") in which she becomes, spiritually, the irreducible vital and shaping essence of life, will become clearer as we proceed. However, there had also been another, earlier, scholarly tradition that had identified Athena as a storm goddess with powers Ruskin assigns to "Athena Chalinitis" of the first lecture, his "Athena the Restrainer," signifying the more obvious physical properties of the air and their spiritual analogues. This storm-and-cloud interpretation had been set forth first by J. F. Lauer (*System der Griechischen Mythologie* [Berlin, 1853], pp. 311 ff.), then by F. L. W. Schwartz (*Der Ursprung der Mythologie* [Berlin, 1860], ff. 83 ff.), and Theodor Benfey (*Nachrichten von der Königl Gesellschaft der Wissenschaften* [Göttingen, 1868], p. 24) and was to be most elaborately developed (a decade after *The Queen*) by W. H. Roscher (*Ausfuhrliches Lexikon der Griechischen und Römischen Mythologie*, 6 vols. [Leipzig, 1884–86], 1:675–87).

52.   For useful introductory materials and selections from the major mythologists of the period see Burton Feldman and Robert D. Richardson, *The Rise of Modern Mythology* 1680–1860 (Bloomington: Indiana Univ. Press, 1972). For relevant passages from Keightly see Fitch, "The Golden Furrow: John Ruskin and the Greek Religion" (Ph. D. diss., University of Pennsylvania, 1965), pp. 286–312; Thomas Keightley, *The Mythology of Greece and Italy*, 3d ed. (London, 1854), p. iii.

53.   G. W. Cox, *Mythology of the Aryan Nations*, 2 vols. (London, 1870), 2: p. 60.

54.   As a doctrinaire solar mythologist, Cox was Max Müller's leading disciple in England. Two earlier works, *A Manual of Mythology in the form of Question and Answer* and *Tales from Ancient Greece* (both published in 1868) also show the solarist influence; they are, however, nontechnical handbooks intended for the young. For a survey of the career of solar mythology in England see Richard Dorson, "The Eclipse of Solar Mythology" rptd. ed. *Myth: A Symposium* Thomas Sebeok, (Bloomington: Indiana University Press, 1958); also Burton Feldman and Robert D. Richardson, *The Rise of Modern Mythology, 1680–1860* pp. 242; 276–87; 400–401; 480–87.

55.   Cox, *Mythology*, 2:286–87.

56.   Ibid., p. 287.

57.   Ibid., p. 288.

58.   Ruskin's Athena resembles in several important respects the forms of the "archetype of the anima," an aspect of the unconscious ("the anima is the *archetype of Life itself*") described by C. G. Jung in his famous "Archetypes of the Collective Unconscious." See my Introduction, pp. 15–17. There is some further speculation along this line in the following chapter as we consider Ruskin's mental breakdown; see pp. 586–93.

59.   *Works*, 19:295.

60.   Ibid., pp. 295–96.

61.   Ibid., p. 296.

62.   Ibid., p. 298.

63.   Ibid., p. 299 (italics mine).

64.   Ibid., p. 300.

65.   Ibid., p. 346. "It . . . will only be possible for me at all after marking the relative intention of the Apolline myths—to trace for you the Greek conception of Athena as the guide of moral passion." His letter to *The Asiatic* (18 May 1871) indicates that he had intended by that time to have issued a parallel volume on the Apolline myths "and, perhaps, one on the Earth-Gods." (*Arrows of the Chace*, in *Works*, 34:504). A summarizing note on the Greek religion to the second lecture ("Traffic") of *The Crown of Wild Olive* shows the relative position and authority he assigned to the two deities: "It was essentially [a religion] of rightness and strength, founded on Forethought: the principal character of Greek art is not beauty, but design: and the Dorian Apollo-worship and Athenian Virgin-

worship are both expressions of adoration of divine wisdom and purity. Next to these great deities, rank, in power over the national mind, Dionysus and Ceres, the givers of human strength and life; then, for heroic examples, Hercules. There is no Venus-worship among the Greeks in the great times: and the muses are essentially teachers of Truth, and of its harmonies" (*Works*, 18: 446, n.).

66. *Works*, 19:300.
67. Ibid., p. 301 and cf. 18:348.
68. Ibid., 28:732.
69. Ibid., 19:302–3.
70. Ibid., p. 303.
71. Ibid., p. 304.
72. Ibid., pp. 306–7.
73. Ibid., p. 309.
74. Ibid., p. 310.
75. Ibid.
76. Ibid., p. 312. Ruskin's allusion is to *Lycidas*, 1. 96.
77. Ibid., p. 313.
78. Ibid., p. 314.
79. Ibid., pp. 314–15. *Inferno* 13. 11. 10, 94–108.
80. *Works*, 19:315.
81. Ibid., p. 317.
82. Ibid., p. 320.
83. Ibid., p. 324.
84. Ibid., p. 325.
85. Ibid., p. 326.
86. Ibid., pp. 326–27.
87. Ibid., 7:185–86.
88. Ibid., 19:327.
89. Ibid.
90. Ibid., p. 328.
91. Ibid., p. 333.
92. Ibid., pp. 336–37.
93. Ibid., p. 337.
94. Ibid., p. 340.
95. Ibid., p. 342.
96. Ibid., p. 346.
97. Ibid.
98. Ibid., p. 351 (italics omitted).
99. Ibid., p. 390.
100. Ibid., p. 391 (first italics mine).
101. Ibid., p. 400.
102. Ibid., p. 399.
103. Ibid., p. 400.
104. Ibid., pp. 406–8, paragraphs 132–33. He also added "The Hercules of Camarina," a brief lecture on Greek art as represented by certain coins. The lecture was delivered at the Art School of South Lambeth on 15 March 1869. In it Ruskin asserts that Greek art never represents ugliness because the Greeks knew no terror: "The Greeks never have ugly dreams. They cannot draw anything ugly when they try." Their art can represent "pensiveness; amazement; often deepest grief and desolateness. All these, but terror never." It is therefore even in its style a message of courage in the face of existential uncertainty. "Everylasting calm in the presence of all fate; and joy such as they could win, not indeed in perfect beauty, but in beauty at perfect rest! A kind of art this, surely, to be looked at, and thought upon sometimes with profit, even in these latter days" (ibid., p. 418).
105. Ibid., p. 351.
106. Ibid., pp. 351–53.

107. Ibid., p. 353.
108. Ibid., pp. 353–54.
109. Ibid., p. 354.
110. Ibid., pp. 355–56.
111. Ibid., p. 356.
112. Ibid., pp. 356–57 and 18:342.
113. Ibid., p. 357.
114. Ibid.
115. Ibid.
116. Ibid., p. 359 (italics mine).
117. Ibid., p. 361.
118. Ibid., p. 360.
119. Ibid., p. 361.
120. Ibid., p. 363.
121. Rosenberg, *The Darkening Glass* p. 169.
122. *Works*, 19:362.
123. Ibid., pp. 364–65.
124. Ibid., 18:346.
125. Ibid., 19:358.
126. Ibid., p. 367.
127. Ibid., p. 369.
128. Ibid., p. 378.
129. Ibid., 18:346.
130. Ibid., 20:265.
131. Ibid., 19:385.
132. Ibid., 20:142 (italics mine).
133. Ibid., 19:381–83.
134. Ibid., 34:68.
135. Ibid., p. 79 (italics mine).
136. Ibid., p. 72.

Chapter 14: My Message Is Not Mine

1. *Notes . . . on His Drawings by Turner*, in *Works*, 13:409, 459.
2. "Arthur Burgess" (1887), *Works*, 14:355.
3. In *Modern Painters*, volume 2, he first speaks of imagination as including only "the healthy, voluntary, and necessary action of the highest powers of the human mind on subjects properly demanding and justifying their exertion" (*Works*, 4:222). This conflicts with his view of imagination as a visionary or seeing capacity, which has "no reasoning in it" (ibid., p. 251) and is "ungovernable," knowing no laws, its appearances having "the character of dreams" (ibid., 11:178). And yet on the following page Ruskin must insist— for he is discussing the "Grotesque Renaisance"—that "if the mind be imperfect or ill-trained, the vision is seen in a broken mirror, with strange distortions and discrepancies, all the passions of the heart breathing upon it in cross ripples, till hardly a trace of it remains unbroken" (ibid., p. 179). Later, in his *Lectures on Art* while he notes the unvoluntariness of great artistic vision he insists that it is *"always, the sign of some mental limitation or derangement"* (ibid., 20:55). Yet in *Fors*, Letter 88 (in ibid., 29:381 [1880]), he insists that he could recognize the "transitional moment" when his own mind slipped from "the not morbid, however dangerous, states of more or less excited temper, and too much quickened thought" to "the state of morbid inflammation of the brain which gives rise to false vision." And in *The Pleasures of England* (1884) he returns to the earliest

position quoted above and explains in a note that "healthy, voluntary, and necessary" action of imagination means that "all healthy minds possess imagination, and use it at will under fixed laws of truthful perception and memory" (Ibid., 33:482 and Ruskin's note).

4. *Works*, 22:138.

5. In his lecture entitled "The Range of Intellectual Conception Proportioned to the Rank in Animated Life" (1871) Ruskin had observed that the capacity of control and selection of vision distinguishes the use of vision in art from the submission to it in insanity: "And even we painters, who dare not call ourselves capable of thought, are capable of choice in more or less salutary vision. In the degree in which we lose such power of choice in vision, so that the spectral phenomena which are the materials of our industry present themselves under forms beyond our control, we become insane; and although for all our best work a certain degree of this insanity is necessary, and the first occurring conceptions are uncommanded, as in dreams, we have, when in health, always instantaneous power of accepting some, refusing others, perfecting the outlines and colours of those we wish to keep, and arranging them in such relations as we choose" (*Works*, 34:110–11).

6. Ruskin to Acland, 5 August, 1871 as quoted in *Works*, 22:xviii.

7. Ruskin to Lady Mount-Temple, Letter of 27 July, 1871, *Letters of John Ruskin to Lord and Lady Mount-Temple*, ed. John Lewis Bradley (Columbus: Ohio State University Press, 1964), pp. 309–10.

8. "Mr. Ruskin's Illness Described by Himself," *British Medical Journal*, 1900. Reprinted in *Works*, 38:172–73.

9. *Diaries*, 3:870 (1875).

10. Ibid., p. 941.

11. Ibid., p. 975. (1878).

12. Passages like the following show Ruskin closely associating the subjective and objective senses of impurity: "Found Rhone utterly destroyed; had three hours of a dismal walk as ever man had in this world, in the deep sorrow and horror of it, and perception of guilt and misery of all round me, and of my own" (ibid., p. 961 [1877]).

13. Charles T. Dougherty, "Of Ruskin's Gardens" in Bernice Slote, ed., *Myth and Symbol* (Lincoln: University of Nebraska Press, 1963), p. 150.

14. *Aion* (1951) in *Psyche and Symbol*, ed. Violet S. de Lazlo (New York: Doubleday, 1958), p. 36.

15. Ibid., pp. 38–39.

16. "Protestantism: The Pleasures of Truth" (1884), in *Works*, 33:507.

17. Ruskin to Charles Eliot Norton 23 July, 1878, in *Works*, 38:252–53.

18. *Works*, 28:770.

19. In the entry of 6 May, 1877, for instance: "Woke at 1/2 past three, with many disturbing thoughts, but got my mind into the right train by St. Ursula's help, and slept till near 7." And the following day: "More light in thought and soul, always by St. Ursula's help." *Diaries*, 3:950–51.

20. *Works*, 29:30-31. The flowers in the window are in Carpaccio's "The Dream of Saint Ursula." For Ruskin's fullest description of the painting (and his copy of it) see *Fors*, Letter 20 (1872), in *Works*, 27: 342–45. The "Irish friend who sent the dianthus was Lady Castletown" (*Diaries*, 3: 920).

21. Professor Daniel Oliver. See *Diaries*, 3:921 and n.

22. Ibid., p. 921. Lacerta was Ruskin's nickname for Mrs. La Touche.

23. Readings in *Modern Painters*, Lecture 12 (1878), in *Works*, 22: 534–35.

24. For a list of Ruskin's descriptions of and various allusions to this painting see *Works*, 24:li.

25. Helen Gill Viljoen, ed., *The Brantwood Diary of John Ruskin* (New Haven: Yale University Press, 1971), p. 228.

26. *Diaries*, 3:887.

27. Ibid., p. 851.
28. Viljoen, *Brantwood Diary*, p. 307.
29. Ibid., p. 493.
30. M. H. Abrams, *Natural Supernaturalism* (New York: Norton, 1971).
31. "For Jung, the *self* connotes the totality of the psyche, embracing both consiousness and the unconscious and including the individual's rootedness in the matrix of the collective unconscious" (Jacques Maritain, *Creative Intuition in Art and Poetry*, Bollingen Series 25 [New York: Pantheon Books, 1953] p. 115).
32. Jung, *Aion*, in *Psyche and Symbol*, p. 22.
33. Abrams, *Natural Supernaturalism*, pp. 95–96. This phrase is meant to convey the general concept discussed by Abrams as "The Theodicy of the Private Life" in Wordsworth. Abrams observes that in the *Confessions* Augustine "transfers the locus of the primary concern with evil from the providential history of mankind to the providential history of the individual self." In Wordsworth this narrative pattern becomes secularized as the "distinctive Romantic genre of the *Bildungsgeschichte*"; however, in Wordsworth, as in Ruskin, crises of personal spiritual development are incorporated into a larger mythology projecting the interactions of mind and nature.
34. *Works*, 13:528.
35. Viljoen, *Brantwood Diary*, pp. 92–93.
36. Ibid., p. 93, n. 38.
37. Ibid., p. 92. Santa Vigri, also Beata Vigri, was another of Ruskin's tutelary feminine spirits. Like Ursula, she became linked in his mind with Rose La Touche. Professor Viljoen's note (ibid., p. 104) identifies Vigri as "the family name of the only woman painter ever canonized—St. Catharine of Bologna (1413–63)." Ruskin apparently recognized striking similarities between her personality and Rose's.
38. Ibid., 100–102.
39. Ruskin to George Richmond, 31 May 1878 *Works*, 37:246–47.
40. *Brantwood Diary*, pp. 220–21.
41. Ruskin to John Brown, 29 March 1881, *Works*, 37:347–48.
42. Ruskin to Charles Eliot Norton, 24 March 1881, *Works*, 37:345.
43. Ruskin to Gladstone, 15 February 1881, as quoted in "1881 Introduction," Viljoen, *Brantwood Diary*, p. 261.
44. Ruskin to Susan Beever, Easter Day, 9 April 1882, in *Works*, 37:389.
45. Ruskin to Mrs. La Touche, 5 April 1882, first published in Viljoen, *Brantwood Diary*, pp. 484–85.
46. Viljoen, *Brantwood Diary*, pp. 294–95 and n. 21 (italics mine).
47. Ibid., pp. 296–99.
48. Jung, "Transformation Symbolism in the Mass" (1955) in *Psyche and Symbol*, p. 209.
49. Jung, *Aion*, ibid., p. 42.
50. Jung, "Transformation Symbolism in the Mass," ibid., p. 212.
51. M. E. Harding, *Psychic Energy*, Bollingen Series no. 10 (New York: Pantheon Books, 1947), p. 339.
52. Ibid., p. 246.
53. Ibid., pp. 250–51.
54. Ibid., p. 261.
55. Ibid., p. 259.
56. Ibid.
57. Ruskin to George MacDonald, 11 August 1872, in Greville MacDonald, *Reminiscences of a Specialist* (1932), as quoted in Derrick Leon, *Ruskin: The Great Victorian* (London: Routledge and Kegan Paul, 1949), pp. 494–95 (italics at "her entire soul, etc." mine).
58. Ruskin to MacDonald, 8 September 1872 (quoted by Leon, *Ruskin*, pp. 496–97).
59. A. Carlyle, *New Letters of Thomas Carlyle*, 2:293, as quoted in Leon, *Ruskin*, p. 498.

60. *Diaries*, 3:795.
61. Ibid., pp. 795–96.
62. Ibid., p. 796.
63. In the third lecture of *Val d'Arno* (1873), in *Works*, 23:49.
64. *Works*, 29:160.
65. General Index, in *Works*, 39:249. The index reveals how the Guild's principles evolved in the master's mind and were set down from time to time as they occurred to him during the composition of the *Fors* letters. These principles appear in contractual form in the "Memorandum of Association of the Guild of St. George" and the "Articles of Association of the Guild of St. George" (1878) (*Works*, 30:5–11).
66. *Works*, 28:xvi.
67. Ibid., 33:119.
68. Ibid., 28:532.
69. Ibid., p. 614.
70. Ibid., 22:202–5.
71. Ibid., pp. 194–95.
72. Ibid., p. 198.
73. Ibid., p. 200.
74. Ibid., p. 222.
75. Ibid., pp. 240–41 (italics mine).
76. Ibid., p. 145.
77. *Works*, 25:40. Similarly in *The Eagle's Nest* he explained that the "natural history of anything, or of any creature," would have three divisions. "We have first to collect and examine the traditions respecting the thing, so that we may know what the effect of its existence has hitherto been on the minds of man." Then it is to be examined or described in its "actual state, with utmost veracity of observation." And lastly it is to be studied in terms of the laws of chemistry and physics (*Works*, 22:244–45).
78. *Works*, 26:167.
79. Ibid., 28:106.
80. Ibid., 29:197.
81. Ibid., p. 338.
82. Ibid., 28:235.
83. Ibid., 27:232.
84. Ibid., 29:198.
85. Ibid., p. 383.
86. Ibid., p. 365.
87. Ibid., 27:132–33.
88. Ibid., 28:463–64.
89. Ibid., p. 488.
90. Ibid., 29:71–72.
91. Ibid., 27:657, and cf. p. 83.
92. Ibid., p. 84.
93. Ibid., 28:328.
94. Ibid., p. 133.
95. Ibid., p. 332.
96. Ibid., 27:129.
97. Ibid., p. xxxiii.
98. Ibid., 29:382 (italics mine).
99. Ibid., 27:481.
100. Ibid., p. 483.
101. "The Place of Dragons," by James Reddie Anderson, edited by Ruskin, *Works*, 24:380.
102. In *Fors*, Letter 26 (1873), Ruskin explains that "the name of St. George, the 'Earthworker,' or 'Husbandman,' connected him instantly, in Greek thoughts, not only

with the ancient dragon, Erichthonius, but with the Spirit of agriculture, called 'Thrice-warrior' to whom the dragon was a harnessed creature of toil." *Works,* 27:482.

103.   *Works,* 27:510, and cf. 403.
104.   Ibid., p. 510 and plate 12.
105.   Ibid., pp. 408–09.
106.   Ibid., p. 413. and cf. 21:103.
107.   Ibid., p. 428.
108.   Ibid., p. 408.
109.   Ibid., 29:30.
110.   Ibid., 28:746.
111.   Ibid., 29:54.
112.   Ibid., p. 385.
113.   Ibid., pp. 90–91.
114.   Ibid., p. 91.
115.   Ibid., 23:xlvii.
116.   Ibid., 20:246–47.
117.   Ibid., pp. 122–23.
118.   Ibid., pp. 123–24.
119.   Ibid., p. 126.
120.   Ibid.
121.   Ibid., p. 127.
122.   Ibid., pp. 139–40.
123.   Ibid., p. 140.
124.   Ibid.
125.   Ibid., p. 142.
126.   Ibid.
127.   Ibid., pp. 142–43.
128.   Ibid., p. 153.
129.   Ibid., p. 153-54.
130.   Ibid., p. 169.
131.   Ibid.
132.   Ibid., p. 170.
133.   Ibid., p. 171.
134.   Ibid., pp. 171–72.
135.   Ibid., p. 269.
136.   Ibid., p. 265.
137.   Ibid., p. 244.
138.   Ibid., pp. 276–77.
139.   Ibid., p. 348.
140.   Ibid., p. 354.
141.   Ibid., p. 333.
142.   Ibid., p. 362.
143.   Ibid., 22: 46.
144.   Ibid., p. 47.
145.   Ibid., p. 231.
146.   Ibid., p. 436.
147.   Ibid., pp. 400, 405.
148.   Ibid., p. 396.
149.   Ibid., p. 400.
150.   Ibid., p. 403.
151.   Ibid., p. 405 (italics mine).
152.   Ibid., p. 328.
153.   Ibid., p. 353.
154.   Ibid., p. 354.
155.   Ibid., pp. 415–16.

156. Ibid., p. 415.
157. Ibid., p. 417.
158. Ibid., p. 413.
159. Ibid., p. 412.
160. Ibid., p. 413.
161. Ibid., pp. 414–15.
162. Ibid., pp. 440–41.
163. Ibid., p. 441.
164. Ibid., p. 449.
165. Ibid., p. 329.
166. Ibid., p. 360.
167. Ibid., p. 351.
168. Ibid., p. 350.
169. Ibid., p. 349.
170. Ibid., p. 489.
171. Ibid., p. 414.
172. Ibid., p. 489–90.
173. Ibid., p. 490.
174. *Fors Clavigera,* Letter 22 (1872), *Works,* 27:371–72.
175. *Works,* 22:83, 407.
176. Ibid., 23:342, n.
177. Ibid., p. 198.
178. Ibid., pp. 199–200.
179. Ibid., p. 199.
180. Ibid., p. 200.
181. Ibid., p. 341.
182. Ibid., p. 342.
183. Ibid., p. 322.
184. Ibid., p. 350.
185. Ibid., p. 477.
186. Ibid., p. 465.
187. Ibid., p. 474.
188. Ibid., p. 475.
189. Ibid., p. 476.
190. Ibid., p. 342, n.
191. Ibid., pp. 275–76.
192. Ibid., 31:17, n.
193. Ibid., pp. 16–17.
194. Ibid., 19:325.
195. Ibid., 33:131.
196. Ibid., pp. 131–32.
197. Ibid., pp. 119–20.
198. *Valle Crucis,* in *Works,* 33:238.
199. *Works,* 35:315.
200. Ibid., p. 289.
201. Ibid., 33:456.
202. Ibid., p. 457.
203. Article in *The World,* 19 November 1884, quoted in *Works,* 33:liv.
204. *Works,* 34:266–67.
205. Ibid., 268.
206. Ibid.
207. Ibid., pp. 269–70.
208. Ibid., p. 271.
209. Ibid., p. 272.
210. Ibid., p. 276.

211. Ibid., p. 281.
212. Ibid., pp. 335–36.
213. Ibid., pp. 370–71.
214. Ibid., 33:293.
215. Ibid., p. 294.
216. Ibid.
217. Ibid., p. 296.
218. Ibid., p. 297.
219. Ibid., p. 320.
220. Ibid., p. 320–21.
221. Ibid., p. 387.
222. Ibid., p. 388.
223. Ibid., p. 444.
224. Ibid., 34:78.

Selected Bibliography

I. Editions of Ruskin's Writings

The Works of John Ruskin. Ed. by E. T. Cook and Alexander Wedderburn. 39 vols. Library Edition. London: George Allen, 1903–12.
The Genius of Ruskin: Selections from His Writings. Ed. by John D. Rosenberg. Boston, 1963.
Praeterita. Ed. by Sir Kenneth Clark. London, 1949.
Ruskin Today. Selections ed. by Sir Kenneth Clark. London, 1964.
The Art Criticism of John Ruskin. Ed. by Robert L. Herbert. New York, 1964.
The Literary Criticism of John Ruskin. Ed. by Harold Bloom. New York, 1965.
The Stones of Venice. Ed. and introd. by Jan Morris. Boston, 1981.
Unto This Last and "Traffic." Ed. by John L. Bradley. New York, 1967.

II. Editions of Ruskin's Letters, Diaries, and Drawings

Letters in *Works*, Library Edition, vols. 36, 37 and, as *Arrows of the Chace*, in vol. 34.
Ruskin's Letters from Venice 1851–1852. Ed. by John L. Bradley. (Yale Studies in English, Vol. 129.) New Haven, 1955.
The Letters of John Ruskin to Lord and Lady Mount-Temple. Ed. by John L. Bradley. Columbus, Ohio, 1964.
The Ruskin Family Letters: The Correspondence of John James Ruskin, His Wife, and Their Son, John, 1801–1843. Ed. by Van Akin Burd. 2 vols. Ithaca, N.Y., 1974.
The Winnington Letters: John Ruskin's Correspondence with Margaret Alexis Bell and the Children at Winnington Hall. Ed. by Van Akin Burd. Cambridge, Mass., 1969.
The Letters of John Ruskin to Charles Eliot Norton. Ed. by Charles Eliot Norton. 2 vols. Boston, 1905.
The Gulf of Years: Letters from John Ruskin to Kathleen Olander. Ed. by Rayner Unwin. London, 1953.
The Diaries of John Ruskin. Ed. by Joan Evans and John H. Whitehouse. 3 vols. Oxford, 1955–59.
The Brantwood Diary of John Ruskin. Ed. and annotated by Helen Gill Viljoen. New Haven, 1971.
The Drawings of John Ruskin. Selected and assessed by Paul H. Walton. Oxford, 1972.

III. Bibliographies

Beetz, K. H. *John Ruskin: A Bibliography 1900–1974.* Metuchen, N. J.: Scarecrow Press, 1976.
Cook, E. T. and A. Wedderburn, eds. *Works.* Library Edition, vol. 38 contains a full bibliography to 1910.
Townsend, Francis G. "John Ruskin" in *Victorian Prose: A Guide to Research.* Ed. by David J. DeLaura. New York: The Modern Language Association of America, 1973.

IV.   Biographies and Biographical Studies

Abse, Joan. *John Ruskin: The Passionate Moralist*. New York, 1981.
Burd, Van Akin. *John Ruskin and Rose La Touche: Her Unpublished Diaries of 1861 and 1867*. Oxford, 1979.
Collingwood, W. G. *The Life and Work of John Ruskin*. 2 vols. London, 1893; rev., 1900.
Cook, E. T. *The Life of Ruskin. 2 vols. London, 1911*.
Evans, Joan. *John Ruskin*. London, 1954.
Harrison, Frederic. *John Ruskin*. London, 1902.
James, Sir William. *The Order of Release*. London, 1947.
Leon, Derrick. *Ruskin: The Great Victorian*. London, 1949.
Lutyens, Mary. *Millais and the Ruskins*. New York, 1969.
MacDonald, Greville. *Reminiscences of a Specialist*. London, 1932.
Quennell, Peter. *John Ruskin: The Portrait of a Prophet*. London, 1949.
Viljoen, Helen Gill. *Ruskin's Scottish Heritage: A Prelude*. Urbana, Ill., 1956.
Whitehouse, J. H. *Vindication of Ruskin*. London, 1950.
Wilenski, R. H. *John Ruskin: An Introduction to Further Study of His Life and Work*. London, 1933.

V.   Critical Studies of Ruskin

Alexander, Edward. *Matthew Arnold, John Ruskin, and the Modern Temper*. Columbus, Ohio, 1973.
Ball, Patricia M. *The Science of Aspects: The Changing Role of Fact in the Work of Coleridge, Ruskin and Hopkins*. London, 1971.
Bloom, Harold. "Ruskin as Literary Critic," in *The Ringers in the Tower: Studies in Romantic Tradition*. Chicago, 1971.
Buckley, Jerome H. "The Moral Aesthetic," in *The Victorian Temper: A Study in Literary Culture*. Cambridge, Mass., 1951.
Burd, Van Akin. "Another Light on the Writing of *Modern Painters*." *Publications of the Modern Language Association* 68 (September 1953): 755–63.
———— "Ruskin's Quest for a Theory of Imagination." *Modern Language Quarterly* 17 (March 1956): 60–72.
Collingwood, R. G. "Ruskin's Philosophy," in his *Essays in the Philosophy of Art*. Ed. by Alan Donagan. Bloomington, Ind., 1964.
Conner, Patrick. *Savage Ruskin*. Detroit, 1979.
Fain, John T. *Ruskin and the Economists*. Nashville, Tenn., 1956.
Fellows, Jay. *The Failing Distance: The Autobiographical Impulse in John Ruskin*. Baltimore, 1975.
Garrigan, Kristine Ottesen. *Ruskin on Architecture: His Thought and Influence*. Madison, Wisc., 1973.
Hewison, Robert. *John Ruskin: The Argument of the Eye*. Princeton, 1976.
Herrmann, L. *Ruskin and Turner*. London, 1968.
Hobson, John A. *John Ruskin: Social Reformer*. Boston, 1898.
Hough, Graham. "Ruskin," in *The Last Romantics*. London, 1949.
Ladd, Henry. *The Victorian Morality of Art: An Analysis of Ruskin's Aesthetic*. New York, 1932.

Landow, George P. *The Aesthetic and Critical Theories of John Ruskin.* Princeton, 1971.

LeRoy, Gaylord C. "John Ruskin," in *Perplexed Prophets: Six Nineteenth-Century British Authors.* Philadelphia, 1953.

McLaughlin, Elizabeth. *Ruskin and Gandhi.* Lewisburg, Pa., 1974.

Maurois, Andre. "Proust et Ruskin." *Essays and Studies by Members of the English Association* 17 (1931): 25–32.

Millett, Kate. "The Debate Over Women: Ruskin Versus Mill." *Victorian Studies* 14 (September 1970): 63–82. Challenged by David Sonstroem in "Millett Versus Ruskin: A Defense of Ruskin's 'Of Queens' Gardens.' " *Victorian Studies* 20 (Spring, 1977): 283–97.

Painter, George D. "Salvation through Ruskin," in *Proust: The Early Years.* Boston, 1959.

Roe, Frederic William. *The Social Philosophy of Carlyle and Ruskin.* New York, 1936.

Rosenberg, John D. *The Darkening Glass: A Portrait of Ruskin's Genius.* New York, 1961.

_____ "Style and Sensibility in Ruskin's Prose," in *The Art of Victorian Prose.* Ed. by George Levine and William Madden. New York, 1968.

Sherburne, James Clark. *John Ruskin, or the Ambiguities of Abundance: A Study in Social and Economic Criticism.* Cambridge, Mass., 1972.

Sizeranne, Robert de la. *Ruskin and the Religion of Beauty.* Tr. by the Countess of Galloway. London, 1899.

Townsend, Francis G. *Ruskin and the Landscape Feeling: A Critical Analysis of His Thought During the Crucial Years of His Life, 1843–56.* (Illinois Studies in Language and Literature, Vol. 35, No. 3.) Urbana, Ill., 1951.

VI. Ruskin and Mythology

Burstein, Janet. "Victorian Mythography and the Progress of the Intellect." *Victorian Studies* 18 (March 1975): 309–24.

Dougherty, Charles T. "Of Ruskin's Gardens," in *Myth and Symbol: Critical Approaches and Applications.* Ed. by Bernice Slote. Lincoln, Neb., 1963.

Jenkyns, Richard. *The Victorians and Ancient Greece.* Cambridge, Mass., 1980.

Kirchoff, Frederick. "A Note on Ruskin's Mythography." *Victorian Newsletter* 50 (Fall 1976): 24–27.

Kissane, James. "Victorian Mythology." *Victorian Studies* 6 (September 1962): 5–27.

Miller, J. Hillis. "Myth as 'Hieroglyph' in Ruskin." *Studies in the Literary Imagination* 8 (Fall, 1976): 15–18.

VII. Mythology and Mythography

Abrams, M. H. *Natural Supernaturalism: Tradition and Revolution in Romantic Literature.* New York, 1971.

Bodkin, Maude. *Archetypal Patterns in Poetry.* Oxford, 1934.

Bush, Douglas. *Mythology and the Romantic Tradition.* Cambridge, Mass., 1937.

Campbell, Joseph. *The Hero with a Thousand Faces.* New York, 1949.

_____ *The Masks of God.* 4 vols. New York, 1959.

Cassirer, Ernst. *Essay on Man.* New Haven, 1944.

———— *Language and Myth.* Tr. by Susanne Langer. New York, 1946.

———— *The Philosophy of Symbolic Forms.* Tr. by Ralph Manheim. New Haven, 1955.

Chase, Richard. *Quest for Myth.* Baton Rouge, La., 1949.

Eliade, Mircea. *The Myth of the Eternal Return.* Tr. by Willard Trask. New York, 1954.

———— *Myths, Dreams, and Mysteries.* Tr. by Philip Mairet. New York, 1960.

Feldman, Burton and Robert D. Richardson, eds. *The Rise of Modern Mythology 1680–1860.* Bloomington, Ind., 1972.

Fontenrose, Joseph. *Python: a Study of Delphic Myth and its Origins.* Berkeley, 1959.

Frazer, Sir James G. *The Golden Bough.* 12 vols. London, 1907–15.

———— *The Worship of Nature.* London, 1926.

Freud, Sigmund. *Totem and Taboo.* Tr. by A. A. Brill. New York, 1918.

Fromm, Erich. *The Forgotten Language.* New York, 1951.

Frye, Northrop. *Anatomy of Criticism.* Princeton, 1957.

———— "The Romantic Myth," in *A Study of English Romanticism.* New York, 1968.

Graves, Robert. *The Greek Myths.* Baltimore, 1955.

Harrison, Jane. *Prolegomena to the Study of Greek Religion.* Cambridge, 1903.

Jung, C. G. *The Archetypes of the Collective Unconscious.* Tr. by R. F. C. Hull. New York, 1959.

———— and Kerenyi. *Essays on a Science of Mythology.* Tr. by R. F. C. Hull. New York, 1949.

Kirk, G. S. *Myth, its Meaning and Functions in Ancient and Other Cultures.* Berkeley, 1970.

———— *The Nature of Greek Myths.* Baltimore, 1974.

Lévi-Strauss, C. *Structural Anthropology.* New York, 1963.

Lévy-Bruhl, Lucien. *Primitive Mentality.* Tr. by Lillian A. Clare. London, 1923.

Malinowski, Bronislaw. *Magic, Science and Religion.* Glencoe, Ill., 1926.

———— *Myth in Primitive Psychology.* London, 1926.

Manuel F. E. *The Eighteenth Century Confronts the Gods.* Cambridge, Mass., 1959.

Murray, G. *Five Stages of Greek Religion.* Oxford, 1925.

Murray, H. A. "The Possible Nature of a 'Mythology' to Come," in *Myth and Myth-Making.* Ed. by H. A. Murray. New York, 1960.

Rank, Otto. *The Myth of the Birth of the Hero.* New York, 1914.

Reik, Theodor. *Ritual.* New York, 1931.

———— *Myth and Guilt.* London, 1958.

Richards, I. A. *Coleridge on Imagination.* London, 1926.

Roheim. Geza. *Animism, Magic, and the Divine King.* London, 1930.

———— *Psychoanalysis and Anthropology.* New York, 1950.

Rose, H. J. *A Handbook of Greek Mythology,* 6th ed. London, 1958.

Sebeok, Thomas A., ed. *Myth: A Symposium.* Bloomington, Ind., 1958.

Slote, Bernice, ed. *Myth and Symbol.* Lincoln, Neb., 1963.

Tucker, Robert. *Philosophy and Myth in Marx.* Cambridge, 1961.

Vickery, John B. *Myth and Literature: Contemporary Theory and Practice.* Lincoln, Neb., 1966.

Watts, Alan. *Myth and Ritual in Christianity.* New York, 1953.
Weston, Jessie L. *From Ritual to Romance.* Cambridge, 1920.
Wheelwright, Philip. *The Burning Fountain.* Bloomington, Ind., 1954.
_____ *Metaphor and Reality.* Bloomington, Ind., 1962.

VIII. Nineteenth Century Mythological Science

Baehr, C. C. *Symbolik des mosaischen Kultes.* Heidelberg, 1837–39.
Benfey, T. *Nachrichten von der Königl Gesellschaft der Wissenschaften.* Göttingen, 1868.
Braun, J. B. *Naturgeschichte der Sage, etc.* Munich, 1864–1865.
Bréal, M. *Hercule et Cacus, étude de Mythologie comparée,* Paris, 1863.
Brown, R., Jr. *Poseidon.* London, 1872.
_____ *The Great Dionysiak Myth.* London, 1877.
_____ *The Unicorn.* London, 1881.
_____ *Myth of Kirike.* London, 1883.
_____ *Semetic Influence on Hellenic Mythology.* London, 1885.
Buttman, P. K. *Mythologus.* Berlin, 1828–1829.
Carlyle, T. "The Life of Heyne." *Foreign Review* 4, 1828.
Cox, G. W. *An Introduction to the Science of Comparative Mythology and Folklore.* New York, 1881.
_____ *Mythology of the Aryan Nations.* 2 vols. London, 1870.
_____ *Tales from Ancient Greece.* London, 1868.
_____ *A Manual of Mythology in the Form of Question and Answer.* London, 1868.
Creuzer, Freidrich. *Symbolik und Mythologie der alten Völker, besonders der Griechen.* 4 vols. Leipzig, 1810-1812.
Decharme, P. *Mythologie de la Grece Antique.* Paris, 1886.
Dorson, R. M. "The Eclipse of Solar Mythology," *Journal of American Folklore.* LXVIII: 399, 1955.
Farnell, L. R. *Cults of the Greek States.* 4 vols. London, 1896.
Gorres, J. J. *Mythengeschichte der alten Welt.* Heidelberg, 1810.
Graves, R. *The Greek Myths.* London, 1955.
Grote, G. *History of Greece.* New York, 1865–1867, I.
Herder, J. G. *Ideen zur Philosophie der Geschichte der Menschheit.* Riga and Leipzig, 1784–91.
Heyne, C. G. Vorrede to Martin Gottfried Hermann's *Handbuch der Mythologie aus Homer und Hesiod als Grundlage zu einer richtigen Fabellehre des Alterthums.* Berlin, 1789.
Jordan, L. H. *Comparative Religion: its Genesis and Growth.* Edinburgh, 1905.
Hermann, J. G. *De Antiq. Graecorum Mythologia.* Heidelberg, 1818.
_____ *Uber das Wesen und die Behandlung der Mythologie.* Leipzig, 1819.
Keightley, T. *The Mythology of Ancient Greece and Italy.* 2nd ed. London, 1838.
_____ *The Mythology of Ancient Greece and Italy,* 3rd ed. London, 1854.
_____ *The Mythology of Ancient Greece and Italy,* 3rd ed. New York, 1866.
Kelly, W. K. *Curiosities of Indo-European Tradition and Folk-Lore.* London, 1863.
Kuhn, A. *Die Herabkunft des Feuers und des Göttertranks.* Berlin, 1859.
Lang, A. *Modern Mythology.* London, 1897.

———— *Myth, Ritual and Religion*. 2 vols. London, 1887.

———— *Myth, Ritual and Religion*. 2 vols. London, 1906.

Lauer, J. F. *System der Gr. Mythologie*. Berlin, 1853.

Littledale, R. F. "The Oxford Solar Myth", in M. Müller *Comparative Mythology, An Essay*, ed. Abraham Smyth Palmer, London, 1909.

Lobeck, C. A. *Aglaophamus sine de theologiae mysticae Graecorum causio*. Königsberg, 1828.

Mannhard, W. *Die Götterwelt der deutschen und nördischen Völker*. Berlin, 1860.

Movers, F. C. *Die Phonizier*. Bonn, 1841–1856.

Müller E., ed., Karl Otfried Müller's *Kleine Deutsche Schriften*. 2 vols. Breslau, 1847–1848.

Müller, F. M. *Auld Lang Syne*. London, 1898.

———— *Chips from a German Workshop*. 5 vols. London, 1869–1881.

———— "Comparative Mythology," *Oxford Essays*. London, 1856.

———— *Lectures on the Science of Language*, 2nd ed. Series. London, 1864.

———— *Natural Religion*. London, 1889.

———— *The Science of Thought*. London, 1861.

Müller, K. O. *Introduction to a Scientific System of Mythology*, tr. John Leitch, London, 1844.

———— *Minerva Poliadis Sacra et Aedes in Arce Athenarium*. Göttingen, 1820.

———— *The History and Antiquities of the Doric Race (Die Dorier)*, tr. Henry Tufnell and George Lewis. London, 1839.

Peile, John. *Introduction to Greek and Latin Etymology*. London, 1869.

Preller, L. *Griechischen. Mythologie*. 2 vols. Berlin, 1860.

———— *Römische Mythologie*. Berlin, 1858.

Prichard, J. C. *The Eastern Origin of the Celtic Nations*. London, 1831.

Raingeard, P. *Hermes Psychagogue*. Rennes, 1934.

Roscher, W. H. *Die Gorgonen und Verwandtes*. Leipzig, 1879.

———— *Ausfuhrliches Lexicon der Griechischen und Römischen Mythologie*. 6 vols. Leipzig, 1884–1886.

Rose, J. H. *A Handbook of Greek Mythology*. London, 1928.

Sandys, J. E. *A History of Classical Scholarship*. Cambridge, 1908.

Schelling, F. W. J. *Philosophie der Mythologie*. Stuttgart, 1856.

Schrader, P. *Prehistoric Antiquities of the Aryan Peoples*, London, 1890.

Schwartz, F. L. W. *Der Ursprung der Mythologie dargelegt an griechischer und deutscher Sage*. Berlin, 1860.

Tylor, E. B. *Researches into the Early History of Mankind*. London, 1865.

———— *Primitive Culture*, 2 vols. London, 1871.

Vico. G. B. *The New Science*, tr. Thomas G. Bergin and Max H. Fisch. Ithaca, 1948.

Voelcker, K. H. W. *Mythologie des Japetischen Geschlectes*. Giessen, 1824.

Voss, J. H. *Antisymbolik*. Stuttgart, 1824–1826.

———— *Mythologische Briefe*. Stuttgart, 1827–1834.

Welcker, F. G. *Griechische Götterlehre*. 3 vols. Göttingen, 1857–1862.

Winning, W. B. *A Manual of Comparative Philology*. London, 1838.

Index

Abrams, M. H., 11, 49, 223, 277, 585, *Natural Supernaturalism*, 49
Abse, Joan, 445, 450, 593, 696
Acheron, smoke of, 22, 644
Achilles, 236, 248, 315, 321, 495, 554
Acland, Henry, 306, 431, 450, 579
Acrisius, 349
Admetus, 342
Aeglé, 406, 415-17, 421, 423, 549, *See also* Hesperides, the.
Aeneas, 396
Aeolus, 556, 558, 559
Aeschylus, 89, 251, 321
aesthetics: analogy of painting and poetry in R.'s, 65-66, archetypal conflict, in, 26-28, 49, 224, 278-79, 319, 322-23, 360-61, 378-79, 390-93, 398-99, 432, 615-20; beauty, faculty of perceiving, distinguished from aesthesis by R., 87, 93; beauty received by theoretic and imaginative faculties, 93, 225; color sacredness of, 177, 278-79, 319, 322-23, 415-17, 436, 614-16; conception leads execution in art, 183, 227, 496; conventionalism in, 432, 442, 496; demand for perfection a misconception in, 183; distance and relation to observer in, 163-64; expression vs. limitation in, 70-71, 102, 227-39; greatness of style, 231-32; Greek humanism, influence of on R.'s after 1858, 319-23, 370-85, 372-85, 394-427, 614-36; Greek sculpture, vitality of, in R.'s later view, 620-27; grotesque, noble and debased forms of, 197-202, 237; ideas conveyable by art, 66; infinity in, 27, 68-69, 94, 265-66, 269; light in, 28, 94-95, 224, 253, 266, 269-70, 277-78, 616-20; and national ethics, 508-09; obscurity necessary in, 279; organicism in, 26-27, 49-50, 95-96, 224, 226, 268, 362-65, 434-37; physicotheology in, 50-92, 94, 222, 225; Pre-Raphaelite, 216-17, 219-20, 279-80, 431-33; scriptural history in, 25, 49, 50, 223-24; superhuman figures, problem of representing, 103-4, 231, 233; symbols, function of, 227-28, 270-92; taste and morality in, 115, 501-2; truth vs. imitation in, 67-71, 225-28; typical beauty, 94-95, 109, 225; vital beauty, 95-96, 109, 132-

35, 225, 432, 567-68. *See also* architecture, imagination, landscape, myth, nature, organicism.
Aglaia, 468, 511-13, 515. *See also* Graces, the.
Agnew, Joan. *See* Severn, Mrs. Arthur.
Agonia, 314, 561
agriculture, machinery vs. natural forces, 479
air: as poisoned, 10, 46, 575, 595; pollution of, 535, 569, 574-75; as vital or forming power, 569-74. *See also* Athena, clouds, pollution, plague-cloud, plague-wind, skies, storms.
Alecto, 512-13. *See also* Furies, the.
alienation, 49, 59, 93, 137, 370, 453, 585; and myth of the fall, 223
allegory: and imagination, 51, 242-43; and immediate perception, 51, 222, 246, 263-64; and interpretation of myth, 51, 246-47; and natural theology, 50-51, 222, 225; and symbol, 51, 190, 202, 222, 225; and typology, 50-51, 93-95, 222, 225, 263, 267, 443; uses of, in R., 51, 222, 225, 443, 519-31. *See also* archetype, Greek religion, myth, symbol.
anatomy, 593, 601, 612, 622, 625, 629
Anderson, J. R., 608-09
Andromeda, 415, 608
angel(s), 18, 72, 249, 347, 496, 530, 560, 611
Angelico, 30, 91-93, 102, 185, 232, 234-35, 384, 413, 629, 632
"Angel of the Sea, The," ch. in *Modern Painters* (R): 341, 344-55, 398, 556, 559
animation, 32, 51, 74, 97, 241-45, 256, 259, 262, 327, 330, 350, 537-39, 600
animatism, 539
animism, 246, 356, 399, 528, 538-39, 541
anthropomorphism, 242, 248-251, 374
Aphrodite, 391, 404, 624, 628
apocalypse: as crisis in the unity of the world, or in organic vision, 10-11, 28, 49-50, 53, 54, 57, 289-92, 297-98, 391, 393, 414, 421, 457, 498-501, 526-28, 537, 542-45, 564-70, 572-75, 577, 599, 634-66, 639-41, 644-75; as divine or demonic intention revealed in nature or human activity, 12, 26-28, 34-35, 45-46, 53, 59, 80-82, 143-44, 169, 174-77, 187-91, 200-2, 262,

———— and Jerolyn Lyle. "The Occupational Standing of Negroes by Areas and Industries," *Journal of Human Resources* 6 (fall 1971): 411–433.

Bersani, Catherine. "La Femme et La Fonction Publique," *Droit Social* 1 (Jan. 1976): 51–52.

Bibb, Robert, and William Form. "The Effects of Industrial, Occupational and Sex Stratification on Wages in Blue Collar Markets," *Social Forces* 55 (June 1977): 974–996.

Bird, Caroline. *The Two-Paycheck Marriage.* New York: Rawson, Wade, 1979.

Blackstone, William T., and Robert D. Heslep, eds. *Social Justice and Preferential Treatment: Women and Racial Minorities in Education and Business.* Athens, Ga.: University of Georgia, 1977.

Blau, Francine D. "The Data on Women Workers, Past, Present and Future." In Ann H. Stromberg and Shirley Harkness, eds., *Women Working: Theories and Facts in Perspective*, pp. 29–62. Palo Alto, Calif.: Mayfield, 1978.

————. *Equal Pay in the Office.* Lexington, Mass.: D. C. Heath, 1977.

Blau, Peter, et al. "Occupational Choice—A Conceptual Framework," *Industrial and Labor Relations Review* 9 (July 1956): 531–543.

Blaxall, Martha, and Barbara Reagan. *Women and the Workplace.* Chicago: University of Chicago Press, 1976.

Blinder, Allan, "Wage Discrimination: Reduced Form and Structural Estimates," *Journal of Human Resources* 8 (fall 1973): 436–455.

Blumberg, Grace Ganz. "Federal Income Tax and Social Security Law." In *American Workers in a Full Employment Economy: A Compendium of Papers Submitted to the Subcommittee on Economic Growth and Stabilization of the Joint Economic Committee*, pp. 237–248. Washington, D.C.: Government Printing Office, 1977.

Blumrosen, Alfred W. "The Duty of Fair Recruitment under the Civil Rights Act of 1964," *Rutgers Law Review* 22 (spring 1968): 465–527.

————. "Quotas, Common Sense and Law in Labor Relations: Three Dimensions of Equal Opportunity," *Rutgers Law Review* 27 (spring 1974): 675–703.

————. "Strangers in Paradise: *Griggs v. Duke Power Co.* and the Concept of Employment Discrimination," *Michigan Law Review* 71 (Nov. 1972): 59–110.

Borris, Maria. *Die Benachteiligung der Maedchen in Schulen der Bundes-Republik.* Frankfurt-am-Main: Europaeischer Verlangsanstalt, 1972.

Boutellier, Jacques, et al. *Male and Female Wage Differentials in France: Theory and Measurement.* Monograph no. 5, International Institute of Social Economics. Hull: Emmasglen Ltd., 1975.

Bowen, Peter. "White-Collar Jobs and the Unionization of Women." Paper presented at the International Symposium on Women and Industrial Relations, International Institute for Labour Studies, Vienna, Sept. 1978.

Bowen, William G., and T. Aldrich Finegan. *The Economics of Labor Force Participation.* Princeton, N.J.: Princeton University Press, 1969.

British Information Service. *Occupations and Conditions of Work*. London: Her Majesty's Stationery Office, 1975.

Brown, E. H. P. *The Inequality of Pay*. Berkeley: University of California Press, 1978.

Burns, John E., and Catherine G. Burns. "An Analysis of the Equal Pay Act," *Labor Law Journal* 24 (Feb. 1973): 92.

Canadian Broadcasting Corporation. *Women in the CBC*. Ottawa: Canadian Broadcasting Corporation, 1975.

Central Arbitration Committee. *First Annual Report, 1976*. London: Her Majesty's Stationery Office, 1977.

Chiplin, Brian. "The Evaluation of Sex Discrimination: Some Problems and a Suggested Re-orientation." Paper presented at the Conference on Women in the Labor Market, Columbia University, Sept. 1977.

——— and Peter J. Sloane. "Equal Pay in Great Britain." In Barrie O. Pettman, ed., *Equal Pay for Women: Progress and Problems in Seven Countries*, pp. 9–34. Bradford, Eng.: MCB, 1975.

——— and Peter J. Sloane. *Sex Discrimination in the Labour Market (Great Britain)*. London: Macmillan, 1976.

Cohen, Malcom S. "Sex Differences in Compensation," *Journal of Human Resources* 6 (fall 1971): 434–447.

Collins, Randall. "A Conflict Theory of Sexual Stratification," *Social Problems* 19 (summer 1971): 3–21.

Comité du Travail Féminin, Ministère du Travail. *Bilan de l'Application de la Loi du 22 Décembre 1972 sur l'Égalité de Rémunération entre Hommes et Femmes*. Paris: Ministère du Travail, Sept. 1976.

———, assisted by G. Bécane-Pascaud. *Les Femmes aux Postes de Direction de la Fonction Publique*. Paris: Ministère du Travail, 1974.

Commission of the European Communities. *The Employment of Women and the Problems It Raises in the Member States of the European Community*. Abridged version of Mrs. E. Sullerot's report. Brussels: Commission of the European Communities, 1972.

———. *Men and Women of Europe: Comparative Attitudes to a Number of Problems of our Society*. Brussels: Commission of the European Communities, 1975.

———. *Report of the Commission to the Council on the Application as at 12 February 1978 of the Principle of Equal Pay for Men and Women*. (Brussels: Commission of the European Communities, 1979.

———. *Report on the Development of the Social Situation in the Communities in 1976*. Brussels and Luxembourg: European Coal and Steel Community, European Economic Community, European Atomic Energy Community, 1977.

———. *Vocational Guidance and Training for Women Workers*. Brussels and Luxembourg: European Coal and Steel Community, European Economic Community, European Atomic Energy Community, 1976.

Cook, Alice H. "Equal Pay: A Multinational History and Comparison." Unpubished manuscript, Ithaca, N.Y., Jan. 1, 1975.

————. "Women in Trade Unions." Paper presented at the International Symposium on Women and Industrial Relations, International Institute for Labour Studies, Vienna, Sept. 1978.

————. *The Working Mother: A Study of Problems and Programs in Nine Countries.* Ithaca, N.Y.: School of Industrial and Labor Relations, Cornell University, 1975.

————. "Working Women: European Experience and American Need." In *American Women Workers in a Full Employment Economy: A Compendium of Papers Submitted to the Subcommittee on Economic Growth and Stabilization of the Joint Economic Committee,* pp. 271–306. Washington, D.C.: Government Printing Office, 1977.

Cook, Gail C. A., ed. *Opportunity for Choice: A Goal for Women in Canada.* Ottawa: Statistics Canada and C. D. Howe, 1976.

———— and Mary Eberts. "Policies Affecting Work." In Gail C. A. Cook, ed., *Opportunity for Choice: A Goal for Women in Canada,* pp. 143–187. Ottawa: Statistics Canada and C. D. Howe, 1976.

Coote, Anna, and Tess Gill. *Women's Rights: A Practical Guide.* 2nd ed. Middlesex, Eng.: Penguin Books, 1977.

Corazzini, Arthur J. "Equality of Employment Opportunity in the Federal White-collar Civil Service," *Journal of Human Resources* 7 (Fall 1972): 424–445.

Corcoran, Mary. "Work Experience, Labor Force Withdrawals and Women's Empirical Results Using the 1976 Panel Study of Income Dynamics." Paper presented at the Conference on Women in the Labor Market, Columbia University, Sept. 1977.

Cornu, R. B. *Women and Employment in the United Kingdom, Ireland, and Denmark.* Brussels: Commission of the European Communities, 1974.

Coussins, Jean. *Amending the Equal Pay Act and the Sex Discrimination Act.* London: National Council for Civil Liberties, 1977.

————. *The Equality Report.* London: National Civil Liberties League, 1976.

Crowe, Patricia Ward. "Complainant Reactions to the Massachusetts Commission Against Discrimination," *Law and Society Review* 12 (winter 1978): 217–235.

Darling, Martha. *The Role of Women in the Economy.* Paris: Organisation for Economic Co-operation and Development, 1975.

Däubler-Gmelin, Herta. *Frauenarbeitslosigkeit oder Frauen zurueck an den Herd?* Hamburg: Rowohlt Taschenbuch, 1977.

Diekershoff, Sybille, and Karl Heinz Diekershoff. *Bildungs under Weiterbildungsbereitschaft von Frauen bis zu 45 Jahren.* Band 42, Schriftenreihe des Bundesministers fuer Jugend, Familie und Gesundheit. Stuttgart/Berlin/Koeln/Mainz: Verlag W. Kohlhammer, 1976.

Directorate-General of Social Affairs, Commission of the European Communities. "Progress with Regard to the Implementation of Council Directive" (75/117/EEC). Preliminary draft, Feb. 10, 1975.

Dunlap, Mary C. "The Legal Road to Equal Employment Opportunity: A Critical View." In *American Workers in a Full Employment Economy:*

A Compendium of Papers Submitted to the Subcommittee on Economic Growth and Stabilization of the Joint Economic Committee, pp. 61–74. Washington, D.C.: Government Printing Office, 1977.

Eastwood, Mary Jane. "Employment Discrimination and Title VII of the Civil Rights Act of 1964," *Harvard Law Review* 84 (March 1971): 1109–1180.

Edgeworth, F. Y. "Equal Pay to Men and Women for Equal Work," *Economic Journal* 32 (Dec. 1922): 431–457.

Edgren, Gösta, Karol-Olof Faxén, and Clas-Erik Odhner. *Wage Formation and the Economy*. London: George Allen & Unwin, 1973.

Edwards, H. T. "Arbitration of Employment Discrimination Cases: A Proposal for Employer and Union Representatives," *Labor Law Journal* 27 (May 1976): 265–277.

—— and Barry Zaretsky. "Preferential Remedies for Employment Discrimination," *Michigan Law Review* 74 (Nov. 1975): 1–47.

Epstein, Irwin, and Tony Tripodi. *Research Techniques for Program Planning, Monitoring and Evaluation*. New York: Columbia University Press, 1977.

"Equal Pay and Sex Discrimination: Outcome of Applications to Industrial Tribunals in 1976," *Department of Employment Gazette* 85 (May 1977): 457–460.

Ett Friare val Jämstalldhetsprogram för Skolan: Rapport Fran S Ö-projektet "Könsrollerna i Skolan." Stockholm: Liber Läromedel, 1975.

European Trade Union Confederation. *Women at Work*. Brussels: European Trade Union Confederation, 1976.

Evaluating the Impact of Affirmative Action: A Look at the Federal Contract Compliance Program (a Symposium). Industrial and Labor Relations Review 29 (1976).

Farley, Lin. *Sexual Shake-Down: The Sexual Harassment of Women on the Job*. New York: McGraw-Hill, 1978.

Fawcett, M. G. "Equal Pay for Equal Work," *Economic Journal* 26 (March 1918): 1–6.

Fiss, Owen. "A Theory of Fair Employment Laws," *University of Chicago Law Review* 38 (winter 1971): 235–314.

Fonda, Nichola, and Peter Moss, eds. *Mothers in Employment*. London: Brunel University, 1976.

Forsebäck, Lennart. *Industrial Relations and Employment in Sweden*. Stockholm: The Swedish Institute, 1976.

Freeman, Howard E., ed. *Policy Studies Review Annual 2, 1978*. Beverly Hills: Sage Publications, 1978.

Freeman, Jo. *The Politics of Women's Liberation*. New York: David MacKay, 1975.

Fuchs, Victor R. "Differences in Hourly Earnings between Men and Women," *Monthly Labor Review* 94 (May 1971): 9–15.

Furstenberg, Friedrich. "Die Vertretung der Frauen und ihrer Interessen im Betriebsrat am Beispiel der Bundesrepublik Deutschland und Osterreichs."

Paper presented at the International Symposium on Women and Industrial Relations, International Institute for Labour Studies, Vienna, Sept. 1978.

Garfinkle, Stewart. "The Outcome of a Spell of Unemployment," *Monthly Labor Review* 100 (January 1977): 54–57.

Gaudart, Dorothea. "Women and Industrial Relations." Paper presented at the International Symposium on Women and Industrial Relations, International Institute for Labour Studies, Vienna, Sept. 1978.

———— and W. Schultz. *Maedchenbildung—Wozu?* Band 1. Vienna, 1971.

Getman, Julius. "The Emerging Constitutional Principle of Sexual Equality." In Philip Kurland, ed., *The Supreme Court Review—1972*, pp. 157–180. Chicago: University of Chicago Press, 1973.

Giele, Janet Zollinger. "Changing Sex Roles and Family Structure," *Social Policy* 9 (Jan./Feb. 1979): 32–43.

———— and Hilda Kahne. "Meeting Work and Family Responsibilities: Proposals for Flexibility." In *Women in Mid-Life—Security and Fulfillment: A Compendium of Papers Submitted to the Subcommittee on Retirement Income and Employment, Select Committee on Aging*, pp. 158–177. Washington, D.C.: Government Printing Office, 1978.

———— and Audrey Chapman Smock, eds. *Women: Roles and Status in Eight Countries*. New York: John Wiley & Sons, 1977.

Ginsburg, Ruth. "Gender in the Supreme Court: The 1973 and 1974 Terms." In Philip Kurland, ed., *The Supreme Court Review—1975*, pp. 1–24. Chicago: University of Chicago Press, 1976.

Girard, Robert A., and Louis L. Jaffe. "Some General Observations on the Administration of State Fair Employment Practice Laws," *Buffalo Law Review* 14 (1964): 114–115.

Gitt, Cynthia, and Marjorie Gelb. "Beyond the Equal Pay Act: Expanding Wage Differential Protections under Title VII," *Loyola University Law Journal* (Chicago) 8 (summer 1977): 723–766.

Glazer, Nathan. *Affirmative Discrimination: Ethnic Inequality and Public Policy*. New York: Basic Books, 1975.

Gleiche Chancen fuer Frauen? Berichte und Erfahrungen in Briefen an die Praesidentin des Deutschen Bundestages. Heidelberg and Karlsruhe: G. F. Mueller, Juristischer Verlag, 1977.

Glucklich, P., C. R. J. Hall, M. Povall, and M. W. Snell. "Equal Pay Experience in 25 Firms," *Department of Employment Gazette* 84 (Dec. 1976): 1337–1340.

Gordon, Nancy. *The Treatment of Women in the Public Pension Systems of Five Countries*. Washington, D.C.: The Urban Institute, 1978.

Gould, Carol C., and Marx W. Wartofsky. *Women and Philosophy: Toward a Theory of Liberation*. New York: G. P. Putnam's Sons, 1976.

Gould, William B. *Black Workers in White Unions: Job Discrimination in the United States*. Ithaca, N.Y.: Cornell University Press, 1977.

Gross, Barry R., ed. *Reverse Discrimination*. Buffalo, N.Y.: Prometheus Books, 1977.

Gross, Edward. "Plus Ca Change . . . ? The Sexual Structure of Occupations over Time," *Social Problems* 16 (1968): 198–208.

Gunderson, M. "Equal Pay in Canada: History, Progress and Problems." In Barrie O. Pettman, ed., *Equal Pay for Women: Progress and Problems in Seven Countries.* (Bradford, Eng.: MCB Ltd., 1975).

————. "Male-Female Wage Differentials and the Impact of Equal Pay Legislation," *The Review of Economics and Statistics* 57 (1975): 462–469.

————. "Work Patterns." In Gail C. A. Cook, ed., *Opportunity for Choice: A Goal for Women in Canada,* pp. 93–142. Ottawa: Statistics Canada and C. D. Howe, 1976.

Halimi, Gisèle. *Le Programme Commun des Femmes.* Paris: Grasset, 1978.

Hartmann, Heidi. "Capitalism, Patriarchy and Job Segregation by Sex." In Martha Blaxall and Barbara Reagan, eds., *Women and the Workplace.* Chicago: University of Chicago Press, 1976.

Hausman, Leonard J., et al. *Equal Rights and Industrial Relations.* San Francisco: Industrial Relations Research Association Series, 1977.

Hay, Howard C., "The Use of Statistics to Disprove Employment Discrimination," *Labor Law Journal* 29 (July 1978): 430–440.

Heckman, James, and Kenneth Wolpin. "Does the Contract Compliance Program Work?" *Industrial and Labor Relations Review* 29 (July 1976): 544–564.

Helberger, Christof, and Hans-Jürgen Krupp. *Die Einstufungsgrundsätze der Tätigkeiten Hinsichtlich des Grundsätzes des gleichen Arbeitsentgeltes für Männer und Frauen.* Art. 119 des EWG—Vertrages. Frankfurt: Forschungsbericht in Auftrag der Europ, Gemeinschaften, 1973.

Helwiz, Gisela, *Zwischen Familie und Beruf: Die Stellung der Frau in beiden deutschen Staaten.* Band 10. Cologne: Koeln Bibliothek Wissenschaft und Politik, 1974.

Hill, Herbert. *Black Labor and the American Legal System.* Vol. 1: *Race, Work, and the Law.* Washington, D.C.: Bureau of National Affairs, 1977.

Holter, Harriet, and Hildur Ve. Henriksen. "Social Policy and the Family in Norway." In Jean Lipman-Blumen and Jessie Bernard, eds., *Sex Roles and Social Policy: A Complex Social Science Equation,* pp. 199–224. Sage Studies in International Sociology, no. 14. Beverly Hills, Calif.: Sage Publications, 1979.

Hoskins, Dalmer, and Lenore E. Bixby. *Women and Social Security: Law and Policy in Five Countries.* U.S. Department of Health, Education and Welfare, Social Security Administration, Office of Research and Statistics, Research Report no. 42. Washington, D.C.: Government Printing Office, 1973.

Howe, Louise Kapp. *Pink Collar Workers.* New York: G. P. Putnam's Sons, 1977.

Hunt, Audrey. *The Elderly at Home.* OPCS. London: HMSO, 1978.

————. *The Home Help Service in England and Wales.* OPCS. London: Her Majesty's Stationery Office, 1970.

———. *Management Attitudes and Practices towards Women at Work*. OPCS. London: Her Majesty's Stationery Office, 1978.

Iglitzin, Lynne B., and Ruth Ross, eds. *Women in the World: A Comparative Study*. Santa Barbara, Calif.: Clio Books, 1976.

International Labour Office. *Equality of Opportunity and Treatment for Women Workers*. International Labour Conference, 60th Session, 1975, Report VIII. Geneva: International Labour Office, 1975.

———. *Equal Remuneration: General Survey by the Committee of Experts on the Application of Conventions and Recommendations*. International Labour Conference, 60th Session, 1975, Report III, Part 4B. Geneva: International Labour Office, 1975.

———. *Job Evaluation*. Geneva: International Labour Office, 1960.

———. *Women Workers and Society*. Geneva: International Labour Office, 1976.

International Social Security Association. *Women and Social Security*. Studies and Research, no. 5. Geneva: ISSA, 1973.

Jenkins, Issie L. "Equal Employment Opportunity in the United States: Title VII of the Civil Rights Act of 1964, as Amended, Its History and Operation." In *Issues and Options: Equal Pay/Equal Opportunity*. Toronto: Ministry of Labour, 1978.

Johnson, J. A. "Equal Pay Act of 1963: A Practical Analysis," *Drake Law Review* 24 (summer 1975): 570–610.

Johnston, T. L. *Collective Bargaining in Sweden: A Study of the Labour Market and its Institutions*. Cambridge, Mass.: Harvard University Press, 1962.

Joint Economic Committee, U. S. Congress. *Economic Planning in Five Western European Countries: An Overview*. Paper no. 1. Washington, D.C.: Government Printing Office, 1976.

Joint Female Labour Council. *Woman in Sweden in the Light of Statistics*. Stockholm: Arbetsmarknadens Kvinnonämnd: Aug. 1973.

Jones, James E. "The Development of Modern Equal Employment Opportunity and Affirmative Action Law: A Brief Chronological Overview," *Howard Law Journal* 20, no. 1 (1977): 74–99.

Jonung, Christina. *Occupational Segregation by Sex in Sweden: Problems and Policies*. Lund, Sweden: Nationaleconomiska Institutionen, Lund Universitet, 1977.

———. "Policies of 'Positive Discrimination' in Scandinavia in Respect of Women's Employment." Paper presented at the International Symposium on Women and Industrial Relations, International Institute for Labour Studies, Vienna, Sept. 1978.

———. "Sexual Equality in the Swedish Labor Market," *Monthly Labor Review* 101 (Oct. 1978): 31–35.

Jowell, Jeffrey. *Law and Bureaucracy*. New York: Dunellen, and Port Washington, N.Y.: Kennicat Press, 1975.

Kahne, Hilda. "Economic Research on Women and Families," *Signs: Journal of Women in Culture and Society* 3 (spring 1978): 652–655.

Kamerman, Sheila B., and Alfred J. Kahn, eds. *Family Policy: Government and Families in Fourteen Countries.* New York: Columbia University Press, 1978.

Kanter, Rosabeth. "Access to Opportunity and Power: Measuring Racism/ Sexism Inside Organizations." In R. Alvarez, ed., *Social Indicators of Institutional Discrimination: Management and Research Tools.* San Francisco: Jossey-Bass, 1978.

———. *Men and Women of the Corporation.* New York: Basic Books, 1977.

———. "Some Effects of Proportions on Group Life: Skewed Sex Ratios and Responses to Token Women," *American Journal of Sociology* 82 (March 1977): 966–990.

Kenneally, Shirley. *Women and American Trade Unions.* Monographs in Women's Studies. St. Albans, Vt.: Eden Press, 1978.

Kiefer, Nicholas M. "Training Programs and the Employment and Earnings of Women." Paper presented at the Conference on Women in the Labor Market, Columbia University, Sept. 1977.

Klapper, Michael J. "The Limitations of the Equal Pay Principle," *Industrial and Labor Relations Forum* 11 (spring 1975): 65–105.

Kohen, Andrew I., Susan C. Breinich, and Patricia Shields. *Women and the Economy: A Bibliography and Review of the Literature on Sex Differentiation in the Labor Market.* Washington, D.C.: Government Printing Office, 1975.

Krebs, Edith. "Women Workers and Trade Unions in Austria: An Interim Report." In *Women Workers and Society.* Geneva: International Labour Office, 1976.

Labour Party Study Group. "Discrimination Against Women." In *Opposition Green Paper: Discrimination against Women.* London: The Labour Party, 1972.

Land, Hilary. "Sex Role Stereotyping in the Social Security and Income Tax Systems." In Jane Chetwynd and Oonagh Hartnett, eds., *The Sex Role System.* London: Routledge and Kegan Paul, 1977.

Landes, William. "The Economics of Fair Employment Laws," *Journal of Political Economy* 16 (July/Aug. 1978): 507–552.

Larsen, C. A. "Equal Pay for Women in the United Kingdom," *International Labour Review* 103 (Jan. 1971): 1–11.

Lazear, Edward. "Male-Female Wage Differentials: Has the Government Had Any Effect?" Paper presented at the Conference on Women in the Labor Market, Columbia University, Sept. 1977.

LeCoultre, Denise. "L'Amenagement du Temps de Travail et ses Répercussions pour les Femmes." Paper presented at the International Symposium on Women and Industrial Relations, International Institute for Labour Studies, Vienna, Sept. 1978.

———. "La Notion du Temps dans notre Environnement." Paper prepared for the Colloque Travail et Emploi: Vers Quelle Société? Centre Européen Féminin de Recherche sur l'Evolution de la Société, Lisbon, Portugal, Jan. 1979.

Lester, Anthony, and Geoffrey Bindman. *Race and Law in Great Britain.* Cambridge, Mass.: Harvard University Press, 1972.

Levine, Marvin, and Anthony Montcalmo. "The Equal Employment Opportunity Commission: Progress, Problems, Prospects," *Labor Law Journal* 22 (Dec. 1971): 771–779.

Liljeström, Rita, Gunilla Fürst Mellström, and Gillan Liljeström Svensson. *Roles in Transition: Report of an Investigation Made for the Advisory Council on Equality between Men and Women.* Stockholm: LiberFörlag/ Almänna Förlaget, 1978.

Lloyd, Cynthia B., ed. *Sex, Discrimination and the Division of Labor.* New York: Columbia University Press, 1975.

Lockard, Duane. *Toward Equal Opportunity: A Study of State and Local Antidiscrimination Laws.* New York: MacMillan, 1968.

Loewisch, W., W. Gitter, and A. Mennel. "Welche rechtlichen Massnahmen sind vordringlich um die tatsaechliche Gleichstellung der Frauen mit den Maennern im Arbeitsleben zu gewachrleisten?" In *Gutachten fuer den 50 Deutschen Juristentag.* Muenchen, Federal Republic of Germany: C. H. Beck' sche Verlagsbuchhandlung, 1974.

Loranger, Julie. "Canadian Policies for the Promotion of Women's Employment Conditions in the Public Service." Paper presented at the International Symposium on Women and Industrial Relations, International Institute for Labour Studies, Vienna, Sept. 1978.

Lundberg, Bergliot. *Försöksverksamhet Med Sex Timmars Arbetsdag.* Stockholm: Jämställdhetskommittén, 1978.

———. *Kvinnor Till Mer Kvalificerade Jobb.* Stockholm: Jämställdhetskommittén, 1978.

Lustgarten, Lawrence S. "Problems of Proof in Employment Discrimination Cases," *Industrial Law Journal* 6 (Dec. 1977): 213–214.

Lyle, Jerolyn R. *Affirmative Action Programs for Women: A Survey of Innovative Programs.* Sponsored by the Equal Employment Opportunity Commission. Washington, D.C.: Government Printing Office, 1973.

——— and Jane L. Ross. *Women in Industry: Employment Patterns of Women in Corporate America.* Lexington, Mass.: D. C. Heath, Lexington Books, 1974.

Lynch, Kathleen A. "Women in Europe," *European Community* (Nov. 1975), pp. 10–14.

McCarthy, Margaret. "Women in Trade Unions Today." In Lucy Middleton, ed., *Women in the Labour Movement.* London: Groom Helm, 1977.

MacDonald, Lynn. "Wages of Work: A Widening Gap between Women and Men." In Marylee Stephenson, ed., *Women in Canada.* Rev. ed. Don Mills, Ontario: General Publishing, 1977.

Mackie, L., and P. Pattullo. *Women at Work.* London: Tavistock, 1977.

Madden, J. F. *The Economics of Sex Discrimination.* Lexington, Mass.: D. C. Heath, 1973.

Marshall, J. P. "Sex Discrimination and State Responsibility," *Social and Economic Administration* 9 (autumn 1975): 153–163.

Marshall, Ray. "The Economics of Racial Discrimination: A Survey," *Journal of Economic Literature* 12 (Sept. 1974): 849–871.

————, Charles Knapp, Malcom Ligget, and Robert Glover. *The Impact of Legal and Administrative Remedies to Overcome Discrimination in Employment.* Austin, Texas: Center for the Study of Human Resources, 1976.

Mayhew, Leon H. *Law and Equal Opportunity: A Study of the Massachusetts Commission against Discrimination.* Cambridge, Mass.: Harvard University Press, 1968.

Meidner, Rudolf. *Co-ordination and Solidarity: An Approach to Wages Policy.* Stockholm: Prisma, 1974.

———— and Berndt Öhman. *Fifteen Years of Wage-Policy.* Stockholm: Swedish Trade Union Confederation–LO, 1971.

Meier, Gretl S. *Job Sharing: A New Pattern for Quality of Work and Life.* Kalamazoo, Mich.: The W. E. Upjohn Institute for Employment Research, 1979.

Michel, Andrée. *Travail Féminin: Un Point de Vue.* Paris: La Documentation Francaise, 1975.

Miller, Jeffrey M. "Innovations in Working Patterns." Report of the U.S. Trade Union Seminar on Alternative Work Patterns in Europe, May 1978.

Ministry of Health and Social Affairs, International Secretariat. *Parental Insurance in Sweden: Some Data.* Stockholm: Departementens Offsetcentral, 1977.

Mott, Frank L., et al. *Women, Work, and Family: Dimensions of Change in American Society.* Lexington, Mass.: D. C. Heath, 1978.

Murphy, Thomas E. "Female Wage Discrimination: A Study of the Equal Pay Act, 1963–1970," *Cincinnati Law Review* 39 (1970): 615–644.

Myrdal, Alva. *Towards Equality.* First report of the Working Group on Equality set up by the Swedish Social Democratic Party and the Swedish Confederation of Trade Unions. Stockholm: Bokförlaget Prisma, 1971.

Nagel, Stuart S., ed. *Policy Studies Review Annual, Vol. 1, 1977.* Beverly Hills, Calif.: Sage Publications, 1977.

National Commission for Manpower Policy. *Reexamining European Manpower Policies.* Washington, D.C.: Government Printing Office, 1976.

National Research Council, Committee on Occupation Classification and Analysis, Assembly of Behavioral and Social Sciences. *Job Evaluation: An Analytic Review.* Interim report to the Equal Employment Opportunity Commission. Washington, D.C.: National Academy of Sciences, 1979.

Niemann, H. J. *Arbeitsmotivation und Arbeitschaltung bei Auszubildenden: Eine empirische Leitstudie.* Frankfurt: Rationalisierungs-Kuratorium der Deutschen Wirtschaft RKW, 1976.

Niemi, Albert W., Jr. "Sexist Earning Differences: The Cost of Female Sexuality," *American Journal of Economics and Sociology* 36 (Jan. 1977): 33–40.

Nordic Committee on Social Security Statistics. *Social Security in the Nordic Countries.* Statistical Reports of the Nordic Countries. Copenhagen: Nordic Committee on Social Security, 1976.

Oakley, Ann. "Sex Discrimination Legislation," *British Journal of Law and Society* 2 (winter 1975): 211–217.

————. *The Sociology of Housework*. New York: Pantheon, 1974.

————. *Women's Work*. New York: Pantheon, 1974.

Office of Manpower Economics. *Equal Pay: First Report on the Implementation of the Equal Pay Act 1970*. London: Her Majesty's Stationery Office, 1972.

Office of Research, Equal Employment Opportunity Commission. *Employment Problems of Women: A Classic Example of Discrimination*. Washington, D.C.: Government Printing Office, 1972.

O'Neill, Onora. "How Do We Know When Opportunities Are Equal?" In Mary Vetterling-Braggin, Frederick A. Elliston, and Jane English, eds., *Feminism and Philosophy*, pp. 177–189. Totowa, N.J.: Littlefields, Adams, 1977.

Ontario Ministry of Labor. *Issues and Options: Equal Pay/Equal Opportunity*. Toronto: Ministry of Labor, 1978.

Oppenheimer, Valerie Kincade. *The Female Labor Force in the United States*. Population Monograph Series, no. 5. Berkeley: University of California Press, 1970.

Ostry, Sylvia. *The Female Worker in Canada*. Ottawa: Queen's Printer, 1968.

Peck, C. J. "Equal Employment Opportunity Commission: Developments in the Administrative Process, 1965–1975," *Washington Law Review* 51 (Oct. 1976): 831–865.

Philosophy and Public Affairs. *Equality and Preferential Treatment*. Princeton, N.J.: Princeton University Press, 1977.

Pichault, Camille. "The Belgian Commission on the Employment of Women," *International Labour Review* 115 (March-April 1977): 157–174.

Pinl, Claudia. *Das Arbeitnehmer-Patriarchat: Die Frauenpolitik der Gewerkschaften*. Cologne: Kepenheuer & Witsh, 1977.

Ratner, Ronnie Steinberg. *A Modest Magna Charta: Wage and Hour Standards Laws in the United States, 1900–1973—A Social Indicators Approach*. New Brunswick, N.J.: Rutgers University Press, forthcoming.

————. "Report on the Wellesley Conference on Equal Pay and Equal Opportunity Policy for Women: United States, Canada, and Western Europe." May 1979. Prepared under a grant from the German Marshall Fund of the United States, the Women's Bureau of the U.S. Department of Labor, and the European Economic Community.

————. "Themes in Equal Employment Policy: Fruitful Areas for Research and Exchange." Paper prepared for the Colloque Travail et Emploi: Vers Quelle Société? Centre Européen Féminin de Recherche sur l'Evolution de la Société, Lisbon, Portugal, Jan. 1979.

———— with Françoise J. Carré. "Compendium of Statistics and Institutional Information: Labor Force, Demographic, Legal and General Data on Western Europe, Canada and the United States." Paper prepared for Conference on Equal Pay and Equal Opportunity Policy in the United States, Canada, and Europe, May 1–4, 1978, Wellesley College.

Remick, Helen. "Strategies for Creating Sound, Bias-free Job Evaluation Plans." In *Job Evaluation and EEO: The Emerging Issues.* New York: Industrial Relations Counselors, 1979.

Rendel, Margherita. "Legislating for Equal Pay and Opportunity for Women in Britain," *Signs: Journal of Women in Culture and Society* 3 (summer 1978): 897–908.

Reynolds, Lloyd G. *Labor Economics and Labor Relations.* Englewood Cliffs, N.J.: Prentice Hall, 1978.

Rheinstein, Max, and Mary Ann Glendon. "West German Marriage and Family Law Reform," *University of Chicago Law Review* 45 (spring 1978): 519–552.

Roberts, Benjamin C., Hideaki Okamoto, and George C. Lodge. *Collective Bargaining and Employee Participation in Western Europe, North America and Japan.* New York: The Trilateral Commission, 1979.

Robinson, Olive, and John Wallace. "Equal Pay and Equality of Opportunity," *International Journal of Social Economics* 2, no. 2 (1975): 87–105.

Rodgers, Harrell, Jr., and Charles S. Bullock III, *Law and Social Change: Civil Rights Laws and Their Consequences.* New York: McGraw-Hill, 1972.

Rohmert, Walter, and Joseph Rutenfranz. *Arbeitswissenschafliche Beurteilung der Belastung und Beanspruchung an Unterschiedlichen Industriellen Arbeitsplätzen.* Bonn: Gutachten für den Bundesminister für Arbeit und Sozialordnung, 1975.

Rosenbloom, David H. *Federal Equal Employment Opportunity.* (New York: Praeger, 1977.

Rosenblum, Marc. "The External Measures of Labor Supply: Recent Issues and Trends." Paper prepared for Conference on Affirmative Action Planning, Cornell University, Oct. 31, 1977.

Ross, A. H., and F. V. McDermott, Jr. "Equal Pay Act of 1963: A Decade of Enforcement," *Boston College Industrial and Commercial Law Review* 16 (Nov. 1974): 1–73.

Sachs, Albie, and Joan Wilson. *Sexism and the Law: A Study of Male Beliefs and Legal Bias in Britain and in the United States.* London: Martin Robertson, 1978.

Sandberg, Elisabet. *Equality Is the Goal.* Stockholm: The Swedish Institute, 1975.

Sawhill, Isabel. "The Economics of Discrimination against Women: Some New Findings," *Journal of Human Resources* 8 (summer 1973): 383–396.

Schfei, Marie, and Dorothea Brueck. *Wege zur Selbstbestimmung: Sozialpolitik als Mittel der Emanzipation.* (Roads to Self-determination: Social Policy as Means to Emancipation. Cologne and Frankfurt: Europaeische Verlagsanstalt, 1976.

Schlei, Barbara Lindemann, and Paul Grossman. *Employment Discrimination Law.* Washington, D.C.: The Bureau of National Affairs, 1976.

Schöpp-Schilling, Hanna Beate. *The Changing Roles of Women and Men in the Family and in Society.* Berlin: Aspen Institute for Humanistic Studies, 1978.

Secretary of State for the Home Department. *Equality for Women*. London: Her Majesty's Stationery Office, 1974.

Seear, B. N. *Re-Entry of Women to the Labour Market after an Interruption in Employment*. Paris: Organisation for Economic Cooperation and Development, 1971.

Seidman, Ann, ed. *Working Women: A Study of Women in Paid Jobs*. Westview Special Studies on Women in Contemporary Society. Boulder, Colo.: Westview Press, 1978.

Sexton, Patricia Cayo. *Women and Work*. Employment and Training Administration, R & D Monograph no. 46. Washington, D.C.: Government Printing Office, 1977.

Shaeffer, Ruth Gilbert. *Nondiscrimination in Employment: Changing Perspectives, 1963–1972*. Conference Board Report no. 589. New York: The Conference Board, 1973.

——. *Nondiscrimination in Employment, 1973–1975: A Broadening and Deepening National Effort*. Conference Board Report no. 677. New York: The Conference Board, 1976.

—— and Helen Axel. *Improving Job Opportunities for Women: A Chartbook Focusing on the Progress in Business*. Conference Board Report no. 744. New York: The Conference Board, 1978.

—— and Edith F. Lynton. *Corporate Experiences in Improving Women's Job Opportunities*. Conference Board Report no. 755. New York: The Conference Board, 1979.

Sindler, Allan P. *Bakke, DeFunis, and Minority Admissions: The Quest for Equal Opportunity*. New York: Longman, 1978.

Singelman, Joachim. "The Sectoral Transformation of the Labor Force in Seven Industrialized Countries." Unpublished Ph.D. dissertation, University of Texas at Austin, 1974.

Smith, Ralph E. *The Impact of Macroeconomic Conditions on Employment Opportunities for Women*. U.S. Congress, Joint Economic Committee, Series on Achieving the Goals of the Employment Act of 1946. Washington, D.C.: Government Printing Office, 1977.

——., ed. *The Subtle Revolution: Women at Work*. Washington: D.C.: The Urban Institute, forthcoming.

——. *Women in the Labor Force in 1990*. Washington, D.C.: The Urban Institute, 1979.

—— and Jean E. Vanski. *The Jobless Rate: Another Dimension of the Employment Picture*. Urban Institute Paper no. 350-76; Washington, D.C.: The Urban Institute, 1975.

Smuts, Robert. *Women and Work in America*. New York: Columbia University Press, 1959.

Somers, G. G., and W. D. Wood, eds. *Cost-Benefit Analysis of Manpower Policies: Proceedings of a North American Conference*. Kingston, Ontario: Industrial Relations Centre, Queen's University, 1969.

Sovern, Michael I. *Legal Restraints on Racial Discrimination in Employment*. New York: The Twentieth Century Fund, 1966.

Staines, Graham L., et al. "Trends in Occupational Sex Discrimination: 1969–1973," *Industrial Relations* (Berkeley) 15 (Feb. 1976): 88–98.

Statistical Office of the European Community. *Labour Force Sample Survey, 1975.* Luxembourg: Eurostat, 1976.

Statistics Canada, Labour Force Survey Division. *Statistics Canada: The Labour Force, 1977.* Ottawa: Ministry of Industry, Trade and Commerce, Dec. 1977.

Statistiska Centralbyran Utredningsinstitutet. *Arbetskrafts Undersökningén Arsmedeltal, 1976.* Stockholm: LiberFörlag/Allmänna Fölaget, 1977.

Steiner, Shari. *The Female Factor.* New York: G. P. Putnam's Sons, 1977.

Stevenson, Mary Huff. "Internal Labor Markets and the Employment of Women in Complex Organizations." Working Paper, Wellesley College Center for Research on Women, Jan. 1977.

————. "Relative Wages and Sex Segregation by Occupation." In Cynthia B. Lloyd, ed., *Sex, Discrimination, and the Division of Labor.* New York: Columbia University Press, 1975.

Stigler, Barbara. *Die Mitbestimmung der Arbeiterin: Frauen zwischen traditioneller Familienbindung und gewerkschaftlichem Engagement im Betrieb.* (Codetermination of Women Workers: Women between Traditional Family Ties and Trade Union Engagement in the Plant.) Schriftenreihe des Forschungsinstituts der Friedrich-Ebert Stifung, Vol. 123. Bonn and Bad Godesberg: Verlag Neue Gesellschaft, 1976.

Stone, Morris, and Earl R. Baderschneider. *Arbitration of Discrimination Grievances: A Case Book.* New York: American Arbitration Association, 1974.

Stone, Olive M. "The Status of Women—Great Britain," *The American Journal of Comparative Law* 20 (fall 1972): 592–621.

Street, Harry, et al. *Anti-Discrimination Legislation: The Street Report.* Sponsored by the Race Relations Board and the National Committee for Commonwealth Immigrants. London: Political and Economic Planning, 1967.

Sullerot, Evelynne. *Les Conditions de Travail des Femmes Salariées dans les Six Etats Membres de la Communeauté Européenne—France.* Brussels: Commission des Communeautés Européennes, 1972.

————. *L'Emploi des Femmes et ses Problèmes dans les Etats Membres de la Communeauté Européenne.* Brussels: Commission des Communeautés Européennes, 1972.

————. "Equality of Remuneration for Men and Women in the Member States of the EEC." In *Women Workers and Society: International Perspectives,* pp. 94–97. Geneva: International Labour Office, 1976.

Sweet, James A. *Women in the Labor Force.* New York: Seminar Press, 1973.

Taggart, Robert. *Job Creation: What Works?* Salt Lake City: Olympus, 1977.

Talbert, Joan, and Christine E. Bose. "Wage-Attainment Processes: The Retail Clerk Case," *American Journal of Sociology* 83 (Sept. 1977): 403–424.

Task Force on Equal Pay, Canadian Human Rights Commission. *Equal Pay for Work of Equal Value.* Ottawa: Canadian Human Rights Commission, 1978.

Thurow, Lester C. *Generating Inequality: Mechanisms of Distribution in the U.S. Economy.* New York: Basic Books, 1975.

Treiman, D., and K. Terrell. "Sex and the Process of Status Attainment: A Comparison of Working Women and Men," *American Sociological Review* 40 (1975): 174–200.

———. "Women, Work and Wages—Trends in the Female Occupational Structure." In K. Land and S. Speilerman, eds., *Social Indicators Models.* New York: Russell Sage, 1975.

Tsuchigane, Robert, and Norton Dodge. *Economic Discrimination against Women in the United States.* Lexington, Mass.: D. C. Heath, 1974.

United Kingdom, Department of Employment. *Women and Work: Overseas Practice.* Manpower Paper no. 12. London: Her Majesty's Stationery Office, 1975.

United Nations, Center for Social Development and Humanitarian Affairs. *Law and the Status of Women: An International Symposium,* ed. Columbia Human Rights Law Review. New York: Columbia University School of Law, 1977.

United Nations, Department of Economic and Social Affairs, Statistical Office. *Demographic Yearbook, 1973.* 25th issue. New York: United Nations, 1974.

———. *Demographic Yearbook, 1974.* 26th issue. New York: United Nations, 1975.

———. *Demographic Yearbook, 1975.* 27th issue. New York: United Nations, 1976.

———. *Levels and Trends of Fertility throughout the World, 1950–1970.* Population Studies no. 59. New York: United Nations, 1977.

United Nations, Secretariat of the Interregional Seminar on National Machinery to Accelerate the Integration of Women in Development and to Eliminate Discrimination on Grounds of Sex. "Countries Having National Commissions or Similar Machinery to Accelerate the Integration of Women in Development and to Eliminate Discrimination on Grounds of Sex: Background Paper." Ottawa, Aug. 26, 1974.

United States Commission on Civil Rights. *The Challenge Ahead: Equal Opportunity in Referral Unions.* Washington, D.C.: Government Printing Office, 1976.

———. *The Federal Civil Rights Enforcement Effort, 1974: To Eliminate Employment Discrimination,* vol. 5. Washington, D.C.: Government Printing Office, 1975.

———. *The Federal Civil Rights Enforcement Effort, 1977. To Eliminate Discrimination,* sequel. Washington, D.C.: Government Printing Office, 1977.

———. *Last Hired, First Fired.* Informal hearing before the United States Commission on Civil Rights, Oct. 12, 1976. Washington, D.C.: Government Printing Office, 1976.

United States Congress, House Committee on Interstate and Foreign Commerce, Subcommittee on Communications. *Enforcement of Equal Oppor-*

tunity and Antidiscrimination Laws in Public Broadcasting. Hearings, Aug. 9–10, 1976, 94th Congress, 2nd Session. Washington, D.C.: Government Printing Office, 1977.

United States Congress, Joint Economic Committee. *Economic Problems of Women*. Hearings, pts. 1–3, July 10–30, 1973, 93rd Congress, 1st Session. Washington, D.C.: Government Printing Office, 1973.

United States Department of Labor, Bureau of Labor Statistics. *International Comparisons of Unemployment*. Bulletin no. 1979. Washington, D.C.: Government Printing Office, 1979.

United States Department of Labor, Employment and Training Administration. *From Learning to Earning: A Transnational Comparison of Transition Services*. R & D Monograph no. 63. Washington, D.C.: Government Printing Office, 1979.

———. *Women and Work*. R & D Monograph no. 45. Washington, D.C.: Government Printing Office, 1977.

United States Department of Labor, Employment Standards Administration, Office of Federal Contract Compliance Programs, Task Force. *Preliminary Report on the Revitalization of the Federal Contract Compliance Programs*. Washington, D.C.: Government Printing Office, 1977.

United States Department of Labor, National Commission on Employment and Unemployment Statistics. *Counting the Labor Force*. Washington, D.C.: Government Printing Office, 1979.

Vangsnes, Karl. "Equal Pay in Norway," *International Labor Review* 103 (April 1971): 379–392.

Vetterling-Braggin, Mary, Frederick A. Elliston, and Jane English, eds. *Feminism and Philosophy*. Totowa, N.J.: Littlefield, Adams, 1977.

Vogel-Polsky, Eliane. *Les Conditions de Travail des Femmes Salariées dans les Six Etats Membres de la Communeauté Européenne—Belgique*. Brussels: Commission des Communeautés Européennes, 1972.

Wallace, Phyllis A., ed. *Equal Employment Opportunity and the AT&T Case*. Cambridge, Mass.: The MIT Press, 1976.

——— and Annette M. LaMond, eds. *Women, Minorities and Employment Discrimination*. Lexington, Mass.: D. C. Heath, 1977.

Wallin, Gunvor. "The Status of Women—Sweden," *The American Journal of Comparative Law* 20 (fall 1972): 622–629.

Weiss, Jane A., and Francisco O. Ramirez. "Female Participation in the Occupational System: A Comparative Institutional Analysis," *Social Problems* 23 (June 1976): 593–608.

Werneke, Diane. "The Impact of the Recent Economic Slowdown on the Employment Opportunities of Women." Working paper, World Employment Programme Research, International Labour Office, Geneva, May 1977.

Wertheimer, Barbara. *We Were There: The Story of Working Women in America*. New York: Pantheon, 1977.

——— and Anne Nelson. *Trade Union Women: A Study of Their Participation in New York City Locals*. New York: Praeger, 1975.

Williams, Gregory. "The Changing U.S. Labor Force and Occupational Differentiation by Sex: A Longitudinal Analysis." Unpublished paper, 1977.

Windmuller, John P., ed. *Industrial Democracy in International Perspective.* Richard D. Lambert and Alan W. Heston, eds., *The Annals of the American Academy of Political and Social Science,* no. 431 (May 1977).

Winkelstraeter, Lisel. *Frauenentlohnung kritisch betrachtet.* (A Critical View of Women's Wages.) Hanover, 1975.

Zander, Michael, Brian Abel-Smith, and Rosalind Brooke. *Legal Problems and the Citizen.* London: Heinemann, 1973.

Zellner, Harriet. "The Determinants of Occupational Segregation." In Cynthia B. Lloyd, ed., *Sex, Discrimination and the Division of Labor.* New York: Columbia University Press, 1975.

CONTRIBUTORS

BARBARA BERGMANN is Professor of Economics at the University of Maryland. She has served on the staff of the Council of Economic Advisors and the Brookings Institution. Dr. Bergmann has published articles in the fields of unemployment, labor market discrimination, and the economics of sex roles and on computer simulation models.

ALICE H. COOK is Professor Emerita at the New York State School of Industrial and Labor Relations, Cornell University, and a Board Member of the Women's Studies Program at Cornell. She has received grants from the Ford Foundation for a study of the problems of working mothers in nine countries and from the German Marshall Fund of the United States for a study of women and trade unions in four European countries. Dr. Cook has also been a Fulbright Fellow in Japan (1963–1964) and a Visiting Scholar at Stanford University (1976) and is currently completing a report on "The Impact of Equal Employment Opportunity on Collective Bargaining and the Merit System in Public Employment in Hawaii" as a consultant to the Industrial Relations Center, University of Hawaii. Her publications include *The Working Mother* and "Working Women: European Experience and American Need," in *American Workers in a Full-Employment Economy*, a Compendium of Papers for the Joint Economic Committee, Congress of the U.S., 1977.

HERTA DÄUBLER-GMELIN is a lawyer who has been a member of the West German Parliament since 1972. Her specific interests include legal policy, labor policy, and furthering equal opportunity for women. Dr. Däubler-Gmelin is affiliated with the Social Democratic Party and currently is vice-chairman of the Legal Committee of the German Parliament. She is the author of *Frauenarbeitslosigkeit oder Frauen zurueck an den herd?* (Women's Unemployment or Women Back to the Kitchen?).

MARCIA D. GREENBERGER is the founder of The Women's Rights Project, Center for Law and Social Policy, which was organized to provide legal representation of women's interests, with a special emphasis on federal governmental action. As an attorney, she has handled several lawsuits and administrative matters concerning government enforcement of civil rights legislation designed to protect women, including employment discrimination laws.

CHRISTOF HELBERGER is University Lecturer at the Department of Economic Sciences at the University of Frankfurt/Main, Federal Republic of

Germany, and a member of the research group "Sozial-politisches Ent-scheidungs—und Indikatorensystem." His current research is concerned with the distribution of income and the development of social indicators, especially the effect of remuneration systems on the economic position of women.

JEFFREY JOWELL is Professor of Public Law at University College, London, England. His book *Law and Bureaucracy* contains a case study of the Massachusetts Commission Against Discrimination. Professor Jowell's research on this and other U.S. state anti-discrimination commissions was instrumental in persuading the government of the United Kingdom to provide conciliation machinery in the first U.K. legislation in 1964. He has written extensively about the enforcement of anti-discrimination laws in Britain and the United States.

ROSABETH MOSS KANTER is Professor of Sociology and of Organization and Management at Yale University and a founding partner of Good-measure, an organizational consulting firm with clients among major U.S. and Canadian corporations. She is author of *Men and Women in the Corporation, Life in Organizations, Work and Family in the United States, Another Voice,* and *Commitment and Community.*

HILARY LAND is Lecturer in Social Administration at the University of Bristol. Before joining the faculty of Social Administration in 1970, she worked on a study of poverty in the United Kingdom, which included a study of large families, and on a study of the development of social policy, including the history of family allowances. Dr. Land, who is active in the women's movement, is currently writing a book on family work and the state. The work on her chapter was completed before October 1978, when she joined the Central Policy Review Staff in the Cabinet Office, United Kingdom.

RITA LILJESTRÖM is an Associate Professor of Sociology at Göteborg University, Sweden. She is the author of the following books: *Uppväxtvillkor,* on behalf of The Child Center Commission (1973); *Samhället och barns utveckling,* for the Child Environment Commission (1975); *Roles in Transition,* a report of an investigation for the Advisory Council on Equality between Men and Women (1978); and *Kultur och arbete,* for the Commission on Future Studies (1979).

MARGUERITE J. LORÉE is Associate Professor of English at the Paris IX University Center for Research on American Business and American Contemporary Civilization (CERLACA) and Research Associate with the Study Group of Sex Roles and Family of the Sociology Department of the National Center for Scientific Research (CNRS), France. Her current research involves the employment status and opportunities of professional and managerial women in France and the United States.

LORNA R. MARSDEN is Associate Dean, School of Graduate Studies, University of Toronto, Canada. She is past president of the National Action Committee on the Status of Women. Dr. Marsden is a feminist and sociologist interested in social change in Canada, especially as it relates to how legislation, organizational policies, and other institutional structures constrain the livelihood of women.

DIPAK NANDY is the Deputy Chief Executive of the Equal Opportunities Commission, United Kingdom. He was the first Director of the Runnymede Trust (1968–1973) and a Visiting Fellow of the Adlai Stevenson Institute of International Affairs, Chicago (1970–1973). Mr. Nandy formmerly was a Lecturer at the Universities of Leicester and Kent.

RONNIE STEINBERG RATNER is Research Director of the Center for Women in Government at the State University of New York at Albany. She was Research Director for the International Conference on Equal Pay and Equal Opportunity Policy: Western Europe, Canada, and the United States. She has been a Russell Sage Foundation Fellow in Law and Society at Yale Law School and a Visiting Scholar at Harvard Law School. Dr. Ratner, a sociologist, studied equality policy in Sweden under a grant from the Swedish Bicentennial Fund (1978) and is the recipient of an individual grant to study equal opportunity policy in the United States from the Ford Foundation. She is completing a report for the Organization of Economic Cooperation and Development on *Labor Market Inequality and Equal Opportunity Policy: A Cross-national Comparison.* Her book, *The Growth of Wage and Hour Standards Laws in the United States, 1900–1973: A Social Indicators Approach*, will be published by Rutgers University Press in 1980.

HELEN REMICK is Director of the Office of Affirmative Action for Women at the University of Washington, Seattle, Washington. She holds a doctorate in psychology. Her past work experience includes positions as assistant professor, coordinator of women's center, lecturer, secretary, bookkeeper, retail sales clerk, receptionist, and clerk typist.

PETER C. ROBERTSON is Director of the Office of Policy Implementation, Equal Employment Opportunity Commission, United States. He is an attorney who has worked for the EEOC for twelve years. Mr. Robertson has been an administrative assistant to a congressman and director of a state government Human Rights Commission. He recently has announced his resignation from government to work as a consultant/lawyer on employment discrimination, affirmative action, and related issues.

BERIT ROLLÉN is the Head of the Department for Labor Market Services of the National Labour Market Board, Sweden. She was a member of the former Advisory Council to the Prime Minister on Equality between Men and Women, press secretary to former Prime Minister Olaf Palme, and political assistant to the Assistant Minister of Labour in the Social-Democratic government. Ms. Rollén has been a journalist on economic affairs for several Swedish newspapers and magazines and has written extensively on political and women's issues.

NANCY SEEAR, a Liberal Life Peer and a freelance lecturer and writer, recently retired from her position as Reader in Personnel Management at the London School of Economics and Political Science. Baronness Seear is director of two research projects on women's employment and author of several articles and books on the same subject.

RUTH GILBERT SHAEFFER is Senior Research Associate, Organization Development, at the Conference Board, New York. She holds a Ph.D. in economics and social sciences from Massachusetts Institute of Technology. Dr. Shaeffer's areas of research specialization are staffing the organization and nondiscrimination in employment. Her recent studies include *Corporate Experiences in Improving Women's Job Opportunities* (with Edith F. Lynton), *Improving Job Opportunities for Women: A Chartbook Focusing on the Progress in Business* (with Helen Axel), and two reports in the series *Nondiscrimination in Employment*.

RALPH SMITH is an economist at the National Commission for Employment Policy, United States. He was with the Urban Institute from 1969 to 1978, where he wrote a number of studies in labor economics. From 1975 through 1978, as a Senior Research Associate on the Institute's Women and Family Policy Program, Dr. Smith wrote *The Impact of Macroeconomic Conditions on Employment Opportunities for Women* and *Women in the Labor Force in 1990* and edited *The Subtle Revolution: Women at Work*.

BARBARA M. WERTHEIMER is Associate Professor at the New York State School of Industrial and Labor Relations, Cornell University, and Director of the Institute for Education and Research on Women and Work. She is a Commissioner of the National Commission on Working Women, United States, and of the New York City Commission on the Status of Women, and a founding member of the Coalition of Labor Union Women. Professor Wertheimer was responsible for designing and implementing the Trade Union Women's Studies Program she describes in her chapter. The Institute on Women and Work is responsible for a variety of education programs and research projects designed to advance women in their jobs and in their labor union organizations. She is the author of *Trade Union Women: Their Participation in New York City Locals* (with Anne H. Nelson), *We Were There: The Story of Working Women in America*, as well as numerous articles and monographs dealing with women and work.

INDEX